TAKING SIDES

Clashing Views on

Legal Issues

FIFTEENTH EDITION

Selected, Edited, and with Introductions by

M. Ethan Katsh
University of Massachusetts—Amherst

Connect
Learn
Succeed™

TAKING SIDES: CLASHING VIEWS ON LEGAL ISSUES, FIFTEENTH EDITION

Published by McGraw-Hill, a business unit of The McGraw-Hill Companies, Inc., 1221 Avenue of the Americas, New York, NY 10020. Copyright © 2012 by The McGraw-Hill Companies, Inc. All rights reserved. Previous edition(s) © 2010, 2008, and 2006. Printed in the United States of America. No part of this publication may be reproduced or distributed in any form or by any means, or stored in a database or retrieval system, without the prior written consent of The McGraw-Hill Companies, Inc., including, but not limited to, in any network or other electronic storage or transmission, or broadcast for distance learning.

Some ancillaries, including electronic and print components, may not be available to customers outside the United States.

Taking Sides® is a registered trademark of the McGraw-Hill Companies, Inc.
Taking Sides is published by the **Contemporary Learning Series** group within the McGraw-Hill Higher Education division.

1 2 3 4 5 6 7 8 9 0 DOC/DOC 1 0 9 8 7 6 5 4 3 2 1

MHID: 0-07-805028-6
ISBN: 978-0-07-805028-2
ISSN: 1098-5395

Managing Editor: *Larry Loeppke*
Senior Developmental Editor: *Jade Benedict*
Permissions Coordinator: *Rita Hingtgen*
Senior Marketing Communications Specialist: *Mary Klein*
Marketing Specialist: *Alice Link*
Project Manager: *Erin Melloy*
Design Coordinator: *Brenda A. Rolwes*
Cover Graphics: *Rick D. Noel*
Buyer: *Nicole Baumgartner*
Media Project Manager: *Sridevi Palani*

Compositor: MPS Limited, a Macmillan Company
Cover Image: © Royalty-Free/CORBIS

www.mhhe.com

Editors/Academic Advisory Board

Members of the Academic Advisory Board are instrumental in the final selection of articles for each edition of *TAKING SIDES*. Their review of articles for content, level, and appropriateness provides critical direction to the editors and staff. We think that you will find their careful consideration well reflected in this volume.

TAKING SIDES: Clashing Views on LEGAL ISSUES
Fifteenth Edition

EDITOR
M. Ethan Katsh
University of Massachusetts—Amherst

Preface

The study of law should be introduced as part of a liberal education, to train and enrich the mind. . . . I am convinced that, like history, economics, and metaphysics—and perhaps even to a greater degree than these—the law could be advantageously studied with a view to the general development of the mind.

—Justice Louis D. Brandeis

The general study of law in colleges, universities, and even high schools has grown rapidly during the last 30 years. Accompanying this development has been the publication of new curriculum materials that go beyond the analyses of legal cases and doctrines that make up much of professional law study in law schools. This book is part of the effort to view and study law as an institution that continuously interacts with other social institutions. Law should be examined from an interdisciplinary perspective and be accessible to all students.

This book focuses on a series of controversial issues involving law and the legal system. It is, we believe, an appropriate starting point for law study because controversy and conflict are inherent in law. Law is based on an adversary approach to conflict resolution, in which two advocates representing opposing sides are pitted against each other. Judicial decisions often contain both majority and dissenting opinions, which reveal some of the arguments that went on in the judges' chambers. Perhaps most relevant to a discussion of the place of controversy in the legal system is the First Amendment guarantee of freedom of speech and of the press, which presumes that we all benefit by a vigorous debate of important issues.

Since many of the issues in *Taking Sides* are often in the news, you probably already have opinions on them. What you should remember, however, is that there is usually more to learn about any given issue, and the topics discussed here are best approached with an open mind. You should not be surprised if your views change as you read the selections.

Organization of the book This book contains 40 selections presented in a pro and con format that debate 20 legal issues. Each issue has an *Introduction*, which sets the stage for the debate as it is argued in the YES and NO selections. Each issue concludes with a *Postscript* that makes some final observations, points the way to other questions related to the issue, and provides some *Suggestions for Further Reading* on the issue. Also, the *Internet References* page that accompanies each part opener contains a list of Internet site addresses (URLs) that should prove useful as starting points for further research. At the back of the book is a listing of all the *Contributors to This Volume,* which provides information on the legal scholars, commentators, and judges whose views are debated here.

Changes to this edition   The five new issues are as follows: Issue 3, "Are Violent Video Games Protected by the First Amendment?"; Issue 7, "Is the Eighth Amendment Protection Violated If Prisoners Are Deprived of Basic Sustenance, Including Adequate Medical Care?"; Issue 8, "Should Judges Be Elected Rather Than Appointed?"; Issue 10, "Does the First Amendment Protect Picketing a Funeral Even When It Intentionally Inflicts Emotional Distress on the Family?" and Issue 15, "Can Noise Coming from Inside an Apartment and Which the Police Believe Involves the Destruction of Drugs Constitute 'Exigent Circumstances' That Allow Police Officers to Enter and Search a Home Without a Warrant?"

A word to the instructor   *An Instructor's Resource Guide with Test Questions* (multiple-choice and essay) is available through the publisher for the instructor using *Taking Sides* in the classroom. A general guidebook, *Using Taking Sides in the Classroom,* which discusses methods and techniques for integrating the pro-con approach into any classroom setting, is also available. An online version of *Using Taking Sides in the Classroom* and a correspondence service for *Taking Sides* adopters can be found at http://www.mhhe.com/cls.

   Taking Sides: Clashing Views on Legal Issues is only one title in the *Taking Sides* series. If you are interested in seeing the table of contents for any of the other titles, please visit the *Taking Sides* Web site at http://www.mhhe.com/cls.

Acknowledgments   This edition has benefitted greatly from the research conducted by Gabriel Katsh, a Ph.D. candidate in the Department of Government, Harvard University, and Professor Jordan Singer of the New England School of Law.

M. Ethan Katsh
University of Massachusetts—Amherst

To Emma and Marley

Contents In Brief

Contents

Justice Ginsburg believes that the copyright laws are violated by a company when its software is used primarily for illegal file sharing, and lawful uses in the future are unlikely. Justice Breyer does not want the copyright laws to hinder technological innovation and is more willing to take into account the potential use of the software for lawful file sharing.

Supreme Court Justice Anthony Kennedy rules that if a prison deprives prisoners of basic sustenance, including adequate medical care, the courts have a responsibility to remedy the resulting violation of the Eighth Amendment. Justice Antonin Scalia believes that a ruling that may result in the release of 40,000 prisoners is unwarranted and unprecedented.

UNIT 3   LAW AND THE STATE   161

Professor Michael Dimino claims that electing judges is no worse than appointing them and that it is appropriate for citizens to have a say in who will be making decisions that affect them. Professor Charles Geyh criticizes the practice of electing judges and argues that it reduces judicial independence and accountability.

Supreme Court Justice Clarence Thomas affirms the right of religious groups to use school facilities after the school day ends, maintaining that restricting such use is a violation of free speech rights. Supreme Court Justice David Souter, dissenting from the Court's opinion, contends that the use of school facilities by religious groups blurs the line between public classroom instruction and private religious indoctrination and therefore violates the Establishment Clause of the Constitution.

Chief Justice John Roberts holds that picketing a soldier's funeral in a way that may be hurtful to those attending is still protected by the First Amendment. Justice Samuel Alito argues that intentionally inflicting severe emotional injury on private persons should not be considered to be protected speech.

Supreme Court Chief Justice John Roberts rules that a student's First Amendment rights are not violated by restrictions on speech that can reasonably be regarded as encouraging illegal drug use. Supreme Court Justice John Paul Stevens argues that an ambiguous reference to drugs does not justify limiting a student's speech.

Supreme Court Justice David Souter holds that a search in school requires a reasonable belief that evidence of wrongdoing will be found and that the search is not excessively intrusive in light of the age and sex of the student. Supreme Court Justice Clarence Thomas argues that the

Fourth Amendment was not violated when there is reasonable suspicion that the student is in possession of drugs banned by school policy and the search is in an area where small pills could be concealed.

Supreme Court Justice Anthony Kennedy holds that the Constitution prohibits the execution of a person who was under the age of 18 at the time of the offense. Supreme Court Justice Antonin Scalia believes that the Constitution does not preclude the execution of a juvenile.

Supreme Court Justice Sandra Day O'Connor rules that a decision in a case involving the theft of $150 worth of merchandise that resulted in two consecutive terms of 25 years to life in prison for a "third strike" conviction was not "grossly disproportional" to the crime nor "contrary to, or an unreasonable application of, clearly established federal law." Supreme Court Justice David Souter argues that under several prior Supreme Court decisions, the "third strike" punishment in this case was grossly disproportional to the crime committed.

Justice Samuel Alito holds that a warrant is unnecessary when "exigent circumstances" exist and the police have not created them. Justice Ruth Bader Ginsburg believes that the "exigent circumstances" must exist before the police arrive and that in this case a warrant should have been obtained before entry into the apartment.

UNIT 4   LAW AND THE COMMUNITY   337

Massachusetts Supreme Judicial Court Chief Justice Margaret Marshall rules that prohibiting same-sex couples from marrying causes hardship to a segment of the population for no rational reason. Massachusetts Supreme Judicial Court Justice Robert Cordy, in dissent, holds that a statute banning same-sex marriage is a valid exercise of the state's police power.

Supreme Court Justice Clarence Thomas argues that the University of Michigan Law School's admissions policy discriminates on the basis of race and is therefore in violation of the Fourteenth Amendment's equal protection clause. Supreme Court Justice Sandra Day O'Connor holds that the admissions policy of the University of Michigan Law School, which makes race one factor among many in the process of creating a diverse student body, does not violate the Constitution's guarantee of equal protection under the law.

Correlation Guide

The *Taking Sides* series presents current issues in a debate-style format designed to stimulate student interest and develop critical thinking skills. Each issue is thoughtfully framed with an issue summary, an issue introduction, and a postscript. The pro and con essays—selected for their liveliness and substance—represent the arguments of leading scholars and commentators in their fields.

Taking Sides: Clashing Views on Legal Issues, 15/e is an easy-to-use reader that presents issues on important topics such as *wiretaps on U.S. citizens, file sharing,* and *same-sex couples.* For more information on *Taking Sides* and other *McGraw-Hill Contemporary Learning Series* titles, visit www.mhhe.com/cls.

This convenient guide matches the issues in **Taking Sides: Clashing Views on Legal Issues, 15/e** with the corresponding chapters in three of our best-selling McGraw-Hill Criminal Justice textbooks by Adler et al., Masters et al., and Bohm/Haley.

Taking Sides: Legal Issues, 15/e	Criminal Justice: An Introduction, 6/e by Adler et al.	CJ: Realities and Challenges, 2/e by Masters et al.	Criminal Justice, 7/e by Bohm/Haley
Issue 1: Should U.S. Citizens Who Are Declared to Be "Enemy Combatants" Be Able to Contest Their Detention Before a Judge?	**Chapter 10:** Criminal Prosecution and Adjudication	**Chapter 4:** Criminal Law and Defenses	**Chapter 9:** Sentencing, Appeals, and the Death Penalty
Issue 2: Does the President Possess Constitutional Authority to Order Wiretaps on U.S. Citizens?	**Chapter 4:** The Criminal Law	**Chapter 4:** Criminal Law and Defenses	**Chapter 4:** The Rule of Law
Issue 3: Are Violent Video Games Protected by the First Amendment?	**Chapter 3:** Explaining Criminal Behavior	**Chapter 3:** Causes of Crime	**Chapter 3:** Explaining Crime
Issue 4: Is It Constitutional to Ban Partial-Birth Abortions Without Providing for an Exception to Protect the Health of the Mother?	**Chapter 3:** Explaining Criminal Behavior		**Chapter 4:** The Rule of Law
Issue 5: Are Restrictions on Physician-Assisted Suicide Constitutional?	**Chapter 3:** Explaining Criminal Behavior	**Chapter 4:** Criminal Law and Defenses	**Chapter 4:** The Rule of Law
Issue 6: Does the Sharing of Music Files Through the Internet Violate Copyright Laws?	**Chapter 7:** The Rule of Law in Law Enforcement	**Chapter 2:** Types of Crime	**Chapter 4:** The Rule of Law
Issue 7: Is the Eighth Amendment Protection Against Cruel and Unusual Punishment Violated If Prisoners are Deprived of Basic Sustenance, Including Adequate Medical Care?	**Chapter 12:** Corrections: Yesterday and Today	**Chapter 12:** Jails and Prisons	**Chapter 7:** Policing America: Issues and Ethics
Issue 8: Should Judges be Elected Rather than Appointed?	**Chapter 8:** The Origin and Role of the Courts **Chapter 9:** Lawyers and Judges	**Chapter 8:** The Courts	**Chapter 8:** The Administration of Justice

(Continued)

Taking Sides: Legal Issues, 15/e	Criminal Justice: An Introduction, 6/e by Adler et al.	CJ: Realities and Challenges, 2/e by Masters et al.	Criminal Justice, 7/e by Bohm/Haley
Issue 9: Do Religious Groups Have a Right to Use Public School Facilities After Hours?		**Chapter 16:** Contemporary Challenges in Criminal Justice	
Issue 10: Does the First Amendment Protect Picketing a Funeral Even when it Intentionally Inflicts Emotional Distress on the Family?	**Chapter 6:** Police Functions and Police Culture	**Chapter 7:** Legal and Special Issues in Policing **Chapter 16:** Contemporary Challenges in Criminal Justice	**Chapter 7:** Policing America: Issues and Ethics
Issue 11: Can a School Punish a Student for Speech at a School-supervised Event Off of School Grounds When That Speech Could be Viewed as Promoting Illegal Drug Use?	**Chapter 15:** Justice for Juveniles and Victims	**Chapter 16:** Contemporary Challenges in Criminal Justice	
Issue 12: Is a Strip Search of Middle School Students That is Aimed at Finding Drugs Prohibited Under the Fourth Amendment?	**Chapter 15:** Justice for Juveniles and Victims	**Chapter 7:** Legal and Special Issues in Policing	**Chapter 7:** Policing America: Issues and Ethics
Issue 13: Does the "Cruel and Unusual Punishment" Clause of the Eighth Amendment Bar the Imposition of the Death Penalty on Juveniles?	**Chapter 15:** Justice for Juveniles and Victims	**Chapter 15:** Juvenile Justice	**Chapter 9:** Sentencing, Appeals, and the Death Penalty
Issue 14: Is a Sentence of Life in Prison for Stealing $150 Worth of Videotapes Constitutional?	**Chapter 11:** Sentencing	**Chapter 10:** Sentencing	**Chapter 9:** Sentencing, Appeals, and the Death Penalty
Issue 15: Can Noise Coming from Inside a Home Which the Police Believe Involves the Destruction of Drugs Justify the Entry and Search of the Premises Without A Warrant?	**Chapter 6:** Police Functions and Police Culture	**Chapter 6:** Policing Operations **Chapter 7:** Legal and Special Issues in Policing	**Chapter 7:** Policing America: Issues and Ethics
Issue 16: Is the Fourth Amendment Search and Seizure Guaranty Violated by the Use of High-technology Thermal Imaging Devices?	**Chapter 4:** The Criminal Law **Chapter 7:** The Rule of Law in Law Enforcement	**Chapter 7:** Legal and Special Issues in Policing	**Chapter 7:** Policing America: Issues and Ethics
Issue 17: Is There a Constitutional Right to Possess a Firearm for Private Use?	**Chapter 4:** The Criminal Law	**Chapter 7:** Legal and Special Issues in Policing	**Chapter 7:** Policing America: Issues and Ethics
Issue 18: Are Blanket Prohibitions on Cross Burnings Unconstitutional?	**Chapter 3:** Explaining Criminal Behavior **Chapter 4:** The Criminal Law	**Chapter 4:** Criminal Law and Defenses	**Chapter 5:** History and Structure of American Law Enforcement
Issue 19: Should Same-Sex Couples Receive Constitutional Protection?	**Chapter 8:** The Origin and Role of the Courts	**Chapter 16:** Contemporary Challenges in Criminal Justice	**Chapter 8:** The Administration of Justice
Issue 20: Do Race-Conscious Programs in Public University Admissions Policies Violate the Fourteenth Amendment's Guarantee of Equal Protection Under the Law?	**Chapter 8:** The Origin and Role of the Courts	**Chapter 2:** Types of Crime	**Chapter 8:** The Administration of Justice

Topic Guide

This topic guide suggests how the selections in this book relate to the subjects covered in your course. You may want to use the topics listed on these pages to search the Web more easily. On the following pages, a number of Web sites have been gathered specifically for this book. They are arranged to reflect the issues of this Taking Sides reader. You can link to these sites by going to http://www.mhhe.com/cls.

All the articles that relate to each topic are listed below the bold-faced term.

Abortion

Issue 4. Is It Constitutional to Ban "Partial-Birth" Abortions Without Providing for an Exception to Protect the Health of the Mother?

Copyright

Issue 6. Does the Sharing of Music Files Through the Internet Violate Copyright Laws?

Criminal Justice System

Issue 7. Is the Eighth Amendment Protection Violated If Prisoners Are Deprived of Basic Sustenance, Including Adequate Medical Care?
Issue 11. Can a School Punish a Student for Speech at a School-Supervised Event Off School Grounds When That Speech Could Be Viewed As Promoting Illegal Drug Use?
Issue 12. Is a Strip Search of Middle School Students That Is Aimed at Finding Drugs Prohibited Under the Fourth Amendment?

Drugs

Issue 11. Can a School Punish a Student for Speech at a School-Supervised Event Off School Grounds When That Speech Could Be Viewed As Promoting Illegal Drug Use?
Issue 15. Can Noise Coming from Inside an Apartment and Which the Police Believe Involves the Destruction of Drugs Constitute "Exigent Circumstances" That Allow Police Officers to Enter and Search a Home Without a Warrant?

Elections and Electoral Systems

Issue 8. Should Judges Be Elected Rather Than Appointed?

Free Speech

Issue 3. Are Violent Video Games Protected by the First Amendment?
Issue 10. Does the First Amendment Protect Picketing a Funeral Even When It Intentionally Inflicts Emotional Distress on the Family?
Issue 18. Are Blanket Prohibitions on Cross Burnings Unconstitutional?

File Sharing

Issue 6. Does the Sharing of Music Files Through the Internet Violate Copyright Laws?

Gaming

Issue 3. Are Violent Video Games Protected by the First Amendment?

Interest groups

Issue 17. Is There a Constitutional Right to Possess a Firearm for Private Use?

Immigration

Issue 1. Should U.S. Citizens Who Are Declared to Be "Enemy Combatants" Be Able to Contest Their Detention Before a Judge?

Internet

Issue 6. Does the Sharing of Music Files Through the Internet Violate Copyright Laws?

Judges

Issue 8. Should Judges Be Elected Rather Than Appointed?

Juvenile Justice

Issue 13. Does the "Cruel and Unusual Punishment" Clause of the Eighth Amendment Bar the Imposition of the Death Penalty on Juveniles?

Legislatures, State

Issue 19. Should Same-Sex Couples Receive Constitutional Protection?

Marriage

Issue 19. Should Same-Sex Couples Receive Constitutional Protection?

Media

Issue 3. Are Violent Video Games Protected by the First Amendment?

Physician-Assisted Suicide

Issue 5. Are Restrictions on Physician-Assisted Suicide Constitutional?

Privacy

Issue 2. Does the President Possess Constitutional Authority to Order Wiretaps on U.S. Citizens?
Issue 11. Can a School Punish a Student for Speech at a School-Supervised Event Off School Grounds When That Speech Could Be Viewed As Promoting Illegal Drug Use?

Public Schools

Issue 9. Do Religious Groups Have a Right to Use Public School Facilities After Hours?
Issue 12. Is a Strip Search of Middle School Students That Is Aimed at Finding Drugs Prohibited Under the Fourth Amendment?

Race

Issue 20. Do Race-Conscious Programs in Public University Admissions Policies Violate the Fourteenth Amendment's Guarantee of Equal Protection Under the Law?

Sentencing

Issue 13. Does the "Cruel and Unusual Punishment" Clause of the Eighth Amendment Bar the Imposition of the Death Penalty on Juveniles?
Issue 14. Is a Sentence of Life in Prison for Stealing $150 Worth of Videotapes Constitutional?

Terrorism

Issue 1. Should U.S. Citizens Who Are Declared to Be "Enemy Combatants" Be Able to Contest Their Detention Before a Judge?

Technology

Issue 16. Is the Fourth Amendment Search and Seizure Guaranty Violated by the Use of High-Technology Thermal Imaging Devices?

Introduction

The Role of Law

M. Ethan Katsh

More than 200 years ago, Edmund Burke, the influential British statesman and orator, commented that "in no other country, perhaps, in the world, is the law so general a study as it is in the United States." Today, in America, general knowledge about law is at a disappointing level. In one study, 69 percent of those surveyed mistakenly believed that when it was first written, the U.S. Constitution outlawed slavery. In a 2010 survey, nearly two-thirds of the people questioned could not name even one member of the U.S. Supreme Court and only 1 percent knew all nine justices. In contrast, several years ago, a whopping majority—75 percent—knew that there are three Rice Krispies characters, and 66 percent proudly cited their names (Snap, Crackle, and Pop).

One purpose of this volume is to provide information about some specific and important legal issues. In your local newspaper today, there is probably at least one story concerning an issue in this book. The quality of your life will be directly affected by how many of these issues are resolved. But affirmative action (Issue 20), abortion (Issue 4), copyrighted material on the Internet (Issue 6), and other issues in this book are often the subject of superficial, misleading, or inaccurate statements. *Taking Sides* is designed to encourage you to become involved in the public debate on these issues and to raise the level of the discussion on them.

The issues that are debated in this book represent some of the most important challenges our society faces. Issue 1, for example, raises questions about the rights of persons suspected of planning terrorist acts. How they are dealt with will influence what kind of society we will have in the future. Although it is important to look at and study them separately, it is equally necessary to think about their relationship to each other and about the fact that there is a tool called "law," which is being called upon to solve a series of difficult conflicts. The study of discrete legal issues should enable you to gain insight into some broad theoretical questions about law. This introduction, therefore, will focus on several basic characteristics of law and the legal process that you should keep in mind as you read this book.

The Nature of Law

The eminent legal anthropologist E. Adamson Hoebel once noted that the search for a definition of law is as difficult as the search for the Holy Grail. Law is certainly complicated, and trying to define it precisely can be frustrating. What follows, therefore, is not a definition of law but a framework or perspective for looking at and understanding law.

Law As a Body of Rules

One of the common incorrect assumptions about law is that it is merely a body of rules invoked by those who need them and then applied by a judge. Under this view, the judge is essentially a machine whose task is simply to find and apply the right rule to the dispute in question. This perspective makes the mistake of equating law with the rules of law. It is sometimes even assumed that there exists somewhere in the libraries or computers of lawyers and judges one book or file with all the rules or laws in it, which can be consulted to answer legal questions. As may already be apparent, such a resource could not exist. Rules alone do not supply the solutions to many legal problems. The late Supreme Court Justice William O. Douglas once wrote, "The law is not a series of calculating machines where definitions and answers come tumbling out when the right levers are pushed." As you read the debates about the issues in this book, you will see that much more goes into a legal argument than the recitation of rules.

Law As a Process

A more meaningful way of thinking about law is to look at it as a process or system, keeping in mind that legal rules are one of the elements in the process. This approach requires a considerably broader vision of law: to think not only of the written rules but also of the judges, the lawyers, the police, and all the other people in the system. It requires an even further consideration of all the things that influence these people, such as their values and economic status.

"Law," one legal commentator has stated, "is very like an iceberg; only one-tenth of its substance appears above the social surface in the explicit form of documents, institutions, and professions, while the nine-tenths of its substance that supports its visible fragment leads a sub-aquatic existence, living in the habits, attitudes, emotions and aspirations of men."[1]

In reading the discussions of controversial issues in this book, try to identify what forces are influencing the content of the rules and the position of the writers. Three of the most important influences on the nature of law are economics, moral values, and public opinion.

Law and Economics

Laws that talk about equality, such as the Fourteenth Amendment, which guarantees that no state shall "deny to any person . . . equal protection of the laws," suggest that economic status is irrelevant in the making and application of the law. As Anatole France, the nineteenth-century French satirist, once wrote, however, "The law, in its majestic equality, forbids the rich as well as the poor to sleep under bridges, to beg in streets, and to steal bread." Sometimes the purpose and effect of the law cannot be determined merely from the words of the law.

Critics of law in capitalistic societies assert that poverty results from the manipulation of the law by the wealthy and powerful. It is possible to look at several issues in this book and make some tentative judgments about the influence of economic power on law. For example, what role does economics play in the debate over the sharing of music files through the Internet (Issue 6)? Is the controversy over providing incentives for creators and musicians or maximizing profits for record companies?

Law and Values

The relationship between law and values has been a frequent theme of legal writers and a source of debate. Clearly, there is in most societies some relationship between law and morality. One writer has summarized the relationship as follows:

1. *There is a moral order in society.* Out of the many different and often conflicting values of the individuals and institutions that make up society may emerge a dominant moral position, a core of the moral order. The position of this core is dynamic, and as it changes, the moral order of society moves in the direction of that change.
2. *There is a moral content to the law.* The moral content of law also changes over time, and as it changes, the law moves in the direction of that change.
3. *The moral content of the law and moral order in society are seldom identical.*
4. *A natural and necessary affinity exists between the two "bodies" of law and moral order.*
5. *When there is a gap between the moral order of society and the law, some movement to close the gap is likely.* The law will move closer to the moral order of society, or the moral order will move closer to the law, or each will move toward the other. The likelihood of the movement to close the gap between law and moral order depends upon the size of the gap between the two bodies and the perceived significance of the subject matter concerning which the gap exists.[2]

Law and morality will not be identical in a pluralistic society, but there will also be attempts by dominant groups to insert their views of what is right into the legal code. The First Amendment prohibition against establishment of religion and the guarantee of freedom of religion are designed to protect those whose beliefs are different. Yet there have also been many historical examples of legal restrictions or limitations being imposed on minorities or of laws being ineffective because of the resistance of powerful groups. Prayers in the public schools, for example, which have been forbidden since the early 1960s, are still said in a few local communities.

Of the topics in this book, the insertion of morality into legal discussions has occurred most frequently in the abortion debate (Issue 4). It is probably fair to say that this issue remains high on the agenda of public debate because it involves strongly held values and beliefs. The nature of the debate is also colored by strong feelings that are held by the parties. Although empirical evidence about public health and abortion does exist, the debate is generally more emotional than objective.

Public Opinion and the Law

It is often claimed that the judicial process is insulated from public pressures. Judges are elected or appointed for long terms or for life, and the theory is that they will, therefore, be less subject to the force of public opinion. As a result, the law should be uniformly applied in different places, regardless of the nature of the community. It is fair to say that the judicial process is less responsive to public sentiment than is the political process, but that is not really saying much. What is important is that the legal process is not totally immune from public pressure. The force of public opinion is not applied directly through lobbying, but it would be naive to think that the force of what large numbers of people believe and desire never gets reflected in what happens in court. The most obvious examples are trials in which individuals are tried as much for their dissident beliefs as for their actions. Less obvious is the fact that the outcomes of cases may be determined in some measure by popular will. Judicial complicity in slavery and the internment of Japanese Americans during World War II are blatant examples of this.

Many of the issues selected for this volume are controversial because a large group is opposed to some practice sanctioned by the courts. Does this mean that the judges have taken a courageous stand and ignored public opinion? Not necessarily. Only in a few of the issues have courts adopted an uncompromising position. In most of the other issues, the trend of court decisions reflects a middle-of-the-road approach that could be interpreted as trying to satisfy everyone but those at the extremes. For example, in affirmative action (Issue 20), the *Bakke* decision, while generally approving of affirmative action, was actually won by Bakke and led to the abolition of all such programs that contained rigid quotas.

Assessing Influences on the Law

This summary of what can influence legal decisions is not meant to suggest that judges consciously ask what the public desires when interpretations of law are made. There are subtle forces at work on judges that may not be obvious in any particular opinion but that can be discerned in a line of cases over a period of time. This may be explicitly denied by judges, such as in this statement by Justice Harry A. Blackmun in his majority opinion for the landmark *Roe v. Wade* abortion case: "Our task, of course, is to resolve the issue by constitutional measurement, free of emotion and predilection." However, a reading of that opinion raises the question of whether or not Blackmun succeeds in being totally objective in his interpretation of law and history.

Do these external and internal influences corrupt the system, create injustice, inject bias and discrimination, and pervert the law? Or do these influences enable judges to be flexible, to treat individual circumstances, and to fulfill the spirit of the law? Both of these ends are possible and do occur. What is important to realize is that there are so many points in the legal system where discretion is employed that it is hopeless to think that we could be governed by rules alone. "A government of laws, not men," aside from the sexism of the language, is not a realistic possibility, and it is not an alternative that many would find satisfying either.

On the other hand, it is also fair to say that the law, in striving to get the public to trust in it, must persuade citizens that it is more than the whim of those who are in power. Although it cannot be denied that the law may be used in self-serving ways, there are also mechanisms at work that are designed to limit abuses of discretionary power. One quality of law that is relevant to this problem is that the legal process is fundamentally a conservative institution, which is, by nature, resistant to radical change. Lawyers are trained to give primary consideration in legal arguments to precedent—previous cases involving similar facts. As attention is focused on how the present case is similar to or different from past cases, some pressure is exerted on new decisions to be consistent with old ones and on the law to be stable. Thus, the way in which a legal argument is constructed tends to reduce the influence of currently popular psychological, sociological, philosophical, or anthropological theories. Prior decisions will reflect ideologies, economic considerations, and ethical values that were influential when these decisions were made, and, if no great change has occurred in the interim, the law will tend to preserve the status quo, both perpetuating old injustices and protecting traditional freedoms.

Legal Procedure

The law's great concern with the procedure of decision making is one of its more basic and important characteristics. Any discussion of the law that did not note the importance of procedure would be inadequate. Legal standards are often phrased not in terms of results but in terms of procedure. For example, it is not unlawful to convict the innocent if the right procedures are used (and it *is* unlawful to convict the guilty if the wrong procedures are followed). The law feels that it cannot guarantee that the right result will always be reached and that only the guilty will be caught, so it minimizes the risk of reaching the wrong result or convicting the innocent by specifying procedural steps to be followed. Lawyers, more than most people, are satisfied if the right procedures are followed even if there is something disturbing about the outcome. Law, therefore, has virtually eliminated the word *justice* from its vocabulary and has substituted the phrase *due process,* meaning that the proper procedures, such as right to counsel, right to a public trial, and right to cross-examine witnesses, have been followed. This concern with method is one of the pillars upon which law is based. It is one of the characteristics of law that distinguishes it from nonlegal methods of dispute resolution, where the atmosphere will be more informal and there may be no set procedures.

Conclusion

Law is a challenging area of study because many questions may not be amenable to simple solutions. The legal approach to problem solving is usually methodical and often slow. We frequently become frustrated with this process, and, in fact, it may be an inappropriate way to deal with some problems. For the issues in this book, however, an approach that pays careful attention to the many different aspects of these topics will be the most rewarding. Many of the readings provide historical, economic, and sociological data as well as information about law. The issues examined in *Taking Sides* involve basic cultural institutions such as religion, schools, and the family as well as basic cultural values such as privacy, individualism, and equality. While the law takes a narrow approach to problems, reading these issues should broaden your outlook on the problems discussed and, perhaps, encourage you to do further reading on those topics that are of particular interest to you.

Notes

1. Iredell Jenkins, *Social Order and the Limits of Law* (Princeton University Press, 1980), p. xi.
2. Lynn Wardle, "The Gap Between Law and Moral Order: An Examination of the Legitimacy of the Supreme Court Abortion Decisions," *Brigham Young University Law Review* (1980), pp. 811–835.

Internet References . . .

FindLaw Special Coverage "War on Terrorism"

http://news.findlaw.com/legalnews/us/terrorism/cases/index.html

The Rule of Law and the Global War on Terrorism: Detainees, Interrogations, and Military Commissions

http://www.washburnlaw.edu/ruleoflaw

Federal Bureau of Investigation: Counterterrorism

http://www.fbi.gov/terrorinfo/counterrorism/waronterrorhome.htm

Resources on Terrorism

http://sanford.duke.edu/centers/tcths/research/terrorismwebpages.php

Law and Terrorism

*T*he events of September 11, 2001, and the subsequent war on terror have had a significant impact on the law. We are continuously being confronted with choices about what we want law to do and how we want law to do it. These choices touch many deeply held values, affect our identity as individuals and as a country, and pose questions that we are likely to visit and revisit for some time.

- Should U.S. Citizens Who Are Declared to Be "Enemy Combatants" Be Able to Contest Their Detention Before a Judge?

- Does the President Possess Constitutional Authority to Order Wiretaps on U.S. Citizens?

ISSUE 1

Should U.S. Citizens Who Are Declared to Be "Enemy Combatants" Be Able to Contest Their Detention Before a Judge?

YES: Sandra Day O'Connor, from Majority Opinion, *Hamdi v. Rumsfeld*, U.S. Supreme Court (June 28, 2004)

NO: Clarence Thomas, from Minority Opinion, *Hamdi v. Rumsfeld*, U.S. Supreme Court (June 28, 2004)

ISSUE SUMMARY

YES: Supreme Court Justice Sandra Day O'Connor finds that the Authorization for Use of Military Force passed by Congress does not authorize the indefinite detainment of a person found to be an "enemy combatant."

NO: Justice Clarence Thomas believes that the detention of an "enemy combatant" is permitted under the federal government's war powers.

T he factual background to this issue is well known. On September 11, 2001, the al Qaeda terrorist network launched a coordinated attack on the United States, striking the twin towers of the World Trade Center in New York City and the Pentagon. They failed to strike a third target in Washington, D.C., presumably the White House or the U.S. Capitol. Approximately 3,000 people were killed with thousands more injured. The attacks' immediate economic damages were calculated in the hundreds of millions of dollars. Their long-term effects, both human and economic, are still accumulating. It was the deadliest foreign attack on U.S. soil in this nation's history.

President George W. Bush took swift retaliatory action in response to the al Qaeda attacks. With the Authorization for Use of Military Force (AUMF), Pub. L. No. 107-40, secs. 1–2, 115 Stat. 224, Congress provided overwhelming bipartisan support for the president's use of "all necessary and appropriate force against those nations, organizations, or persons *he* determines planned, authorized, committed, or aided the terrorist attacks or harbored such organizations or person" (emphasis added). In addition to the power to commit military forces to battle, President Bush also claimed the authority to detain, indefinitely, those persons he designated as "enemy combatants"; a somewhat ambiguous term that includes suspected terrorists and their accomplices. Yaser Esam Hamdi was captured by Northern Alliance forces on the battlefields of Afghanistan in late 2001 and was eventually turned over to the American military. Hamdi was designated an "enemy combatant" and therefore subject to detention away from the battlefield for the duration of "hostilities."

Although he claimed to have been a noncombatant, Hamdi was held by the Department of Defense, without access to legal counsel for more than a year. Ultimately, Hamdi's father, acting as his "next friend," petitioned a federal district court for a writ of *habeas corpus*, alleging that his son had been wrongfully seized and was being unlawfully held by the U.S. government. In the course of the litigation, a central legal question that emerged was what level of review the courts should give to the government's determination of facts. In a time of war, should the courts simply defer to the executive branch because of national security concerns?

The legal challenge to Hamdi's detention moved back and forth between federal district court and the U.S. Court of Appeals. The U.S. government was ordered to grant a federal public defender's request to gain access to Hamdi in order to facilitate a due process challenge to his continued detention. Federal District Court Judge Robert Doumar characterized the government's factual declarations regarding Hamdi's original seizure as little more than their "say-so." He went on to insist that if the Court were to accept the government's factual claims alone as sufficient justification for Hamdi's continued detention, "it would in effect be abdicating any semblance of the most minimal level of judicial review. In effect, this Court would be acting as little more than a rubber-stamp" (*Hamdi v. Rumsfeld*, 243 F. Supp. 2d 527, 535 (E.D., Va. 2002)). On appeal, however, the Fourth Circuit Court of Appeals rejected the lower court's analysis, urging instead the need for limited judicial review during times of war. Fourth Circuit Judge J. Harvey Wilkinson, citing separation of powers concerns and the need to defer to the war-making powers of the executive and legislative branches, observed that, "[t]he safeguards that all Americans have come to expect in criminal prosecutions do not translate neatly to the arena of armed conflict. In fact, if deference to the executive branch is not exercised with respect to military judgments in the field, it is difficult to see where deference would ever obtain" (*Hamdi v. Rumsfeld*, 316 F.3d 450 (4th Cir. 2003)). With this decision, the Fourth Circuit Court denied further inquiry into the facts alleged by the U.S. government that justified Hamdi's status as an "enemy combatant." The U.S. Supreme Court granted review in this case, and the separation of powers question again would assume center stage. In a time of war, when an American citizen's individual liberties are in question, what role should the courts take in reviewing actions by the executive and legislative branches in their prosecution of that war?

YES

Sandra Day O'Connor

Majority Opinion,
Hamdi v. Rumsfeld

JUSTICE O'CONNOR announced the judgment of the Court and delivered an opinion, in which the CHIEF JUSTICE, JUSTICE KENNEDY, and JUSTICE BREYER join.

At this difficult time in our Nation's history, we are called upon to consider the legality of the Government's detention of a United States citizen on United States soil as an "enemy combatant" and to address the process that is constitutionally owed to one who seeks to challenge his classification as such. The United States Court of Appeals for the Fourth Circuit held that petitioner's detention was legally authorized and that he was entitled to no further opportunity to challenge his enemy-combatant label. We now vacate and remand. We hold that although Congress authorized the detention of combatants in the narrow circumstances alleged here, due process demands that a citizen held in the United States as an enemy combatant be given a meaningful opportunity to contest the factual basis for that detention before a neutral decisionmaker.

I

. . . This case arises out of the detention of a man whom the Government alleges took up arms with the Taliban during this conflict. . . . The Government contends that Hamdi is an "enemy combatant," and that this status justifies holding him in the United States indefinitely—without formal charges or proceedings—unless and until it makes the determination that access to counsel or further process is warranted. . . .

The petition contends that Hamdi's detention was not legally authorized. *Id.*, at 105. It argues that, "[a]s an American citizen, . . . Hamdi enjoys the full protections of the Constitution," and that Hamdi's detention in the United States without charges, access to an impartial tribunal, or assistance of counsel "violated and continue[s] to violate the Fifth and Fourteenth Amendments to the United States Constitution. . . .

[The] District Court had failed to extend appropriate deference to the Government's security and intelligence interests. 296 F. 3d 278, 279, 283 (2002). It directed the District Court to consider "the most cautious procedures first," *id.*, at 284, and to conduct a deferential inquiry into Hamdi's status. . . .

From Supreme Court of the United States, June 28, 2004.

The Fourth Circuit emphasized that the "vital purposes" of the detention of uncharged enemy combatants—preventing those combatants from rejoining the enemy while relieving the military of the burden of litigating the circumstances of wartime captures halfway around the globe—were interests "directly derived from the war powers of Articles I and II." *Id.*, at 465–466. In that court's view, because "Article III contains nothing analogous to the specific powers of war so carefully enumerated in Articles I and II," *id.*, at 463, separation of powers principles prohibited a federal court from "delv[ing] further into Hamdi's status and capture," *id.*, at 473. Accordingly, the District Court's more vigorous inquiry "went far beyond the acceptable scope of review.". . .

II

The threshold question before us is whether the Executive has the authority to detain citizens who qualify as "enemy combatants." There is some debate as to the proper scope of this term, and the Government has never provided any court with the full criteria that it uses in classifying individuals as such. It has made clear, however, that, for purposes of this case, the "enemy combatant" that it is seeking to detain is an individual who, it alleges, was "'part of or supporting forces hostile to the United States or coalition partners'" in Afghanistan and who "'engaged in an armed conflict against the United States'" there. Brief for Respondents 3. We therefore answer only the narrow question before us: whether the detention of citizens falling within that definition is authorized.

The Government maintains that no explicit congressional authorization is required, because the Executive possesses plenary authority to detain pursuant to Article II of the Constitution. We do not reach the question whether Article II provides such authority, however, because we agree with the Government's alternative position, that Congress has in fact authorized Hamdi's detention, through the AUMF. . . .

The AUMF authorizes the President to use "all necessary and appropriate force" against "nations, organizations, or persons" associated with the September 11, 2001, terrorist attacks. 115 Stat. 224. There can be no doubt that individuals who fought against the United States in Afghanistan as part of the Taliban, an organization known to have supported the al Qaeda terrorist network responsible for those attacks, are individuals Congress sought to target in passing the AUMF. We conclude that detention of individuals falling into the limited category we are considering, for the duration of the particular conflict in which they were captured, is so fundamental and accepted an incident to war as to be an exercise of the "necessary and appropriate force" Congress has authorized the President to use.

The capture and detention of lawful combatants and the capture, detention, and trial of unlawful combatants, by "universal agreement and practice," are "important incident[s] of war.". . .

There is no bar to this Nation's holding one of its own citizens as an enemy combatant. . . .

Hamdi objects, nevertheless, that Congress has not authorized the *indefinite* detention to which he is now subject. . . . We take Hamdi's objection to be not to the lack of certainty regarding the date on which the conflict will end, but to the substantial prospect of perpetual detention. We recognize that the national security underpinnings of the "war on terror," although crucially important, are broad and malleable. As the Government concedes, "given its unconventional nature, the current conflict is unlikely to end with a formal cease-fire agreement." *Ibid.* The prospect Hamdi raises is therefore not far-fetched. If the Government does not consider this unconventional war won for two generations, and if it maintains during that time that Hamdi might, if released, rejoin forces fighting against the United States, then the position it has taken throughout the litigation of this case suggests that Hamdi's detention could last for the rest of his life. . . .

III

Even in cases in which the detention of enemy combatants is legally authorized, there remains the question of what process is constitutionally due to a citizen who disputes his enemy-combatant status. Hamdi argues that he is owed a meaningful and timely hearing and that "extra-judicial detention [that] begins and ends with the submission of an affidavit based on third-hand hearsay" does not comport with the Fifth and Fourteenth Amendments. . . .

A

. . . All agree that, absent suspension, the writ of habeas corpus remains available to every individual detained within the United States. U. S. Const., Art. I, §9, cl. 2. . . . Only in the rarest of circumstances has Congress seen fit to suspend the writ. . . . At all other times, it has remained a critical check on the Executive, ensuring that it does not detain individuals except in accordance with law. . . . All agree suspension of the writ has not occurred here. Thus, it is undisputed that Hamdi was properly before an Article III court to challenge his detention under 28 U. S. C. §2241. . . .

C

The Government's second argument requires closer consideration. This is the argument that further factual exploration is unwarranted and inappropriate in light of the extraordinary constitutional interests at stake. Under the Government's most extreme rendition of this argument, "[r]espect for separation of powers and the limited institutional capabilities of courts in matters of military decision-making in connection with an ongoing conflict" ought to eliminate entirely any individual process, restricting the courts to investigating only whether legal authorization exists for the broader detention scheme. At most, the Government argues, courts should review its determination that a citizen is an enemy combatant under a very deferential "some evidence" standard. *Id.,* at 34 ("Under the some evidence standard, the focus is exclusively on the factual basis supplied by the Executive to support its own determination."). . . .

In response, Hamdi emphasizes that this Court consistently has recognized that an individual challenging his detention may not be held at the will of the Executive without recourse to some proceeding before a neutral tribunal to determine whether the Executive's asserted justifications for that detention have basis in fact and warrant in law. . . . He argues that the Fourth Circuit inappropriately "ceded power to the Executive during wartime to define the conduct for which a citizen may be detained, judge whether that citizen has engaged in the proscribed conduct, and imprison that citizen indefinitely," . . . and that due process demands that he receive a hearing in which he may challenge the Mobbs Declaration and adduce his own counter evidence. . . .

Both of these positions highlight legitimate concerns. And both emphasize the tension that often exists between the autonomy that the Government asserts is necessary in order to pursue effectively a particular goal and the process that a citizen contends he is due before he is deprived of a constitutional right. The ordinary mechanism that we use for balancing such serious competing interests, and for determining the procedures that are necessary to ensure that a citizen is not deprived of life, liberty, or property, . . .

1

It is beyond question that substantial interests lie on both sides of the scale in this case. Hamdi's "private interest . . . affected by the official action," *ibid.*, is the most elemental of liberty interests—the interest in being free from physical detention by one's own government. . . . "In our society liberty is the norm," and detention without trial "is the carefully limited exception.". . .

Nor is the weight on this side of the *Mathews* scale offset by the circumstances of war or the accusation of treasonous behavior, for "[i]t is clear that commitment for *any* purpose constitutes a significant deprivation of liberty that requires due process protection," . . . Indeed, as *amicus* briefs from media and relief organizations emphasize, the risk of erroneous deprivation of a citizen's liberty in the absence of sufficient process here is very real. . . . Moreover, as critical as the Government's interest may be in detaining those who actually pose an immediate threat to the national security of the United States during ongoing international conflict, history and common sense teach us that an unchecked system of detention carries the potential to become a means for oppression and abuse of others who do not present that sort of threat. . . . We reaffirm today the fundamental nature of a citizen's right to be free from involuntary confinement by his own government without due process of law, and we weigh the opposing governmental interests against the curtailment of liberty that such confinement entails.

2

On the other side of the scale are the weighty and sensitive governmental interests in ensuring that those who have in fact fought with the enemy during a war do not return to battle against the United States. . . . Without doubt, our Constitution recognizes that core strategic matters of warmaking belong in the hands of those who are best positioned and most politically accountable for making them. . . .

3

Striking the proper constitutional balance here is of great importance to the Nation during this period of ongoing combat. But it is equally vital that our calculus not give short shrift to the values that this country holds dear or to the privilege that is American citizenship. It is during our most challenging and uncertain moments that our Nation's commitment to due process is most severely tested; and it is in those times that we must preserve our commitment at home to the principles for which we fight abroad. . . .

With due recognition of these competing concerns, we believe that neither the process proposed by the Government nor the process apparently envisioned by the District Court below strikes the proper constitutional balance when a United States citizen is detained in the United States as an enemy combatant. That is, "the risk of erroneous deprivation" of a detainee's liberty interest is unacceptably high under the Government's proposed rule, while some of the "additional or substitute procedural safeguards" suggested by the District Court are unwarranted in light of their limited "probable value" and the burdens they may impose on the military in such cases. *Mathews*, 424 U. S., at 335.

We therefore hold that a citizen-detainee seeking to challenge his classification as an enemy combatant must receive notice of the factual basis for his classification, and a fair opportunity to rebut the Government's factual assertions before a neutral decisionmaker. . . . "For more than a century the central meaning of procedural due process has been clear: 'Parties whose rights are to be affected are entitled to be heard; and in order that they may enjoy that right they must first be notified.' It is equally fundamental that the right to notice and an opportunity to be heard 'must be granted at a meaningful time and in a meaningful manner.'" . . . These essential constitutional promises may not be eroded.

At the same time, the exigencies of the circumstances may demand that, aside from these core elements, enemy combatant proceedings may be tailored to alleviate their uncommon potential to burden the Executive at a time of ongoing military conflict. . . .

We think it unlikely that this basic process will have the dire impact on the central functions of warmaking that the Government forecasts. . . .

In sum, while the full protections that accompany challenges to detentions in other settings may prove unworkable and inappropriate in the enemy-combatant setting, the threats to military operations posed by a basic system of independent review are not so weighty as to trump a citizen's core rights to challenge meaningfully the Government's case and to be heard by an impartial adjudicator.

D

In so holding, we necessarily reject the Government's assertion that separation of powers principles mandate a heavily circumscribed role for the courts in such circumstances. . . . We have long since made clear that a state of war is not a blank check for the President when it comes to the rights of the Nation's citizens. . . . Whatever power the United States Constitution envisions for the

Executive in its exchanges with other nations or with enemy organizations in times of conflict, it most assuredly envisions a role for all three branches when individual liberties are at stake. . . . Likewise, we have made clear that, unless Congress acts to suspend it, the Great Writ of habeas corpus allows the Judicial Branch to play a necessary role in maintaining this delicate balance of governance, serving as an important judicial check on the Executive's discretion in the realm of detentions. . . .

Minority Opinion, *Hamdi v. Rumsfeld*

J USTICE THOMAS, dissenting.

The Executive Branch, acting pursuant to the powers vested in the President by the Constitution and with explicit congressional approval, has determined that Yaser Hamdi is an enemy combatant and should be detained. This detention falls squarely within the Federal Government's war powers, and we lack the expertise and capacity to second-guess that decision. As such, petitioners' habeas challenge should fail, and there is no reason to remand the case. The plurality reaches a contrary conclusion by failing adequately to consider basic principles of the constitutional structure as it relates to national security and foreign affairs and by using the balancing scheme of *Mathews v. Eldridge,* 424 U. S. 319 (1976). I do not think that the Federal Government's war powers can be balanced away by this Court. Arguably, Congress could provide for additional procedural protections, but until it does, we have no right to insist upon them. But even if I were to agree with the general approach the plurality takes, I could not accept the particulars. The plurality utterly fails to account for the Government's compelling interests and for our own institutional inability to weigh competing concerns correctly. I respectfully dissent.

I

"It is 'obvious and unarguable' that no governmental interest is more compelling than the security of the Nation." *Haig v. Agee,* 453 U. S. 280, 307 (1981). . . . The national security, after all, is the primary responsibility and purpose of the Federal Government. . . . But because the Founders understood that they could not foresee the myriad potential threats to national security that might later arise, they chose to create a Federal Government that necessarily possesses sufficient power to handle any threat to the security of the Nation. The power to protect the Nation

> "ought to exist without limitation . . . *[b]ecause it is impossible to foresee or define the extent and variety of national exigencies, or the correspondent extent & variety of the means which may be necessary to satisfy them.* The circumstances that endanger the safety of nations are infinite; and for this reason no constitutional shackles can wisely be imposed on the power to which the care of it is committed." *Id.,* at 147.

From Supreme Court of the United States, June 28, 2004.

. . . The Founders intended that the President have primary responsibility—along with the necessary power—to protect the national security and to conduct the Nation's foreign relations. They did so principally because the structural advantages of a unitary Executive are essential in these domains. "Energy in the executive is a leading character in the definition of good government. It is essential to the protection of the community against foreign attacks." The Federalist No. 70. The principle "ingredien[t]" for "energy in the executive" is "unity.". . . This is because "[d]ecision, activity, secrecy, and dispatch will generally characterise the proceedings of one man, in a much more eminent degree, than the proceedings of any greater number."

These structural advantages are most important in the national-security and foreign-affairs contexts. "Of all the cares or concerns of government, the direction of war most peculiarly demands those qualities which distinguish the exercise of power by a single hand.". . . Also for these reasons, John Marshall explained that "[t]he President is the sole organ of the nation in its external relations, and its sole representative with foreign nations.". . . To this end, the Constitution vests in the President "[t]he executive Power," Art. II, §1, provides that he "shall be Commander in Chief of the" armed forces, §2, and places in him the power to recognize foreign governments, §3.

This Court has long recognized these features and has accordingly held that the President has *constitutional* authority to protect the national security and that this authority carries with it broad discretion. . . .

The Court has acknowledged that the President has the authority to "employ [the Nation's Armed Forces] in the manner he may deem most effectual to harass and conquer and subdue the enemy.". . . With respect to foreign affairs as well, the Court has recognized the President's independent authority and need to be free from interference. . . .

Congress, to be sure, has a substantial and essential role in both foreign affairs and national security. But it is crucial to recognize that *judicial* interference in these domains destroys the purpose of vesting primary responsibility in a unitary Executive. I cannot improve on Justice Jackson's words, speaking for the Court:

> "The President, both as Commander-in-Chief and as the Nation's organ for foreign affairs, has available intelligence services whose reports are not and ought not to be published to the world. It would be intolerable that courts, without the relevant information, should review and perhaps nullify actions of the Executive taken on information properly held secret. Nor can courts sit *in camera* in order to be taken into executive confidences. But even if courts could require full disclosure, the very nature of executive decisions as to foreign policy is political, not judicial. Such decisions are wholly confided by our Constitution to the political departments of the government, Executive and Legislative. They are delicate, complex, and involve large elements of prophecy. They are and should be undertaken only by those directly responsible to the people whose welfare they advance or imperil. They are decisions of a kind for which the Judiciary has neither aptitude,

facilities nor responsibility and which has long been held to belong in the domain of political power not subject to judicial intrusion or inquiry." *Ibid.*

Several points . . . are worth emphasizing. First, with respect to certain decisions relating to national security and foreign affairs, the courts simply lack the relevant information and expertise to second-guess determinations made by the President based on information properly withheld. Second, even if the courts could compel the Executive to produce the necessary information, such decisions are simply not amenable to judicial determination because "[t]hey are delicate, complex, and involve large elements of prophecy." Third, the Court . . . has correctly recognized the primacy of the political branches in the foreign-affairs and national-security contexts.

For these institutional reasons and because "Congress cannot anticipate and legislate with regard to every possible action the President may find it necessary to take or every possible situation in which he might act," it should come as no surprise that "[s]uch failure of Congress . . . does not, 'especially . . . in the areas of foreign policy and national security,' imply 'congressional disapproval' of action taken by the Executive.". . . . Rather, in these domains, the fact that Congress has provided the President with broad authorities does not imply—and the Judicial Branch should not infer—that Congress intended to deprive him of particular powers not specifically enumerated. See *Dames & Moore*, 453 U. S., at 678. As far as the courts are concerned, "the enactment of legislation closely related to the question of the President's authority in a particular case which evinces legislative intent to accord the President broad discretion may be considered to 'invite' 'measures on independent presidential responsibility.'" *Ibid.* (quoting *Youngstown*, 343 U. S., at 637 (Jackson, J., concurring)). . . .

I acknowledge that the question whether Hamdi's executive detention is lawful is a question properly resolved by the Judicial Branch, though the question comes to the Court with the strongest presumptions in favor of the Government. The plurality agrees that Hamdi's detention is lawful if he is an enemy combatant. But the question whether Hamdi is actually an enemy combatant is "of a kind for which the Judiciary has neither aptitude, facilities nor responsibility and which has long been held to belong in the domain of political power not subject to judicial intrusion or inquiry.". . . That is, although it is appropriate for the Court to determine the judicial question whether the President has the asserted authority . . . we lack the information and expertise to question whether Hamdi is actually an enemy combatant, a question the resolution of which is committed to other branches.[1] . . .

II

"The war power of the national government is 'the power to wage war successfully.'". . . The Authorization for Use of Military Force (AUMF), 115 Stat. 224, authorizes the President to "use all necessary and appropriate force against those nations, organizations, or persons he determines planned, authorized, committed, or aided the terrorist attacks" of September 11, 2001. Indeed, the Court has previously concluded that language materially identical to . . .

The plurality, however, qualifies its recognition of the President's authority to detain enemy combatants in the war on terrorism in ways that are at odds with our precedent. . . . [We] are bound by the political branches' determination that the United States is at war. . . . [The] power to detain does not end with the cessation of formal hostilities. . . .

Accordingly, the President's action here is "supported by the strongest of presumptions and the widest latitude of judicial interpretation.". . . The question becomes whether the Federal Government (rather than the President acting alone) has power to detain Hamdi as an enemy combatant. More precisely, we must determine whether the Government may detain Hamdi given the procedures that were used.

III

I agree with the plurality that the Federal Government has power to detain those that the Executive Branch determines to be enemy combatants. See *ante*, at 10. But I do not think that the plurality has adequately explained the breadth of the President's authority to detain enemy combatants, an authority that includes making virtually conclusive factual findings. In my view, the structural considerations discussed above, as recognized in our precedent, demonstrate that we lack the capacity and responsibility to second-guess this determination. . . .

The Court has held that an executive, acting pursuant to statutory and constitutional authority may, consistent with the Due Process Clause, unilaterally decide to detain an individual if the executive deems this necessary for the public safety *even if he is mistaken.*

. . . In *Luther v. Borden,* 7 How. 1 (1849), . . . the Court also addressed the natural concern that placing "this power in the President is dangerous to liberty, and may be abused." The Court noted that "[a]ll power may be abused if placed in unworthy hands," and explained that "it would be difficult . . . to point out any other hands in which this power would be more safe, and at the same time equally effectual." Putting that aside, the Court emphasized that this power "is conferred upon him by the Constitution and laws of the United States, and must therefore be respected and enforced in its judicial tribunals." Finally, the Court explained that if the President abused this power "it would be in the power of Congress to apply the proper remedy. But the courts must administer the law as they find it." *Id.,* at 45. . . .

The Government's asserted authority to detain an individual that the President has determined to be an enemy combatant, at least while hostilities continue, comports with the Due Process Clause. As these cases also show, the Executive's decision that a detention is necessary to protect the public need not and should not be subjected to judicial second-guessing. Indeed, at least in the context of enemy-combatant determinations, this would defeat the unity, secrecy, and dispatch that the Founders believed to be so important to the warmaking function. . . .

Accordingly, I conclude that the Government's detention of Hamdi as an enemy combatant does not violate the Constitution. By detaining Hamdi, the President, in the prosecution of a war and authorized by Congress, has acted well within his authority. Hamdi thereby received all the process to which he was due under the circumstances. I therefore believe that this is no occasion to balance the competing interests, as the plurality unconvincingly attempts to do.

IV

Although I do not agree with the plurality that the balancing approach of *Mathews v. Eldridge,* 424 U. S. 319 (1976), is the appropriate analytical tool with which to analyze this case,[2] I cannot help but explain that the plurality misapplies its chosen framework, one that if applied correctly would probably lead to the result I have reached. . . .

Undeniably, Hamdi has been deprived of a serious interest, one actually protected by the Due Process Clause. Against this, however, is the Government's overriding interest in protecting the Nation. If a deprivation of liberty can be justified by the need to protect a town, the protection of the Nation, *a fortiori*, justifies it.

I acknowledge that under the plurality's approach, it might, at times, be appropriate to give detainees access to counsel and notice of the factual basis for the Government's determination. See *ante*, at 25–27. But properly accounting for the Government's interests also requires concluding that access to counsel and to the factual basis would not always be warranted. . . .

Notes

1. Although I have emphasized national-security concerns, the President's foreign-affairs responsibilities are also squarely implicated by this case. The Government avers that Northern Alliance forces captured Hamdi, and the District Court demanded that the Government turn over information relating to statements made by members of the Northern Alliance. See 316 F. 3d 450, 462 (CA4 2003).
2. Evidently, neither do the parties, who do not cite *Mathews* even once.

POSTSCRIPT

Should U.S. Citizens Who Are Declared to Be "Enemy Combatants" Be Able to Contest Their Detention Before a Judge?

Although the events of September 11th were unique in American history, many of the legal questions they entail are not. In a time of war, how do democracies negotiate the difficult balance between the security of the many and protection of individual liberties? What should be the role of the courts in maintaining this balance? A look back in our own history is instructive.

On April 27, 1861, President Abraham Lincoln first suspended the writ of *habeas corpus,* nearly two weeks after Fort Sumpter fell to Confederate forces. He would do so again two more times before the end of the Civil War, in response to the profound nature of the threat posed to the nation's security by the war. Lambdin Milligan, Indiana lawyer and sympathizer of the Southern cause, was one of several thousand civilians arrested during this period. Sentenced to death for insurrectionary activities by a military commission, Milligan ultimately challenged his conviction before the U.S. Supreme Court. Rendering its decision after the war had come to an end, the Court overturned Milligan's conviction, holding that he had been denied his constitutional rights to a jury trial in a court of law (not the military tribunal that convicted him). Writing for the Court, Justice Davis observed: "During the late wicked Rebellion, the temper of the times did not allow that calmness in deliberation and discussion so necessary to a correct conclusion of a purely judicial question. *Then,* considerations of safety were mingled with the exercise of power; and feelings and interests prevailed which are happily terminated. *Now* that the public safety is assured, this question, as well as all others, can be discussed and decided without passion or the admixture of any element not required to form a legal judgment." (*Ex parte Milligan,* 24 Wall. [71 U.S.] 2, 1866)

Although Justice Davis would concede that constitutional protections of individual rights are "elastic," narrowing in a time of crisis, expanding in a time of calm, he would go on to insist on the absolute necessity for judicial review of executive action, even in time of war. The scope of such judicial review would remain in question. However, in one of the next great crises to confront this nation, World War II, a majority of the Supreme Court would uphold the constitutionality of the forced internment of innocent American citizens of Japanese descent (*Korematsu v. United States,* 323 U.S. 214, 1944). In doing so, the Court articulated the need on the part of the judiciary, in the name of security, to defer to the military and the executive branch in times of

15

national emergency. *Korematsu v. United States* was not a unanimous decision, however, and three justices wrote stinging dissents accusing the majority of sanctioning racism, overlooking a clear violation of citizens' constitutional rights, and shirking the Court's time-honored responsibility to protect U.S. citizens from unjust executive detention. Although never reversed, the *Korematsu* decision was in later years repudiated. In 1980, Congress established a Commission on Wartime Relocation and Internment of Civilians to study the Japanese internment during World War II. In its report, *Personal Justice Denied*, the Commission found that the internment program "was done out of fear," rather than the claimed military necessity, and "inflicted tremendous human cost" without any benefit. In 1993, President Clinton issued a formal apology to Japanese Americans interned during the war, stating that "[i]n retrospect, we understand that the nation's actions were rooted deeply in racial prejudice, wartime hysteria, and a lack of political leadership." Clinton later awarded Fred Korematsu the Presidential Medal of Freedom.

The literature dealing with this issue is enormous. One place to begin is with Michael Ignatieff's *The Lesser Evil: Political Ethics in an Age of Terror* (Princeton University Press, 2004), which provides a rich historical and comparative analysis of the unique problems democracies face when confronted by external military threats. Also valuable is the influential work of Louis Fisher; see *Military Tribunals and Presidential Power* (University Press of Kansas, 2005); and *Presidential War Power* (University Press of Kansas, 2004). In addition, [former] Supreme Court Chief Justice William Rehnquist authored an interesting history of the issue; see *All the Laws but One: Civil Liberties in Wartime* (Vintage, 2000). Finally, the New York City Bar Association's Committee on Federal Courts analyzes the *Hamdi* decision and its implications for U.S. detention policy in its report "The Indefinite Detention of 'Enemy Combatants': Balancing Due Process and National Security in the Context of the War on Terror." March 2004 (updated edition), http://www.abcny.org/pdf/report/IC WL06i.pdf.

ISSUE 2

Does the President Possess Constitutional Authority to Order Wiretaps on U.S. Citizens?

YES: U.S. Department of Justice, from "Legal Authorities Supporting the Activities of the National Security Agency Described by the President" (January 19, 2006)

NO: Letter to Congress, from 14 Law Professors and Former Government Attorneys to Congressional Leaders (January 2, 2006)

ISSUE SUMMARY

YES: The Department of Justice argues that the Constitution gives the president the right to engage in electronic surveillance, with or without congressional approval or judicial oversight. It further claims that the NSA wiretapping program ordered by President Bush does not violate federal law, specifically the Foreign Intelligence Surveillance Act (FISA), because such surveillance falls under the auspices of the military response to the 9/11 attacks that was authorized by Congress.

NO: Several lawyers with expertise in constitutional law or experience in the federal government argue that the NSA wiretapping program violates FISA and the Fourth Amendment of the U.S. Constitution. They further argue that the president does not have any inherent ability either to engage in warrantless wiretapping or to violate federal law that limits such surveillance.

After discovering that President Nixon had used the FBI and other law enforcement mechanisms to spy on political opponents, the Senate voted in 1975 to establish a committee, chaired by Senator Frank Church, to investigate the government's recent intelligence gathering and whether it had involved any "illegal, improper, or unethical activities . . . by any agency of the Federal Government" (S. Res. 21, 1975). The Church Committee found, as many had speculated, that the FBI and CIA had engaged in massive spying on American citizens with little or no judicial oversight.

In issuing its numerous recommendations to Congress for how it should address the abuses that intelligence-gathering agencies had perpetrated, the Church Committee stated that it "believe[d] that there should be no electronic surveillance within the United States which is not subject to a judicial warrant procedure." The Supreme Court largely agreed: By the time of the Church Committee report, it had already ruled that most electronic surveillance, such as wiretapping phone calls, required a warrant. In *United States v. United States District Court* (1972), the majority declared that "Fourth Amendment freedoms cannot properly be guaranteed if domestic security surveillances may be conducted solely within the discretion of the Executive Branch . . . the Government's concerns do not justify departure in this case from the customary Fourth Amendment requirement of judicial approval prior to initiation of a search or surveillance."

However, in its decision in *United States v. U.S. District Court,* the Court was careful to disclaim that it was not passing judgment "on the scope of the President's surveillance power with respect to the activities of *foreign* powers, within or without this country" [emphasis added]. Congress similarly had avoided the subject of "foreign intelligence surveillance" in federal legislation on electronic surveillance. Thus, while there were constitutional and statutory restrictions on how law enforcement could conduct surveillance on criminal suspects and "domestic" national security threats, there were no guidelines on measures that the government undertook in the name of foreign intelligence surveillance.

To address this issue, Congress in 1978 passed the Foreign Intelligence Surveillance Act. FISA established a special court, the Foreign Intelligence Surveillance Court (FISC), that meets in secret to issue warrants for wiretapping and searches that relate to threats from "a foreign power or an agent of a foreign power," including potential acts of "sabotage and international terrorism" (FISA, codified as 50 USC 1801(e)(1)). FISA also established civil and criminal penalties for any government official who "engages in electronic surveillance under color of law except as authorized by statute" (50 USC 1809(a)(1)). Congress believed that in passing FISA and in establishing a method whereby intelligence agencies could obtain warrants secretly and without any public record, it had balanced the Church Committee and the Supreme Court's concerns about civil liberties with the need of those agencies to collect information vital to national security.

In a 2002 presidential order, President Bush authorized the National Security Agency (NSA) to engage in warrantless wiretapping as part of its antiterrorism surveillance. Although, because of the secret nature of the program, its true extent is unknown, the *New York Times,* in breaking the story, reported that the NSA has monitored "the international telephone calls and international e-mail messages of hundreds, perhaps thousands, of people inside the United States." The president has since acknowledged the program's existence, and the Department of Justice released a memorandum, from which the attached "Yes" reading is excerpted, defending the legality of the program. In response, civil libertarians have criticized it as a dangerous invasion of the privacy of ordinary Americans, and many legal scholars, such as those who wrote this issue's "No" reading, have argued that it is both illegal and unconstitutional.

YES ↵   U.S. Department of Justice

Legal Authorities Supporting the Activities of the National Security Agency Described by the President

As the President has explained, since shortly after the attacks of September 11, 2001, he has authorized the National Security Agency ("NSA") to intercept international communications into and out of the United States of persons linked to al Qaeda or related terrorist organizations. The purpose of these intercepts is to establish an early warning system to detect and prevent another catastrophic terrorist attack on the United States. This paper addresses, in an unclassified form, the legal basis for the NSA activities described by the President ("NSA activities"). . . .

In its first legislative response to the terrorist attacks of September 11th, Congress authorized the President to "use all necessary and appropriate force against those nations, organizations, or persons he determines planned, authorized, committed, or aided the terrorist attacks" of September 11th in order to prevent "any future acts of international terrorism against the United States." Authorization for Use of Military Force, Pub. L. No. 107–40, § 2(a), 115 Stat. 224, 224 (Sept. 18, 2001) (reported as a note to 50 U.S.C.A. § 1541) ("AUMF"). History conclusively demonstrates that warrantless communications intelligence targeted at the enemy in time of armed conflict is a traditional and fundamental incident of the use of military force authorized by the AUMF. The Supreme Court's interpretation of the AUMF in *Hamdi v. Rumsfeld*, 542 U.S. 507 (2004), confirms that Congress in the AUMF gave its express approval to the military conflict against al Qaeda and its allies and thereby to the President's use of all traditional and accepted incidents of force in this current military conflict—including warrantless electronic surveillance to intercept enemy communications both at home and abroad. This understanding of the AUMF demonstrates Congress's support for the President's authority to protect the Nation and, at the same time, adheres to Justice O'Connor's admonition that "a state of war is not a blank check for the President," *Hamdi*, 542 U.S. at 536 (plurality opinion), particularly in view of the narrow scope of the NSA activities. . . .

Memorandum released by the U.S. Department of Justice, January 19, 2006.

Background

A. The Attacks of September 11, 2001

On September 14, 2001, the President declared a national emergency "by reason of the terrorist attacks at the World Trade Center, New York, New York, and the Pentagon, and the continuing and immediate threat of further attacks on the United States." Proclamation No. 7463, 66 Fed. Reg. 48,199 (Sept. 14, 2001). The same day, Congress passed a joint resolution authorizing the President "to use all necessary and appropriate force against those nations, organizations, or persons he determines planned, authorized, committed, or aided the terrorist attacks" of September 11th, which the President signed on September 18th. AUMF § 2(a). Congress also expressly acknowledged that the attacks rendered it "necessary and appropriate" for the United States to exercise its right "to protect United States citizens both at home and abroad," and in particular recognized that "the President has authority under the Constitution to take action to deter and prevent acts of international terrorism against the United States." *Id.* pmbl. Congress emphasized that the attacks "continue to pose an unusual and extraordinary threat to the national security and foreign policy of the United States." *Id.* The United States also launched a large-scale military response, both at home and abroad. In the United States, combat air patrols were immediately established over major metropolitan areas and were maintained 24 hours a day until April 2002. The United States also immediately began plans for a military response directed at al Qaeda's base of operations in Afghanistan. Acting under his constitutional authority as Commander in Chief, and with the support of Congress, the President dispatched forces to Afghanistan and, with the assistance of the Northern Alliance, toppled the Taliban regime.

As the President made explicit in his Military Order of November 13, 2001, authorizing the use of military commissions to try terrorists, the attacks of September 11th "created a state of armed conflict." Military Order § l(a), 66 Fed. Reg. 57,833 (Nov. 13, 2001). Indeed, shortly after the attacks, NATO—for the first time in its 46-year history—invoked article 5 of the North Atlantic Treaty, which provides that an "armed attack against one or more of [the parties] shall be considered an attack against them all." . . . The President also determined in his Military Order that al Qaeda and related terrorists organizations "possess both the capability and the intention to undertake further terrorist attacks against the United States that, if not detected and prevented, will cause mass deaths, mass injuries, and massive destruction of property, and may place at risk the continuity of the operations of the United States Government," and concluded that "an extraordinary emergency exists for national defense purposes." Military Order, § l(c), (g), 66 Fed. Reg. at 57,833–34.

B. The NSA Activities

Against this unfolding background of events in the fall of 2001, there was substantial concern that al Qaeda and its allies were preparing to carry out another attack within the United States. Al Qaeda had demonstrated its ability to introduce agents into the United States undetected and to perpetrate devastating attacks, and it was suspected that additional agents were likely already in position within the Nation's borders. As the President has explained, unlike a conventional enemy, al Qaeda has infiltrated "our cities and communities and communicated from here in America to plot and plan with bin Laden's lieutenants in Afghanistan, Pakistan and elsewhere." Press Conference of President Bush (Dec. 19, 2005). . . . To this day, finding al Qaeda sleeper agents in the United States remains one of the paramount concerns in the War on Terror. As the President has explained, "[t]he terrorists want to strike America again, and they hope to inflict even more damage than they did on September the 11th." *Id.*

The President has acknowledged that, to counter this threat, he has authorized the NSA to intercept international communications into and out of the United States of persons linked to al Qaeda or related terrorist organizations. The same day, the Attorney General elaborated and explained that in order to intercept a communication, there must be "a reasonable basis to conclude that one party to the communication is a member of al Qaeda, affiliated with al Qaeda, or a member of an organization affiliated with al Qaeda." Press Briefing by Attorney General Alberto Gonzales and General Michael Hayden, Principal Deputy Director for National Intelligence . . . (Dec. 19, 2005) (statement of Attorney General Gonzales). The purpose of these intercepts is to establish an early warning system to detect and prevent another catastrophic terrorist attack on the United States. The President has stated that the NSA activities "ha[ve] been effective in disrupting the enemy, while safeguarding our civil liberties." President's Press Conference. . . .

Analysis

I. The President Has Inherent Constitutional Authority to Order Warrantless Foreign Intelligence Surveillance

As Congress expressly recognized in the AUMF, "the President has authority under the Constitution to take action to deter and prevent acts of international terrorism against the United States," AUMF pmbl., especially in the context of the current conflict. Article II of the Constitution vests in the President all executive power of the United States, including the power to act as Commander in Chief of the Armed Forces, *see* U.S. Const. art. II, § 2, and authority over the conduct of the Nation's foreign affairs. . . .

To carry out these responsibilities, the President must have authority to gather information necessary for the execution of his office. The Founders, after all, intended the federal Government to be clothed with all authority necessary to protect the Nation. . . . Because of the structural advantages of the Executive Branch, the Founders also intended that the President would have the primary responsibility and necessary authority as Commander in Chief and Chief Executive to protect the Nation and to conduct the Nation's foreign affairs. . . . Thus, it has been long recognized that the President has the authority to use secretive means to collect intelligence necessary for the conduct of foreign affairs and military campaigns. . . .

In reliance on these principles, a consistent understanding has developed that the President has inherent constitutional authority to conduct warrantless searches and surveillance within the United States for foreign intelligence purposes. Wiretaps for such purposes thus have been authorized by Presidents at least since the administration of Franklin Roosevelt in 1940. *See, e.g., United States v. United States District Court,* 444 F.2d 651, 669–71 (6th Cir. 1971) (reproducing as an appendix memoranda from Presidents Roosevelt, Truman, and Johnson). In a Memorandum to Attorney General Jackson, President Roosevelt wrote on May 21, 1940:

> You are, therefore, authorized and directed in such cases as you may approve, after investigation of the need in each case, to authorize the necessary investigation agents that they are at liberty to secure information by listening devices directed to the conversation or other communications of persons suspected of subversive activities against the Government of the United States, including suspected spies. You are requested furthermore to limit these investigations so conducted to a minimum and limit them insofar as possible to aliens.

. . . In *United States v. United States District Court,* 407 U.S. 297 (1972) (the *"Keith"* case), the Supreme Court concluded that the Fourth Amendment's warrant requirement applies to investigations of wholly *domestic* threats to security—such as domestic political violence and other crimes. But the Court in the *Keith* case made clear that it was not addressing the President's authority to conduct *foreign* intelligence surveillance without a warrant and that it was expressly reserving that question: "[T]he instant case requires no judgment on the scope of the President's surveillance power with respect to the activities of foreign powers, within or without this country." *Id.* at 308; *see also id.* at 321–22 & n. 20 ("We have not addressed, and express no opinion as to, the issues which may be involved with respect to activities of foreign powers or their agents."). That *Keith* does not apply in the context of protecting against a foreign attack has been confirmed by the lower courts. After *Keith,* each of the three courts of appeals that have squarely considered the question have concluded—expressly taking the Supreme Court's decision into account—that the President has inherent authority to conduct warrantless surveillance in the foreign intelligence context. *See, e.g., Truong Dinh Hung,* 629 F.2d at 913–14; *Butenko,* 494 F.2d at 603; *Brown,* 484 F.2d 425–26.

From a constitutional standpoint, foreign intelligence surveillance such as the NSA activities differs fundamentally from the domestic security surveillance at issue in *Keith.* As the Fourth Circuit observed, the President has uniquely strong constitutional powers in matters pertaining to foreign affairs and national security. "Perhaps most crucially, the executive branch not only has superior expertise in the area of foreign intelligence, it is also constitutionally designated as the pre-eminent authority in foreign affairs." *Truong,* 629 F.2d at 914. . . .

The present circumstances that support recognition of the President's inherent constitutional authority to conduct the NSA activities are considerably stronger than were the circumstances at issue in the earlier courts of appeals cases that recognized this power. All of the cases described above addressed inherent executive authority under the foreign affairs power to conduct surveillance in a peacetime context. The courts in these cases therefore had no occasion even to consider the fundamental authority of the President, as Commander in Chief, to gather intelligence in the context of an ongoing armed conflict in which the United States already had suffered massive civilian casualties and in which the intelligence gathering efforts at issue were specifically designed to thwart further armed attacks. Indeed, intelligence gathering is particularly important in the current conflict, in which the enemy attacks largely through clandestine activities and which, as Congress recognized, "pose[s] an unusual and extraordinary threat," AUMF pmbl. . . .

II. The AUMF Confirms and Supplements the President's Inherent Power to Use Warrantless Surveillance Against the Enemy in the Current Armed Conflict

In the Authorization for Use of Military Force enacted in the wake of September 11th, Congress confirms and supplements the President's constitutional authority to protect the Nation, including through electronic surveillance, in the context of the current post–September 11th armed conflict with al Qaeda and its allies. The broad language of the AUMF affords the President, at a minimum, discretion to employ the traditional incidents of the use of military force. The history of the President's use of warrantless surveillance during armed conflicts demonstrates that the NSA surveillance described by the President is a fundamental incident of the use of military force that is necessarily included in the AUMF. . . .

The AUMF passed by Congress on September 14, 2001, does not lend itself to a narrow reading. Its expansive language authorizes the President "to use *all necessary and appropriate force* against those nations, organizations, or persons *he determines* planned, authorized, committed, or aided the terrorist attacks that occurred on September 11, 2001." AUMF § 2(a) (emphases added). In the field of foreign affairs, and particularly that of war powers and national security, congressional enactments are to be broadly construed where they indicate support for authority long asserted and exercised by the Executive Branch. . . . Although Congress's war powers under Article I, Section 8 of the Constitution empower Congress to legislate regarding the raising, regulation, and material support of the Armed Forces and related matters, rather than the prosecution of military campaigns, the AUMF indicates Congress's endorsement of the President's use of his constitutional war powers. This authorization transforms the struggle against al Qaeda and related terrorist organizations from what Justice Jackson called "a zone of twilight," in which the President and the Congress may have concurrent powers whose "distribution is uncertain," *Youngstown Sheet & Tube Co. v. Sawyer,* 343 U.S. 579, 637 (1952) (Jackson, J., concurring), into a situation in which the President's authority is at is maximum because "it includes all that he possesses in his own right plus all that Congress can delegate," *id.* at 635. With regard to these fundamental tools of warfare—and, as demonstrated below, warrantless electronic surveillance against the declared enemy is one such tool—the AUMF places the President's authority at its zenith under *Youngstown.* . . .

Warrantless Electronic Surveillance Aimed at Intercepting Enemy
Communications Has Long Been Recognized as a Fundamental
Incident of the Use of Military Force

The history of warfare—including the consistent practice of Presidents since the earliest days of the Republic—demonstrates that warrantless intelligence surveillance against the enemy is a fundamental incident of the use of military force, and this history confirms the statutory authority provided by the AUMF. Electronic surveillance is a fundamental tool of war that must be included in any natural reading of the AUMF's authorization to use "all necessary and appropriate force."

As one author has explained:

> It is *essential* in warfare for a belligerent to be as fully informed as possible about the enemy—his strength, his weaknesses, measures taken by him and measures contemplated by him. This applies not only to military matters, but . . . anything which bears on and is material to his ability to wage the war in which he is engaged. *The laws of war recognize and sanction this aspect of warfare.*

Morris Greenspan, *The Modern Law of Land Warfare* 325 (1959) (emphases added). . . .

In accordance with these well-established principles, the Supreme Court has consistently recognized the President's authority to conduct intelligence activities. *See, e.g., Totten v. United States,* 92 U.S. 105, 106 (1876) (recognizing President's authority to hire spies); *Tenet v. Doe,* 544 U.S. 1 (2005) (reaffirming *Totten* and counseling against judicial interference with such matters); *see also Chicago & S. Air Lines v. Waterman S.S. Corp.,* 333 U.S. 103, 111 (1948) ("The President, both as Commander-in-Chief and as the Nation's organ for foreign affairs, has available intelligence services whose reports neither are not and ought not to be published to the world."); *United States v. Curtiss-Wright Export Corp.,* 299 U.S. 304, 320 (1936) (The President "has his confidential sources of information. He has his agents in the form of diplomatic, consular, and other officials."). Chief Justice John Marshall even described the gathering of intelligence as a military duty. *See Tatum v. Laird,* 444 F.2d 947, 952–53 (D.C. Cir. 1971) ("As Chief Justice John Marshall said of Washington, 'A general must be governed by his intelligence and must regulate his measures by his information. It is his duty to obtain correct information. . . .'") (quoting Foreword, U.S. Army Basic Field Manual, Vol. X, circa 1938), *rev'd on other grounds,* 408 U.S. 1 (1972). . . .

The interception of communications, in particular, has long been accepted as a fundamental method for conducting wartime surveillance. *See, e.g.,* Greenspan, *supra,* at 326 (accepted and customary means for gathering intelligence "include air reconnaissance and photography; ground reconnaissance; observation of enemy positions; *interception of enemy messages, wireless and other;* examination of captured documents; . . . and interrogation of prisoners and civilian inhabitants") (emphasis added). Indeed, since its independence, the United States has intercepted communications for wartime intelligence purposes and, if necessary, has done so within its own borders.

During the Revolutionary War, for example, George Washington received and used to his advantage reports from American intelligence agents on British military strength, British strategic intentions, and British estimates of American strength.

More specifically, warrantless electronic surveillance of wartime communications has been conducted in the United States since electronic communications have existed, *i.e.,* since at least the Civil War, when "[t]elegraph wiretapping was common, and an important intelligence source for both sides." G.J.A. O'Toole, *The Encyclopedia of American Intelligence and Espionage* 498 (1988). Confederate General J.E.B. Stuart even "had his own personal wiretapper travel along with him in the field" to intercept military telegraphic communications. . . .

In light of the long history of prior wartime practice, the NSA activities fit squarely within the sweeping terms of the AUMF. The use of signals intelligence to identify and pinpoint the enemy is a traditional component of wartime military operations—or, to use the terminology of *Hamdi,* a "fundamental and accepted . . . incident to war," 542 U.S. at 518 (plurality opinion)—employed to defeat the enemy and to prevent enemy attacks in the United States. Here, as in other conflicts, the enemy may use public communications networks, and some of the enemy may already be in the United States. Although those factors may be present in this conflict to a greater degree than in the past, neither is novel. Certainly, both factors were well known at the time Congress enacted the AUMF. Wartime interception of international communications made by the enemy thus should be understood, no less than the wartime detention at issue in *Hamdi,* as one of the basic methods of engaging and defeating the enemy that Congress authorized in approving "*all* necessary and appropriate force" that the President would need to defend the Nation. AUMF § 2(a) (emphasis added).

◦◦◦

III. The NSA Activities Are Consistent with the Foreign Intelligence Surveillance Act

The President's exercise of his constitutional authority to conduct warrantless wartime electronic surveillance of the enemy, as confirmed and supplemented by statute in the AUMF, is fully consistent with the requirements of the Foreign Intelligence Surveillance Act ("FISA").[1] FISA is a critically important tool in the War on Terror. The United States makes full use of the authorities available under FISA to gather foreign intelligence information, including authorities to intercept communications, conduct physical searches, and install and use pen registers and trap and trace devices. While FISA establishes certain procedures that must be followed for these authorities to be used (procedures that usually involve applying for and obtaining an order from a special court), FISA also expressly contemplates that a later legislative enactment could authorize electronic surveillance outside the procedures set forth in FISA itself. The AUMF constitutes precisely such an enactment. To the extent there is any ambiguity on this point, the canon of constitutional avoidance requires that such ambiguity be resolved in favor of the President's authority to conduct the communications intelligence activities he has described. Finally, if FISA could not be read to allow the President to authorize the NSA activities during the current congressionally authorized armed conflict with al Qaeda, FISA would be unconstitutional as applied in this narrow context.

A. The Requirements of FISA

FISA was enacted in 1978 to regulate "electronic surveillance," particularly when conducted to obtain "foreign intelligence information," as those terms are defined in section 101 of FISA, 50 U.S.C. § 1801. As a general matter, the statute requires that the Attorney General approve an application for an order from a special court composed of Article III judges and created by FISA—the Foreign Intelligence Surveillance Court ("FISC"). See 50 U.S.C. §§ 1803–1804. The application must demonstrate, among other things, that there is probable cause to believe that the target is a foreign power or an agent of a foreign power. See id. § 1805(a)(3)(A). It must also contain a certification from the Assistant to the President for National Security Affairs or an officer of the United States appointed by the President with the advice and consent of the Senate and having responsibilities in the area of national security or defense that the information sought is foreign intelligence information and cannot reasonably be obtained by normal investigative means. See id. § 1804(a)(7). FISA further requires the Government to state the means that it proposes to use to obtain the information and the basis for its belief that the facilities at which the surveillance will be directed are being used or are about to be used by a foreign power or an agent of a foreign power. See id. § 1804(a)(4), (a)(8).

FISA was the first congressional measure that sought to impose restrictions on the Executive Branch's authority to engage in electronic surveillance for foreign intelligence purposes, an authority that, as noted above, had been repeatedly recognized by the federal courts. . . .

In addition, Congress addressed, to some degree, the manner in which FISA might apply after a formal declaration of war by expressly allowing warrantless surveillance for a period of fifteen days following such a declaration. Section 111 of FISA allows the President to "authorize electronic surveillance without a court order under this subchapter to acquire foreign intelligence information for a period not to exceed fifteen calendar days following a declaration of war by the Congress." 50 U.S.C. § 1811.

The legislative history of FISA shows that Congress understood it was legislating on fragile constitutional ground and was pressing or even exceeding constitutional limits in regulating the President's authority in the field of foreign intelligence. The final House Conference Report, for example, recognized that the statute's restrictions might well impermissibly infringe on the President's constitutional powers. That report includes the extraordinary acknowledgment that "[t]he conferees agree that the establishment by this act of exclusive means by which the President may conduct electronic surveillance does not foreclose a different decision by the Supreme Court." H.R. Conf. Rep. No. 95-1720, at 35, reprinted in 1978 U.S.C.C.A.N. 4048, 4064. But, invoking Justice Jackson's concurrence in the *Steel Seizure* case, the Conference Report explained that Congress intended in FISA to exert whatever power Congress constitutionally had over the subject matter to restrict foreign intelligence surveillance and to leave the President solely with whatever inherent constitutional authority he might be able to invoke against Congress's express wishes. . . .

B. FISA Contemplates and Allows Surveillance Authorized "by Statute"

Congress did not attempt through FISA to prohibit the Executive Branch from using electronic surveillance. Instead, Congress acted to bring the exercise of that power under more stringent congressional control. *See, e.g.,* H. Conf. Rep. No. 95-1720, at 32, *reprinted in* 1978 U.S.C.C.A.N. 4048, 4064. Congress therefore enacted a regime intended to supplant the President's reliance on his own constitutional authority. Consistent with this overriding purpose of bringing the use of electronic surveillance under *congressional* control and with the commonsense notion that the Congress that enacted FISA could not bind future Congresses, FISA expressly contemplates that the Executive Branch may conduct electronic surveillance outside FISA's express procedures if and when a subsequent statute authorizes such surveillance.

Thus, section 109 of FISA prohibits any person from intentionally "engag[ing] . . . in electronic surveillance under color of law *except as authorized by statute.*" 50 U.S.C. § 1809(a)(1) (emphasis added). Because FISA's prohibitory provision broadly exempts surveillance "authorized by statute," the provision demonstrates that Congress did not attempt to regulate through FISA electronic surveillance authorized by Congress through a subsequent enactment. The use of the term "statute" here is significant because it strongly suggests that *any* subsequent authorizing statute, not merely one that amends FISA itself, could legitimately authorize surveillance outside FISA's standard procedural requirements. . . . In enacting FISA, therefore, Congress contemplated the possibility that the President might be permitted to conduct electronic surveillance pursuant to a later-enacted statute that did not incorporate all of the procedural requirements set forth in FISA or that did not expressly amend FISA itself. . . .

C. The AUMF Is a "Statute" Authorizing Surveillance Outside the Confines of FISA

The AUMF qualifies as a "statute" authorizing electronic surveillance within the meaning of section 109 of FISA.

First, because the term "statute" historically has been given broad meaning, the phrase "authorized by statute" in section 109 of FISA must be read to include joint resolutions such as the AUMF. . . .

Second, the longstanding history of communications intelligence as a fundamental incident of the use of force and the Supreme Court's decision in *Hamdi v. Rumsfeld* strongly suggest that the AUMF satisfies the requirement of section 109 of FISA for statutory authorization of electronic surveillance. As explained above, it is not necessary to demarcate the outer limits of the AUMF to conclude that it encompasses electronic surveillance targeted at the enemy. Just as a majority of the Court concluded in *Hamdi* that the AUMF authorizes detention of U.S. citizens who are enemy combatants without expressly mentioning the President's long-recognized power to detain, so too does it authorize the use of electronic surveillance without specifically mentioning the President's equally long-recognized power to engage in communications intelligence targeted at the enemy. . . .

D. The Canon of Constitutional Avoidance Requires Resolving in Favor of the President's Authority any Ambiguity About Whether FISA Forbids the NSA Activities

As explained above, the AUMF fully authorizes the NSA activities. Because FISA contemplates the possibility that subsequent statutes could authorize electronic surveillance without requiring FISA's standard procedures, the NSA activities are also consistent with FISA and related provisions in title 18. Nevertheless, some might argue that sections 109 and 111 of FISA, along with section 2511(2)(f)'s "exclusivity" provision and section 2511(2)(e)'s liability exception for officers engaged in FISA-authorized surveillance, are best read to suggest that FISA requires that subsequent authorizing legislation specifically amend FISA in order to free the Executive from FISA's enumerated procedures. As detailed above, this is not the better reading of FISA. But even if these provisions were ambiguous, any doubt as to whether the AUMF and FISA should be understood to allow the President to make tactical military decisions to authorize surveillance outside the parameters of FISA must be resolved to avoid the serious constitutional questions that a contrary interpretation would raise.

It is well established that the first task of any interpreter faced with a statute that may present an unconstitutional infringement on the powers of the President is to determine whether the statute may be construed to avoid the constitutional difficulty. "[I]f an otherwise acceptable construction of a statute would raise serious constitutional problems, and where an alternative interpretation of the statute is 'fairly possible,' we are obligated to construe the statute to avoid such problems." *INS v. St. Cyr,* 533 U.S. 289, 299–300 (2001) (citations omitted); *Ashwander v. TVA,* 297 U.S. 288, 345–48 (1936) (Brandeis, J., concurring). Moreover, the canon of constitutional avoidance has particular importance in the realm of national security, where the President's constitutional authority is at its highest. . . . Thus, courts and the Executive Branch typically construe a general statute, even one that is written in unqualified terms, to be implicitly limited so as not to infringe on the President's Commander in Chief powers.

Reading FISA to prohibit the NSA activities would raise two serious constitutional questions, both of which must be avoided if possible: (1) whether the signals intelligence collection the President determined was necessary to undertake is such a core exercise of Commander in Chief control over the Armed Forces during armed conflict that Congress cannot interfere with it at all and (2) whether the particular restrictions imposed by FISA are such that their application would impermissibly impede the President's exercise of his constitutionally assigned duties as Commander in Chief. Constitutional avoidance principles require interpreting FISA, at least in the context of the military conflict authorized by the AUMF, to avoid these questions, if "fairly possible." Even if Congress intended FISA to use the full extent of its constitutional authority to "occupy the field" of "electronic surveillance," as FISA used that term, during peacetime, the legislative history indicates that Congress had not reached a definitive conclusion about its regulation during wartime. *See* H.R. Conf. Rep. No. 95-1720, at 34, *reprinted in* 1978 U.S.C.C.A.N. at 4063 (noting that the purpose of the fifteen-day period following a declaration of war in section 111 of FISA was to "allow time for consideration of any amendment to this act that may be appropriate during a wartime emergency"). Therefore, it is not clear that Congress, in fact, intended to test the limits of its constitutional authority in the context of wartime electronic surveillance.

Whether Congress may interfere with the President's constitutional authority to collect foreign intelligence information through interception of communications reasonably believed to be linked to the enemy poses a difficult constitutional question. As explained in Part I, it had long been accepted at the time of FISA's enactment that the President has inherent constitutional authority to conduct warrantless electronic surveillance for foreign intelligence purposes. Congress recognized at the time that the enactment of a statute purporting to eliminate the President's ability, even during peacetime, to conduct warrantless electronic surveillance to collect foreign intelligence was near or perhaps beyond the limit of Congress's Article I powers. The NSA activities, however, involve signals intelligence performed in the midst of a congressionally authorized armed conflict undertaken to prevent further hostile attacks on the United States. The NSA activities lie at the very core of the Commander in Chief power, especially in light of the AUMF's explicit authorization for the President to take *all* necessary and appropriate military action to stop al Qaeda from striking again. The constitutional principles at stake here thus involve not merely the President's well-established inherent authority to conduct warrantless surveillance for foreign intelligence purposes during peacetime, but also the powers and duties expressly conferred on him as Commander in Chief by Article II. . . .

IV. The NSA Activities Are Consistent with the Fourth Amendment

The Fourth Amendment prohibits "unreasonable searches and seizures" and directs that "no Warrants shall issue, but upon probable cause, supported by Oath or affirmation, and particularly describing the place to be searched, and the persons or things to be seized." U.S. Const. amend. IV. The touchstone for review of government action under the Fourth Amendment is whether the search is "reasonable." *See, e.g., Vernonia Sch. Dist. v. Acton,* 515 U.S. 646, 653 (1995).

As noted above, . . . all of the federal courts of appeals to have addressed the issue have affirmed the President's inherent constitutional authority to collect foreign intelligence without a warrant. *See In re Sealed Case,* 310 F.3d at 742. Properly understood, foreign intelligence collection in general, and the NSA activities in particular, fit within the "special needs" exception to the warrant requirement of the Fourth Amendment. Accordingly, the mere fact that no warrant is secured prior to the surveillance at issue in the NSA activities does not suffice to render the activities unreasonable. Instead, reasonableness in this context must be assessed under a general balancing approach, "'by assessing, on the one hand, the degree to which it intrudes upon an individual's privacy and, on the other, the degree to which it is needed for the promotion of legitimate governmental interests.'" *United States v. Knights,* 534 U.S. 112, 118–19 (2001) (quoting *Wyoming v. Houghton,* 526 U.S. 295, 300 (1999)). The NSA activities are reasonable because the Government's interest, defending the Nation from another foreign attack in time of armed conflict, outweighs the individual privacy interests at stake, and because they seek to intercept only international communications where one party is linked to al Qaeda or an affiliated terrorist organization.

A. The Warrant Requirement of the Fourth Amendment
Does Not Apply to the NSA Activities
In "the criminal context," the Fourth Amendment reasonableness requirement "usually requires a showing of probable cause" and a warrant. *Board of Educ. v. Earls,* 536 U.S. 822, 828 (2002). The requirement of a warrant supported by probable cause, however, is not universal. Rather, the Fourth Amendment's "central requirement is one of reasonableness," and the rules the Court has developed to implement that requirement "[s]ometimes . . . require warrants." *Illinois v. McArthur,* 531 U.S. 326, 330 (2001). . . .

In particular, the Supreme Court repeatedly has made clear that in situations involving "special needs" that go beyond a routine interest in law enforcement, the warrant requirement is inapplicable. . . . It is difficult to encapsulate in a nutshell all of the different circumstances the Court has found to qualify as "special needs" justifying warrantless searches. But one application in which the Court has found the warrant requirement inapplicable is in circumstances in which the Government faces an increased need to be able to react swiftly and flexibly, or when there are at stake interests in public safety beyond the interests in ordinary law enforcement. One important factor in establishing "special needs" is whether the Government is responding to an emergency that goes beyond the need for general crime control. . . .

Thus, the Court has permitted warrantless searches of property of students in public schools, *see New Jersey v. T.L.O.,* 469 U.S. 325, 340 (1985) (noting that warrant requirement would "unduly interfere with the maintenance of the swift and informal disciplinary procedures needed in the schools"), to screen athletes and students involved in extracurricular activities at public schools for drug use, *see Vernonia,* 515 U.S. at 654–55; *Earls,* 536 U.S. at 829–38, to conduct drug testing of railroad personnel involved in train accidents, *see Skinner v. Railway Labor Executives' Ass'n,* 489 U.S. 602, 634 (1989), and to search probationers' homes, *see Griffin,* 483 U.S. 868. Many special needs doctrine and related cases have upheld *suspicionless* searches or seizures. *See, e.g., Illinois v. Lidster,* 540 U.S. 419, 427 (2004) (implicitly relying on special needs doctrine to uphold use of automobile checkpoint to obtain information about recent hit-and-run accident); *Earls,* 536 U.S. at 829–38 (suspicionless drug testing of public school students involved in extracurricular activities); *Michigan Dep't of State Police v. Sitz*, 496 U.S. 444, 449–55 (1990) (road block to check all motorists for signs of drunken driving); *United States v. Martinez-Fuerte*, 428 U.S. 543 (1976) (road block near the border to check vehicles for illegal immigrants); *cf. In re Sealed Case*, 310 F.3d at 745–46 (noting that suspicionless searches and seizures in one sense are a greater encroachment on privacy than electronic surveillance under FISA because they are not based on any particular suspicion, but "[o]n the other hand, wiretapping is a good deal more intrusive than an automobile stop accompanied by questioning"). To fall within the "special needs" exception to the warrant requirement, the purpose of the search must be distinguishable from ordinary general crime control. *See, e.g., Ferguson v. Charleston*, 532 U.S. 67 (2001); *City of Indianapolis v. Edmond*, 531 U.S. 32, 41 (2000).

Foreign intelligence collection, especially in the midst of an armed conflict in which the adversary has already launched catastrophic attacks within the United States, fits squarely within the area of "special needs, beyond the normal need for law enforcement" where the Fourth Amendment's touchstone of reasonableness can be satisfied without resort to a warrant. *Vernonia*, 515 U.S. at 653. The Executive Branch has long maintained that collecting foreign intelligence is far removed from the ordinary criminal law enforcement action to which the warrant requirement is particularly suited. . . .

In particular, the NSA activities are undertaken to prevent further devastating attacks on our Nation, and they serve the highest government purpose through means other than traditional law enforcement. The NSA activities are designed to enable the Government to act quickly and flexibly (and with secrecy) to find agents of al Qaeda and its affiliates—an international terrorist group which has already demonstrated a capability to infiltrate American communities without being detected—in time to disrupt future terrorist attacks against the United States. As explained by the Foreign Intelligence Surveillance Court of Review, the nature of the "emergency" posed by al Qaeda "takes the matter out of the realm of ordinary crime control." *In re Sealed Case*, 310 F.3d at 746. Thus, under the "special needs" doctrine, no warrant is required by the Fourth Amendment for the NSA activities.

B. The NSA Activities Are Reasonable

As the Supreme Court has emphasized repeatedly, "[t]he touchstone of the Fourth Amendment is reasonableness, and the reasonableness of a search is determined by assessing, on the one hand, the degree to which it intrudes upon an individual's privacy and, on the other, the degree to which it is needed for the promotion of legitimate governmental interests." . . . Under the standard balancing of interests analysis used for gauging reasonableness, the NSA activities are consistent with the Fourth Amendment.

With respect to the individual privacy interests at stake, there can be no doubt that, as a general matter, interception of telephone communications implicates a significant privacy interest of the individual whose conversation is intercepted. The Supreme Court has made clear at least since *Katz v. United States*, 389 U.S. 347 (1967), that individuals have a substantial and constitutionally protected reasonable expectation of privacy that their telephone conversations will not be subject to governmental eavesdropping. Although the individual privacy interests at stake may be substantial, it is well recognized that a variety of governmental interests—including routine law enforcement and foreign-intelligence gathering—can overcome those interests.

On the other side of the scale here, the Government's interest in engaging in the NSA activities is the most compelling interest possible—securing the Nation from foreign attack in the midst of an armed conflict. One attack already has taken thousands of lives and placed the Nation in state of armed conflict. Defending the Nation from attack is perhaps the most important function of the federal Government—and one of the few express obligations of the federal Government enshrined in the Constitution. *See* U.S. Const. art. IV, § 4 ("The United States shall guarantee to every State in this Union a Republican Form of Government, *and shall protect each of them against Invasion* . . . .") (emphasis added); *The Prize Cases,* 67 U.S. (2 Black) 635, 668 (1863) ("If war be made by invasion of a foreign nation, the President is not only authorized but bound to resist force by force."). As the Supreme Court has declared, "[i]t is 'obvious and unarguable' that no governmental interest is more compelling than the security of the Nation." *Haig v. Agee,* 453 U.S. 280, 307 (1981).

The Government's overwhelming interest in detecting and thwarting further al Qaeda attacks is easily sufficient to make reasonable the intrusion into privacy involved in intercepting one-end foreign communications where there is "a reasonable basis to conclude that one party to the communication is a member of al Qaeda, affiliated with al Qaeda, or a member of an organization affiliated with al Qaeda." . . .

Conclusion

For the foregoing reasons, the President—in light of the broad authority to use military force in response to the attacks of September 11th and to prevent further catastrophic attack expressly conferred on the President by the Constitution and confirmed and supplemented by Congress in the AUMF—has legal authority to authorize the NSA to conduct the signals intelligence activities he has described. Those activities are authorized by the Constitution and by statute, and they violate neither FISA nor the Fourth Amendment.

Note

1. To avoid revealing details about the operation of the program, it is assumed for purposes of this paper that the activities described by the President constitute "electronic surveillance," as defined by FISA, 50 U.S.C. § 1801(f).

Letter to Congress from 14 Law Professors and Former Government Attorneys to Congressional Leaders

Dear Members of Congress:

We are scholars of constitutional law and former government officials. We write in our individual capacities as citizens concerned by the Bush Administration's National Security Agency domestic spying program, as reported in the New York Times, and in particular to respond to the Justice Department's December 22, 2005, letter to the majority and minority leaders of the House and Senate Intelligence Committees setting forth the administration's defense of the program. Although the program's secrecy prevents us from being privy to all of its details, the Justice Department's defense of what it concedes was secret and warrantless electronic surveillance of persons within the United States fails to identify any plausible legal authority for such surveillance. Accordingly the program appears on its face to violate existing law.

The basic legal question here is not new. In 1978, after an extensive investigation of the privacy violations associated with foreign intelligence surveillance programs, Congress and the President enacted the Foreign Intelligence Surveillance Act (FISA). Pub. L. 95–511, 92 Stat. 1783. FISA comprehensively regulates electronic surveillance within the United States, striking a careful balance between protecting civil liberties and preserving the "vitally important government purpose" of obtaining valuable intelligence in order to safeguard national security. S. Rep. No. 95-604, pt. 1, at 9 (1977).

With minor exceptions, FISA authorizes electronic surveillance only upon certain specified showings, and only if approved by a court. The statute specifically allows for warrantless *wartime* domestic electronic surveillance— but only for the first fifteen days of a war. 50 U.S.C. § 1811. It makes criminal any electronic surveillance not authorized by statute, *id.* § 1809; and it expressly establishes FISA and specified provisions of the federal criminal code (which govern wiretaps for criminal investigation) as the "*exclusive* means by which electronic surveillance . . . may be conducted," 18 U.S.C. § 2511(2)(f) (emphasis added).[1]

The Department of Justice (DOJ) concedes that the NSA program was not authorized by any of the above provisions. It maintains, however, that the program did not violate existing law because Congress implicitly authorized

Letter to Congress from 14 Law Professors and Former Government Attorneys to Congressional Leaders (January 2, 2006).

the NSA program when it enacted the Authorization for Use of Military Force (AUMF) against al Qaeda, Pub. L. No. 107–40, 115 Stat. 224 (2001). But the AUMF cannot reasonably be construed to implicitly authorize warrantless electronic surveillance in the United States during wartime, where Congress has expressly and specifically addressed that precise question in FISA and limited any such warrantless surveillance to the first fifteen days of war.

The DOJ also invokes the President's inherent constitutional authority as Commander in Chief to collect "signals intelligence" targeted at the enemy, and maintains that construing FISA to prohibit the President's actions would raise constitutional questions. But even conceding that the President in his role as Commander in Chief may generally collect signals intelligence on the enemy abroad, Congress indisputably has authority to regulate electronic surveillance within the United States, as it has done in FISA. Where Congress has so regulated, the President can act in contravention of statute only if his authority is *exclusive,* and not subject to the check of statutory regulation. The DOJ letter pointedly does not make that extraordinary claim.

Moreover, to construe the AUMF as the DOJ suggests would itself raise serious constitutional questions under the Fourth Amendment. The Supreme Court has never upheld warrantless wiretapping within the United States. Accordingly, the principle that statutes should be construed to avoid serious constitutional questions provides an additional reason for concluding that the AUMF does not authorize the President's actions here.

I. Congress Did Not Implicitly Authorize the NSA Domestic Spying Program in the AUMF, and in Fact Expressly Prohibited It in FISA

The DOJ concedes . . . that the NSA program involves "electronic surveillance," which is defined in FISA to mean the interception of the *contents* of telephone, wire, or email communications that occur, at least in part, in the United States. 50 U.S.C. §§ 1801(f)(1)–(2), 1801(n). NSA engages in such surveillance without judicial approval, and apparently without the substantive showings that FISA requires—e.g., that the subject is an "agent of a foreign power." *Id.* § 1805(a). The DOJ does not argue that FISA itself authorizes such electronic surveillance; and, as the DOJ letter acknowledges, 18 U.S.C. § 1809 makes criminal any electronic surveillance not authorized by statute.

The DOJ nevertheless contends that the surveillance is authorized by the AUMF, signed on September 18, 2001, which empowers the President to use "all necessary and appropriate force against" al Qaeda. According to the DOJ, collecting "signals intelligence" on the enemy, even if it involves tapping U.S. phones without court approval or probable cause, is a "fundamental incident of war" authorized by the AUMF. This argument fails for four reasons.

First, and most importantly, the DOJ's argument rests on an unstated general "implication" from the AUMF that directly contradicts *express* and *specific* language in FISA. Specific and "carefully drawn" statutes prevail over general statutes where there is a conflict. *Morales v. TWA, Inc.,* 504 U.S. 374,

384–85 (1992) (quoting *International Paper Co. v. Ouelette,* 479 U.S. 481, 494 (1987)). In FISA, Congress has directly and specifically spoken on the question of domestic warrantless wiretapping, including during wartime, and it could not have spoken more clearly.

As noted above, Congress has comprehensively regulated all electronic surveillance in the United States, and authorizes such surveillance only pursuant to specific statutes designated as the *"exclusive* means by which electronic surveillance . . . and the interception of domestic wire, oral, and electronic communications may be conducted." 18 U.S.C. § 2511(2)(f) (emphasis added). Moreover, FISA *specifically* addresses the question of domestic wiretapping during wartime. In a provision entitled "Authorization during time of war," FISA dictates that "[n]otwithstanding any other law, the President, through the Attorney General, may authorize electronic surveillance without a court order under this subchapter to acquire foreign intelligence information *for a period not to exceed fifteen calendar days following a declaration of war by the Congress."* 50 U.S.C. § 1811 (emphasis added). Thus, even where Congress has declared war—a more formal step than an authorization such as the AUMF—the law limits warrantless wiretapping to the first fifteen days of the conflict. Congress explained that if the President needed further warrantless surveillance during wartime, the fifteen days would be sufficient for Congress to consider and enact further authorization.[2] Rather than follow this course, the President acted unilaterally and secretly in contravention of FISA's terms. The DOJ letter remarkably does not even *mention* FISA's fifteen-day war provision, which directly refutes the President's asserted "implied" authority. . . .

Second, the DOJ's argument would require the conclusion that Congress implicitly and *sub silentio* repealed 18 U.S.C. § 2511(2)(f), the provision that identifies FISA and specific criminal code provisions as "the *exclusive* means by which electronic surveillance . . . may be conducted." Repeals by implication are strongly disfavored; they can be established only by "overwhelming evidence," *J.E.M. Ag. Supply, Inc. v. Pioneer Hi-Bred Int'l, Inc.,* 534 U.S. 124, 137 (2001), and "'the only permissible justification for a repeal by implication is when the earlier and later statutes are irreconcilable,'" *id.* at 141–142 (quoting *Morton v. Mancari,* 417 U.S. 535, 550 (1974)). The AUMF and § 2511(2)(f) are not irreconcilable, and there is *no* evidence, let alone overwhelming evidence, that Congress intended to repeal § 2511(2)(f).

Third, Attorney General Alberto Gonzales has admitted that the administration did not seek to amend FISA to authorize the NSA spying program because it was advised that Congress would reject such an amendment.[3] The administration cannot argue on the one hand that Congress authorized the NSA program in the AUMF, and at the same time that it did not ask Congress for such authorization because it feared Congress would say no.[4]

Finally, the DOJ's reliance upon *Hamdi v. Rumsfeld,* 542 U.S. 507 (2004), to support its reading of the AUMF, . . . is misplaced. A plurality of the Court in *Hamdi* held that the AUMF authorized military detention of enemy combatants captured on the battlefield abroad as a "fundamental incident of waging war." *Id.* at 519. The plurality expressly limited this holding to individuals who were "part of or supporting forces hostile to the United States or coalition partners *in Afghanistan and who engaged in an armed conflict against the United States there." Id.* at 516 (emphasis added). It is one thing, however, to say that foreign battlefield capture of enemy combatants is an incident of waging war that Congress intended to authorize. It is another matter entirely to treat unchecked warrantless *domestic* spying as included in that authorization, especially where an existing statute specifies that other laws are the "exclusive means" by which electronic surveillance may be conducted and provides that even a declaration of war authorizes such spying only for a fifteen-day emergency period.

II. Construing FISA to Prohibit Warrantless Domestic Wiretapping Does Not Raise Any Serious Constitutional Question, Whereas Construing the AUMF to Authorize Such Wiretapping Would Raise Serious Questions Under the Fourth Amendment

The DOJ argues that FISA and the AUMF should be construed to permit the NSA program's domestic surveillance because otherwise there might be a "conflict between FISA and the President's Article II authority as Commander-in-Chief." DOJ Letter at 4. The statutory scheme described above is not ambiguous, and therefore the constitutional avoidance doctrine is not even implicated. *See United States v. Oakland Cannabis Buyers' Coop.*, 532 U.S. 483, 494 (2001) (the "canon of constitutional avoidance has no application in the absence of statutory ambiguity"). But were it implicated, it would work against the President, not in his favor. Construing FISA and the AUMF according to their plain meanings raises no serious constitutional questions regarding the President's duties under Article II. Construing the AUMF to *permit* unchecked warrantless wiretapping without probable cause, however, would raise serious questions under the Fourth Amendment.

A. FISA's Limitations Are Consistent with the President's Article II Role

We do not dispute that, absent congressional action, the President might have inherent constitutional authority to collect "signals intelligence" about the enemy abroad. Nor do we dispute that, had Congress taken no action in this area, the President might well be constitutionally empowered to conduct domestic surveillance directly tied and narrowly confined to that goal—subject, of course, to Fourth Amendment limits. Indeed, in the years before FISA was enacted, the federal law involving wiretapping specifically provided that "[n]othing contained in this chapter or in section 605 of the Communications Act of 1934 shall limit the constitutional power of the President . . . to obtain foreign intelligence information deemed essential to the security of the United States." 18 U.S.C. § 2511(3) (1976).

But FISA specifically *repealed* that provision. FISA § 201(c), 92 Stat. 1797, and replaced it with language dictating that FISA and the criminal code are the "exclusive means" of conducting electronic surveillance. In doing so, Congress did not deny that the President has constitutional power to conduct electronic surveillance for national security purposes; rather, Congress properly concluded that "even if the President has the inherent authority *in the absence of legislation* to authorize warrantless electronic surveillance for foreign intelligence purposes, Congress has the power to regulate the conduct of such surveillance by legislating a reasonable procedure, which then becomes the exclusive means by which such surveillance may be conducted." H.R. Rep. No. 95-1283, pt. 1, at 24 (1978) (emphasis added). This analysis, Congress noted, was "supported by two successive Attorneys General." *Id.*

To say that the President has inherent authority does not mean that his authority is exclusive, or that his conduct is not subject to statutory regulations enacted (as FISA was) pursuant to Congress's Article I powers. As Justice Jackson famously explained in his influential opinion in *Youngstown Sheet & Tube Co. v. Sawyer,* 343 U.S. at 635 (Jackson, J., concurring), the Constitution "enjoins upon its branches separateness but interdependence, autonomy but reciprocity. Presidential powers are not fixed but fluctuate, depending upon their disjunction or conjunction with those of Congress." For example, the President in his role as Commander in Chief directs military operations. But the Framers gave Congress the power to prescribe rules for the regulation of the armed and naval forces, Art. I, § 8, cl. 14, and if a duly enacted statute prohibits the military from engaging in torture or cruel, inhuman, and degrading treatment, the President must follow that dictate. As Justice Jackson wrote, when the President acts in defiance of "the expressed or implied will of Congress," his power is "at its lowest ebb." 343 U.S. at 637. In this setting, Jackson wrote, "Presidential power [is] most vulnerable to attack and in the least favorable of possible constitutional postures." *Id.* at 640.

Congress plainly has authority to regulate domestic wiretapping by federal agencies under its Article I powers, and the DOJ does not suggest otherwise. Indeed, when FISA was enacted, the Justice Department agreed that Congress had power to regulate such conduct, and could require judicial approval of foreign intelligence surveillance. FISA does not prohibit foreign intelligence surveillance, but merely imposes reasonable regulation to protect legitimate privacy rights. (For example, although FISA generally requires judicial approval for electronic surveillance of persons within the United States, it permits the executive branch to install a wiretap immediately so long as it obtains judicial approval within 72 hours. 50 U.S.C. § 1805(f).)

Just as the President is bound by the statutory prohibition on torture, he is bound by the statutory dictates of FISA. The DOJ once infamously argued that the President as Commander in Chief could ignore even the criminal prohibition on torture,[5] and, more broadly still, that statutes may not "place *any* limits on the President's determinations as to any terrorist threat, the amount of military force to be used in response, or the method, timing, and nature of the response."[6] But the administration withdrew the August 2002 torture memo after it was disclosed, and for good reason the DOJ does not advance these extreme arguments here. Absent a serious question about FISA's constitutionality, there is no reason even to consider construing the AUMF to have implicitly overturned the carefully designed regulatory regime that FISA establishes. *See, e.g., Reno v. Flores,* 507 U.S. 292, 314 n.9 (1993) (constitutional avoidance canon applicable only if the constitutional question to be avoided is a serious one, "not to eliminate all possible contentions that the statute *might* be unconstitutional") (emphasis in original; citation omitted).[7]

B. Construing the AUMF to Authorize Warrantless Domestic Wiretapping Would Raise Serious Constitutional Questions

The principle that ambiguous statutes should be construed to avoid serious constitutional questions works against the administration, not in its favor. Interpreting the AUMF and FISA to permit unchecked domestic wiretapping for the duration of the conflict with al Qaeda would certainly raise serious constitutional questions. The Supreme Court has never upheld such a sweeping power to invade the privacy of Americans at home without individualized suspicion or judicial oversight.

The NSA surveillance program permits wiretapping within the United States without *either* of the safeguards presumptively required by the Fourth Amendment for electronic surveillance—individualized probable cause and a warrant or other order issued by a judge or magistrate. The Court has long held that wiretaps generally require a warrant and probable cause. *Katz v. United States,* 389 U.S. 347 (1967). And the only time the Court considered the question of national security wiretaps, it held that the Fourth Amendment prohibits domestic security wiretaps without those safeguards. *United States v. United States Dist. Court,* 407 U.S. 297 (1972). Although the Court in that case left open the question of the Fourth Amendment validity of warrantless wiretaps for foreign intelligence purposes, its precedents raise serious constitutional questions about the kind of open-ended authority the President has asserted with respect to the NSA program. *See id.* at 316–18 (explaining difficulty of guaranteeing Fourth Amendment freedoms if domestic surveillance can be conducted solely in the discretion of the executive branch).

Indeed, serious Fourth Amendment questions about the validity of warrantless wiretapping led Congress to enact FISA, in order to "provide the secure framework by which the executive branch may conduct legitimate electronic surveillance for foreign intelligence purposes within the context of this nation's commitment to privacy and individual rights." S. Rep. No. 95-604, pt. 1, at 15 (1977) (citing, *inter alia, Zweibon v. Mitchell,* 516 F.2d 594 (D.C. Cir. 1975), in which "the court of appeals held that a warrant must be obtained before a wiretap is installed on a domestic organization that is neither the agent of, nor acting in collaboration with, a foreign power").

Relying on *In re Sealed Case No. 02-001,* the DOJ argues that the NSA program falls within an exception to the warrant and probable cause requirement for reasonable searches that serve "special needs" above and beyond ordinary law enforcement. But the existence of "special needs" has never been found to permit warrantless wiretapping. "Special needs" generally excuse the warrant and individualized suspicion requirements only where those requirements are impracticable and the intrusion on privacy is minimal. . . . Wiretapping is not a minimal intrusion on privacy, and the experience of FISA shows that foreign intelligence surveillance can be carried out through warrants based on individualized suspicion.

The court in *Sealed Case* upheld FISA itself, which requires warrants issued by Article III federal judges upon an individualized showing of probable cause that the subject is an "agent of a foreign power." The NSA domestic spying program, by contrast, includes none of these safeguards. It does not require individualized judicial approval, and it does not require a showing that the target is an "agent of a foreign power." According to Attorney General Gonzales, the NSA may wiretap any person in the United States who so much as receives a communication from anyone abroad, if the administration deems either of the parties to be affiliated with al Qaeda, a member of an organization affiliated with al Qaeda, "working in support of al Qaeda," or "part of" an organization or group "that is supportive of al Qaeda." Under this reasoning, a U.S. citizen living here who received a phone call from another U.S. citizen who attends a mosque that the administration believes is "supportive" of al Qaeda could be wiretapped without a warrant. The absence of meaningful safeguards on the NSA program at a minimum raises serious questions about the validity of the program under the Fourth Amendment, and therefore supports an interpretation of the AUMF that does not undercut FISA's regulation of such conduct.

∼◎∼

In conclusion, the DOJ letter fails to offer a plausible legal defense of the NSA domestic spying program. If the Administration felt that FISA was insufficient, the proper course was to seek legislative amendment, as it did with other aspects of FISA in the Patriot Act, and as Congress expressly contemplated when it enacted the wartime wiretap provision in FISA. One of the crucial features of a constitutional democracy is that it is always open to the President— or anyone else—to seek to change the law. But it is also beyond dispute that, in such a democracy, the President cannot simply violate criminal laws behind closed doors because he deems them obsolete or impracticable.[8]

We hope you find these views helpful to your consideration of the legality of the NSA domestic spying program.

Notes

1. More detail about the operation of FISA can be found in Congressional Research Service, "Presidential Authority to Conduct Warrantless Electronic Surveillance to Gather Foreign Intelligence Information" (Jan. 5, 2006). This letter was drafted prior to release of the CRS Report, which corroborates the conclusions drawn here.

2. "The Conferees intend that this [15-day] period will allow time for consideration of any amendment to this act that may be appropriate during

a wartime emergency. . . . The conferees expect that such amendment would be reported with recommendations within 7 days and that each House would vote on the amendment within 7 days thereafter." H.R. Conf. Rep. No. 95-1720, at 34 (1978).

3. Attorney General Gonzales stated, "We have had discussions with Congress in the past—certain members of Congress—as to whether or not FISA could be amended to allow us to adequately deal with this kind of threat, and we were advised that that would be difficult, if not impossible." Press Briefing by Attorney General Alberto Gonzales and General Michael Hayden, Principal Deputy Director for National Intelligence (Dec. 19, 2005). . . .

4. The administration had a convenient vehicle for seeking any such amendment in the USA PATRIOT Act of 2001, Pub. L. No. 107–56, 115 Stat. 272, enacted in October 2001. The Patriot Act amended FISA in several respects, including in sections 218 (allowing FISA wiretaps in criminal investigations) and 215 (popularly known as the "libraries provision"). Yet the administration did not ask Congress to amend FISA to authorize the warrantless electronic surveillance at issue here.

5. *See* Memorandum from Jay S. Bybee, Assistant Attorney General, Department of Justice Office of Legal Counsel, to Alberto R. Gonzales, Counsel to the President, Re: *Standards of Conduct for Interrogation under 18 U.S.C. §§ 2340-2340A* (Aug. 1, 2002), at 31.

6. Memorandum from John C. Yoo, Deputy Assistant Attorney General, Office of Legal Counsel, to the Deputy Counsel to the President, Re: *The President's Constitutional Authority to Conduct Military Operations against Terrorists and Nations Supporting Them* (Sept. 25, 2001) . . . (emphasis added).

7. Three years ago, the FISA Court of Review suggested in dictum that Congress cannot "encroach on the President's constitutional power" to conduct foreign intelligence surveillance. *In re Sealed Case No. 02-001,* 310 F.3d 717, 742 (FIS Ct. Rev. 2002) (per curiam). The FISA Court of Review, however, did not hold that FISA was unconstitutional, nor has any other court suggested that FISA's modest regulations constitute an impermissible encroachment on presidential authority. The FISA Court of Review relied upon *United States v. Truong Dihn Hung,* 629 F.2d 908 (4th Cir. 1980)—but that court did not suggest that the President's powers were beyond congressional control. To the contrary, the *Truong* court indicated that FISA's restrictions *were* constitutional. *See* 629 F.2d at 915 n.4 (noting that "the imposition of a warrant requirement, beyond the constitutional minimum described in this opinion, *should be left to the intricate balancing performed in the course of the legislative process by Congress and the President"*) (emphasis added).

8. During consideration of FISA, the House of Representatives noted that "the decision as to the standards governing when and how foreign intelligence electronic surveillance should be conducted is and should be a political decision, in the best sense of the term, because it involves the weighing of important public policy concerns—civil liberties and national security. Such a political decision is one properly made by the political branches of Government together, not adopted by one branch on its own and with no regard for the other. Under our Constitution legislation is the embodiment of just such political decisions." H. Rep.

95-1283, pt. I, at 21–22. Attorney General Griffin Bell supported FISA in part because "no matter how well intentioned or ingenious the persons in the Executive branch who formulate these measures, the crucible of the legislative process will ensure that the procedures will be affirmed by that branch of government which is more directly responsible to the electorate." Foreign Intelligence Surveillance Act of 1978: Hearings Before the Subcomm. on Intelligence and the Rights of Americans of the Senate Select Comm. on Intelligence, 95th Cong., 2d Sess. 12 (1977).

POSTSCRIPT

Does the President Possess Constitutional Authority to Order Wiretaps on U.S. Citizens?

While the Bush administration claimed to have stopped the NSA wiretapping program in 2007, the controversy over the constitutionality of the government's surveillance programs has continued, even into the new Obama Administration. When the NSA program was first disclosed in 2005, critics—such as the law professors who wrote the "NO" reading in this chapter—made two separate claims as to why the president could not legally engage in warrantless wiretapping: first, it violated Fourth Amendment prohibitions against "unreasonable search and seizure," which is generally interpreted to require warrants for surveillance on Americans within the United States, and second, it violated the framework set up by Congress in FISA to regulate foreign-intelligence wiretapping. The latter issue has largely become moot because of changes to FISA. In 2007 and 2008, Congress amended FISA to loosen the warrant requirement. The changed law allows the government to engage in some forms of warrantless wiretapping that could lead it to listen in to the conversations of Americans within the United States, as long as it does not *intentionally* target domestic conversations for warrantless wiretapping. If the government intends to wiretap conversations involving someone within the United States, or has good reason to believe one of the speakers is within the United States, it is still required to obtain a warrant from the Foreign Intelligence Surveillance Court (FISC).

With FISA no longer providing strict limits on the government's ability to wiretap without warrants, the primary legal challenges to the government's surveillance programs have shifted to the constitutional issues, including whether the FISA amendments themselves violate the Fourth Amendment by sanctioning domestic warrantless wiretapping. As mentioned in the readings in this chapter, one court, the Foreign Intelligence Surveillance Court of Review (FISCR), an appeals court set up under FISA to hear challenges to FISC decisions, has previously held that domestic foreign-intelligence surveillance falls under one of the limited exceptions that the courts have carved out to the general Fourth Amendment warrant requirement (see *In re Sealed Case No. 02-001*, 310 F.3d 717, 2002). However, this claim has not been endorsed by courts in other jurisdictions, or, most importantly, by the Supreme Court. An ACLU challenge to the 2008 FISA amendment, *Amnesty International USA, et al. v. Clapper,* is currently making its way through the federal court system and could eventually reach the Supreme Court, especially if the courts hearing that case decide, contrary to the FISCR, that domestic warrantless wiretapping is inherently unconstitutional.

Interesting readings on this issue include "Symposium: 'Torture and the War on Terror': NSA Wiretapping Controversy: A Debate Between Professor David D. Cole and Professor Ruth Wedgwood," 37 *Case W. Res. J. Int'l L.* 509 (2006); Fletcher N. Baldwin, Jr., and Robert B. Shaw, "Down to the Wire: Assessing the Constitutionality of the National Security Agency's Warrantless Wiretapping Program: Exit the Rule of Law," 17 *J. Law & Pub. Pol'y* 429 (2006); and Peter P. Swire, "The System of Foreign Intelligence Surveillance Law," *George Washington Law Review,* vol. 72 (2004) http://ssrn.com/abstract=586616.

Internet References . . .

Cornell Legal Information Institute

This is a reliable and useful site for primary legal information and documents.

http://www.law.cornell.edu

FindLaw

This is a good place to begin looking for court decisions, statutes, law reviews, and other primary legal resources.

http://www.findlaw.com

American Civil Liberties Union

The American Civil Liberties Union (ACLU) Web site is a significant repository of information related to individual rights.

http://www.aclu.org

American Bar Association Section on Individual Rights and Responsibilities

This is a source of information about law and individual rights.

http://www.abanet.org/irr/home.html

Law and the Individual

*T*he American legal and political systems are oriented around protection of the individual. The law does not provide absolute protection for the individual, however, because legitimate state interests are often recognized as being controlling. This unit examines issues that affect individual choice and the dignity of the individual.

- Are Violent Video Games Protected by the First Amendment?

- Is It Constitutional to Ban "Partial-Birth" Abortions Without Providing for an Exception to Protect the Health of the Mother?

- Are Restrictions on Physician-Assisted Suicide Constitutional?

- Does the Sharing of Music Files Through the Internet Violate Copyright Laws?

- Is the Eighth Amendment Protection Violated If Prisoners Are Deprived of Basic Sustenance, Including Adequate Medical Care?

ISSUE 3

Are Violent Video Games Protected by the First Amendment?

YES: Antonin Scalia, from Majority Opinion, *Brown v. Entertainment Merchants Association,* U.S. Supreme Court (June 27, 2011)

NO: Stephen Breyer, from Dissenting Opinion, *Brown v. Entertainment Merchants Association,* U.S. Supreme Court (June 27, 2011)

ISSUE SUMMARY

YES: Supreme Court Justice Antonin Scalia argues that legislation creating a whole new category of speech that is banned only for children violates the First Amendment.

NO: Justice Stephen Breyer believes that the California law restricting the purchase of video games by minors is clear.

This edition of Taking Sides contains three issues that revolve around the use of new information technologies: one dealing with file sharing and copyright (Issue 6), one focusing on searches and seizures (Issue 15), and this one concerned with violent video games. This reflects the growing role that these technologies are playing in daily life. The more we use the Internet, the more we can expect future editions of this book to have even more links to technology-related legal issues.

Cyberspace is, increasingly, the "place" where people shop, socialize, learn, and so forth. It has been equated with such physical places as a library, a shopping mall, a school, a conference center, an arcade, and a casino, because we can read, buy, learn, converse, play games, and gamble online. Looked at most simply, cyberspace allows information to be distributed and exchanged extremely quickly, over great distances, and at much lower costs than existed before. As a result, its continuing growth in our lives should not be surprising.

What cyberspace is not is a harmonious place or a problem-free environment. This, too, should not be surprising since there is an enormous amount of activity in cyberspace, there is a great deal of money being spent there, and there are numerous relationships being formed there. When so much is happening so fast, you have conditions in which there will be a demand for law.

Much of the activity that occurs in cyberspace may involve activities that we are familiar with. Buying something online, for example, may seem like purchasing something from a catalog or on the phone. For law, the question is whether we need new rules, new frameworks for thinking about traditional rules, and new processes for dealing with disputes that arise online.

Supreme Court Justice Oliver Wendell Holmes once wrote that "the life of the law is not logic; it is experience." What Holmes meant is that outside forces shape the law at the same time that the law is shaping those forces. The emergence of powerful information technologies certainly qualifies as an "experience," for all of us as well as for the law. It is, in all likelihood, one of the most powerful experiences the law has encountered in a long time and this presents us with a broad range of interesting and significant issues to explore.

The readings that follow involve a challenge to a law enacted by the California legislature in 2005. It imposed a fine of up to $1000 upon any person who distributed a violent video game in California without labeling it "18," or who sold or rented a labeled violent video game to a person under the age of 18. The law defined a violent video game as one in which a player

   a. "kill[s], maim[s], dismember[s], or sexually assault[s] an image of a human being;"
   b. "[a] reasonable person, considering the game as a whole, would find [the game] appeals to a deviant or morbid interest of minors;"
   c. "[the game] is patently offensive to prevailing standards in the community as to what is suitable for minors"; and
   d. "the game, as a whole, . . . lack[s] serious literary, artistic, political, or scientific value for minors."

This language was chosen with care and is very similar to the language that the Supreme Court used in carving out an exception to the First Amendment for obscenity. In *Miller v. United States,* the Court had ruled that the test for determining whether a work was obscene was

   a. whether the average person, applying contemporary community standards, would find that the work, taken as a whole, appealed to the prurient interest;
   b. whether the work depicted or described, in a patently offensive way, sexual conduct or excretory functions specifically defined by applicable state law; and
   c. whether the work, taken as a whole, lacked serious literary, artistic, political, or scientific value.

In *Miller v. United States,* the Court was dealing with obscenity, a category difficult to define but one which everyone agrees is not protected by the First Amendment. It was trying to distinguish obscenity from pornography, which, for adults, is protected by the First Amendment.

Although the distribution of pornography to adults is a protected activity, child pornography is not and is illegal under all circumstances. The challenge here is that video games are not obscene and the court is being asked to recognize a new exception to the First Amendment. It is being asked to do this when children are involved and reach a result that parallels pornography in allowing an activity for adults while regulating that same activity for children.

YES ↩

Antonin Scalia

Majority Opinion, *Brown v. Entertainment Merchants Association*

J USTICE SCALIA delivered the opinion of the Court.

We consider whether a California law imposing restrictions on violent video games comports with the First Amendment.

. . .

II

California correctly acknowledges that video games qualify for First Amendment protection. The Free Speech Clause exists principally to protect discourse on public matters, but we have long recognized that it is difficult to distinguish politics from entertainment, and dangerous to try. "Everyone is familiar with instances of propaganda through fiction. What is one man's amusement, teaches another's doctrine." *Winters v. New York,* 333 U.S. 507, 510 (1948). Like the protected books, plays, and movies that preceded them, video games communicate ideas—and even social messages—through many familiar literary devices (such as characters, dialogue, plot, and music) and through features distinctive to the medium (such as the player's interaction with the virtual world). That suffices to confer First Amendment protection. Under our Constitution, "esthetic and moral judgments about art and literature . . . are for the individual to make, not for the Government to decree, even with the mandate or approval of a majority." *United States v. Playboy Entertainment Group, Inc.,* 529 U.S. 803, 818 (2000). And whatever the challenges of applying the Constitution to ever-advancing technology, "the basic principles of freedom of speech and the press, like the First Amendment's command, do not vary" when a new and different medium for communication appears. *Joseph Burstyn, Inc. v. Wilson,* 343 U.S. 495, 503 (1952).

The most basic of those principles is this: "[A]s a general matter, . . . government has no power to restrict expression because of its message, its ideas, its subject matter, or its content." *Ashcroft v. American Civil Liberties Union,* 535 U.S. 564, 573 (2002). There are of course exceptions. "'From 1791 to the present,' . . . the First Amendment has 'permitted restrictions upon the content of speech in a few limited areas,' and has never 'include[d] a freedom to disregard these traditional limitations.'" *United States v. Stevens,* 559 U.S. ___, ___ (2010) (slip op., at 5) (quoting *R. A. V. v. St. Paul,* 505 U.S. 377, 382–383 (1992)). These limited areas—such as obscenity, *Roth v. United States,* 354 U.S. 476, 483 (1957), incitement, *Brandenburg v. Ohio,* 395 U.S. 444, 447–449 (1969) (*per curiam*), and fighting words, *Chaplinsky v. New Hampshire,* 315 U.S. 568, 572 (1942)—represent "well-defined and narrowly limited classes of speech, the prevention and punishment of which have never been thought to raise any Constitutional problem," *id.,* at 571–572.

Last Term, in *Stevens,* we held that new categories of unprotected speech may not be added to the list by a legislature that concludes certain speech is too harmful to be tolerated. *Stevens* concerned a federal statute purporting to criminalize the creation, sale, or possession of certain depictions of animal cruelty. See 18 U.S. C. §48 (amended 2010). The statute covered depictions "in which a living animal is intentionally maimed, mutilated, tortured, wounded, or killed" if that harm to the animal was illegal where the "the creation, sale, or possession t[ook] place," §48(c)(1). A saving clause largely borrowed from our obscenity jurisprudence, see *Miller v. California,* 413 U.S. 15, 24 (1973), exempted depictions with "serious religious, political, scientific, educational, journalistic, historical, or artistic value," §48(b). We held that statute to be an impermissible content-based restriction on speech. There was no American tradition of forbidding the *depiction of* animal cruelty—though States have long had laws against *committing* it.

The Government argued in *Stevens* that lack of a historical warrant did not matter; that it could create new categories of unprotected speech by applying a "simple balancing test" that weighs the value of a particular category of speech against its social costs and then punishes that category of speech if it fails the test. . . . We emphatically rejected that "startling and dangerous" proposition. . . . "Maybe there are some categories of speech that have been historically unprotected, but have not yet been specifically identified or discussed as such in our case law." . . . But without persuasive evidence that a novel restriction on content is part of a long (if heretofore unrecognized) tradition of proscription, a legislature may not revise the "judgment [of] the American people," embodied in the First Amendment, "that the benefits of its restrictions on the Government outweigh the costs." . . .

That holding controls this case. As in *Stevens,* California has tried to make violent-speech regulation look like obscenity regulation by appending a saving clause required for the latter. That does not suffice. Our cases have been clear that the obscenity exception to the First Amendment does not cover whatever a legislature finds shocking, but only depictions of "sexual conduct," *Miller, supra,* at 24. See also *Cohen v. California,* 403 U.S. 15, 20 (1971); *Roth, supra,* at 487, and n. 20.

Stevens was not the first time we have encountered and rejected a State's attempt to shoehorn speech about violence into obscenity. In *Winters,* we considered a New York criminal statute "forbid[ding] the massing of stories of bloodshed and lust in such a way as to incite to crime against the person," 333 U.S., at 514. The New York Court of Appeals upheld the provision as a law against obscenity. "[T]here can be no more precise test of written indecency or obscenity," it said, "than the continuing and changeable experience of the community as to what types of books are likely to bring about the corruption of public morals or other analogous injury to the public order." *Id.,* at 514. That is of course the same expansive view of governmental power to abridge the freedom of speech based on interest-balancing that we rejected in *Stevens.* Our opinion in *Winters,* which concluded that the New York statute failed a heightened vagueness standard applicable to restrictions upon speech entitled to First Amendment protection, 333 U.S., at 517–519, made clear that violence is not part of the obscenity that the Constitution permits to be regulated. The speech reached by the statute contained "no indecency or obscenity in any sense heretofore known to the law." *Id.,* at 519.

Because speech about violence is not obscene, it is of no consequence that California's statute mimics the New York statute regulating obscenity-for-minors that we upheld in *Ginsberg v. New York,* 390 U.S. 629 (1968). That case approved a prohibition on the sale to minors of *sexual* material that would be obscene from the perspective of a child.[1] We held that the legislature could "adjus[t] the definition of obscenity 'to social realities by permitting the appeal of this type of material to be assessed in terms of the sexual interests . . .' of . . . minors." *Id.,* at 638 (quoting *Mishkin v. New York,* 383 U.S. 502, 509 (1966)). And because "obscenity is not protected expression," the New York statute could be sustained so long as the legislature's judgment that the proscribed materials were harmful to children "was not irrational." 390 U.S., at 641.

The California Act is something else entirely. It does not adjust the boundaries of an existing category of unprotected speech to ensure that a definition designed for adults is not uncritically applied to children. California does not argue that it is empowered to prohibit selling offensively violent works *to adults*—and it is wise not to, since that is but a hair's breadth from the argument rejected in *Stevens.* Instead, it wishes to create a wholly new category of content-based regulation that is permissible only for speech directed at children.

That is unprecedented and mistaken. "[M]inors are entitled to a significant measure of First Amendment protection, and only in relatively narrow and well-defined circumstances may government bar public dissemination of protected materials to them." *Erznoznik v. Jacksonville,* 422 U.S. 205, 212–213 (1975) (citation omitted). No doubt a State possesses legitimate power to protect children from harm, *Ginsberg, supra,* at 640–641; *Prince v. Massachusetts,* 321 U.S. 158, 165 (1944), but that does not include a free-floating power to restrict the ideas to which children may be exposed. "Speech that is neither obscene as to youths nor subject to some other legitimate proscription cannot be suppressed solely to protect the young from ideas or images that a legislative body thinks unsuitable for them." *Erznoznik, supra,* at 213–214.[2]

California's argument would fare better if there were a longstanding tradition in this country of specially restricting children's access to depictions of violence, but there is none. Certainly the *books* we give children to read—or read to them when they are younger—contain no shortage of gore. Grimm's Fairy Tales, for example, are grim indeed. As her just deserts for trying to poison Snow White, the wicked queen is made to dance in red hot slippers "till she fell dead on the floor, a sad example of envy and jealousy." The Complete Brothers Grimm Fairy Tales 198 (2006 ed.). Cinderella's evil stepsisters have their eyes pecked out by doves. *Id.,* at 95. And Hansel and Gretel (children!) kill their captor by baking her in an oven. *Id.,* at 54.

High-school reading lists are full of similar fare. Homer's Odysseus blinds Polyphemus the Cyclops by grinding out his eye with a heated stake. The Odyssey of Homer, Book IX, p. 125 (S. Butcher & A. Lang transls. 1909) ("Even so did we seize the fiery-pointed brand and whirled it round in his eye, and the blood flowed about the heated bar. And the breath of the flame singed his eyelids and brows all about, as the ball of the eye burnt away, and the roots thereof crackled in the flame"). In the Inferno, Dante and Virgil watch corrupt politicians struggle to stay submerged beneath a lake of boiling pitch, lest they be skewered by devils above the surface. Canto XXI, pp. 187–189 (A. Mandelbaum transl. Bantam Classic ed. 1982). And Golding's Lord of the Flies recounts how a schoolboy called Piggy is savagely murdered *by other children* while marooned on an island. W. Golding, Lord of the Flies 208–209 (1997 ed.).[3]

This is not to say that minors' consumption of violent entertainment has never encountered resistance. In the 1800's, dime novels depicting crime and "penny dreadfuls" (named for their price and content) were blamed in some quarters for juvenile delinquency. See Brief for Cato Institute as *Amicus Curiae* 6–7. When motion pictures came along, they became the villains instead. "The days when the police looked upon dime novels as the most dangerous of textbooks in the school for crime are drawing to a close. . . . They say that the moving picture machine . . . tends even more than did the dime novel to turn the thoughts of the easily influenced to paths which sometimes lead to prison." Moving Pictures as Helps to Crime, N. Y. Times, Feb. 21, 1909, quoted in Brief for Cato Institute, at 8. For a time, our Court did permit broad censorship of movies because of their capacity to be "used for evil," see *Mutual Film Corp. v. Industrial Comm'n of Ohio,* 236 U.S. 230, 242 (1915), but we eventually reversed course, *Joseph Burstyn, Inc.,* 343 U.S., at 502; see also *Erznoznik, supra,* at 212–214 (invalidating a drive-in movies restriction designed to protect children). Radio dramas were next, and then came comic books. Brief for Cato Institute, at 10–11. Many in the late 1940's and early 1950's blamed comic books for fostering a "preoccupation with violence and horror" among the young, leading to a rising juvenile crime rate. See Note, Regulation of Comic Books, 68 Harv. L. Rev. 489, 490 (1955). But efforts to convince Congress to restrict comic books failed. Brief for Comic Book Legal Defense Fund as *Amicus Curiae* 11–15.[4] And, of course, after comic books came television and music lyrics.

California claims that video games present special problems because they are "interactive," in that the player participates in the violent action on screen and determines its outcome. The latter feature is nothing new: Since at least the publication of The Adventures of You: Sugarcane Island in 1969, young readers of choose-your-own adventure stories have been able to make decisions that determine the plot by following instructions about which page to turn to. Cf. *Interactive Digital Software Assn. v. St. Louis County,* 329 F. 3d 954, 957–958 (CA8 2003). As for the argument that video games enable participation in the violent action, that seems to us more a matter of degree than of kind. As Judge Posner has observed, all literature is interactive. "[T]he better it is, the more interactive. Literature when it is successful draws the reader into the story, makes him identify with the characters, invites him to judge them and quarrel with them, to experience their joys and sufferings as the reader's own." *American Amusement Machine Assn. v. Kendrick,* 244 F. 3d 572, 577 (CA7 2001) (striking down a similar restriction on violent video games).

JUSTICE ALITO has done considerable independent research to identify . . . video games in which "the violence is astounding," "Victims are dismembered, decapitated, disemboweled, set on fire, and chopped into little pieces. . . . Blood gushes, splatters, and pools.". . . JUSTICE ALITO recounts all these disgusting video games in order to disgust us—but disgust is not a valid basis for restricting expression. And the same is true of JUSTICE ALITO's description, . . . of those video games he has discovered that have a racial or ethnic motive for their violence—"'ethnic cleansing' [of] . . . African Americans, Latinos, or Jews." To what end does he relate this? Does it somehow increase the "aggressiveness" that California wishes to suppress? Who knows? But it does arouse the reader's ire, and the reader's desire to put an end to this horrible message. Thus, ironically, JUSTICE ALITO's argument highlights the precise danger posed by the California Act: that the *ideas* expressed by speech—whether it be violence, or gore, or racism—and not its objective effects, may be the real reason for governmental proscription.

III

Because the Act imposes a restriction on the content of protected speech, it is invalid unless California can demonstrate that it passes strict scrutiny—that is, unless it is justified by a compelling government interest and is narrowly drawn to serve that interest. *R. A. V.,* 505 U.S., at 395. The State must specifically identify an "actual problem" in need of solving, *Playboy,* 529 U.S., at 822–823, and the curtailment of free speech must be actually necessary to the solution, see *R. A. V., supra,* at 395. That is a demanding standard. "It is rare that a regulation restricting speech because of its content will ever be permissible." *Playboy, supra,* at 818.

California cannot meet that standard. At the outset, it acknowledges that it cannot show a direct causal link between violent video games and harm to minors. Rather, relying upon our decision in *Turner Broadcasting System, Inc. v. FCC,* 512 U.S. 622 (1994), the State claims that it need not produce such proof because the legislature can make a predictive judgment that such a link exists, based on competing psychological studies. But reliance on *Turner Broadcasting* is misplaced. That decision applied *intermediate scrutiny* to a content-neutral regulation. . . . California's burden is much higher, and because it bears the risk of uncertainty, . . . ambiguous proof will not suffice.

The State's evidence is not compelling. California relies primarily on the research of Dr. Craig Anderson and a few other research psychologists whose studies purport to show a connection between exposure to violent video games and harmful effects on children. These studies have been rejected by every court to consider them, and with good reason: They do not prove that violent video games *cause* minors to *act* aggressively (which would at least be a beginning). Instead, "[n]early all of the research is based on correlation, not evidence of causation, and most of the studies suffer from significant, admitted flaws in methodology." *Video Software Dealers Assn.* 556 F. 3d, at 964. They show at best some correlation between exposure to violent entertainment and minuscule real-world effects, such as children's feeling more aggressive or making louder noises in the few minutes after playing a violent game than after playing a nonviolent game.[5]

Even taking for granted Dr. Anderson's conclusions that violent video games produce some effect on children's feelings of aggression, those effects are both small and indistinguishable from effects produced by other media. In his testimony in a similar lawsuit, Dr. Anderson admitted that the "effect sizes" of children's exposure to violent video games are "about the same" as that produced by their exposure to violence on television. . . . And he admits that the *same* effects have been found when children watch cartoons starring Bugs Bunny or the Road Runner, *id.*, at 1304, or when they play video games like Sonic the Hedgehog that are rated "E" (appropriate for all ages), . . . or even when they "vie[w] a picture of a gun.". . .[6]

Of course, California has (wisely) declined to restrict Saturday morning cartoons, the sale of games rated for young children, or the distribution of pictures of guns. The consequence is that its regulation is wildly underinclusive when judged against its asserted justification, which in our view is alone enough to defeat it. Underinclusiveness raises serious doubts about whether the government is in fact pursuing the interest it invokes, rather than disfavoring a particular speaker or viewpoint. . . . Here, California has singled out the purveyors of video games for disfavored treatment—at least when compared to booksellers, cartoonists, and movie producers—and has given no persuasive reason why.

The Act is also seriously underinclusive in another respect—and a respect that renders irrelevant the contentions of the concurrence and the dissents that video games are qualitatively different from other portrayals of violence. The California Legislature is perfectly willing to leave this dangerous, mind-altering material in the hands of children so long as one parent (or even an aunt or uncle) says it's OK. And there are not even any requirements as to how this parental or avuncular relationship is to be verified; apparently the child's or putative parent's, aunt's, or uncle's say-so suffices. That is not how one addresses a serious social problem.

California claims that the Act is justified in aid of parental authority: By requiring that the purchase of violent video games can be made only by adults, the Act ensures that parents can decide what games are appropriate. At the outset, we note our doubts that punishing third parties for conveying protected speech to children *just in case* their parents disapprove of that speech is a proper governmental means of aiding parental authority. Accepting that position would largely vitiate the rule that "only in relatively narrow and well-defined circumstances may government bar public dissemination of protected materials to [minors]." *Erznoznik*, 422 U.S., at 212–213.

But leaving that aside, California cannot show that the Act's restrictions meet a substantial need of parents who wish to restrict their children's access to violent video games but cannot do so. The video-game industry has in place a voluntary rating system designed to inform consumers about the content of games. The system, implemented by the Entertainment Software Rating Board (ESRB), assigns age-specific ratings to each video game submitted: EC (Early Childhood); E (Everyone); E10+ (Everyone 10 and older); T (Teens); M (17 and older); and AO (Adults Only—18 and older). . . . The Video Software Dealers Association encourages retailers to prominently display information about the ESRB system in their stores; to refrain from renting or selling adults-only games to minors; and to rent or sell "M" rated games to minors only with parental consent. . . . In 2009, the Federal Trade Commission (FTC) found that, as a result of this system, "the video game industry outpaces the movie and music industries" in "(1) restricting target-marketing of mature-rated products to children; (2) clearly and prominently disclosing rating information; and (3) restricting children's access to mature-rated products at retail." FTC, Report to Congress, Marketing Violent Entertainment to Children 30 (Dec. 2009). . . . This system does much to ensure that minors cannot purchase seriously violent games on their own, and that parents who care about the matter can readily evaluate the games their children bring home. Filling the remaining modest gap in concerned-parents' control can hardly be a compelling state interest.[7]

And finally, the Act's purported aid to parental authority is vastly overinclusive. Not all of the children who are forbidden to purchase violent video games on their own have parents who *care* whether they purchase violent video games. While some of the legislation's effect may indeed be in support of what some parents of the restricted children actually want, its entire effect is only in support of what the State thinks parents *ought* to want. This is not the narrow tailoring to "assisting parents" that restriction of First Amendment rights requires.

ᴄᴏ⟐ᴏ

California's effort to regulate violent video games is the latest episode in a long series of failed attempts to censor violent entertainment for minors. While we have pointed out above that some of the evidence brought forward to support the harmfulness of video games is unpersuasive, we do not mean to demean or disparage the concerns that underlie the attempt to regulate them—concerns that may and doubtless do prompt a good deal of parental oversight. We have no business passing judgment on the view of the California Legislature that violent video games (or, for that matter, any other forms of speech) corrupt the young or harm their moral development. Our task is only to say whether or not such works constitute a "well-defined and narrowly limited clas[s] of speech, the prevention and punishment of which have never been thought to raise any Constitutional problem," *Chaplinsky*, 315 U.S., at 571–572 (the answer plainly is no); and if not, whether the regulation of such works is justified by that high degree of necessity we have described as a compelling state interest (it is not). Even where the protection of children is the object, the constitutional limits on governmental action apply.

California's legislation straddles the fence between (1) addressing a serious social problem and (2) helping concerned parents control their children. Both ends are legitimate, but when they affect First Amendment rights they must be pursued by means that are neither seriously underinclusive nor seriously overinclusive. . . . As a means of protecting children from portrayals of violence, the legislation is seriously underinclusive, not only because it excludes portrayals other than video games, but also because it permits a parental or avuncular veto. And as a means of assisting concerned parents it is seriously overinclusive because it abridges the First Amendment rights of young people whose parents (and aunts and uncles) think violent video games are a harmless pastime. And the overbreadth in achieving one goal is not cured by the underbreadth in achieving the other. Legislation such as this, which is neither fish nor fowl, cannot survive strict scrutiny.

We affirm the judgment below.

It is so ordered.

Notes

1. The statute in *Ginsberg* restricted the sale of certain depictions of "nudity, sexual conduct, sexual excitement, or sado-masochistic abuse," that were "'[h]armful to minors.'" A depiction was harmful to minors if it:

   "(i)   predominantly appeals to the prurient, shameful or morbid interests of minors, and

   "(ii) is patently offensive to prevailing standards in the adult community as a whole with respect to what is suitable material for minors, and

   "(iii) is utterly without redeeming social importance for minors." 390 U.S., at 646 (Appendix A to opinion of the Court) (quoting N. Y. Penal Law §484–h(1)(f)).

2. JUSTICE THOMAS ignores the holding of *Erznoznik,* and denies that persons under 18 have any constitutional right to speak or be spoken to without their parents' consent. He cites no case, state or federal, supporting this view, and to our knowledge there is none. Most of his dissent is devoted to the proposition that parents have traditionally had the power to control what their children hear and say. This is true enough. And it perhaps follows from this that the state has the power to *enforce* parental prohibitions—to require, for example, that the promoters of a rock concert exclude those minors whose parents have advised the promoters that their children are forbidden to attend. But it does not follow that the state has the power to prevent children from hearing or saying anything *without their parents' prior consent.* The latter would mean, for example, that it could be made criminal to admit persons under 18 to a political rally without their parents' prior written consent—even a political rally in support of laws against corporal punishment of children, or laws in favor of greater rights for minors. And what is good for First Amendment rights of speech must be good for First Amendment rights of religion as well: It could be made criminal to admit a person under 18 to church, or to give a

person under 18 a religious tract, without his parents' prior consent. Our point is not, as JUSTICE THOMAS believes, *post,* at 16, n. 2, merely that such laws are "undesirable." They are obviously an infringement upon the religious freedom of young people and those who wish to proselytize young people. Such laws do not enforce *parental* authority over children's speech and religion; they impose *governmental* authority, subject only to a parental veto. In the absence of any precedent for state control, uninvited by the parents, over a child's speech and religion (JUSTICE THOMAS cites none), and in the absence of any justification for such control that would satisfy strict scrutiny, those laws must be unconstitutional. This argument is not, as JUSTICE THOMAS asserts, "circular," . . . It is the absence of any historical warrant or compelling justification for such restrictions, not our *ipse dixit,* that renders them invalid.

3. JUSTICE ALITO accuses us of pronouncing that playing violent video games "is not different in 'kind' " from reading violent literature. *Post,* at 2. Well of course it is different in kind, but not in a way that causes the provision and viewing of violent video games, unlike the provision and reading of books, not to be expressive activity and hence not to enjoy First Amendment protection. Reading Dante is unquestionably more cultured and intellectually edifying than playing Mortal Kombat. But these cultural and intellectual differences are not *constitutional* ones. Crudely violent video games, tawdry TV shows, and cheap novels and magazines are no less forms of speech than The Divine Comedy, and restrictions upon them must survive strict scrutiny—a question to which we devote our attention in Part III, *infra.* Even if we can see in them "nothing of any possible value to society . . . , they are as much entitled to the protection of free speech as the best of literature." *Winters v. New York,* 333 U.S. 507, 510 (1948).

4. The crusade against comic books was led by a psychiatrist, Frederic Wertham, who told the Senate Judiciary Committee that "as long as the crime comic books industry exists in its present forms there are no secure homes." Juvenile Delinquency (Comic Books): Hearings before the Subcommittee to Investigate Juvenile Delinquency, 83d Cong., 2d Sess., 84 (1954). Wertham's objections extended even to Superman comics, which he described as "particularly injurious to the ethical development of children." *Id.,* at 86. Wertham's crusade did convince the New York Legislature to pass a ban on the sale of certain comic books to minors, but it was vetoed by Governor Thomas Dewey on the ground that it was unconstitutional given our opinion in *Winters, supra.* See *People v. Bookcase, Inc.,* 14 N. Y. 2d 409, 412–413, 201 N. E. 2d 14, 15–16 (1964).

5. One study, for example, found that children who had just finished playing violent video games were more likely to fill in the blank letter in "explo_e" with a "d" (so that it reads "explode") than with an "r" ("explore"). App. 496, 506 (internal quotation marks omitted). The prevention of this phenomenon, which might have been anticipated with common sense, is not a compelling state interest.

6. JUSTICE ALITO is mistaken in thinking that we fail to take account of "new and rapidly evolving technology." . . . The studies in question pertain to that new and rapidly evolving technology, and fail to show, with the degree of certitude that strict scrutiny requires, that this subject-matter restriction on speech is justified. Nor is JUSTICE ALITO correct in attributing to us the

view that "violent video games really present no serious problem." . . . Perhaps they do present a problem, and perhaps none of us would allow our own children to play them. But there are all sorts of "problems"—some of them surely more serious than this one—that cannot be addressed by governmental restriction of free expression: for example, the problem of encouraging anti-Semitism (*National Socialist Party of America v. Skokie*, 432 U.S. 43 (1977) (*per curiam*)), the problem of spreading a political philosophy hostile to the Constitution (*Noto v. United States*, 367 U.S. 290 (1961)), or the problem of encouraging disrespect for the Nation's flag (*Texas v. Johnson*, 491 U.S. 397 (1989)).

JUSTICE BREYER would hold that California has satisfied strict scrutiny based upon his own research into the issue of the harmfulness of violent video games. . . . (Appendixes to dissenting opinion) (listing competing academic articles discussing the harmfulness *vel non* of violent video games). The vast preponderance of this research is outside the record—and in any event we do not see how it could lead to JUSTICE BREYER's conclusion, since he admits he cannot say whether the studies on his side are right or wrong. . . . Similarly, JUSTICE ALITO says he is not "sure" whether there are any constitutionally dispositive differences between video games and other media. . . . If that is so, then strict scrutiny plainly has not been satisfied.

7. JUSTICE BREYER concludes that the remaining gap is compelling because, according to the FTC's report, some "20% of those under 17 are still able to buy M-rated games." *Post,* at 18 (citing FTC Report 28). But some gap in compliance is unavoidable. The sale of alcohol to minors, for example, has long been illegal, but a 2005 study suggests that about 18% of retailers still sell alcohol to those under the drinking age. . . . Even if the sale of violent video games to minors could be deterred further by increasing regulation, the government does not have a compelling interest in each marginal percentage point by which its goals are advanced.

NO

Dissenting Opinion, *Brown v. Entertainment Merchants Association*

J USTICE BREYER, dissenting.

California imposes a civil fine of up to $1,000 upon any person who distributes a violent video game in California without labeling it "18," or who sells or rents a labeled violent video game to a person under the age of 18. Representatives of the video game and software industries, claiming that the statute violates the First Amendment on its face, seek an injunction against its enforcement. Applying traditional First Amendment analysis, I would uphold the statute as constitutional on its face and would consequently reject the industries' facial challenge.

I

A

California's statute defines a violent video game as: A game in which a player "kill[s], maim[s], dismember[s], or sexually assault[s] an image of a human being,"
and

> "[a] reasonable person, considering the game as a whole, would find
> [the game] appeals to a deviant or morbid interest of minors,"

and

> "[the game] is patently offensive to prevailing standards in the com-
> munity as to what is suitable for minors,"

and

> "the game, as a whole, . . . lack[s] serious literary, artistic, political, or
> scientific value for minors." Cal. Civ. Code Ann. §1746(d)(1).

The statute in effect forbids the sale of such a game to minors unless they are accompanied by a parent; it requires the makers of the game to affix a label

Supreme Court of the United States, June 27, 2011.

identifying it as a game suitable only for those aged 18 and over; it exempts retailers from liability unless such a label is properly affixed to the game; and it imposes a civil fine of up to $1,000 upon a violator. . . .

B

A facial challenge to this statute based on the First Amendment can succeed only if "a substantial number of its applications are unconstitutional, judged in relation to the statute's plainly legitimate sweep." *United States v. Stevens,* 559 U.S. __, __ (2010). . . . Moreover, it is more difficult to mount a facial First Amendment attack on a statute that seeks to regulate activity that involves action as well as speech. See *Broadrick v. Oklahoma,* 413 U.S. 601, 614–615 (1973). Hence, I shall focus here upon an area within which I believe the State can legitimately apply its statute, namely sales to minors under the age of 17 (the age cutoff used by the industry's own ratings system), of highly realistic violent video games, which a reasonable game maker would know meet the Act's criteria. That area lies at the heart of the statute. I shall assume that the number of instances in which the State will enforce the statute within that area is comparatively large, and that the number outside that area (for example, sales to 17-year-olds) is comparatively small. And the activity the statute regulates combines speech with action (a virtual form of target practice).

C

In determining whether the statute is unconstitutional, I would apply both this Court's "vagueness" precedents and a strict form of First Amendment scrutiny. In doing so, the special First Amendment category I find relevant is not (as the Court claims) the category of "depictions of violence," . . . but rather the category of "protection of children." This Court has held that the "power of the state to control the conduct of children reaches beyond the scope of its authority over adults." *Prince v. Massachusetts,* 321 U.S. 158, 170 (1944). And the " 'regulatio[n] of communication addressed to [children] need not conform to the requirements of the [F]irst [A]mendment in the same way as those applicable to adults.' " *Ginsberg v. New York,* 390 U.S. 629, 638, n. 6 (1968) (quoting Emerson, Toward a General Theory of the First Amendment, 72 Yale L. J. 877, 939 (1963)).

The majority's claim that the California statute, if upheld, would create a "new categor[y] of unprotected speech," . . . is overstated. No one here argues that depictions of violence, even extreme violence, *automatically* fall outside the First Amendment's protective scope as, for example, do obscenity and depictions of child pornography. We properly speak of *categories* of expression that lack protection when, like "child pornography," the category is broad, when it applies automatically, and when the State can prohibit everyone, including adults, from obtaining access to the material within it. But where, as here, careful analysis must precede a narrower judicial conclusion (say, denying protection to a shout of "fire" in a crowded theater, or to an effort to teach a terrorist group how to peacefully petition the United Nations), we do not normally describe the result as creating a "new category of unprotected speech." See *Schenck v. United States*, 249 U.S. 47, 52 (1919); *Holder v. Humanitarian Law Project*, 561 U.S. __ (2010).

Thus, in *Stevens,* after rejecting the claim that *all* depictions of animal cruelty (a category) fall outside the First Amendment's protective scope, we went on to decide whether the particular statute at issue violates the First Amendment under traditional standards; and we held that, because the statute was overly broad, it was invalid. Similarly, here the issue is whether, applying traditional First Amendment standards, this statute does, or does not, pass muster.

II

In my view, California's statute provides "fair notice of what is prohibited," and consequently it is not impermissibly vague. *United States v. Williams*, 553 U.S. 285, 304 (2008). *Ginsberg* explains why that is so. The Court there considered a New York law that forbade the sale to minors of a

> "picture, photograph, drawing, sculpture, motion picture film, or similar visual representation or image of a person or portion of the human body which depicts nudity . . . ,"

that

> "predominately appeals to the prurient, shameful or morbid interest of minors,"

and

> "is patently offensive to prevailing standards in the adult community as a whole with respect to what is suitable material for minors,"

and

> "is utterly without redeeming social importance for minors." 390 U.S., at 646–647.

This Court upheld the New York statute in *Ginsberg* (which is sometimes unfortunately confused with a very different, earlier case, *Ginzburg v. United States,* 383 U.S. 463 (1966)). The five-Justice majority, in an opinion written by Justice Brennan, wrote that the statute was sufficiently clear. 390 U.S., at 643–645. No Member of the Court voiced any vagueness objection. See *id.*, at 648–650 (Stewart, J., concurring in result); *id.*, at 650–671 (Douglas, J., joined by Black, J., dissenting); *id.*, at 671–675 (Fortas, J., dissenting).

Comparing the language of California's statute . . . with the language of New York's statute (set forth immediately above), it is difficult to find any vagueness-related difference. Why are the words "kill," "maim," and "dismember" any more difficult to understand than the word "nudity?" JUSTICE ALITO objects that these words do "not perform the narrowing function" that this

Court has required in adult obscenity cases, where statutes can only cover " 'hard core' " depictions. . . . But the relevant comparison is not to adult obscenity cases but to *Ginsberg,* which dealt with "nudity," a category no more "narrow" than killing and maiming. And in any event, *narrowness* and *vagueness* do not necessarily have anything to do with one another. All that is required for vagueness purposes is that the terms "kill," "maim," and "dismember" give fair notice as to what they cover, which they do.

The remainder of California's definition copies, almost word for word, the language this Court used in *Miller v. California,* 413 U.S. 15 (1973), in permitting a *total ban* on material that satisfied its definition (one enforced with *criminal* penalties). The California law's reliance on "community standards" adheres to *Miller,* and in *Fort Wayne Books, Inc. v. Indiana,* 489 U.S. 46, 57–58 (1989), this Court specifically upheld the use of *Miller's* language against charges of vagueness. California only departed from the *Miller* formulation in two significant respects: It substituted the word "deviant" for the words "prurient" and "shameful," and it three times added the words "for minors." The word "deviant" differs from "prurient" and "shameful," but it would seem no less suited to defining and narrowing the reach of the statute. And the addition of "for minors" to a version of the *Miller* standard was approved in *Ginsberg,* 390 U.S., at 643, even though the New York law "dr[ew] no distinction between young children and adolescents who are nearing the age of majority," *ante,* at 8 (opinion of ALITO, J.).

Both the *Miller* standard and the law upheld in *Ginsberg* lack perfect clarity. But that fact reflects the difficulty of the Court's long search for words capable of protecting expression without depriving the State of a legitimate constitutional power to regulate. As is well known, at one point Justice Stewart thought he could do no better in defining obscenity than, "I know it when I see it." *Jacobellis v. Ohio,* 378 U.S. 184, 197 (1964) (concurring opinion). And Justice Douglas dissented from *Miller's* standard, which he thought was still too vague. 413 U.S., at 39–40. Ultimately, however, this Court accepted the "community standards" tests used in *Miller* and *Ginsberg.* They reflect the fact that sometimes, even when a precise standard proves elusive, it is easy enough to identify instances that fall within a legitimate regulation. And they seek to draw a line, which, while favoring free expression, will nonetheless permit a legislature to find the words necessary to accomplish a legitimate constitutional objective . . . (the Constitution does not always require " 'perfect clarity and precise guidance,' " even when " 'expressive activity' " is involved).

What, then, is the difference between *Ginsberg* and *Miller* on the one hand and the California law on the other? It will often be easy to pick out cases at which California's statute directly aims, involving, say, a character who shoots out a police officer's knee, douses him with gasoline, lights him on fire, urinates on his burning body, and finally kills him with a gunshot to the head. (Footage of one such game sequence has been submitted in the record.) . . . As in *Miller* and *Ginsberg,* the California law clearly *protects* even the most violent games that possess serious literary, artistic, political, or scientific value. §1746(d) (1)(A)(iii). And it is easier here than in *Miller* or *Ginsberg* to separate the sheep from the goats at the statute's border. That is because here the industry itself has promulgated standards and created a review process, in which adults who "typically have experience with children" assess what games are inappropriate for minors. . . .

There is, of course, one obvious difference: The *Ginsberg* statute concerned depictions of "nudity," while California's statute concerns extremely violent video games. But for purposes of vagueness, why should that matter? JUSTICE ALITO argues that the *Miller* standard sufficed because there are "certain generally accepted norms concerning expression related to sex," whereas there are no similarly "accepted standards regarding the suitability of violent entertainment." . . . But there is no evidence that is so. The Court relied on "community standards" in *Miller* precisely because of the difficulty of articulating "accepted norms" about depictions of sex. I can find no difference—historical or otherwise—that is *relevant* to the vagueness question. Indeed, the majority's examples of literary descriptions of violence, on which JUSTICE ALITO relies, do not show anything relevant at all.

After all, one can find in literature as many (if not more) descriptions of physical love as descriptions of violence. Indeed, sex "has been a theme in art and literature throughout the ages." *Ashcroft v. Free Speech Coalition,* 535 U.S. 234, 246 (2002). For every Homer, there is a Titian. For every Dante, there is an Ovid. And for all the teenagers who have read the original versions of Grimm's Fairy Tales, I suspect there are those who know the story of Lady Godiva.

Thus, I can find no meaningful vagueness-related differences between California's law and the New York law upheld in *Ginsberg.* And if there remain any vagueness problems, the state courts can cure them through interpretation. See *Erznoznik v. Jacksonville,* 422 U.S. 205, 216 (1975) ("[S]tate statute should not be deemed facially invalid unless it is not readily subject to a narrowing construction by the state courts"). Cf. *Ginsberg, supra,* at 644 (relying on the fact that New York Court of Appeals would read a knowledge requirement into the statute); *Berry v. Santa Barbara,* 40 Cal. App. 4th 1075, 1088–1089, 47 Cal. Rptr. 2d 661, 669 (1995) (reading a knowledge requirement into a statute). Consequently, for purposes of this facial challenge, I would not find the statute unconstitutionally vague.

III

Video games combine physical action with expression. Were physical activity to predominate in a game, government could appropriately intervene, say by requiring parents to accompany children when playing a game involving actual target practice, or restricting the sale of toys presenting physical dangers to children. See generally Consumer Product Safety Improvement Act of 2008, 122 Stat. 3016 ("Title I—Children's Product Safety"). But because video games also embody important expressive and artistic elements, I agree with the Court that the First Amendment significantly limits the State's power to regulate. And I would determine whether the State has exceeded those limits by applying a strict standard of review.

Like the majority, I believe that the California law must be "narrowly tailored" to further a "compelling interest," without there being a "less restrictive" alternative that would be "at least as effective." *Reno v. American Civil Liberties Union,* 521 U.S. 844, 874, 875, 879 (1997). I would not apply this strict standard "mechanically." *United States v. Playboy Entertainment Group, Inc.,* 529 U.S. 803, 841 (2000) (BREYER, J., joined by Rehnquist, C. J., and O'Connor and SCALIA, JJ., dissenting). Rather, in applying it, I would evaluate the degree to which the statute injures speech-related interests, the nature of the potentially-justifying "compelling interests," the degree to which the statute furthers that interest, the nature and effectiveness of possible alternatives, and, in light of this evaluation, whether, overall, "the statute works speech-related harm . . . out of proportion to the benefits that the statute seeks to provide." . . .

First Amendment standards applied in this way are difficult but not impossible to satisfy. Applying "strict scrutiny" the Court has upheld restrictions on speech that, for example, ban the teaching of peaceful dispute resolution to a group on the State Department's list of terrorist organizations, *Holder,* 561 U.S., at ___ (slip op., at 22–34); but cf. *id.,* at ___ (slip op., at 1) (BREYER, J., dissenting), and limit speech near polling places, *Burson, supra,* at 210–211 (plurality opinion). And applying less clearly defined but still rigorous standards, the Court has allowed States to require disclosure of petition signers, *Doe v. Reed,* 561 U.S. ___ (2010), and to impose campaign contribution limits that were "'closely drawn' to match a 'sufficiently important interest,'" *Nixon v. Shrink Missouri Government PAC,* 528 U.S. 377, 387–388 (2000).

Moreover, although the Court did not specify the "level of scrutiny" it applied in *Ginsberg,* we have subsequently described that case as finding a "compelling interest" in protecting children from harm sufficient to justify limitations on speech. See *Sable Communications of Cal., Inc. v. FCC,* 492 U.S. 115, 126 (1989). Since the Court in *Ginsberg* specified that the statute's prohibition applied to material that was *not* obscene, 390 U.S., at 634, I cannot dismiss *Ginsberg* on the ground that it concerned obscenity. . . . Nor need I depend upon the fact that the Court in *Ginsberg* insisted only that the legislature have a "rational" basis for finding the depictions there at issue harmful to children. . . . For in this case, California has substantiated its claim of harm with considerably stronger evidence.

A

California's law imposes no more than a modest restriction on expression. The statute prevents no one from playing a video game, it prevents no adult from buying a video game, and it prevents no child or adolescent from obtaining a game provided a parent is willing to help. §1746.1(c). All it prevents is a child or adolescent from buying, without a parent's assistance, a gruesomely violent video game of a kind that the industry *itself* tells us it wants to keep out of the hands of those under the age of 17. . . .

Nor is the statute, if upheld, likely to create a precedent that would adversely affect other media, say films, or videos, or books. A typical video game involves a significant amount of physical activity. See *ante,* at 13–14 (ALITO, J., concurring in judgment). . . . And pushing buttons that achieve an interactive, virtual form of target practice (using images of human beings as targets), while containing an expressive component, is not just like watching a typical movie.

B

The interest that California advances in support of the statute is compelling. As this Court has previously described that interest, it consists of both (1) the "basic" parental claim "to authority in their own household to direct the rearing of their children," which makes it proper to enact "laws designed to aid discharge of [parental] responsibility," and (2) the State's "independent interest in the well-being of its youth." *Ginsberg,* 390 U.S., at 639–640. . . . (" '[O]ne can well distinguish laws which do not impose a morality on children, but which support the right of parents to deal with the morals of their children as they see fit' " (quoting Henkin, Morals and the Constitution: The Sin of Obscenity, 63 Colum. L. Rev. 391, 413, n. 68 (1963))). And where these interests work in tandem, it is not fatally "underinclusive" for a State to advance its interests in protecting children against the special harms present in an interactive video game medium through a default rule that still allows parents to provide their children with what their parents wish.

Both interests are present here. As to the need to help parents guide their children, the Court noted in 1968 that " 'parental control or guidance cannot always be provided.' " 390 U.S., at 640. Today, 5.3 million grade-school-age children of working parents are routinely home alone. See Dept. of Commerce, Census Bureau, Who's Minding the Kids? Child Care Arrangements: Spring 2005/Summer 2006, p. 12 (2010). . . . Thus, it has, if anything, become more important to supplement parents' authority to guide their children's development.

As to the State's independent interest, we have pointed out that juveniles are more likely to show a " 'lack of maturity' " and are "more vulnerable or susceptible to negative influences and outside pressures," and that their "character . . . is not as well formed as that of an adult." *Roper v. Simmons,* 543 U.S. 551, 569–570 (2005). And we have therefore recognized "a compelling interest in protecting the physical and psychological well-being of minors." *Sable Communications, supra,* at 126.

At the same time, there is considerable evidence that California's statute significantly furthers this compelling interest. That is, in part, because video games are excellent teaching tools. Learning a practical task often means developing habits, becoming accustomed to performing the task, and receiving positive reinforcement when performing that task well. Video games can help develop habits, accustom the player to performance of the task, and reward the player for performing that task well. Why else would the Armed Forces incorporate video games into its training? See CNN, War Games: Military Training Goes High-Tech (Nov. 22, 2001). . . .

When the military uses video games to help soldiers train for missions, it is using this medium for a beneficial purpose. But California argues that when the teaching features of video games are put to less desirable ends, harm can ensue. In particular, extremely violent games can harm children by rewarding them for being violently aggressive in play, and thereby often teaching them to be violently aggressive in life. And video games can cause more harm in this respect than can typically passive media, such as books or films or television programs.

There are many scientific studies that support California's views. Social scientists, for example, have found *causal* evidence that playing these games results in harm. Longitudinal studies, which measure changes over time, have found that increased exposure to violent video games causes an increase in aggression over the same period. . . .

Experimental studies in laboratories have found that subjects randomly assigned to play a violent video game subsequently displayed more characteristics of aggression than those who played nonviolent games. See, *e.g.,* Anderson et al., Violent Video Games: Specific Effects of Violent Content on Aggressive Thoughts and Behavior, 36 Advances in Experimental Soc. Psychology 199 (2004).

Surveys of 8th and 9th grade students have found a correlation between playing violent video games and aggression. See, *e.g.,* Gentile, Lynch, Linder, & Walsh, The Effects of Violent Video Game Habits On Adolescent Hostility, Aggressive Behaviors, and School Performance, 27 J. Adolescence 5 (2004).

Cutting-edge neuroscience has shown that "virtual violence in video game playing results in those neural patterns that are considered characteristic for aggressive cognition and behavior." Weber, Ritterfeld, & Mathiak, Does Playing Violent Video Games Induce Aggression? Empirical Evidence of a Functional Magnetic Resonance Imaging Study, 8 Media Psychology 39, 51 (2006).

And "meta-analyses," *i.e.,* studies of all the studies, have concluded that exposure to violent video games "was positively associated with aggressive behavior, aggressive cognition, and aggressive affect," and that "playing violent video games is a *causal* risk factor for long-term harmful outcomes." Anderson et al., Violent Video Game Effects on Aggression, Empathy, and Prosocial Behavior in Eastern and Western Countries: A Meta-Analytic Review, 136 Psychological Bulletin 151, 167, 169 (2010) (emphasis added).

Some of these studies take care to explain in a common-sense way why video games are potentially more harmful than, say, films or books or television. In essence, they say that the closer a child's behavior comes, not to watching, but to *acting* out horrific violence, the greater the potential psychological harm. See Bushman & Huesmann, Aggression, in 2 Handbook of Social Pscyhology 833, 851 (S. Fiske, D. Gilbert, & G. Lindzey eds., 5th ed. 2010) (video games stimulate more aggression because "[p]eople learn better when they are actively involved," players are "more likely to identify with violent characters," and "violent games directly reward violent behavior"); Polman, de Castro, & van Aken, Experimental Study of the Differential Effects of Playing Versus Watching Violent Video Games on Children's Aggressive Behavior, 34 Aggressive Behavior 256 (2008) (finding greater aggression resulting from playing, as opposed to watching, a violent game); C. Anderson, D. Gentile, & K. Buckley, Violent Video Game Effects on Children and Adolescents 136–137 (2007) (three studies finding greater effects from games as opposed to television). See also *infra,* at 15–16 (statements of expert public health associations agreeing that interactive games can be more harmful than "passive" media like television); *ante,* at 12–17 (ALITO, J., concurring in judgment).

Experts debate the conclusions of all these studies. Like many, perhaps most, studies of human behavior, each study has its critics, and some of those critics have produced studies of their own in which they reach different conclusions. (I list both sets of research in the appendixes.) I, like most judges, lack the social science expertise to say definitively who is right. But associations of public health professionals who do possess that expertise have reviewed many of these studies and found a significant risk that violent video games, when compared with more passive media, are particularly likely to cause children harm.

Eleven years ago, for example, the American Academy of Pediatrics, the American Academy of Child & Adolescent Psychiatry, the American Psychological Association, the American Medical Association, the American Academy of Family Physicians, and the American Psychiatric Association released a joint statement, which said:

> "[O]ver 1000 studies . . . point overwhelmingly to a causal connection between media violence and aggressive behavior in some children . . . [and, though less research had been done at that time, preliminary studies indicated that] the impact of violent interactive entertainment (video games and other interactive media) on young people . . . may be *significantly more severe* than that wrought by television, movies, or music." Joint Statement on the Impact of Entertainment Violence on Children (2000) (emphasis added). . . .

Five years later, after more research had been done, the American Psychological Association adopted a resolution that said:

> "[C]omprehensive analysis of violent interactive video game research suggests such exposure . . . increases aggressive behavior, . . . increases aggressive thoughts, . . . increases angry feelings, . . . decreases helpful behavior, and . . . increases physiological arousal." Resolution on Violence in Video Games and Interactive Media (2005). . . .

The Association added:

> "[T]he practice, repetition, and rewards for acts of violence may be *more conducive* to increasing aggressive behavior among children and youth than passively watching violence on TV and in films." *Ibid.* (emphasis added).

Four years after that, in 2009, the American Academy of Pediatrics issued a statement in significant part about interactive media. It said:

> "Studies of these rapidly growing and ever-more-sophisticated types of media have indicated that the effects of child-initiated virtual violence may be *even more profound than those of passive media* such as television. In many games the child or teenager is 'embedded' in the game and uses a 'joystick' (handheld controller) that enhances both the experience and the aggressive feelings." Policy Statement—Media Violence, 124 Pediatrics 1495, 1498 (2009) (emphasis added).

It added:

> "Correlational and experimental studies have revealed that violent video games lead to increases in aggressive behavior and aggressive thinking and decreases in prosocial behavior. Recent longitudinal studies . . . have revealed that in as little as 3 months, high exposure to violent video games increased physical aggression. Other recent longitudinal studies . . . have revealed similar effects across 2 years." *Ibid.* (footnotes omitted).

Unlike the majority, I would find sufficient grounds in these studies and expert opinions for this Court to defer to an elected legislature's conclusion that the video games in question are particularly likely to harm children. This Court has always thought it owed an elected legislature some degree of deference in respect to legislative facts of this kind, particularly when they involve technical matters that are beyond our competence, and even in First Amendment cases. . . . The majority, in reaching its own, opposite conclusion about the validity of the relevant studies, grants the legislature no deference at all. . . .

C

I can find no "less restrictive" alternative to California's law that would be "at least as effective." . . . The majority points to a voluntary alternative: The industry tries to prevent those under 17 from buying extremely violent games by labeling those games with an "M" (Mature) and encouraging retailers to restrict their sales to those 17 and older. . . . But this voluntary system has serious enforcement gaps. When California enacted its law, a Federal Trade Commission (FTC) study had found that nearly 70% of unaccompanied 13- to 16-year-olds were able to buy M-rated video games. FTC, Marketing Violent Entertainment to Children 27 (2004). . . . Subsequently the voluntary program has become more effective. But as of the FTC's most recent update to Congress, 20% of those under 17 are still able to buy M-rated video games, and, breaking down sales by store, one finds that this number rises to nearly 50% in the case of one large national chain. FTC, Marketing Violent Entertainment to Children 28 (2009). . . . And the industry could easily revert back to the substantial noncompliance that existed in 2004, particularly after today's broad ruling reduces the industry's incentive to police itself.

The industry also argues for an alternative technological solution, namely "filtering at the console level." Brief for Respondents 53. But it takes only a quick search of the Internet to find guides explaining how to circumvent any such technological controls. YouTube viewers, for example, have watched one of those guides (called "How to bypass parental controls on the Xbox 360") more than 47,000 times. . . .

IV

The upshot is that California's statute, as applied to its heartland of applications (*i.e.*, buyers under 17; extremely violent, realistic video games), imposes a restriction on speech that is modest at most. That restriction is justified by a compelling interest (supplementing parents' efforts to prevent their children from purchasing potentially harmful violent, interactive material). And there is no equally effective, less restrictive alternative. California's statute is consequently constitutional on its face—though litigants remain free to challenge the statute as applied in particular instances, including any effort by the State to apply it to minors aged 17.

I add that the majority's different conclusion creates a serious anomaly in First Amendment law. *Ginsberg* makes clear that a State can prohibit the sale to minors of depictions of nudity; today the Court makes clear that a State cannot prohibit the sale to minors of the most violent interactive video games. But what sense does it make to forbid selling to a 13-year-old boy a magazine with an image of a nude woman, while protecting a sale to that 13-year-old of an interactive video game in which he actively, but virtually, binds and gags the woman, then tortures and kills her? What kind of First Amendment would permit the government to protect children by restricting sales of that extremely violent video game *only* when the woman—bound, gagged, tortured, and killed—is also topless?

This anomaly is not compelled by the First Amendment. It disappears once one recognizes that extreme violence, where interactive, and *without literary, artistic, or similar justification,* can prove at least as, if not more, harmful to children as photographs of nudity. And the record here is more than adequate to support such a view. That is why I believe that *Ginsberg* controls the outcome here *a fortiori*. And it is why I believe California's law is constitutional on its face.

This case is ultimately less about censorship than it is about education. Our Constitution cannot succeed in securing the liberties it seeks to protect unless we can raise future generations committed cooperatively to making our system of government work. Education, however, is about choices. Sometimes, children need to learn by making choices for themselves. Other times, choices are made for children—by their parents, by their teachers, and by the people acting democratically through their governments. In my view, the First Amendment does not disable government from helping parents make such a choice here—a choice not to have their children buy extremely violent, interactive video games, which they more than reasonably fear pose only the risk of harm to those children.

For these reasons, I respectfully dissent.

POSTSCRIPT

Are Violent Video Games Protected by the First Amendment?

Computer games are rated by an organization called the Entertainment Software Rating Board (ESRB). Each game contains a symbol suggesting age appropriateness and a description of content that influenced the rating. Looking up Mortal Kombat, for example, one of the most popular games sold in the United States, reveals a rating of M (Mature), meaning that it should not be played by anyone under 17. It is accompanied by the following content descriptor: "Blood and Gore, Intense Violence, Partial Nudity, Strong Language" and the following paragraph explaining the rating.

> . . . Players use swords, guns, chains, spikes, and supernatural attacks (e.g., fire, ice, lightning) to defeat a cast of human-like characters. After an opponent is defeated at the end of a match, players have the option to perform finishing moves called 'Fatalities.' Many of these finishing moves depict over-the-top instances of violence: impalement, bone-crushing body snaps, execution-style gunshots to the head; large blood-splatter effects occur during these sequences, staining characters' bodies and the ground. Several of these exaggerated finishing moves depict characters getting dismembered, ripped or sliced in half, stabbed, set on fire, or set to explode. . . . http://www.esrb.org/ratings/synopsis.jsp?Certificate=30816&searchkeyword=mortal%20kombat

Justice Scalia wrote in his majority opinion that

> California claims that video games present special problems because they are "interactive," in that the player participates in the violent action on screen and determines its outcome. The latter feature is nothing new: Since at least the publication of The Adventures of You: Sugarcane Island in 1969, young readers of choose-your-own-adventure stories have been able to make decisions that determine the plot by following instructions about which page to turn to . . . As for the argument that video games enable participation in the violent action, that seems to us more a matter of degree than of kind. As Judge Posner has observed, all literature is interactive. "[T]he better it is, the more interactive. Literature when it is successful draws the reader into the story, makes him identify with the characters, invites him to judge them and quarrel with them, to experience their joys and sufferings as the reader's own."

Is the interactive quality of violent video games "nothing new" and to be reasonably equated with the kind of interaction between reader and character that occurs when one is immersed in a novel? Or would Justice Scalia have been better off writing only that without much stronger evidence of harm, removing First Amendment protection is unwarranted.

In a concurring opinion, Justice Alito wrote

> In considering the application of unchanging constitutional principles to new and rapidly evolving technology, this Court should proceed with caution. We should make every effort to understand the new technology. We should take into account the possibility that developing technology may have important societal implications that will become apparent only with time. We should not jump to the conclusion that new technology is fundamentally the same as some older thing with which we are familiar. And we should not hastily dismiss the judgment of legislators, who may be in a better position than we are to assess the implications of new technology. The opinion of the Court exhibits none of this caution.

A fascinating comparison of the research contained in the brief submitted by the state of California and that submitted by the video game industry is Sacks, Bushman, and Anderson, "Do Violent Video Games Harm Children? Comparing the Scientific Amicus Curiae 'Experts' in *Brown V. Entertainment Merchants Association*" 106 Nw. U. L. Rev. Colloquy 1 (2011), http://www.law .northwestern.edu/lawreview/colloquy/2011/15/LRColl2011n15PollardSacks.pdf. It argues that the California case for video games causing harm is much stronger than that of the opposition. Several interesting articles on the topic of "Do Children Have The Same First Amendment Rights As Adults?" are in the 2004 Chicago-Kent Law Review. An interesting case involving "virtual" child pornography is *Ashcroft v. Free Speech Coalition,* 535 U.S. 234 (2002).

ISSUE 4

Is It Constitutional to Ban "Partial-Birth" Abortions Without Providing for an Exception to Protect the Health of the Mother?

YES: **Anthony Kennedy**, from Majority Opinion, *Gonzales v. Carhart*, U.S. Supreme Court (April 18, 2007)

NO: **Ruth Bader Ginsburg**, from Dissenting Opinion, *Gonzales v. Carhart*, U.S. Supreme Court (April 18, 2007)

ISSUE SUMMARY

YES: Justice Anthony Kennedy rules that the federal Partial-Birth Abortion Ban Act of 2003 was constitutional even without a "health exception" for the woman.

NO: In dissent, Justice Ruth Bader Ginsburg argues that the law clearly contravenes the Court's holding in prior cases that any regulation limiting a woman's access to abortion, even postviability, must include a health exception.

$\mathbf{A}$bortion is an issue that has never left the spotlight, even though it has been more than three decades since the Supreme Court ruled, in *Roe v. Wade* (410 U.S. 113, 1973), that laws banning the procedure violated the Constitution. The Supreme Court has repeatedly upheld and reaffirmed its decision in *Roe* that the Due Process Clause of the Fourteenth Amendment provides a right to privacy that encompasses a woman's right to choose whether to terminate a pregnancy. However, the Court did not say in *Roe* that this right was absolute.

The recognition in *Roe* and *Planned Parenthood v. Casey* (505 U.S. 833, 1992) that the government has a "legitimate interest" in "protecting the potentiality of human life" has led to considerable litigation surrounding the extent to which both state and federal legislatures can pass laws regulating abortion. The difficulty of deciding which types of laws cross the ill-defined line that separates legitimate governmental action from unconstitutional interference in a private decision is evident in the Supreme Court's mixed holdings in post-*Roe* abortion cases. For instance, can states mandate that doctors perform all second-trimester abortions in hospitals? No, according to the Court's decision in *Planned Parenthood of Kansas City, MO, v. Ashcroft,* 462 U.S. 476 (1983). Can states mandate that a second doctor be present at all late-term abortions? Yes, according to the same ruling.

Adding to this confusion was the Court's decision in *Planned Parenthood v. Casey* to reaffirm *Roe's* "central holding" while modifying some of its methodology for determining which laws violate a woman's right to choose. In *Casey,* the Court stated that in many of its rulings since *Roe,* it had gone "too far" and "[struck] down . . . some abortion regulations which in no real sense deprived women of the ultimate decision." Part of the problem, according to the Court, was its use of *Roe's* "trimester approach," under which "almost no regulation at all [wa]s permitted during the first trimester of pregnancy; regulations designed to protect the woman's health, but not to further the State's interest in potential life, [were] permitted during the second trimester; and during the third trimester, when the fetus is viable, prohibitions [were] permitted provided the life or health of the mother [wa]s not at stake." The Court announced in *Casey* that it would adopt a new standard to determine the constitutionality of abortion regulations—whether they posed an "undue burden" to a woman's exercise of her right to choose—and it overruled some of its previous abortion decisions, for example, its holding in two cases that states could not require doctors to provide certain information to all women seeking abortions.

In 2000, the Court faced one of its most significant post-*Casey* abortion cases, *Stenberg v. Carhart. Stenberg* required the Court to weigh in, using its "undue burden" standard, on the constitutionality of a Nebraska state law banning certain types of late-term abortions that critics have dubbed "partial-birth" abortions.

Nevertheless, the Court, in a 5–4 opinion, held the Nebraska law unconstitutional for two reasons. First, it lacked an exception, required by *Roe* and *Casey,* to allow for the banned procedure when necessary to safeguard the mother's health. Second, the language was so broad that it could be read to outlaw the most common types of second-trimester abortions, "thereby unduly burdening the right to choose abortion itself."

In 2007, the Court once again addressed the constitutionality of a law prohibiting partial-birth abortions. This time, however, the Court—again in a 5–4 decision—upheld the ban. According to Justice Anthony Kennedy's decision for the five-justice majority, the law at issue—the federal Partial-Birth Abortion Ban Act of 2003—was sufficiently different from the Nebraska statute in *Stenberg* that the Court could not conclude that it posed an "undue burden." However, in her dissent, Justice Ruth Bader Ginsburg argued that the law clearly contravenes the Court's holding, in both *Roe* and *Casey,* that any regulation limiting a woman's access to abortion, even postviability, must include a health exception.

YES ↙

Anthony Kennedy

Majority Opinion, *Gonzales v. Carhart*

JUSTICE KENNEDY delivered the opinion of the Court.

These cases require us to consider the validity of the Partial-Birth Abortion Ban Act of 2003 (Act), 18 U.S. C. §1531 (2000 ed., Supp. IV), a federal statute regulating abortion procedures. In recitations preceding its operative provisions the Act refers to the Court's opinion in *Stenberg v. Carhart*, 530 U.S. 914 (2000), which also addressed the subject of abortion procedures used in the later stages of pregnancy. Compared to the state statute at issue in *Stenberg*, the Act is more specific concerning the instances to which it applies and in this respect more precise in its coverage. We conclude the Act should be sustained against the objections lodged by the broad, facial attack brought against it. . . .

In 2003, after this Court's decision in *Stenberg*, Congress passed the Act at issue here. H. R. Rep. No. 108–58, at 12–14. On November 5, 2003, President Bush signed the Act into law. It was to take effect the following day. 18 U.S. C. §1531(a) (2000 ed., Supp. IV).

The Act responded to *Stenberg* in two ways. First, Congress made factual findings. Congress determined that this Court in *Stenberg* "was required to accept the very questionable findings issued by the district court judge," but that Congress was "not bound to accept the same factual findings," Congress found, among other things, that "[a] moral, medical, and ethical consensus exists that the practice of performing a partial-birth abortion . . . is a gruesome and inhumane procedure that is never medically necessary and should be prohibited." . . .

Second, and more relevant here, the Act's language differs from that of the Nebraska statute struck down in *Stenberg*. . . .

C

The District Court in *Carhart* concluded the Act was unconstitutional for two reasons. First, it determined the Act was unconstitutional because it lacked an exception allowing the procedure where necessary for the health of the mother. 331 F. Supp. 2d, at 1004–1030. Second, the District Court found the Act deficient because it covered not merely intact D&E but also certain other D&Es. *Id.*, at 1030–1037.

The Court of Appeals for the Eighth Circuit addressed only the lack of a health exception. 413 F. 3d, at 803–804. The court began its analysis with what

From U.S. Supreme Court, April 18, 2007.

it saw as the appropriate question—"whether 'substantial medical authority' supports the medical necessity of the banned procedure." *Id.*, at 796 (quoting *Stenberg*, 530 U.S., at 938). This was the proper framework, according to the Court of Appeals, because "when a lack of consensus exists in the medical community, the Constitution requires legislatures to err on the side of protecting women's health by including a health exception." 413 F. 3d, at 796. The court rejected the Attorney General's attempt to demonstrate changed evidentiary circumstances since *Stenberg* and considered itself bound by *Stenberg's* conclusion that a health exception was required. 413 F. 3d, at 803 (explaining "[t]he record in [the] case and the record in *Stenberg* [were] similar in all significant respects"). It invalidated the Act. *Ibid.* . . .

II

The principles set forth in the joint opinion in *Planned Parenthood of Southeastern Pa. v. Casey*, 505 U.S. 833 (1992), did not find support from all those who join the instant opinion. See *id.*, at 979–1002 (SCALIA, J., joined by THOMAS, J., *inter alios*, concurring in judgment in part and dissenting in part). Whatever one's views concerning the *Casey* joint opinion, it is evident a premise central to its conclusion—that the government has a legitimate and substantial interest in preserving and promoting fetal life—would be repudiated were the Court now to affirm the judgments of the Courts of Appeals.

   Casey involved a challenge to *Roe v. Wade*, 410 U.S. 113 (1973). The opinion contains this summary:

> "It must be stated at the outset and with clarity that *Roe's* essential holding, the holding we reaffirm, has three parts. First is a recognition of the right of the woman to choose to have an abortion before viability and to obtain it without undue interference from the State. Before viability, the State's interests are not strong enough to support a prohibition of abortion or the imposition of a substantial obstacle to the woman's effective right to elect the procedure. Second is a confirmation of the State's power to restrict abortions after fetal viability, if the law contains exceptions for pregnancies which endanger the woman's life or health. And third is the principle that the State has legitimate interests from the outset of the pregnancy in protecting the health of the woman and the life of the fetus that may become a child. These principles do not contradict one another; and we adhere to each." 505 U.S., at 846 (opinion of the Court).

Though all three holdings are implicated in the instant cases, it is the third that requires the most extended discussion; for we must determine whether the Act furthers the legitimate interest of the Government in protecting the life of the fetus that may become a child.

   To implement its holding, *Casey* rejected both *Roe's* rigid trimester framework and the interpretation of *Roe* that considered all previability regulations of abortion unwarranted. 505 U.S., at 875–876, 878 (plurality opinion). On this point *Casey* overruled the holdings in two cases because they undervalued the State's interest in potential life. See *id.*, at 881–883 (joint opinion) (overruling *Thornburgh v. American College of Obstetricians and Gynecologists*, 476 U.S. 747 (1986) and *Akron v. Akron Center for Reproductive Health, Inc.*, 462 U.S. 416 (1983)).

We assume the following principles for the purposes of this opinion. Before viability, a State "may not prohibit any woman from making the ultimate decision to terminate her pregnancy." 505 U.S., at 879 (plurality opinion). It also may not impose upon this right an undue burden, which exists if a regulation's "purpose or effect is to place a substantial obstacle in the path of a woman seeking an abortion before the fetus attains viability." *Id.*, at 878. On the other hand, "[r]egulations which do no more than create a structural mechanism by which the State, or the parent or guardian of a minor, may express profound respect for the life of the unborn are permitted, if they are not a substantial obstacle to the woman's exercise of the right to choose." *Id.*, at 877. *Casey*, in short, struck a balance. The balance was central to its holding. We now apply its standard to the cases at bar. . . .

IV

Under the principles accepted as controlling here, the Act, as we have interpreted it, would be unconstitutional "if its purpose or effect is to place a substantial obstacle in the path of a woman seeking an abortion before the fetus attains viability." *Casey*, 505 U.S., at 878 (plurality opinion). The abortions affected by the Act's regulations take place both previability and postviability; so the quoted language and the undue burden analysis it relies upon are applicable. The question is whether the Act, measured by its text in this facial attack, imposes a substantial obstacle to late-term, but previability, abortions. The Act does not on its face impose a substantial obstacle, and we reject this further facial challenge to its validity.

A

The Act's purposes are set forth in recitals preceding its operative provisions. A description of the prohibited abortion procedure demonstrates the rationale for the congressional enactment. The Act proscribes a method of abortion in which a fetus is killed just inches before completion of the birth process. Congress stated as follows: "Implicitly approving such a brutal and inhumane procedure by choosing not to prohibit it will further coarsen society to the humanity of not only newborns, but all vulnerable and innocent human life, making it increasingly difficult to protect such life." Congressional Findings (14)(N), in notes following 18 U. S. C. §1531 (2000 ed., Supp. IV), p. 769. The Act expresses respect for the dignity of human life.

Congress was concerned, furthermore, with the effects on the medical community and on its reputation caused by the practice of partial-birth abortion. The findings in the Act explain:

> "Partial-birth abortion . . . confuses the medical, legal, and ethical duties of physicians to preserve and promote life, as the physician acts

directly against the physical life of a child, whom he or she had just delivered, all but the head, out of the womb, in order to end that life." Congressional Findings (14)(J), *ibid.*

There can be no doubt the government "has an interest in protecting the integrity and ethics of the medical profession." *Washington v. Glucksberg,* 521 U.S. 702, 731 (1997); see also *Barsky v. Board of Regents of Univ. of N. Y.,* 347 U.S. 442, 451 (1954) (indicating the State has "legitimate concern for maintaining high standards of professional conduct" in the practice of medicine). Under our precedents it is clear the State has a significant role to play in regulating the medical profession.

Casey reaffirmed these governmental objectives. The government may use its voice and its regulatory authority to show its profound respect for the life within the woman. A central premise of the opinion was that the Court's precedents after *Roe* had "undervalue[d] the State's interest in potential life." 505 U.S., at 873 (plurality opinion); see also *id.,* at 871. The plurality opinion indicated "[t]he fact that a law which serves a valid purpose, one not designed to strike at the right itself, has the incidental effect of making it more difficult or more expensive to procure an abortion cannot be enough to invalidate it." *Id.,* at 874. This was not an idle assertion. The three premises of *Casey* must coexist. See *id.,* at 846 (opinion of the Court). The third premise, that the State, from the inception of the pregnancy, maintains its own regulatory interest in protecting the life of the fetus that may become a child, cannot be set at naught by interpreting *Casey's* requirement of a health exception so it becomes tantamount to allowing a doctor to choose the abortion method he or she might prefer. Where it has a rational basis to act, and it does not impose an undue burden, the State may use its regulatory power to bar certain procedures and substitute others, all in furtherance of its legitimate interests in regulating the medical profession in order to promote respect for life, including life of the unborn.

The Act's ban on abortions that involve partial delivery of a living fetus furthers the Government's objectives. No one would dispute that, for many, D&E is a procedure itself laden with the power to devalue human life. Congress could nonetheless conclude that the type of abortion proscribed by the Act requires specific regulation because it implicates additional ethical and moral concerns that justify a special prohibition. Congress determined that the abortion methods it proscribed had a "disturbing similarity to the killing of a newborn infant," Congressional Findings (14)(L), in notes following 18 U. S. C. §1531 (2000 ed., Supp. IV), p. 769, and thus it was concerned with "draw[ing] a bright line that clearly distinguishes abortion and infanticide." Congressional Findings (14)(G), *ibid.* The Court has in the past confirmed the validity of drawing boundaries to prevent certain practices that extinguish life and are close to actions that are condemned. *Glucksberg* found reasonable the State's "fear that permitting assisted suicide will start it down the path to voluntary and perhaps even involuntary euthanasia." 521 U.S., at 732–735, and n. 23. . . .

B

The Act's furtherance of legitimate government interests bears upon, but does not resolve, the next question: whether the Act has the effect of imposing an unconstitutional burden on the abortion right because it does not allow use of the barred procedure where "'necessary, in appropriate medical judgment, for [the] preservation of the . . . health of the mother.'" *Ayotte*, 546 U.S., at 327–328 (quoting *Casey*, *supra*, at 879 (plurality opinion)). The prohibition in the Act would be unconstitutional, under precedents we here assume to be controlling, if it "subject[ed] [women] to significant health risks." *Ayotte*, *supra*, at 328; see also *Casey*, *supra*, at 880 (opinion of the Court). In *Ayotte* the parties agreed a health exception to the challenged parental-involvement statute was necessary "to avert serious and often irreversible damage to [a pregnant minor's] health." 546 U.S., at 328. Here, by contrast, whether the Act creates significant health risks for women has been a contested factual question. The evidence presented in the trial courts and before Congress demonstrates both sides have medical support for their position.

Respondents presented evidence that intact D&E may be the safest method of abortion, for reasons similar to those adduced in *Stenberg*. See 530 U.S., at 932. Abortion doctors testified, for example, that intact D&E decreases the risk of cervical laceration or uterine perforation because it requires fewer passes into the uterus with surgical instruments and does not require the removal of bony fragments of the dismembered fetus, fragments that may be sharp. Respondents also presented evidence that intact D&E was safer both because it reduces the risks that fetal parts will remain in the uterus and because it takes less time to complete. Respondents, in addition, proffered evidence that intact D&E was safer for women with certain medical conditions or women with fetuses that had certain anomalies. . . .

These contentions were contradicted by other doctors who testified in the District Courts and before Congress. They concluded that the alleged health advantages were based on speculation without scientific studies to support them. They considered D&E always to be a safe alternative. See, *e.g.*, *Carhart*, *supra*, at 930–940; *Nat. Abortion Federation*, 330 F. Supp. 2d, at 470–474; *Planned Parenthood*, 320 F. Supp. 2d, at 983.

There is documented medical disagreement whether the Act's prohibition would ever impose significant health risks on women. See, *e.g.*, *id.*, at 1033 ("[T]here continues to be a division of opinion among highly qualified experts regarding the necessity or safety of intact D & E"); see also *Nat. Abortion Federation*, *supra*, at 482. The three District Courts that considered the Act's constitutionality appeared to be in some disagreement on this central factual question. The District Court for the District of Nebraska concluded "the banned procedure is, sometimes, the safest abortion procedure to preserve the health of women." *Carhart*, *supra*, at 1017. The District Court for the Northern District of California reached a similar conclusion. *Planned Parenthood*, *supra*, at 1002 (finding intact D&E was "under certain circumstances . . . significantly safer than D & E by disarticulation"). The District Court for the Southern District of New York was more skeptical of the purported health benefits of intact D&E. It found the Attorney General's "expert witnesses reasonably and effectively refuted [the plaintiffs'] proffered bases for the opinion that [intact D&E] has safety advantages over other second-trimester abortion procedures." *Nat. Abortion Federation*, 330 F. Supp. 2d, at 479. In addition it did "not believe that many of [the plaintiffs'] purported reasons for why [intact D&E] is medically necessary [were] credible; rather [it found them to be] theoretical or false." *Id.*, at 480. The court nonetheless invalidated the Act because it determined "a significant body of medical opinion . . . holds that D & E has safety advantages over induction and that [intact D&E] has some safety advantages (however hypothetical and unsubstantiated by scientific evidence) over D & E for some women in some circumstances." *Ibid.*

The question becomes whether the Act can stand when this medical uncertainty persists. The Court's precedents instruct that the Act can survive this facial attack. The Court has given state and federal legislatures wide discretion to pass legislation in areas where there is medical and scientific uncertainty. . . .

This traditional rule is consistent with *Casey*, which confirms the State's interest in promoting respect for human life at all stages in the pregnancy. Physicians are not entitled to ignore regulations that direct them to use reasonable alternative procedures. The law need not give abortion doctors unfettered choice in the course of their medical practice, nor should it elevate their status above other physicians in the medical community. In *Casey* the controlling opinion held an informed-consent requirement in the abortion context was "no different from a requirement that a doctor give certain specific information about any medical procedure." 505 U.S., at 884 (joint opinion). The opinion stated "the doctor-patient relation here is entitled to the same solicitude it receives in other contexts." *Ibid.*; see also *Webster v. Reproductive Health Services,* 492 U.S. 490, 518–519 (1989) (plurality opinion) (criticizing *Roe's* trimester framework because, *inter alia,* it "left this Court to serve as the country's *ex officio* medical board with powers to approve or disapprove medical and operative practices and standards throughout the United States" (internal quotation marks omitted)); *Mazurek v. Armstrong,* 520 U.S. 968, 973 (1997) (*per curiam*) (upholding a restriction on the performance of abortions to licensed physicians despite the respondents' contention "all health evidence contradicts the claim that there is any health basis for the law" (internal quotation marks omitted)).

Medical uncertainty does not foreclose the exercise of legislative power in the abortion context any more than it does in other contexts. . . . The medical uncertainty over whether the Act's prohibition creates significant health risks provides a sufficient basis to conclude in this facial attack that the Act does not impose an undue burden.

The conclusion that the Act does not impose an undue burden is supported by other considerations. Alternatives are available to the prohibited procedure. As we have noted, the Act does not proscribe D&E. One District Court found D&E to have extremely low rates of medical complications. *Planned Parenthood, supra,* at 1000. Another indicated D&E was "generally the safest method of abortion during the second trimester." *Carhart,* 331 F. Supp. 2d, at 1031; see also *Nat. Abortion Federation, supra,* at 467–468 (explaining that "[e]xperts testifying for both sides" agreed D&E was safe). In addition the Act's prohibition only applies to the delivery of "a living fetus." 18 U. S. C. §1531(b)(1)(A) (2000 ed., Supp. IV). If the intact D&E procedure is truly necessary in some circumstances, it appears likely an injection that kills the fetus is an alternative under the Act that allows the doctor to perform the procedure.

The instant cases, then, are different from *Planned Parenthood of Central Mo. v. Danforth,* 428 U.S. 52, 77–79 (1976), in which the Court invalidated a ban on saline amniocentesis, the then-dominant second-trimester abortion method. The Court found the ban in *Danforth* to be "an unreasonable or arbitrary regulation designed to inhibit, and having the effect of inhibiting, the vast majority of abortions after the first 12 weeks." *Id.,* at 79. Here the Act allows, among other means, a commonly used and generally accepted method, so it does not construct a substantial obstacle to the abortion right.

In reaching the conclusion the Act does not require a health exception we reject certain arguments made by the parties on both sides of these cases. On the one hand, the Attorney General urges us to uphold the Act on the basis of the congressional findings alone. . . . Although we review congressional factfinding under a deferential standard, we do not in the circumstances here place dispositive weight on Congress' findings. The Court retains an independent constitutional duty to review factual findings where constitutional rights are at stake. . . .

As respondents have noted, and the District Courts recognized, some recitations in the Act are factually incorrect. . . . Whether or not accurate at the time, some of the important findings have been superseded. Two examples suffice. Congress determined no medical schools provide instruction on the prohibited procedure. Congressional Findings (14)(B), in notes following 18 U. S. C. §1531 (2000 ed., Supp. IV), p. 769. The testimony in the District Courts, however, demonstrated intact D&E is taught at medical schools. . . . Congress also found there existed a medical consensus that the prohibited procedure is never medically necessary. Congressional Findings (1), in notes following 18 U. S. C. §1531 (2000 ed., Supp. IV), p. 767. The evidence presented in the District Courts contradicts that conclusion. See, *e.g., Carhart, supra,* at 1012–1015; *Nat. Abortion Federation, supra,* at 488–489; *Planned Parenthood, supra,* at 1025–1026. Uncritical deference to Congress' factual findings in these cases is inappropriate.

On the other hand, relying on the Court's opinion in *Stenberg,* respondents contend that an abortion regulation must contain a health exception "if 'substantial medical authority supports the proposition that banning a particular procedure could endanger women's health.'" Brief for Respondents in No. 05-380, p. 19 (quoting 530 U.S., at 938); see also Brief for Respondent Planned Parenthood et al. in No. 05-1382, at 12 (same). As illustrated by respondents' arguments and the decisions of the Courts of Appeals, *Stenberg* has been interpreted to leave no margin of error for legislatures to act in the face of medical uncertainty. *Carhart,* 413 F. 3d, at 796; *Planned Parenthood,* 435 F. 3d, at 1173; see also *Nat. Abortion Federation,* 437 F. 3d, at 296 (Walker, C. J., concurring) (explaining the standard under *Stenberg* "is a virtually insurmountable evidentiary hurdle").

A zero tolerance policy would strike down legitimate abortion regulations, like the present one, if some part of the medical community were disinclined to follow the proscription. This is too exacting a standard to impose on the legislative power, exercised in this instance under the Commerce Clause, to regulate the medical profession. Considerations of marginal safety, including the balance of risks, are within the legislative competence when the regulation is rational and in pursuit of legitimate ends. When standard medical options are available, mere convenience does not suffice to displace them; and if some procedures have different risks than others, it does not follow that the State is altogether barred from imposing reasonable regulations. The Act is not invalid on its face where there is uncertainty over whether the barred procedure is ever necessary to preserve a woman's health, given the availability of other abortion procedures that are considered to be safe alternatives. . . .

⌑

Respondents have not demonstrated that the Act, as a facial matter, is void for vagueness, or that it imposes an undue burden on a woman's right to abortion based on its overbreadth or lack of a health exception. For these reasons the judgments of the Courts of Appeals for the Eighth and Ninth Circuits are reversed.

It is so ordered.

Ruth Bader Ginsburg   ➡ **NO**

Dissenting Opinion,
Gonzales v. Carhart

JUSTICE GINSBURG, with whom JUSTICE STEVENS, JUSTICE SOUTER, and JUSTICE BREYER join, dissenting.

In *Planned Parenthood of Southeastern Pa. v. Casey*, 505 U.S. 833, 844 (1992), the Court declared that "[l]iberty finds no refuge in a jurisprudence of doubt." There was, the Court said, an "imperative" need to dispel doubt as to "the meaning and reach" of the Court's 7-to-2 judgment, rendered nearly two decades earlier in *Roe v. Wade*, 410 U.S. 113 (1973). Responsive to that need, the Court endeavored to provide secure guidance to "[s]tate and federal courts as well as legislatures throughout the Union," by defining "the rights of the woman and the legitimate authority of the State respecting the termination of pregnancies by abortion procedures." *Ibid.*

Taking care to speak plainly, the *Casey* Court restated and reaffirmed *Roe's* essential holding. 505 U.S., at 845–846. First, the Court addressed the type of abortion regulation permissible prior to fetal viability. It recognized "the right of the woman to choose to have an abortion before viability and to obtain it without undue interference from the State." *Id.*, at 846. Second, the Court acknowledged "the State's power to restrict abortions *after fetal viability,* if the law contains exceptions for pregnancies which endanger the woman's life *or health.*" *Ibid.* (emphasis added). Third, the Court confirmed that "the State has legitimate interests from the outset of the pregnancy in protecting *the health of the woman* and the life of the fetus that may become a child." *Ibid.* (emphasis added).

In reaffirming *Roe*, the *Casey* Court described the centrality of "the decision whether to bear . . . a child," *Eisenstadt v. Baird*, 405 U.S. 438, 453 (1972), to a woman's "dignity and autonomy," her "personhood" and "destiny," her "conception of . . . her place in society." 505 U.S., at 851–852. Of signal importance here, the *Casey* Court stated with unmistakable clarity that state regulation of access to abortion procedures, even after viability, must protect "the health of the woman." *Id.*, at 846.

Seven years ago, in *Stenberg v. Carhart*, 530 U.S. 914 (2000), the Court invalidated a Nebraska statute criminalizing the performance of a medical procedure that, in the political arena, has been dubbed "partial-birth abortion."[1] With fidelity to the *Roe-Casey* line of precedent, the Court held the Nebraska statute unconstitutional in part because it lacked the requisite protection for the preservation of a woman's health. . . .

From U.S. Supreme Court, April 18, 2007.

Today's decision is alarming. It refuses to take *Casey* and *Stenberg* seriously. It tolerates, indeed applauds, federal intervention to ban nationwide a procedure found necessary and proper in certain cases by the American College of Obstetricians and Gynecologists (ACOG). It blurs the line, firmly drawn in *Casey,* between previability and postviability abortions. And, for the first time since *Roe,* the Court blesses a prohibition with no exception safeguarding a woman's health.

I dissent from the Court's disposition. Retreating from prior rulings that abortion restrictions cannot be imposed absent an exception safeguarding a woman's health, the Court upholds an Act that surely would not survive under the close scrutiny that previously attended state-decreed limitations on a woman's reproductive choices.

I

A

As *Casey* comprehended, at stake in cases challenging abortion restrictions is a woman's "control over her [own] destiny." 505 U.S., at 869 (plurality opinion). . . . "There was a time, not so long ago," when women were "regarded as the center of home and family life, with attendant special responsibilities that precluded full and independent legal status under the Constitution." *Id.,* at 896–897 (quoting *Hoyt v. Florida,* 368 U.S. 57, 62 (1961)). Those views, this Court made clear in *Casey*, "are no longer consistent with our understanding of the family, the individual, or the Constitution." 505 U.S., at 897. Women, it is now acknowledged, have the talent, capacity, and right "to participate equally in the economic and social life of the Nation." *Id.,* at 856. Their ability to realize their full potential, the Court recognized, is intimately connected to "their ability to control their reproductive lives." *Ibid.* Thus, legal challenges to undue restrictions on abortion procedures do not seek to vindicate some generalized notion of privacy; rather, they center on a woman's autonomy to determine her life's course, and thus to enjoy equal citizenship stature. . . .

In keeping with this comprehension of the right to reproductive choice, the Court has consistently required that laws regulating abortion, at any stage of pregnancy and in all cases, safeguard a woman's health.

We have thus ruled that a State must avoid subjecting women to health risks not only where the pregnancy itself creates danger, but also where state regulation forces women to resort to less safe methods of abortion. See *Planned Parenthood of Central Mo. v. Danforth,* 428 U.S. 52, 79 (1976) (holding unconstitutional a ban on a method of abortion that "force[d] a woman . . . to terminate her pregnancy by methods more dangerous to her health"). See also *Stenberg,* 530 U.S., at 931 ("[Our cases] make clear that a risk to . . . women's health is the same whether it happens to arise from regulating a particular method of abortion, or from barring abortion entirely."). Indeed, we have applied the rule that abortion regulation must safeguard a woman's health to the particular procedure at issue here—intact dilation and evacuation (D&E).

In *Stenberg,* we expressly held that a statute banning intact D&E was unconstitutional in part because it lacked a health exception. We noted that there existed a "division of medical opinion" about the relative safety of intact D&E, but we made clear that as long as "substantial medical authority supports the proposition that banning a particular abortion procedure could endanger women's health," a health exception is required, *id.,* at 938. We explained:

> "The word 'necessary' in *Casey's* phrase 'necessary, in appropriate medical judgment, for the preservation of the life or health of the [pregnant woman],' cannot refer to an absolute necessity or to absolute proof. Medical treatments and procedures are often considered appropriate (or inappropriate) in light of estimated comparative health risks (and health benefits) in particular cases. Neither can that phrase require unanimity of medical opinion. Doctors often differ in their estimation of comparative health risks and appropriate treatment. And *Casey's* words 'appropriate medical judgment' must embody the judicial need to tolerate responsible differences of medical opinion . . . ." *Id.,* at 937 (citation omitted).

Thus, we reasoned, division in medical opinion "at most means uncertainty, a factor that signals the presence of risk, not its absence." *Ibid.* "[A] statute that altogether forbids [intact D&E] . . . consequently must contain a health exception." *Id.,* at 938. . . .

B

In 2003, a few years after our ruling in *Stenberg,* Congress passed the Partial-Birth Abortion Ban Act—without an exception for women's health.[2] . . . The congressional findings on which the Partial-Birth Abortion Ban Act rests do not withstand inspection, as the lower courts have determined and this Court is obliged to concede. . . . See *National Abortion Federation v. Ashcroft,* 330 F. Supp. 2d 436, 482 (SDNY 2004) ("Congress did not . . . carefully consider the evidence before arriving at its findings."), aff'd *sub nom. National Abortion Federation v. Gonzales,* 437 F. 3d 278 (CA2 2006). See also *Planned Parenthood Federation of Am. v. Ashcroft,* 320 F. Supp. 2d 957, 1019 (ND Cal. 2004) ("[N]one of the six physicians who testified before Congress had ever performed an intact D&E. Several did not provide abortion services at all; and one was not even an obgyn. . . . [T]he oral testimony before Congress was not only unbalanced, but intentionally polemic."), aff'd, 435 F. 3d 1163 (CA9 2006); *Carhart v. Ashcroft,* 331 F. Supp. 2d 805, 1011 (Neb. 2004) ("Congress arbitrarily relied upon the opinions of doctors who claimed to have no (or very little) recent and relevant experience with surgical abortions, and disregarded the views of doctors who had significant and relevant experience with those procedures."), aff'd, 413 F. 3d 791 (CA8 2005).

Many of the Act's recitations are incorrect. . . . For example, Congress determined that no medical schools provide instruction on intact D&E. . . . But in fact, numerous leading medical schools teach the procedure. . . .

More important, Congress claimed there was a medical consensus that the banned procedure is never necessary. . . . But the evidence "very clearly demonstrate[d] the opposite." *Planned Parenthood*, 320 F. Supp. 2d, at 1025. See also *Carhart*, 331 F. Supp. 2d, at 1008–1009 ("[T]here was no evident consensus in the record that Congress compiled. There was, however, a substantial body of medical opinion presented to Congress in opposition. If anything . . . the congressional record establishes that there was a 'consensus' in favor of the banned procedure."); *National Abortion Federation*, 330 F. Supp. 2d, at 488 ("The congressional record itself undermines [Congress'] finding" that there is a medical consensus that intact D&E "is never medically necessary and should be prohibited." (internal quotation marks omitted)).

Similarly, Congress found that "[t]here is no credible medical evidence that partial-birth abortions are safe or are safer than other abortion procedures." Congressional Findings (14)(B), in notes following 18 U. S. C. §1531 (2000 ed., Supp. IV), p. 769. But the congressional record includes letters from numerous individual physicians stating that pregnant women's health would be jeopardized under the Act, as well as statements from nine professional associations, including ACOG, the American Public Health Association, and the California Medical Association, attesting that intact D&E carries meaningful safety advantages over other methods. See *National Abortion Federation*, 330 F. Supp. 2d, at 490. See also *Planned Parenthood*, 320 F. Supp. 2d, at 1021 ("Congress in its findings . . . chose to disregard the statements by ACOG and other medical organizations."). No comparable medical groups supported the ban. In fact, "all of the government's own witnesses disagreed with many of the specific congressional findings." *Id.*, at 1024.

C

In contrast to Congress, the District Courts made findings after full trials at which all parties had the opportunity to present their best evidence. The courts had the benefit of "much more extensive medical and scientific evidence . . . concerning the safety and necessity of intact D&Es." *Planned Parenthood*, 320 F. Supp. 2d, at 1014. . . .

During the District Court trials, "numerous" "extraordinarily accomplished" and "very experienced" medical experts explained that, in certain circumstances and for certain women, intact D&E is safer than alternative procedures and necessary to protect women's health. *Carhart*, 331 F. Supp. 2d, at 1024–1027; see *Planned Parenthood*, 320 F. Supp. 2d, at 1001 ("[A]ll of the doctors who actually perform intact D&Es concluded that in their opinion and clinical judgment, intact D&Es remain the safest option for certain individual women under certain individual health circumstances, and are significantly safer for these women than other abortion techniques, and are thus medically necessary."); cf. *ante*, at 31 ("Respondents presented evidence that intact D&E may be the safest method of abortion, for reasons similar to those adduced in *Stenberg*.").

According to the expert testimony plaintiffs introduced, the safety advantages of intact D&E are marked for women with certain medical conditions, for example, uterine scarring, bleeding disorders, heart disease, or compromised immune systems. . . . Further, plaintiffs' experts testified that intact D&E is significantly safer for women with certain pregnancy-related conditions, such as placenta previa and accreta, and for women carrying fetuses with certain abnormalities, such as severe hydrocephalus. . . .

Based on thoroughgoing review of the trial evidence and the congressional record, each of the District Courts to consider the issue rejected Congress' findings as unreasonable and not supported by the evidence. . . . The trial courts concluded, in contrast to Congress' findings, that "significant medical authority supports the proposition that in some circumstances, [intact D&E] is the safest procedure." *Id.*, at 1033. . . .

The District Courts' findings merit this Court's respect. Today's opinion supplies no reason to reject those findings. Nevertheless, despite the District Courts' appraisal of the weight of the evidence, and in undisguised conflict with *Stenberg*, the Court asserts that the Partial-Birth Abortion Ban Act can survive "when . . . medical uncertainty persists." *Ante*, at 33. This assertion is bewildering. Not only does it defy the Court's longstanding precedent affirming the necessity of a health exception, with no carve-out for circumstances of medical uncertainty, see *supra*, at 4–5; it gives short shrift to the records before us, carefully canvassed by the District Courts. Those records indicate that "the majority of highly-qualified experts on the subject believe intact D&E to be the safest, most appropriate procedure under certain circumstances." *Planned Parenthood*, 320 F. Supp. 2d, at 1034. . . .

The Court acknowledges some of this evidence, *ante*, at 31, but insists that, because some witnesses disagreed with the ACOG and other experts' assessment of risk, the Act can stand. . . . In this insistence, the Court brushes under the rug the District Courts' well-supported findings that the physicians who testified that intact D&E is never necessary to preserve the health of a woman had slim authority for their opinions. They had no training for, or personal experience with, the intact D&E procedure, and many performed abortions only on rare occasions. See *Planned Parenthood*, 320 F. Supp. 2d, at 980; *Carhart*, 331 F. Supp. 2d, at 1025; cf. *National Abortion Federation*, 330 F. Supp. 2d, at 462–464. Even indulging the assumption that the Government witnesses were equally qualified to evaluate the relative risks of abortion procedures, their testimony could not erase the "significant medical authority support[ing] the proposition that in some circumstances, [intact D&E] would be the safest procedure." *Stenberg*, 530 U.S., at 932.

II

A

The Court offers flimsy and transparent justifications for upholding a nationwide ban on intact D&E *sans* any exception to safeguard a women's health. Today's ruling, the Court declares, advances "a premise central to [*Casey*'s] conclusion"—*i.e.*, the Government's "legitimate and substantial interest in preserving and promoting fetal life." *Ante*, at 14. But the Act scarcely furthers that interest: The law saves not a single fetus from destruction, for it targets only a *method* of performing abortion. . . . In short, the Court upholds a law that, while doing nothing to "preserv[e] . . . fetal life," *ante,* at 14, bars a woman from choosing intact D&E although her doctor "reasonably believes [that procedure] will best protect [her]." *Stenberg,* 530 U.S., at 946 (STEVENS, J., concurring).

As another reason for upholding the ban, the Court emphasizes that the Act does not proscribe the nonintact D&E procedure. See *ante,* at 34. But why not, one might ask. Nonintact D&E could equally be characterized as "brutal," *ante,* at 26, involving as it does "tear[ing] [a fetus] apart" and "ripp[ing] off" its limbs, *ante,* at 4, 6. "[T]he notion that either of these two equally gruesome procedures . . . is more akin to infanticide than the other, or that the State furthers any legitimate interest by banning one but not the other, is simply irrational." *Stenberg,* 530 U.S., at 946–947 (STEVENS, J., concurring).

Delivery of an intact, albeit nonviable, fetus warrants special condemnation, the Court maintains, because a fetus that is not dismembered resembles an infant. . . . But so, too, does a fetus delivered intact after it is terminated by injection a day or two before the surgical evacuation, . . . or a fetus delivered through medical induction or cesarean. . . . Yet, the availability of those procedures—along with D&E by dismemberment—the Court says, saves the ban on intact D&E from a declaration of unconstitutionality. . . . Never mind that the procedures deemed acceptable might put a woman's health at greater risk. . . .

Ultimately, the Court admits that "moral concerns" are at work, concerns that could yield prohibitions on any abortion. . . . ("Congress could . . . conclude that the type of abortion proscribed by the Act requires specific regulation because it implicates additional ethical and moral concerns that justify a special prohibition."). Notably, the concerns expressed are untethered to any ground genuinely serving the Government's interest in preserving life. By allowing such concerns to carry the day and case, overriding fundamental rights, the Court dishonors our precedent. See, *e.g., Casey,* 505 U.S., at 850 ("Some of us as individuals find abortion offensive to our most basic principles of morality, but that cannot control our decision. Our obligation is to define the liberty of all, not to mandate our own moral code."); *Lawrence v. Texas,* 539 U.S. 558, 571 (2003) (Though "[f]or many persons [objections to homosexual conduct] are not trivial concerns but profound and deep convictions accepted as ethical and moral principles," the power of the State may not be used "to enforce these views on the whole society through operation of the criminal law." (citing *Casey,* 505 U.S., at 850)).

Revealing in this regard, the Court invokes an antiabortion shibboleth for which it concededly has no reliable evidence: Women who have abortions come to regret their choices, and consequently suffer from "[s]evere depression and loss of esteem." *Ante,* at 29.[3] Because of women's fragile emotional state and because of the "bond of love the mother has for her child," the Court worries, doctors may withhold information about the nature of the intact D&E procedure. *Ante,* at 28–29.[4] The solution the Court approves, then, is *not* to require doctors to inform women, accurately and adequately, of the different procedures and their attendant risks. Cf. *Casey,* 505 U.S., at 873 (plurality opinion) ("States are free to enact laws to provide a reasonable framework for a woman to make a decision that has such profound and lasting

meaning."). Instead, the Court deprives women of the right to make an auton-
omous choice, even at the expense of their safety.[5]

This way of thinking reflects ancient notions about women's place in
the family and under the Constitution—ideas that have long since been dis-
credited. Compare, *e.g., Muller v. Oregon,* 208 U.S. 412, 422–423 (1908) ("protective" legislation imposing hours-of-work limitations on women only held
permissible in view of women's "physical structure and a proper discharge of
her maternal funct[ion]"); *Bradwell v. State,* 16 Wall. 130, 141 (1873) (Bradley,
J., concurring) ("Man is, or should be, woman's protector and defender. The
natural and proper timidity and delicacy which belongs to the female sex evidently unfits it for many of the occupations of civil life. . . . The paramount
destiny and mission of woman are to fulfil[l] the noble and benign offices of
wife and mother."), with *United States v. Virginia,* 518 U.S. 515, 533, 542, n. 12
(1996) (State may not rely on "overbroad generalizations" about the "talents,
capacities, or preferences" of women; "[s]uch judgments have . . . impeded . . .
women's progress toward full citizenship stature throughout our Nation's
history"); *Califano v. Goldfarb,* 430 U.S. 199, 207 (1977) (gender-based Social
Security classification rejected because it rested on "archaic and overbroad
generalizations" "such as assumptions as to [women's] dependency" (internal
quotation marks omitted)).

Though today's majority may regard women's feelings on the matter as
"self-evident," *ante,* at 29, this Court has repeatedly confirmed that "[t]he destiny of the woman must be shaped . . . on her own conception of her spiritual
imperatives and her place in society." *Casey,* 505 U.S., at 852. See also *id.,* at
877 (plurality opinion) ("[M]eans chosen by the State to further the interest in
potential life must be calculated to inform the woman's free choice, not hinder
it."); *supra,* at 3–4.

B

In cases on a "woman's liberty to determine whether to [continue] her pregnancy," this Court has identified viability as a critical consideration. See *Casey,*
505 U.S., at 869–870 (plurality opinion). "[T]here is no line [more workable]
than viability," the Court explained in *Casey,* for viability is "the time at which
there is a realistic possibility of maintaining and nourishing a life outside the
womb, so that the independent existence of the second life can in reason and
all fairness be the object of state protection that now overrides the rights of the
woman. . . . In some broad sense it might be said that a woman who fails to
act before viability has consented to the State's intervention on behalf of the
developing child." *Id.,* at 870.

Today, the Court blurs that line, maintaining that "[t]he Act [legiti-
mately] appl[ies] both previability and postviability because . . . a fetus is a
living organism while within the womb, whether or not it is viable outside
the womb." *Ante,* at 17. Instead of drawing the line at viability, the Court
refers to Congress' purpose to differentiate "abortion and infanticide" based
not on whether a fetus can survive outside the womb, but on where a fetus is
anatomically located when a particular medical procedure is performed. . . .

One wonders how long a line that saves no fetus from destruction will hold in face of the Court's "moral concerns." . . . The Court's hostility to the right *Roe* and *Casey* secured is not concealed. Throughout, the opinion refers to obstetrician-gynecologists and surgeons who perform abortions not by the titles of their medical specialties, but by the pejorative label "abortion doctor." . . . A fetus is described as an "unborn child," and as a "baby," . . . second-trimester, previability abortions are referred to as "late-term," . . . and the reasoned medical judgments of highly trained doctors are dismissed as "preferences" motivated by "mere convenience." . . . Instead of the heightened scrutiny we have previously applied, the Court determines that a "rational" ground is enough to uphold the Act, *ante,* at 28, 37. And, most troubling, *Casey's* principles, confirming the continuing vitality of "the essential holding of *Roe,*" are merely "assume[d]" for the moment, *ante,* at 15, 31, rather than "retained" or "reaffirmed," *Casey,* 505 U.S., at 846.

III

A

The Court further confuses our jurisprudence when it declares that "facial attacks" are not permissible in "these circumstances," *i.e.,* where medical uncertainty exists. *Ante,* at 37; see *ibid.* ("In an as-applied challenge the nature of the medical risk can be better quantified and balanced than in a facial attack."). This holding is perplexing given that, in materially identical circumstances we held that a statute lacking a health exception was unconstitutional on its face. *Stenberg,* 530 U.S., at 930; see *id.,* at 937 (in facial challenge, law held unconstitutional because "significant body of medical opinion believes [the] procedure may bring with it greater safety for *some patients*" (emphasis added)). . . .

Without attempting to distinguish *Stenberg* and earlier decisions, the majority asserts that the Act survives review because respondents have not shown that the ban on intact D&E would be unconstitutional "in a large fraction of relevant cases." *Ante,* at 38 (citing *Casey,* 505 U.S., at 895). But *Casey* makes clear that, in determining whether any restriction poses an undue burden on a "large fraction" of women, the relevant class is *not* "all women," nor "all pregnant women," nor even all women "seeking abortions." 505 U.S., at 895. Rather, a provision restricting access to abortion, "must be judged by reference to those [women] for whom it is an actual rather than an irrelevant restriction," *ibid.* Thus the absence of a health exception burdens *all* women for whom it is relevant—women who, in the judgment of their doctors, require an intact D&E because other procedures would place their health at risk. . . . It makes no sense to conclude that this facial challenge fails because respondents have not shown that a health exception is necessary for a large fraction of second-trimester abortions, including those for which a health exception is unnecessary: The very purpose of a health *exception* is to protect women in *exceptional* cases.

B

If there is anything at all redemptive to be said of today's opinion, it is that the Court is not willing to foreclose entirely a constitutional challenge to the Act. "The Act is open," the Court states, "to a proper as-applied challenge in a discrete case.". . . But the Court offers no clue on what a "proper" lawsuit might look like. . . . Nor does the Court explain why the injunctions ordered by the District Courts should not remain in place, trimmed only to exclude instances in which another procedure would safeguard a woman's health at least equally well. Surely the Court cannot mean that no suit may be brought until a woman's health is immediately jeopardized by the ban on intact D&E. A woman "suffer[ing] from medical complications," *ante,* at 38, needs access to the medical procedure at once and cannot wait for the judicial process to unfold. See *Ayotte,* 546 U.S., at 328.

The Court appears, then, to contemplate another lawsuit by the initiators of the instant actions. In such a second round, the Court suggests, the challengers could succeed upon demonstrating that "in discrete and well-defined instances a particular condition has or is likely to occur in which the procedure prohibited by the Act must be used." *Ante,* at 37. One may anticipate that such a preenforcement challenge will be mounted swiftly, to ward off serious, sometimes irremediable harm, to women whose health would be endangered by the intact D&E prohibition.

The Court envisions that in an as-applied challenge, "the nature of the medical risk can be better quantified and balanced." . . . But it should not escape notice that the record already includes hundreds and hundreds of pages of testimony identifying "discrete and well-defined instances" in which recourse to an intact D&E would better protect the health of women with particular conditions. . . . Record evidence also documents that medical exigencies, unpredictable in advance, may indicate to a well-trained doctor that intact D&E is the safest procedure. . . .

The Court's allowance only of an "as-applied challenge in a discrete case," *ante,* at 38—jeopardizes women's health and places doctors in an untenable position. Even if courts were able to carve-out exceptions through piecemeal litigation for "discrete and well-defined instances," *ante,* at 37, women whose circumstances have not been anticipated by prior litigation could well be left unprotected. In treating those women, physicians would risk criminal prosecution, conviction, and imprisonment if they exercise their best judgment as to the safest medical procedure for their patients. The Court is thus gravely mistaken to conclude that narrow as-applied challenges are "the proper manner to protect the health of the woman." . . .

IV

As the Court wrote in *Casey,* "overruling *Roe*'s central holding would not only reach an unjustifiable result under principles of *stare decisis,* but would seriously weaken the Court's capacity to exercise the judicial power and to function as the Supreme Court of a Nation dedicated to the rule of law."

505 U.S., at 865. "[T]he very concept of the rule of law underlying our own Constitution requires such continuity over time that a respect for precedent is, by definition, indispensable." *Id.*, at 854. See also *id.*, at 867 ("[T]o over-rule under fire in the absence of the most compelling reason to reexamine a watershed decision would subvert the Court's legitimacy beyond any serious question.").

Though today's opinion does not go so far as to discard *Roe* or *Casey*, the Court, differently composed than it was when we last considered a restrictive abortion regulation, is hardly faithful to our earlier invocations of "the rule of law" and the "principles of *stare decisis*." Congress imposed a ban despite our clear prior holdings that the State cannot proscribe an abortion procedure when its use is necessary to protect a woman's health. . . . Although Congress' findings could not withstand the crucible of trial, the Court defers to the legislative override of our Constitution-based rulings. . . . A decision so at odds with our jurisprudence should not have staying power.

In sum, the notion that the Partial-Birth Abortion Ban Act furthers any legitimate governmental interest is, quite simply, irrational. The Court's defense of the statute provides no saving explanation. In candor, the Act, and the Court's defense of it, cannot be understood as anything other than an effort to chip away at a right declared again and again by this Court—and with increasing comprehension of its centrality to women's lives. . . . When "a statute burdens constitutional rights and all that can be said on its behalf is that it is the vehicle that legislators have chosen for expressing their hostility to those rights, the burden is undue." *Stenberg*, 530 U.S., at 952 (GINSBURG, J., concurring) (quoting *Hope Clinic v. Ryan*, 195 F. 3d 857, 881 (CA7 1999) (Posner, C. J., dissenting)).

◦◦◦

For the reasons stated, I dissent from the Court's disposition and would affirm the judgments before us for review.

Notes

1. The term "partial-birth abortion" is neither recognized in the medical literature nor used by physicians who perform second-trimester abortions. See *Planned Parenthood Federation of Am. v. Ashcroft*, 320 F. Supp. 2d 957, 964 (ND Cal. 2004), aff'd, 435 F. 3d 1163 (CA9 2006). The medical community refers to the procedure as either dilation & extraction (D&X) or intact dilation and evacuation (intact D&E). See, *e.g., ante*, at 5; *Stenberg v. Carhart*, 530 U.S. 914, 927 (2000).

2. The Act's sponsors left no doubt that their intention was to nullify our ruling in *Stenberg*, 530 U.S. 914. See, *e.g.*, 149 Cong. Rec. 5731 (2003) (statement of Sen. Santorum) ("Why are we here? We are here because the Supreme Court defended the indefensible. . . . We have responded to the Supreme Court."). See also 148 Cong. Rec. 14273 (2002) (statement of Rep. Linder) (rejecting proposition that Congress has "no right to legislate a ban on this horrible practice because the Supreme Court says [it] cannot").

3. The Court is surely correct that, for most women, abortion is a painfully difficult decision. See *ante,* at 28. But "neither the weight of the scientific evidence to date nor the observable reality of 33 years of legal abortion in the United States comports with the idea that having an abortion is any more dangerous to a woman's long-term mental health than delivering and parenting a child that she did not intend to have. . . ." Cohen, Abortion and Mental Health: Myths and Realities, 9 Guttmacher Policy Rev. 8 (2006); see generally Bazelon, Is There a Post-Abortion Syndrome? *N. Y. Times Magazine,* Jan. 21, 2007, p. 40. See also, *e.g.,* American Psychological Association, APA Briefing Paper on the Impact of Abortion (2005) (rejecting theory of a postabortion syndrome and stating that "[a]ccess to legal abortion to terminate an unwanted pregnancy is vital to safeguard both the physical and mental health of women"); Schmiege & Russo, Depression and Unwanted First Pregnancy: Longitudinal Cohort Study, 331 *British Medical J.* 1303 (2005) (finding no credible evidence that choosing to terminate an unwanted first pregnancy contributes to risk of subsequent depression); Gilchrist, Hannaford, Frank, & Kay, Termination of Pregnancy and Psychiatric Morbidity, 167 *British J. of Psychiatry* 243, 247–248 (1995) (finding, in a cohort of more than 13,000 women, that the rate of psychiatric disorder was no higher among women who terminated pregnancy than among those who carried pregnancy to term); Stodland, The Myth of the Abortion Trauma Syndrome, 268 *JAMA* 2078, 2079 (1992) ("Scientific studies indicate that legal abortion results in fewer deleterious sequelae for women compared with other possible outcomes of unwanted pregnancy. There is no evidence of an abortion trauma syndrome."); American Psychological Association, Council Policy Manual: (N)(I)(3), Public Interest (1989) (declaring assertions about widespread severe negative psychological effects of abortion to be "without fact"). But see Cougle, Reardon, & Coleman, Generalized Anxiety Following Unintended Pregnancies Resolved Through Childbirth and Abortion: A Cohort Study of the 1995 National Survey of Family Growth, 19 *J. Anxiety Disorders* 137, 142 (2005) (advancing theory of a postabortion syndrome but acknowledging that "no causal relationship between pregnancy outcome and anxiety could be determined" from study); Reardon et al., Psychiatric Admissions of Low-Income Women following Abortion and Childbirth, 168 *Canadian Medical Assn. J.* 1253, 1255–1256 (May 13, 2003) (concluding that psychiatric admission rates were higher for women who had an abortion compared with women who delivered); cf. Major, Psychological Implications of Abortion—Highly Charged and Rife with Misleading Research, 168 *Canadian Medical Assn. J.* 1257, 1258 (May 13, 2003) (critiquing Reardon study for failing to control for a host of differences between women in the delivery and abortion samples).

4. Notwithstanding the "bond of love" women often have with their children, see *ante,* at 28, not all pregnancies, this Court has recognized, are wanted, or even the product of consensual activity. See *Casey,* 505 U.S., at 891 ("[O]n an average day in the United States, nearly 11,000 women are severely assaulted by their male partners. Many of these incidents involve sexual assault."). See also Glander, Moore, Michielutte, & Parsons, The Prevalence of Domestic Violence Among Women Seeking Abortion, 91 Obstetrics & Gynecology 1002 (1998); Holmes, Resnick, Kilpatrick, & Best, Rape-Related Pregnancy; Estimates and Descriptive Characteristics from

a National Sample of Women, 175 Am. J. Obstetrics & Gynecology 320 (Aug. 1996).

5. Eliminating or reducing women's reproductive choices is manifestly *not* a means of protecting them. When safe abortion procedures cease to be an option, many women seek other means to end unwanted or coerced pregnancies. See, *e.g.,* World Health Organization, Unsafe Abortion: Global and Regional Estimates of the Incidence of Unsafe Abortion and Associated Mortality in 2000, pp. 3, 16 (4th ed. 2004) ("Restrictive legislation is associated with a high incidence of unsafe abortion" worldwide; unsafe abortion represents 13% of all "maternal" deaths); Henshaw, Unintended Pregnancy and Abortion: A Public Health Perspective, in A Clinician's Guide to Medical and Surgical Abortion 11, 19 (M. Paul, E. Lichtenberg, L. Borgatta, D. Grimes, & P. Stubblefield eds. 1999) ("Before legalization, large numbers of women in the United States died from unsafe abortions."); H. Boonstra, R. Gold, C. Richards, & L. Finer, Abortion in Women's Lives 13, and fig. 2.2 (2006) ("as late as 1965, illegal abortion still accounted for an estimated . . . 17% of all officially reported pregnancy-related deaths"; "[d]eaths from abortion declined dramatically after legalization").

POSTSCRIPT

Is It Constitutional to Ban "Partial-Birth" Abortions Without Providing for an Exception to Protect the Health of the Mother?

In claiming that the Court's decision in *Gonzales v. Carhart* is "in undisguised conflict with *Stenberg*" and "surely would not survive under the close scrutiny that previously attended state-decreed limitations on a woman's reproductive choices," Justice Ginsburg hints at one factor that could explain the Court's divergent opinions in these two cases: the change in the composition of the Supreme Court between 2000 and 2007. In 2005, Justice Sandra Day O'Connor, who was generally pro-choice and even coauthored the Court's decision in *Casey,* announced she was planning to retire. She was soon replaced by Justice Samuel Alito, who sided with the Court's majority in *Gonzales v. Carhart.*

Former Justice Potter Stewart once lamented that a "basic change in the law upon a ground no firmer than a change in our membership invites the popular misconception that this institution is little different from the two political branches of the Government. No misconception could do more lasting injury to this Court and to the system of law which it is our abiding mission to serve" (Dissenting Opinion, *Michell v. W. T. Grant Co.,* 416 U.S. 600, 1974). The need to maintain a consistent approach to legal issues and downplay the effect of justices' own value systems on its decision-making process is part of the reason the Supreme Court has adopted the principle of *stare decisis* as one of its central tenets.

Stare decisis, Latin for "to stand by decisions," is the concept that the Court will restrain itself when possible from overruling previous decisions that have set important legal precedents. As former Justice Byron White once described it, "The rule of stare decisis is essential if case-by-case judicial decisionmaking is to be reconciled with the principle of the rule of law, for when governing legal standards are open to revision in every case, deciding cases becomes a mere exercise of judicial will, with arbitrary and unpredictable results" (Dissenting Opinion, *Akron v. Akron Reproductive Health,* 462 U.S. 416, 1983). According to Justice O'Connor in her *Casey* decision, stare decisis was a key reason why the Court should hesitate to overrule *Roe:*

> The obligation to follow precedent begins with necessity, and a contrary necessity marks its outer limit . . . no judicial system could do society's work if it eyed each issue afresh in every case that raised it. . . . Indeed, the very concept of the rule of law underlying our own Constitution requires such continuity over time that a respect for precedent is, by definition, indispensable.

Nevertheless, there are, of course, times when the Court has found it both prudent and necessary to overrule precedent, especially in constitutional cases. Whereas Congress can overcome the Court's judgments on statutory issues by passing new laws, the difficulty of amending the Constitution has made the Supreme Court more willing to review its constitutional holdings when previous decisions have proven difficult in practice or no longer seem defensible on principle. For instance, the Court has shown willingness to revisit periodically its decisions on what constitutes "cruel and unusual punishment" under the Eighth Amendment, citing as its justification former Chief Justice Warren's assertion that "the words of the Amendment are not precise. . . . their scope is not static. The Amendment must draw its meaning from the evolving standards of decency that mark the progress of a maturing society" (*Trop v. Dulles,* 356 U.S. 86, 1958). Of course, one could make a similar pronouncement about many of the amendments to the Constitution, making the Supreme Court's determination of which of its decisions are worthy of adherence, and which should be overruled, an important part of its constitutional jurisprudence.

A good place to begin to study the contemporary legal debates surrounding abortion is N. E. H. Hull and Peter Charles Hoffer's Roe v. Wade: *The Abortion Rights Controversy in American History* (University Press of Kansas, 2001) and *The Abortion Rights Controversy in America: A Legal Reader* (N. E. H. Hull, William James Hoffer, & Peter Hoffer, eds., University of North Carolina Press, 2004). A unique recent contribution to the literature on the Supreme Court's abortion jurisprudence is *What* Roe v. Wade *Should Have Said: The Nation's Top Legal Experts Rewrite America's Most Controversial Decision* (Jack Balkin, ed., New York University Press, 2005). For analyses of *Gonzales v. Carhart* and how it fits into the Supreme Court's abortion jurisprudence since *Roe,* see Robert J. Pushaw, "Partial-Birth Abortion and the Perils of Constitutional Common Law," 31 *Harvard Journal of Law & Public Policy* 519 (2008) and David J. Garrow, "Significant Risks: *Gonzales v. Carhart* and the Future of Abortion Law," 2007 *Supreme Court Review* 1 (2008).

ISSUE 5

Are Restrictions on Physician-Assisted Suicide Constitutional?

YES: William H. Rehnquist, from Majority Opinion, *Washington et al. v. Glucksberg et al.*, U.S. Supreme Court (June 26, 1997)

NO: Stephen Reinhardt, from Opinion for the Court, *Compassion in Dying v. State of Washington*, U.S. Court of Appeals for the Ninth Circuit (1996)

ISSUE SUMMARY

YES: Former Supreme Court Chief Justice William H. Rehnquist rules that although patients have the right to refuse life-sustaining treatment, physician-assisted suicide is not constitutionally protected.

NO: Judge Stephen Reinhardt argues that forbidding physician-assisted suicide in the cases of competent, terminally ill patients violates the due process clause of the Constitution.

In 1990 the Supreme Court issued its landmark ruling in *Cruzan v. Director, Missouri Department of Health*, 497 U.S. 261 (1990). Nancy Beth Cruzan had sustained severe and irreversible injuries in an automobile accident; her condition was one commonly characterized as a "persistent vegetative state." She displayed no discernible cognitive functioning and was kept alive through the use of artificial hydration and feeding equipment. Four years after the accident, Nancy's parents began proceedings in a Missouri state trial court so that they could withdraw all artificial means of life support.

Cruzan was one of an estimated 10,000 persons in the United States in a vegetative state. She had left no explicit directions on whether or not she wanted to continue to be fed and receive treatment if she were ever to be in such a condition. Should her parents have been allowed to make life-and-death decisions under such circumstances? How clear should an incompetent person's wishes be before the parents are allowed to make a decision? The trial court granted the parents' request to withdraw life support. However, the State of Missouri intervened, claiming an "unqualified governmental interest in preserving the sanctity of human life." Although the state recognized the legal validity of "living wills," in which a person indicates what he or she would like done if the individual were no longer able to make treatment decisions, it argued that in the absence of a living will, "clear and convincing" evidence of the patient's wishes was required to authorize the removal of life-sustaining devices. Agreeing with the state, the Missouri Supreme Court reversed the trial court order directing the withdrawal of life-support equipment.

In *Cruzan* the U.S. Supreme Court granted *certiorari* to hear, for the first time, a constitutional question concerning a "right to die." Upholding the constitutionality of Missouri's evidentiary requirements, the decision of the Missouri Supreme Court was affirmed. Chief Justice William H. Rehnquist delivered the opinion of the Court and wrote that while a "right to die" might be exercised by an individual who was able to make his or her own decisions, "clear and convincing" evidence of the individual's wishes was needed before a court could allow parents or someone else to make a decision to stop treatment or care. The postscript to this issue describes what the consequences of this were for Cruzan and her parents.

The issues raised in the *Cruzan* case illustrate a basic distinction made by the law. The law prohibits active euthanasia, in which death results from some positive act, such as a lethal injection. "Mercy killings" fall into this category and can be prosecuted as acts of homicide. The law is more tolerant of passive euthanasia, in which death results from the failure to act or on the removal of life-saving equipment. In *Cruzan*, the Court noted that the Anglo-American legal tradition has generally recognized the right of competent adults to refuse medical treatment and has viewed the act of forcing of treatment on an unconsenting person, violating his or her "bodily integrity," as akin to battery. But if people have a right to refuse life-saving treatment, resulting in their death, shouldn't they also have a right to hasten their death, for instance, through the use of prescription drugs? This controversial moral and legal issue is taken up by an appeals court and the Supreme Court in the following readings.

YES ↵

William H. Rehnquist

Majority Opinion, *Washington v. Glucksberg*

CHIEF JUSTICE REHNQUIST delivered the opinion of the Court.

The question presented in this case is whether Washington's prohibition against "causing" or "aiding" a suicide offends the Fourteenth Amendment to the United States Constitution. We hold that it does not.

It has always been a crime to assist a suicide in the State of Washington. In 1854, Washington's first Territorial Legislature outlawed "assisting another in the commission of self-murder." Today, Washington law provides: "A person is guilty of promoting a suicide attempt when he knowingly causes or aids another person to attempt suicide." Wash. Rev. Code 9A.36.060(1)(1994). "Promoting a suicide attempt" is a felony, punishable by up to five years' imprisonment and up to a $10,000 fine. §§ 9A.36.060(2) and 9A.20.021(1)(c). At the same time, Washington's Natural Death Act, enacted in 1979, states that the "withholding or withdrawal of life-sustaining treatment" at a patient's direction "shall not, for any purpose, constitute a suicide." Wash. Rev. Code § 70.122.070(1).[1]

Petitioners in this case are the State of Washington and its Attorney General. Respondents Harold Glucksberg, M.D., Abigail Halperin, M.D., Thomas A. Preston, M.D., and Peter Shalit, M.D., are physicians who practice in Washington. These doctors occasionally treat terminally ill, suffering patients, and declare that they would assist these patients in ending their lives if not for Washington's assisted-suicide ban. In January 1994, respondents, along with three gravely ill, pseudonymous plaintiffs who have since died and Compassion in Dying, a non-profit organization that counsels people considering physician-assisted suicide, sued in the United States District Court, seeking a declaration that Wash. Rev. Code 9A.36.060(1) (1994) is, on its face, unconstitutional. *Compassion in Dying v. Washington, 850 F. Supp. 1454, 1459 (WD Wash. 1994).*

The plaintiffs asserted "the existence of a liberty interest protected by the Fourteenth Amendment which extends to a personal choice by a mentally competent, terminally ill adult to commit physician-assisted suicide." Relying primarily on *Planned Parenthood v. Casey, 505 U.S. 833 (1992),* and *Cruzan v. Director, Missouri Dept. of Health, 497 U.S. 261 (1990),* the District Court agreed, *850 F. Supp., at 1459–1462,* and concluded that Washington's assisted-suicide ban is unconstitutional because it "places an undue burden on the exercise of [that] constitutionally protected liberty interest." The District Court also decided that the Washington statute violated the Equal Protection Clause's requirement that "'all persons similarly situated . . . be treated alike.'"

From Supreme Court of the United States, June 26, 1997.

A panel of the Court of Appeals for the Ninth Circuit reversed, emphasizing that "in the two hundred and five years of our existence no constitutional right to aid in killing oneself has ever been asserted and upheld by a court of final jurisdiction." *Compassion in Dying v. Washington, 49 F.3d 586, 591 (1995).* The Ninth Circuit reheard the case en banc, reversed the panel's decision, and affirmed the District Court. *Compassion in Dying v. Washington, 79 F.3d 790, 798 (1996).* Like the District Court, the en banc Court of Appeals emphasized our *Casey* and *Cruzan* decisions. The court also discussed what it described as "historical" and "current societal attitudes" toward suicide and assisted suicide, and concluded that "the Constitution encompasses a due process liberty interest in controlling the time and manner of one's death—that there is, in short, a constitutionally-recognized 'right to die.'" After "weighing and then balancing" this interest against Washington's various interests, the court held that the State's assisted-suicide ban was unconstitutional "as applied to terminally ill competent adults who wish to hasten their deaths with medication prescribed by their physicians." The court did not reach the District Court's equal-protection holding. We granted certiorari, and now reverse.

I

We begin, as we do in all due-process cases, by examining our Nation's history, legal traditions, and practices. In almost every State—indeed, in almost every western democracy—it is a crime to assist a suicide. The States' assisted-suicide bans are not innovations. Rather, they are longstanding expressions of the States' commitment to the protection and preservation of all human life.

More specifically, for over 700 years, the Anglo-American common-law tradition has punished or otherwise disapproved of both suicide and assisting suicide. In the 13th century, Henry de Bracton, one of the first legal-treatise writers, observed that "just as a man may commit felony by slaying another so may he do so by slaying himself." Bracton on Laws and Customs of England 423 (f. 150) (G. Woodbine ed., S. Thorne transl., 1968). The real and personal property of one who killed himself to avoid conviction and punishment for a crime were forfeit to the king; however, thought Bracton, "if a man slays himself in weariness of life or because he is unwilling to endure further bodily pain . . . [only] his movable goods [were] confiscated." Thus, "the principle that suicide of a sane person, for whatever reason, was a punishable felony was . . . introduced into English common law."

For the most part, the early American colonies adopted the common-law approach. For example, the legislators of the Providence Plantations, which would later become Rhode Island, declared, in 1647, that "self-murder is by all agreed to be the most unnatural, and it is by this present Assembly declared, to be that, wherein he that doth it, kills himself out of a premeditated hatred against his own life or other humor: . . . his goods and chattels are the king's custom, but not his debts nor lands; but in case he be an infant, a lunatic, mad or distracted man, he forfeits nothing." The Earliest Acts and Laws of the Colony of Rhode Island and Providence Plantations 1647–1719, p. 19 (J. Cushing ed. 1977). Virginia also required ignominious burial for suicides, and their estates were forfeit to the crown. A. Scott, Criminal Law in Colonial Virginia 108, and n. 93, 198, and n. 15 (1930).

Over time, however, the American colonies abolished these harsh common-law penalties. William Penn abandoned the criminal-forfeiture sanction in Pennsylvania in 1701, and the other colonies (and later, the other States) eventually followed this example. *Cruzan, 497 U.S. at 294* (SCALIA, J., concurring). . . .

[T]he movement away from the common law's harsh sanctions did not represent an acceptance of suicide; rather, as Chief Justice Swift observed, this change reflected the growing consensus that it was unfair to punish the suicide's family for his wrongdoing. Nonetheless, although States moved away from Blackstone's treatment of suicide, courts continued to condemn it as a grave public wrong.

That suicide remained a grievous, though nonfelonious, wrong is confirmed by the fact that colonial and early state legislatures and courts did not retreat from prohibiting assisting suicide. Swift, in his early 19th century treatise on the laws of Connecticut, stated that "if one counsels another to commit suicide, and the other by reason of the advice kills himself, the advisor is guilty of murder as principal." Z. Swift, *A Digest of the Laws of the State of Connecticut* 270 (1823). This was the well established common-law view.

And the prohibitions against assisting suicide never contained exceptions for those who were near death. Rather, "the life of those to whom life had become a burden—of those who [were] hopelessly diseased or fatally wounded—nay, even the lives of criminals condemned to death, [were] under the protection of law, equally as the lives of those who [were] in the full tide of life's enjoyment, and anxious to continue to live." *Blackburn v. State, 23 Ohio St. 146, 163 (1872).*

The earliest American statute explicitly to outlaw assisting suicide was enacted in New York in 1828, and many of the new States and Territories followed New York's example. Between 1857 and 1865, a New York commission led by Dudley Field drafted a criminal code that prohibited "aiding" a suicide and, specifically, "furnishing another person with any deadly weapon or poisonous drug, knowing that such person intends to use such weapon or drug in taking his own life." By the time the Fourteenth Amendment was ratified, it was a crime in most States to assist a suicide. The Field Penal Code was adopted in the Dakota Territory in 1877, in New York in 1881, and its language served as a model for several other western States' statutes in the late 19th and early 20th centuries. California, for example, codified its assisted-suicide prohibition in 1874, using language similar to the Field Code's. In this century, the Model Penal Code also prohibited "aiding" suicide, prompting many States to enact or revise their assisted-suicide bans. . . .

Though deeply rooted, the States' assisted-suicide bans have in recent years been reexamined and, generally, reaffirmed. Because of advances in medicine and technology, Americans today are increasingly likely to die in institutions, from chronic illnesses. Public concern and democratic action are therefore sharply focused on how best to protect dignity and independence at the end of life, with the result that there have been many significant changes in state laws and in the attitudes these laws reflect. Many States, for example, now permit "living wills," surrogate health-care decisionmaking, and the withdrawal or refusal of life-sustaining medical treatment. At the same time, however, voters and legislators continue for the most part to reaffirm their States' prohibitions on assisting suicide.

The Washington statute at issue in this case, Wash. Rev. Code § 9A.36.060 (1994), was enacted in 1975 as part of a revision of that State's criminal code. Four years later, Washington passed its Natural Death Act, which specifically stated that the "withholding or withdrawal of life-sustaining treatment . . . shall not, for any purpose, constitute a suicide" and that "nothing in this chapter shall be construed to condone, authorize, or approve mercy killing. . . ." In 1991, Washington voters rejected a ballot initiative which, had it passed, would have permitted a form of physician-assisted suicide. Washington then added a provision to the Natural Death Act expressly excluding physician-assisted suicide.

California voters rejected an assisted-suicide initiative similar to Washington's in 1993. On the other hand, in 1994, voters in Oregon enacted, also through ballot initiative, that State's "Death With Dignity Act," which legalized physician-assisted suicide for competent, terminally ill adults. Since the Oregon vote, many proposals to legalize assisted suicide have been and continue to be introduced in the States' legislatures, but none has been enacted. And just last year, Iowa and Rhode Island joined the overwhelming majority of States explicitly prohibiting assisted suicide. See Iowa Code Ann. §§ 707A.2, 707A.3 (Supp. 1997); R. I. Gen. Laws §§ 11-60-1, 11-60-3 (Supp. 1996). Also, on April 30, 1997, President Clinton signed the Federal Assisted Suicide Funding Restriction Act of 1997, which prohibits the use of federal funds in support of physician-assisted suicide. . . .

Attitudes toward suicide itself have changed since Bracton, but our laws have consistently condemned, and continue to prohibit, assisting suicide. Despite changes in medical technology and notwithstanding an increased emphasis on the importance of end-of-life decisionmaking, we have not retreated from this prohibition. Against this backdrop of history, tradition, and practice, we now turn to respondents' constitutional claim.

II

. . . In a long line of cases, we have held that, in addition to the specific freedoms protected by the Bill of Rights, the "liberty" specially protected by the Due Process Clause includes the rights to marry, *Loving v. Virginia, 388 U.S. 1 (1967)*; to have children, *Skinner v. Oklahoma ex rel. Williamson, 316 U.S. 535 (1942)*; to direct the education and upbringing of one's children, *Meyer v. Nebraska, 262 U.S. 390 (1923); Pierce v. Society of Sisters, 268 U.S. 510 (1925)*; to marital privacy, *Griswold v. Connecticut, 381 U.S. 479 (1965)*; to use contraception, ibid; *Eisenstadt v. Baird, 405 U.S. 438 (1972)*; to bodily integrity, *Rochin v. California, 342 U.S. 165 (1952)*, and to abortion, Casey, supra. We have also assumed, and strongly suggested, that the Due Process Clause protects the traditional right to refuse unwanted lifesaving medical treatment. *Cruzan, 497 U.S. at 278–279.*

But we "have always been reluctant to expand the concept of substantive due process because guideposts for responsible decisionmaking in this unchartered area are scarce and open-ended." *Collins, 503 U.S. at 125.* By extending constitutional protection to an asserted right or liberty interest, we, to a great extent, place the matter outside the arena of public debate and legislative action. We must therefore "exercise the utmost care whenever we are asked to break new ground in this field," ibid, lest the liberty protected by the Due Process Clause be subtly transformed into the policy preferences of the members of this Court, *Moore, 431 U.S. at 502* (plurality opinion).

Our established method of substantive-due-process analysis has two primary features: First, we have regularly observed that the Due Process Clause specially protects those fundamental rights and liberties which are, objectively, "deeply rooted in this Nation's history and tradition," *id., at 503* (plurality opinion); *Snyder v. Massachusetts, 291 U.S. 97, 105 (1934)* ("so rooted in the traditions and conscience of our people as to be ranked as fundamental"), and "implicit in the concept of ordered liberty," such that "neither liberty nor justice would exist if they were sacrificed," *Palko v. Connecticut, 302 U.S. 319, 325, 326 (1937).* Second, we have required in substantive-due-process cases a "careful description" of the asserted fundamental liberty interest. Our Nation's history, legal traditions, and practices thus provide the crucial "guideposts for responsible decisionmaking," that direct and restrain our exposition of the Due Process Clause. As we stated recently in Flores, the Fourteenth Amendment "forbids the government to infringe . . . 'fundamental' liberty interests at all, no matter what process is provided, unless the infringement is narrowly tailored to serve a compelling state interest." *507 U.S. at 302.*

JUSTICE SOUTER, relying on Justice Harlan's dissenting opinion in Poe v. Ullman, would largely abandon this restrained methodology, and instead ask "whether [Washington's] statute sets up one of those 'arbitrary impositions' or 'purposeless restraints' at odds with the Due Process Clause of the Fourteenth Amendment," post, at 1 (quoting *Poe, 367 U.S. 497, 543 (1961)* (Harlan, J., dissenting)). In our view, however, the development of this Court's substantive-due-process jurisprudence, described briefly above, has been a process whereby the outlines of the "liberty" specially protected by the Fourteenth Amendment—never fully clarified, to be sure, and perhaps not capable of being fully clarified—have at least been carefully refined by concrete examples involving fundamental rights found to be deeply rooted in our legal tradition. This approach tends to rein in the subjective elements that are necessarily present in due-process judicial review. In addition, by establishing a threshold requirement—that a challenged state action implicate a fundamental right—before requiring more than a reasonable relation to a legitimate state interest to justify the action, it avoids the need for complex balancing of competing interests in every case.

Turning to the claim at issue here, the Court of Appeals stated that "properly analyzed, the first issue to be resolved is whether there is a liberty interest in determining the time and manner of one's death," or, in other words, "is there a right to die?" Similarly, respondents assert a "liberty to choose how to die" and a right to "control of one's final days," and describe the asserted liberty as "the right to choose a humane, dignified death," and "the liberty to shape death." As noted above, we have a tradition of carefully formulating the interest at stake in substantive-due-process cases. For example, although

Cruzan is often described as a "right to die" case, see *79 F.3d, at 799;* post, at 9 (STEVENS, J., concurring in judgment) (*Cruzan* recognized "the more specific interest in making decisions about how to confront an imminent death"), we were, in fact, more precise: we assumed that the Constitution granted competent persons a "constitutionally protected right to refuse lifesaving hydration and nutrition." *Cruzan, 497 U.S. at 279; id., at 287* (O'CONNOR, J., concurring) ("[A] liberty interest in refusing unwanted medical treatment may be inferred from our prior decisions"). The Washington statute at issue in this case prohibits "aiding another person to attempt suicide," Wash. Rev. Code § 9A.36.060(1) (1994), and, thus, the question before us is whether the "liberty" specially protected by the Due Process Clause includes a right to commit suicide which itself includes a right to assistance in doing so.

We now inquire whether this asserted right has any place in our Nation's traditions. Here, as discussed above, we are confronted with a consistent and almost universal tradition that has long rejected the asserted right, and continues explicitly to reject it today, even for terminally ill, mentally competent adults. To hold for respondents, we would have to reverse centuries of legal doctrine and practice, and strike down the considered policy choice of almost every State.

Respondents contend, however, that the liberty interest they assert is consistent with this Court's substantive-due-process line of cases, if not with this Nation's history and practice. Pointing to *Casey* and *Cruzan,* respondents read our jurisprudence in this area as reflecting a general tradition of "self-sovereignty," and as teaching that the "liberty" protected by the Due Process Clause includes "basic and intimate exercises of personal autonomy" ("It is a promise of the Constitution that there is a realm of personal liberty which the government may not enter"). According to respondents, our liberty jurisprudence, and the broad, individualistic principles it reflects, protects the "liberty of competent, terminally ill adults to make end-of-life decisions free of undue government interference." Brief for Respondents 10. The question presented in this case, however, is whether the protections of the Due Process Clause include a right to commit suicide with another's assistance. With this "careful description" of respondents' claim in mind, we turn to *Casey* and *Cruzan.*

In *Cruzan,* we considered whether Nancy Beth Cruzan, who had been severely injured in an automobile accident and was in a persistive vegetative state, "had a right under the United States Constitution which would require the hospital to withdraw life-sustaining treatment" at her parents' request. We began with the observation that "at common law, even the touching of one person by another without consent and without legal justification was a battery." We then discussed the related rule that "informed consent is generally required for medical treatment." After reviewing a long line of relevant state cases, we concluded that "the common-law doctrine of informed consent is viewed as generally encompassing the right of a competent individual to refuse medical treatment." Next, we reviewed our own cases on the subject, and stated that "the principle that a competent person has a constitutionally protected liberty interest in refusing unwanted medical treatment may be inferred from our prior decisions." Therefore, "for purposes of [that] case, we assumed that the United States Constitution would grant a competent person a constitutionally protected right to refuse lifesaving hydration and nutrition." We concluded that, notwithstanding this right, the Constitution permitted Missouri to require clear and convincing evidence of an incompetent patient's wishes concerning the withdrawal of life-sustaining treatment.

Respondents contend that in *Cruzan* we "acknowledged that competent, dying persons have the right to direct the removal of life-sustaining medical treatment and thus hasten death," Brief for Respondents 23, and that "the constitutional principle behind recognizing the patient's liberty to direct the withdrawal of artificial life support applies at least as strongly to the choice to hasten impending death by consuming lethal medication." Similarly, the Court of Appeals concluded that "*Cruzan,* by recognizing a liberty interest that includes the refusal of artificial provision of life-sustaining food and water, necessarily recognized a liberty interest in hastening one's own death." *79 F.3d, at 816.*

The right assumed in *Cruzan,* however, was not simply deduced from abstract concepts of personal autonomy. Given the common-law rule that forced medication was a battery, and the long legal tradition protecting the decision to refuse unwanted medical treatment, our assumption was entirely consistent with this Nation's history and constitutional traditions. The decision to commit suicide with the assistance of another may be just as personal and profound as the decision to refuse unwanted medical treatment, but it has never enjoyed similar legal protection. Indeed, the two acts are widely and reasonably regarded as quite distinct. In *Cruzan* itself, we recognized that most States outlawed assisted suicide—and even more do today—and we certainly gave no intimation that the right to refuse unwanted medical treatment could be somehow transmuted into a right to assistance in committing suicide.

Respondents also rely on *Casey*. There, the Court's opinion concluded that "the essential holding of Roe v. Wade should be retained and once again reaffirmed." *Casey, 505 U.S. at 846.* We held, first, that a woman has a right, before her fetus is viable, to an abortion "without undue interference from the State"; second, that States may restrict post-viability abortions, so long as exceptions are made to protect a woman's life and health; and third, that the State has legitimate interests throughout a pregnancy in protecting the health of the woman and the life of the unborn child. Ibid. In reaching this conclusion, the opinion discussed in some detail this Court's substantive-due-process tradition of interpreting the Due Process Clause to protect certain fundamental rights and "personal decisions relating to marriage, procreation, contraception, family relationships, child rearing, and education," and noted that many of those rights and liberties "involve the most intimate and personal choices a person may make in a lifetime."

The Court of Appeals, like the District Court, found *Casey* "'highly instructive'" and "'almost prescriptive'" for determining "'what liberty interest may inhere in a terminally ill person's choice to commit suicide'":

> "Like the decision of whether or not to have an abortion, the decision how and when to die is one of 'the most intimate and personal choices a person may make in a lifetime,' a choice 'central to personal dignity and autonomy.'" *79 F.3d, at 813–814.*

Similarly, respondents emphasize the statement in *Casey* that:

"At the heart of liberty is the right to define one's own concept of existence, of meaning, of the universe, and of the mystery of human life.
Beliefs about these matters could not define the attributes of personhood
were they formed under compulsion of the State." *Casey, 505 U.S. at 851.*

. . . By choosing this language, the Court's opinion in *Casey* described,
in a general way and in light of our prior cases, those personal activities and
decisions that this Court has identified as so deeply rooted in our history and
traditions, or so fundamental to our concept of constitutionally ordered liberty,
that they are protected by the Fourteenth Amendment. The opinion moved
from the recognition that liberty necessarily includes freedom of conscience and
belief about ultimate considerations to the observation that "though the abortion decision may originate within the zone of conscience and belief, it is more
than a philosophic exercise." *Casey, 505 U.S. at 852.* . . . That many of the rights
and liberties protected by the Due Process Clause sound in personal autonomy
does not warrant the sweeping conclusion that any and all important, intimate,
and personal decisions are so protected, *San Antonio Independent School Dist. v.
Rodriguez, 411 U.S. 1, 33–35 (1973),* and *Casey* did not suggest otherwise.

The history of the law's treatment of assisted suicide in this country has
been and continues to be one of the rejection of nearly all efforts to permit it.
That being the case, our decisions lead us to conclude that the asserted "right"
to assistance in committing suicide is not a fundamental liberty interest protected by the Due Process Clause. The Constitution also requires, however, that
Washington's assisted-suicide ban be rationally related to legitimate government
interests. See *Heller v. Doe, 509 U.S. 312, 319–320 (1993); Flores, 507 U.S. at 305.*
This requirement is unquestionably met here. As the court below recognized,
Washington's assisted-suicide ban implicates a number of state interests.

First, Washington has an "unqualified interest in the preservation of
human life." *Cruzan, 497 U.S. at 282.* The State's prohibition on assisted suicide, like all homicide laws, both reflects and advances its commitment to
this interest. ("The interests in the sanctity of life that are represented by the
criminal homicide laws are threatened by one who expresses a willingness to
participate in taking the life of another"). This interest is symbolic and aspira-
tional as well as practical:

"While suicide is no longer prohibited or penalized, the ban against
assisted suicide and euthanasia shores up the notion of limits in human
relationships. It reflects the gravity with which we view the decision to
take one's own life or the life of another, and our reluctance to encourage or promote these decisions." New York Task Force 131–132.

Respondents admit that "the State has a real interest in preserving the
lives of those who can still contribute to society and enjoy life." Brief for
Respondents 35, n.23. The Court of Appeals also recognized Washington's
interest in protecting life, but held that the "weight" of this interest depends
on the "medical condition and the wishes of the person whose life is at stake."

79 F.3d, at 817. Washington, however, has rejected this sliding-scale approach and, through its assisted-suicide ban, insists that all persons' lives, from beginning to end, regardless of physical or mental condition, are under the full protection of the law. See *United States v. Rutherford, 442, U.S. 544, 558 (1979)* (". . . Congress could reasonably have determined to protect the terminally ill, no less than other patients, from the vast range of self-styled panaceas that inventive minds can devise"). As we have previously affirmed, the States "may properly decline to make judgments about the 'quality' of life that a particular individual may enjoy," *Cruzan, 497 U.S. at 282.* This remains true, as *Cruzan* makes clear, even for those who are near death.

Relatedly, all admit that suicide is a serious public-health problem, especially among persons in otherwise vulnerable groups.

Those who attempt suicide—terminally ill or not—often suffer from depression or other mental disorders. Research indicates, however, that many people who request physician-assisted suicide withdraw that request if their depression and pain are treated. The New York Task Force, however, expressed its concern that, because depression is difficult to diagnose, physicians and medical professionals often fail to respond adequately to seriously ill patients' needs. Thus, legal physician-assisted suicide could make it more difficult for the State to protect depressed or mentally ill persons, or those who are suffering from untreated pain, from suicidal impulses.

The State also has an interest in protecting the integrity and ethics of the medical profession. In contrast to the Court of Appeals' conclusion that "the integrity of the medical profession would [not] be threatened in any way [by physician-assisted suicide]," *79 F.3d, at 827,* the American Medical Association, like many other medical and physicians' groups, has concluded that "physician-assisted suicide is fundamentally incompatible with the physician's role as healer." American Medical Association, Code of Ethics § 2.211 (1994); see Council on Ethical and Judicial Affairs, Decisions Near the End of Life, *267 JAMA 2229, 2233 (1992)* ("The societal risks of involving physicians in medical interventions to cause patients' deaths is too great"); New York Task Force 103–109 (discussing physicians' views). And physician-assisted suicide could, it is argued, undermine the trust that is essential to the doctor-patient relationship by blurring the time-honored line between healing and harming.

Next, the State has an interest in protecting vulnerable groups—including the poor, the elderly, and disabled persons—from abuse, neglect, and mistakes. The Court of Appeals dismissed the State's concern that disadvantaged persons might be pressured into physician-assisted suicide as "ludicrous on its face." *79 F.3d, at* 825. We have recognized, however, the real risk of subtle coercion and undue influence in end-of-life situations. *Cruzan, 497 U.S. at 281.* Similarly, the New York Task Force warned that "legalizing physician-assisted suicide would pose profound risks to many individuals who are ill and vulnerable. . . . The risk of harm is greatest for the many individuals in our society whose autonomy and well-being are already compromised by poverty, lack of access to good medical care, advanced age, or membership in a stigmatized social group." If physician-assisted suicide were permitted, many might resort to it to spare their families the substantial financial burden of end-of-life health-care costs.

The State's interest here goes beyond protecting the vulnerable from coercion; it extends to protecting disabled and terminally ill people from prejudice, negative and inaccurate stereotypes, and "societal indifference." *49 F.3d, at 592.* The state's assisted-suicide ban reflects and reinforces its policy that the lives of terminally ill, disabled, and elderly people must be no less valued than the lives of the young and healthy, and that a seriously disabled person's suicidal impulses should be interpreted and treated the same way as anyone else's.

Finally, the State may fear that permitting assisted suicide will start it down the path to voluntary and perhaps even involuntary euthanasia. The Court of Appeals struck down Washington's assisted-suicide ban only "as applied to competent, terminally ill adults who wish to hasten their deaths by obtaining medication prescribed by their doctors." *79 F.3d, at 838.* Washington insists, however, that the impact of the court's decision will not and cannot be so limited. If suicide is protected as a matter of constitutional right, it is argued, "every man and woman in the United States must enjoy it."

The Court of Appeals' decision, and its expansive reasoning, provide ample support for the State's concerns. The court noted, for example, that the "decision of a duly appointed surrogate decision maker is for all legal purposes the decision of the patient himself," *79 F.3d, at 832, n.120;* that "in some instances, the patient may be unable to self-administer the drugs and . . . administration by the physician . . . may be the only way the patient may be able to receive them," *id., at 831;* and that not only physicians, but also family members and loved ones, will inevitably participate in assisting suicide. *Id., at 838, n.140.* Thus, it turns out that what is couched as a limited right to "physician-assisted suicide" is likely, in effect, a much broader license, which could prove extremely difficult to police and contain. Washington's ban on assisting suicide prevents such erosion.

This concern is further supported by evidence about the practice of euthanasia in the Netherlands. The Dutch government's own study revealed that in 1990, there were 2,300 cases of voluntary euthanasia (defined as "the deliberate termination of another's life at his request"), 400 cases of assisted suicide, and more than 1,000 cases of euthanasia without an explicit request. In addition to these latter 1,000 cases, the study found an additional 4,941 cases where physicians administered lethal morphine overdoses without the patients' explicit consent. Physician-Assisted Suicide and Euthanasia in the Netherlands: A Report of Chairman Charles T. Canady, at 12–13 (citing Dutch study). This study suggests that, despite the existence of various reporting procedures, euthanasia in the Netherlands has not been limited to competent, terminally ill adults who are enduring physical suffering, and that regulation of the practice may not have prevented abuses in cases involving vulnerable persons, including severely disabled neonates and elderly persons suffering from dementia. The New York Task Force, citing the Dutch experience, observed that "assisted suicide and euthanasia are closely linked," New York Task Force 145, and concluded that the "risk of . . . abuse is neither speculative nor distant." Washington, like most other States, reasonably ensures against this risk by banning, rather than regulating, assisting suicide.

We need not weigh exactingly the relative strengths of these various interests. They are unquestionably important and legitimate, and Washington's ban on assisted suicide is at least reasonably related to their promotion and protection. We therefore hold that Wash. Rev. Code § 9A.36.060(1)(1994) does not violate the Fourteenth Amendment, either on its face or "as applied to competent, terminally ill adults who wish to hasten their deaths by obtaining medication prescribed by their doctors." *79 F.3d, at 838.*

Throughout the Nation, Americans are engaged in an earnest and profound debate about the morality, legality, and practicality of physician-assisted suicide. Our holding permits this debate to continue, as it should in a democratic society. The decision of the en banc Court of Appeals is reversed, and the case is remanded for further proceedings consistent with this opinion.

Note

1. Under Washington's Natural Death Act, "adult persons have the fundamental right to control the decisions relating to the rendering of their own health care, including the decision to have life-sustaining treatment withheld or withdrawn in instances of a terminal condition or permanent unconscious condition." Wash. Rev. Code § 70.122.010 (1994). In Washington, "any adult person may execute a directive directing the withholding or withdrawal of life-sustaining treatment in a terminal condition or permanent unconscious condition," § 70.122.030, and a physician who, in accordance with such a directive, participates in the withholding or withdrawal of life-sustaining treatment is immune from civil, criminal, or professional liability. § 70.122.051.

Stephen Reinhardt

→ **NO**

Majority Opinion, *Compassion in Dying v. State of Washington*

I.

This case raises an extraordinarily important and difficult issue. It compels us to address questions to which there are no easy or simple answers, at law or otherwise. It requires us to confront the most basic of human concerns—the mortality of self and loved ones—and to balance the interest in preserving human life against the desire to die peacefully and with dignity. People of good will can and do passionately disagree about the proper result, perhaps even more intensely than they part ways over the constitutionality of restricting a woman's right to have an abortion. Heated though the debate may be, we must determine whether and how the United States Constitution applies to the controversy before us, a controversy that may touch more people more profoundly than any other issue the courts will face in the foreseeable future.

Today, we are required to decide whether a person who is terminally ill has a constitutionally-protected liberty interest in hastening what might otherwise be a protracted, undignified, and extremely painful death. If such an interest exists, we must next decide whether or not the state of Washington may constitutionally restrict its exercise by banning a form of medical assistance that is frequently requested by terminally ill people who wish to die. We first conclude that there is a constitutionally-protected liberty interest in determining the time and manner of one's own death, an interest that must be weighed against the state's legitimate and countervailing interests, especially those that relate to the preservation of human life. After balancing the competing interests, we conclude by answering the narrow question before us: We hold that insofar as the Washington statute prohibits physicians from prescribing life-ending medication for use by terminally ill, competent adults who wish to hasten their own deaths, it violates the Due Process Clause of the Fourteenth Amendment.

II. Preliminary Matters and History of the Case

. . . The plaintiffs do not challenge Washington statute RCW 9A.36.060 in its entirety. Specifically they do not object to the portion of the Washington statute that makes it unlawful for a person knowingly to cause another to

From Supreme Court of the United States, 1996.

commit suicide. Rather, they only challenge the statute's "or aids" provision. They challenge that provision both on its face and as applied to terminally ill, mentally competent adults who wish to hasten their own deaths with the help of medication prescribed by their doctors. The plaintiffs contend that the provision impermissibly prevents the exercise by terminally ill patients of a constitutionally-protected liberty interest in violation of the Due Process Clause of the Fourteenth Amendment, and also that it impermissibly distinguishes between similarly situated terminally ill patients in violation of the Equal Protection Clause. . . .

III. Overview of Legal Analysis: Is There a Due Process Violation?

In order to answer the question whether the Washington statute violates the Due Process Clause insofar as it prohibits the provision of certain medical assistance to terminally ill, competent adults who wish to hasten their own deaths, we first determine whether there is a liberty interest in choosing the time and manner of one's death—a question sometimes phrased in common parlance as: Is there a right to die? Because we hold that there is, we must then determine whether prohibiting physicians from prescribing life-ending medication for use by terminally ill patients who wish to die violates the patients' due process rights.

The mere recognition of a liberty interest does not mean that a state may not prohibit the exercise of that interest in particular circumstances, nor does it mean that a state may not adopt appropriate regulations governing its exercise. Rather, in cases like the one before us, the courts must apply a balancing test under which we weigh the individual's liberty interests against the relevant state interests in order to determine whether the state's actions are constitutionally permissible. . . .

Defining the Liberty Interest and Other Relevant Terms

. . . While some people refer to the liberty interest implicated in right-to-die cases as a liberty interest in committing suicide, we do not describe it that way. We use the broader and more accurate terms, "the right to die," "determining the time and manner of one's death," and "hastening one's death" for an important reason. The liberty interest we examine encompasses a whole range of acts that are generally not considered to constitute "suicide." Included within the liberty interest we examine, is for example, the act of refusing or terminating unwanted medical treatment . . . a competent adult has a liberty interest in refusing to be connected to a respirator or in being disconnected from one, even if he is terminally ill and cannot live without mechanical assistance. The law does not classify the death of a patient that results from the granting of his wish to decline or discontinue treatment as "suicide." Nor does the law label the acts of those who help the patient carry out that wish, whether by physically disconnecting the respirator or by removing an intravenous tube, as assistance in suicide.

Accordingly, we believe that the broader terms—"the right to die," "controlling the time and manner of one's death," and "hastening one's death"—more accurately describe the liberty interest at issue here. . . .

Like the Court in *Roe [v. Wade]*, we begin with ancient attitudes. In Greek and Roman times, far from being universally prohibited, suicide was often considered commendable in literature, mythology, and practice. . . .

While Socrates counseled his disciples against committing suicide, he willingly drank the hemlock as he was condemned to do, and his example inspired others to end their lives. Plato, Socrates' most distinguished student, believed suicide was often justifiable.

He suggested that if life itself became immoderate, then suicide became a rational, justifiable act. Painful disease, or intolerable constraint were sufficient reasons to depart. And this when religious superstitions faded was philosophic justification enough.

Many contemporaries of Plato were even more inclined to find suicide a legitimate and acceptable act. In *Roe*, while surveying the attitudes of the Greeks toward abortion, the Court stated that "only the Pythagorean school of philosophers frowned on the related act of suicide," 410 U.S. at 131; it then noted that the Pythagorean school represented a distinctly minority view. *Id.*

The Stoics glorified suicide as an act of pure rational will. Cato, who killed himself to avoid dishonor when Ceasar crushed his military aspirations, was the most celebrated of the many suicides among the Stoics. Montaigne wrote of Cato: "This was a man chosen by nature to show the heights which can be attained by human steadfastness and constancy. . . . Such courage is above philosophy."

Like the Greeks, the Romans often considered suicide to be acceptable or even laudable.

To live nobly also meant to die nobly and at the right time. Everything depended on a dominant will and a rational choice. . . .

Suicide was a crime under the English common law, at least in limited circumstances, probably as early as the thirteenth century. Bracton, incorporating Roman Law as set forth in Justinian's Digest, declared that if someone commits suicide to avoid conviction of a felony, his property escheats to his lords. Bracton said "[i]t ought to be otherwise if he kills himself through madness or unwillingness to endure suffering." Despite his general fidelity to Roman law, Bracton did introduce a key innovation: "[I]f a man slays himself in weariness of life or because he is unwilling to endure further bodily pain . . . he may have a successor, but his movable goods [personal property] are confiscated. He does not lose his inheritance [real property], only his movable goods." Bracton's innovation was incorporated into English common law, which has thus treated suicides resulting from the inability to "endure further bodily pain" with compassion and understanding ever since a common law scheme was firmly established. . . .

English attitudes toward suicide, including the tradition of ignominious burial, carried over to America where they subsequently underwent a transformation. By 1798, six of the 13 original colonies had abolished all penalties for suicide either by statute or state constitution. There is no evidence that any court ever imposed a punishment for suicide or attempted suicide under common law in post-revolutionary America. By the time the Fourteenth Amendment was adopted in 1868, suicide was generally not punishable, and in only nine of the 37 states is it clear that there were statutes prohibiting assisting suicide.

The majority of states have not criminalized suicide or attempted suicide since the turn of the century. The New Jersey Supreme Court declared in 1901 that since suicide was not punishable it should not be considered a crime. "[A]ll will admit that in some cases it is ethically defensible," the court said, as when a woman kills herself to escape being raped or "when a man curtails weeks or months of agony of an incurable disease." *Campbell v. Supreme Conclave Improved Order Heptasophs,* 66 N.J.L. 274, 49 A. 550, 553 (1901). Today, no state has a statute prohibiting suicide or attempted suicide; nor has any state had such a statute for at least 10 years. A majority of states do, however, still have laws on the books against assisting suicide.

Current Societal Attitudes

Clearly the absence of a criminal sanction alone does not show societal approbation of a practice. Nor is there any evidence that Americans approve of suicide in general. In recent years, however, there has been increasingly widespread support for allowing the terminally ill to hasten their deaths and avoid painful, undignified, and inhumane endings to their lives. Most Americans simply do not appear to view such acts as constituting suicide, and there is much support in reason for that conclusion.

Polls have repeatedly shown that a large majority of Americans—sometimes nearing 90%—fully endorse recent legal changes granting terminally ill patients, and sometimes their families, the prerogative to accelerate their death by refusing or terminating treatment. Other polls indicate that a majority of Americans favor doctor-assisted suicide for the terminally ill. In April, 1990, the Roper Report found that 64% of Americans believed that the terminally ill should have the right to request and receive physician aid-in-dying. Another national poll, conducted in October 1991, shows that "nearly two out of three Americans favor doctor-assisted suicide and euthanasia for terminally ill patients who request it." A 1994 Harris poll found 73% of Americans favor legalizing physician-assisted suicide. Three states have held referenda on proposals to allow physicians to help terminally ill, competent adults commit suicide with somewhat mixed results. In Oregon, voters approved the carefully-crafted referendum by a margin of 51 to 49 percent in November of 1994. In Washington and California where the measures contained far fewer practical safeguards, they narrowly failed to pass. . . . Accounts of doctors who have helped their patients end their lives have appeared both in professional journals and in the daily press. . . .

Liberty Interest Under Casey

In *[Planned Parenthood v.] Casey,* the Court surveyed its prior decisions affording "constitutional protection to personal decisions relating to marriage,

procreation, contraception, family relationships, child rearing, and education," *id.* at 2807 and then said:

> These matters, involving the most intimate and personal choices a
> person may make in a lifetime, choices central to personal dignity
> and autonomy, are central to the liberty protected by the Fourteenth
> Amendment. At the heart of liberty is the right to define one's own
> concept of existence, of meaning, of the universe, and of the mystery of
> human life. Beliefs about these matters could not define the attributes
> of personhood were they formed under compulsion of the State. The
> district judge in this case found the Court's reasoning in *Casey* "highly
> instructive" and "almost prescriptive" for determining "what liberty
> interest may inhere in a terminally ill person's choice to commit sui-
> cide." Compassion In Dying, 850 F. Supp. at 1459. We agree.

Like the decision of whether or not to have an abortion, the decision
how and when to die is one of "the most intimate and personal choices a
person may make in a lifetime," a choice "central to personal dignity and
autonomy." A competent terminally ill adult, having lived nearly the full
measure of his life, has a strong liberty interest in choosing a dignified and
humane death rather than being reduced at the end of his existence to a child-
like state of helplessness, diapered, sedated, incontinent. How a person dies
not only determines the nature of the final period of his existence, but in
many cases, the enduring memories held by those who love him.

Prohibiting a terminally ill patient from hastening his death may have
an even more profound impact on that person's life than forcing a woman
to carry a pregnancy to term. The case of an AIDS patient treated by Dr. Peter
Shalit, one of the physician-plaintiffs in this case, provides a compelling illus-
tration. In his declaration, Dr. Shalit described his patient's death this way:

> One patient of mine, whom I will call Smith, a fictitious name, lin-
> gered in the hospital for weeks, his lower body so swollen from oozing
> Kaposi's lesions that he could not walk, his genitals so swollen that he
> required a catheter to drain his bladder, his fingers gangrenous from
> clotted arteries. Patient Smith's friends stopped visiting him because it
> gave them nightmares. Patient Smith's agonies could not be relieved by
> medication or by the excellent nursing care he received. Patient Smith
> begged for assistance in hastening his death. As his treating doctor, it
> was my professional opinion that patient Smith was mentally compe-
> tent to make a choice with respect to shortening his period of suffering
> before inevitable death. I felt that I should accommodate his request.
> However, because of the statute, I was unable to assist him and he died
> after having been tortured for weeks by the end-phase of his disease.

For such patients, wracked by pain and deprived of all pleasure, a state-
enforced prohibition on hastening their deaths condemns them to unrelieved
misery or torture. Surely, a person's decision whether to endure or avoid such an
existence constitutes one of the most, if not the most, "intimate and personal

choices a person may make in a life-time," a choice that is "central to personal dignity and autonomy." *Casey,* 112 S.Ct. at 2807. . . .

Cruzan stands for the proposition that there is a due process liberty interest in rejecting unwanted medical treatment, including the provision of food and water by artificial means. Moreover, the Court majority clearly recognized that granting the request to remove the tubes through which Cruzan received artificial nutrition and hydration would lead inexorably to her death. *Cruzan,* 497 U.S. at 267–68, 283. Accordingly, we conclude that *Cruzan,* by recognizing a liberty interest that includes the refusal of artificial provision of life-sustaining food and water, necessarily recognizes a liberty interest in hastening one's own death.

Summary

Casey and *Cruzan* provide persuasive evidence that the Constitution encompasses a due process liberty interest in controlling the time and manner of one's death—that there is, in short, a constitutionally recognized "right to die." Our conclusion is strongly influenced by, but not limited to, the plight of mentally competent, terminally ill adults. We are influenced as well by the plight of others, such as those whose existence is reduced to a vegetative state or a permanent and irreversible state of unconsciousness.

Our conclusion that there is a liberty interest in determining the time and manner of one's death does not mean that there is a concomitant right to exercise that interest in all circumstances or to do so free from state regulation. To the contrary, we explicitly recognize that some prohibitory and regulatory state action is fully consistent with constitutional principles.

In short, finding a liberty interest constitutes a critical first step toward answering the question before us. The determination that must now be made is whether the state's attempt to curtail the exercise of that interest is constitutionally justified.

V. Relevant Factors and Interests

To determine whether a state action that impairs a liberty interest violates an individual's substantive due process rights we must identify the factors relevant to the case at hand, assess the state's interests and the individual's liberty interest in light of those factors, and then weigh and balance the competing interests. The relevant factors generally include: 1) the importance of the various state interests, both in general and in the factual context of the case; 2) the manner in which those interests are furthered by the state law or regulation; 3) the importance of the liberty interest, both in itself and in the context in which it is being exercised; 4) the extent to which that interest is burdened by the challenged state action; and, 5) the consequences of upholding or overturning the statute or regulation. . . .

B. The Means by Which the State Furthers Its Interests

In applying the balancing test, we must take into account not only the strength of the state's interests but also the means by which the state has chosen to further those interests.

1. Prohibition—A Total Ban for the Terminally Ill

Washington's statute prohibiting assisted suicide has a drastic impact on the terminally ill. By prohibiting physician assistance, it bars what for many terminally ill patients is the only palatable, and only practical, way to end their lives. Physically frail, confined to wheelchairs or beds, many terminally ill patients do not have the means or ability to kill themselves in the multitude of ways that healthy individuals can. Often, for example, they cannot even secure the medication or devices they would need to carry out their wishes.

Some terminally ill patients stockpile prescription medicine, which they can use to end their lives when they decide the time is right. The successful use of the stockpile technique generally depends, however, on the assistance of a physician, whether tacit or unknowing (although it is possible to end one's life with over-the-counter medication). Even if the terminally ill patients are able to accumulate sufficient drugs, given the pain killers and other medication they are taking, most of them would lack the knowledge to determine what dose of any given drug or drugs they must take, or in what combination. Miscalculation can be tragic. It can lead to an even more painful and lingering death. Alternatively, if the medication reduces respiration enough to restrict the flow of oxygen to the brain but not enough to cause death, it can result in the patient's falling into a comatose or vegetative state.

Thus for many terminally ill patients, the Washington statute is effectively a prohibition. While technically it only prohibits one means of exercising a liberty interest, practically it prohibits the exercise of that interest as effectively as prohibiting doctors from performing abortions prevented women from having abortions in the days before *Roe*.

2. Regulation—A Permissible Means of Promoting State Interests

State laws or regulations governing physician-assisted suicide are both necessary and desirable to ensure against errors and abuse, and to protect legitimate state interests. Any of several model statutes might serve as an example of how these legitimate and important concerns can be addressed effectively.

By adopting appropriate, reasonable, and properly drawn safeguards Washington could ensure that people who choose to have their doctors prescribe lethal doses of medication are truly competent and meet all of the requisite standards. Without endorsing the constitutionality of any particular procedural safeguards, we note that the state might, for example, require: witnesses to ensure voluntariness; reasonable, though short, waiting periods to prevent rash decisions; second medical opinions to confirm a patient's terminal status and also to confirm that the patient has been receiving proper treatment, including adequate comfort care; psychological examinations to ensure that the patient is not suffering from momentary or treatable depression; reporting procedures that will aid in the avoidance of abuse. Alternatively, such safeguards could be adopted by interested medical associations and other organizations involved in the provision of health care, so long as they meet the state's needs and concerns. . . .

NO / Stephen Reinhardt   **115**

E. The Consequences of Upholding or Overturning the Statutory Provision

In various earlier sections of this opinion, we have discussed most of the consequences of upholding or overturning the Washington statutory provision at issue, because in this case those consequences are best considered as part of the discussion of the specific factors or interests. The one remaining consequence of significance is easy to identify: Whatever the outcome here, a host of painful and agonizing issues involving the right to die will continue to confront the courts. More important, these problems will continue to plague growing numbers of Americans of advanced age as well as their families, dependents, and loved ones. The issue is truly one which deserves the most thorough, careful, and objective attention from all segments of society.

VI. Application of the Balancing Test and Holding

Weighing and then balancing a constitutionally-protected interest against the state's countervailing interests, while bearing in mind the various consequences of the decision, is quintessentially a judicial role. Despite all of the efforts of generations of courts to categorize and objectify, to create multi-part tests and identify weights to be attached to the various factors, in the end balancing entails the exercise of judicial judgment rather than the application of scientific or mathematical formulae. No legislative body can perform the task for us. Nor can any computer. In the end, mindful of our constitutional obligations, including the limitations imposed on us by that document, we must rely on our judgment, guided by the facts and the law as we perceive them.

As we have explained, in this case neither the liberty interest in choosing the time and manner of death nor the state's countervailing interests are static. The magnitude of each depends on objective circumstances and generally varies inversely with the other. The liberty interest in hastening death is at its strongest when the state's interest in protecting life and preventing suicide is at its weakest, and vice-versa.

The liberty interest at issue here is an important one and, in the case of the terminally ill, is at its peak. Conversely, the state interests, while equally important in the abstract, are for the most part at a low point here. We recognize that in the case of life and death decisions the state has a particularly strong interest in avoiding undue influence and other forms of abuse. Here, that concern is ameliorated in large measure because of the mandatory involvement in the decision-making process of physicians, who have a strong bias in favor of preserving life, and because the process itself can be carefully regulated and rigorous safeguards adopted. Under these circumstances, we believe that the possibility of abuse, even when considered along with the other state interests, does not outweigh the liberty interest at issue.

The state has chosen to pursue its interests by means of what for terminally ill patients is effectively a total prohibition, even though its most important interests could be adequately served by a far less burdensome measure.

The consequences of rejecting the as-applied challenge would be disastrous for the terminally ill, while the adverse consequences for the state would be of a far lesser order. This, too, weighs in favor of upholding the liberty interest.

We consider the state's interests in preventing assisted suicide as being different only in degree and not in kind from its interests in prohibiting a number of other medical practices that lead directly to a terminally ill patient's death. Moreover, we do not consider those interests to be significantly greater in the case of assisted suicide than they are in the case of those other medical practices, if indeed they are greater at all. However, even if the difference were one of kind and not degree, our result would be no different. For no matter how much weight we could legitimately afford the state's interest in preventing suicide, that weight, when combined with the weight we give all the other state's interests, is insufficient to outweigh the terminally ill individual's interest in deciding whether to end his agony and suffering by hastening the time of his death with medication prescribed by his physician. The individual's interest in making that vital decision is compelling indeed, for no decision is more painful, delicate, personal, important, or final than the decision how and when one's life shall end. If broad general state policies can be used to deprive a terminally ill individual of the right to make that choice, it is hard to envision where the exercise of arbitrary and intrusive power by the state can be halted. In this case, the state has wide power to regulate, but it may not ban the exercise of the liberty interest, and that is the practical effect of the program before us. Accordingly, after examining one final legal authority, we hold that the "or aids" provision of Washington statute RCW 9A.36.06 is unconstitutional as applied to terminally ill competent adults who wish to hasten their deaths with medication prescribed by their physicians. . . .

VII. Conclusion

We hold that a liberty interest exists in the choice of how and when one dies, and that the provision of the Washington statute banning assisted suicide, as applied to competent, terminally ill adults who wish to hasten their deaths by obtaining medication prescribed by their doctors, violates the Due Process Clause. We recognize that this decision is a most difficult and controversial one, and that it leaves unresolved a large number of equally troublesome issues that will require resolution in the years ahead. We also recognize that other able and dedicated jurists, construing the Constitution as they believe it must be construed, may disagree not only with the result we reach but with our method of constitutional analysis. Given the nature of the judicial process and the complexity of the task of determining the rights and interests comprehended by the Constitution, good faith disagreements within the judiciary should not surprise or disturb anyone who follows the development of the law. For these reasons, we express our hope that whatever debate may accompany the future exploration of the issues we have touched on today will be conducted in an objective, rational, and constructive manner that will increase, not diminish, respect for the Constitution.

There is one final point we must emphasize. Some argue strongly that decisions regarding matters affecting life or death should not be made by the courts. Essentially, we agree with that proposition. In this case, by permitting the individual to exercise the right to choose we are following the constitutional mandate to take such decisions out of the hands of the government, both state and federal, and to put them where they rightly belong, in the hands of the people. We are allowing individuals to make the decisions that so profoundly affect their very existence—and precluding the state from intruding excessively into that critical realm. The Constitution and the courts stand as a bulwark between individual freedom and arbitrary and intrusive governmental power. Under our constitutional system, neither the state nor the majority of the people in a state can impose its will upon the individual in a matter so highly "central to personal dignity and autonomy," *Casey,* 112 S.Ct. at 2807. Those who believe strongly that death must come without physician assistance are free to follow that creed, be they doctors or patients. They are not free, however, to force their views, their religious convictions, or their philosophies on all the other members of a democratic society, and to compel those whose values differ with theirs to die painful, protracted, and agonizing deaths.

Affirmed.

POSTSCRIPT

Are Restrictions on Physician-Assisted Suicide Constitutional?

Nancy Cruzan died six months after the U.S. Supreme Court's ruling on her right to die. Two months after the Court's decision, the Cruzans asked for a court hearing to present new evidence from three of their daughter's coworkers. At the hearing, the coworkers testified that they recalled her saying she would never want to live "like a vegetable." At the same hearing, Cruzan's doctor called her existence a "living hell" and recommended removal of the tube. Her court-appointed guardian concurred. The judge then ruled that there was clear evidence of Cruzan's wishes and gave permission for the feeding tube to be removed. She died on December 26, 1990.

The fundamental concern of courts in right-to-die cases—indeed in most civil liberties cases—is the fear of what will happen in the next case. In other words, a judge may avoid doing what seems reasonable in one case if his ruling could be used to reach a less desirable result in a future case with slightly different facts. Lawyers refer to this as the "slippery slope." If euthanasia is justified in a case where the patient is conscious and competent, it may be allowed in a later case where, perhaps due to the pain the patient is in, competency is not perfectly clear.

The most recent "right to die" case in the news involved Terry Schiavo, a severely brain-damaged forty-two-year-old woman. Schiavo's husband, Michael Schiavo, wanted the feeding tube removed from his wife, and the courts supported his right to make this decision. Schiavo's parents bitterly opposed Michael Schiavo's decision. On March 18, 2005, the feeding tube was removed, and Terry Schiavo passed away on March 30, 2005. Detailed information about the issues in the case can be found at http://www6.miami.edu/ethics2/schiavo/schiavo.html.

The legal issues involved in assisting suicide are covered in a symposium in the *Ohio Northern Law Review,* p. 559 (vol. 20, 1994). Other interesting writings in this area include "Physician-Assisted Suicide and the Right to Die With Assistance," 105 *Harvard Law Review* 2021 (1992); Yale Kamisar, "When Is There a Constitutional 'Right to Die'? When Is There No Constitutional 'Right to Live'?" 25 *Georgia Law Review* 1203 (1991); John A. Robertson, "Assessing Quality of Life: A Response to Professor Kamisar," 25 *Georgia Law Review* 1243 (1991); and A. W. Alschuler, "The Right to Die," 141 *New Law Journal* 1637 (1991). Finally, the legal debate around physician-assisted suicide is put into a broader moral context in Linda Emanuel (ed.), *Regulating How We Die: The Ethical, Medical and*

Legal Issues Surrounding Physician-Assisted Suicide (Harvard University Press, 1998); Gerald Dworkin, R. G. Frey, & Sissela Bok, *Euthanasia and Physician-Assisted Suicide* (Cambridge University Press, 1998); and Ronald Dworkin, *Life's Dominion: An Argument About Abortion, Euthanasia, and Individual Freedom* (Vintage, 1994).

ISSUE 6

Does the Sharing of Music Files Through the Internet Violate Copyright Laws?

YES: Ruth Bader Ginsburg, from Concurring Opinion, *Metro-Goldwyn-Mayer Studios v. Grokster,* U.S. Supreme Court (June 27, 2005)

NO: Stephen Breyer, from Concurring Opinion, *Metro-Goldwyn-Mayer Studios v. Grokster,* U.S. Supreme Court (June 27, 2005)

ISSUE SUMMARY

YES: Justice Ginsburg believes that the copyright laws are violated by a company when its software is used primarily for illegal file sharing, and lawful uses in the future are unlikely.

NO: Justice Breyer does not want the copyright laws to hinder technological innovation and is more willing to take into account the potential use of the software for lawful file sharing.

When the first edition of *Taking Sides: Legal Issues* was published, it would have been impossible to think of a copyright issue that was controversial and newsworthy enough to include. Today, however, the issue of file sharing and copyright may be the issue in this book that most directly touches the daily activities of readers. Several decades ago, it would have been difficult for ordinary citizens to commit a copyright violation that would provoke a response from the copyright owner. Today, every person who downloads music from a free file-sharing site exposes himself or herself to some measure of risk.

On June 27, 2005, the final day of its 2004–2005 term, the U.S. Supreme Court issued its decision in the case of *MGM Studios v. Grokster*. Those awaiting the decision hoped that it would clarify an important question, namely whether software that allowed users to exchange music and other copyrighted files was a violation of the copyright laws. The producers of such software did not themselves copy anything, but they made it possible for many millions of users to copy and circulate copyrighted files.

The decision in *MGM Studios v. Grokster* was unanimous and held that Grokster could be held liable for violating the copyright laws. The Court did not, however, go so far as to state that all file-sharing programs would violate the copyright laws. The justices were willing to hold Grokster liable since Grokster, in addition to making its software available, encouraged users to copy copyrighted files. But what if a developer simply made software available online that could be used for file sharing but did not actively encourage file sharing of copyrighted works? What if a developer made available software that in fact was used by many to exchange copyrighted works but was also used to exchange nonprotected works?

While *Grokster* was the first file-sharing case for the U.S. Supreme Court, it was not the first case involving a technology that made possible the copying of copyrighted works. The landmark case in this area is *Sony v. Universal City Studios,* 464 U.S. 417 (1984), a case questioning whether the VCR manufactured by Sony violated the copyrighted laws. The decision in that case was very close, 5–4, and held that machines that were being used to violate the copyright law but that also were being used in ways that didn't violate the copyright laws could not be banned.

In the *Sony* case, five of the justices felt that if only 10 percent of the copying done with the VCR might be lawful, that was sufficient to keep the technology from being banned. But what if the lawful copying were less than 10 percent? The *Sony* court suggested that a technology that could be used both for lawful and unlawful copying does not violate the copyright laws if it is "capable of substantial non-infringing use." But how much use qualifies as being "substantial"? And is this an appropriate standard in a case where tens of millions of unlawful copies are being made, but the technology is still "capable" of broad lawful use?

On the above questions, the Court was not unanimous. The two concurring opinions differed greatly on what the standard should be for a company that produces software that is used unlawfully, an issue that the Court will have to decide in some future case. In the first reading, Justice Ruth Bader Ginsburg writes that without evidence of noninfringing uses, a company that distributes a product used to violate the copyright law should be held responsible. Justice Stephen Breyer, on the other hand, emphasizes the need to encourage the development of new technologies, something that will not happen if creators are worried that their creations will be held to violate the copyright law. Thus, Justice Breyer believes that it is sufficient in a case like this merely to show a capability of future noninfringing use in order to escape liability under the copyright laws.

YES

Ruth Bader Ginsburg

Concurring Opinion, Metro-Goldwyn-Mayer Studios Inc., et al., v. Grokster, Ltd., et al.

JUSTICE GINSBURG, with whom THE CHIEF JUSTICE AND JUSTICE KENNEDY join, concurring.

I concur in the Court's decision, which vacates in full the judgment of the Court of Appeals for the Ninth Circuit, and write separately to clarify why I conclude that the Court of Appeals misperceived, and hence misapplied, our holding in *Sony Corp. of America v. Universal City Studios, Inc.,* 464 U.S. 417 (1984). There is here at least a "genuine issue as to [a] material fact," Fed. Rule Civ. Proc. 56(c), on the liability of Grokster or StreamCast, not only for actively inducing copyright infringement, but also or alternatively, based on the distribution of their software products, for contributory copyright infringement. On neither score was summary judgment for Grokster and StreamCast warranted.

At bottom, however labeled, the question in this case is whether Grokster and StreamCast are liable for the direct infringing acts of others. Liability under our jurisprudence may be predicated on actively encouraging (or inducing) infringement through specific acts (as the Court's opinion develops) or on distributing a product distributees use to infringe copyrights, if the product is not capable of "substantial" or "commercially significant" noninfringing uses. *Sony,* 464 U.S., at 442. While the two categories overlap, they capture different culpable behavior. Long coexisting, both are now codified in patent law. Compare 35 U. S. C. §271(b) (active inducement liability), with §271(c) (contributory liability for distribution of a product not "suitable for substantial noninfringing use").

In *Sony,* 464 U.S. 417, the Court considered Sony's liability for selling the Betamax video cassette recorder. It did so enlightened by a full trial record. Drawing an analogy to the staple article of commerce doctrine from patent law, the *Sony* Court observed that the "sale of an article . . . adapted to [a patent] infringing use" does not suffice "to make the seller a contributory infringer" if the article "is also adapted to other and lawful uses." *Id.,* at 441 (quoting *Henry v. A. B. Dick Co.,* 224 U.S. 1, 48 (1912), overruled on other grounds, *Motion Picture Patents Co. v. Universal Film Mfg. Co.,* 243 U.S. 502, 517 (1917)).

Metro-Goldwyn-Mayer Studios Inc., et al., Petitioners *v. Grokster, Ltd., et al.* United States Court of Appeals for the Ninth Circuit Case, Nos. 03-55894, 03-55901, 03-56236. Decision date August 19, 2004.

"The staple article of commerce doctrine" applied to copyright, the Court stated, "must strike a balance between a copyright holder's legitimate demand for effective—not merely symbolic—protection of the statutory monopoly, and the rights of others freely to engage in substantially unrelated areas of commerce." *Sony*, 464 U.S., at 442. "Accordingly," the Court held, "the sale of copying equipment, like the sale of other articles of commerce, does not constitute contributory infringement if the product is widely used for legitimate, unobjectionable purposes. Indeed, it need merely be capable of substantial noninfringing uses." Thus, to resolve the *Sony* case, the Court explained, it had to determine "whether the Betamax is capable of commercially significant noninfringing uses."

To answer that question, the Court considered whether "a significant number of [potential uses of the Betamax were] noninfringing." The Court homed in on one potential use—private, noncommercial time-shifting of television programs in the home (*i.e.*, recording a broadcast TV program for later personal viewing). Time-shifting was noninfringing, the Court concluded, because in some cases trial testimony showed it was authorized by the copyright holder, and in others it qualified as legitimate fair use. Most purchasers used the Betamax principally to engage in time-shifting, a use that "plainly satisfie[d]" the Court's standard. Thus, there was no need in *Sony* to "give precise content to the question of how much [actual or potential] use is commercially significant." *Ibid.*[1] Further development was left for later days and cases.

The Ninth Circuit went astray, I will endeavor to explain, when that court granted summary judgment to Grokster and StreamCast on the charge of contributory liability based on distribution of their software products. Relying on its earlier opinion in *A&M Records, Inc. v. Napster, Inc.*, 239 F. 3d 1004 (CA9 2001), the Court of Appeals held that "if substantial noninfringing use was shown, the copyright owner would be required to show that the defendant had reasonable knowledge of specific infringing files." 380 F. 3d 1154, 1161 (CA9 2004). "A careful examination of the record," the court concluded, "indicates that there is no genuine issue of material fact as to noninfringing use." The appeals court pointed to the band Wilco, which made one of its albums available for free downloading, to other recording artists who may have authorized free distribution of their music through the Internet, and to public domain literary works and films available through Grokster's and StreamCast's software. Although it acknowledged MGM's assertion that "the vast majority of the software use is for copyright infringement," the court concluded that Grokster's and StreamCast's proffered evidence met *Sony*'s requirement that "a product need only be *capable* of substantial noninfringing uses." 380 F. 3d, at 1162.[2]

This case differs markedly from *Sony*. Cf. Peters, Brace Memorial Lecture: Copyright Enters the Public Domain, 51 J. Copyright Soc. 701, 724 (2004) ("The *Grokster* panel's reading of *Sony* is the broadest that any court has given it. . . ."). Here, there has been no finding of any fair use and little beyond anecdotal evidence of noninfringing uses. In finding the Grokster and StreamCast software products capable of substantial noninfringing uses, the District Court and the Court of Appeals appear to have relied largely on declarations submitted by the defendants. These declarations include assertions (some of them hearsay) that a number of copyright owners authorize distribution of their works on the Internet and that some public domain material is available through peer-to-peer networks including those accessed through Grokster's and StreamCast's software. 380 F. 3d, at 1161; 259 F. Supp. 2d 1029, 1035–1036 (CD Cal. 2003); App. 125–171.

The District Court declared it "undisputed that there are substantial noninfringing uses for Defendants' software," thus obviating the need for further proceedings. 259 F. Supp. 2d, at 1035. This conclusion appears to rest almost entirely on the collection of declarations submitted by Grokster and StreamCast. Review of these declarations reveals mostly anecdotal evidence, sometimes obtained second-hand, of authorized copyrighted works or public domain works available online and shared through peer-to-peer networks, and general statements about the benefits of peer-to-peer technology. See, *e.g.,* Decl. of Janis Ian ¶13, App. 128 ("P2P technologies offer musicians an alternative channel for promotion and distribution."); Decl. of Gregory Newby ¶12, *id.,* at 136 ("Numerous authorized and public domain Project Gutenberg eBooks are made available on Morpheus, Kazaa, Gnutella, Grokster, and similar software products."); Decl. of Aram Sinnreich ¶6, *id.,* at 151 ("file sharing seems to have a net positive impact on music sales"); Decl. of John Busher ¶8, *id.,* at 166 ("I estimate that Acoustica generates sales of between $1,000 and $10,000 per month as a result of the distribution of its trialware software through the Gnutella and FastTrack Networks."); Decl. of Patricia D. Hoekman ¶¶3–4, *id.,* at 169–170 (search on Morpheus for "President Bush speeches" found several video recordings, searches for "Declaration of Independence" and "Bible" found various documents and declarant was able to download a copy of the Declaration); Decl. of Sean L. Mayers ¶11, *id.,* at 67 ("Existing open, decentralized peer-to-peer file-sharing networks . . . offer content owners distinct business advantages over alternate online distribution technologies."). Compare Decl. of Brewster Kahle ¶20, *id.,* at 142 ("Those who download the Prelinger films . . . are entitled to redistribute those files, and the Archive welcomes their redistribution by the Morpheus-Grokster-KaZaa community of users."), with Deposition of Brewster Kahle, *id.,* at 396–403 (Sept. 18, 2002) (testifying that he has no knowledge of any person downloading a Prelinger film using Morpheus, Grokster, or Kazaa). Compare also Decl. of Richard Prelinger ¶17, *id.,* at 147 ("[W]e welcome further redistribution of the Prelinger films . . . by individuals using peer-to-peer software products like Morpheus, Kazaa and Grokster."), with Deposition of Richard Prelinger, *id.,* at 410–411 (Oct. 1, 2002) ("Q. What is your understanding of Grokster? A. I have no understanding of Grokster. . . . Q. Do you know whether any user of the Grokster software has made available to share any Prelinger film? A. No."). See also Deposition of Aram Sinnreich, *id.,* at 390 (Sept. 25, 2002) (testimony about the band Wilco based on "[t]he press and industry news groups and scuttlebutt."). These declarations do not support summary judgment in the face of evidence, proffered by MGM, of overwhelming use of Grokster's and StreamCast's software for infringement.[3]

Even if the absolute number of noninfringing files copied using the Grokster and StreamCast software is large, it does not follow that the products are therefore put to substantial noninfringing uses and are thus immune from liability. The number of noninfringing copies may be reflective of, and dwarfed by, the huge total volume of files shared. Further, the District Court and the Court of Appeals did not sharply distinguish between uses of Grokster's and StreamCast's software products (which this case is about) and uses of peer-to-peer technology generally (which this case is not about).

In sum, when the record in this case was developed, there was evidence that Grokster's and StreamCast's products were, and had been for some time, overwhelmingly used to infringe, and that this infringement was the overwhelming source of revenue from the products. Fairly appraised, the evidence was insufficient to demonstrate, beyond genuine debate, a reasonable prospect that substantial or commercially significant noninfringing uses were likely to develop over time. On this record, the District Court should not have ruled dispositively on the contributory infringement charge by granting summary judgment to Grokster and StreamCast.[4]

If, on remand, the case is not resolved on summary judgment in favor of MGM based on Grokster and StreamCast actively inducing infringement, the Court of Appeals, I would emphasize, should reconsider, on a fuller record, its interpretation of *Sony*'s product distribution holding.

Notes

1. JUSTICE BREYER finds in *Sony Corp. of America v. Universal City Studios, Inc.*, 464 U.S. 417 (1984), a "clear" rule permitting contributory liability for copyright infringement based on distribution of a product only when the product "will be used *almost exclusively* to infringe copyrights." *Post*, at 9–10. But cf. *Sony*, 464 U.S., at 442 (recognizing "copyright holder's legitimate demand for effective—not merely symbolic—protection"). *Sony*, as I read it, contains no clear, near-exclusivity test. Nor have Courts of Appeals unanimously recognized JUSTICE BREYER'S clear rule. Compare *A&M Records, Inc. v. Napster, Inc.*, 239 F. 3d 1004, 1021 (CA9 2001) ("[E]vidence of actual knowledge of specific acts of infringement is required to hold a computer system operator liable for contributory copyright infringement."), with *In re Aimster Copyright Litigation*, 334 F. 3d 643, 649–650 (CA7 2003) ("[W]hen a supplier is offering a product or service that has noninfringing as well as infringing uses, some estimate of the respective magnitudes of these uses is necessary for a finding of contributory infringement. . . . But the balancing of costs and benefits is necessary only in a case in which substantial noninfringing uses, present or prospective, are demonstrated."). See also *Matthew Bender & Co., Inc. v. West Pub. Co.*, 158 F. 3d 693, 707 (CA2 1998) ("The Supreme Court applied [the *Sony*] test to prevent copyright holders from leveraging the copyrights in their original work to control distribution of . . . products that might be used incidentally for infringement, but that had substantial noninfringing uses. . . . The same rationale applies here [to products] that have substantial, predominant and noninfringing uses as tools for research and citation."). All Members of the Court agree, moreover, that "the Court of Appeals misapplied *Sony*," at least to the extent it read that decision to limit "secondary liability" to a hardly-ever category, "quite beyond the circumstances to which the case applied." *Ante*, at 16.

2. Grokster and StreamCast, in the Court of Appeals' view, would be entitled to summary judgment unless MGM could show that that the software companies had knowledge of specific acts of infringement and failed to act on that knowledge—a standard the court held MGM could not meet. 380 F. 3d, at 1162–1163.

3. JUSTICE BREYER finds support for summary judgment in this motley collection of declarations and in a survey conducted by an expert retained by MGM. *Post*, at 4–8. That survey identified 75% of the files available through Grokster as copyrighted works owned or controlled by the plaintiffs, and 15% of the files as works likely copyrighted. App. 439. As to the remaining 10% of the files, "there was not enough information to form reasonable conclusions either as to what those files even consisted of, and/or whether they were infringing or non-infringing." App. 479. Even assuming, as JUSTICE BREYER does, that the *Sony* Court would have absolved Sony of contributory liability solely on the basis of the use of the Betamax for authorized time-shifting, *post*, at 3–4, summary judgment is not inevitably appropriate here. *Sony* stressed that the plaintiffs there owned "well below 10%" of copyrighted television programming, 464 U.S., at 443, and found, based on trial testimony from representatives of the four major sports leagues and other individuals authorized to consent to home-recording of their copyrighted broadcasts, that a similar percentage of program copying was authorized, *id.*, at 424. Here, the plaintiffs allegedly control copyrights for 70% or 75% of the material exchanged through the Grokster and StreamCast software, 380 F. 3d, at 1158; App. 439, and the District Court does not appear to have relied on comparable testimony about authorized copying from copyright holders.

4. The District Court's conclusion that "[p]laintiffs do not dispute that Defendants' software is being used, and could be used, for substantial non-infringing purposes," 259 F. Supp. 2d 1029, 1036 (CD Cal. 2003); accord 380 F. 3d, at 1161, is, to say the least, dubious. In the courts below and in this Court, MGM has continuously disputed any such conclusion. Brief for Motion Picture Studio and Recording Company Petitioners 30–38; Brief for MGM Plaintiffs-Appellants in No. 03-55894, etc. (CA9), p. 41; App. 356–357, 361–365.

Stephen Breyer

NO

Concurring Opinion, *Metro-Goldwyn-Mayer Studios Inc., et al., Petitioners v. Grokster, Ltd., et al.*

J USTICE BREYER, with whom JUSTICE STEVENS and JUSTICE O'CONNOR join, concurring.

I agree with the Court that the distributor of a dual-use technology may be liable for the infringing activities of third parties where he or she actively seeks to advance the infringement. I further agree that, in light of our holding today, we need not now "revisit" *Sony Corp. of America v. Universal City Studios, Inc.,* 464 U.S. 417 (1984). Other Members of the Court, however, take up the *Sony* question: whether Grokster's product is "capable of 'substantial' or 'commercially significant' noninfringing uses." (GINSBURG, J., concurring) (quoting *Sony, supra,* at 442). And they answer that question by stating that the Court of Appeals was wrong when it granted summary judgment on the issue in Grokster's favor. I write to explain why I disagree with them on this matter.

I

The Court's opinion in *Sony* and the record evidence (as described and analyzed in the many briefs before us) together convince me that the Court of Appeals' conclusion has adequate legal support.

A

I begin with *Sony*'s standard. In *Sony,* the Court considered the potential copyright liability of a company that did not itself illegally copy protected material, but rather sold a machine—a Video Cassette Recorder (VCR)—that could be used to do so. A buyer could use that machine for *non*infringing purposes, such as recording for later viewing (sometimes called "'time-shifting,'" *Sony,* 464 U.S., at 421) uncopyrighted television programs or copyrighted programs with a copyright holder's permission. The buyer could use the machine for infringing purposes as well, such as building libraries of taped copyrighted programs. Or, the buyer might use the machine to record copyrighted programs under circumstances in which the legal status of the act of recording was uncertain

Metro-Goldwyn-Mayer Studios Inc., et al., Petitioners *v. Grokster, Ltd., et al.* United States Court of Appeals for the Ninth Circuit Case, Nos. 03-55894, 03-55901, 03-56236. Decision date August 19, 2004.

(*i.e.*, where the copying may, or may not, have constituted a "fair use." Sony knew many customers would use its VCRs to engage in unauthorized copying and "'library-building.'" *Id.*, at 458–459 (Blackmun, J., dissenting). But that fact, said the Court, was insufficient to make Sony itself an infringer. And the Court ultimately held that Sony was not liable for its customers' acts of infringement.

In reaching this conclusion, the Court recognized the need for the law, in fixing *secondary* copyright liability, to "strike a balance between a copyright holder's legitimate demand for effective—not merely symbolic—protection of the statutory monopoly, and the rights of others freely to engage in substantially unrelated areas of commerce." *Id.*, at 442. It pointed to patent law's "staple article of commerce" doctrine, under which a distributor of a product is not liable for patent infringement by its customers unless that product is "unsuited for any commercial noninfringing use." *Dawson Chemical Co. v. Rohm & Haas Co.*, 448 U.S. 176, 198 (1980). The Court wrote that the sale of copying equipment, "like the sale of other articles of commerce, does not constitute contributory infringement if the product is widely used for legitimate, unobjectionable purposes. *Indeed, it need merely be capable of substantial noninfringing uses.*" *Sony*, 464 U.S., at 442 (emphasis added). The Court ultimately characterized the legal "question" in the particular case as "whether [Sony's VCR] is *capable of commercially significant noninfringing uses*" (while declining to give "precise content" to these terms). *Ibid.* (emphasis added).

It then applied this standard. The Court had before it a survey (commissioned by the District Court and then prepared by the respondents) showing that roughly 9% of all VCR recordings were of the type—namely, religious, educational, and sports programming—owned by producers and distributors testifying on Sony's behalf who did not object to time-shifting. See Brief for Respondent Universal Studios et al. O. T. 1983, No. 81-1687, pp. 52–53; see also *Sony*, *supra*, at 424 (7.3% of all Sony VCR use is to record sports programs; representatives of the sports leagues do not object). A much higher percentage of VCR *users* had at one point taped an authorized program, in addition to taping unauthorized programs. And the plaintiffs—not a large class of content providers as in this case—owned only a small percentage of the total available *un*authorized programming. See *ante*, at 6–7, and n. 3 (GINSBURG, J., concurring). But of all the taping actually done by Sony's customers, only around 9% was of the sort the Court referred to as authorized.

The Court found that the magnitude of authorized programming was "significant," and it also noted the "significant potential for future authorized copying." 464 U.S., at 444. The Court supported this conclusion by referencing the trial testimony of professional sports league officials and a religious broadcasting representative. It also discussed (1) a Los Angeles educational station affiliated with the Public Broadcasting Service that made many of its programs available for home taping, and (2) Mr. Rogers' Neighborhood, a widely watched children's program. On the basis of this testimony and other similar evidence, the Court determined that producers of this kind had authorized duplication of their copyrighted programs "in significant enough numbers to create a *substantial* market for a noninfringing use of the" VCR. *Id.*, at 447, n. 28 (emphasis added).

The Court, in using the key word "substantial," indicated that these circumstances alone constituted a sufficient basis for rejecting the imposition of secondary liability. See *id.*, at 456 ("Sony demonstrated a significant likelihood that *substantial* numbers of copyright holders" would not object to time-shifting (emphasis added)). Nonetheless, the Court buttressed its conclusion by finding separately that, in any event, *un*authorized time-shifting often constituted not infringement, but "fair use."

B

When measured against *Sony's* underlying evidence and analysis, the evidence now before us shows that Grokster passes *Sony's* test—that is, whether the company's product is capable of substantial or commercially significant noninfringing uses. For one thing, petitioners' (hereinafter MGM) own expert declared that 75% of current files available on Grokster are infringing and 15% are "likely infringing." See App. 436–439, ¶¶6–17 (Decl. of Dr. Ingram Olkin); cf. *ante*, at 4 (opinion of the Court). That leaves some number of files near 10% that apparently are noninfringing, a figure very similar to the 9% or so of authorized time-shifting uses of the VCR that the Court faced in *Sony*.

As in *Sony*, witnesses here explained the nature of the noninfringing files on Grokster's network without detailed quantification. Those files include:

- Authorized copies of music by artists such as Wilco, Janis Ian, Pearl Jam, Dave Matthews, John Mayer, and others. See App. at 152–153, ¶¶9–13 (Decl. of Aram Sinnreich) (Wilco's "lesson has already been adopted by artists still signed to their major labels"); *id.*, at 170, ¶¶5–7 (Decl. of Patricia D. Hoekman) (locating "numerous audio recordings" that were authorized for swapping); *id.*, at 74, ¶10 (Decl. of Daniel B. Rung) (describing Grokster's partnership with a company that hosts music from thousands of independent artists)
- Free electronic books and other works from various online publishers, including Project Gutenberg. See id., at 136, ¶12 (Decl. of Gregory B. Newby) ("Numerous authorized and public domain Project Gutenberg eBooks are made available" on Grokster. Project Gutenberg "welcomes this widespread sharing . . . using these software products[,] since they assist us in meeting our objectives"); *id.*, at 159–160, ¶32 (Decl. of Sinnreich)
- Public domain and authorized software, such as WinZip 8.1. *Id.*, at 170, ¶8 (Decl. of Hoekman); id., at 165, ¶¶4–7 (Decl. of John Busher)
- Licensed music videos and television and movie segments distributed via digital video packaging with the permission of the copyright holder. Id., at 70, ¶24 (Decl. of Sean L. Mayers)

The nature of these and other lawfully swapped files is such that it is reasonable to infer quantities of current lawful use roughly approximate to those at issue in *Sony*. At least, MGM has offered no evidence sufficient to survive summary judgment that could plausibly demonstrate a significant quantitative difference. See *ante*, at 4 (opinion of the Court); see also Brief for Motion Picture Studio and Recording Company Petitioners i (referring to "at least 90% of the total use of the services"); but see *ante*, at 6–7, n. 3 (GINSBURG, J., concurring). To be sure, in quantitative terms these uses account for only a small percentage of the total number of uses of Grokster's product. But the same was true in *Sony*, which characterized the relatively limited authorized copying market as "substantial." (The Court made clear as well in *Sony* that the amount of material then presently available for lawful copying—if not actually copied—was significant, see 464 U.S., at 444, and the same is certainly true in this case.)

Importantly, *Sony* also used the word "capable," asking whether the product is *"capable of"* substantial noninfringing uses. Its language and analysis suggest that a figure like 10%, if fixed for all time, might well prove insufficient, but that such a figure serves as an adequate foundation where there is a reasonable prospect of expanded legitimate uses over time. See *ibid.* (noting a "significant potential for future authorized copying"). And its language also indicates the appropriateness of looking to potential future uses of the product to determine its "capability."

Here the record reveals a significant future market for noninfringing uses of Grokster-type peer-to-peer software. Such software permits the exchange of *any* sort of digital file—whether that file does, or does not, contain copyrighted material. As more and more uncopyrighted information is stored in swappable form, it seems a likely inference that lawful peer-to-peer sharing will become increasingly prevalent. See, *e.g.*, App. 142, ¶20 (Decl. of Brewster Kahle) ("The [Internet Archive] welcomes [the] redistribution [of authorized films] by the Morpheus-Grokster-KaZaa community of users"); *id.*, at 166, ¶8 (Decl. of Busher) (sales figures of $1,000 to $10,000 per month through peer-to-peer networks "will increase in the future as Acoustica's trialware is more widely distributed through these networks"); *id.*, at 156–164, ¶¶21–40 (Decl. of Sinnreich).

And that is just what is happening. Such legitimate noninfringing uses are coming to include the swapping of: *research information* (the initial purpose of many peer-to-peer networks); *public domain films* (*e.g.*, those owned by the Prelinger Archive); *historical recordings and digital educational materials* (*e.g.*, those stored on the Internet Archive); *digital photos* (OurPictures, for example, is starting a P2P photo-swapping service); *"shareware" and "freeware"* (*e.g.*, Linux and certain Windows software); *secure licensed music and movie files* (Intent MediaWorks, for example, protects licensed content sent across P2P networks); *news broadcasts past and present* (the BBC Creative Archive lets users "rip, mix and share the BBC"); *user-created audio and video files* (including "podcasts" that may be distributed through P2P software); *and all manner of free "open content" works collected by Creative Commons* (one can search for Creative Commons material on StreamCast). See Brief for Distributed Computing Industry Association as *Amicus Curiae* 15–26; Merges, A New Dynamism in the Public Domain, 71 U. Chi. L. Rev. 183 (2004). I can find nothing in the record that suggests that this course of events will *not* continue to flow naturally as a consequence of the character of the software taken together with the foreseeable development of the Internet and of information technology. Cf. *ante*, at 1–2 (opinion of the Court) (discussing the significant benefits of peer-to-peer technology).

There may be other now-unforeseen noninfringing uses that develop for peer-to-peer software, just as the home-video rental industry (unmentioned in

Sony) developed for the VCR. But the foreseeable development of such uses, when taken together with an estimated 10% noninfringing material, is sufficient to meet *Sony's* standard. And while *Sony* considered the record following a trial, there are no facts asserted by MGM in its summary judgment filings that lead me to believe the outcome after a trial here could be any different. The lower courts reached the same conclusion.

Of course, Grokster itself may not want to develop these other noninfringing uses. But *Sony's* standard seeks to protect not the Groksters of this world (which in any event may well be liable under today's holding), but the development of technology more generally. And Grokster's desires in this respect are beside the point.

II

The real question here, I believe, is not whether the record evidence satisfies *Sony*. As I have interpreted the standard set forth in that case, it does. And of the Courts of Appeals that have considered the matter, only one has proposed interpreting *Sony* more strictly than I would do—in a case where the product might have failed under *any* standard. *In re Aimster Copyright Litigation*, 334 F. 3d 643, 653 (CA7 2003) (defendant "failed to show that its service is *ever* used for any purpose other than to infringe" copyrights (emphasis added)); see *Matthew Bender & Co., Inc. v. West Pub. Co.*, 158 F. 3d 693, 706–707 (CA2 1998) (court did not *require* that noninfringing uses be "predominant," it merely found that they *were* predominant, and therefore provided no analysis of *Sony's* boundaries); but see *ante*, at 3 n. 1 (GINSBURG, J., concurring); see also *A&M Records v. Napster, Inc.*, 239 F. 3d 1004, 1020 (CA9 2001) (discussing *Sony*); *Cable/Home Communication Corp. v. Network Productions, Inc.*, 902 F. 2d 829, 842–847 (CA11 1990) (same); *Vault Corp. v. Quaid Software, Ltd.*, 847 F. 2d 255, 262 (CA5 1988) (same); cf. *Dynacore Holdings Corp. v. U.S. Philips Corp.*, 363 F. 3d 1263, 1275 (CA Fed. 2004) (same); see also *Doe v. GTE Corp.*, 347 F. 3d 655, 661 (CA7 2003) ("A person may be liable as a contributory infringer if the product or service it sells has no (or only slight) legal use").

Instead, the real question is whether we should modify the *Sony* standard, as MGM requests, or interpret *Sony* more strictly, as I believe JUSTICE GINSBURG's approach would do in practice. Compare *ante*, at 4–8 (concurring) (insufficient evidence in this case of both present lawful uses and of a reasonable prospect that substantial noninfringing uses would develop over time), with *Sony*, 464 U.S., at 442–447 (basing conclusion as to the likely existence of a substantial market for authorized copying upon general declarations, some survey data, and common sense).

As I have said, *Sony* itself sought to "strike a balance between a copyright holder's legitimate demand for effective—not merely symbolic—protection of the statutory monopoly, and the rights of others freely to engage in substantially unrelated areas of commerce." *Id.*, at 442. Thus, to determine whether modification, or a strict interpretation, of *Sony* is needed, I would ask whether MGM has shown that *Sony* incorrectly balanced copyright and new-technology interests. In particular: (1) Has *Sony* (as I interpret it) worked to protect new technology?

(2) If so, would modification or strict interpretation significantly weaken that protection? (3) If so, would new or necessary copyright-related benefits outweigh any such weakening?

A

The first question is the easiest to answer. *Sony*'s rule, as I interpret it, has provided entrepreneurs with needed assurance that they will be shielded from copyright liability as they bring valuable new technologies to market.

Sony's rule is clear.   That clarity allows those who develop new products that are capable of substantial noninfringing uses to know, *ex ante*, that distribution of their product will not yield massive monetary liability. At the same time, it helps deter them from distributing products that have no other real function than—or that are specifically intended for—copyright infringement, deterrence that the Court's holding today reinforces (by adding a weapon to the copyright holder's legal arsenal).

Sony's rule is strongly technology protecting.   The rule deliberately makes it difficult for courts to find secondary liability where new technology is at issue. It establishes that the law will not impose copyright liability upon the distributors of dual-use technologies (who do not themselves engage in unauthorized copying) unless the product in question will be used *almost exclusively* to infringe copyrights (or unless they actively induce infringements as we today describe). *Sony* thereby recognizes that the copyright laws are not intended to discourage or to control the emergence of new technologies, including (perhaps especially) those that help disseminate information and ideas more broadly or more efficiently. Thus *Sony*'s rule shelters VCRs, typewriters, tape recorders, photocopiers, computers, cassette players, compact disc burners, digital video recorders, MP3 players, Internet search engines, and peer-to-peer software. But *Sony*'s rule does not shelter descramblers, even if one could *theoretically* use a descrambler in a noninfringing way. 464 U.S., at 441–442; compare *Cable/Home Communication Corp., supra*, at 837–850 (developer liable for advertising television signal descrambler), with *Vault Corp., supra*, at 262 (primary use infringing but a substantial noninfringing use).

Sony's rule is forward looking.   It does not confine its scope to a static snapshot of a product's current uses (thereby threatening technologies that have undeveloped future markets). Rather, as the VCR example makes clear, a product's market can evolve dramatically over time. And *Sony*—by referring to a *capacity* for substantial noninfringing uses—recognizes that fact. *Sony*'s word "capable" refers to a plausible, not simply a theoretical, likelihood that such uses will come to pass, and that fact anchors *Sony* in practical reality.

Sony's rule is mindful of the limitations facing judges where matters of technology are concerned.   Judges have no specialized technical ability to answer questions about present or future technological feasibility or commercial viability where technology professionals, engineers, and venture capitalists themselves may radically disagree and where answers may differ depending upon whether one focuses upon the time of product development or the time of distribution. Consider, for example, the question whether devices can be added to Grokster's software that will filter out infringing files. MGM tells us this is easy enough to do, as do several *amici* that produce and sell the filtering technology. See, *e.g.*, Brief for Motion Picture Studio Petitioners 11; Brief for Audible Magic Corp. et al. as *Amicus Curiae* 3–10. Grokster says it is not at all easy to do, and not an efficient solution in any event, and several apparently disinterested computer science professors agree. See Brief for Respondents 31; Brief for Computer Science Professors as *Amicus Curiae* 6–10, 14–18. Which account should a judge credit? *Sony* says that the judge will not necessarily have to decide.

Given the nature of the *Sony* rule, it is not surprising that in the last 20 years, there have been relatively few contributory infringement suits—based on a product distribution theory—brought against technology providers (a small handful of federal appellate court cases and perhaps fewer than two dozen District Court cases in the last 20 years). I have found nothing in the briefs or the record that shows that *Sony* has failed to achieve its innovation-protecting objective.

B

The second, more difficult, question is whether a modified *Sony* rule (or a strict interpretation) would significantly weaken the law's ability to protect new technology. Justice Ginsburg's approach would require defendants to produce considerably more concrete evidence—more than was presented here—to earn *Sony*'s shelter. That heavier evidentiary demand, and especially the more dramatic (case-by-case balancing) modifications that MGM and the Government seek, would, I believe, undercut the protection that *Sony* now offers.

To require defendants to provide, for example, detailed evidence—say business plans, profitability estimates, projected technological modifications, and so forth—would doubtless make life easier for copyright holder plaintiffs. But it would simultaneously increase the legal uncertainty that surrounds the creation or development of a new technology capable of being put to infringing uses. Inventors and entrepreneurs (in the garage, the dorm room, the corporate lab, or the boardroom) would have to fear (and in many cases endure) costly and extensive trials when they create, produce, or distribute the sort of information technology that can be used for copyright infringement. They would often be left guessing as to how a court, upon later review of the product and its uses, would decide when necessarily rough estimates amounted to sufficient evidence. They would have no way to predict how courts would weigh the respective values of infringing and noninfringing uses; determine the efficiency and advisability of technological changes; or assess a product's potential future markets. The price of a wrong guess—even if it involves a good-faith effort to assess technical and commercial viability—could be large statutory damages (not less than $750 and up to $30,000 *per infringed work*). 17 U. S. C. §504(c)(1). The additional risk and uncertainty would mean a consequent additional chill of technological development.

C

The third question—whether a positive copyright impact would outweigh any technology-related loss—I find the most difficult of the three. I do not doubt that a more intrusive *Sony* test would generally provide greater revenue security for copyright holders. But it is harder to conclude that the gains on the copyright swings would exceed the losses on the technology roundabouts.

For one thing, the law disfavors equating the two different kinds of gain and loss; rather, it leans in favor of protecting technology. As *Sony* itself makes clear, the producer of a technology which *permits* unlawful copying does not himself *engage* in unlawful copying—a fact that makes the attachment of copyright liability to the creation, production, or distribution of the technology an exceptional thing. See 464 U.S., at 431 (courts "must be circumspect" in construing the copyright laws to preclude distribution of new technologies). Moreover, *Sony* has been the law for some time. And that fact imposes a serious burden upon copyright holders like MGM to show a need for change in the current rules of the game, including a more strict interpretation of the test. See, *e.g.,* Brief for Motion Picture Studio Petitioners 31 (*Sony* should not protect products when the "primary or principal" use is infringing).

In any event, the evidence now available does not, in my view, make out a sufficiently strong case for change. To say this is not to doubt the basic need to protect copyrighted material from infringement. The Constitution itself stresses the vital role that copyright plays in advancing the "useful Arts." Art. I, §8, cl. 8. No one disputes that "reward to the author or artist serves to induce release to the public of the products of his creative genius." *United States v. Paramount Pictures, Inc.,* 334 U.S. 131, 158 (1948). And deliberate unlawful copying is no less an unlawful taking of property than garden-variety theft. See, *e.g.,* 18 U. S. C. §2319 (criminal copyright infringement); §1961(1)(B) (copyright infringement can be a predicate act under the Racketeer Influenced and Corrupt Organizations Act); §1956(c)(7)(D) (money laundering includes the receipt of proceeds from copyright infringement). But these highly general principles cannot by themselves tell us how to balance the interests at issue in *Sony* or whether *Sony*'s standard needs modification. And at certain key points, information is lacking.

Will an unmodified *Sony* lead to a significant diminution in the amount or quality of creative work produced? Since copyright's basic objective is creation and its revenue objectives but a means to that end, this is the underlying copyright question. See *Twentieth Century Music Corp. v. Aiken,* 422 U.S. 151, 156 (1975) ("Creative work is to be encouraged and rewarded, but private motivation must ultimately serve the cause of promoting broad public availability of literature, music, and the other arts"). And its answer is far from clear.

Unauthorized copying likely diminishes industry revenue, though it is not clear by how much. Compare S. Liebowitz, Will MP3 Downloads Annihilate the Record Industry? The Evidence So Far, p. 2 (June 2003) . . . (all Internet materials as visited June 24, 2005, and available in Clerk of Court's case file) (file sharing has caused a decline in music sales), and Press Release, Informa Media Group Report (citing Music on the Internet (5th ed. 2004)) (estimating

total lost sales to the music industry in the range of $2 billion annually) . . .
with F. Oberholzer & K. Strumpf, The Effect of File Sharing on Record Sales:
An Empirical Analysis, p. 24 (Mar. 2004) . . . (academic study concluding that
"file sharing has no statistically significant effect on purchases of the average
album"), and McGuire, Study: File-Sharing No Threat to Music Sales (Mar. 29,
2004) . . . (discussing mixed evidence).

The extent to which related production has actually and resultingly
declined remains uncertain, though there is good reason to believe that
the decline, if any, is not substantial. See, *e.g.*, M. Madden, Pew Internet &
American Life Project, Artists, Musicians, and the Internet, p. 21 . . . (nearly
70% of musicians believe that file sharing is a minor threat or no threat at
all to creative industries); Benkler, Sharing Nicely: On Shareable Goods and
the Emergence of Sharing as a Modality of Economic Production, 114 Yale L.
J. 273, 351–352 (2004) ("Much of the actual flow of revenue to artists—from
performances and other sources—is stable even assuming a complete displace-
ment of the CD market by peer-to-peer distribution. . . . [I]t would be silly to
think that music, a cultural form without which no human society has existed,
will cease to be in our world [because of illegal file swapping]").

More importantly, copyright holders at least potentially have other tools
available to reduce piracy and to abate whatever threat it poses to creative
production. As today's opinion makes clear, a copyright holder may proceed
against a technology provider where a provable specific intent to infringe (of
the kind the Court describes) is present. *Ante*, at 24 (opinion of the Court).
Services like Grokster may well be liable under an inducement theory.

In addition, a copyright holder has always had the legal authority to bring
a traditional infringement suit against one who wrongfully copies. Indeed,
since September 2003, the Recording Industry Association of America (RIAA)
has filed "thousands of suits against people for sharing copyrighted material."
Walker, New Movement Hits Universities: Get Legal Music, *Washington Post*,
Mar. 17, 2005, p. E1. These suits have provided copyright holders with damages; have served as a teaching tool, making clear that much file sharing, if
done without permission, is unlawful; and apparently have had a real and significant deterrent effect. See, *e.g.*, L. Rainie, M. Madden, D. Hess, & G. Mudd,
Pew Internet Project and comScore Media Metrix Data Memo: The state of
music downloading and file-sharing online, pp. 2, 4, 6, 10 (Apr. 2004) . . .
(number of people downloading files fell from a peak of roughly 35 million to
roughly 23 million in the year following the first suits; 38% of current downloaders report downloading fewer files because of the suits); M. Madden & L.
Rainie, Pew Internet Project Data Memo: Music and video downloading moves
beyond P2P, p. 7 (March 2005) . . . (number of downloaders has "inched up"
but "continues to rest well below the peak level"); Groennings, Note, Costs
and Benefits of the Recording Industry's Litigation Against Individuals, 20
Berkeley Technology L. J. 571 (2005); but see Evangelista, Downloading Music
and Movie Files Is as Popular as Ever, San Francisco Chronicle, Mar. 28, 2005,
p. E1 (referring to the continuing "tide of rampant copyright infringement,"
while noting that the RIAA says it believes the "campaign of lawsuits and public education has at least contained the problem").

Further, copyright holders may develop new technological devices that will help curb unlawful infringement. Some new technology, called "digital 'watermarking'" and "digital fingerprint[ing]," can encode within the file information about the author and the copyright scope and date, which "finger-prints" can help to expose infringers. RIAA Reveals Method to Madness, Wired News, Aug. 28, 2003; . . . Besek, Anti-Circumvention Laws and Copyright: A Report from the Kernochan Center for Law, Media and the Arts, 27 Colum. J. L. & Arts 385, 391, 451 (2004). Other technology can, through encryption, potentially restrict users' ability to make a digital copy. See J. Borland, Tripping the Rippers, C/net News.com (Sept. 28, 2001); . . . but see Brief for Bridgemar Services Ltd. as *Amicus Curiae* 5–8 (arguing that peer-to-peer service providers can more easily block unlawful swapping).

At the same time, advances in technology have discouraged unlaw-ful copying by making *lawful* copying (*e.g.*, downloading music with the copyright holder's permission) cheaper and easier to achieve. Several ser-vices now sell music for less than $1 per song. (Walmart.com, for example, charges $0.88 each). Consequently, many consumers initially attracted to the convenience and flexibility of services like Grokster are now migrating to lawful paid services (services with copying permission) where they can enjoy at little cost even greater convenience and flexibility without engag-ing in unlawful swapping. See Wu, When Code Isn't Law, 89 Va. L. Rev. 679, 731–735 (2003) (noting the prevalence of technological problems on unpaid swapping sites); K. Dean, P2P Tilts Toward Legitimacy, Wired.com, Wired News (Nov. 24, 2004); . . . M. Madden & L. Rainie, March 2005 Data Memo, *supra*, at 6–7 (percentage of current downloaders who have used paid services rose from 24% to 43% in a year; number using free services fell from 58% to 41%).

Thus, lawful music downloading services—those that charge the cus-tomer for downloading music and pay royalties to the copyright holder—have continued to grow and to produce substantial revenue. See Brief for Internet Law Faculty as *Amici Curiae* 5–20; Bruno, Digital Entertainment: Piracy Fight Shows Encouraging Signs (Mar. 5, 2005), available at LEXIS, News Library, Billboard File (in 2004, consumers worldwide purchased more than 10 times the number of digital tracks purchased in 2003; global digital music market of $330 million in 2004 expected to double in 2005); Press Release, Informa Media Report, *supra* (global digital revenues will likely exceed $3 billion in 2010); Ashton [International Federation of the Phonographic Industry] Pre-dicts Downloads Will Hit the Mainstream, Music Week, Jan. 29, 2005, p. 6 (legal music sites and portable MP3 players "are helping transform the digital music market" into "an everyday consumer experience"). And more advanced types of *non*-music-oriented P2P networks have also started to develop, draw-ing in part on the lessons of Grokster.

Finally, as *Sony* recognized, the legislative option remains available. Courts are less well suited than Congress to the task of "accommodat[ing] fully the varied permutations of competing interests that are inevitably implicated by such new technology." *Sony*, 464 U.S., at 431; see, *e.g.*, Audio Home Recording Act of 1992, 106 Stat. 4237 (adding 17 U. S. C., ch. 10);

Protecting Innovation and Art While Preventing Piracy: Hearing Before the Senate Comm. on the Judiciary, 108th Cong., 2d Sess. (July 22, 2004).

I do not know whether these developments and similar alternatives will prove sufficient, but I am reasonably certain that, given their existence, a strong demonstrated need for modifying *Sony* (or for interpreting *Sony*'s standard more strictly) has not yet been shown. That fact, along with the added risks that modification (or strict interpretation) would impose upon technological innovation, leads me to the conclusion that we should maintain *Sony*, reading its standard as I have read it. As so read, it requires affirmance of the Ninth Circuit's determination of the relevant aspects of the *Sony* question.

⚜

For these reasons, I disagree with JUSTICE GINSBURG, but I agree with the Court and join its opinion.

POSTSCRIPT

Does the Sharing of Music Files Through the Internet Violate Copyright Laws?

In 1983, Jack Valenti, the president of the Motion Picture Association of America (MPAA), appeared before a House of Representatives Committee and testified that "the VCR is to the motion picture industry and the American public what the Boston strangler is to the woman alone." He felt that if the *Sony* case were decided in favor of Sony, as it was, copying would be rampant, and the movie industry would suffer terribly. As it turned out, however, the VCR may have saved the movie industry by providing new outlets and new sources of revenue. Similarly dire predications are currently being made about the impact of file sharing on the music and film industry. Will more aggressive enforcement of the copyright laws encourage the investment of time and money and lead to more creative activity, or will it interfere with the process of creation and inhibit those trying to express themselves in new ways? Will tolerating file sharing lead to new outlets of expression and new models for creating value?

Copyright is mentioned in the U.S. Constitution. Article I, Section 8 states that the purpose of copyright is "To promote the progress of science and useful arts, by securing for limited times to authors and inventors the exclusive right to their respective writings and discoveries." Copyright, therefore, is for the benefit of society, and rewarding authors and creators is the means to do this. But it should be kept in mind that there will always be a tension between encouraging the use and processing of information, and discouraging it. If there is too little control, there may be a negative effect on creative activity. But if there is too much control and too many restrictions on copying, there will also be interference with creative activity.

Copyright questions are particularly important today because so much economic value and economic activity relates to information and communication. Thus, copyright law has the attention of both the legal community and the public at large. Yet, in addition to the question of whether stricter controls on copying are desirable, is the question of whether the law is capable of restricting copying when the technology is so widespread, when communication across borders is so easy, and when new applications which can be used for copying appear frequently. Copyright owners may have won the Grokster case, but it is not certain that the cases will have a significant impact on the practice or volume of file sharing.

The first file-sharing challenge involved Napster, a Web site that allowed one to obtain copies of music that might have been stored on a machine in some distant country. Typically, when one "surfs" the Web, one is only able to look at files located on a machine called a *server*. If anyone has something they want to make available on the Web, they must find a server and then find a way to put the file containing the information on that server. Every server, in order to be reachable on the Web, has an address, such as www.mhcls.com or 128.119.199.27.

Napster and other "peer-to-peer" software (such as Kazaa and Grokster) made it possible to obtain files that were located on anyone's machine, located anywhere in the world, whether it was a server or not. Obviously, there are many more machines using the Web and connected to the Web than there are servers. Thus, Napster greatly increased the number of files available for download on the Web. Although Napster was put out of business and Grokster lost this case, file sharing and new patterns of file sharing can be expected, and there is little doubt that courts will be faced with more such cases.

Interesting readings about copyright in a digital age are Jessica Litman, *Digital Copyright: Protecting Intellectual Property on the Internet* (2001); Lawrence Lessig's two works, *The Future of Ideas* (2002) and *Free Culture* (2004); Robert P. Merges, Peter S. Menell, and Mark A. Lemley, *Intellectual Property in the New Technological Age,* 2d ed. (2000); and Paul Edward Geller, "Copyright's History and the Future: What's Culture Got To Do with It?", 47 J. Copyright Soc'y U.S.A. 209, 264 (2000). An interesting recent case about how "limited" the term of a copyright should be is *Eldred v. Ashcroft* (2003) http://supct.law.cornell.edu/supct/html/01-618.ZS.html.

ISSUE 7

Is the Eighth Amendment Protection Violated If Prisoners Are Deprived of Basic Sustenance, Including Adequate Medical Care?

YES: **Anthony Kennedy**, from Majority Opinion, *Brown v. Plata*, U.S. Supreme Court (May 23, 2011)

NO: **Antonin Scalia**, from Dissenting Opinion, *Brown v. Plata*, U.S. Supreme Court (May 23, 2011)

ISSUE SUMMARY

YES: Supreme Court Justice Anthony Kennedy rules that if a prison deprives prisoners of basic sustenance, including adequate medical care, the courts have a responsibility to remedy the resulting violation of the Eighth Amendment.

NO: Justice Antonin Scalia believes that a ruling that may result in the release of 40,000 prisoners is unwarranted and unprecedented.

Three of the cases in this edition of Taking Sides deal with the prohibition on cruel and unusual punishment in the Eighth Amendment of the Constitution. Most of the cases that the Supreme Court hears regarding the Cruel and Unusual Punishment clause challenge a type of punishment, such as the death penalty (Issue 13) or a lengthy prison term for a nonviolent crime (Issue 14). This seems to accord with what the Framers originally intended in including the Eighth Amendment in the Bill of Rights. Given the history in Europe of torturous methods of punishment, such as drawing and quartering criminals or burning them at the stake, the Framers added the Eighth Amendment to the Constitution to ensure that such forms of punishment would not reappear in the American criminal justice system. As one critic of the pre–Bill of Rights Constitution argued,

> [Congress is] nowhere restrained from inventing the most *cruel and unheard-of* punishments, and annexing them to crimes; and there is no

constitutional check on [it], but that *racks* and *gibbets* may be amongst the most mild instruments of [its] discipline.[1]

Few would argue that, all else being equal, imprisonment is a form of cruel and unusual punishment. It is a far cry from physical torture to merely segregate someone from the general population, and insofar as it is the default method of punishment in the modern world, it hardly qualifies as "unusual." However, even if imprisonment is generally considered humane, the conditions under which someone is imprisoned could be so gruesome as to bring into question whether the prisoner was being subjected to cruel and unusual punishment. In the 1970s, the Supreme Court made clear that the Eighth Amendment outlawed both inhumane punishments and the inhumane treatment of prisoners while incarcerated:

> The Eighth Amendment's ban on inflicting cruel and unusual punishments, made applicable to the States by the Fourteenth Amendment, [proscribes] more than physically barbarous punishments. It prohibits penalties that . . . transgress today's broad and idealistic concepts of dignity, civilized standards, humanity, and decency. Confinement in a prison or in an isolation cell is a form of punishment subject to scrutiny under Eighth Amendment standards.[2]

Not all the current Supreme Court justices agree with this interpretation of the Eighth Amendment. Justices Antonin Scalia and Clarence Thomas—both "originalists," who believe that the Constitution should be interpreted based on norms at the time it was drafted—see the application of the Eighth Amendment to prison conditions as unwarranted, and the intervention of the judiciary into prison management as impractical. Congress has agreed with the latter sentiment: Concerned with the number of lawsuits challenging prison conditions, it adopted legislation in 1995—the Prison Litigation Reform Act (PLRA)—making it harder for prisoners to file suits for Eighth Amendment violations. Nonetheless, federal courts still hear such challenges and occasionally are forced to take drastic action to remedy constitutional violations. Such was the situation in the recent case of *Brown v. Plata,* in which conditions at several California state prisons were so bad that a federal court took the drastic step of ordering the release of several thousand prisoners. In the YES reading, Justice Kennedy, writing for the majority, defends the legitimacy and necessity of that decision; Justice Scalia, in the NO reading, argues that it is constitutionally unsound and threatens public safety.

---

[1] Quoted in *Harmelin v. Michigan*, 501 U.S. 957, 980 (1991). A gibbet was a device used to publicly display the corpse of an executed criminal, in hopes of deterring others from committing the same crime.
[2] *Hutto v. Finney*, 437 U.S. 678, 685 (1978). Internal citations and quotation marks omitted.

YES ⬅

Anthony Kennedy

Majority Opinion, *Brown v. Plata*

JUSTICE KENNEDY delivered the opinion of the Court.

This case arises from serious constitutional violations in California's prison system. The violations have persisted for years. They remain uncorrected. The appeal comes to this Court from a three-judge District Court order directing California to remedy two ongoing violations of the Cruel and Unusual Punishments Clause, a guarantee binding on the States by the Due Process Clause of the Fourteenth Amendment. The violations are the subject of two class actions in two Federal District Courts. The first involves the class of prisoners with serious mental disorders. That case is *Coleman v. Brown*. The second involves prisoners with serious medical conditions. That case is *Plata v. Brown*. The order of the three-judge District Court is applicable to both cases.

After years of litigation, it became apparent that a remedy for the constitutional violations would not be effective absent a reduction in the prison system population. The authority to order release of prisoners as a remedy to cure a systemic violation of the Eighth Amendment is a power reserved to a three-judge district court, not a single-judge district court. . . . In accordance with that rule, the *Coleman* and *Plata* District Judges independently requested that a three-judge court be convened. The Chief Judge of the Court of Appeals for the Ninth Circuit convened a three-judge court composed of the *Coleman* and *Plata* District Judges and a third, Ninth Circuit Judge. Because the two cases are interrelated, their limited consolidation for this purpose has a certain utility in avoiding conflicting decrees and aiding judicial consideration and enforcement. . . . The State . . . objects to the substance of the three-judge court order, which requires the State to reduce overcrowding in its prisons.

The appeal presents the question whether the remedial order issued by the three-judge court is consistent with requirements and procedures set forth in a congressional statute, the Prison Litigation Reform Act of 1995 (PLRA) . . . The order leaves the choice of means to reduce overcrowding to the discretion of state officials. But absent compliance through new construction, out-of-state transfers, or other means—or modification of the order upon a further showing by the State—the State will be required to release some number of prisoners before their full sentences have been served. High recidivism rates must serve as a warning that mistaken or premature release of even one prisoner can cause injury and harm. The release of prisoners in large numbers— assuming the State finds no other way to comply with the order—is a matter of undoubted, grave concern.

Supreme Court of the United States, May 23, 2011.

At the time of trial, California's correctional facilities held some 156,000 persons. This is nearly double the number that California's prisons were designed to hold, and California has been ordered to reduce its prison population to 137.5% of design capacity. By the three-judge court's own estimate, the required population reduction could be as high as 46,000 persons. Although the State has reduced the population by at least 9,000 persons during the pendency of this appeal, this means a further reduction of 37,000 persons could be required. As will be noted, the reduction need not be accomplished in an indiscriminate manner or in these substantial numbers if satisfactory, alternate remedies or means for compliance are devised. The State may employ measures, including good-time credits and diversion of low-risk offenders and technical parole violators to community-based programs, that will mitigate the order's impact. The population reduction potentially required is nevertheless of unprecedented sweep and extent.

Yet so too is the continuing injury and harm resulting from these serious constitutional violations. For years the medical and mental health care provided by California's prisons has fallen short of minimum constitutional requirements and has failed to meet prisoners' basic health needs. Needless suffering and death have been the well documented result. Over the whole course of years during which this litigation has been pending, no other remedies have been found to be sufficient. Efforts to remedy the violation have been frustrated by severe overcrowding in California's prison system. Short term gains in the provision of care have been eroded by the long-term effects of severe and pervasive overcrowding.

Overcrowding has overtaken the limited resources of prison staff; imposed demands well beyond the capacity of medical and mental health facilities; and created unsanitary and unsafe conditions that make progress in the provision of care difficult or impossible to achieve. The overcrowding is the "primary cause of the violation of a Federal right," 18 U. S. C. §3626(a)(3)(E)(i), specifically the severe and unlawful mistreatment of prisoners through grossly inadequate provision of medical and mental health care.

This Court now holds that the PLRA does authorize the relief afforded in this case and that the court-mandated population limit is necessary to remedy the violation of prisoners' constitutional rights. The order of the three judge court, subject to the right of the State to seek its modification in appropriate circumstances, must be affirmed.

I

A

The degree of overcrowding in California's prisons is exceptional. California's prisons are designed to house a population just under 80,000, but at the time of the three-judge court's decision the population was almost double that. The State's prisons had operated at around 200% of design capacity for at least 11 years. Prisoners are crammed into spaces neither designed nor intended to house inmates. As many as 200 prisoners may live in a gymnasium, monitored by as few as two or three correctional officers. . . . As many as 54 prisoners may share a single toilet. . . .

The Corrections Independent Review Panel, a body appointed by the Governor and composed of correctional consultants and representatives from state agencies, concluded that California's prisons are "'severely overcrowded, imperiling the safety of both correctional employees and inmates. . . .'"

In 2006, then-Governor Schwarzenegger declared a state of emergency in the prisons, as "'immediate action is necessary to prevent death and harm caused by California's severe prison overcrowding.'". . . The consequences of overcrowding identified by the Governor include "'increased, substantial risk for transmission of infectious illness'" and a suicide rate "'approaching an average of one per week.'". . .

Prisoners in California with serious mental illness do not receive minimal, adequate care. Because of a shortage of treatment beds, suicidal inmates may be held for prolonged periods in telephone-booth sized cages without toilets. . . . A psychiatric expert reported observing an inmate who had been held in such a cage for nearly 24 hours, standing in a pool of his own urine, unresponsive and nearly catatonic. Prison officials explained they had "'no place to put him.'". . . Other inmates awaiting care may be held for months in administrative segregation, where they endure harsh and isolated conditions and receive only limited mental health services. Wait times for mental health care range as high as 12 months. . . . In 2006, the suicide rate in California's prisons was nearly 80% higher than the national average for prison populations; and a court-appointed Special Master found that 72.1% of suicides involved "some measure of inadequate assessment, treatment, or intervention, and were therefore most probably foreseeable and/or preventable.". . .

Prisoners suffering from physical illness also receive severely deficient care. California's prisons were designed to meet the medical needs of a population at 100% of design capacity and so have only half the clinical space needed to treat the current population. . . . A correctional officer testified that, in one prison, up to 50 sick inmates may be held together in a 12- by 20-foot cage for up to five hours awaiting treatment. . . . The number of staff is inadequate, and prisoners face significant delays in access to care. . . .

D

The *Coleman* and *Plata* plaintiffs, believing that a remedy for unconstitutional medical and mental health care could not be achieved without reducing overcrowding, moved their respective District Courts to convene a three-judge court empowered under the PLRA to order reductions in the prison population. . . .

The three-judge court heard 14 days of testimony and issued a 184-page opinion, making extensive findings of fact. The court ordered California to reduce its prison population to 137.5% of the prisons' design capacity within two years. Assuming the State does not increase capacity through new construction, the order requires a population reduction of 38,000 to 46,000 persons. Because it appears all but certain that the State cannot complete sufficient construction to comply fully with the order, the prison population will have to be reduced to at least some extent. The court did not order the State to achieve this reduction in any particular manner. Instead, the court ordered the State to formulate a plan for compliance and submit its plan for approval by the court.

The State appealed to this Court. . . .

II

As a consequence of their own actions, prisoners may be deprived of rights that are fundamental to liberty. Yet the law and the Constitution demand recognition of certain other rights. Prisoners retain the essence of human dignity inherent in all persons. Respect for that dignity animates the Eighth Amendment prohibition against cruel and unusual punishment. "'The basic concept underlying the Eighth Amendment is nothing less than the dignity of man.'" *Atkins v. Virginia,* 536 U.S. 304, 311 (2002) (quoting *Trop v. Dulles,* 356 U.S. 86, 100 (1958) (plurality opinion)).

To incarcerate, society takes from prisoners the means to provide for their own needs. Prisoners are dependent on the State for food, clothing, and necessary medical care. A prison's failure to provide sustenance for inmates "may actually produce physical 'torture or a lingering death.'" *Estelle v. Gamble,* 429 U.S. 97, 103 (1976) (quoting *In re Kemmler,* 136 U.S. 436, 447 (1890)); . . . Just as a prisoner may starve if not fed, he or she may suffer or die if not provided adequate medical care. A prison that deprives prisoners of basic sustenance, including adequate medical care, is incompatible with the concept of human dignity and has no place in civilized society.

If government fails to fulfill this obligation, the courts have a responsibility to remedy the resulting Eighth Amendment violation. . . . Courts must be sensitive to the State's interest in punishment, deterrence, and rehabilitation, as well as the need for deference to experienced and expert prison administrators faced with the difficult and dangerous task of housing large numbers of convicted criminals. . . . Courts nevertheless must not shrink from their obligation to "enforce the constitutional rights of all 'persons,' including prisoners." *Cruz v. Beto,* 405 U.S. 319, 321 (1972) *(per curiam).* Courts may not allow constitutional violations to continue simply because a remedy would involve intrusion into the realm of prison administration. . . .

B

[Under the PLRA,] Once a three-judge court has been convened, the court must find additional requirements satisfied before it may impose a population limit. The first of these requirements is that "crowding is the primary cause of the violation of a Federal right." 18 U. S. C. §3626(a)(3)(E)(i).

1

The three-judge court found the primary cause requirement satisfied by the evidence at trial. The court found that overcrowding strains inadequate medical and mental health facilities; overburdens limited clinical and custodial staff; and creates violent, unsanitary, and chaotic conditions that contribute to the constitutional violations and frustrate efforts to fashion a remedy. The three-judge court also found that "until the problem of over-crowding is overcome it will be impossible to provide constitutionally compli-ant care to California's prison population." . . .

The record documents the severe impact of burgeoning demand on the provision of care. At the time of trial, vacancy rates for medical and men-tal health staff ranged as high as 20% for surgeons, 25% for physicians, 39% for nurse practitioners, and 54.1% for psychiatrists. . . . These percentages are based on the number of positions budgeted by the State. Dr. Ronald Shansky, former medical director of the Illinois prison system, concluded that these numbers understate the severity of the crisis because the State has not budg-eted sufficient staff to meet demand. According to Dr. Shansky, "even if the prisons were able to fill all of their vacant health care positions, which they have not been able to do to date, . . . the prisons would still be unable to han-dle the level of need given the current overcrowding.". . . Dr. Craig Haney, a professor of psychology, reported that mental health staff are "managing far larger caseloads than is appropriate or effective.". . . A prison psychiatrist told Dr. Haney that "'we are doing about 50% of what we should be doing.'". . . In the context of physical care Dr. Shansky agreed that "demand for care, par-ticularly for the high priority cases, continues to overwhelm the resources. . . .

Crowding also creates unsafe and unsanitary living conditions that ham-per effective delivery of medical and mental health care. A medical expert described living quarters in converted gymnasiums or dayrooms, where large numbers of prisoners may share just a few toilets and showers, as "'breeding grounds for disease.'". . . Cramped conditions promote unrest and violence, making it difficult for prison officials to monitor and control the prison pop-ulation. On any given day, prisoners in the general prison population may become ill, thus entering the plaintiff class; and overcrowding may prevent immediate medical attention necessary to avoid suffering, death, or spread of disease. After one prisoner was assaulted in a crowded gymnasium, prison staff did not even learn of the injury until the prisoner had been dead for several hours. . . . Living in crowded, unsafe, and unsanitary conditions can cause prisoners with latent mental illnesses to worsen and develop overt symptoms. Crowding may also impede efforts to improve delivery of care. Two prison-ers committed suicide by hanging after being placed in cells that had been identified as requiring a simple fix to remove attachment points that could support a noose. The repair was not made because doing so would involve removing prisoners from the cells, and there was no place to put them. . . . More generally, Jeanne Woodford, the former acting secretary of California's prisons, testified that there "'are simply too many issues that arise from such a large number of prisoners,'" and that, as a result, "'management spends vir-tually all of its time fighting fires instead of engaging in thoughtful decision-making and planning'" of the sort needed to fashion an effective remedy for these constitutional violations. . . .

Increased violence also requires increased reliance on lockdowns to keep order, and lockdowns further impede the effective delivery of care. In 2006, prison officials instituted 449 lockdowns. . . . The average lockdown lasted 12 days, and 20 lockdowns lasted 60 days or longer. . . . During lockdowns, staff must either escort prisoners to medical facilities or bring medical staff to the prisoners. Either procedure puts additional strain on already overburdened medical and custodial staff. Some programming for the mentally ill even may be canceled altogether during lockdowns, and staff may be unable to supervise the delivery of psychotropic medications. . . .

Numerous experts testified that crowding is the primary cause of the constitutional violations. The former warden of San Quentin and former acting secretary of the California prisons concluded that crowding "makes it 'virtually impossible for the organization to develop, much less implement, a plan to provide prisoners with adequate care.'". . .

3

The three-judge court acknowledged that the violations were caused by factors in addition to overcrowding and that reducing crowding in the prisons would not entirely cure the violations. This is consistent with the reports of the *Coleman* Special Master and *Plata* Receiver, both of whom concluded that even a significant reduction in the prison population would not remedy the violations absent continued efforts to train staff, improve facilities, and reform procedures. . . . The three-judge court nevertheless found that overcrowding was the primary cause in the sense of being the foremost cause of the violation. . . .

As this case illustrates, constitutional violations in conditions of confinement are rarely susceptible of simple or straightforward solutions. In addition to overcrowding the failure of California's prisons to provide adequate medical and mental health care may be ascribed to chronic and worsening budget shortfalls, a lack of political will in favor of reform, inadequate facilities, and systemic administrative failures. The *Plata* District Judge, in his order appointing the Receiver, compared the problem to "'a spider web, in which the tension of the various strands is determined by the relationship among all the parts of the web, so that if one pulls on a single strand, the tension of the entire web is redistributed in a new and complex pattern.'". . . Only a multifaceted approach aimed at many causes, including overcrowding, will yield a solution.

The PLRA should not be interpreted to place undue restrictions on the authority of federal courts to fashion practical remedies when confronted with complex and intractable constitutional violations. Congress limited the availability of limits on prison populations, but it did not forbid these measures altogether. . . . The House Report accompanying the PLRA explained:

> "While prison caps must be the remedy of last resort, a court still retains the power to order this remedy despite its intrusive nature and harmful consequences to the public if, but only if, it is truly necessary to prevent an actual violation of a prisoner's federal rights." H. R. Rep. No. 104–21, p. 25 (1995).

Courts should presume that Congress was sensitive to the real-world problems faced by those who would remedy constitutional violations in the prisons and that Congress did not leave prisoners without a remedy for violations of their constitutional rights. . . .

C

The three-judge court was also required to find by clear and convincing evidence that "no other relief will remedy the violation of the Federal right.". . .

The State argues that the violation could have been remedied through a combination of new construction, transfers of prisoners out of State, hiring of medical personnel, and continued efforts by the *Plata* Receiver and *Coleman* Special Master. The order in fact permits the State to comply with the population limit by transferring prisoners to county facilities or facilities in other States, or by constructing new facilities to raise the prisons' design capacity. And the three-judge court's order does not bar the State from undertaking any other remedial efforts. If the State does find an adequate remedy other than a population limit, it may seek modification or termination of the three-judge court's order on that basis. The evidence at trial, however, supports the three-judge court's conclusion that an order limited to other remedies would not provide effective relief. . . .

The common thread connecting the State's proposed remedial efforts [in order to avoid releasing prisoners] is that they would require the State to expend large amounts of money absent a reduction in overcrowding. The Court cannot ignore the political and fiscal reality behind this case. California's Legislature has not been willing or able to allocate the resources necessary to meet this crisis absent a reduction in overcrowding. There is no reason to believe it will begin to do so now, when the State of California is facing an unprecedented budgetary shortfall. As noted above, the legislature recently failed to allocate funds for planned new construction. *Supra,* at 30–31. Without a reduction in overcrowding, there will be no efficacious remedy for the unconstitutional care of the sick and mentally ill in California's prisons. . . .

In reaching its decision, the three-judge court gave "substantial weight" to any potential adverse impact on public safety from its order. The court devoted nearly 10 days of trial to the issue of public safety, and it gave the question extensive attention in its opinion. Ultimately, the court concluded that it would be possible to reduce the prison population "in a manner that preserves public safety and the operation of the criminal justice system.". . .

The PLRA's requirement that a court give "substantial weight" to public safety does not require the court to certify that its order has no possible adverse impact on the public. A contrary reading would depart from the statute's text by replacing the word "substantial" with "conclusive." Whenever a court issues an order requiring the State to adjust its incarceration and criminal justice policy, there is a risk that the order will have some adverse impact on public safety in some sectors. This is particularly true when the order requires release of prisoners before their sentence has been served. Persons incarcerated for even one offense may have committed many other crimes prior to arrest and conviction, and some number can be expected to commit further crimes upon release. Yet the PLRA contemplates that courts will retain authority to issue orders necessary to remedy constitutional violations, including authority to issue population limits when necessary. . . . A court is required to consider the public safety consequences of its order and to structure, and monitor, its ruling in a way that mitigates those consequences while still achieving an effective remedy of the constitutional violation.

This inquiry necessarily involves difficult predictive judgments regarding the likely effects of court orders. Although these judgments are normally made by state officials, they necessarily must be made by courts when those courts fashion injunctive relief to remedy serious constitutional violations in the prisons. These questions are difficult and sensitive, but they are factual questions and should be treated as such. Courts can, and should, rely on relevant and informed expert testimony when making factual findings. It was proper for the three-judge court to rely on the testimony of prison officials from California and other States. Those experts testified on the basis of empirical evidence and extensive experience in the field of prison administration.

The three-judge court credited substantial evidence that prison populations can be reduced in a manner that does not increase crime to a significant degree. Some evidence indicated that reducing overcrowding in California's prisons could even improve public safety. Then-Governor Schwarzenegger, in his emergency proclamation on overcrowding, acknowledged that "'overcrowding causes harm to people and property, leads to inmate unrest and misconduct, . . . and increases recidivism as shown within this state and in others.'" . . . The former warden of San Quentin and acting secretary of the California prison system testified that she "'absolutely believe[s] that we make people worse, and that we are not meeting public safety by the way we treat people.'". . . And the head of Pennsylvania's correctional system testified that measures to reduce prison population may "actually improve on public safety because they address the problems that brought people to jail." . . .

Expert witnesses produced statistical evidence that prison populations had been lowered without adversely affecting public safety in a number of jurisdictions, including certain counties in California, as well as Wisconsin, Illinois, Texas, Colorado, Montana, Michigan, Florida, and Canada. . . . Washington's former secretary of corrections testified that his State had implemented population reduction methods, including parole reform and expansion of good time credits, without any "deleterious effect on crime." . . . In light of this evidence, the three-judge court concluded that any negative impact on public safety would be "substantially offset, and perhaps entirely eliminated, by the public safety benefits" of a reduction in overcrowding. Juris. App. 248a.

The court found that various available methods of reducing overcrowding would have little or no impact on public safety. Expansion of good-time credits would allow the State to give early release to only those prisoners who pose the least risk of reoffending. Diverting low-risk offenders to community programs such as drug treatment, day reporting centers, and electronic monitoring would likewise lower the prison population without releasing violent convicts. The State now sends large numbers of persons to prison for violating a technical term or condition of their parole, and it could reduce the prison population by punishing technical parole violations through community-based programs. This last measure would be particularly beneficial as it would reduce crowding in the reception centers, which are especially hard hit by overcrowding. . . . The court's order took account of public safety concerns by giving the State substantial flexibility to select among these and other means of reducing overcrowding. . . .

III

Establishing the population at which the State could begin to provide constitutionally adequate medical and mental health care, and the appropriate time frame within which to achieve the necessary reduction, requires a degree of judgment. The inquiry involves uncertain predictions regarding the effects of population reductions, as well as difficult determinations regarding the capacity of prison officials to provide adequate care at various population levels. Courts have substantial flexibility when making these judgments. . . .

A

The three-judge court concluded that the population of California's prisons should be capped at 137.5% of design capacity. This conclusion is supported by the record. . . . The medical and mental health care provided by California's prisons falls below the standard of decency that inheres in the Eighth Amendment. This extensive and ongoing constitutional violation requires a remedy, and a remedy will not be achieved without a reduction in overcrowding. The relief ordered by the three-judge court is required by the Constitution and was authorized by Congress in the PLRA. The State shall implement the order without further delay.

The judgment of the three-judge court is affirmed.

It is so ordered.

Antonin Scalia   → **NO**

Dissenting Opinion, *Brown v. Plata*

JUSTICE SCALIA, with whom JUSTICE THOMAS joins, dissenting.

Today the Court affirms what is perhaps the most radical injunction issued by a court in our Nation's history: an order requiring California to release the staggering number of 46,000 convicted criminals.

There comes before us, now and then, a case whose proper outcome is so clearly indicated by tradition and common sense, that its decision ought to shape the law, rather than vice versa. One would think that, before allowing the decree of a federal district court to release 46,000 convicted felons, this Court would bend every effort to read the law in such a way as to avoid that outrageous result. Today, quite to the contrary, the Court disregards stringently drawn provisions of the governing statute, and traditional constitutional limitations upon the power of a federal judge, in order to uphold the absurd.

The proceedings that led to this result were a judicial travesty. I dissent because the institutional reform the District Court has undertaken violates the terms of the governing statute, ignores bedrock limitations on the power of Article III judges, and takes federal courts wildly beyond their institutional capacity.

I

A

The Prison Litigation Reform Act (PLRA) states that "[p]rospective relief in any civil action with respect to prison conditions shall extend no further than necessary to correct the violation of the Federal right of a particular plaintiff or plaintiffs"; that such relief must be "narrowly drawn, [and] exten[d] no further than necessary to correct the violation of the Federal right"; and that it must be "the least intrusive means necessary to correct the violation of the Federal right.". . . In deciding whether these multiple limitations have been complied with, it is necessary to identify with precision what is the "violation of the Federal right of a particular plaintiff or plaintiffs" that has been alleged. What has been alleged here, and what the injunction issued by the Court is tailored (narrowly or not) to remedy is the running of a prison system with inadequate medical facilities. That may result in the denial of needed medical treatment to "a particular [prisoner] or [prisoners]," thereby violating (according to our cases) his or their Eighth Amendment rights. But the mere

Supreme Court of the United States, May 23, 2011.

existence of the inadequate system does not subject to cruel and unusual punishment the entire prison population in need of medical care, including those who receive it.

The Court acknowledges that the plaintiffs "do not base their case on deficiencies in care provided on any one occasion"; rather, "[p]laintiffs rely on systemwide deficiencies in the provision of medical and mental health care that, taken as a whole, subject sick and mentally ill prisoners in California to 'substantial risk of serious harm' and cause the delivery of care in the prisons to fall below the evolving standards of decency that mark the progress of a maturing society." . . . But our judge-empowering "evolving standards of decency" jurisprudence. . . . does not prescribe (or at least has not until today prescribed) rules for the "decent" running of schools, prisons, and other government institutions. It forbids "indecent" treatment of individuals—in the context of this case, the *denial of medical care* to those who need it. And the persons who have a constitutional claim for denial of medical care are those who are denied medical care—not all who face a "substantial risk" (whatever that is) of being denied medical care.

The *Coleman* litigation involves "the class of seriously mentally ill persons in California prisons," . . . and the *Plata* litigation involves "the class of state prisoners with serious medical conditions" . . . The plaintiffs do not appear to claim—and it would absurd to suggest—that every single one of those prisoners has personally experienced "torture or a lingering death," . . . as a consequence of that bad medical system. Indeed, it is inconceivable that anything more than a small proportion of prisoners in the plaintiff classes have personally received sufficiently atrocious treatment that their Eighth Amendment right was violated—which, as the Court recognizes, is why the plaintiffs do not premise their claim on "deficiencies in care provided on any one occasion." . . . Rather, the plaintiffs' claim is that they are all part of a medical system so defective that some number of prisoners will inevitably be injured by incompetent medical care, and that this number is sufficiently high so as to render the system, as a whole, unconstitutional.

But what procedural principle justifies certifying a class of plaintiffs so they may assert a claim of systemic unconstitutionality? I can think of two possibilities, both of which are untenable. The first is that although some or most plaintiffs in the class do not *individually* have viable Eighth Amendment claims, the class as a whole has collectively suffered an Eighth Amendment violation. That theory is contrary to the bedrock rule that the sole purpose of classwide adjudication is to aggregate claims that are individually viable. "A class action, no less than traditional joinder (of which it is a species), merely enables a federal court to adjudicate claims of multiple parties at once, instead of in separate suits. And like traditional joinder, it leaves the parties' legal rights and duties intact and the rules of decision unchanged." . . .

The second possibility is that every member of the plaintiff class *has* suffered an Eighth Amendment violation merely by virtue of being a patient in a poorly-run prison system, and the purpose of the class is merely to aggregate all those individually viable claims. This theory has the virtue of being consistent with procedural principles, but at the cost of a gross substantive departure from our case law. Under this theory, each and every prisoner who happens to be a patient in a system that has systemic weaknesses—such as "hir[ing] any doctor who had a license, a pulse and a pair of shoes," . . . —has suffered cruel or unusual punishment, even if that person cannot make an individualized showing of mistreatment. Such a theory of the Eighth Amendment is preposterous. And we have said as much in the past: "If . . . a healthy inmate who had suffered no deprivation of needed medical treatment were able to claim violation of his constitutional right to medical care . . . simply on the ground that the prison medical facilities were inadequate, the essential distinction between judge and executive would have disappeared: it would have become the function of the courts to assure adequate medical care in prisons." . . .

Whether procedurally wrong or substantively wrong, the notion that the plaintiff class can allege an Eighth Amendment violation based on "systemwide deficiencies" is assuredly wrong. It follows that the remedy decreed here is also contrary to law, since the theory of systemic unconstitutionality is central to the plaintiffs' case. The PLRA requires plaintiffs to establish that the systemwide injunction entered by the District Court was "narrowly drawn" and "extends no further than necessary" to correct "the violation of the Federal right of a particular plaintiff or plaintiffs." If (as is the case) the only viable constitutional claims consist of individual instances of mistreatment, then a remedy reforming the system as a whole goes far beyond what the statute allows.

It is also worth noting the peculiarity that the vast majority of inmates most generously rewarded by the release order—the 46,000 whose incarceration will be ended—do not form part of any aggrieved class even under the Court's expansive notion of constitutional violation. Most of them will not be prisoners with medical conditions or severe mental illness; and many will undoubtedly be fine physical specimens who have developed intimidating muscles pumping iron in the prison gym.

B

Even if I accepted the implausible premise that the plaintiffs have established a systemwide violation of the Eighth Amendment, I would dissent from the Court's endorsement of a decrowding order. That order is an example of what has become known as a "structural injunction." As I have previously explained, structural injunctions are radically different from the injunctions traditionally issued by courts of equity, and presumably part of "the judicial Power" conferred on federal courts by Article III:

> "The mandatory injunctions issued upon termination of litigation usually required 'a single simple act.' . . . Indeed, there was a 'historical prejudice of the court of chancery against rendering decrees which called for more than a single affirmative act.'. . . And where specific performance of contracts was sought, it was the categorical rule that no decree would issue that required ongoing supervision. . . .Compliance with these 'single act' mandates could, in addition to being simple, be

quick; and once it was achieved the contemnor's relationship with the court came to an end, at least insofar as the subject of the order was concerned. Once the document was turned over or the land conveyed, the litigant's obligation to the court, and the court's coercive power over the litigant, ceased. . . . The court did not engage in any ongoing supervision of the litigant's conduct, nor did its order continue to regulate its behavior." *Mine Work ers v. Bagwell,* 512 U.S. 821, 841–842 (1994) (SCALIA, J., concurring).

Structural injunctions depart from that historical practice, turning judges into long-term administrators of complex social institutions such as schools, prisons, and police departments. Indeed, they require judges to play a role essentially indistinguishable from the role ordinarily played by executive officials. Today's decision not only affirms the structural injunction but vastly expands its use, by holding that an entire system is unconstitutional because it *may produce* constitutional violations.

The drawbacks of structural injunctions have been described at great length elsewhere. . . . This case illustrates one of their most pernicious aspects: that they force judges to engage in a form of factfinding-as-policymaking that is outside the traditional judicial role. The factfinding judges traditionally engage in involves the determination of past or present facts based (except for a limited set of materials of which courts may take "judicial notice") exclusively upon a closed trial record. That is one reason why a district judge's factual findings are entitled to clear-error review: because having viewed the trial first hand he is in a better position to evaluate the evidence than a judge reviewing a cold record. In a very limited category of cases, judges have also traditionally been called upon to make some predictive judgments: which custody will best serve the interests of the child, for example, or whether a particular one-shot injunction will remedy the plaintiff's grievance. When a judge manages a structural injunction, however, he will inevitably be required to make very broad empirical predictions necessarily based in large part upon policy views—the sort of predictions regularly made by legislators and executive officials, but inappropriate for the Third Branch.

This feature of structural injunctions is superbly illustrated by the District Court's proceeding concerning the decrowding order's effect on public safety. The PLRA requires that, before granting "[p]rospective relief in [a] civil action with respect to prison conditions," a court must "give substantial weight to any adverse impact on public safety or the operation of a criminal justice system caused by the relief." . . . Here, the District Court discharged that requirement by making the "factual finding" that "the state has available methods by which it could readily reduce the prison population to 137.5% design capacity or less without an adverse impact on public safety or the operation of the criminal justice system." . . . It found the evidence "clear" that prison overcrowding would "perpetuate a criminogenic prison system that itself threatens public safety," . . . and volunteered its opinion that "[t]he population could be reduced even further with the reform of California's antiquated sentencing policies and other related changes to the laws." . . . It "reject[ed] the testimony that inmates released early from prison would commit additional new crimes," finding that "shortening the length of stay through earned credits would give inmates incentives to participate in programming designed to lower recidivism," . . . and that "slowing the flow of technical parole violators to prison, thereby substantially reducing the churning of parolees, would by itself improve both the prison and parole systems, and public safety." . . . It found that "the diversion of offenders to community correctional programs has significant beneficial effects on public safety,". . . and that "additional rehabilitative programming would result in a significant population reduction while improving public safety" . . .

The District Court cast these predictions (and the Court today accepts them) as "factual findings," made in reliance on the procession of expert witnesses that testified at trial. Because these "findings" have support in the record, it is difficult to reverse them under a plain-error standard of review. . . . And given that the District Court devoted nearly 10 days of trial and 70 pages of its opinion to this issue, it is difficult to dispute that the District Court has discharged its statutory obligation to give "substantial weight to any adverse impact on public safety."

But the idea that the three District Judges in this case relied solely on the credibility of the testifying expert witnesses is fanciful. *Of course* they were relying largely on their own beliefs about penology and recidivism. And *of course* different district judges, of different policy views, would have "found" that rehabilitation would not work and that releasing prisoners would increase the crime rate. I am not saying that the District Judges rendered their factual findings in bad faith. I am saying that it is impossible for judges to make "factual findings" without inserting their own policy judgments, when the factual findings *are* policy judgments. What occurred here is no more judicial factfinding in the ordinary sense than would be the factual findings that deficit spending will not lower the unemployment rate, or that the continued occupation of Iraq will decrease the risk of terrorism. Yet, because they have been branded "factual findings" entitled to deferential review, the policy preferences of three District Judges now govern the operation of California's penal system.

It is important to recognize that the dressing-up of policy judgments as factual findings is not an error peculiar to this case. It is an unavoidable concomitant of institutional-reform litigation. When a district court issues an injunction, it must make a factual assessment of the anticipated consequences of the injunction. And when the injunction undertakes to restructure a social institution, assessing the factual consequences of the injunction is necessarily the sort of predictive judgment that our system of government allocates to other government officials.

But structural injunctions do not simply invite judges to indulge policy preferences. They invite judges to indulge *incompetent* policy preferences. Three years of law school and familiarity with pertinent Supreme Court precedents give no insight whatsoever into the management of social institutions. Thus, in the proceeding below the District Court determined that constitutionally adequate medical services could be provided if the prison population was 137.5% of design capacity. This was an empirical finding it was utterly unqualified to make. Admittedly, the court did not generate that number entirely on its own; it heard the numbers 130% and 145% bandied about by various witnesses and decided to split the difference. But the ability of judges to spit back or even average-out numbers spoon-fed to them by expert witnesses does not render them competent decisionmakers in areas in which they are otherwise unqualified. . . .

C

My general concerns associated with judges' running social institutions are magnified when they run prison systems, and doubly magnified when they force prison officials to release convicted criminals. As we have previously recognized:

> "[C]ourts are ill equipped to deal with the increasingly urgent problems of prison administration and reform. . . . [T]he problems of prisons in America are complex and intractable, and, more to the point, they are not readily susceptible of resolution by decree. . . . Running a prison is an inordinately difficult undertaking that requires expertise, planning, and the commitment of resources, all of which are peculiarly within the province of the legislative and executive branches of government. Prison is, moreover, a task that has been committed to the responsibility of those branches, and separation of powers concerns counsel a policy of judicial restraint. Where a state penal system is involved, federal courts have . . . additional reason to accord deference to the appropriate prison authorities." *Turner v. Safley*, 482 U.S. 78, 84–85 (1987) (internal quotation marks omitted).

These principles apply doubly to a prisoner-release order. As the author of today's opinion explained earlier this Term, granting a writ of habeas corpus "'disturbs the State's significant interest in repose for concluded litigation, denies society the right to punish some admitted offenders, and intrudes on state sovereignty to a degree matched by few exercises of federal judicial authority.'" *Harrington v. Richter*, 562 U.S. ___, ___ (2011) (slip op., at 13) (quoting *Harris v. Reed*, 489 U.S. 255, 282 (1989) (KENNEDY, J., dissenting)). Recognizing that habeas relief must be granted sparingly, we have reversed the Ninth Circuit's erroneous grant of habeas relief to individual California prisoners four times this Term alone. . . . And yet here, the Court affirms an order granting the functional equivalent of 46,000 writs of habeas corpus, based on its paean to courts' "substantial flexibility when making these judgments." . . . It seems that the Court's respect for state sovereignty has vanished in the case where it most matters. . . .

III

In view of the incoherence of the Eighth Amendment claim at the core of this case, the nonjudicial features of institutional reform litigation that this case exemplifies, and the unique concerns associated with mass prisoner releases, I do not believe this Court can affirm this injunction. I will state my approach briefly: In my view, a court may not order a prisoner's release unless it determines that the prisoner is suffering from a violation of his constitutional rights, and that his release, and no other relief, will remedy that violation. Thus, if the court determines that a particular prisoner is being denied constitutionally required medical treatment, and the release of that prisoner (and no other remedy) would enable him to obtain medical treatment, then the court can order his release; but a court may not order the release of prisoners who have suffered no violations of their constitutional rights, merely to make it less likely that that will happen to them in the future.

This view follows from the PLRA's text that I discussed at the outset, . . . "[N]arrowly drawn" means that the relief applies only to the "particular [prisoner] or [prisoners]" whose constitutional rights are violated; "extends no further than necessary" means that prisoners whose rights are not violated will not obtain relief; and "least intrusive means necessary to correct the violation of the Federal right" means that no other relief is available.

I acknowledge that this reading of the PLRA would severely limit the circumstances under which a court could issue structural injunctions to remedy allegedly unconstitutional prison conditions, although it would not eliminate them entirely. If, for instance, a class representing all prisoners in a particular institution alleged that the temperature in their cells was so cold as to violate the Eighth Amendment, or that they were deprived of all exercise time, a court could enter a prisonwide injunction ordering that the temperature be raised or exercise time be provided. Still, my approach may invite the objection that the PLRA appears to contemplate structural injunctions in general and mass prisoner-release orders in particular. The statute requires courts to "give substantial weight to any adverse impact on public safety or the operation of a criminal justice system caused by the relief" and authorizes them to appoint Special Masters . . . provisions that seem to presuppose the possibility of a structural remedy. It also sets forth criteria under which courts may issue orders that have "the purpose or effect of reducing or limiting the prisoner population" . . .

I do not believe that objection carries the day. In addition to imposing numerous limitations on the ability of district courts to order injunctive relief with respect to prison conditions, the PLRA states that "[n]othing in this section shall be construed to . . . repeal or detract from otherwise applicable limitations on the remedial powers of the courts." . . . The PLRA is therefore best understood as an attempt to constrain the discretion of courts issuing structural injunctions— not as a mandate for their use. For the reasons I have outlined, structural injunctions, especially prisoner-release orders, raise grave separation-of-powers concerns and veer significantly from the historical role and institutional capability of courts. It is appropriate to construe the PLRA so as to constrain courts from entering injunctive relief that would exceed that role and capability.

* * *

The District Court's order that California release 46,000 prisoners extends "further than necessary to correct the violation of the Federal right of a particular plaintiff or plaintiffs" who have been denied needed medical care. . . . It is accordingly forbidden by the PLRA—besides defying all sound conception of the proper role of judges.

POSTSCRIPT

Is the Eighth Amendment Protection Violated If Prisoners Are Deprived of Basic Sustenance, Including Adequate Medical Care?

Were the courts right to intervene in this case? Or, is Justice Scalia correct that these are issues of public policy, not constitutionalism? As noted in Justice Kennedy's opinion, there was little chance that California would take the initiative to fix the problem absent judicial intervention. The most obvious solution—and one that would avoid the potential dangers associated with releasing prisoners—would be to build new prison facilities and increase the medical services available to prisoners. However, this would require an enormous investment of money and California has long struggled with financial problems, which have been further exacerbated by the recent economic downturn. California's elected officials are limited in their ability to raise taxes because of a 1978 ballot initiative, Proposition 13, which amended the state constitution to limit property tax increases and require supermajorities to increase other tax rates. Meanwhile, California's prison population has exploded over the last two decades, in part because of harsher sentencing laws and a "Three Strikes" policy that mandates a 25-year prison sentence for any defendant convicted of a third felony offense, even for minor, nonviolent crimes (see Issue 14).

Brown v. Plata highlights some of the often-overlooked complexities involved in administering a criminal justice system. The California "Three Strikes" law was passed as a popular ballot initiative, Proposition 184 in 1994, by an overwhelming margin, but another popular measure—Proposition 13— has impeded California from raising the billions of dollars necessary to accommodate the increased prison population that resulted from Proposition 184. Few would want to return to the times of corporal punishment, public executions, or banishment of citizens to penal colonies, but the alternative—a prison system—requires the expenditure of public funds, and taxpayers are often loathe to have their hard-earned tax dollars go to support food and medical care for those who violate the law. If these competing interests cannot be resolved, prison conditions may deteriorate, as they did here, to the point where judicial intervention is the only option. However, even the courts would admit that the solutions at their disposal, such as ordering the release of convicted criminals, are hardly ideal.

For additional background on the Cruel and Unusual Punishment Clause, a good place to begin is Anthony Granucci's classic article '"Nor Cruel and Unusual Punishment Inflicted:' The Original Meaning" 57 *California Law Review* 4 (October 1969). For the application of the Eighth Amendment to prison conditions, see Sharon Dolovich, "Cruelty, Prison Conditions, and the Eighth Amendment" 84 *NYU Law Review* 4 (2009), and Malcolm M. Feeley and Edward L. Rubin, *Judicial Policy Making and the Modern State: How the Courts Reformed American Prisons* (Cambridge University Press, 1999). Human Rights Watch criticizes the PLRA for blocking legitimate lawsuits about abusive prison conditions in its 2009 report *No Equal Justice: The Prison Litigation Reform Act in the United States* (www.hrw.org/en/reports/2009/06/15/no-equal-justice), while the act is defended in Eugene J. Kuzinski, "The End of the Prison Law Firm?: Frivolous Inmate Litigation, Judicial Oversight, and the Prison Litigation Reform Act of 1995" 29 *Rutgers Law Journal* 361 (1997–1998). Finally, for a comparative study of prison conditions in the United States and abroad, see Dirk van Zyl Smit and Frieder Dunkel (eds.), *Imprisonment Today and Tomorrow: International Perspectives on Prisoners' Rights and Prison Conditions,* 2nd ed. (Kluwer Law International, 2001).

Internet References . . .

Thomas: Legislative Information on the Internet

This site of the Library of Congress provides access to federal statutes, pending legislation, and other legal material.

http://thomas.loc.gov

FedWorld

FedWorld is a highly comprehensive site with links to federal agencies and to the reports and information produced by those agencies.

http://www.fedworld.gov

FedNet

FedNet allows you to listen in on congressional hearings and events and also provides links to archives of previously recorded material.

http://www.fednet.net

Death Penalty Information Center

The Death Penalty Information Center provides a wealth of information on a variety of topics related to capital punishment, including a history of the death penalty, race issues, and mental retardation and the death penalty.

http://www.deathpenaltyinfo.org

Law and the State

*T*he use of state power can be seen in various ways, including in the promotion of patriotic and moral values, in efforts to deal with crime, in responses to public opinion, and in choices of policies to be implemented. The majority is not always allowed to rule, and determining when state interests are compelling and legitimate is often difficult. The issues in this section confront some of these challenges.

- Should Judges Be Elected Rather Than Appointed?

- Do Religious Groups Have a Right to Use Public School Facilities After Hours?

- Does the First Amendment Protect Picketing a Funeral Even When It Intentionally Inflicts Emotional Distress on the Family?

- Can a School Punish a Student for Speech at a School-Supervised Event Off of School Grounds When That Speech Could Be Viewed as Promoting Illegal Drug Use?

- Is a Strip Search of Middle School Students That Is Aimed at Finding Drugs Permissible Under the Fourth Amendment?

- Does the "Cruel and Unusual Punishment" Clause of the Eighth Amendment Bar the Imposition of the Death Penalty on Juveniles?

- Is a Sentence of Life in Prison for Stealing $150 Worth of Videotapes Constitutional?

- Can Noise Coming from Inside an Apartment and Which the Police Believe Involves the Destruction of Drugs Constitute "Exigent Circumstances" That Allow Police Officers to Enter and Search a Home Without a Warrant?

- Is the Fourth Amendment Search and Seizure Guaranty Violated by the Use of Thermal Imaging Devices?

ISSUE 8

Should Judges Be Elected Rather Than Appointed?

YES: Michael R. Dimino, Sr., from "The Worst Way of Selecting Judges—Except All the Others That Have Been Tried," *Northern Kentucky L. Rev.*, v. 32, pp. 267–304 (2005)

NO: Charles Gardner Geyh, from "Why Judicial Elections Stink," *Ohio St. L.J.*, v. 64, pp. 43–79 (2003)

ISSUE SUMMARY

YES: Professor Michael Dimino claims that electing judges is no worse than appointing them and that it is appropriate for citizens to have a say in who will be making decisions that affect them.

NO: Professor Charles Geyh criticizes the practice of electing judges and argues that it reduces judicial independence and accountability.

In April 2011, Wisconsin voters went to the polls to choose between two candidates for high state office. For weeks beforehand, special interest groups—mostly from outside the state—had poured millions of dollars into television ads designed to influence the election. One ad told voters that the incumbent, David Prosser, was unwilling to bring sex offenders to justice. Another stated that his challenger, JoAnne Kloppenburg, was antifarmer. In all, more than $5.4 million was spent on the campaign, 80 percent of it from special interests. Prosser won by a margin of less than one-half of 1 percent.

The Prosser–Kloppenburg race drew the kind of national attention that once was reserved for high-stakes Congressional races. But this election was for the state supreme court. The race for a single seat on a seven-judge court in a Midwestern state drew the focus and money of organizations across the country, each of which felt that they had a stake in the outcome.

Most judges do not face such high-cost and high-intensity elections but they face elections just the same. Unlike federal judges in the United States, who enjoy lifetime appointments, nearly 90 percent of state judges must periodically face voters if they want to stay on the bench. In all, 38 states subject some or all of their judges to periodic elections, in one of three forms.

In *partisan elections,* candidates run under a party label, and typically must navigate their party's nominating process in order to be placed on the ballot. Throughout most of the nineteenth and into the twentieth century, partisan elections were the norm across the country. Today they are used in only a handful of states.

Nonpartisan judicial elections are contested races, but the candidates do not run with a party affiliation. Reformers adopted nonpartisan elections out of concern that judges are not ordinary politicians and should not be linked to a party platform. Still, in many states a candidate's party is known even if it does not appear on the ballot.

Merit selection was developed in the 1920s as an alternative to contested elections. Judges are initially appointed by the governor from a slate of candidates recommended by an independent nominating commission. At the end of each term, a judge faces a retention election. Proponents of merit selection argue that the initial appointment process avoids the problems of contested elections, but that retention elections still preserve judicial accountability to the public. Missouri became the first state to adopt the merit selection system in 1940. Since then, more than a dozen states (mostly in the West) have adopted merit selection for some or all of their judges.

The judicial selection debate today focuses on three key issues. The first is balancing judicial independence and judicial accountability. Critics of judicial elections complain that judges will avoid making controversial rulings in order to get reelected, which may unfairly hurt criminal defendants, minority groups and proponents of unpopular expression. Supporters of judicial elections counter that judges should not be completely free to rule any way they want, especially if those rulings fly in the face of community standards. Some even say that judicial rulings should directly reflect the majority will.

The second key issue is judicial ethics. Much of the money that funds judicial races comes from the lawyers and parties that are likely to appear before the candidate if he or she is elected. Can judges set aside their gratitude for campaign funding and deliver completely neutral and fair opinions? Another ethical question is whether a judicial candidate should share his or her positions on controversial issues during the election campaign. The U.S. Supreme Court ruled that such statements are permissible under the First Amendment in *Republican Party of Minnesota v. White,* 536 U.S. 765 (2002). Proponents of judicial elections say that such statements give voters badly needed information about the candidate. Critics of elections say such statements make it impossible for judges to rule fairly.

A final issue is voter knowledge. Voters typically know less about judicial candidates than they do about candidates in higher profile races. As a result, many voters do not vote in judicial elections or, if they do, they vote based on limited information. Again, proponents of elections argue that it is possible to get more information to the voters, and that lack of information should not justify removing the right to vote. Opponents of elections maintain that voter ignorance leads, among other things, to poor-quality judges.

The YES article by professor Michael Dimino and the NO article by professor Charles Geyh address these issues from very different perspectives.

163

YES

Michael R. Dimino, Sr.

The Worst Way of Selecting Judges—Except All the Others That Have Been Tried

Introduction

We all know the defects of judicial elections. The public is too ignorant of the legal system, the candidates, and the law to make wise choices; consequently, judges are elected often because of their famous names, ethnicities, position on the ballot, party affiliation, and the like, rather than through an assessment of merit. Judicial candidates prostrate themselves before the majority, dependent on their votes; consequently, the ability of the judiciary to protect the rights of unpopular individuals and to maintain fidelity to precedent suffers. Candidates campaign by appealing to constituencies; consequently, judges once on the bench do not approach legal issues with entirely open minds. And judges approaching reelection look over their shoulders, cognizant of the political risk they run by performing their jobs honorably. . . .

Nevertheless, I write here in the defense of elections, or at least to urge caution in the face of the seeming torrent of criticism. Just as "you can't beat something with nothing," it is not enough to point to the flaws inhering in elections; those who would do away with them need to show that a different approach is superior.

This Essay critiques the arguments leveled at judicial elections. . . . I argue that the flaws of judicial elections, though often considerable, are shared in large part by alternative selection systems. Beyond, however, being simply equivalent in malignity to other selection methods, elections have—or, rather, may have, depending on the content of judicial-election campaigns—one advantage over other systems that instigated the nineteenth century move to judicial elections and ensures their popularity with the everyday citizenry: the opportunity they provide for a free people to choose those officials who exercise policy-making authority. Democracy may indeed be the worst method of choosing judges . . . except for all the other ones.

From *Northern Kentucky Law Review*, vol. 32, 2005, pp. 267–304. Copyright © 2005 by Michael R. Dimino. Reprinted by permission.

Threats to Judicial Independence

Independent from Whom?

Two motivations inspired the move to judicial elections. First, judges were seen by liberals of the mid-nineteenth century as too conservative, and it was thought that public involvement in the selection of judges would make the bench more liberal. The goal was accountability. Judges were making unpopular decisions, and the public wanted a voice in judicial selection to bring the judiciary back into line. Second, certain reformers thought judicial elections would raise the quality of the bench by making it independent of other parts of the government. According to this theory, judges who were dependent on the legislature or the governor for their positions could not, it was thought, fulfill their duties properly, for they would be constantly worried about the ways other governmental officials would perceive their performance.

Elections were adopted, therefore, to change the philosophies of the courts and to make the judges *more* independent than they were under appointive systems—independent, that is, of other government officials. In essence, the states adopting judicial elections made a conscious choice to trade dependence on a governmental appointing authority for dependence on the people.

Independence in Non-Elective Systems

This history should give us pause before condemning judicial elections as negating the independence of the judiciary, and force us to ask ourselves what we mean by the phrase. In a system most protective of judicial independence, judges would be subservient only to the law. . . . But this is unrealistic in at least two ways. First, there will always be some controls the people and their representatives can place on all aspects of government. Second, faithfulness to a concept as indeterminate as "law" is not terribly constraining. With legal interpretations subject to endless debate among the most honorable jurists, and with the constant threat or presence of some judges who refuse to treat law as constraining in the least, it is evident that a judge who need be responsive to only the law need be responsive to no one. . . .

Critics of judicial elections note with distress the potential for elected judges to decide cases so as to pander to the electorate. As Justice O'Connor opined, "[e]lected judges cannot help being aware that if the public is not satisfied with the outcome of a particular case, it could hurt their reelection prospects." The most colorful (and, as a result, the most famous) statement of this phenomenon was California Supreme Court Justice Otto Kaus's quip that trying to ignore the political impact of decisions was like trying to ignore a crocodile in one's bathtub.

It would appear indisputable, though distasteful to many observers, that elected judges do take public opinion into account. Nevertheless, there is no reason to criticize judicial elections for that fact while ignoring the effect of public opinion on *appointed* judges. . . .

Indeed, appointed judges' departures from the law may be *worse* than elected judges', not in the sense that such departures are more frequent, but because appointed judges may try to curry favor with a different audience. Whereas the incentive on elected judges is to rule consistently with the preferences of the median voter, appointed judges who bend the law in response to political pressure may disproportionately favor the desires of elites, whose opinions may be antagonistic to those of a majority of Americans. . . .

Finding and Making the Law

The single-minded pursuit of judicial independence places excessive faith in the capacity of judges to follow the law. All judicial-selection reformers seek a system where the law prevails. But condemning judicial elections because they invite popular control over the meaning of law requires assuming that judges, left to their own devices, would follow the law better than would judges who are more tightly controlled. No explanation for that assumption has been offered or, perhaps, is possible. So long as there are legal controversies, the proper interpretation of law will be uncertain. Whether one side or another has the "correct" interpretation is unknowable, for we have yet to agree on the proper methodology for determining what constitutes a "correct" legal answer. Thus, because of the uncertainty of the law, insulating judges from influences elevates one vision of the law over another, but may not elevate law over the caprice of judges. . . .

Beyond the practical problems of defining the institutions from whom judges should be independent and in ascertaining the law that the judicial-selection method should protect, judicial-selection reformers face a conceptual problem in doing away with accountability. The problem is the ancient one of guarding the guardians—*Quis custodiet ipsos custodies?* As one commentator stated the quandary, "[t]he trade-off for judicial independence is the risk that judges will pursue personal agendas that are in conflict with their judicial responsibilities."

. . . Are we really comfortable giving judges the power to interpret the law, knowing that some decisions will be wrong, without adequate means to force judges to follow the law correctly? Does anyone doubt that without checks on judicial power, judges will feel freer to alter the law to their own ends?

Of course no one doubts that side effect, and nobody doubts that judicial decisions are correlated with judicial selection methods. Judges decide cases, particularly criminal cases, differently depending on the methods of accountability they face. And reformers fear that the influence of the people will move judicial decisions away from the law and toward mob rule. But for the cure to be better than the diseases caused by judicial elections, states must decide that it is better for judges to pursue their own ends than to have judges pursuing the people's desires. Only reformers' idealism and naïveté make the choice appear to be between systems where judges follow the mob and one where judges follow the law.

The People's Law

. . . We accept that public input into the legislative process is proper, and we view law as a manifestation of the public will. On the other hand, ideals of due process require that individual cases be judged by one or more "neutral" decision-makers. If the Rule of Law requires that like cases be treated alike, then public input would seem to be of little value (and considerable harm) in individual cases.

The problem is that judges are both policy-makers and adjudicators; indeed, judges make policy *through* adjudication. Rules governing judicial accountability, therefore, suffer in a dilemma: either the public is locked-out of a policy-making process that often can be as important as legislative policy-making, or individual litigants need fear that their unpopular, but legally correct, positions will not receive a fair hearing. States, it seems to me, have good arguments on both horns of that dilemma. But it does the judicial-selection debate no good to point out elections' threats to independence without also pointing out their reinforcement of democracy.

Critics of judicial elections and popular accountability of judges minimize the extent to which judges effectuate policy. Justice Ginsburg, for example, claims that "[e]ven when they develop common law or give concrete meaning to constitutional text, judges act only in the context of individual cases, the outcome of which cannot depend on the will of the public." History, social science, and common, modern-day experience, however, demonstrate beyond peradventure that courts have used those "individual cases" to formulate policy affecting far more people than the parties to any one case. Anyone who has been the least bit attuned to the development of public policy over the last fifty years is well aware that massive changes in our nation's approach to problems involving race, criminal justice, family relations and sexual intimacy, tort liability, religion, education, and elections, just to name a few areas, have come about through the actions of courts. And some decisions have been explicit about the degree to which policy considerations shape the holdings. Irrespective of whether these changes have been beneficial, they demonstrate that the judiciary has both the capacity and the will to be more than a passive interpreter of law. . . .

Policy-making courts are a poor fit with a nation accustomed to self-governance. And yet it seems unlikely either that courts will stop making policy or that the people will stop caring. Our long history of legislating from the bench—in both a conservative and a liberal direction—should be enough to demonstrate that courts do more than "lay the article of the Constitution which is invoked beside the statute which is challenged and to decide whether the latter squares with the former." Instead, the courts use their own ideas of good policy to interpret the law, thereby making the judges' policy views critical to citizens interested in shaping the laws governing society. Accordingly, it is hardly surprising that voters expect accountability from those who govern them—whether they wear business suits or judicial gowns.

Ideology and Interest Groups in Judicial Selection

Ideology

Thus far I have considered the supposed threat to judicial independence of judges while on the bench, either due to an impending election, the desire for a positive public reputation, or the like. Critics of elections have argued, however, that particularly in light of *Republican Party v. White,* which invalidated some restrictions on judicial campaign speech, campaigns for judicial office pressure candidates to promise to rule in certain ways, such that even before a judge takes office he has compromised his impartiality.

Judges often approach cases with an inclination about the proper resolution. That inclination may have been gleaned from years of practice, from scholarly examination of a related question, or simply a philosophical feeling (whether that philosophy is political, judicial, social, or something else) that the case should be resolved one way or another. Such an inclination might influence the eventual decision more or less, depending on the type of case and the strength of the inclination. Nevertheless, it is undeniable that such intuitions exist and that the attitudes of the judges forecast their decisions on the bench. . . .

Because I believe the public has a strong interest in staffing its courts with judges faithful to the public's view of the proper jurisprudential philosophy, I view judicial discussion of philosophy—a candidate's *"honestly held views,"* as *White* stressed—as less of a problem than do critics of judicial elections. Whether problematic or not, however, the pre-commitment phenomenon is as prevalent in appointment processes as in elections, and is becoming ever more so as Americans (and their Senators) recognize the policy-making power that appellate judges carry.

Both the President in nominating judges and the Senate in providing "Advice and Consent" have long been keenly aware that the philosophies of judges determine, in large part, the policies that result from the courts. It is no surprise, then, that Presidents have nominated judges whose philosophies match their own, and that Senators look both to their constituents' policy preferences and the Senators' own preferences in deciding how to vote on nominees.

. . . [N]ot only does the Senate consider ideology important as a general matter, but Senators may require commitments of nominees regarding certain issues before confirmation is granted. Thus, one's views of *Roe, Griswold, Brown,* the Pledge of Allegiance, and countless other topics (some more controversial than others) may mean the difference between confirmation and rejection. And nominees, though they may decline to answer such questions as a prudential or political choice, may not rely on ethical canons as tying their hands and forcing them to demur. Nominees, like candidates, enjoy the constitutional right to discuss matters of judicial philosophy.

. . . The "merit selection" process was supposed to rid states of both candidate electioneering and the politics that is necessarily a part in any appointment process, but of course it has done neither. "Merit selection" systems call for the initial selection of a judge who then runs unopposed in a retention election. The procedures for making the initial selection vary by state, but typically involve executive appointment (with all the problems of politics associated therewith), or the use of a nominating commission, which typically chooses a few nominees and leaves to the executive the choice of which nominee to fill the vacancy. Any pretense that the nomination process rids judicial selection of politics evaporates when it is recognized that the members of the commission itself are appointed as part of a political process and they vote along ideological lines, seeking to install judges who favor their policy preferences. If such use of ideology is acceptable, there seems little reason to limit involvement to the elites who are appointed to commissions.

Whatever the form of judicial selection, ideology matters. The question is *whose* ideology should matter. . . . Because it is impossible to determine who is "right" in the substantive dispute (or, more accurately, to convince anyone else that one's substantive position is correct), there is little reason to privilege elite ideology over the rest of the public's. Indeed, democracy would seem to argue for quite the opposite.

Interest Group Involvement

Many of the same points made with regard to the impact ideology has on judicial selection in both appointive and electoral systems also apply to the role played by interest-group support and opposition. Interest groups, many of which are formed precisely to advocate for a certain ideology, have become increasingly active in both state electoral and federal appointive systems of judicial selection. Chambers of Commerce push for pro-business judges. Associations of Trial Lawyers urge the selection of judges favorable to tort victims. District Attorneys' Associations and Associations of Criminal Defense Lawyers advocate for judges sympathetic to their causes. We should not be surprised. As the importance of judicially-crafted public policy has become clear, interest groups have exercised their influence to affect the selection of judges.

Critics of judicial elections decry the involvement of interest groups, saying that candidates should not be pressured to subscribe to interest groups' agendas, and arguing that wealthy interest groups "can overwhelm campaign debate with [their] messages." In the view of the critics, judges should keep open minds on legal questions, and that were judicial elections to become referenda on specific legal questions, the advantage of having a separate judicial branch would be undermined. This argument presents merely a nuanced version of the argument that ideology should be removed from elections altogether. . . .

Even if one . . . concludes that interest group involvement in the judicial-selection process should be avoided, adopting an appointive system is hardly likely to solve the problem. Interest groups have been active in the appointment process on the federal level for generations. . . .

Nevertheless, there are two types of interest groups that present particular concerns in the debate between judicial elections and appointments: political parties and the organized bar. Both interest groups can aid the selection process. Parties provide voters with cues of judges' philosophical outlooks and enable voters to make intelligent choices without extensive research, while the organized bar can help evaluate the professional competence of prospective judges. Though both groups can play a role in judicial selection, whether states use appointments or elections, parties hold a greater influence under elective systems (particularly systems using partisan elections) and the organized bar's influence is greatest when appointments are made by a non-partisan or bipartisan commission ostensibly trying to select meritorious potential judges. As anthropologist Susan Philips has demonstrated by looking at the changes in Pima County (Tucson), Arizona, when the state altered its system of selecting trial judges from elections to appointments, participation in bar activities replaced political-party participation as the principal way of maximizing one's chances to ascend to the bench.

. . . At best, appointment systems do not eliminate the influence of interest groups, but rather change the identities of the groups that do the influencing. The special interests, therefore, provide no reason to dispense with elections.

The Unqualified

Closely related to the complaint that elections excessively empower parties and their bosses is the complaint that voters will select whomever the bosses put before them and, therefore, elections will fill courts with unfit judges. Like the other criticisms leveled at judicial elections, this one has a basis in truth. The public is likely to vote based on visceral reactions to decisions and unlikely to understand the role that a judge plays in upholding the law. Therefore a judge often becomes "politically vulnerable for being legally right" and the judges who succeed in the political game are often not the ones scholars and other elites most respect. Furthermore, ballot position, famous names, ethnicity and other factors are as likely as merit, intelligence, and other "objective" "qualifications" to influence a judge's election, causing elites to lose further respect for the electoral process.

This critique is unfair in two respects. First, the appointments process often selects the unqualified. Second, voters have little choice but to focus on party affiliation (where available) and candidates' demographic characteristics as indications of future judicial rulings where the candidates refuse to answer questions about judicial philosophy or are prohibited from doing so by rules of judicial conduct. In other words, elections might be more likely to reflect a public deliberation on judicial policy if judicial policy were allowed to play center stage in campaigns.

Appointments Not Based on Merit

Appointing authorities, be they Presidents, legislatures, or Governors, do not focus exclusively on merit in selecting individuals for judgeships. Presidents nominating Justices for the Supreme Court of the United States, the most prestigious judicial body in the nation, if not the world, have the ability to choose among the country's entire legal community and could, if they wanted, select the most intelligent, most articulate, and most experienced of America's legal scholars, judges, and practitioners. The fact that this does not happen—that Learned Hand spent fifty-two years on the district court and the court of appeals without a Supreme Court nomination, for example—indicates that factors other than merit influence the selection of Supreme Court Justices. And if the Supreme Court does not contain the most talented members of the legal profession, state courts and lower federal courts would seem even more likely to be filled with individuals whose distinguishing features may not include legal proficiency.

Demographics

These other distinguishing characteristics turn out to be virtually the same ones that voters care about when judicial candidates stand for election. Judicial candidates must be politically connected to get a place on the ballot, but so too must a would-be judge come to the attention of an appointing authority through his work on behalf of the appointer's political party. Judicial candidates benefit from being able to "represent" a particular geographic region, in that favorite-son candidates may receive a home-town bounce at the polls, but so too do appointing officials look to geography in making appointments.

Most controversially, critics of judicial elections allege that members of certain ethnic groups or genders face a disadvantage in elections, because voters will prefer members of their own ethnicity and look more favorably on men than women. Once again, the implied distinction from appointive systems fails. Surely it is unquestionable that ethnicity, religion, and gender play a considerable role in appointing judges. President Eisenhower selected Catholic Democrat, William Brennan to appeal to those groups. President Johnson selected Thurgood Marshall because he believed naming a black man to the Court was "the right thing to do." President Nixon tried to name a Southerner to the Court, succeeding finally with Justice Powell. President Reagan promised to name a woman to the Court (something Nixon had tried but failed to do) and did so with his nomination of Justice O'Connor. President Reagan was attracted to Justice Scalia in part because naming him would place the first Justice of Italian ancestry on the Court. President George H.W. Bush filled Justice Marshall's "black seat" with Justice Thomas. And President George W. Bush is widely rumored to be interested in naming the first Hispanic Justice to the Court. Though certain of these Justices were indisputably qualified for the Court, in each example merit was merely one concern among many, occasionally subordinate to the politics of demography.

Against this background, it is curious indeed to object to *elections* on the ground that ethnicity and other demographic characteristics might make the difference to voters. Of course, one may object to the particular ethnic preferences of voters. That is, one may approve of giving a member of a minority group or a female a preference in the selection process, while disapproving of a preference for a white male. But that criticism accuses voters not of focusing on the wrong criteria, but of coming to the wrong conclusion. Both reasons for opposing elections are strongly elitist. . . .

It's Whom You Know, Not What You Know

Elections have a distinct advantage over other selection systems in that voters are relatively free from the pressures of cronyism that affect judicial selection in appointive systems. Even where party nominees are selected through backroom politicking, and even where the nominees are the ones who know the right party officials, at least the voters are able to choose the more qualified of two different cronies.

When the appointment is made by an executive, however, the possibility of judgeships being rewards for long-time political support or personal friendship is manifest. Senatorial and presidential patronage have long been responsible for hundreds of appointments to lower federal courts, and President Truman made personal friendship the single most important criterion for appointment to the Supreme Court. . . . As one commentator stated, even in states that select their judges by appointment "[p]olitics and cronyism remain the order of the day when it comes to selecting judges."

Voters have neither the expertise nor the inclination to choose the most qualified jurists for their states' courts. Instead, they rely on proxies including party affiliation and loyalty, ethnicity, and gender to indicate the candidates' likely approaches to judging. Such reliance may be distasteful, but eliminating elections does not solve the problem, for appointing authorities use the same criteria.

Who Is to Blame for Public Ignorance?

Few quarrel with the idea that voters know too little about the law and the legal system to make informed choices in judicial elections. Voter ignorance, however, has not stopped us from extending universal suffrage in legislative and executive races, where the public votes with the same visceral, half-informed opinions as determine their votes in judicial races. . . . Given the judicial capacity for, and history of, policy-making, it is unclear why democracy's risks to the judiciary are much worse than their risks to other branches of government. . . .

To the extent that voters lack the information required to make wise choices, that ignorance stems from the muzzle placed on judicial candidates by the same elites who play heightened roles in non-elective selection processes. Until the Supreme Court's 2002 decision in *Republican Party v. White*, states could forbid judicial candidates from making the least enlightening speech on judicial philosophy. As a result, there was virtually no information available for voters to discern differences between candidates, and yet that lack of information was used as a reason for denying the public the capacity to vote on judges. Since the *White* decision, some judicial candidates have been more upfront about their views and informing the public about the judicial system, but some states have resisted *White* and continue to restrict the ability of candidates to talk about the law in any substantive way. So long as information is restricted, elections will not be fully effective, but that is hardly the fault of the voters.

The Problem of Money

Unless campaigns are publicly funded, judges running for election must raise money from private sources, which often include interests that would practice before the judge, were he elected. In this way, elections raise a threat of bias, in that potential donors feel obligated to contribute to a judge's campaign lest he remember their lack of generosity the next time the contributor appears before the judge. Even for those who do not believe that judges in fact consider relative contributions when deciding cases, critics claim that a system of private financing creates the *appearance* that justice is for sale, and argue that elections should be scrapped to eliminate this appearance.

Unquestionably, campaign contributions create a serious risk of undermining public confidence in the impartiality of judicial decisions. Eliminating elections will reduce the dependence of would-be judges on direct donor-to-candidate contributions, but even under an appointive system, money matters. . . .

I do not mean to overstate the point. I do not fear that appointed judges are deciding cases so as to appease friendly interest groups. But neither am I very concerned that elected judges will decide cases to repay generous donors. The worry, to the extent there is one, stems from the requirement of *re*election. Judges about to face reelection may decide cases in certain ways to avoid upsetting potential donors. But if an appointed judge were required to be reconfirmed, there is the same danger that the judge will decide cases so as not to upset interest groups or their contributors. Thus, contributions can induce corruption in both appointive and elective systems, and may cause more of a problem in elective systems only because those systems require judges to undergo the selection process multiple times.

Conclusion

One need not be enamored with judicial elections to conclude that they are no worse than the other available selection systems. I have argued two points which should at least cause readers to think twice before advocating the abandonment of an institution that has kept one branch of government accountable to the people of many states since the Jacksonian era. First, many of the same problems that critics see with judicial elections are present in appointive systems as well. Second, the democratic accountability that was a major impetus for instituting elections continues to present a powerful argument for their continuance.

I do not argue that each of the problems discussed in the body of this Essay are worse, or even as bad, in appointive systems as in electoral ones. Scholars and policy-makers may well conclude that the threats caused by privately financing judicial election campaigns are worse than are the threats caused by the interest group involvement and financing of "campaigns" for and against the confirmation of judicial nominees. Similarly, though one must concede that appointive systems occasionally select cronies and hacks, perhaps states will conclude that the risk of selecting unqualified judges is greater with elections than appointments (though empirical evidence as yet belies such a position).

It is imperative that we examine both the plusses and the minuses of alternative systems before condemning our current ones, and when we do we find that many of the same problems that animate reformers will persist under appointive systems. Additionally, appointments have the considerable disadvantage of creating an "independent" but unaccountable judiciary, whose policy judgments are insulated from popular change. . . .

No system of judicial selection can guard against every danger. Any system of selecting fallible humans, by fallible humans, is bound to face some challenges. In the end, a healthy rule of law depends on both a judiciary and a public dedicated to preserving it. No system of judicial selection can guarantee both. If the public maintains the "spirit of moderation" about which Judge Hand wrote, then judicial elections present no problems. To continue paraphrasing, if the people lack that spirit, an appointive system will not be the salvation. And if the people abdicate their responsibility, blindly delegating legal authority to judges, the rule of law "will perish."

We live in an imperfect world where government is "to be administered by men over men," where human nature foreordains self-interested politics, and where we must choose to risk the tyranny of the majority or the tyranny of the judges. Each of us must decide which risk he fears less.

Charles Gardner Geyh  **NO**

Why Judicial Elections Stink

Judicial Selections as the Critical Landmark in the Independence-Accountability Landscape

. . . One of the primary lessons learned from the groundwork laid by the general judicial independence projects of the mid-nineties is that when one seeks to map serious threats to [judicial] independence, most roads go through judicial selection. It is important to understand why.

Proposals to Hold Judges Accountable for Their Decisions by Means Outside of the Electoral Process Have Been Rejected

Among the states, fundamental respect for an independent judiciary is sufficiently entrenched that states embroiled in cyclical wars waged in the name of judicial accountability are typically deterred from resorting to weaponry more lethal than the ballot box. As Professor Peter Shane has observed, all states have adopted a tripartite system of separated powers in which the judiciary is assigned the task of keeping the political branches within their constitutionally assigned roles through the exercise of judicial review. This shared vision of the judicial role implies a baseline of judicial independence that the courts must possess in order to serve their purpose. . . .

Judicial Elections Have, Perhaps by Default, Become the Primary Vehicle for Retaliation Against Judges on Account of Their Decisions

With most avenues for promoting judicial accountability blocked, court critics have focused their attention on judicial elections as the means of choice to rid the system of unwelcome judges and substitute jurists whose views are more consonant with their own. . . .

. . . It is true that the vast majority of incumbent judges continue to win reelection, but one should not assume that because few judges lose their reelection or retention elections, few judges feel threatened by the specter of a challenge to their incumbency based upon the decisions they render in

From *Ohio State Law Journal*, vol. 64, 2003, pp. 43–79. Copyright © 2003 by Charles Gardner Geyh. Reprinted by permission.

particular cases. Were incumbents to feel no threat, they would presumably perceive no need to campaign aggressively (and spend lavishly) in defense of their seats, which is clearly not the case.

To the contrary, in many jurisdictions the cost of winning reelection is increasing exponentially. If we define a judge's decision-making independence in terms of her capacity to remain impartial and decide cases according to facts as she finds them and law as she construes it to be written, then threats to that independence can occur not only when a judge loses her job for exercising independent judgment, but also when a judge perceives that she may lose her job for doing so. If so, the spiraling costs that incumbents feel they must incur to stave off reelection or retention election challenges may be a better proxy for gauging the escalating threat to decisional independence than the rate of electoral defeat. By the same token, the unprecedented sums that individuals and organizations are contributing to judicial campaigns underscores the primacy, at least in their minds, of judicial elections as a device for promoting judicial accountability.

Increased Activity in the Judicial Election Arena Has Created Important Satellite Issues Affecting Independence and Accountability

To fully appreciate why judicial elections deserve the limelight in the variety show of threats to judicial independence, it is important to understand that the judicial independence "problem" caused by electing judges does not end with the concern that a judge's impartiality in politically sensitive cases may be compromised by the fear of losing her reelection or retention bid. It extends to the perception, if not the reality, that judges are beholden to the burgeoning volume of contributors who make their reelection possible. That perception, in turn, coupled with the premise underlying campaigns to defeat judges who make rulings with which voters disagree—namely, that judges are supposed to make decisions agreeable to their "constituents"— contributes to the view that the judiciary is as "political" a branch of government as the other two, and should be no more independent of the people it serves than the legislature or the governor. And therein lies the potential for the erosion of the public's longstanding respect for an independent judiciary.

The "Axiom of 80"

Efforts to address threats to independence that arise in the context of selecting judges must take into account four political realities, that together constitute what I am calling the "Axiom of 80": (1) Roughly 80% of the public prefers to select its judges by election and does so; (2) Roughly 80% of the electorate does not vote in judicial elections; (3) Roughly 80% of the electorate cannot identify the candidates for judicial office; and (4) Roughly 80% of the public believes that when judges are elected, their decisions are influenced by the campaign contributions they receive.

Eighty Percent of the Public Favors Selecting Judges by Election and Does So

Those who favor judicial elections rightly point out that when we speak of an "independent" judge, we are not using the term in its literal sense. No one suggests that judges should be so completely free from influence or control that they may pursue avocations as outlaws or libertines, whenever the spirit moves them. Rather, the unspoken adverb "appropriately" precedes "independent judge" in our collective understanding, and an appropriately independent judge is one whose autonomy is circumscribed by some measure of accountability to the public she serves. For fans of judicial elections, an appropriately independent judge is properly held accountable to the electorate from time to time, and to the extent that elections diminish a judge's absolute independence, it is a fair price to pay for ensuring accountability.

This view would seem to be widely shared. Elections are, after all, the way we select our leaders in a representative democracy (never mind, for the moment, that judges are not supposed to be our "representatives"). . . . Practitioners of applied academia who regard the toll elections take on judicial independence as too high a price to pay for the accountability they promote, must therefore toil in the shadow of entrenched public support for judicial elections. This support runs as high as 80% in some jurisdictions, and translates into 80% of the nation's judges standing for election.

Eighty Percent of the Electorate Does Not Vote

Despite the overwhelming popularity of judicial elections on a conceptual level, it is not uncommon to find that 80% or more of eligible voters fail to vote in judicial elections. On the one hand, when judicial and political branch candidates share the same ballot, there is a well-documented "roll off" of voters, who cast ballots in the political branch races but not the judicial. On the other hand, when judicial elections do not share the ballot with high-profile political branch contests, voters simply stay home. Although there has been some conjecture that increased spending on judicial campaigns may translate into increased voter interest, such a conclusion is far from clear. In 1997, for example, record spending in a Wisconsin Supreme Court race yielded a meager 21% voter turnout, prompting the executive director of the state elections board to opine that "People come out because they have a reason to come out. And these races don't get people out as much as other things do."

Eighty Percent of the Electorate is Unfamiliar with the Judicial Candidates

In Michigan, a spokesperson for the governor attributed low voter turnout to the fact that "People just don't know who they're voting for." This is a third political reality that may help to explain the second: as much as 80% of the electorate is completely unfamiliar with its candidates for judicial office. Once again, one might hypothesize that as more money is spent on advertising in judicial races, voter ignorance will diminish, but that too is far from clear. . . .

Eighty Percent of the Public Believes that Financial Contributions to Judicial Election Campaigns Buy Influence

Even if increased spending in judicial campaigns has done little to relieve voter apathy and ignorance, this is not to suggest that the public perceives such spending to have had no impact. To the contrary, the public believes that when judges are elected, their decisions are influenced by the money they receive from contributors. In Texas, a 1998 survey sponsored by the state supreme court found that 83% of Texas adults thought that money had an impact on judicial decisions. In Ohio, a 1995 survey reported that nine out of ten residents believed that campaign contributions influenced judicial decisions. And in Pennsylvania, a 1998 poll sponsored by a special commission appointed by the Pennsylvania Supreme Court, found that nine out of ten voters believed that judicial decisions were influenced by large campaign contributions. In short, we have a fourth political reality to complete the Axiom of 80: Eighty percent (closer to ninety, but where's the symmetry in that?) of the public thinks that campaign contributions buy influence with judges.

And so we are confronted with the conundrum of a public that does not vote, would not know the candidates if it did, but which will not relinquish the franchise it declines to exercise, even as it believes that judges are corrupted by the contributors they must solicit if they are to win the elections that the public will not abandon. The Axiom of 80 thus isolates a set of conflicting political realities in judicial elections that fosters neither independence nor accountability. If it is inevitable that judges stand for election, it is equally inevitable that they will be subject to loss of tenure for the rulings they make, and it opens the door to the likelihood that they will appear beholden to financial contributors who make their reelection possible. Widespread voter ignorance and apathy, on the other hand, undercut the likelihood that judges will be held accountable to the public in any meaningful way.

Incremental Reform in the Shadow of the Axiom of 80

The perceived inevitability of judicial elections has had a profound effect on recent developments in judicial selection reform. For the better part of the twentieth century, judicial reformers peddled merit selection systems as the sure-cure for what ailed elected judiciaries. The phrase "merit selection" implies a system in which judges are selected on the basis of qualifications, rather than popularity or partisanship. As to popularity, virtually all merit selection systems feature retention elections, which opens the door to the possibility that the electorate will hinge a judge's continuation in office on her popularity, rather than merit. The presence of retention elections in merit selection systems can only be explained as a concession to the entrenched political necessity of preserving judicial elections in some form, so that merit selection proponents have an answer for detractors who oppose plans that "take away our right to vote."

Even then, it is somewhat disingenuous to say that merit selection systems preserve the right to vote. Retention elections are designed to minimize the risk of non-retention, by stripping elections of features that might inspire voters to become interested enough to oust incumbents. Thus, there is no choice to make between competing candidates or viewpoints, no race to follow, no opportunity to pick a new winner, and no political party to support. I realize that one can (and should) recast the justifications for retention elections in less cynical terms, as an effort to focus voter attention on professional competence, judicial demeanor, etc., which are legitimately related to evaluating the judge's merit. The essential point, however, is that retention elections diminish the scope of voter control over judicial selection—a point not lost on fans of contested judicial elections who have successfully stalled the merit-selection movement across the United States.

. . . Reformers conceded to the political necessity of judicial elections long ago, and now many appear poised to raise the white flag on merit selection systems that split the difference between purely appointive models and contested elections. If the first political reality of the Axiom of 80—the public's entrenched preference for judicial elections—could be conquered and judicial elections ended in favor of true appointive systems, the remaining three political realities, which arise only when judges are elected, would likewise be overcome. Not even the moribund merit selection movement, however, can lay claim to a system that succeeds on that score. On the contrary, retention elections, by virtue of the sterile questions they ask the electorate to decide, breed voter apathy and ignorance, and inspire highly motivated interest groups to launch anti-retention campaigns on the theory that they need only energize a small block of voters to influence election outcomes. That, in turn, requires incumbents to stave off opposition with monies solicited from contributors to whom they then appear beholden.

Having reached the end of the road with merit selection and having accepted elections as a permanent part of the judicial selection landscape, reformers are now embarking on new programs of incremental change. Such programs concede the inevitability of the first political reality, and confine themselves to modest proposals that seek to reduce the independence-threatening effects of judicial elections and address the remaining three Axiom of 80 political realities. . . .

Why Judicial Elections Are Unsalvageable and Incremental Reforms Will Fail

For years, court defenders have called attention to differences between the judiciary and the political branches of government. Judges are supposed to be impartial; governors and legislators are not. Governors and legislators are supposed to represent the views of their constituents; judges are not. Judges are subject to ethical restrictions that limit their ability to clarify their positions or comment on their decisions; governors and legislators are not. . . . Seemingly lost in the incremental reform shuffle, is the obvious point that the fundamental differences between the judiciary and the other branches undermine the legitimacy of judicial elections altogether. . . .

It is one thing to expect voters with no training in the law to decide whether the policies favored by senators and governors (who may not be lawyers either) coincide with their own positions, and quite another to expect them to decide whether the rulings of judges coincide with the law. If we suspend disbelief and assume that voters can actually acquire the expertise needed to assess a judge's familiarity with and fidelity to innumerable laws as reflected in the myriad cases she has decided, then the learning curve will be considerably steeper than that required to divine a political branch candidate's position on the major issues of the day, and decide whether the candidate will be receptive to the concerns of constituents.

Historically, however, it has been impossible for voters to gather the information they need to make intelligent decisions from the candidates themselves. First, judges are not supposed to care what voters think. The Model Code of Judicial Conduct declares that a judge "shall not be swayed by partisan interests, public clamor, or fear of criticism."

Second, Canon 3B(9) forbids judges from making extra-judicial comments on pending or impending cases. Although the prohibition is limited to comments that "might reasonably be expected to affect [a proceeding's] outcome or . . . fairness," the remainder of the section and the accompanying comment strongly suggest that most, if not all, case-specific comments will violate the rule. Although Canon 5A(3)(e) provides that judicial candidates "may respond to personal attacks or attacks on the candidate's record," this provision has not been widely adopted, and the Code makes no attempt to reconcile its terms with Canon 3B(9)'s prohibition of public comments on pending cases.

Third, although not technically forbidding judges to comment on completed cases, Canon 2 provides that judges generally must "act at all times in a manner that promotes public confidence in the integrity and impartiality of the judiciary," and conduct all their extra-judicial activities so that they do not "cast reasonable doubt on the judge's capacity to act impartially as a judge.". . .

Fourth, and finally, voters who look to the candidates to tell them what they plan to do after they are elected have, at least historically, been sorely disappointed. Although the Supreme Court's recent decision in *Republican Party v. White* creates uncertainty as to its continuing vitality, Canon 5 of the Code provides that candidates for judicial office shall not "make pledges or promises of conduct in office other than the faithful and impartial performance of the duties of the office."

In short, if voters are expected to second-guess the decisions of a judge who brings years of specialized training to bear in deciding complex, subtly nuanced issues of law, they need more information than would be required to assess the performance of political branch officials for whom no professional training is required. And yet, voters have had access to far less information from judicial candidates than their political branch counterparts.

Conventional Responses to the Information Shortfall in Judicial Elections

The revelation that the Code of Judicial Conduct has created an information shortfall for voters in judicial elections is hardly new, and has elicited at least two alternative responses, both of which are deficient. The first alternative is to counsel voters against casting their ballots on the basis of whether they agree with a judge's decisions, to urge them instead to look at the judge's entire record for the purpose of assessing the jurist's character, competence and temperament, and to supply voters with information that enables them to make such assessments. The second is to shrug, concede the inadequacy of the information upon which voters cast their ballots, but conclude that it is the only way to ensure judicial accountability.

The primary problem with the first alternative is its futility. Codes of judicial conduct authorize judges to tell the electorate about the incumbents' integrity and demeanor, but permit them to say very little about the cases they decide. Deciding cases, however, is what judges do, and those decisions are important because they can affect people's lives in profound ways. If we make voters go to the trouble of deciding whether a judge should remain in office, it is fatuous to suppose that they can be persuaded to bracket out their views on the merits of the judge's most important decisions and cast their ballots on the basis of an arid assessment of the incumbent's general fitness. Groups interested in judicial election outcomes, sensing pent up voter demand for case-specific information that codes of judicial conduct have foreclosed the candidates from providing themselves, have found it worth their time and energy to spend millions of dollars on campaign advertising attacking or defending the decisions of incumbent judges. The question of whether the electorate is willing to vote without regard to the merits of an incumbent's decisions would thus appear to be one that the marketplace of ideas has already answered in the negative.

The second alternative, on the other hand, overestimates the potential for elections to foster accountability. Up to this point, I have entertained the fiction that voters are capable of assessing the performance of judges on their own. . . . [H]ow can people who have no specialized expertise or training assess the professional competence of one who has such training and expertise, unless someone with the requisite knowledge offers them guidance? In judicial elections, the code of judicial conduct forecloses the candidates from supplying that guidance themselves, and so the task falls to others.

. . . At first blush, lawyers might seem to be the most qualified source of information on the professional competence of judicial candidates, but groups that find themselves at odds with the views of bar organizations on such matters have challenged the assumption that the bar is a disinterested purveyor of information. For their part, bar organizations have challenged their challengers by calling attention to allegedly misleading information that other groups have included in their advertising. Voters are caught in the middle. Incapable of evaluating judicial candidates unassisted, unable to receive such assistance from the candidates themselves, and ill-equipped to evaluate the trustworthiness of information they receive from sources that accuse each other of being unreliable, they are left to vote badly, or not at all. The opportunity for self-interested organizations and single-issue voter groups to influence election outcomes disproportionately is thus correspondingly greater. . . .

Repeated references here to voter ignorance, apathy and incapacity may create the impression that mine is an essentially condescending and elitist perspective. Not so. Rather, my views are rooted in the recognition that the complexities of modern life make specialists of us all, if only because the volume of information available on the universe of subjects relevant to our lives has become so vast that mere mortals can gain mastery over no more than their small corner of it. To delegate judicial selection and oversight of the common law to elected officials who make it their business to be adequately informed on such subjects is thus a pragmatic approach, not an aristocratic one.

A New Response to the Information Shortfall in Judicial Elections: Authorizing Candidates to Provide the Electorate with the Information It Seeks

In *Republican Party v. White*, . . . the Supreme Court of the United States invalidated one of the restrictions on judicial campaign speech responsible for the information shortfall in judicial elections, and in so doing, may have created a new dynamic in court races. The good news is that the information shortfall may soon be overcome. The bad news is that efforts to preserve judicial impartiality may be seriously compromised. To the extent the decision liberates judicial candidates to emulate their counterparts in political branch races by committing themselves to positions on issues they are likely to decide as judges, it will accelerate the downward spiral of politicization that can be arrested only if judicial elections are eliminated. . . .

As the dust settles on the decision in *White*, the Court's bottom line becomes clear: if you don't like what judicial campaign speech does to the impartiality of elected judges, your solution is not to curtail campaign speech. It is to end judicial elections. The point is one that Justice O'Connor underscored forcefully in her concurrence: "Minnesota has chosen to select its judges through contested popular elections instead of through an appointment system," she observed. "In doing so the State has voluntarily taken on the risks to judicial bias," which make its "claim that it needs to significantly restrict judges' speech in order to protect judicial impartiality . . . particularly troubling." "If the State has a problem with judicial impartiality," she concluded, "it is largely one the state brought upon itself by continuing the practice of popularly electing judges."

In the aftermath of *White*, judicial candidates will be under increasing pressure from interest groups and voters to announce their positions on issues likely to come before the court, and candidates who do not comply can anticipate accusations that they are hiding behind debunked ethical rules. The blurring that already exists between judicial and political branch candidates is bound to accelerate. What has distinguished judges from other elected officials is their capacity to uphold the rule of law by deciding cases impartially on the basis of facts as they find them and law as they construe it to be written, without regard to the popularity of the decisions they make. If, however, judicial campaigns are transformed into referenda on past rulings that judges defend from the stump, feature position taking on pending or impending cases that candidates clarify in campaign speeches, and effectively require candidates to commit themselves to deciding future cases in particular ways, that capacity for impartiality will have been seriously compromised. . . .

Toward the Gradual Elimination of Elected Judiciaries

If, for the reasons elaborated upon above, we accept that judicial elections are undesirable in principle, then our focus should be on devising a long-term strategy for phasing them out. The pivotal task for this strategy will be to overcome the public's entrenched acceptance of judicial elections as an essential component of judicial selection. To that end, I propose a six-point strategy.

Patience

. . . Because the gradual elimination of judicial elections is a long-term strategy, it would be ill-advised to abandon short-term plans for incremental reform in the interim. First, it would seem unnecessarily ascetic to deprive ourselves of opportunities for short-term alleviation from the pain of the judicial election bunion, simply because we anticipate complete relief following surgery several years hence. Second . . . if incremental reform of judicial elections is repeatedly tried, but fails to achieve lasting results, it will gradually assist in softening public resistance to the elimination of judicial elections altogether.

Identifying a Theme

. . . To be recognized as a movement, the drive to end judicial elections must be linked to a theme that resonates with the public and gives the campaign persuasive force. For that reason, the theme should *not* trumpet the need for judicial independence or sound judicial administration. Although judicial elections do indeed undermine judicial independence and effective judicial administration, our purpose is not to make the world a safer place for judges. Rather, our purpose is to make the world a safer place for the people whom judges serve. . . .

Capitalizing on Bellwether Events

. . . Groups committed to judicial selection reform have had a veritable buffet of bellwether events to feed upon that illustrate quite poignantly the threat judicial elections pose to impartial justice. The problem, however, is that such groups invariably cite a horrid experience with one form of judicial election as grounds for adopting some other form of judicial election which has had a horrid experience of its own; as a result, these events serve more as millstones than bellwethers. Thus, for example, horror stories emerging from partisan judicial elections in Texas have led to calls for non-partisan judicial elections, which can be countered with horror stories from non-partisan elections in Wisconsin, Ohio and Michigan, which in turn have served as fodder for merit selection proponents to load their cannons, only to have them backfire in the face of retention election disasters in Tennessee and Nebraska. . . .

Professionalizing the Judiciary

If we are to convince the public that judges ought to be selected differently than public officials in the political branches, it is essential to explain why by highlighting the differences between them. One difference to which I alluded earlier is the almost universal requirement that judges be lawyers, which highlights the specialized expertise that states expect judges—as distinguished from legislators and governors—to possess. That distinction could be drawn more vividly for the public's benefit if the credentials of all judicial candidates were publicly reviewed by qualification commissions akin to those endorsed by the American Bar Association. . . .

Enhancing Alternative Means to Promote General Judicial Accountability

One means of promoting accountability worth exploring concerns adverse publicity. In his testimony before the original ABA Commission on Separation of Powers and Judicial Independence, Senior Judge and Former Dean Louis Pollack made the obvious but important point that judges are no more desirous of having their foibles publicized than anyone else. Characterizing "intimidation" as "too strong" a term to describe the impact of criticism on judges, Judge Pollack nevertheless acknowledged that from a judge's perspective, "it would be nice to make a decision that doesn't necessarily get closer than about page 23 to anybody's attention who is reading the next day's newspapers." . . .

Judicial discipline is another means to hold judges accountable for a variety of inappropriate behaviors ranging from chronic delays in decisionmaking, to abusiveness toward lawyers, litigants, and staff, to inebriation on the bench, to gender and racial bias. Mechanisms for judicial discipline are already in place among the states, but the availability and use of such mechanisms have not been adequately publicized. The net effect is that meritorious disciplinary complaints may never be filed, and disciplinary actions taken may never come to the public's attention. It bears reemphasis that adverse publicity of the misconduct and resulting disciplinary action can be just as chastening as the disciplinary action itself. As one federal judge observed in the context of an interview concerning judicial discipline and misconduct, "the threat of newspaper coverage is a big deterrent. Every judge worries about something coming out in the newspaper."

Restructuring the Judicial Selection Process to Provide Prospective Accountability for a Judge's Political and Judicial Philosophy

. . . To provide a means for assessing political acceptability in the absence of elections, I would propose a modified federal model of judicial selection for the states. Like the federal model, state judges could be nominated by the governor and confirmed by the state senate or some other subset of the state legislature. Judges so selected would then serve during good behavior. Two modifications of the federal model are in order.

First, as discussed above, technical merit is a necessary (but not sufficient) credential for judicial office. A professional judiciary must possess the competence, experience, character, and temperament needed to do the job well. Accordingly, nominees for whom legislative confirmation is sought should be limited to those approved by independent judicial qualification commissions akin to those proposed by the American Bar Association.

Second, the federal model of judicial selection is currently enveloped in a fog of uncertainty as to just how "political" the appointments process should be—a fog that should be lifted before the model is exported to the states. The federal appointments process has always been "political" in at least three senses of the term: it is, by design, a process conducted by the "political" branches of government; it has, from its inception, been vulnerable to partisan "political" manipulation; and it is subject to majoritarian "political" influence from constituents of political branch officeholders. More recently, federal judicial selection has become political in yet another way, as the judicial and political philosophy of would-be judges has become a more prominent issue for president and Senate alike. . . .

Dyed in the wool advocates of judicial elections often contend that appointive systems akin to the one I propose are no better and probably worse than elections. An appointive process, the argument goes, simply moves the point at which partisan politics matters, from the moment of election to the moment of appointment; and unlike appointive systems, which often profess to be apolitical when they are not, elections are at least honest about being openly political.

On the latter point, I not only concede that the appointments process can be at least as political as elections, but argue that its inherently political character is a virtue that serves to promote prospective judicial accountability. More fundamentally, however, the assertion that an appointment process does no more than change the moment at which politics matters misses the essential point that the moment at which politics matters is very important. Suppose that you are a defendant who stands accused of committing a violent crime. Which judge is likelier to give you an impartial hearing: one appointed for life twenty years before by a governor committed to "getting tough on crime?" Or one at risk of being voted out of office next month by an electorate committed to "getting tough on crime?" Simply put, a politicized process for determining whether an individual will become a judge is less threatening to that person's capacity to be impartial and uphold the rule of law than a politicized process for determining whether that same person will be permitted to remain a judge.

Conclusion

. . . [I]n our current climate, proposing an end to judicial elections is akin to tilting at windmills, but the N.A.A.C.P's strategy to end Jim Crow laws must have seemed equally far-fetched in the 1940s. To make this more than a daydream, we must approach judicial selection not merely as a project or a campaign, but as a movement—a movement to recapture impartial justice and the rule of law. With each judicial campaign cycle will come a new round of election-related disasters that can serve to stoke the fires of reform. To succeed, the appointive system that we offer in its stead must ensure not just an appropriately independent, but also an accountable judiciary. . . .

POSTSCRIPT

Should Judges Be Elected Rather Than Appointed?

Another U.S. Supreme Court opinion further changed the judicial election landscape in 2010. In *Citizens United v. Federal Election Commission*, 130 S.Ct. 876 (2010), the Court held that the First Amendment prevents legislatures from limiting independent political broadcasts by corporations and unions. As a result, both corporations and unions are free to spend as much as they like in support of—or against—candidates in judicial elections.

Some states have implemented a system of public financing for judicial elections. Candidates who choose to take public financing are allocating a certain amount of public dollars in return for a pledge not to raise money independently. Public financing has been successful at curbing candidate fundraising in states like North Carolina and Wisconsin. However, in light of *Citizens United,* no public financing scheme can prevent independent expenditures outside of the candidates' control.

Another increasingly popular reform is judicial performance evaluation (JPE), in which an official state commission evaluates sitting judges seeking retention and provides those evaluations to voters before Election Day. JPE is designed to educate voters about their judges and allow them to make more informed decisions at the ballot box. JPE commissions are typically bipartisan and consist both of lawyers and nonlawyers. Judges are never evaluated directly on the outcomes of their decisions; rather, the evaluation focuses on whether each judge treated litigants fairly, explained his or her decisions clearly, and demonstrated knowledge of applicable law and rules.

As you might expect, much has been written on all sides of the judicial selection debate. Several law journals have published entire symposium issues with competing perspectives, including the *Fordham Urban Law Journal* (vol. 34, no. 1, 2007) and the *Nevada Law Journal* (vol. 4, no. 1, 2003). For an additional view favoring judicial elections, see Chris W. Bonneau and Melinda Gann Hall, *In Defense of Judicial Elections* (2009). For perspectives favoring merit selection, see Thomas R. Phillips, *The Merits of Merit Selection, 32 Harv. J.L. & Pub. Pol'y* 67 (2009); Norman L. Greene, *Perspectives on Judicial Selection, 56 Mercer L. Rev.* 949 (2005); and Rachel Paine Caufield, *What Makes Merit Selection Different?,* 15 *Roger Williams L. Rev.* 765 (2010).

Up-to-date information on the selection mechanism(s) used in each state is available through the American Judicature Society at http://www.judicialselection .us. Similarly, up-to-date information on JPE programs in each state is available from the Institute for the Advancement of the American Legal System at http:// www.du.edu/legalinstitute/jpe_publications.html. For a general introduction to JPE programs, see Rebecca Love Kourlis and Jordan M. Singer, *Using Judicial Performance Evaluation to Promote Judicial Accountability*, 90 *Judicature* 200 (2007).

Finally, many commentators have recently weighed in on the impact of money and negative advertising in judicial elections. The most comprehensive resource is *The New Politics of Judicial Elections 2000–2009: Decade of Change* (Charles Hall, ed., 2010), which tracks the amount and sources of funding for judicial races, and the way the money is spent.

ISSUE 9

Do Religious Groups Have a Right to Use Public School Facilities After Hours?

YES: Clarence Thomas, from Majority Opinion, *Good News Club, et al., v. Milford Central School*, U.S. Supreme Court (June 11, 2001)

NO: David Souter, from Dissenting Opinion, *Good News Club, et al., v. Milford Central School*, U.S. Supreme Court (June 11, 2001)

ISSUE SUMMARY

YES: Supreme Court Justice Clarence Thomas affirms the right of religious groups to use school facilities after the school day ends, maintaining that restricting such use is a violation of free speech rights.

NO: Supreme Court Justice David Souter, dissenting from the Court's opinion, contends that the use of school facilities by religious groups blurs the line between public classroom instruction and private religious indoctrination and therefore violates the Establishment Clause of the Constitution.

An Easter egg hunt on the White House lawn. Christmas as a national holiday. Prayers opening legislative sessions of state legislatures. If you were a judge and the above practices were challenged as being unconstitutional, how would you rule?

The First Amendment to the Constitution states that "Congress shall make no law respecting an establishment of religion, or prohibiting the free exercise thereof." Interpreting these words and applying them in particular cases has been exceedingly difficult for the courts. What, for example, does "respecting an establishment of religion" mean? Is any governmental involvement or support for religion, direct or indirect, small or great, barred by this phrase?

While the courts have struggled to keep church and state separate, they have also recognized that it would be impossible to have an absolute prohibition on the celebration of religious values and holidays. Therefore, cases continue to be brought, challenging the courts to determine how the words of the Constitution and the standards of prior cases should be applied to the facts of each new case.

The clearest and most well known of the establishment-of-religion cases are the school prayer decisions. In 1963, in *School District of Abington Township, Pennsylvania, v. Schempp, 374* U.S. 203, the Supreme Court ruled that it was unconstitutional to require students to open the school day by reading biblical passages and reciting the Lord's Prayer. A year earlier, in *Engel v. Vitale,* 370 U.S. 421 (1962), the Supreme Court had ruled that public recitation of the New York Regent's Prayer in New York public schools was unconstitutional. This prayer read, "Almighty God, we acknowledge our dependence upon Thee, and we beg thy blessings upon us, our parents, our teachers, and our country."

While banning prayer in the schools, the courts have upheld some questionable practices, such as Sunday closing laws and the loaning of secular textbooks to parochial schools. Yet they have struck down other statutes, such as a Kentucky law that required posting the Ten Commandments in the classroom (see *Stone v. Graham,* 101 S. Ct. 192, 1980). More generally, the Court has upheld prayers at the beginning of legislative sessions and tuition tax credits for parochial schools. Yet it has held unconstitutional statutes requiring a moment of silence in public schools (*Wallace v. Jaffree,* 105 S. Ct. 2479, 1985) and the teaching of "creation science" whenever evolution is taught (*Edwards v. Aguillard,* 107 S. Ct. 2573, 1987).

The many cases involving religion that have been considered by the Supreme Court in the past 30 years indicate that the task of defining precisely what role religion should have in government-sponsored activities is extraordinarily difficult. Religion has not been banned from public life. "In God We Trust" appears on U.S. coins, prayers are said at presidential inaugurations, Christmas is a national holiday, the lighting of the national Christmas tree at the White House is a newsworthy event, and tax exemptions are given to religious institutions. It is probably still accurate, as Supreme Court justice William O. Douglas once wrote, that "we are a religious people whose institutions presuppose a Supreme Being." It is also true, however, that many religious activities may not be sponsored by the government.

The following case is one of the most recent Supreme Court decisions to consider the intersection between the free exercise of religion and the establishment of religion. Justice Clarence Thomas finds that the plaintiff, the Good News Club, has as much a right as anyone else to use school grounds. Justice David Souter dissents.

YES ↵

Clarence Thomas

Majority Opinion, *Good News Club v. Milford Central School*

J USTICE THOMAS delivered the opinion of the Court.

This case presents two questions. The first question is whether Milford Central School violated the free speech rights of the Good News Club when it excluded the Club from meeting after hours at the school. The second question is whether any such violation is justified by Milford's concern that permitting the Club's activities would violate the Establishment Clause. We conclude that Milford's restriction violates the Club's free speech rights and that no Establishment Clause concern justifies that violation.

I

The State of New York authorizes local school boards to adopt regulations governing the use of their school facilities. In particular, N. Y. Educ. Law §414 (McKinney 2000) enumerates several purposes for which local boards may open their schools to public use. In 1992, respondent Milford Central School (Milford) enacted a community use policy adopting seven of §414's purposes for which its building could be used after school. Two of the stated purposes are relevant here. First, district residents may use the school for "instruction in any branch of education, learning or the arts." Second, the school is available for "social, civic and recreational meetings and entertainment events, and other uses pertaining to the welfare of the community, provided that such uses shall be nonexclusive and shall be opened to the general public."

Stephen and Darleen Fournier reside within Milford's district and therefore are eligible to use the school's facilities as long as their proposed use is approved by the school. Together they are sponsors of the local Good News Club, a private Christian organization for children ages 6 to 12. Pursuant to Milford's policy, in September 1996 the Fourniers submitted a request to Dr. Robert McGruder, interim superintendent of the district, in which they sought permission to hold the Club's weekly afterschool meetings in the school cafeteria. The next month, McGruder formally denied the Fourniers' request on the ground that the proposed use—to have "a fun time of singing songs, hearing a Bible lesson and memorizing scripture,"—was "the equivalent of religious worship." According to McGruder, the community use policy,

From Supreme Court of the United States, June 11, 2001.

which prohibits use "by any individual or organization for religious purposes," foreclosed the Club's activities.

In response to a letter submitted by the Club's counsel, Milford's attorney requested information to clarify the nature of the Club's activities. The Club sent a set of materials used or distributed at the meetings and the following description of its meeting:

> "The Club opens its session with Ms. Fournier taking attendance. As she calls a child's name, if the child recites a Bible verse the child receives a treat. After attendance, the Club sings songs. Next Club members engage in games that involve, *inter alia,* learning Bible verses. Ms. Fournier then relates a Bible story and explains how it applies to Club members' lives. The Club closes with prayer. Finally, Ms. Fournier distributes treats and the Bible verses for memorization."

McGruder and Milford's attorney reviewed the materials and concluded that "the kinds of activities proposed to be engaged in by the Good News Club were not a discussion of secular subjects such as child rearing, development of character and development of morals from a religious perspective, but were in fact the equivalent of religious instruction itself." In February 1997, the Milford Board of Education adopted a resolution rejecting the Club's request to use Milford's facilities "for the purpose of conducting religious instruction and Bible study."

In March 1997, petitioners, the Good News Club, Ms. Fournier, and her daughter Andrea Fournier (collectively, the Club), filed an action under 42 U.S.C. §1983 against Milford in the United States District Court for the Northern District of New York. The Club alleged that Milford's denial of its application violated its free speech rights under the First and Fourteenth Amendments, its right to equal protection under the Fourteenth Amendment, and its right to religious freedom under the Religious Freedom Restoration Act of 1993, 107 Stat. 1488, 42 U.S.C. §2000bb *et seq.*

The Club moved for a preliminary injunction to prevent the school from enforcing its religious exclusion policy against the Club and thereby to permit the Club's use of the school facilities. On April 14, 1997, the District Court granted the injunction. The Club then held its weekly afterschool meetings from April 1997 until June 1998 in a high school resource and middle school special education room.

In August 1998, the District Court vacated the preliminary injunction and granted Milford's motion for summary judgment. 21 F. Supp. 2d 147 (NDNY 1998). The court found that the Club's "subject matter is decidedly religious in nature, and not merely a discussion of secular matters from a religious perspective that is otherwise permitted under [Milford's] use policies." Because the school had not permitted other groups that provided religious instruction to use its limited public forum, the court held that the school could deny access to the Club without engaging in unconstitutional viewpoint discrimination. The court also rejected the Club's equal protection claim.

The Club appealed, and a divided panel of the United States Court of Appeals for the Second Circuit affirmed. 202 F. 3d 502 (2000). First, the court rejected the Club's contention that Milford's restriction against allowing religious instruction in its facilities is unreasonable. Second, it held that, because the subject matter of the Club's activities is "quintessentially religious," and the activities "fall outside the bounds of pure 'moral and character development,'" Milford's policy of excluding the Club's meetings was constitutional subject discrimination, not unconstitutional viewpoint discrimination. Judge Jacobs filed a dissenting opinion in which he concluded that the school's restriction did constitute viewpoint discrimination under *Lamb's Chapel v. Center Moriches Union Free School Dist.*, 508 U.S. 384 (1993).

There is a conflict among the Courts of Appeals on the question whether speech can be excluded from a limited public forum on the basis of the religious nature of the speech. Compare *Gentala v. Tucson*, 244 F. 3d 1065 (CA9 2001) (en banc) (holding that a city properly refused National Day of Prayer organizers' application to the city's civic events fund for coverage of costs for city services); *Campbell v. St. Tammany's School Bd.*, 206 F. 3d 482 (CA5 2000) (holding that a school's policy against permitting religious instruction in its limited public forum did not constitute viewpoint discrimination), cert. pending, No. 00-1194; *Bronx Household of Faith v. Community School Dist. No. 10*, 127 F. 3d 207 (CA2 1997) (concluding that a ban on religious services and instruction in the limited public forum was constitutional), with *Church on the Rock v. Albuquerque*, 84 F. 3d 1273 (CA10 1996) (holding that a city's denial of permission to show the film *Jesus* in a senior center was unconstitutional viewpoint discrimination); and *Good News/Good Sports Club v. School Dist. of Ladue*, 28 F. 3d 1501 (CA8 1994) (holding unconstitutional a school use policy that prohibited Good News Club from meeting during times when the Boy Scouts could meet). We granted certiorari to resolve this conflict. 531 U.S. 923 (2000).

II

The standards that we apply to determine whether a State has unconstitutionally excluded a private speaker from use of a public forum depend on the nature of the forum. See *Perry Ed. Assn. v. Perry Local Educators' Assn.*, 460 U.S. 37, 44 (1983). If the forum is a traditional or open public forum, the State's restrictions on speech are subject to stricter scrutiny than are restrictions in a limited public forum. *Id.*, at 45–46. We have previously declined to decide whether a school district's opening of its facilities pursuant to N. Y. Educ. Law §414 creates a limited or a traditional public forum. See *Lamb's Chapel, supra*, at 391–392. Because the parties have agreed that Milford created a limited public forum when it opened its facilities in 1992, we need not resolve the issue here. Instead, we simply will assume that Milford operates a limited public forum.

When the State establishes a limited public forum, the State is not required to and does not allow persons to engage in every type of speech. The State may be justified "in reserving [its forum] for certain groups or for the discussion of certain topics." *Rosenberger v. Rector and Visitors of Univ. of Va.*, 515 U.S. 819, 829 (1995); see also *Lamb's Chapel, supra*, at 392–393. The State's power to restrict speech, however, is not without limits. The restriction must not discriminate against speech on the basis of viewpoint, *Rosenberger, supra,* at 829, and the restriction must be "reasonable in light of the purpose served by the forum," *Cornelius v. NAACP Legal Defense & Ed. Fund, Inc.,* 473 U.S. 788, 806 (1985).

III

Applying this test, we first address whether the exclusion constituted viewpoint discrimination. We are guided in our analysis by two of our prior opinions, *Lamb's Chapel* and *Rosenberger.* In *Lamb's Chapel,* we held that a school district violated the Free Speech Clause of the First Amendment when it excluded a private group from presenting films at the school based solely on the films' discussions of family values from a religious perspective. Likewise, in *Rosenberger,* we held that a university's refusal to fund a student publication because the publication addressed issues from a religious perspective violated the Free Speech Clause. Concluding that Milford's exclusion of the Good News Club based on its religious nature is indistinguishable from the exclusions in these cases, we hold that the exclusion constitutes viewpoint discrimination. Because the restriction is viewpoint discriminatory, we need not decide whether it is unreasonable in light of the purposes served by the forum.

Milford has opened its limited public forum to activities that serve a variety of purposes, including events "pertaining to the welfare of the community." Milford interprets its policy to permit discussions of subjects such as child rearing, and of "the development of character and morals from a religious perspective." Brief for Appellee in No. 98-9494 (CA2), p. 6. For example, this policy would allow someone to use Aesop's Fables to teach children moral values. Additionally, a group could sponsor a debate on whether there should be a constitutional amendment to permit prayer in public schools, and the Boy Scouts could meet "to influence a boy's character, development and spiritual growth." In short, any group that "promote[s] the moral and character development of children" is eligible to use the school building.

Just as there is no question that teaching morals and character development to children is a permissible purpose under Milford's policy, it is clear that the Club teaches morals and character development to children. For example, no one disputes that the Club instructs children to overcome feelings of jealousy, to treat others well regardless of how they treat the children, and to be obedient, even if it does so in a nonsecular way. Nonetheless, because Milford found the Club's activities to be religious in nature—"the equivalent of religious instruction itself," 202 F. 3d, at 507—it excluded the Club from use of its facilities.

Applying *Lamb's Chapel,*[1] we find it quite clear that Milford engaged in viewpoint discrimination when it excluded the Club from the afterschool forum. In *Lamb's Chapel,* the local New York school district similarly had adopted §414's "social, civic or recreational use" category as a permitted use in its limited public forum. The district also prohibited use "by any group for religious purposes." 508 U.S., at 387. Citing this prohibition, the school district excluded a church that wanted to present films teaching family values from a Christian perspective. We held that, because the films "no doubt dealt with a subject otherwise permissible" under the rule, the teaching of family values, the district's exclusion of the church was unconstitutional viewpoint discrimination. *Id.*, at 394.

Like the church in *Lamb's Chapel* the Club seeks to address a subject otherwise permitted under the rule, the teaching of morals and character, from a religious standpoint. Certainly, one could have characterized the film presentations in *Lamb's Chapel* as a religious use, as the Court of Appeals did, *Lamb's Chapel v. Center Moriches Union Free School Dist.*, 959 F. 2d 381, 388–389 (CA2 1992). And one easily could conclude that the films' purpose to instruct that "'society's slide toward humanism . . . can only be counterbalanced by a loving home where Christian values are instilled from an early age,'" *id.*, at 384, was "quintessentially religious," 202 F. 3d, at 510. The only apparent difference between the activity of Lamb's Chapel and the activities of the Good News Club is that the Club chooses to teach moral lessons from a Christian perspective through live storytelling and prayer, whereas Lamb's Chapel taught lessons through films. This distinction is inconsequential. Both modes of speech use a religious viewpoint. Thus, the exclusion of the Good News Club's activities, like the exclusion of Lamb's Chapel's films, constitutes unconstitutional viewpoint discrimination.

Our opinion in *Rosenberger* also is dispositive. In *Rosenberger,* a student organization at the University of Virginia was denied funding for printing expenses because its publication, Wide Awake, offered a Christian viewpoint. Just as the Club emphasizes the role of Christianity in students' morals and character, Wide Awake "'challenge[d] Christians to live, in word and deed, according to the faith they proclaim and . . . encourage[d] students to consider what a personal relationship with Jesus Christ means.'" 515 U.S., at 826. Because the university "select[ed] for disfavored treatment those student journalistic efforts with religious editorial viewpoints," we held that the denial of funding was unconstitutional. *Id.*, at 831. Although in *Rosenberger* there was no prohibition on religion as a subject matter, our holding did not rely on this factor. Instead, we concluded simply that the university's denial of funding to print Wide Awake was viewpoint discrimination, just as the school district's refusal to allow Lamb's Chapel to show its films was viewpoint discrimination. Given the obvious religious content of Wide Awake, we cannot say that the Club's activities are any more "religious" or deserve any less First Amendment protection than did the publication of Wide Awake in *Rosenberger.*

Despite our holdings in *Lamb's Chapel* and *Rosenberger,* the Court of Appeals, like Milford, believed that its characterization of the Club's activities as religious in nature warranted treating the Club's activities as different in kind from the other activities permitted by the school. See 202 F. 3d, at 510 (the Club "is doing something other than simply teaching moral values"). The "Christian viewpoint" is unique, according to the court, because it contains an "additional layer" that other kinds of viewpoints do not. *Id.*, at 509. That is, the Club "is focused on teaching children how to cultivate their relationship with God through Jesus Christ," which it characterized as "quintessentially religious." *Id.*, at 510. With these observations, the court concluded that, because the Club's activities "fall outside the bounds of pure 'moral and character development,'" the exclusion did not constitute viewpoint discrimination. *Id.,* at 511.

We disagree that something that is "quintessentially religious" or "decidedly religious in nature" cannot also be characterized properly as the teaching of morals and character development from a particular viewpoint. See 202 F. 3d, at 512 (Jacobs, J., dissenting) ("[W]hen the subject matter is morals and character, it is quixotic to attempt a distinction between religious viewpoints and religious subject matters"). What matters for purposes of the Free Speech Clause is that we can see no logical difference in kind between the invocation of Christianity by the Club and the invocation of teamwork, loyalty, or patriotism by other associations to provide a foundation for their lessons. It is apparent that the unstated principle of the Court of Appeals' reasoning is its conclusion that any time religious instruction and prayer are used to discuss morals and character, the discussion is simply not a "pure" discussion of those issues. According to the Court of Appeals, reliance on Christian principles taints moral and character instruction in a way that other foundations for thought or viewpoints do not. We, however, have never reached such a conclusion. Instead, we reaffirm our holdings in *Lamb's Chapel* and *Rosenberger* that speech discussing otherwise permissible subjects cannot be excluded from a limited public forum on the ground that the subject is discussed from a religious viewpoint. Thus, we conclude that Milford's exclusion of the Club from use of the school, pursuant to its community use policy, constitutes impermissible viewpoint discrimination.

IV

Milford argues that, even if its restriction constitutes viewpoint discrimination, its interest in not violating the Establishment Clause outweighs the Club's interest in gaining equal access to the school's facilities. In other words, according to Milford, its restriction was required to avoid violating the Establishment Clause. We disagree.

We have said that a state interest in avoiding an Establishment Clause violation "may be characterized as compelling," and therefore may justify content-based discrimination. *Widmar v. Vincent,* 454 U.S. 263, 271 (1981). However, it is not clear whether a State's interest in avoiding an Establishment Clause violation would justify viewpoint discrimination. See *Lamb's Chapel,* 508 U.S., at 394–395 (noting the suggestion in *Widmar* but ultimately not finding an Establishment Clause problem). We need not, however, confront the issue in this case, because we conclude that the school has no valid Establishment Clause interest.

We rejected Establishment Clause defenses similar to Milford's in two previous free speech cases, *Lamb's Chapel* and *Widmar.* In particular, in *Lamb's Chapel,* we explained that "[t]he showing of th[e] film series would not have been during school hours, would not have been sponsored by the school, and would have been open to the public, not just to church members." 508 U.S., at 395. Accordingly, we found that "there would have been no realistic danger that the community would think that the District was endorsing religion or any particular creed." *Ibid.* Likewise, in *Widmar,* where the university's forum was already available to other groups, this Court concluded that there was no Establishment Clause problem. 454 U.S., at 272–273, and n. 13.

The Establishment Clause defense fares no better in this case. As in *Lamb's Chapel,* the Club's meetings were held after school hours, not sponsored by the school, and open to any student who obtained parental consent, not just to Club members. As in *Widmar,* Milford made its forum available to other organizations. The Club's activities are materially indistinguishable from those in *Lamb's Chapel* and *Widmar.* Thus, Milford's reliance on the Establishment Clause is unavailing.

Milford attempts to distinguish *Lamb's Chapel* and *Widmar* by emphasizing that Milford's policy involves elementary school children. According to Milford, children will perceive that the school is endorsing the Club and will feel coercive pressure to participate, because the Club's activities take place on school grounds, even though they occur during nonschool hours. This argument is unpersuasive.

First, we have held that "a significant factor in upholding governmental programs in the face of Establishment Clause attack is their *neutrality* towards religion." *Rosenberger,* 515 U.S., at 839 (emphasis added). See also *Mitchell v. Helms,* 530 U.S. 793 (2000) (slip op., at 10) (plurality opinion) ("In distinguishing between indoctrination that is attributable to the State and indoctrination that is not, [the Court has] consistently turned to the principle of neutrality, upholding aid that is offered to a broad range of groups or persons without regard to their religion" (emphasis added)); (O'CONNOR, J., concurring in judgment) ("[N]eutrality is an important reason for upholding government-aid programs against Establishment Clause challenges"). Milford's implication that granting access to the Club would do damage to the neutrality principle defies logic. For the "guarantee of neutrality is respected, not offended, when the government, following neutral criteria and evenhanded policies, extends benefits to recipients whose ideologies and viewpoints, including religious ones, are broad and diverse." *Rosenberger, supra,* at 839. The Good News Club seeks nothing more than to be treated neutrally and given access to speak about the same topics as are other groups. Because allowing the Club to speak on school grounds would ensure neutrality, not threaten it, Milford faces an uphill battle in arguing that the Establishment Clause compels it to exclude the Good News Club.

Second, to the extent we consider whether the community would feel coercive pressure to engage in the Club's activities, cf. *Lee v. Weisman,* 505 U.S. 577, 592–593 (1992), the relevant community would be the parents, not the elementary school children. It is the parents who choose whether their children will attend the Good News Club meetings. Because the children cannot attend without their parents' permission, they cannot be coerced into engaging in the Good News Club's religious activities. Milford does not suggest that the parents of elementary school children would be confused about whether the school was endorsing religion. Nor do we believe that such an argument could be reasonably advanced.

Third, whatever significance we may have assigned in the Establishment Clause context to the suggestion that elementary school children are more impressionable than adults, cf., *e.g.*, *Lee, supra*, at 592; *School Dist. of Grand Rapids v. Ball*, 473 U.S. 373, 390 (1985) (stating that "symbolism of a union between church and state is most likely to influence children of tender years, whose experience is limited and whose beliefs consequently are the function of environment as much as of free and voluntary choice"), we have never extended our Establishment Clause jurisprudence to foreclose private religious conduct during nonschool hours merely because it takes place on school premises where elementary school children may be present.

None of the cases discussed by Milford persuades us that our Establishment Clause jurisprudence has gone this far. For example, Milford cites *Lee v. Weisman* for the proposition that "there are heightened concerns with protecting freedom of conscience from subtle coercive pressure in the elementary and secondary public schools," 505 U.S., at 592. In *Lee*, however, we concluded that attendance at the graduation exercise was obligatory. *Id.*, at 586. See also *Santa Fe Independent School Dist. v. Doe*, 530 U.S. 290 (2000) (holding the school's policy of permitting prayer at football games unconstitutional where the activity took place during a school-sponsored event and not in a public forum). We did not place independent significance on the fact that the graduation exercise might take place on school premises, *Lee, supra*, at 583. Here, where the school facilities are being used for a nonschool function and there is no government sponsorship of the Club's activities, *Lee* is inapposite.

Equally unsupportive is *Edwards v. Aguillard*, 482 U.S. 578 (1987), in which we held that a Louisiana law that proscribed the teaching of evolution as part of the public school curriculum, unless accompanied by a lesson on creationism, violated the Establishment Clause. In *Edwards*, we mentioned that students are susceptible to pressure in the classroom, particularly given their possible reliance on teachers as role models. See *id.*, at 584. But we did not discuss this concern in our application of the law to the facts. Moreover, we did note that mandatory attendance requirements meant that State advancement of religion in a school would be particularly harshly felt by impressionable students. But we did not suggest that, when the school was not actually advancing religion, the impressionability of students would be relevant to the Establishment Clause issue. Even if *Edwards* had articulated the principle Milford believes it did, the facts in *Edwards* are simply too remote from those here to give the principle any weight. *Edwards* involved the content of the curriculum taught by state teachers during the schoolday to children required to attend. Obviously, when individuals who are not schoolteachers are giving lessons after school to children permitted to attend only with parental consent, the concerns expressed in *Edwards* are not present.

Fourth, even if we were to consider the possible misperceptions by schoolchildren in deciding whether Milford's permitting the Club's activities would violate the Establishment Clause, the facts of this case simply do not support Milford's conclusion. There is no evidence that young children are permitted to loiter outside classrooms after the schoolday has ended. Surely even young children are aware of events for which their parents must sign permission forms. The meetings were held in a combined high school resource room and middle school special education room, not in an elementary school classroom. The instructors are not schoolteachers. And the children in the group are not all the same age as in the normal classroom setting; their ages range from 6 to 12. In sum, these circumstances simply do not support the theory that small children would perceive endorsement here.

Finally, even if we were to inquire into the minds of schoolchildren in this case, we cannot say the danger that children would misperceive the endorsement of religion is any greater than the danger that they would perceive a hostility toward the religious viewpoint if the Club were excluded from the public forum. This concern is particularly acute given the reality that Milford's building is not used only for elementary school children. Students, from kindergarten through the 12th grade, all attend school in the same building. There may be as many, if not more, upperclassmen than elementary school children who occupy the school after hours. For that matter, members of the public writ large are permitted in the school after hours pursuant to the community use policy. Any bystander could conceivably be aware of the school's use policy and its exclusion of the Good News Club, and could suffer as much from viewpoint discrimination as elementary school children could suffer from perceived endorsement. Cf. *Rosenberger,* 515 U.S., at 835–836 (expressing the concern that viewpoint discrimination can chill individual thought and expression).

We cannot operate, as Milford would have us do, under the assumption that any risk that small children would perceive endorsement should counsel in favor of excluding the Club's religious activity. We decline to employ Establishment Clause jurisprudence using a modified heckler's veto, in which a group's religious activity can be proscribed on the basis of what the youngest members of the audience might misperceive. Cf. *Capitol Square Review and Advisory Bd. v. Pinette,* 515 U.S. 753, 779–780 (1995) (O'CONNOR, J., concurring in part and concurring in judgment) ("[B]ecause our concern is with the political community writ large, the endorsement inquiry is *not about the perceptions of particular individuals* or saving isolated nonadherents from . . . discomfort. . . . It is for this reason that the reasonable observer in the endorsement inquiry must be deemed aware of the history and context of the community and forum in which the religious [speech takes place]" (emphasis added)). There are countervailing constitutional concerns related to rights of other individuals in the community. In this case, those countervailing concerns are the free speech rights of the Club and its members. Cf. *Rosenberger, supra,* at 835 ("Vital First Amendment speech principles are at stake here"). And, we have already found that those rights have been violated, not merely perceived to have been violated, by the school's actions toward the Club.

We are not convinced that there is any significance in this case to the possibility that elementary school children may witness the Good News Club's activities on school premises, and therefore we can find no reason to depart from our holdings in *Lamb's Chapel* and *Widmar.* Accordingly, we conclude that permitting the Club to meet on the school's premises would not have violated the Establishment Clause.

V

When Milford denied the Good News Club access to the school's limited public forum on the ground that the Club was religious in nature, it discriminated against the Club because of its religious viewpoint in violation of the Free Speech Clause of the First Amendment. Because Milford has not raised a valid Establishment Clause claim, we do not address the question whether such a claim could excuse Milford's viewpoint discrimination.

⋅⚙⋅

The judgment of the Court of Appeals is reversed, and the case is remanded for further proceedings consistent with this opinion.

It is so ordered.

Note

1. We find it remarkable that the Court of Appeals majority did not cite *Lamb's Chapel,* despite its obvious relevance to the case. We do not necessarily expect a court of appeals to catalog every opinion that reverses one of its precedents. Nonetheless, this oversight is particularly incredible because the majority's attention was directed to it at every turn. See, *e.g.,* 202 F. 3d 502, 513 (CA2 2000) (JACOBS, J., dissenting) ("I cannot square the majority's analysis in this case with *Lamb's Chapel*"); 21 F. Supp. 2d, at 150; App. O9-O11 (District Court stating "that *Lamb's Chapel* and *Rosenberger* pinpoint the critical issue in this case"); Brief for Appellee in No. 98-9494 (CA2) at 36–39; Brief for Appellants in No. 98-9494 (CA2), pp. 15, 36.

David Souter   ➡ **NO**

Dissenting Opinion of
David Souter

JUSTICE SOUTER, with whom JUSTICE GINSBURG joins, dissenting.

The majority rules on two issues. First, it decides that the Court of Appeals failed to apply the rule in *Lambs's Chapel v. Center Moriches Union Free School Dist.,* 508 U.S. 384 (1993), which held that the government may not discriminate on the basis of viewpoint in operating a limited public forum. The majority applies that rule and concludes that Milford violated *Lambs's Chapel* in denying Good News the use of the school. The majority then goes on to determine that it would not violate the Establishment Clause of the First Amendment for the Milford School District to allow the Good News Club to hold its intended gatherings of public school children in Milford's elementary school. The majority is mistaken on both points. The Court of Appeals unmistakably distinguished this case from *Lamb's Chapel,* though not by name, and accordingly affirmed the application of a policy, unchallenged in the District Court, that Milford's public schools may not be used for religious purposes. As for the applicability of the Establishment Clause to the Good News Club's intended use of Milford's school, the majority commits error even in reaching the issue, which was addressed neither by the Court of Appeals nor by the District Court. I respectfully dissent.

I

Lamb's Chapel, a case that arose (as this one does) from application of N.Y. Educ. Law §414 (McKinney 2000) and local policy implementing it, built on the accepted rule that a government body may designate a public forum subject to a reasonable limitation on the scope of permitted subject matter and activity, so long as the government does not use the forum-defining restrictions to deny expression to a particular viewpoint on subjects open to discussion. Specifically, *Lamb's Chapel* held that the government could not "permit school property to be used for the presentation of all views about family issues and child rearing except those dealing with the subject matter from a religious standpoint." 508 U.S., at 393–394.

This case, like *Lamb's Chapel,* properly raises no issue about the reasonableness of Milford's criteria for restricting the scope of its designated public forum. Milford has opened school property for, among other things, "instruction in

From Supreme Court of the United States, June 11, 2001.

any branch of education, learning or the arts" and for "social, civic and recreational meetings and entertainment events and other uses pertaining to the welfare of the community, provided that such uses shall be nonexclusive and shall be opened to the general public." App. to Pet. for Cert. D1–D3. But Milford has done this subject to the restriction that "[s]chool premises shall not be used . . . for religious purposes." As the District Court stated, Good News did "not object to the reasonableness of [Milford]'s policy that prohibits the use of [its] facilities for religious purposes."

The sole question before the District Court was, therefore, whether, in refusing to allow Good News's intended use, Milford was misapplying its unchallenged restriction in a way that amounted to imposing a viewpoint-based restriction on what could be said or done by a group entitled to use the forum for an educational, civic, or other permitted purpose. The question was whether Good News was being disqualified when it merely sought to use the school property the same way that the Milford Boy and Girl Scouts and the 4-H Club did. The District Court held on the basis of undisputed facts that Good News's activity was essentially unlike the presentation of views on secular issues from a religious standpoint held to be protected in *Lamb's Chapel,* see App. to Pet. for Cert. C29–C31, and was instead activity precluded by Milford's unchallenged policy against religious use, even under the narrowest definition of that term.

The Court of Appeals understood the issue the same way. See 202 F. 3d 502, 508 (CA2 2000) (Good News argues that "to exclude the Club because it teaches morals and values from a Christian perspective constitutes unconstitutional viewpoint discrimination"); *id.,* at 509 ("The crux of the Good News Club's argument is that the Milford school's application of the Community Use Policy to exclude the Club from its facilities is not viewpoint neutral"). The Court of Appeals also realized that the *Lamb's Chapel* criterion was the appropriate measure: "The activities of the Good News Club do not involve merely a religious perspective on the secular subject of morality." 202 F. 3d, at 510. Cf. *Lamb's Chapel, supra,* at 393 (district could not exclude "religious standpoint" in discussion on childrearing and family values, an undisputed "use for social or civic purposes otherwise permitted" under the use policy).[1] The appeals court agreed with the District Court that the undisputed facts in this case differ from those in *Lamb's Chapel,* as night from day. A sampling of those facts shows why both courts were correct.

Good News's classes open and close with prayer. In a sample lesson considered by the District Court, children are instructed that "[t]he Bible tells us how we can have our sins forgiven by receiving the Lord Jesus Christ. It tells us how to live to please Him. . . . If you have received the Lord Jesus as your Saviour from sin, you belong to God's special group—His family." The lesson plan instructs the teacher to "lead a child to Christ," and, when reading a Bible verse, to "[e]mphasize that this verse is from the Bible, God's Word" and is "important—and true—because God said it." The lesson further exhorts the teacher to "[b]e sure to give an opportunity for the 'unsaved' children in your class to respond to the Gospel" and cautions against "neglect[ing] this responsibility."

While Good News's program utilizes songs and games, the heart of the meeting is the "challenge" and "invitation," which are repeated at various times throughout the lesson. During the challenge, "saved" children who "already believe in the Lord Jesus as their Savior" are challenged to "'stop and ask God for the strength and the "want" . . . to obey Him.'" *Ibid*. They are instructed that

> "[i]f you know Jesus as your Savior, you need to place God first in your life. And if you don't know Jesus as Savior and if you would like to, then we will—we will pray with you separately, individually. . . . And the challenge would be, those of you who know Jesus as Savior, you can rely on God's strength to obey Him." *Ibid*.

During the invitation, the teacher "invites" the "unsaved" children "'to trust the Lord Jesus to be your Savior from sin,'" and "'receiv[e] [him] as your Savior from sin.'" *Id.*, at C21. The children are then instructed that

> "[i]f you believe what God's Word says about your sin and how Jesus died and rose again for you, you can have His forever life today. Please bow your heads and close your eyes. If you have never believed on the Lord Jesus as your Savior and would like to do that, please show me by raising your hand. If you raised your hand to show me you want to believe on the Lord Jesus, please meet me so I can show you from God's Word how you can receive His everlasting life." *Ibid*.

It is beyond question that Good News intends to use the public school premises not for the mere discussion of a subject from a particular, Christian point of view, but for an evangelical service of worship calling children to commit themselves in an act of Christian conversion.[2] The majority avoids this reality only by resorting to the bland and general characterization of Good News's activity as "teaching of morals and character, from a religious standpoint." See *ante*, at 9. If the majority's statement ignores reality, as it surely does, then today's holding may be understood only in equally generic terms. Otherwise, indeed, this case would stand for the remarkable proposition that any public school opened for civic meetings must be opened for use as a church, synagogue, or mosque. . . .

This Court has accepted the independent obligation to obey the Establishment Clause as sufficiently compelling to satisfy strict scrutiny under the First Amendment. See *id.*, at 271 ("[T]he interest of the [government] in complying with its constitutional obligations may be characterized as compelling"); *Lamb's Chapel*, 508 U.S., at 394. Milford's actions would offend the Establishment Clause if they carried the message of endorsing religion under the circumstances, as viewed by a reasonable observer. See *Capitol Square Review and Advisory Bd. v. Pinette*, 515 U.S. 753, 777 (1995) (O'CONNOR, J., concurring). The majority concludes that such an endorsement effect is out of the question in Milford's case, because the context here is "materially indistinguishable" from the facts in *Lamb's Chapel* and *Widmar*. *Ante*, at 13. In fact, the majority is in no position to say that, for the principal grounds on which we based our Establishment Clause holdings in those cases are clearly absent here.

In *Widmar,* we held that the Establishment Clause did not bar a religious student group from using a public university's meeting space for worship as well as discussion. As for the reasonable observers who might perceive government endorsement of religion, we pointed out that the forum was used by university students, who "are, of course, young adults," and, as such, "are less impressionable than younger students and should be able to appreciate that the University's policy is one of neutrality toward religion." 454 U.S., at 274, n. 14. To the same effect, we remarked that the "large number of groups meeting on campus" negated "any reasonable inference of University support from the mere fact of a campus meeting place." *Ibid.* Not only was the forum "available to a broad class of nonreligious as well as religious speakers," but there were, in fact, over 100 recognized student groups at the University, and an "absence of empirical evidence that religious groups [would] dominate [the University's] open forum." *Id.,* at 274–275; see also *id.,* at 274 ("The provision of benefits to so broad a spectrum of groups is an important index of secular effect"). And if all that had not been enough to show that the university-student use would probably create no impression of religious endorsement, we pointed out that the university in that case had issued a student handbook with the explicit disclaimer that "the University's name will not 'be identified in any way with the aims, policies, programs, products, or opinions of any organization or its members.'" *Id.,* at 274, n. 14.

Lamb's Chapel involved an evening film series on childrearing open to the general public (and, given the subject matter, directed at an adult audience). See 508 U.S., at 387, 395. There, school property "had repeatedly been used by a wide variety of private organizations," and we could say with some assurance that "[u]nder these circumstances . . . there would have been no realistic danger that the community would think that the District was endorsing religion or any particular creed. . . ." *Id.,* at 395.

What we know about this case looks very little like *Widmar* or *Lamb's Chapel.* The cohort addressed by Good News is not university students with relative maturity, or even high school pupils, but elementary school children as young as six.[3] The Establishment Clause cases have consistently recognized the particular impressionability of schoolchildren, see *Edwards v. Aguillard,* 482 U.S. 578, 583–584 (1987), and the special protection required for those in the elementary grades in the school forum, see *County of Allegheny v. American Civil Liberties Union, Greater Pittsburgh Chapter,* 492 U.S. 573, 620, n. 69 (1989). We have held the difference between college students and grade school pupils to be a "distinction [that] warrants a difference in constitutional results," *Edwards v. Aguillard, supra,* at 584, n. 5 (internal quotation marks and citation omitted).

Nor is Milford's limited forum anything like the sites for wide-ranging intellectual exchange that were home to the challenged activities in *Widmar* and *Lamb's Chapel.* See also *Rosenberger,* 515 U.S., at 850, 836–837. In Widmar, the nature of the university campus and the sheer number of activities offered precluded the reasonable college observer from seeing government endorsement in any one of them, and so did the time and variety of community use in the *Lamb's Chapel* case. See also *Rosenberger,* 515 U.S., at 850 ("Given this wide array of nonreligious, antireligious and competing religious viewpoints in the forum supported by the University, any perception that the University endorses one particular viewpoint would be illogical"); *id.,* at 836–837, 850 (emphasizing the array of university-funded magazines containing "widely divergent viewpoints" and the fact that believers in Christian evangelism competed on equal footing in the University forum with aficionados of "Plato, Spinoza, and Descartes," as well as "Karl Marx, Bertrand Russell, and Jean-Paul Sartre"); *Board of Ed. of Westside Community Schools (Dist. 66) v. Mergens,* 496 U.S. 226, 252 (1990) (plurality opinion) ("To the extent that a religious club is merely one of many different student-initiated voluntary clubs, students should perceive no message of government endorsement of religion").

The timing and format of Good News's gatherings, on the other hand, may well affirmatively suggest the *imprimatur* of officialdom in the minds of the young children. The club is open solely to elementary students (not the entire community, as in *Lamb's Chapel*), only four outside groups have been identified as meeting in the school, and Good News is, seemingly, the only one whose instruction follows immediately on the conclusion of the official school day. See Brief for National School Boards Association et al. as *Amici Curiae* 6. Although school is out at 2:56 p.m., Good News apparently requested use of the school beginning at 2:30 on Tuesdays "during the school year," so that instruction could begin promptly at 3:00, at which time children who are compelled by law to attend school surely remain in the building. Good News's religious meeting follows regular school activities so closely that the Good News instructor must wait to begin until "the room is clear," and "people are out of the room," before starting proceedings in the classroom located next to the regular third- and fourth-grade rooms. In fact, the temporal and physical continuity of Good News's meetings with the regular school routine seems to be the whole point of using the school. When meetings were held in a community church, 8 or 10 children attended; after the school became the site, the number went up three-fold.

Even on the summary judgment record, then, a record lacking whatever supplementation the trial process might have led to, and devoid of such insight as the trial and appellate judges might have contributed in addressing the Establishment Clause, we can say this: there is a good case that Good News's exercises blur the line between public classroom instruction and private religious indoctrination, leaving a reasonable elementary school pupil unable to appreciate that the former instruction is the business of the school while the latter evangelism is not. Thus, the facts we know (or think we know) point away from the majority's conclusion, and while the consolation may be that nothing really gets resolved when the judicial process is so truncated, that is not much to recommend today's result.

Notes

1. It is true, as the majority notes, *ante,* at 8, n. 3, that the Court of Appeals did not cite *Lamb's Chapel* by name. But it followed it in substance, and it did cite an earlier opinion written by the author of the panel opinion here, *Bronx Household of Faith v. Community School Dist. No. 10,* 127 F. 3d 207 (CA2 1997), which discussed *Lamb's Chapel* at length.

2. The majority rejects Milford's contention that Good News's activities fall outside the purview of the limited forum because they constitute "religious worship" on the ground that the Court of Appeals made no such determination regarding the character of the club's program, see *ante,* at 11, n. 4. This distinction is merely semantic, in light of the Court of Appeals's conclusion that "[i]t is difficult to see how the Club's activities differ materially from the 'religious worship' described" in other case law, 202 F. 3d, at 510, and the record below.

JUSTICE STEVENS distinguishes between proselytizing and worship, *ante,* at 1 (dissenting opinion), and distinguishes each from discussion reflecting a religious point of view. I agree with Justice Stevens that Good News's activities may be characterized as proselytizing and therefore as outside the purpose of Milford's limited forum, *ante,* at 5. Like the Court of Appeals, I also believe Good News's meetings have elements of worship that put the club's activities further afield of Milford's limited forum policy, the legitimacy of which was unchallenged in the summary judgment proceeding.

3. It is certainly correct that parents are required to give permission for their children to attend Good News's classes, see *ante,* at 14, (as parents are often required to do for a host of official school extracurricular activities), and correct that those parents would likely not be confused as to the sponsorship of Good News's classes. But the proper focus of concern in assessing effects includes the elementary school pupils who are invited to meetings, Lodging, Exh. X2, who see peers heading into classrooms for religious instruction as other classes end, and who are addressed by the "challenge" and "invitation."

The fact that there may be no evidence in the record that individual students were confused during the time the Good News Club met on school premises pursuant to the District Court's preliminary injunction is immaterial, cf. Brief for Petitioners 38. As JUSTICE O'CONNOR explained in *Capitol Square Review and Advisory Bd. v. Pinette,* 515 U.S. 753 (1995), the endorsement test does not focus "on the actual perception of individual observers, who naturally have differing degrees of knowledge," but on "the perspective of a hypothetical observer." *Id.,* at 779–780 (opinion concurring in part and concurring in judgment).

POSTSCRIPT

Do Religious Groups Have a Right to Use Public School Facilities After Hours?

Why should church and state be separate? Is there any danger to be feared from public religious displays? It is probably fair to say that behind the debates over this issue and the ongoing controversy over prayer in the schools are differing interpretations of the benefits and dangers of religion in public life. Does religion bring us to a higher level of existence, one that can help us shape our society for the better, or is it a system that will oppress dissidents, nonbelievers, and members of minority faiths? Almost everyone has an opinion on this question, and most can find some historical support for their positions. Ironically, the same historical circumstance may even be used to support opposing points of view. For example, at a congressional hearing on school prayer, the following testimony was introduced:

> *When I was educated in German public schools, they provided as part of the regular curriculum separate religious instruction for children of the three major faiths. At that time, all children in public schools from the ages of 6 to 18 were required not merely to recite a prayer at the beginning of each school session but to receive religious instruction twice a week. That system continued in the following decades.*

> —Statement by Joachim Prinz, quoted in testimony of Nathan Dershowitz, Hearings on Prayer in Public Schools and Buildings, Committee on the Judiciary, House of Representatives, August 19,1980

Did that program effectively teach morality to the German people? If it did, it would be difficult to explain the rise of Hitler and the total moral collapse and even depravity of many Germans, which resulted in the torture and death of millions of Jews and other minorities.

Another witness, however, testifying in support of prayer in the schools, quoted the report of the President's Commission on the Holocaust, which stated,

> *The Holocaust could not have occurred without the collapse of certain religious norms; increasing secularity fueled a devaluation of the image of the human being created in the likeness of God.*

> —Statement of Judah Glasner, Hearings on Prayer in Public Schools and Buildings, Committee on the Judiciary, House of Representatives, July 30,1980

Relevant cases concerning religion in the public schools are *McCollum v. Board of Education*, 333 U.S. 203 (1948), about religious instruction on school property; *Zorach v. Clauson*, 343 U.S. 306 (1952), regarding free time from school for religious instruction off school property; and *Board of Education of the Westside Community Schools v. Mergens*, 110 S. Ct. 2356 (1990), regarding the use of school premises for an after-school religious club. *Rosenberger v. University of Virginia*, 115 S. Ct. 2510 (1995) involved funding of a student newspaper by a religious group. Recent cases involving the constitutionality of the pledge of allegiance are discussed by Steven G. Gey in "'Under God,' the Pledge of Allegiance, and Other Constitutional Trivia," 81 *North Carolina Law Review* 1865 (2003). For broader discussions about the separation of church and state in America, see Martha Nussbaum, *Liberty of Conscience: In Defense of America's Tradition of Religious Equality* (Basic Books, 2008); Christopher L. Eisengruber & Lawrence G. Sager, *Religious Freedom and the Constitution* (Harvard University Press, 2007); and Peter Irons, *God on Trial: Landmark Cases from America's Religious Battlefields* (Penguin, 2007).

In June 2005, the Supreme Court decided two cases involving the placing of the Ten Commandments in public places. In a Kentucky case, *McCreary County v. ACLU of Kentucky* (545 U.S. 844), the Court found the purpose for the display to be religious and prohibited it. In a Texas case, *Van Orden v. Perry* (545 U.S. 677), the Court found a secular purpose to the display and allowed it. Both decisions were by a 5–4 vote, indicating a significant difference of opinion among the justices and the possibility for further cases involving this issue in the future.

ISSUE 10

Does the First Amendment Protect Picketing a Funeral Even When It Intentionally Inflicts Emotional Distress on the Family?

YES: John Roberts, from Majority Opinion, *Snyder v. Phelps,* U.S. Supreme Court (March 2, 2011)

NO: Samuel Alito, from Dissenting Opinion, *Snyder v. Phelps,* U.S. Supreme Court (March 2, 2011)

ISSUE SUMMARY

YES: Chief Justice John Roberts holds that picketing a soldier's funeral in a way that may be hurtful to those attending is still protected by the First Amendment.

NO: Justice Samuel Alito argues that intentionally inflicting severe emotional injury on private persons should not be considered to be protected speech.

T he main concern of the Framers in adding the free-speech clause of the First Amendment to the Constitution was that the government might criminalize speech with which it disagrees. The Amendment itself is framed explicitly as a limitation on the government to pass laws regulating speech; instead of stating merely that people have a right to free speech, it emphasizes that *"Congress shall make no law . . .* abridging the freedom of speech" (emphasis added). Later, after the addition of the Fourteenth Amendment to the Constitution, the Supreme Court interpreted the clause to apply to state governments as well. As it wrote in the 1925 case *Gitlow v. New York,* "we may and do assume that freedom of speech and of the press which are protected by the First Amendment from abridgment by Congress are among the fundamental personal rights and 'liberties' protected by the due process clause of the Fourteenth Amendment from impairment by the States."[1]

---

[1] 268 U.S. 652, 666 (1925).

Criminal laws are not the only way that the government could suppress the free speech of citizens. As seen in Issue 11, the regulation of speech in public schools—institutions funded and run by the government—can pose First Amendment problems as well. In addition, civil laws—those that allow one individual to sue another for causing him or her harm—define certain types of speech as *torts* or civil wrongs that make the speaker liable to pay monetary damages to the harmed party. Someone who publicly spreads lies to ruin another's reputation can be sued for slander; if those lies are published, the writer may be sued for libel. Recognizing the importance of free speech in American history, U.S. courts have interpreted the First Amendment as setting a high bar to these type of suits—often much higher than in other countries. In an internationally watched trial in 2004, historian Deborah Lipstadt was sued in England by writer David Irving for defamation after publishing a book calling him a Holocaust denier. Even though Lipstadt lived in America and the book was first published here, Irving waited until a British edition of the book came out because English laws make it much easier to sue for libel. Lipstadt was eventually completely exonerated, but not until after a lengthy and expensive trial; had Irving sued in the United States, the case likely would have been thrown out on free-speech grounds before ever going to trial.

In the case from which this chapter's readings are drawn, the Supreme Court had to address whether an extremist group could be held liable for civil damages after being sued for protesting the funeral of a fallen soldier. The Westboro Baptist Church (WBC), a tiny religious sect whose members consist almost exclusively of its founder, Fred Phelps, and his family, has for years attracted attention—and widespread condemnation—for its public demonstrations against organizations and individuals it views as disagreeing with its fundamentalist ideology. Its hateful rhetoric against gays, Jews, and Catholics, among others, has offended such a broad audience that a recent documentary about the Phelpses was titled *The Most Hated Family in America*. In expressing its extreme opposition to homosexuality, the WBC has chosen to protest at events that have little overt connection to gay rights, including pop music concerts, football games, and law school graduation ceremonies. After a protest at a military funeral, the father of a fallen soldier sued the WBC for several torts, including defamation of his deceased son. In the YES reading, Chief Justice John G. Roberts, Jr., writing for an eight-justice majority, argues that the lawsuit must be dismissed because the Phelps family has a First Amendment right to express their views through the funeral protest. Justice Samuel Alito, the lone dissenter, argues in the NO reading that the First Amendment should not cover the Phelpses' actions.

YES ↵

John Roberts

Majority Opinion, *Snyder v. Phelps*

CHIEF JUSTICE ROBERTS delivered the opinion of the Court.

A jury held members of the Westboro Baptist Church liable for millions of dollars in damages for picketing near a soldier's funeral service. The picket signs reflected the church's view that the United States is overly tolerant of sin and that God kills American soldiers as punishment. The question presented is whether the First Amendment shields the church members from tort liability for their speech in this case.

I

A

Fred Phelps founded the Westboro Baptist Church in Topeka, Kansas, in 1955. The church's congregation believes that God hates and punishes the United States for its tolerance of homosexuality, particularly in America's military. The church frequently communicates its views by picketing, often at military funerals. In the more than 20 years that the members of Westboro Baptist have publicized their message, they have picketed nearly 600 funerals. . . .

Marine Lance Corporal Matthew Snyder was killed in Iraq in the line of duty. Lance Corporal Snyder's father selected the Catholic church in the Snyders' hometown of Westminster, Maryland, as the site for his son's funeral. Local newspapers provided notice of the time and location of the service.

Phelps became aware of Matthew Snyder's funeral and decided to travel to Maryland with six other Westboro Baptist parishioners (two of his daughters and four of his grandchildren) to picket. On the day of the memorial service, the Westboro congregation members picketed on public land adjacent to public streets near the Maryland State House, the United States Naval Academy, and Matthew Snyder's funeral. The Westboro picketers carried signs that were largely the same at all three locations. They stated, for instance: "God Hates the USA/Thank God for 9/11," "America is Doomed," "Don't Pray for the USA," "Thank God for IEDs," "Thank God for Dead Soldiers," "Pope in Hell," "Priests Rape Boys," "God Hates Fags," "You're Going to Hell," and "God Hates You."

The church had notified the authorities in advance of its intent to picket at the time of the funeral, and the picketers complied with police instructions in staging their demonstration. The picketing took place within a

Supreme Court of the United States, March 2, 2011.

10- by 25-foot plot of public land adjacent to a public street, behind a temporary fence. . . . That plot was approximately 1,000 feet from the church where the funeral was held. Several buildings separated the picket site from the church. . . . The Westboro picketers displayed their signs for about 30 minutes before the funeral began and sang hymns and recited Bible verses. None of the picketers entered church property or went to the cemetery. They did not yell or use profanity, and there was no violence associated with the picketing. . . .

The funeral procession passed within 200 to 300 feet of the picket site. Although Snyder testified that he could see the tops of the picket signs as he drove to the funeral, he did not see what was written on the signs until later that night, while watching a news broadcast covering the event. . . .

B

Snyder filed suit against Phelps, Phelps's daughters, and the Westboro Baptist Church (collectively Westboro or the church) in the United States District Court for the District of Maryland under that court's diversity jurisdiction. Snyder alleged five state tort law claims: defamation, publicity given to private life, intentional infliction of emotional distress, intrusion upon seclusion, and civil conspiracy. Westboro moved for summary judgment contending, in part, that the church's speech was insulated from liability by the First Amendment. . . .

The District Court awarded Westboro summary judgment on Snyder's claims for defamation and publicity given to private life, concluding that Snyder could not prove the necessary elements of those torts. . . . A trial was held on the remaining claims. At trial, Snyder described the severity of his emotional injuries. He testified that he is unable to separate the thought of his dead son from his thoughts of Westboro's picketing, and that he often becomes tearful, angry, and physically ill when he thinks about it. . . . Expert witnesses testified that Snyder's emotional anguish had resulted in severe depression and had exacerbated preexisting health conditions.

A jury found for Snyder on the intentional infliction of emotional distress, intrusion upon seclusion, and civil conspiracy claims, and held Westboro liable for $2.9 million in compensatory damages and $8 million in punitive damages. Westboro filed several post-trial motions, including a motion contending that the jury verdict was grossly excessive and a motion seeking judgment as a matter of law on all claims on First Amendment grounds. The District Court remitted the punitive damages award to $2.1 million, but left the jury verdict otherwise intact. . . .

In the Court of Appeals, Westboro's primary argument was that the church was entitled to judgment as a matter of law because the First Amendment fully protected Westboro's speech. The Court of Appeals agreed. . . . The court reviewed the picket signs and concluded that Westboro's statements were entitled to First Amendment protection because those statements were on matters of public concern, were not provably false, and were expressed solely through hyperbolic rhetoric. . . .

We granted certiorari. . . .

II

To succeed on a claim for intentional infliction of emotional distress in Maryland, a plaintiff must demonstrate that the defendant intentionally or recklessly engaged in extreme and outrageous conduct that caused the plaintiff to suffer severe emotional distress. . . . The Free Speech Clause of the First Amendment—"Congress shall make no law . . . abridging the freedom of speech"—can serve as a defense in state tort suits, including suits for intentional infliction of emotional distress. . . .

Whether the First Amendment prohibits holding Westboro liable for its speech in this case turns largely on whether that speech is of public or private concern, as determined by all the circumstances of the case. "[S]peech on 'matters of public concern' . . . is 'at the heart of the First Amendment's protection.'" *Dun & Bradstreet, Inc. v. Greenmoss Builders, Inc.,* 472 U.S. 749, 758–759 (1985) (opinion of Powell, J.) (quoting *First Nat. Bank of Boston v. Bellotti,* 435 U.S. 765, 776 (1978)). The First Amendment reflects "a profound national commitment to the principle that debate on public issues should be uninhibited, robust, and wide-open." *New York Times Co. v. Sullivan,* 376 U.S. 254, 270 (1964). That is because "speech concerning public affairs is more than self-expression; it is the essence of self-government." *Garrison v. Louisiana,* 379 U. S. 64, 74–75 (1964). Accordingly, "speech on public issues occupies the highest rung of the hierarchy of First Amendment values, and is entitled to special protection." *Connick v. Myers,* 461 U.S. 138, 145 (1983) (internal quotation marks omitted).

"'[N]ot all speech is of equal First Amendment importance,'" however, and where matters of purely private significance are at issue, First Amendment protections are often less rigorous. . . . That is because restricting speech on purely private matters does not implicate the same constitutional concerns as limiting speech on matters of public interest: "[T]here is no threat to the free and robust debate of public issues; there is no potential interference with a meaningful dialogue of ideas"; and the "threat of liability" does not pose the risk of "a reaction of self-censorship" on matters of public import. . . .

We noted a short time ago, in considering whether public employee speech addressed a matter of public concern, that "the boundaries of the public concern test are not well defined." *San Diego v. Roe,* 543 U.S. 77, 83 (2004) (*per curiam*). Although that remains true today, we have articulated some guiding principles, principles that accord broad protection to speech to ensure that courts themselves do not become inadvertent censors.

Speech deals with matters of public concern when it can "be fairly considered as relating to any matter of political, social, or other concern to the community," . . . when it "is a subject of legitimate news interest; that is, a subject of general interest and of value and concern to the public." . . . The arguably "inappropriate or controversial character of a statement is irrelevant to the question whether it deals with a matter of public concern." . . .

Our opinion in *Dun & Bradstreet,* on the other hand, provides an example of speech of only private concern. In that case we held, as a general matter, that information about a particular individual's credit report "concerns no public issue." . . . The content of the report, we explained, "was speech solely in the individual interest of the speaker and its specific business audience.". . . That was confirmed by the fact that the particular report was sent to only five subscribers to the reporting service, who were bound not to disseminate it further. . . . To cite another example, we concluded in *San Diego v. Roe* that, in the context of a government employer regulating the speech of its employees, videos of an employee engaging in sexually explicit acts did not address a public concern; the videos "did nothing to inform the public about any aspect of the [employing agency's] functioning or operation." . . .

Deciding whether speech is of public or private concern requires us to examine the "'content, form, and context'" of that speech, "'as revealed by the whole record.'" . . . As in other First Amendment cases, the court is obligated "to 'make an independent examination of the whole record' in order to make sure that 'the judgment does not constitute a forbidden intrusion on the field of free expression.'" . . . In considering content, form, and context, no factor is dispositive, and it is necessary to evaluate all the circumstances of the speech, including what was said, where it was said, and how it was said.

The "content" of Westboro's signs plainly relates to broad issues of interest to society at large, rather than matters of "purely private concern." *Dun & Bradstreet, supra,* at 759. The placards read "God Hates the USA/Thank God for 9/11," "America is Doomed," "Don't Pray for the USA," "Thank God for IEDs," "Fag Troops," "Semper Fi Fags," "God Hates Fags," "Maryland Taliban," "Fags Doom Nations," "Not Blessed Just Cursed," "Thank God for Dead Soldiers," "Pope in Hell," "Priests Rape Boys," "You're Going to Hell," and "God Hates You." . . . While these messages may fall short of refined social or political commentary, the issues they highlight—the political and moral conduct of the United States and its citizens, the fate of our Nation, homosexuality in the military, and scandals involving the Catholic clergy—are matters of public import. The signs certainly convey Westboro's position on those issues, in a manner designed, unlike the private speech in *Dun & Bradstreet,* to reach as broad a public audience as possible. And even if a few of the signs—such as "You're Going to Hell" and "God Hates You"—were viewed as containing messages related to Matthew Snyder or the Snyders specifically, that would not change the fact that the overall thrust and dominant theme of Westboro's demonstration spoke to broader public issues.

Apart from the content of Westboro's signs, Snyder contends that the "context" of the speech—its connection with his son's funeral—makes the speech a matter of private rather than public concern. The fact that Westboro spoke in connection with a funeral, however, cannot by itself transform the nature of Westboro's speech. Westboro's signs, displayed on public land next to a public street, reflect the fact that the church finds much to condemn in modern society. Its speech is "fairly characterized as constituting speech on a matter of public concern," . . . the funeral setting does not alter that conclusion.

Snyder argues that the church members in fact mounted a personal attack on Snyder and his family, and then attempted to "immunize their conduct by claiming that they were actually protesting the United States' tolerance of homosexuality or the supposed evils of the Catholic Church." . . . We are not concerned in this case that Westboro's speech on public matters was in any way contrived to insulate speech on a private matter from liability. Westboro had been actively engaged in speaking on the subjects addressed in its picketing long before it became aware of Matthew Snyder, and there can be no serious claim that Westboro's picketing did not represent its "honestly believed" views on public issues. . . . There was no preexisting relationship or conflict between Westboro and Snyder that might suggest Westboro's speech on public matters was intended to mask an attack on Snyder over a private matter. . . .

Snyder goes on to argue that Westboro's speech should be afforded less than full First Amendment protection "not only because of the words" but also because the church members exploited the funeral "as a platform to bring their message to a broader audience." . . . There is no doubt that Westboro chose to stage its picketing at the Naval Academy, the Maryland State House, and Matthew Snyder's funeral to increase publicity for its views and because of the relation between those sites and its views—in the case of the military funeral, because Westboro believes that God is killing American soldiers as punishment for the Nation's sinful policies.

Westboro's choice to convey its views in conjunction with Matthew Snyder's funeral made the expression of those views particularly hurtful to many, especially to Matthew's father. The record makes clear that the applicable legal term—"emotional distress"—fails to capture fully the anguish Westboro's choice added to Mr. Snyder's already incalculable grief. But Westboro conducted its picketing peacefully on matters of public concern at a public place adjacent to a public street. Such space occupies a "special position in terms of First Amendment protection." *United States v. Grace,* 461 U.S. 171, 180 (1983). "[W]e have repeatedly referred to public streets as the archetype of a traditional public forum," noting that "'[t]ime out of mind' public streets and sidewalks have been used for public assembly and debate." *Frisby v. Schultz,* 487 U.S. 474, 480 (1988).[1]

That said, "[e]ven protected speech is not equally permissible in all places and at all times." . . . Westboro's choice of where and when to conduct its picketing is not beyond the Government's regulatory reach—it is "subject to reasonable time, place, or manner restrictions" that are consistent with the standards announced in this Court's precedents. . . . Maryland now has a law imposing restrictions on funeral picketing, . . . as do 43 other States and the Federal Government. . . . To the extent these laws are content neutral, they raise very different questions from the tort verdict at issue in this case. Maryland's law, however, was not in effect at the time of the events at issue here, so we have no occasion to consider how it might apply to facts such as those before us, or whether it or other similar regulations are constitutional.[2]

We have identified a few limited situations where the location of targeted picketing can be regulated under provisions that the Court has determined to be content neutral. In *Frisby,* for example, we upheld a ban on such picketing "before or about" a particular residence, 487 U.S., at 477. In *Madsen v. Women's Health Center, Inc.,* we approved an injunction requiring a buffer zone between protesters and an abortion clinic entrance, 512 U.S. 753, 768 (1994). The facts here are obviously quite different, both with respect to the activity being regulated and the means of restricting those activities.

Simply put, the church members had the right to be where they were. Westboro alerted local authorities to its funeral protest and fully complied with police guidance on where the picketing could be staged. The picketing was conducted under police supervision some 1,000 feet from the church, out of the sight of those at the church. The protest was not unruly; there was no shouting, profanity, or violence.

The record confirms that any distress occasioned by Westboro's picketing turned on the content and viewpoint of the message conveyed, rather than any interference with the funeral itself. A group of parishioners standing at the very spot where Westboro stood, holding signs that said "God Bless America" and "God Loves You," would not have been subjected to liability. It was what Westboro said that exposed it to tort damages.

Given that Westboro's speech was at a public place on a matter of public concern, that speech is entitled to "special protection" under the First Amendment. Such speech cannot be restricted simply because it is upsetting or arouses contempt. "If there is a bedrock principle underlying the First Amendment, it is that the government may not prohibit the expression of an idea simply because society finds the idea itself offensive or disagreeable." *Texas v. Johnson*, 491 U.S. 397, 414 (1989). Indeed, "the point of all speech protection . . . is to shield just those choices of content that in someone's eyes are misguided, or even hurtful." *Hurley v. Irish-American Gay, Lesbian and Bisexual Group of Boston, Inc.*, 515 U.S. 557, 574 (1995).

The jury here was instructed that it could hold Westboro liable for intentional infliction of emotional distress based on a finding that Westboro's picketing was "outrageous." "Outrageousness," however, is a highly malleable standard with "an inherent subjectiveness about it which would allow a jury to impose liability on the basis of the jurors' tastes or views, or perhaps on the basis of their dislike of a particular expression." . . . In a case such as this, a jury is "unlikely to be neutral with respect to the content of [the] speech," posing "a real danger of becoming an instrument for the suppression of . . . 'vehement, caustic, and some times unpleasan[t]'" expression. . . . Such a risk is unacceptable; "in public debate [we] must tolerate insulting, and even outrageous, speech in order to provide adequate 'breathing space' to the freedoms protected by the First Amendment." . . . What Westboro said, in the whole context of how and where it chose to say it, is entitled to "special protection" under the First Amendment, and that protection cannot be overcome by a jury finding that the picketing was outrageous.

For all these reasons, the jury verdict imposing tort liability on Westboro for intentional infliction of emotional distress must be set aside. . . .

IV

Our holding today is narrow. We are required in First Amendment cases to carefully review the record, and the reach of our opinion here is limited by the particular facts before us. As we have noted, "the sensitivity and significance of the interests presented in clashes between First Amendment and [state law] rights counsel relying on limited principles that sweep no more broadly than the appropriate context of the instant case." . . .

Westboro believes that America is morally flawed; many Americans might feel the same about Westboro. Westboro's funeral picketing is certainly hurtful and its contribution to public discourse may be negligible. But Westboro addressed matters of public import on public property, in a peaceful manner, in full compliance with the guidance of local officials. The speech was indeed planned to coincide with Matthew Snyder's funeral, but did not itself disrupt that funeral, and Westboro's choice to conduct its picketing at that time and place did not alter the nature of its speech.

Speech is powerful. It can stir people to action, move them to tears of both joy and sorrow, and—as it did here—inflict great pain. On the facts before us, we cannot react to that pain by punishing the speaker. As a Nation we have chosen a different course—to protect even hurtful speech on public issues to ensure that we do not stifle public debate. That choice requires that we shield Westboro from tort liability for its picketing in this case.

The judgment of the United States Court of Appeals for the Fourth Circuit is affirmed.

It is so ordered.

Notes

1. The dissent is wrong to suggest that the Court considers a public street "a free-fire zone in which otherwise actionable verbal attacks are shielded from liability." . . . The fact that Westboro conducted its picketing adjacent to a public street does not insulate the speech from liability, but instead heightens concerns that what is at issue is an effort to communicate to the public the church's views on matters of public concern. That is why our precedents so clearly recognize the special significance of this traditional public forum.

2. The Maryland law prohibits picketing within 100 feet of a funeral service or funeral procession; Westboro's picketing would have complied with that restriction.

Dissenting Opinion,
Snyder v. Phelps

J USTICE ALITO, dissenting.

Our profound national commitment to free and open debate is not a license for the vicious verbal assault that occurred in this case.

Petitioner Albert Snyder is not a public figure. He is simply a parent whose son, Marine Lance Corporal Matthew Snyder, was killed in Iraq. Mr. Snyder wanted what is surely the right of any parent who experiences such an incalculable loss: to bury his son in peace. But respondents, members of the Westboro Baptist Church, deprived him of that elementary right. They first issued a press release and thus turned Matthew's funeral into a tumultuous media event. They then appeared at the church, approached as closely as they could without trespassing, and launched a malevolent verbal attack on Matthew and his family at a time of acute emotional vulnerability. As a result, Albert Snyder suffered severe and lasting emotional injury. The Court now holds that the First Amendment protected respondents' right to brutalize Mr. Snyder. I cannot agree.

I

Respondents and other members of their church have strong opinions on certain moral, religious, and political issues, and the First Amendment ensures that they have almost limitless opportunities to express their views. They may write and distribute books, articles, and other texts; they may create and disseminate video and audio recordings; they may circulate petitions; they may speak to individuals and groups in public forums and in any private venue that wishes to accommodate them; they may picket peacefully in countless locations; they may appear on television and speak on the radio; they may post messages on the Internet and send out e-mails. And they may express their views in terms that are "uninhibited," "vehement," and "caustic." *New York Times Co. v. Sullivan*, 376 U.S. 254, 270 (1964).

It does not follow, however, that they may intentionally inflict severe emotional injury on private persons at a time of intense emotional sensitivity by launching vicious verbal attacks that make no contribution to public debate. To protect against such injury, "most if not all jurisdictions" permit recovery in tort for the intentional infliction of emotional distress (or IIED). . . .

Supreme Court of the United States, March 2, 2011.

This is a very narrow tort with requirements that "are rigorous, and difficult to satisfy." . . . To recover, a plaintiff must show that the conduct at issue caused harm that was truly severe. . . .

A plaintiff must also establish that the defendant's conduct was "'so outrageous in character, and so extreme in degree, as to go beyond all possible bounds of decency, and to be regarded as atrocious, and utterly intolerable in a civilized community.'" . . .

Although the elements of the IIED tort are difficult to meet, respondents long ago abandoned any effort to show that those tough standards were not satisfied here. On appeal, they chose not to contest the sufficiency of the evidence. . . . They did not dispute that Mr. Snyder suffered "'wounds that are truly severe and incapable of healing themselves.'" . . . Nor did they dispute that their speech was "'so outrageous in character, and so extreme in degree, as to go beyond all possible bounds of decency, and to be regarded as atrocious, and utterly intolerable in a civilized community.'" . . . Instead, they maintained that the First Amendment gave them a license to engage in such conduct. They are wrong.

II

It is well established that a claim for the intentional infliction of emotional distress can be satisfied by speech. . . . And although this Court has not decided the question, I think it is clear that the First Amendment does not entirely preclude liability for the intentional infliction of emotional distress by means of speech.

This Court has recognized that words may "by their very utterance inflict injury" and that the First Amendment does not shield utterances that form "no essential part of any exposition of ideas, and are of such slight social value as a step to truth that any benefit that may be derived from them is clearly outweighed by the social interest in order and morality." *Chaplinsky v. New Hampshire*, 315 U.S. 568, 572 (1942); see also *Cantwell v. Connecticut*, 310 U.S. 296, 310 (1940) ("[P]ersonal abuse is not in any proper sense communication of information or opinion safeguarded by the Constitution"). When grave injury is intentionally inflicted by means of an attack like the one at issue here, the First Amendment should not interfere with recovery.

III

In this case, respondents brutally attacked Matthew Snyder, and this attack, which was almost certain to inflict injury, was central to respondents' well-practiced strategy for attracting public attention.

On the morning of Matthew Snyder's funeral, respondents could have chosen to stage their protest at countless locations. They could have picketed the United States Capitol, the White House, the Supreme Court, the Pentagon, or any of the more than 5,600 military recruiting stations in this country. They could have returned to the Maryland State House or the United States Naval Academy, where they had been the day before. They could have selected any public road where pedestrians are allowed. (There are more than 4,000,000 miles of public roads in the United States.) They could have staged their protest in a public park. (There are more than 20,000 public parks in this country.) They could have chosen any Catholic church where no funeral was taking place. (There are nearly 19,000 Catholic churches in the United States.) But of course, a small group picketing at any of these locations would have probably gone unnoticed.

The Westboro Baptist Church, however, has devised a strategy that remedies this problem. As the Court notes, church members have protested at nearly 600 military funerals. . . . They have also picketed the funerals of police officers, firefighters, and the victims of natural disasters, accidents, and shocking crimes. And in advance of these protests, they issue press releases to ensure that their protests will attract public attention.

This strategy works because it is expected that respondents' verbal assaults will wound the family and friends of the deceased and because the media is irresistibly drawn to the sight of persons who are visibly in grief. The more outrageous the funeral protest, the more publicity the Westboro Baptist Church is able to obtain. Thus, when the church recently announced its intention to picket the funeral of a 9-year-old girl killed in the shooting spree in Tucson—proclaiming that she was "better off dead"—their announcement was national news, and the church was able to obtain free air time on the radio in exchange for canceling its protest. Similarly, in 2006, the church got air time on a talk radio show in exchange for canceling its threatened protest at the funeral of five Amish girls killed by a crazed gunman.

In this case, respondents implemented the Westboro Baptist Church's publicity-seeking strategy. Their press release stated that they were going "to picket the funeral of Lance Cpl. Matthew A. Snyder" because "God Almighty killed Lance Cpl. Snyder. He died in shame, not honor—for a fag nation cursed by God . . . . Now in Hell—sine die." . . . This announcement guaranteed that Matthew's funeral would be transformed into a raucous media event and began the wounding process. It is well known that anticipation may heighten the effect of a painful event.

On the day of the funeral, respondents, true to their word, displayed placards that conveyed the message promised in their press release. Signs stating "God Hates You" and "Thank God for Dead Soldiers" reiterated the message that God had caused Matthew's death in retribution for his sins. . . . Others, stating "You're Going to Hell" and "Not Blessed Just Cursed," conveyed the message that Matthew was "in Hell—sine die." . . .

Even if those who attended the funeral were not alerted in advance about respondents' intentions, the meaning of these signs would not have been missed. Since respondents chose to stage their protest at Matthew Snyder's funeral and not at any of the other countless available venues, a reasonable person would have assumed that there was a connection between the messages on the placards and the deceased. Moreover, since a church funeral is an event that naturally brings to mind thoughts about the afterlife, some of respondents' signs—e.g., "God Hates You," "Not Blessed Just Cursed," and "You're Going to Hell"—would have likely been interpreted as referring to God's judgment of the deceased.

Other signs would most naturally have been understood as suggesting—falsely—that Matthew was gay. Homosexuality was the theme of many of the signs. There were signs reading "God Hates Fags," "Semper Fi Fags," "Fags Doom Nations," and "Fag Troops." . . . Another placard depicted two men engaging in anal intercourse. A reasonable bystander seeing those signs would have likely concluded that they were meant to suggest that the deceased was a homosexual. . . .

In light of this evidence, it is abundantly clear that respondents, going far beyond commentary on matters of public concern, specifically attacked Matthew Snyder because (1) he was a Catholic and (2) he was a member of the United States military. Both Matthew and petitioner were private figures, and this attack was not speech on a matter of public concern. While commentary on the Catholic Church or the United States military constitutes speech on matters of public concern, speech regarding Matthew Snyder's purely private conduct does not. . . .

IV

The Court concludes that respondents' speech was protected by the First Amendment for essentially three reasons, but none is sound.

First—and most important—the Court finds that "the overall thrust and dominant theme of [their] demonstration spoke to" broad public issues. . . . As I have attempted to show, this portrayal is quite inaccurate; respondents' attack on Matthew was of central importance. But in any event, I fail to see why actionable speech should be immunized simply because it is interspersed with speech that is protected. The First Amendment allows recovery for defamatory statements that are interspersed with nondefamatory statements on matters of public concern, and there is no good reason why respondents' attack on Matthew Snyder and his family should be treated differently.

Second, the Court suggests that respondents' personal attack on Matthew Snyder is entitled to First Amendment protection because it was not motivated by a private grudge, . . . but I see no basis for the strange distinction that the Court appears to draw. Respondents' motivation—"to increase publicity for its views," . . .—did not transform their statements attacking the character of a private figure into statements that made a contribution to debate on matters of public concern. Nor did their publicity-seeking motivation soften the sting of their attack. And as far as culpability is concerned, one might well think that wounding statements uttered in the heat of a private feud are less, not more, blameworthy than similar statements made as part of a cold and calculated strategy to slash a stranger as a means of attracting public attention.

Third, the Court finds it significant that respondents' protest occurred on a public street, but this fact alone should not be enough to preclude IIED liability. To be sure, statements made on a public street may be less likely to satisfy the elements of the IIED tort than statements made on private property, but there is no reason why a public street in close proximity to the scene of a funeral should be regarded as a free-fire zone in which otherwise actionable verbal attacks are shielded from liability. If the First Amendment permits the

States to protect their residents from the harm inflicted by such attacks—and the Court does not hold otherwise—then the location of the tort should not be dispositive. A physical assault may occur without trespassing; it is no defense that the perpetrator had "the right to be where [he was]." . . . And the same should be true with respect to unprotected speech. Neither classic "fighting words" nor defamatory statements are immunized when they occur in a public place, and there is no good reason to treat a verbal assault based on the conduct or character of a private figure like Matthew Snyder any differently.

One final comment about the opinion of the Court is in order. The Court suggests that the wounds inflicted by vicious verbal assaults at funerals will be prevented or at least mitigated in the future by new laws that restrict picketing within a specified distance of a funeral. . . . It is apparent, however, that the enactment of these laws is no substitute for the protection provided by the established IIED tort; according to the Court, the verbal attacks that severely wounded petitioner in this case complied with the new Maryland law regulating funeral picketing. . . . And there is absolutely nothing to suggest that Congress and the state legislatures, in enacting these laws, intended them to displace the protection provided by the well-established IIED tort.

The real significance of these new laws is not that they obviate the need for IIED protection. Rather, their enactment dramatically illustrates the fundamental point that funerals are unique events at which special protection against emotional assaults is in order. At funerals, the emotional well-being of bereaved relatives is particularly vulnerable. . . . Exploitation of a funeral for the purpose of attracting public attention "intrud[es] upon their . . . grief," . . . and may permanently stain their memories of the final moments before a loved one is laid to rest. Allowing family members to have a few hours of peace without harassment does not undermine public debate. I would therefore hold that, in this setting, the First Amendment permits a private figure to recover for the intentional infliction of emotional distress caused by speech on a matter of private concern. . . .

VI

Respondents' outrageous conduct caused petitioner great injury, and the Court now compounds that injury by depriving petitioner of a judgment that acknowledges the wrong he suffered.

In order to have a society in which public issues can be openly and vigorously debated, it is not necessary to allow the brutalization of innocent victims like petitioner. I therefore respectfully dissent.

POSTSCRIPT

Does the First Amendment Protect Picketing a Funeral Even When It Intentionally Inflicts Emotional Distress on the Family?

If the WBC members had physically attacked Mr. Snyder, there would be no question that they could be sued for their actions (and, additionally, arrested). However, this case illustrates that it is much more difficult for society to regulate the harm caused by words than by actions. Justice Alito attempts to undermine the majority's opinion protecting the WBC from tort liability by arguing the Mr. Snyder was the victim of a "vicious verbal assault." The First Amendment, Alito argues, is not a license for "the brutalization of innocent victims." However, while not denying that speech can "inflict great pain," Chief Justice Roberts refuses to accept the analogy between assault and hateful speech. The First Amendment would mean little, he suggests, if it only protected speech that had no possibility of offending someone. If society attempted to protect people from the harm caused by speech in the same way it protects people from the harm caused by a physical attack, then there would be no end to the type of speech regulations that could be enacted in the name of public safety. As Roberts points out, the First Amendment exists precisely to ensure that the government cannot impose its views of appropriate speech on citizens. On this view, the existence of hate speech is unfortunate, but it is the price we must pay if we are to live in a free society.

Free speech and the First Amendment are the subjects of an enormous number of books and law articles; some good recent works to being with include C. Edwin Baker, *Human Liberty and Freedom of Speech* (Oxford University Press, 1992); Mark Graber, *Transforming Free Speech: The Ambiguous Legacy of Civil Libertarianism* (University of California Press, 1991); Cass Sunstein, *Democracy and the Problem of Free Speech* (Free Press, 1995); and Eric Barendt, *Freedom of Speech*, 2nd ed. (Oxford University Press, 2007). For background on torts and the laws governing civil suits between individuals, see M. Stuart Madden (ed.), *Exploring Tort Law* (Cambridge University Press, 2005) and G. Edward White, *Tort Law in America: An Intellectual History* (Oxford University Press, 2003). The particulars of *Snyder v. Phelps* and the legal issued involved are discussed in the following law review articles, although all were written before the Supreme Court handed down its decision: Eugene Volokh, "Freedom of Speech and the Intentional Infliction of Emotional Distress Tort" 2010 *Cardozo Law Review De Novo* 300 (2010); Clay

Calvert, "Dying for Privacy: Pitting Public Access Against Familial Interests in the Era of the Internet" 105 *Northwestern University Law Review Colloquy* 18 (August 2010); and Christina Wells, "Regulating Offensiveness: *Snyder v. Phelps*, Emotion, and the First Amendment" 1 *California Law Review Circuit* 71 (October 2010).

ISSUE 11

Can a School Punish a Student for Speech at a School-Supervised Event Off of School Grounds When That Speech Could Be Viewed as Promoting Illegal Drug Use?

YES: John Roberts, from Majority Opinion, *Deborah Morse, et. al., v. Joseph Frederick*, U.S. Supreme Court (June 25, 2007)

NO: John Paul Stevens, from Dissenting Opinion, *Deborah Morse, et al., v. Joseph Frederick*, U.S. Supreme Court (June 25, 2007)

ISSUE SUMMARY

YES: Supreme Court Chief Justice John Roberts rules that a student's First Amendment rights are not violated by restrictions on speech that can reasonably be regarded as encouraging illegal drug use.

NO: Supreme Court Justice John Paul Stevens argues that an ambiguous reference to drugs does not justify limiting a student's speech.

There are several selections in this book that involve student rights, and some link to drug use. In two of the issues, the legal question concerns privacy. In one of them, the Court had to consider whether a strip search of a student thought to be in possession of a drug violated the Fourth Amendment. In another, the Court focused on the issue of drug testing and under what circumstances drug testing could be required even when actual drug use by the student is not suspected. The issue under consideration here is different in that the primary legal issue is the First Amendment and freedom of expression.

In this case, some students at a school-supervised event occurring outside the school building held up a banner stating, "BONG HITS 4 JESUS." The principal requested that the students fold up the banner, but one student refused and was suspended. The student sued, claiming that his First Amendment rights of free speech had been violated. The school claimed that the sign could reasonably be interpreted to be encouraging drug use and that this justified a restriction on the student's speech.

This is a case that not only was decided by a 5–4 vote at the Supreme Court but that involved a significant disagreement in the lower courts. The District Court, the first court to hear the case, had found no violation of free speech rights. The Court of Appeals reversed, finding that while the banner may have expressed approval of marijuana use, there was no threat of the speech causing any disruption and, therefore, the suspension was unwarranted.

The only points of agreement in these lower-court opinions seem to have been that while students in public schools do have First Amendment rights, they also do not enjoy all the rights of someone who is speaking outside the school context. The challenge for the Supreme Court was to clarify when and in what circumstances the rights of a student might be limited. As you read the case, consider whether the Court is successful in achieving this goal.

Relatively few cases are cited in the opinions, largely because there have been relatively few cases involving free speech in schools. This was the first Supreme Court decision in more than 20 years and only the fourth case in 40 years that focused on the First Amendment rights of students. In the first of these, *Tinker v. Des Moines Independent Community School District* (1969), the Court ruled in favor of students who were protesting the Vietnam War by wearing armbands to school. In the two cases from the 1980s, *Bethel School District v. Fraser* (1986) and *Hazelwood School District v. Kuhlmeier* (1988), the Court ruled against the students. The first of these involved a speech that contained many sexual innuendos by a student. The second involved censorship of the school newspaper.

YES ↵

John Roberts

Majority Opinion, *Deborah Morse, et al., v. Joseph Frederick*

CHIEF JUSTICE ROBERTS delivered the opinion of the Court.

At a school-sanctioned and school-supervised event, a high school principal saw some of her students unfurl a large banner conveying a message she reasonably regarded as promoting illegal drug use. Consistent with established school policy prohibiting such messages at school events, the principal directed the students to take down the banner. One student—among those who had brought the banner to the event—refused to do so. The principal confiscated the banner and later suspended the student. The Ninth Circuit held that the principal's actions violated the First Amendment, and that the student could sue the principal for damages.

Our cases make clear that students do not "shed their constitutional rights to freedom of speech or expression at the schoolhouse gate." *Tinker v. Des Moines Independent Community School Dist.*, 393 U.S. 503, 506 (1969). At the same time, we have held that "the constitutional rights of students in public school are not automatically coextensive with the rights of adults in other settings," *Bethel School Dist. No. 403 v. Fraser*, 478 U.S. 675, 682 (1986), and that the rights of students "must be 'applied in light of the special characteristics of the school environment.'" *Hazelwood School Dist. v. Kuhlmeier*, 484 U.S. 260, 266 (1988) (quoting *Tinker, supra*, at 506). Consistent with these principles, we hold that schools may take steps to safeguard those entrusted to their care from speech that can reasonably be regarded as encouraging illegal drug use. We conclude that the school officials in this case did not violate the First Amendment by confiscating the pro-drug banner and suspending the student responsible for it.

I

On January 24, 2002, the Olympic Torch Relay passed through Juneau, Alaska, on its way to the winter games in Salt Lake City, Utah. The torchbearers were to proceed along a street in front of Juneau-Douglas High School (JDHS) while school was in session. Petitioner Deborah Morse, the school principal, decided to permit staff and students to participate in the Torch Relay as an approved social event or class trip. . . . Students were allowed to leave class to observe

From Supreme Court of the United States, June 25, 2007.

the relay from either side of the street. Teachers and administrative officials monitored the students' actions.

Respondent Joseph Frederick, a JDHS senior, was late to school that day. When he arrived, he joined his friends (all but one of whom were JDHS students) across the street from the school to watch the event. Not all the students waited patiently. Some became rambunctious, throwing plastic cola bottles and snowballs and scuffling with their classmates. As the torchbearers and camera crews passed by, Frederick and his friends unfurled a 14-foot banner bearing the phrase: "BONG HiTS 4 JESUS." . . . The large banner was easily readable by the students on the other side of the street.

Principal Morse immediately crossed the street and demanded that the banner be taken down. Everyone but Frederick complied. Morse confiscated the banner and told Frederick to report to her office, where she suspended him for 10 days. Morse later explained that she told Frederick to take the banner down because she thought it encouraged illegal drug use, in violation of established school policy. Juneau School Board Policy No. 5520 states: "The Board specifically prohibits any assembly or public expression that . . . advocates the use of substances that are illegal to minors. . . ." *Id.*, at 53a. In addition, Juneau School Board Policy No. 5850 subjects "[p]upils who participate in approved social events and class trips" to the same student conduct rules that apply during the regular school program. *Id.*, at 58a.

Frederick administratively appealed his suspension, but the Juneau School District Superintendent upheld it, limiting it to time served (8 days). In a memorandum setting forth his reasons, the superintendent determined that Frederick had displayed his banner "in the midst of his fellow students, during school hours, at a school-sanctioned activity." *Id.*, at 63a. He further explained that Frederick "was not disciplined because the principal of the school 'disagreed' with his message, but because his speech appeared to advocate the use of illegal drugs." *Id.*, at 61a.

The superintendent continued:

> "The common-sense understanding of the phrase 'bong hits' is that it is a reference to a means of smoking marijuana. Given [Frederick's] inability or unwillingness to express any other credible meaning for the phrase, I can only agree with the principal and countless others who saw the banner as advocating the use of illegal drugs. [Frederick's] speech was not political. He was not advocating the legalization of marijuana or promoting a religious belief. He was displaying a fairly silly message promoting illegal drug usage in the midst of a school activity, for the benefit of television cameras covering the Torch Relay. [Frederick's] speech was potentially disruptive to the event and clearly disruptive of and inconsistent with the school's educational mission to educate students about the dangers of illegal drugs and to discourage their use." *Id.*, at 61a–62a.

Relying on our decision in *Fraser,* . . . the superintendent concluded that the principal's actions were permissible because Frederick's banner was "speech or action that intrudes upon the work of the schools." . . . The Juneau School District Board of Education upheld the suspension.

Frederick then filed suit under 42 U. S. C. §1983, alleging that the school board and Morse had violated his First Amendment rights. He sought declaratory and injunctive relief, unspecified compensatory damages, punitive damages, and attorney's fees. The District Court granted summary judgment for the school board and Morse, ruling that they were entitled to qualified immunity and that they had not infringed Frederick's First Amendment rights. The court found that Morse reasonably interpreted the banner as promoting illegal drug use—a message that "directly contravened the Board's policies relating to drug abuse prevention." . . . Under the circumstances, the court held that "Morse had the authority, if not the obligation, to stop such messages at a school-sanctioned activity." . . .

The Ninth Circuit reversed. Deciding that Frederick acted during a "school-authorized activit[y]," and "proceed[ing] on the basis that the banner expressed a positive sentiment about marijuana use," the court nonetheless found a violation of Frederick's First Amendment rights because the school punished Frederick without demonstrating that his speech gave rise to a "risk of substantial disruption." 439 F. 3d 1114, 1118, 1121–1123 (2006). The court further concluded that Frederick's right to display his banner was so "clearly established" that a reasonable principal in Morse's position would have understood that her actions were unconstitutional, and that Morse was therefore not entitled to qualified immunity. . . .

We granted certiorari on two questions: whether Frederick had a First Amendment right to wield his banner, and, if so, whether that right was so clearly established that the principal may be held liable for damages. . . . We resolve the first question against Frederick, and therefore have no occasion to reach the second.

II

At the outset, we reject Frederick's argument that this is not a school speech case—as has every other authority to address the question. . . . The event occurred during normal school hours. It was sanctioned by Principal Morse "as an approved social event or class trip," . . . and the school district's rules expressly provide that pupils in "approved social events and class trips are subject to district rules for student conduct." . . . Teachers and administrators were interspersed among the students and charged with supervising them. The high school band and cheerleaders performed. Frederick, standing among other JDHS students across the street from the school, directed his banner toward the school, making it plainly visible to most students. Under these circumstances, we agree with the superintendent that Frederick cannot "stand in the midst of his fellow students, during school hours, at a school-sanctioned activity and claim he is not at school." . . . There is some uncertainty at the outer boundaries as to when courts should apply school-speech precedents, see *Porter v. Ascension Parish School Bd.*, 393 F. 3d 608, 615, n. 22 (CA5 2004), but not on these facts.

III

The message on Frederick's banner is cryptic. It is no doubt offensive to some, perhaps amusing to others. To still others, it probably means nothing at all. Frederick himself claimed "that the words were just nonsense meant to attract television cameras." 439 F. 3d, at 1117–1118. But Principal Morse thought the banner would be interpreted by those viewing it as promoting illegal drug use, and that interpretation is plainly a reasonable one.

As Morse later explained in a declaration, when she saw the sign, she thought that "the reference to a 'bong hit' would be widely understood by high school students and others as referring to smoking marijuana." . . . She further believed that "display of the banner would be construed by students, District personnel, parents and others witnessing the display of the banner, as advocating or promoting illegal drug use"—in violation of school policy. . . . ("I told Frederick and the other members of his group to put the banner down because I felt that it violated the [school] policy against displaying . . . material that advertises or promotes use of illegal drugs").

We agree with Morse. At least two interpretations of the words on the banner demonstrate that the sign advocated the use of illegal drugs. First, the phrase could be interpreted as an imperative: "[Take] bong hits . . ."—a message equivalent, as Morse explained in her declaration, to "smoke marijuana" or "use an illegal drug." Alternatively, the phrase could be viewed as celebrating drug use—"bong hits [are a good thing]," or "[we take] bong hits"—and we discern no meaningful distinction between celebrating illegal drug use in the midst of fellow students and outright advocacy or promotion. See *Guiles v. Marineau,* 461 F. 3d 320, 328 (CA2 2006) (discussing the present case and describing the sign as "a clearly pro-drug banner").

The pro-drug interpretation of the banner gains further plausibility given the paucity of alternative meanings the banner might bear. The best Frederick can come up with is that the banner is "meaningless and funny." 439 F. 3d, at 1116. The dissent similarly refers to the sign's message as "curious," *post,* at 1, "ambiguous," *ibid.,* "nonsense," *post,* at 2, "ridiculous," *post,* at 6, "obscure," *post,* at 7, "silly," *post,* at 12, "quixotic," *post,* at 13, and "stupid," *ibid.* Gibberish is surely a possible interpretation of the words on the banner, but it is not the only one, and dismissing the banner as meaningless ignores its undeniable reference to illegal drugs.

The dissent mentions Frederick's "credible and uncontradicted explanation for the message—he just wanted to get on television." . . . But that is a description of Frederick's *motive* for displaying the banner; it is not an interpretation of what the banner says. The *way* Frederick was going to fulfill his ambition of appearing on television was by unfurling a pro-drug banner at a school event, in the presence of teachers and fellow students.

Elsewhere in its opinion, the dissent emphasizes the importance of political speech and the need to foster "national debate about a serious issue," . . . as if to suggest that the banner is political speech. But not even Frederick argues that the banner conveys any sort of political or religious message. Contrary to the dissent's suggestion, . . . this is plainly not a case about political debate over the criminalization of drug use or possession.

IV

The question thus becomes whether a principal may, consistent with the First Amendment, restrict student speech at a school event, when that speech is reasonably viewed as promoting illegal drug use. We hold that she may.

In *Tinker,* this Court made clear that "First Amendment rights, applied in light of the special characteristics of the school environment, are available to teachers and students." 393 U.S., at 506. *Tinker* involved a group of high school students who decided to wear black armbands to protest the Vietnam War. School officials learned of the plan and then adopted a policy prohibiting students from wearing armbands. When several students nonetheless wore armbands to school, they were suspended. *Id.,* at 504. The students sued, claiming that their First Amendment rights had been violated, and this Court agreed.

Tinker held that student expression may not be suppressed unless school officials reasonably conclude that it will "materially and substantially disrupt the work and discipline of the school." . . . The essential facts of *Tinker* are quite stark, implicating concerns at the heart of the First Amendment. The students sought to engage in political speech, using the armbands to express their "disapproval of the Vietnam hostilities and their advocacy of a truce, to make their views known, and, by their example, to influence others to adopt them." . . . Political speech, of course, is "at the core of what the First Amendment is designed to protect." *Virginia v. Black,* 538 U.S. 343, 365 (2003). The only interest the Court discerned underlying the school's actions was the "mere desire to avoid the discomfort and unpleasantness that always accompany an unpopular viewpoint," or "an urgent wish to avoid the controversy which might result from the expression." *Tinker,* 393 U.S., at 509, 510. That interest was not enough to justify banning "a silent, passive expression of opinion, unaccompanied by any disorder or disturbance." *Id.,* at 508.

This Court's next student speech case was *Fraser,* 478 U.S. 675. Matthew Fraser was suspended for delivering a speech before a high school assembly in which he employed what this Court called "an elaborate, graphic, and explicit sexual metaphor." . . . Analyzing the case under *Tinker,* the District Court and Court of Appeals found no disruption, and therefore no basis for disciplining Fraser. 478 U.S., at 679–680. This Court reversed, holding that the "School District acted entirely within its permissible authority in imposing sanctions upon Fraser in response to his offensively lewd and indecent speech." . . .

The mode of analysis employed in *Fraser* is not entirely clear. The Court was plainly attuned to the content of Fraser's speech, citing the "marked distinction between the political 'message' of the armbands in *Tinker* and the sexual content of [Fraser's] speech." . . . But the Court also reasoned that school boards have the authority to determine "what manner of speech in the classroom or in school assembly is inappropriate." *Id.,* at 683. Cf. *id.,* at 689 (Brennan, J., concurring in judgment) ("In the present case, school officials sought only to ensure that a high school assembly proceed in an orderly manner. There is no suggestion that school officials attempted to regulate [Fraser's] speech because they disagreed with the views he sought to express").

We need not resolve this debate to decide this case. For present purposes, it is enough to distill from *Fraser* two basic principles. First, *Fraser's* holding demonstrates that "the constitutional rights of students in public school are not automatically coextensive with the rights of adults in other settings." . . . Had Fraser delivered the same speech in a public forum outside the school context, it would have been protected. See *Cohen v. California*, 403 U.S. 15 (1971); *Fraser, supra*, at 682–683. In school, however, Fraser's First Amendment rights were circumscribed "in light of the special characteristics of the school environment." *Tinker, supra*, at 506. Second, *Fraser* established that the mode of analysis set forth in *Tinker* is not absolute. Whatever approach *Fraser* employed, it certainly did not conduct the "substantial disruption" analysis prescribed by *Tinker, supra*, at 514. See *Kuhlmeier*, 484 U.S., at 271, n. 4 (disagreeing with the proposition that there is "no difference between the First Amendment analysis applied in *Tinker* and that applied in *Fraser*," and noting that the holding in *Fraser* was not based on any showing of substantial disruption).

Our most recent student speech case, *Kuhlmeier*, concerned "expressive activities that students, parents, and members of the public might reasonably perceive to bear the imprimatur of the school." 484 U.S., at 271. Staff members of a high school newspaper sued their school when it chose not to publish two of their articles. The Court of Appeals analyzed the case under *Tinker*, ruling in favor of the students because it found no evidence of material disruption to classwork or school discipline. 795 F. 2d 1368, 1375 (CA8 1986). This Court reversed, holding that "educators do not offend the First Amendment by exercising editorial control over the style and content of student speech in school-sponsored expressive activities so long as their actions are reasonably related to legitimate pedagogical concerns." *Kuhlmeier, supra*, at 273.

Kuhlmeier does not control this case because no one would reasonably believe that Frederick's banner bore the school's imprimatur. The case is nevertheless instructive because it confirms both principles cited above. *Kuhlmeier* acknowledged that schools may regulate some speech "even though the government could not censor similar speech outside the school." *Id.*, at 266. And, like *Fraser*, it confirms that the rule of *Tinker* is not the only basis for restricting student speech.

Drawing on the principles applied in our student speech cases, we have held in the Fourth Amendment context that "while children assuredly do not 'shed their constitutional rights . . . at the schoolhouse gate,' . . . the nature of those rights is what is appropriate for children in school." *Vernonia School Dist. 47J v. Acton*, 515 U.S. 646, 655–656 (1995) (quoting *Tinker, supra*, at 506). In particular, "the school setting requires some easing of the restrictions to which searches by public authorities are ordinarily subject." *New Jersey v. T. L. O.*, 469 U.S. 325, 340 (1985). See *Vernonia, supra*, at 656 ("Fourth Amendment rights, no less than First and Fourteenth Amendment rights, are different in public schools than elsewhere . . ."); *Board of Ed. of Independent School Dist. No. 92 of Pottawatomie Cty. v. Earls*, 536 U.S. 822, 829–830 (2002) ("'special needs' inhere in the public school context"; "[w]hile schoolchildren do not shed their constitutional rights when they enter the schoolhouse, Fourth Amendment rights . . . are different in public schools than elsewhere; the 'reasonableness' inquiry cannot disregard the schools' custodial and tutelary responsibility for children" (quoting *Vernonia*, 515 U.S., at 656; citation and some internal quotation marks omitted).

Even more to the point, these cases also recognize that deterring drug use by schoolchildren is an "important—indeed, perhaps compelling" interest. *Id.*, at 661. Drug abuse can cause severe and permanent damage to the health and well-being of young people:

> "School years are the time when the physical, psychological, and addictive effects of drugs are most severe. Maturing nervous systems are more critically impaired by intoxicants than mature ones are; childhood losses in learning are lifelong and profound; children grow chemically dependent more quickly than adults, and their record of recovery is depressingly poor. And of course the effects of a drug-infested school are visited not just upon the users, but upon the entire student body and faculty, as the educational process is disrupted." *Id.*, at 661–662 (citations and internal quotation marks omitted).

Just five years ago, we wrote: "The drug abuse problem among our Nation's youth has hardly abated since *Vernonia* was decided in 1995. In fact, evidence suggests that it has only grown worse." *Earls, supra,* at 834, and n. 5.

The problem remains serious today. See generally 1 National Institute on Drug Abuse, National Institutes of Health, Monitoring the Future: National Survey Results on Drug Use, 1975–2005, Secondary School Students (2006). About half of American 12th graders have used an illicit drug, as have more than a third of 10th graders and about one-fifth of 8th graders. *Id.*, at 99. Nearly one in four 12th graders has used an illicit drug in the past month. *Id.*, at 101. Some 25% of high schoolers say that they have been offered, sold, or given an illegal drug on school property within the past year. Dept. of Health and Human Services, Centers for Disease Control and Prevention, Youth Risk Behavior Surveillance—United States, 2005, 55 Morbidity and Mortality Weekly Report, Surveillance Summaries, No. SS-5, p. 19 (June 9, 2006).

Congress has declared that part of a school's job is educating students about the dangers of illegal drug use. It has provided billions of dollars to support state and local drug-prevention programs, . . . and required that schools receiving federal funds under the Safe and Drug-Free Schools and Communities Act of 1994 certify that their drug prevention programs "convey a clear and consistent message that . . . the illegal use of drugs [is] wrong and harmful." 20 U. S. C. §7114(d)(6) (2000 ed., Supp. IV).

Thousands of school boards throughout the country—including JDHS—have adopted policies aimed at effectuating this message. . . . Those school boards know that peer pressure is perhaps "the single most important factor leading schoolchildren to take drugs," and that students are more likely to use drugs when the norms in school appear to tolerate such behavior. . . . Student speech celebrating illegal drug use at a school event, in the presence of school administrators and teachers, thus poses a particular challenge for school officials working to protect those entrusted to their care from the dangers of drug abuse.

The "special characteristics of the school environment," *Tinker*, 393 U.S., at 506, and the governmental interest in stopping student drug abuse—reflected in the policies of Congress and myriad school boards, including JDHS—allow schools to restrict student expression that they reasonably regard as promoting illegal drug use. *Tinker* warned that schools may not prohibit student speech because of "undifferentiated fear or apprehension of disturbance" or "a mere desire to avoid the discomfort and unpleasantness that always accompany an unpopular viewpoint." *Id.*, at 508, 509. The danger here is far more serious and palpable. The particular concern to prevent student drug abuse at issue here, embodied in established school policy, . . . extends well beyond an abstract desire to avoid controversy.

Petitioners urge us to adopt the broader rule that Frederick's speech is prescribable because it is plainly "offensive" as that term is used in *Fraser*. . . . We think this stretches *Fraser* too far; that case should not be read to encompass any speech that could fit under some definition of "offensive." After all, much political and religious speech might be perceived as offensive to some. The concern here is not that Frederick's speech was offensive, but that it was reasonably viewed as promoting illegal drug use.

Although accusing this decision of doing "serious violence to the First Amendment" by authorizing "viewpoint discrimination," *post*, at 2, 5 (opinion of STEVENS, J.), the dissent concludes that "it might well be appropriate to tolerate some targeted viewpoint discrimination in this unique setting," *post*, at 6–7. Nor do we understand the dissent to take the position that schools are required to tolerate student advocacy of illegal drug use at school events, even if that advocacy falls short of inviting "imminent" lawless action. See *post*, at 7 ("[I]t is possible that our rigid imminence requirement ought to be relaxed at schools"). And even the dissent recognizes that the issues here are close enough that the principal should not be held liable in damages, but should instead enjoy qualified immunity for her actions. . . . Stripped of rhetorical flourishes, then, the debate between the dissent and this opinion is less about constitutional first principles than about whether Frederick's banner constitutes promotion of illegal drug use. We have explained our view that it does. The dissent's contrary view on that relatively narrow question hardly justifies sounding the First Amendment bugle.

❦

School principals have a difficult job, and a vitally important one. When Frederick suddenly and unexpectedly unfurled his banner, Morse had to decide to act—or not act—on the spot. It was reasonable for her to conclude that the banner promoted illegal drug use—in violation of established school policy—and that failing to act would send a powerful message to the students in her charge, including Frederick, about how serious the school was about the dangers of illegal drug use. The First Amendment does not require schools to tolerate at school events student expression that contributes to those dangers.

The judgment of the United States Court of Appeals for the Ninth Circuit is reversed, and the case is remanded for further proceedings consistent with this opinion.

It is so ordered.

→ **NO**

Dissenting Opinion, *Deborah Morse, et al., v. Joseph Frederick*

JUSTICE STEVENS, with whom JUSTICE SOUTER and JUSTICE GLNSBURG join, dissenting.

A significant fact barely mentioned by the Court sheds a revelatory light on the motives of both the students and the principal of Juneau-Douglas High School (JDHS). On January 24, 2002, the Olympic Torch Relay gave those Alaska residents a rare chance to appear on national television. As Joseph Frederick repeatedly explained, he did not address the curious message—"BONG HiTS 4 JESUS"—to his fellow students. He just wanted to get the camera crews' attention. Moreover, concern about a nationwide evaluation of the conduct of the JDHS student body would have justified the principal's decision to remove an attention-grabbing 14-foot banner, even if it had merely proclaimed "Glaciers Melt!"

I agree with the Court that the principal should not be held liable for pulling down Frederick's banner. See *Harlow v. Fitzgerald,* 457 U.S. 800, 818 (1982). I would hold, however, that the school's interest in protecting its students from exposure to speech "reasonably regarded as promoting illegal drug use," *ante,* at 1, cannot justify disciplining Frederick for his attempt to make an ambiguous statement to a television audience simply because it contained an oblique reference to drugs. The First Amendment demands more, indeed, much more.

The Court holds otherwise only after laboring to establish two uncontroversial propositions: first, that the constitutional rights of students in school settings are not coextensive with the rights of adults, . . . and second, that deterring drug use by schoolchildren is a valid and terribly important interest. . . . As to the first, I take the Court's point that the message on Frederick's banner is not *necessarily* protected speech, even though it unquestionably would have been had the banner been unfurled elsewhere. As to the second, I am willing to assume that the Court is correct that the pressing need to deter drug use supports JDHS's rule prohibiting willful conduct that expressly "advocates the use of substances that are illegal to minors." App. to Pet. for Cert. 53a. But it is a gross non sequitur to draw from these two unremarkable propositions the remarkable conclusion that the school may suppress student speech that was never meant to persuade anyone to do anything.

From Supreme Court of the United States, June 25, 2007.

In my judgment, the First Amendment protects student speech if the message itself neither violates a permissible rule nor expressly advocates conduct that is illegal and harmful to students. This nonsense banner does neither, and the Court does serious violence to the First Amendment in upholding—indeed, lauding—a school's decision to punish Frederick for expressing a view with which it disagreed.

I

In December 1965, we were engaged in a controversial war, a war that "divided this country as few other issues ever have." *Tinker v. Des Moines Independent Community School Dist.*, 393 U.S. 503, 524 (1969) (Black, J., dissenting). Having learned that some students planned to wear black armbands as a symbol of opposition to the country's involvement in Vietnam, officials of the Des Moines public school district adopted a policy calling for the suspension of any student who refused to remove the armband. As we explained when we considered the propriety of that policy, "[t]he school officials banned and sought to punish petitioners for a silent, passive expression of opinion, unaccompanied by any disorder or disturbance on the part of petitioners." *Id.*, at 508. The district justified its censorship on the ground that it feared that the expression of a controversial and unpopular opinion would generate disturbances. Because the school officials had insufficient reason to believe that those disturbances would "materially and substantially interfere with the requirements of discipline in the operation of the school," we found the justification for the rule to lack any foundation and therefore held that the censorship violated the First Amendment. . . .

Justice Harlan dissented, but not because he thought the school district could censor a message with which it disagreed. Rather, he would have upheld the district's rule only because the students never cast doubt on the district's anti-disruption justification by proving that the rule was motivated "by other than legitimate school concerns—for example, a desire to prohibit the expression of an unpopular point of view while permitting expression of the dominant opinion." *Id.*, at 526.

Two cardinal First Amendment principles animate both the Court's opinion in *Tinker* and Justice Harlan's dissent. First, censorship based on the content of speech, particularly censorship that depends on the viewpoint of the speaker, is subject to the most rigorous burden of justification:

> "Discrimination against speech because of its message is presumed to be unconstitutional. . . . When the government targets not subject matter, but particular views taken by speakers on a subject, the violation of the First Amendment is all the more blatant. View-point discrimination is thus an egregious form of content discrimination. The government must abstain from regulating speech when the specific motivating ideology or the opinion or perspective of the speaker is the rationale for the restriction." *Rosenberger v. Rector and Visitors of Univ. of Va.*, 515 U.S. 819, 828–829 (1995) (citation omitted).

Second, punishing someone for advocating illegal conduct is constitutional only when the advocacy is likely to provoke the harm that the government seeks to avoid. See *Brandenburg v. Ohio*, 395 U.S. 444, 449 (1969) *(per curiam)* (distinguishing "mere advocacy" of illegal conduct from "incitement to imminent lawless action").

However necessary it may be to modify those principles in the school setting, *Tinker* affirmed their continuing vitality. 393 U.S., at 509 ("In order for the State in the person of school officials to justify prohibition of a particular expression of opinion, it must be able to show that its action was caused by something more than a mere desire to avoid the discomfort and unpleasantness that always accompany an unpopular viewpoint. Certainly where there is no finding and no showing that engaging in that conduct would materially and substantially interfere with the requirements of appropriate discipline in the operation of the school, the prohibition cannot be sustained" (internal quotation marks omitted)). As other federal courts have long recognized, under *Tinker*,

> "regulation of student speech is generally permissible only when the speech would substantially disrupt or interfere with the work of the school or the rights of other students. . . . *Tinker* requires a specific and significant fear of disruption, *not just some remote apprehension of disturbance.*" *Saxe v. State College Area School Dist.*, 240 F. 3d 200, 211 (CA3 2001) (ALITO, J.) (emphasis added).

Yet today the Court fashions a test that trivializes the two cardinal principles upon which *Tinker* rests. . . . ("[S]chools [may] restrict student expression that they reasonably regard as promoting illegal drug use"). The Court's test invites stark viewpoint discrimination. In this case, for example, the principal has unabashedly acknowledged that she disciplined Frederick because she disagreed with the pro-drug viewpoint she ascribed to the message on the banner . . . —a viewpoint, incidentally, that Frederick has disavowed. . . . Unlike our recent decision in *Tennessee Secondary School Athletic Assn. v. Brentwood Academy*, 551 U.S. —, — (2007) . . . (ALITO, J., concurring), the Court's holding in this case strikes at "the heart of the First Amendment" because it upholds a punishment meted out on the basis of a listener's disagreement with her understanding (or, more likely, misunderstanding) of the speaker's viewpoint. "If there is a bedrock principle underlying the First Amendment, it is that the Government may not prohibit the expression of an idea simply because society finds the idea itself offensive or disagreeable." *Texas v. Johnson*, 491 U.S. 397, 414 (1989).

It is also perfectly clear that "promoting illegal drug use" . . . comes nowhere close to proscribable "incitement to imminent lawless action." *Brandenburg*, 395 U.S., at 447. Encouraging drug use might well increase the likelihood that a listener will try an illegal drug, but that hardly justifies censorship:

> "Every denunciation of existing law tends in some measure to increase the probability that there will be violation of it. Condonation of a breach enhances the probability. Expressions of approval add to the probability. . . . Advocacy of law-breaking heightens it still further. But

even advocacy of violation, however reprehensible morally, is not a justification for denying free speech where the advocacy falls short of incitement and there is nothing to indicate that the advocacy would be immediately acted upon." *Whitney v. California*, 274 U.S. 357, 376 (1927) (Brandeis, J., concurring).

No one seriously maintains that drug advocacy (much less Frederick's ridiculous sign) comes within the vanishingly small category of speech that can be prohibited because of its feared consequences. Such advocacy, to borrow from Justice Holmes, "ha[s] no chance of starting a present conflagration." *Gitlow v. New York*, 268 U.S. 652, 673 (1925) (dissenting opinion).

II

The Court rejects outright these twin foundations of *Tinker* because, in its view, the unusual importance of protecting children from the scourge of drugs supports a ban on all speech in the school environment that promotes drug use. Whether or not such a rule is sensible as a matter of policy, carving out pro-drug speech for uniquely harsh treatment finds no support in our case law and is inimical to the values protected by the First Amendment. . . .

I will nevertheless assume for the sake of argument that the school's concededly powerful interest in protecting its students adequately supports its restriction on "any assembly or public expression that . . . advocates the use of substances that are illegal to minors . . . ." App. to Pet. for Cert. 53a. Given that the relationship between schools and students "is custodial and tutelary, permitting a degree of supervision and control that could not be exercised over free adults," *Vernonia School Dist. 47J v. Acton*, 515 U.S. 646, 655 (1995), it might well be appropriate to tolerate some targeted viewpoint discrimination in this unique setting. And while conventional speech may be restricted only when likely to "incit[e] imminent lawless action," *Brandenburg*, 395 U.S., at 449, it is possible that our rigid imminence requirement ought to be relaxed at schools. See *Bethel School Dist. No. 403 v. Fraser*, 478 U.S. 675, 682 (1986) ("[T]he constitutional rights of students in public school are not automatically coextensive with the rights of adults in other settings").

But it is one thing to restrict speech that *advocates* drug use. It is another thing entirely to prohibit an obscure message with a drug theme that a third party subjectively—and not very reasonably—thinks is tantamount to express advocacy. Cf. *Masses Publishing Co. v. Patten*, 244 F. 535, 540, 541 (SDNY 1917) (Hand, J.) (distinguishing sharply between "agitation, legitimate as such" and "the direct advocacy" of unlawful conduct). Even the school recognizes the paramount need to hold the line between, on the one hand, non-disruptive speech that merely expresses a viewpoint that is unpopular or contrary to the school's preferred message, and on the other hand, advocacy of an illegal or unsafe course of conduct. The district's prohibition of drug advocacy is a gloss on a more general rule that is otherwise quite tolerant of non-disruptive student speech:

"Students will not be disturbed in the exercise of their constitutionally guaranteed rights to assemble peaceably and to express ideas and opinions, privately or publicly, provided that their activities do not infringe on the rights of others and do not interfere with the operation of the educational program.

"The Board will not permit the conduct on school premises of any willful activity . . . that interferes with the orderly operation of the educational program or offends the rights of others. The Board specifically prohibits . . . any assembly or public expression that . . . advocates the use of substances that are illegal to minors. . . ." App. to Pet. for Cert. 53a; see also *ante,* at 3 (quoting rule in part).

There is absolutely no evidence that Frederick's banner's reference to drug paraphernalia "willful[ly]" infringed on anyone's rights or interfered with any of the school's educational programs.[1] On its face, then, the rule gave Frederick wide berth "to express [his] ideas and opinions" so long as they did not amount to "advoca[cy]" of drug use. . . . If the school's rule is, by hypothesis, a valid one, it is valid only insofar as it scrupulously preserves adequate space for constitutionally protected speech. When First Amendment rights are at stake, a rule that "sweep[s] in a great variety of conduct under a general and indefinite characterization" may not leave "too wide a discretion in its application." *Cantwell v. Connecticut,* 310 U.S. 296, 308 (1940). Therefore, just as we insisted in *Tinker* that the school establish some likely connection between the armbands and their feared consequences, so too JDHS must show that Frederick's supposed advocacy stands a meaningful chance of making otherwise-abstemious students try marijuana.

But instead of demanding that the school make such a showing, the Court punts. Figuring out just *how* it punts is tricky; "[t]he mode of analysis [it] employ[s] is not entirely clear," see *ante,* at 9. On occasion, the Court suggests it is deferring to the principal's "reasonable" judgment that Frederick's sign qualified as drug advocacy.[2] At other times, the Court seems to say that *it* thinks the banner's message constitutes express advocacy.[3] Either way, its approach is indefensible.

To the extent the Court defers to the principal's ostensibly reasonable judgment, it abdicates its constitutional responsibility. The beliefs of third parties, reasonable or otherwise, have never dictated which messages amount to proscribable advocacy. Indeed, it would be a strange constitutional doctrine that would allow the prohibition of only the narrowest category of speech advocating unlawful conduct, . . . yet would permit a listener's perceptions to determine which speech deserved constitutional protection.[4]

Such a peculiar doctrine is alien to our case law. In *Abrams v. United States,* 250 U.S. 616 (1919), this Court affirmed the conviction of a group of Russian "rebels, revolutionists, [and] anarchists," . . . on the ground that the leaflets they distributed were thought to "incite, provoke, and encourage resistance to the United States," *id.,* at 617 (internal quotation marks omitted). Yet Justice Holmes' dissent—which has emphatically carried the day—never inquired into the reasonableness of the United States' judgment that the leaflets would likely undermine the war effort. The dissent instead ridiculed that judgment: "nobody can suppose that the surreptitious publishing of a silly leaflet by an unknown man, without more, would present any immediate danger that its opinions would hinder the success of the government arms or have any appreciable tendency to do so." *Id.*, at 628. In *Thomas v. Collins,* 323 U.S. 516 (1945) (opinion for the Court by Rutledge, J.), we overturned the conviction of a union organizer who violated a restraining order forbidding him from exhorting workers. In so doing, we held that the distinction between advocacy and incitement could not depend on how one of those workers might have understood the organizer's speech. That would "pu[t] the speaker in these circumstances wholly at the mercy of the varied understanding of his hearers and consequently of whatever inference may be drawn as to his intent and meaning." *Id.*, at 535. In *Cox v. Louisiana,* 379 U.S. 536, 543 (1965), we vacated a civil rights leader's conviction for disturbing the peace, even though a Baton Rouge sheriff had "deem[ed]" the leader's "appeal to . . . students to sit in at the lunch counters to be 'inflammatory.'" We never asked if the sheriffs in-person, on-the-spot judgment was "reasonable." Even in *Fraser,* we made no inquiry into whether the school administrators reasonably thought the student's speech was obscene or profane; we rather satisfied ourselves that "[t]he pervasive sexual innuendo in Fraser's speech was plainly offensive to both teachers and students—indeed, to any mature person." 478 U.S., at 683. Cf. *Bose Corp. v. Consumers Union of United States, Inc.,* 466 U.S. 485, 499 (1984) ("[I]n cases raising First Amendment issues we have repeatedly held that an appellate court has an obligation to make an independent examination of the whole record in order to make sure that the judgment does not constitute a forbidden intrusion on the field of free expression" (internal quotation marks omitted)).[5]

To the extent the Court independently finds that "BONG HiTS 4 JESUS" *objectively* amounts to the advocacy of illegal drug use—in other words, that it can *most* reasonably be interpreted as such—that conclusion practically refutes itself. This is a nonsense message, not advocacy. The Court's feeble effort to divine its hidden meaning is strong evidence of that . . . (positing that the banner might mean, alternatively, "'[Take] bong hits,'" "'bong hits [are a good thing],'" or "'[we take] bong hits'"). Frederick's credible and uncontradicted explanation for the message—he just wanted to get on television—is also relevant because a speaker who does not intend to persuade his audience can hardly be said to be advocating anything.[6] But most importantly, it takes real imagination to read a "cryptic" message (the Court's characterization, not mine, see *ibid.*, at 6) with a slanting drug reference as an incitement to drug use. Admittedly, some high school students (including those who use drugs) are dumb. Most students, however, do not shed their brains at the schoolhouse gate, and most students know dumb advocacy when they see it. The notion that the message on this banner would actually persuade either the average student or even the dumbest one to change his or her behavior is most implausible. That the Court believes such a silly message can be proscribed as advocacy underscores the novelty of its position, and suggests that the principle it articulates has no stopping point.

Even if advocacy could somehow be wedged into Frederick's obtuse reference to marijuana, that advocacy was at best subtle and ambiguous. There is abundant precedent, including another opinion THE CHIEF JUSTICE announces today, for the proposition that when the "First Amendment is implicated, the tie goes to the speaker," *Federal Election Comm'n v. Wisconsin*

Right to Life, Inc., 551 U.S. _____ (2007) (slip op., at 21) and that "when it comes to defining what speech qualifies as the functional equivalent of express advocacy . . . we give the benefit of the doubt to speech, not censorship," *post,* at 29. If this were a close case, the tie would have to go to Frederick's speech, not to the principal's strained reading of his quixotic message.

Among other things, the Court's ham-handed, categorical approach is deaf to the constitutional imperative to permit unfettered debate, even among high-school students, about the wisdom of the war on drugs or of legalizing marijuana for medicinal use.[7] See *Tinker,* 393 U.S., at 511 ("[Students] may not be confined to the expression of those sentiments that are officially approved"). If Frederick's stupid reference to marijuana can in the Court's view justify censorship, then high school students everywhere could be forgiven for zipping their mouths about drugs at school lest some "reasonable" observer censor and then punish them for promoting drugs. . . .

Consider, too, that the school district's rule draws no distinction between alcohol and marijuana, but applies evenhandedly to all "substances that are illegal to minors." App. to Pet. for Cert. 53a; see also App. 83 (expressly defining "'drugs'" to include "all alcoholic beverages"). Given the tragic consequences of teenage alcohol consumption—drinking causes far more fatal accidents than the misuse of marijuana—the school district's interest in deterring teenage alcohol use is at least comparable to its interest in preventing marijuana use. Under the Court's reasoning, must the First Amendment give way whenever a school seeks to punish a student for any speech mentioning beer, or indeed anything else that might be deemed risky to teenagers? While I find it hard to believe the Court would support punishing Frederick for flying a "WINE SiPS 4 JESUS" banner—which could quite reasonably be construed either as a protected religious message or as a pro-alcohol message—the breathtaking sweep of its opinion suggests it would.

III

Although this case began with a silly, nonsensical banner, it ends with the Court inventing out of whole cloth a special First Amendment rule permitting the censorship of any student speech that mentions drugs, at least so long as someone could perceive that speech to contain a latent pro-drug message. Our First Amendment jurisprudence has identified some categories of expression that are less deserving of protection than others—fighting words, obscenity, and commercial speech, to name a few. Rather than reviewing our opinions discussing such categories, I mention two personal recollections that have no doubt influenced my conclusion that it would be profoundly unwise to create special rules for speech about drug and alcohol use.

The Vietnam War is remembered today as an unpopular war. During its early stages, however, "the dominant opinion" that Justice Harlan mentioned in his *Tinker* dissent regarded opposition to the war as unpatriotic, if not treason. 393 U.S., at 526. That dominant opinion strongly supported the prosecution of several of those who demonstrated in Grant Park during the 1968 Democratic Convention in Chicago, see *United States v. Dellinger,* 472 F. 2d 340 (CA7 1972), and the vilification of vocal opponents of the war like Julian

Bond, cf. *Bond v. Floyd,* 385 U.S. 116 (1966). In 1965, when the Des Moines students wore their armbands, the school district's fear that they might "start an argument or cause a disturbance" was well founded. *Tinker,* 393 U.S., at 508. Given that context, there is special force to the Court's insistence that "our Constitution says we must take that risk; and our history says that it is this sort of hazardous freedom—this kind of openness—that is the basis of our national strength and of the independence and vigor of Americans who grow up and live in this relatively permissive, often disputatious, society." *Id.,* at 508–509 (citation omitted). As we now know, the then-dominant opinion about the Vietnam War was not etched in stone.

Reaching back still further, the current dominant opinion supporting the war on drugs in general, and our anti-marijuana laws in particular, is reminiscent of the opinion that supported the nationwide ban on alcohol consumption when I was a student. While alcoholic beverages are now regarded as ordinary articles of commerce, their use was then condemned with the same moral fervor that now supports the war on drugs. The ensuing change in public opinion occurred much more slowly than the relatively rapid shift in Americans' views on the Vietnam War, and progressed on a state-by-state basis over a period of many years. But just as prohibition in the 1920's and early 1930's was secretly questioned by thousands of otherwise law-abiding patrons of bootleggers and speakeasies, today the actions of literally millions of otherwise law-abiding users of marijuana,[8] and of the majority of voters in each of the several States that tolerate medicinal uses of the product,[9] lead me to wonder whether the fear of disapproval by those in the majority is silencing opponents of the war on drugs. Surely our national experience with alcohol should make us wary of dampening speech suggesting—however inarticulately—that it would be better to tax and regulate marijuana than to persevere in a futile effort to ban its use entirely.

Even in high school, a rule that permits only one point of view to be expressed is less likely to produce correct answers than the open discussion of countervailing views. *Whitney,* 274 U.S., at 377 (Brandeis, J., concurring); *Abrams,* 250 U.S., at 630 (Holmes, J., dissenting); *Tinker,* 393 U.S., at 512. In the national debate about a serious issue, it is the expression of the minority's viewpoint that most demands the protection of the First Amendment. Whatever the better policy may be, a full and frank discussion of the costs and benefits of the attempt to prohibit the use of marijuana is far wiser than suppression of speech because it is unpopular.

I respectfully dissent.

Notes

[1.] It is also relevant that the display did not take place "on school premises," as the rule contemplates. App. to Pet. for Cert. 53a. While a separate district rule does make the policy applicable to "social events and class trips," *id.,* at 58a, Frederick might well have thought that the Olympic Torch Relay was neither a "social event" (for example, prom) nor a "class trip."

[2.] See *ante,* at 1 (stating that the principal "reasonably regarded" Frederick's banner as "promoting illegal drug use"); *ante,* at 6 (explaining that "Principal

Morse thought the banner would be interpreted by those viewing it as promoting illegal drug use, and that interpretation is plainly a reasonable one"); *ante,* at 8 (asking whether "a principal may . . . restrict student speech . . . when that speech is reasonably viewed as promoting illegal drug use"); *ante,* at 14 (holding that "schools [may] restrict student expression that they reasonably regard as promoting illegal drug use"); see also *ante,* at 1 (ALITO, J., concurring) ("[A] public school may restrict speech that a reasonable observer would interpret as advocating illegal drug use").

[3.] See *ante,* at 7 ("We agree with Morse. At least two interpretations of the words on the banner demonstrate that the sign advocated the use of illegal drugs"); *ante,* at 15 (observing that "[w]e have explained our view" that "Frederick's banner constitutes promotion of illegal drug use").

[4.] The reasonableness of the view that Frederick's message was unprotected speech is relevant to ascertaining whether qualified immunity should shield the principal from liability, not to whether her actions violated Frederick's constitutional rights. Cf. *Saucier v. Katz,* 533 U.S. 194, 202 (2001) ("The relevant, dispositive inquiry in determining whether a right is clearly established is whether it would be clear to a reasonable officer that his conduct was unlawful in the situation he confronted").

[5.] This same reasoning applies when the interpreter is not just a listener, but a legislature. We have repeatedly held that "[d]eference to a legislative finding" that certain types of speech are inherently harmful "cannot limit judicial inquiry when First Amendment rights are at stake," reasoning that "the judicial function commands analysis of whether the specific conduct charged falls within the reach of the statute and if so whether the legislation is consonant with the Constitution." *Landmark Communications, Inc. v. Virginia,* 435 U.S. 829, 843, 844 (1978); see also *Whitney v. California,* 274 U.S. 357, 378–379 (1927) (Brandeis, J., concurring) ("[A legislative declaration] does not preclude enquiry into the question whether, at the time and under the circumstances, the conditions existed which are essential to validity under the Federal Constitution. . . . Whenever the fundamental rights of free speech and assembly are alleged to have been invaded, it must remain open to a defendant to present the issue whether there actually did exist at the time a clear danger; whether the danger, if any, was imminent; and whether the evil apprehended was so substantial as to justify the stringent restriction interposed by the legislature"). When legislatures are entitled to no deference as to whether particular speech amounts to a "clear and present danger," *id.,* at 379, it is hard to understand why the Court would so blithely defer to the judgment of a single school principal.

[6.] In affirming Frederick's suspension, the JDHS superintendent acknowledged that Frederick displayed his message "for the benefit of television cameras covering the Torch Relay." App. to Pet. for Cert. 62a.

[7.] The Court's opinion ignores the fact that the legalization of marijuana is an issue of considerable public concern in Alaska. The State Supreme Court held in 1975 that Alaska's constitution protects the right of adults to possess less than four ounces of marijuana for personal use. *Ravin v. State,* 537 P. 2d 494 (Alaska). In 1990, the voters of Alaska attempted to undo that decision by voting for a ballot initiative recriminalizing marijuana possession. Initiative Proposal No. 2, §§1–2 (effective Mar. 3,

1991), 11 Alaska Stat., p. 872 (Lexis 2006). At the time Frederick unfurled his banner, the constitutionality of that referendum had yet to be tested. It was subsequently struck down as unconstitutional. See *Noy v. State,* 83 P. 3d 538 (Alaska App. 2003). In the meantime, Alaska voters had approved a ballot measure decriminalizing the use of marijuana for medicinal purposes, 1998 Ballot Measure No. 8 (approved Nov. 3, 1998), 11 Alaska Stat., p. 882 (codified at Alaska Stat. §§11.71.090, 17.37.010–17.37.080), and had rejected a much broader measure that would have decriminalized marijuana possession and granted amnesty to anyone convicted of marijuana-related crimes, see 2000 Ballot Measure No. 5 (failed Nov. 7, 2000), 11 Alaska Stat., p. 886.

[8.] See *Gonzales v. Raich,* 545 U.S. 1, 21, n. 31 (2005) (citing a Government estimate "that in 2000 American users spent $10.5 *billion* on the purchase of marijuana").

[9.] *Id.,* at 5 (noting that "at least nine States . . . authorize the use of marijuana for medicinal purposes").

POSTSCRIPT

Can a School Punish a Student for Speech at a School-Supervised Event Off of School Grounds When That Speech Could Be Viewed as Promoting Illegal Drug Use?

*H*azelwood gave school administrators fairly broad authority to intervene in school newspapers, and *Fraser* was a case about the spoken word. In addition to these cases, one dealing with press and the other with speech, the Vietnam-era case of *Tinker v. Des Moines* involved an armband, a kind of silent protest. The future is likely to generate more cases about control of expression involving students and different kinds of cases. The reason for this is simple, namely that there are new ways to communicate, the number of new forms of communication are growing, and whether something communicated electronically occurred in school or out of school may not be clear. While the three most important precedents involve armbands, speech, and a printed newspaper, three very traditional modes of expression, we are now in an era of ever-increasing forms of communication. We have cell phones that have the processing power of some computers, bloggers who wish to be recognized as journalists, and virtual worlds like SecondLife that allow us to reshape our identities.

In *Morse v. Frederick,* the Court could have provided some clarification of the important question of when school officials can punish students for off-campus behavior. There have been increasing numbers of such cases in recent years. The earliest cases tended to involve underground newspapers, which were critical of teachers or administrators and were not written and published in or during school. More recent cases have involved new problems like cyberbullying and the creation of Web sites or Facebook pages which criticize teachers or use offensive language.

Consider, for example, the following:

- Anthony Latour was expelled from school because of four rap songs he wrote over a four-year period. The songs, which contained profanity and violent imagery, were put on the Internet. The District Court ruled in favor of the student. *Latour v. Riverside Beaver Sch. Dist.*
- Justin Layshock posted a parody profile of his school's principal on MySpace. The profile was created outside of school but proved to be so popular that the computer system in school could not be used for several days. In *Layshock v. Hermitage School District,* the District

Court for the Western District of Pennsylvania (www.citmedialaw .org/threats/hermitage-school-district-v-layshock) the Federal District Court ruled that Justin Layshock's rights were not violated when he was suspended because of the disruption caused in the school. A copy of the Web site can be found at http://www.aclupa.org/downloads/Justinswebsite .pdf.

Some Web sites touching on these examples are http://www.aclu.org/ studentsrights/index.html, http://www.citmedialaw.org, and http://www.aclupa.org/ legal/legaldocket/middleschoolrapperexpelled/. An actual picture of the armband worn by John Tinker is at http://www.bandofrights.org. Recent articles include Rita J. Verga, "Policing Their Space: The First Amendment Parameters of School Discipline of Student Cyberspeech," 23 *Santa Clara Computer & High Tech. L. J.* 727 (May, 2007); Mary-Rose Papandrea, "Student Speech Rights in the Digital Age," 60 *Fla. L. Rev.* 1027 (2008); and Brannon P. Denning and Molly C. Taylor, "*Morse v. Frederick* and the Regulation of Student Cyberspeech" 35 *Hastings Const. L. Q.* 835 (2008).

ISSUE 12

Is a Strip Search of Middle School Students That Is Aimed at Finding Drugs Prohibited Under the Fourth Amendment?

YES: David Souter, from Majority Opinion, *Safford Unified School District, et al., v. April Redding,* U.S. Supreme Court (June 25, 2009)

NO: Clarence Thomas, from Dissenting Opinion, *Safford Unified School District, et al., v. April Redding,* U.S. Supreme Court (June 25, 2009)

ISSUE SUMMARY

YES: Supreme Court Justice David Souter holds that a search in school requires a reasonable belief that evidence of wrongdoing will be found and that the search is not excessively intrusive in light of the age and sex of the student.

NO: Supreme Court Justice Clarence Thomas argues that the Fourth Amendment was not violated when there is reasonable suspicion that the student is in possession of drugs banned by school policy and the search is in an area where small pills could be concealed.

The Fourth Amendment to the Constitution requires authorities to obtain a search warrant before conducting a search. In order to do this, they must persuade a judge that probable cause exists that a crime has been committed and that the evidence sought will be found in the place to be searched. The warrant requirement is the key constitutional element restricting the power of the police to decide unilaterally to invade the privacy of someone's home.

There are exceptions to this requirement. For example, warrants are not required when a person is searched after an arrest or when the object seized is in plain view. Nor is a warrant needed if the invasion of privacy is less intrusive than a full-scale search. Patting down the outside of someone's clothing when the police believe the person might have a weapon only requires "reasonable suspicion." In such situations, the police do not need to meet the standard of probable cause but also may not extensively search the person.

Public schools are another context in which searches have been allowed even when probable cause was not present. For example, the Court has held that search warrants are not required for school officials to search school lockers if there are reasonable grounds for believing that the search will reveal evidence of criminal behavior (*New Jersey v. T. L. O., A Juvenile,* 105 S. Ct. 733, [1985]). In the case here, the Supreme Court was asked to rule on a search that was extremely intrusive and where the grounds for believing that the search would turn up drugs were questionable.

The Supreme Court is not required to accept a case for review, and in recent decades, it has been deciding fewer and fewer cases. When it does decide to hear a case, it requires the parties to prepare and submit their legal arguments in writing and then to appear at an oral argument to answer questions that the justices might have. Often, observers at the oral argument make predictions about how the justices will vote based on the questions they ask and the comments they make at the oral argument.

The oral argument in the *Redding* case had many of the male members of the Court asking questions that appeared to be insensitive to the feelings of a 13-year-old girl subjected to a strip search. Justice Breyer, for example, asked, "Why is this a major thing to say strip down to your underclothes, which children do when they change for gym?" Justice Souter commented that if he were the principal in a school, he "would rather have the kid embarrassed by a strip search . . . than have some other kids dead because the stuff is distributed at lunchtime and things go awry." One correspondent at the Court wrote after the oral argument "after today's argument, it's plain the court will overturn a Ninth Circuit Court of Appeals' opinion finding a school's decision to strip search a 13-year-old girl unconstitutional. That the school in question was looking for a prescription pill with the mind-altering force of a pair of Advil— and couldn't be bothered to call the child's mother first—hardly matters."

As it turned out, the case was decided 8–1 in favor of Ms. Redding, and the majority opinion was written by Justice Souter. For some, this was an example of the justices, and the law, being influenced by public opinion. For others, who have seen many decisions that would not have been predicted given the questioning at the oral argument, the outcome in this case was much less of a surprise.

YES ↵

David Souter

Majority Opinion, *Safford Unified School District, et al., v. April Redding*

J USTICE SOUTER delivered the opinion of the Court.

The issue here is whether a 13-year-old student's Fourth Amendment right was violated when she was subjected to a search of her bra and underpants by school officials acting on reasonable suspicion that she had brought forbidden prescription and over-the-counter drugs to school. Because there were no reasons to suspect the drugs presented a danger or were concealed in her underwear, we hold that the search did violate the Constitution, but because there is reason to question the clarity with which the right was established, the official who ordered the unconstitutional search is entitled to qualified immunity from liability.

I

The events immediately prior to the search in question began in 13-year-old Savana Redding's math class at Safford Middle School one October day in 2003. The assistant principal of the school, Kerry Wilson, came into the room and asked Savana to go to his office. There, he showed her a day planner, unzipped and open flat on his desk, in which there were several knives, lighters, a permanent marker, and a cigarette. Wilson asked Savana whether the planner was hers; she said it was, but that a few days before she had lent it to her friend, Marissa Glines. Savana stated that none of the items in the planner belonged to her.

Wilson then showed Savana four white prescription-strength ibuprofen 400-mg pills, and one over-the-counter blue naproxen 200-mg pill, all used for pain and inflammation but banned under school rules without advance permission. He asked Savana if she knew anything about the pills. Savana answered that she did not. Wilson then told Savana that he had received a report that she was giving these pills to fellow students; Savana denied it and agreed to let Wilson search her belongings. Helen Romero, an administrative assistant, came into the office, and together with Wilson they searched Savana's backpack, finding nothing.

At that point, Wilson instructed Romero to take Savana to the school nurse's office to search her clothes for pills. Romero and the nurse, Peggy

From Supreme Court of the United States, June 25, 2009.

Schwallier, asked Savana to remove her jacket, socks, and shoes, leaving her in stretch pants and a T-shirt (both without pockets), which she was then asked to remove. Finally, Savana was told to pull her bra out and to the side and shake it, and to pull out the elastic on her underpants, thus exposing her breasts and pelvic area to some degree. No pills were found.

Savana's mother filed suit against Safford Unified School District #1, Wilson, Romero, and Schwallier for conducting a strip search in violation of Savana's Fourth Amendment rights. The individuals (hereinafter petitioners) moved for summary judgment, raising a defense of qualified immunity. The District Court for the District of Arizona granted the motion on the ground that there was no Fourth Amendment violation, and a panel of the Ninth Circuit affirmed. 504 F. 3d 828 (2007).

A closely divided Circuit sitting en banc, however, reversed. Following the two-step protocol for evaluating claims of qualified immunity, see *Saucier v. Katz,* 533 U.S. 194, 200 (2001), the Ninth Circuit held that the strip search was unjustified under the Fourth Amendment test for searches of children by school officials set out in *New Jersey v. T. L. O.,* 469 U.S. 325 (1985). 531 F. 3d 1071, 1081–1087 (2008). The Circuit then applied the test for qualified immunity, and found that Savana's right was clearly established at the time of the search: "'[t]hese notions of personal privacy are "clearly established" in that they inhere in all of us, particularly middle school teenagers, and are inherent in the privacy component of the Fourth Amendment's proscription against unreasonable searches.'" *Id.,* at 1088–1089 (quoting *Brannum v. Overton Cty. School Bd.,* 516 F. 3d 489, 499 (CA6 2008)). The upshot was reversal of summary judgment as to Wilson, while affirming the judgments in favor of Schwallier, the school nurse, and Romero, the administrative assistant, since they had not acted as independent decisionmakers. 531 F. 3d, at 1089.

We granted certiorari, 555 U.S. ___ (2009), and now affirm in part, reverse in part, and remand.

II

The Fourth Amendment "right of the people to be secure in their persons . . . against unreasonable searches and seizures" generally requires a law enforcement officer to have probable cause for conducting a search. "Probable cause exists where 'the facts and circumstances within [an officer's] knowledge and of which [he] had reasonably trustworthy information [are] sufficient in themselves to warrant a man of reasonable caution in the belief that' an offense has been or is being committed," *Brinegar v. United States,* 338 U.S. 160, 175–176 (1949) (quoting *Carroll v. United States,* 267 U.S. 132, 162 (1925)), and that evidence bearing on that offense will be found in the place to be searched.

In *T. L. O.,* we recognized that the school setting "requires some modification of the level of suspicion of illicit activity needed to justify a search," 469 U.S., at 340, and held that for searches by school officials "a careful balancing of governmental and private interests suggests that the public interest is best served by a Fourth Amendment standard of reasonableness that stops short of probable cause". . . We have thus applied a standard of reasonable suspicion to determine the legality of a school administrator's search of a student, . . . and have held that a school search "will be permissible in its scope when the measures adopted are reasonably related to the objectives of the search and not excessively intrusive in light of the age and sex of the student and the nature of the infraction." . . .

A number of our cases on probable cause have an implicit bearing on the reliable knowledge element of reasonable suspicion, as we have attempted to flesh out the knowledge component by looking to the degree to which known facts imply prohibited conduct, see, *e.g., Adams v. Williams,* 407 U.S. 143, 148 (1972); *id.,* at 160, n. 9 (Marshall, J., dissenting), the specificity of the information received, see, *e.g., Spinelli v. United States,* 393 U.S. 410, 416–417 (1969), and the reliability of its source, see, *e.g., Aguilar v. Texas, 378* U.S. 108, 114 (1964). At the end of the day, however, we have realized that these factors cannot rigidly control, *Illinois v. Gates,* 462 U.S. 213, 230 (1983), and we have come back to saying that the standards are "fluid concepts that take their substantive content from the particular contexts" in which they are being assessed. *Ornelas v. United States,* 517 U.S. 690, 696 (1996).

Perhaps the best that can be said generally about the required knowledge component of probable cause for a law enforcement officer's evidence search is that it raise a "fair probability," *Gates,* 462 U.S., at 238, or a "substantial chance," *id.,* at 244, n. 13, of discovering evidence of criminal activity. The lesser standard for school searches could as readily be described as a moderate chance of finding evidence of wrongdoing.

III

A

In this case, the school's policies strictly prohibit the nonmedical use, possession, or sale of any drug on school grounds, including "'[a]ny prescription or over-the-counter drug, except those for which permission to use in school has been granted pursuant to Board policy.'" . . .[1] A week before Savana was searched, another student, Jordan Romero (no relation of the school's administrative assistant), told the principal and Assistant Principal Wilson that "certain students were bringing drugs and weapons on campus," and that he had been sick after taking some pills that "he got from a classmate." . . . On the morning of October 8, the same boy handed Wilson a white pill that he said Marissa Glines had given him. He told Wilson that students were planning to take the pills at lunch.

Wilson learned from Peggy Schwallier, the school nurse, that the pill was Ibuprofen 400 mg, available only by prescription. Wilson then called Marissa out of class. Outside the classroom, Marissa's teacher handed Wilson the day planner, found within Marissa's reach, containing various contraband items. Wilson escorted Marissa back to his office.

In the presence of Helen Romero, Wilson requested Marissa to turn out her pockets and open her wallet. Marissa produced a blue pill, several white ones, and a razor blade. Wilson asked where the blue pill came from, and Marissa answered, "'I guess it slipped in when *she* gave me the IBU 400s.'" . . . When Wilson asked whom she meant, Marissa replied, "'Savana Redding.'" . . . Wilson then enquired about the day planner and its contents; Marissa denied knowing anything about them. Wilson did not ask Marissa any followup questions to determine whether there was any likelihood that Savana presently had pills: neither asking when Marissa received the pills from Savana nor where Savana might be hiding them.

Schwallier did not immediately recognize the blue pill, but information provided through a poison control hotline . . . indicated that the pill was a 200-mg dose of an anti-inflammatory drug, generically called naproxen, available over the counter. At Wilson's direction, Marissa was then subjected to a search of her bra and underpants by Romero and Schwallier, as Savana was later on. The search revealed no additional pills.

It was at this juncture that Wilson called Savana into his office and showed her the day planner. Their conversation established that Savana and Marissa were on friendly terms: while she denied knowledge of the contraband, Savana admitted that the day planner was hers and that she had lent it to Marissa. Wilson had other reports of their friendship from staff members, who had identified Savana and Marissa as part of an unusually rowdy group at the school's opening dance in August, during which alcohol and cigarettes were found in the girls' bathroom. Wilson had reason to connect the girls with this contra band, for Wilson knew that Jordan Romero had told the principal that before the dance, he had been at a party at Savana's house where alcohol was served. Marissa's statement that the pills came from Savana was thus sufficiently plausible to warrant suspicion that Savana was involved in pill distribution.

This suspicion of Wilson's was enough to justify a search of Savana's backpack and outer clothing.[2] If a student is reasonably suspected of giving out contraband pills, she is reasonably suspected of carrying them on her person and in the carryall that has become an item of student uniform in most places today. If Wilson's reasonable suspicion of pill distribution were not understood to support searches of outer clothes and backpack, it would not justify any search worth making. And the look into Savana's bag, in her presence and in the relative privacy of Wilson's office, was not excessively intrusive, any more than Romero's subsequent search of her outer clothing.

B

Here it is that the parties part company, with Savana's claim that extending the search at Wilson's behest to the point of making her pull out her underwear was constitutionally unreasonable. The exact label for this final step in the intrusion is not important, though strip search is a fair way to speak of it. Romero and Schwallier directed Savana to remove her clothes down to her underwear, and then "pull out" her bra and the elastic band on her underpants. . . . Although Romero and Schwallier stated that they did not see anything when Savana followed their instructions, . . . we would not define strip search and its Fourth Amendment consequences in a way that would guarantee litigation about who was looking and how much was seen. The very fact of Savana's pulling her underwear away from her body in the presence of the two officials who were able to see her necessarily exposed her breasts and pelvic area to some degree, and both subjective and reasonable societal expectations of personal privacy support the treatment of such a search as categorically distinct, requiring distinct elements of justification on the part of school authorities for going beyond a search of outer clothing and belongings.

Savana's subjective expectation of privacy against such a search is inherent in her account of it as embarrassing, frightening, and humiliating. The reasonableness of her expectation (required by the Fourth Amendment standard) is indicated by the consistent experiences of other young people similarly searched, whose adolescent vulnerability intensifies the patent intrusiveness of the exposure. See Brief for National Association of Social Workers et al. as *Amici Curiae* 6–14; Hyman & Perone, The Other Side of School Violence: Educator Policies and Practices that may Contribute to Student Misbehavior, 36 J. School Psychology 7, 13 (1998) (strip search can "result in serious emotional damage"). The common reaction of these adolescents simply registers the obviously different meaning of a search exposing the body from the experience of nakedness or near undress in other school circumstances. Changing for gym is getting ready for play; exposing for a search is responding to an accusation reserved for suspected wrongdoers and fairly understood as so degrading that a number of communities have decided that strip searches in schools are never reasonable and have banned them no matter what the facts may be, see, *e.g.*, New York City Dept. of Education, Reg. No. A-432, p. 2 (2005), . . . ("Under no circumstances shall a strip-search of a student be conducted").

The indignity of the search does not, of course, outlaw it, but it does implicate the rule of reasonableness as stated in *T. L. O.*, that "the search as actually conducted [be] reasonably related in scope to the circumstances which justified the interference in the first place." 469 U.S., at 341 (internal quotation marks omitted). The scope will be permissible, that is, when it is "not excessively intrusive in light of the age and sex of the student and the nature of the infraction." *Id.*, at 342.

Here, the content of the suspicion failed to match the degree of intrusion. Wilson knew beforehand that the pills were prescription-strength ibuprofen and over-the-counter naproxen, common pain relievers equivalent to two Advil, or one Aleve. . . . He must have been aware of the nature and limited threat of the specific drugs he was searching for, and while just about anything can be taken in quantities that will do real harm, Wilson had no reason to suspect that large amounts of the drugs were being passed around, or that individual students were receiving great numbers of pills.

Nor could Wilson have suspected that Savana was hiding common painkillers in her underwear. Petitioners suggest, as a truth universally acknowledged, that "students . . . hid[e] contraband in or under their clothing," Reply Brief for Petitioners 8, and cite a smattering of cases of students with contraband in their underwear, *id.*, at 8–9. But when the categorically extreme intrusiveness of a search down to the body of an adolescent requires some justification in suspected facts, general background possibilities fall short; a reasonable search that extensive calls for suspicion that it will pay off. But nondangerous school contraband does not raise the specter of stashes in intimate places, and there is no evidence in the record of any general practice among Safford Middle School students of hiding that sort of thing in underwear; neither Jordan nor Marissa suggested to Wilson that Savana was doing that, and the preceding search of Marissa that Wilson ordered yielded nothing. Wilson never even determined when Marissa had received the pills from Savana; if it had been a few days before, that would weigh heavily against any reasonable conclusion that Savana presently had the pills on her person, much less in her underwear.

In sum, what was missing from the suspected facts that pointed to Savana was any indication of danger to the students from the power of the drugs or their quantity, and any reason to suppose that Savana was carrying pills in her underwear. We think that the combination of these deficiencies was fatal to finding the search reasonable.

In so holding, we mean to cast no ill reflection on the assistant principal, for the record raises no doubt that his motive throughout was to eliminate drugs from his school and protect students from what Jordan Romero had gone through. Parents are known to overreact to protect their children from danger, and a school official with responsibility for safety may tend to do the same. The difference is that the Fourth Amendment places limits on the official, even with the high degree of deference that courts must pay to the educator's professional judgment.

We do mean, though, to make it clear that the *T. L. O.* concern to limit a school search to reasonable scope requires the support of reasonable suspicion of danger or of resort to underwear for hiding evidence of wrongdoing before a search can reasonably make the quantum leap from outer clothes and backpacks to exposure of intimate parts. The meaning of such a search, and the degradation its subject may reasonably feel, place a search that intrusive in a category of its own demanding its own specific suspicions.

IV

A school official searching a student is "entitled to qualified immunity where clearly established law does not show that the search violated the Fourth Amendment." *Pearson v. Callahan*, 555 U.S. _, _ (2009) (slip op., at 18). To be established clearly, however, there is no need that "the very action in question [have] previously been held unlawful." *Wilson v. Layne*, 526 U.S. 603, 615 (1999). The unconstitutionality of outrageous conduct obviously will be unconstitutional, this being the reason, as Judge Posner has said, that "[t]he easiest cases don't even arise." *K. H. v. Morgan*, 914 F. 2d 846, 851 (CA7 1990). But even as to action less than an outrage, "officials can still be on notice that their conduct violates established law . . . in novel factual circumstances." *Hope v. Pelzer*, 536 U.S. 730, 741 (2002).

T. L. O. directed school officials to limit the intrusiveness of a search, "in light of the age and sex of the student and the nature of the infraction," 469 U.S., at 342, and as we have just said at some length, the intrusiveness of the strip search here cannot be seen as justifiably related to the circumstances. But we realize that the lower courts have reached divergent conclusions regarding how the *T. L. O.* standard applies to such searches.

A number of judges have read *T. L. O.* as the en banc minority of the Ninth Circuit did here. The Sixth Circuit upheld a strip search of a high school student for a drug, without any suspicion that drugs were hidden next to her body. *Williams v. Ellington,* 936 F. 2d 881, 882–883, 887 (1991). And other courts considering qualified immunity for strip searches have read *T. L. O.* as "a series of abstractions, on the one hand, and a declaration of seeming deference to the judgments of school officials, on the other," *Jenkins v. Talladega City Bd. of Ed.,* 115 F. 3d 821, 828 (CA11 1997) (en banc), which made it impossible "to establish clearly the contours of a Fourth Amendment right . . . [in] the wide variety of possible school settings different from those involved in *T. L. O."* itself. *Ibid.* See also *Thomas v. Roberts,* 323 F. 3d 950 (CA11 2003) (granting qualified immunity to a teacher and police officer who conducted a group strip search of a fifth grade class when looking for a missing $26).

We think these differences of opinion from our own are substantial enough to require immunity for the school officials in this case. We would not suggest that entitlement to qualified immunity is the guaranteed product of disuniform views of the law in the other federal, or state, courts, and the fact that a single judge, or even a group of judges, disagrees about the contours of a right does not automatically render the law unclear if we have been clear. That said, however, the cases viewing school strip searches differently from the way we see them are numerous enough, with well-reasoned majority and dissenting opinions, to counsel doubt that we were sufficiently clear in the prior statement of law. We conclude that qualified immunity is warranted.

V

The strip search of Savana Redding was unreasonable and a violation of the Fourth Amendment, but petitioners Wilson, Romero, and Schwallier are nevertheless protected from liability through qualified immunity. Our conclusions here do not resolve, however, the question of the liability of petitioner Safford Unified School District #1 under *Monell v. New York City Dept. of Social Servs.,* 436 U.S. 658, 694 (1978), a claim the Ninth Circuit did not address. The judgment of the Ninth Circuit is therefore affirmed in part and reversed in part, and this case is remanded for consideration of the *Monell* claim.

It is so ordered.

Notes

[1.] When the object of a school search is the enforcement of a school rule, a valid search assumes, of course, the rule's legitimacy. But the legitimacy of the rule usually goes without saying as it does here. The Court said plainly in *New Jersey v. T. L. O.,* 469 U.S. 325, 342, n. 9 (1985), that standards of conduct for schools are for school administrators to determine without

second-guessing by courts lacking the experience to appreciate what may
be needed. Except in patently arbitrary instances, Fourth Amendment
analysis takes the rule as a given, as it obviously should do in this case.
There is no need here either to explain the imperative of keeping drugs
out of schools, or to explain the reasons for the school's rule banning all
drugs, no matter how benign, without advance permission. Teachers are
not pharmacologists trained to identify pills and powders, and an effective drug ban has to be enforceable fast. The plenary ban makes sense, and
there is no basis to claim that the search was unreasonable owing to some
defect or shortcoming of the rule it was aimed at enforcing.

[2.] 'There is no question here that justification for the school officials' search
was required in accordance with the *T. L. O.* standard of reasonable suspicion, for it is common ground that Savana had a reasonable expectation
of privacy covering the personal things she chose to carry in her backpack,
cf. 469 U.S., at 339, and that Wilson's decision to look through it was a
"search" within the meaning of the Fourth Amendment.

Clarence Thomas

→ **NO**

Dissenting Opinion, *Safford Unified School District, et al., v. April Redding*

JUSTICE THOMAS, concurring in the judgment in part and dissenting in part.
I agree with the Court that the judgment against the school officials with respect to qualified immunity should be reversed. . . . Unlike the majority, however, I would hold that the search of Savana Redding did not violate the Fourth Amendment. The majority imposes a vague and amorphous standard on school administrators. It also grants judges sweeping authority to second-guess the measures that these officials take to maintain discipline in their schools and ensure the health and safety of the students in their charge. This deep intrusion into the administration of public schools exemplifies why the Court should return to the common-law doctrine of *in loco parentis* under which "the judiciary was reluctant to interfere in the routine business of school administration, allowing schools and teachers to set and enforce rules and to maintain order." *Morse v. Frederick,* 551 U.S. 393, 414 (2007) (THOMAS, J., concurring). But even under the prevailing Fourth Amendment test established by *New Jersey v. T. L. O.,* 469 U.S. 325 (1985), all petitioners, including the school district, are entitled to judgment as a matter of law in their favor.

I

"Although the underlying command of the Fourth Amendment is always that searches and seizures be reasonable, what is reasonable depends on the context within which a search takes place." *Id.,* at 337. Thus, although public school students retain Fourth Amendment rights under this Court's precedent, see *id.,* at 333–337, those rights "are different . . . than elsewhere; the 'reasonableness' inquiry cannot disregard the schools' custodial and tutelary responsibility for children," *Vernonia School Dist. 47J v. Acton,* 515 U.S. 646, 656 (1995); see also *T. L. O.,* 469 U.S., at 339 (identifying "the substantial interest of teachers and administrators in maintaining discipline in the classroom and on school grounds"). For nearly 25 years this Court has understood that "[m]aintaining order in the classroom has never been easy, but in more recent years, school disorder has often taken particularly ugly forms: drug use and violent crime in the schools have become major social problems." . . . In schools, "[e]vents

From Supreme Court of the United States, June 25, 2009.

calling for discipline are frequent occurrences and sometimes require immediate, effective action." *Goss v. Lopez,* 419 U.S. 565, 580 (1975); see also *T. L. O.,* 469 U.S., at 340 (explaining that schools have a "legitimate need to maintain an environment in which learning can take place").

For this reason, school officials retain broad authority to protect students and preserve "order and a proper educational environment" under the Fourth Amendment. . . . This authority requires that school officials be able to engage in the "close supervision of schoolchildren, as well as . . . enforc[e] rules against conduct that would be perfectly permissible if undertaken by an adult." . . . Seeking to reconcile the Fourth Amendment with this unique public school setting, the Court in *T. L. O.* held that a school search is "reasonable" if it is "'justified at its inception'" and "'reasonably related in scope to the circumstances which justified the interference in the first place.'" . . . The search under review easily meets this standard.

A

A "search of a student by a teacher or other school official will be 'justified at its inception' when there are reasonable grounds for suspecting that the search will turn up evidence that the student has violated or is violating either the law or the rules of the school." *T. L. O., supra,* at 341–342 (footnote omitted). As the majority rightly concedes, this search was justified at its inception because there were reasonable grounds to suspect that Redding possessed medication that violated school rules. . . . A finding of reasonable suspicion "does not deal with hard certainties, but with probabilities." *United States v. Cortez,* 449 U.S. 411, 418 (1981); see also *T. L. O., supra,* at 346 ("[T]he requirement of reasonable suspicion is not a requirement of absolute certainty"). To satisfy this standard, more than a mere "hunch" of wrongdoing is required, but "considerably" less suspicion is needed than would be required to "satisf[y] a preponderance of the evidence standard." *United States v. Arvizu,* 534 U.S. 266, 274 (2002) (internal quotation marks omitted).

Furthermore, in evaluating whether there is a reasonable "particularized and objective" basis for conducting a search based on suspected wrongdoing, government officials must consider the "totality of the circumstances." . . . School officials have a specialized understanding of the school environment, the habits of the students, and the concerns of the community, which enables them to "'formulat[e] certain common-sense conclusions about human behavior.'" *United States v. Sokolow,* 490 U.S. 1, 8 (1989) (quoting *Cortez, supra,* at 418). And like police officers, school officials are "entitled to make an assessment of the situation in light of [this] specialized training and familiarity with the customs of the [school]." See *Arvizu, supra,* at 276.

Here, petitioners had reasonable grounds to suspect that Redding was in possession of prescription and nonprescription drugs in violation of the school's prohibition of the "non-medical use, possession, or sale of a drug" on school property or at school events. 531 F. 3d 1071, 1076 (CA9 2008) (en banc); see also *id.,* at 1107 (Hawkins, J., dissenting) (explaining that the school policy defined "drugs" to include "'[a]ny prescription or over-the-counter drug, except those for which permission to use in school has been granted'"). As an initial matter, school officials were aware that a few years earlier, a student had become "seriously ill" and "spent several days in intensive care" after ingesting prescription medication obtained from a classmate. . . . Fourth Amendment searches do not occur in a vacuum; rather, context must inform the judicial inquiry. . . . In this instance, the suspicion of drug possession arose at a middle school that had "a history of problems with students using and distributing prohibited and illegal substances on campus." . . .

The school's substance-abuse problems had not abated by the 2003–2004 school year, which is when the challenged search of Redding took place. School officials had found alcohol and cigarettes in the girls' bathroom during the first school dance of the year and noticed that a group of students including Redding and Marissa Glines smelled of alcohol. . . . Several weeks later, another student, Jordan Romero, reported that Redding had hosted a party before the dance where she served whiskey, vodka, and tequila. . . . Romero had provided this report to school officials as a result of a meeting his mother scheduled with the officials after Romero "bec[a]me violent" and "sick to his stomach" one night and admitted that "he had taken some pills that he had got[ten] from a classmate." . . . At that meeting, Romero admitted that "certain students were bringing drugs and weapons on campus." . . . One week later, Romero handed the assistant principal a white pill that he said he had received from Glines. . . . He reported "that a group of students [were] planning on taking the pills at lunch." . . .

School officials justifiably took quick action in light of the lunchtime deadline. The assistant principal took the pill to the school nurse who identified it as prescription-strength 400-mg Ibuprofen. . . . A subsequent search of Glines and her belongings produced a razor blade, a Naproxen 200-mg pill, and several Ibuprofen 400-mg pills. . . . When asked, Glines claimed that she had received the pills from Redding. . . . A search of Redding's planner, which Glines had borrowed, then uncovered "several knives, several lighters, a cigarette, and a permanent marker." . . . Thus, as the majority acknowledges, . . . the totality of relevant circumstances justified a search of Redding for pills.

B

The remaining question is whether the search was reasonable in scope. Under *T. L. O.*, "a search will be permissible in its scope when the measures adopted are reasonably related to the objectives of the search and not excessively intrusive in light of the age and sex of the student and the nature of the infraction." 469 U.S., at 342. The majority concludes that the school officials' search of Redding's underwear was not "'reasonably related in scope to the circumstances which justified the interference in the first place,'" . . . notwithstanding the officials' reasonable suspicion that Redding "was involved in pill distribution." . . . According to the majority, to be reasonable, this school search required a showing of "danger to the students from the power of the drugs or their quantity" or a "reason to suppose that [Redding] was carrying pills in her underwear." . . . Each of these additional requirements is an unjustifiable departure from bedrock Fourth Amendment law in the school setting, where this Court has heretofore read the Fourth Amendment to grant considerable leeway to school officials. Because the school officials searched in a location where the pills could have been hidden, the search was reasonable in scope under *T. L. O.*

1

The majority finds that "subjective and reasonable societal expectations of personal privacy support . . . treat[ing]" this type of search, which it labels a "strip search," as "categorically distinct, requiring distinct elements of justification on the part of school authorities for going beyond a search of clothing and belongings." . . . Thus, in the majority's view, although the school officials had reasonable suspicion to believe that Redding had the pills on her person, . . . they needed some greater level of particularized suspicion to conduct this "strip search." There is no support for this contortion of the Fourth Amendment.

The Court has generally held that the reasonableness of a search's scope depends only on whether it is limited to the area that is capable of concealing the object of the search. See, *e.g., Wyoming v. Houghton*, 526 U.S. 295, 307 (1999) (Police officers "may inspect passengers' belongings found in the car that are capable of concealing the object of the search"); *Florida v. Jimeno*, 500 U.S. 248, 251 (1991) ("The scope of a search is generally defined by its expressed object"); *United States v. Johns*, 469 U.S. 478, 487 (1985) (search reasonable because "there is no plausible argument that the object of the search could not have been concealed in the packages"); *United States v. Ross*, 456 U.S. 798, 820 (1982) ("A lawful search . . . generally extends to the entire area in which the object of the search may be found").[1]

In keeping with this longstanding rule, the "nature of the infraction" referenced in *T. L. O.* delineates the proper scope of a search of students in a way that is identical to that permitted for searches outside the school—*i.e.,* the search must be limited to the areas where the object of that infraction could be concealed. See *Horton v. California*, 496 U.S. 128, 141 (1990) ("Police with a warrant for a rifle may search only places where rifles might be" (internal quotation marks omitted)); *Ross, supra,* at 824 ("[P]robable cause to believe that undocumented aliens are being transported in a van will not justify a warrantless search of a suitcase"). A search of a student therefore is permissible in scope under *T. L. O.* so long as it is objectively reasonable to believe that the area searched could conceal the contraband. The dissenting opinion below correctly captured this Fourth Amendment standard, noting that "if a student brought a baseball bat on campus in violation of school policy, a search of that student's shirt pocket would be patently unjustified." 531 F. 3d, at 1104 (opinion of Hawkins, J.).

The analysis of whether the scope of the search here was permissible under that standard is straightforward. Indeed, the majority does not dispute that "general background possibilities" establish that students conceal "contraband in their underwear." . . . It acknowledges that school officials had reasonable suspicion to look in Redding's backpack and outer clothing because if "Wilson's reasonable suspicion of pill distribution were not understood to support searches of outer clothes and backpack, it would not justify any search worth making." . . . The majority nevertheless concludes that proceeding any further with the search was unreasonable. See *ante,* at 8–10; see also *ante,* at 1 (Ginsburg, J., concurring in part and dissenting in part) ("Any reasonable search for the pills would have ended when inspection of Redding's backpack and jacket pockets yielded nothing"). But there is no support for this conclusion. The reasonable suspicion that Redding possessed the pills for distribution purposes did not dissipate simply because the search of her backpack turned up nothing. It was eminently reasonable to conclude that the backpack was empty because Redding was secreting the pills in a place she thought no one would look. See *Ross, supra,* at 820 ("Contraband goods rarely are strewn" about in plain view; "by their very nature such goods must be withheld from public view").

Redding would not have been the first person to conceal pills in her undergarments. See Hicks, Man Gets 17-Year Drug Sentence, [Corbin, KY] Times-Tribune, Oct. 7, 2008, p. 1 (Drug courier "told officials she had the [Oxycontin] pills concealed in her crotch"); Conley, Whitehaven: Traffic Stop Yields Hydrocodone Pills, [Memphis] Commercial Appeal, Aug. 3, 2007, p. B3 ("An additional 40 hydrocodone pills were found in her pants"); Caywood, Police Vehicle Chase Leads to Drug Arrests, [Worcester] Telegram & Gazette, June 7, 2008, p. A7 (25-year-old "allegedly had a cigar tube stuffed with pills tucked into the waistband of his pants"); Hubartt, 23-Year-Old Charged With Dealing Ecstasy, The [Fort Wayne] Journal Gazette, Aug. 8, 2007, p. C2 ("[W]hile he was being put into a squad car, his pants fell down and a plastic bag containing pink and orange pills fell on the ground"); Sebastian Residents Arrested in Drug Sting, Vero Beach Press Journal, Sept. 16, 2006, p. B2 (Arrestee "told them he had more pills 'down my pants'"). Nor will she be the last after today's decision, which announces the safest place to secrete contraband in school.

2

The majority compounds its error by reading the "nature of the infraction" aspect of the *T. L. O.* test as a license to limit searches based on a judge's assessment of a particular school policy. According to the majority, the scope of the search was impermissible because the school official "must have been aware of the nature and limited threat of the specific drugs he was searching for" and because he "had no reason to suspect that large amounts of the drugs were being passed around, or that individual students were receiving great numbers of pills." . . . Thus, in order to locate a rationale for finding a Fourth Amendment violation in this case, the majority retreats from its observation that the school's firm no-drug policy "makes sense, and there is no basis to claim that the search was unreasonable owing to some defect or shortcoming of the rule it was aimed at enforcing." . . .

Even accepting the majority's assurances that it is not attacking the rule's reasonableness, it certainly is attacking the rule's importance. This approach directly conflicts with *T. L. O.* in which the Court was "unwilling to adopt a standard under which the legality of a search is dependent upon a judge's evaluation of the relative importance of school rules." 469 U.S., at 342, n. 9. Indeed, the Court in *T. L. O.* expressly rejected the proposition that the majority seemingly endorses—that "some rules regarding student conduct are by nature too 'trivial' to justify a search based upon reasonable suspicion." . . .

The majority's decision in this regard also departs from another basic principle of the Fourth Amendment: that law enforcement officials can enforce with the same vigor all rules and regulations irrespective of the perceived importance of any of those rules. "In a long line of cases, we have said that when an officer has probable cause to believe a person committed even a minor crime in his presence, the balancing of private and public interests is not in doubt. The arrest is constitutionally reasonable." *Virginia v. Moore,* 553 U.S. __, __ (2008) (slip op., at 6). The Fourth Amendment rule for searches is the same: Police officers are entitled to search regardless of the perceived triviality of the underlying law. As we have explained, requiring police to make "sensitive, case-by-case determinations of government need," *Atwater v. Lago Vista,* 532 U.S. 318, 347 (2001), for a particular prohibition before conducting a search would "place police in an almost impossible spot," *id.,* at 350.

The majority has placed school officials in this "impossible spot" by questioning whether possession of Ibuprofen and Naproxen causes a severe enough threat to warrant investigation. Had the suspected infraction involved a street drug, the majority implies that it would have approved the scope of the search. . . . In effect, then, the majority has replaced a school rule that draws no distinction among drugs with a new one that does. As a result, a full search of a student's person for prohibited drugs will be permitted only if the Court agrees that the drug in question was sufficiently dangerous. Such a test is unworkable and unsound. School officials cannot be expected to halt searches based on the possibility that a court might later find that the particular infraction at issue is not severe enough to warrant an intrusive investigation.[2]

A rule promulgated by a school board represents the judgment of school officials that the rule is needed to maintain "school order" and "a proper educational environment." *T. L. O.,* 469 U.S., at 343, n. 9. Teachers, administrators, and the local school board are called upon both to "protect the . . . safety of students and school personnel" and "maintain an environment conducive to learning." *Id.,* at 353 (Blackmun, J., concurring in judgment). They are tasked with "watch[ing] over a large number of students" who "are inclined to test the outer boundaries of acceptable conduct and to imitate the misbehavior of a peer if that misbehavior is not dealt with quickly." *Id.,* at 352. In such an environment, something as simple as a "water pistol or peashooter can wreak [havoc] until it is taken away." *Ibid.* The danger posed by unchecked distribution and consumption of prescription pills by students certainly needs no elaboration.

Judges are not qualified to second-guess the best manner for maintaining quiet and order in the school environment. . . . It is a mistake for judges to assume the responsibility for deciding which school rules are important enough to allow for invasive searches and which rules are not.

3

Even if this Court were authorized to second-guess the importance of school rules, the Court's assessment of the importance of this district's policy is flawed. It is a crime to possess or use prescription-strength Ibuprofen without a prescription. See Ariz. Rev. Stat. Ann. §13–3406(A)(1) (West Supp. 2008) ("A person shall not knowingly . . . [p]ossess or use a prescription-only drug unless the person obtains the prescription-only drug pursuant to a valid prescription of a prescriber who is licensed pursuant to [state law]"). By prohibiting unauthorized prescription drugs on school grounds—and conducting a search to ensure students abide by that prohibition—the school rule here was consistent with a routine provision of the state criminal code. It hardly seems unreasonable for school officials to enforce a rule that, in effect, proscribes conduct that amounts to a crime. . . .

Admittedly, the Ibuprofen and Naproxen at issue in this case are not the prescription painkillers at the forefront of the prescription-drug-abuse problem. See Prescription for Danger 3 ("Pain relievers like Vicodin and OxyContin are the prescription drugs most commonly abused by teens"). But they are not without their own dangers. As nonsteroidal anti-inflammatory drugs (NSAIDs), they pose a risk of death from overdose. The Pill Book 821, 827 (H. Silverman, ed., 13th ed. 2008) (observing that Ibuprofen and Naproxen are NSAIDs and "[p]eople have died from NSAID overdoses"). Moreover, the side-effects caused by the use of NSAIDs can be magnified if they are taken in combination with other drugs. See, *e.g.,* Reactions Weekly, p. 18 (Issue no. 1235, Jan. 17, 2009) ("A 17-year-old girl developed allergic interstitial nephritis and renal failure while receiving escitalopram and ibuprofen"); *id.,* at 26 (Issue no. 1232, Dec. 13, 2008) ("A 16-month-old boy developed iron deficiency anaemia and hypoalbuminaemia during treatment with naproxen"); *id.,* at 15 (Issue no. 1220, Sept. 20, 2008) (18-year-old "was diagnosed with pill-induced oeso-phageal perforation" after taking ibuprofen "and was admitted to the [intensive care unit]"); *id.,* at 20 (Issue no. 1170, Sept. 22, 2007) ("A 12-year-old boy developed anaphylaxis following ingestion of ibuprofen").

If a student with a previously unknown intolerance to Ibuprofen or Naproxen were to take either drug and become ill, the public outrage would likely be directed toward the school for failing to take steps to prevent the unmonitored use of the drug. In light of the risks involved, a school's decision to establish and enforce a school prohibition on the possession of any unauthorized drug is thus a reasonable judgment.

꤮

In determining whether the search's scope was reasonable under the Fourth Amendment, it is therefore irrelevant whether officials suspected Redding of possessing prescription-strength Ibuprofen, nonprescription-strength Naproxen, or some harder street drug. Safford prohibited its possession on school property. Reasonable suspicion that Redding was in possession of drugs in violation of these policies, therefore, justified a search extending to any area where small pills could be concealed. The search did not violate the Fourth Amendment. . . .

Notes

[1.] The Court has adopted a different standard for searches involving an "intrusio[n] into the human body." *Schmerber v. California,* 384 U.S. 757, 770 (1966). The search here does not implicate the Court's cases governing bodily intrusions, however, because it did not involve a "physical intrusion, penetrating beneath the skin," *Skinner v. Railway Labor Executives' Assn.,* 489 U.S. 602, 616 (1989).

[2.] JUSTICE GINSBURG suggests that requiring Redding to "sit on a chair outside [the assistant principal's] office for over two hours" and failing to call her parents before conducting the search constitutes an "[a] buse of authority" that "should not be shielded by official immunity." See *ante,* at 1–2. But the school was under no constitutional obligation to call Redding's parents before conducting the search: "[R]easonableness under the Fourth Amendment does not require employing the least intrusive means, because the logic of such elaborate less-restrictive-alternative arguments could raise insuperable barriers to the exercise of virtually all search-and-seizure powers." *Board of Ed. of Independent School Dist. No. 92 of Pottawatomie Cty. v. Earls,* 536 U.S. 822, 837 (2002) (internal quotation marks and brackets omitted). For the same reason, the Constitution did not require school officials to ask "followup questions" after they had already developed reasonable suspicion that Redding possessed drugs. See *ante,* at 6, 10 (majority opinion); *ante,* at 1 (opinion of GINSBURG, J.). In any event, the suggestion that requiring Redding to sit in a chair for two hours amounted to a deprivation of her constitutional rights, or that school officials are required to engage in detailed interrogations before conducting searches for drugs, only reinforces the conclusion that the Judiciary is ill-equipped to second-guess the daily decisions made by public administrators. Cf. *Beard v. Banks,* 548 U.S. 521, 536–537 (2006) (THOMAS, J., concurring in judgment).

POSTSCRIPT

Is a Strip Search of Middle School Students That Is Aimed at Finding Drugs Prohibited Under the Fourth Amendment?

The *Redding* case is an example of a physical intrusion using physical means. Technological advances, however, are posing new challenges. We are developing technological capabilities to do things at a distance and to obtain information that previously would have required entering a physical location. Law enforcement's ability to invade privacy at a distance is increasing, and the Supreme Court is likely to be faced with cases in which data is collected without the student or citizen being aware of it. The Court has already upheld some novel search techniques outside of school, and most searches permitted outside of school are likely to be permitted in school. Consider the following:

- *Dow Chemical v. United States*, 476 U.S. 227 (1986)—The Court allowed aerial pictures taken by the Environmental Protection Agency (EPA) even though the company had refused to allow inspectors to enter.
- *Florida v. Riley*, 488 U.S. 445, 450 (1989)—The Court allowed a search in which a police officer in a helicopter looked into a greenhouse from a height of 400 feet and observed through openings in the roof what he thought was marijuana.
- *California v. Ciraolo*, 476 U.S. 207, 213–214 (1986)—The Court held that police officers were not "searching" when they flew over the defendant's property and observed marijuana growing.
- *Smith v. Maryland*, 442 U.S. 735, 742–744 (1979)—The Court allowed the authorities to look at "pen registers," or records of telephone numbers dialed, without a warrant.

One exception to the trend is *Danny Lee Kyllo v. United States*, 533 U.S. 27 (2001), where the Court held that the use without a warrant of thermal imaging devices which reveal information "that would previously have been unknowable without physical intrusion" violates the Fourth Amendment. The police had used the thermal imaging technology on the assumption that to grow marijuana indoors, one needs to provide a lot of light so plants can photosynthesize.

In *United States v. Place*, 462 U.S. 696 (1983), the Court allowed the use of dogs when the sniff "discloses only the presence or absence of narcotics." We are in an era in which there are many electronic substitutes for such dogs. We are also in an era in which we can be tracked via cameras in many locations and GPS systems in cell phones. We are, in other words, in an era in which the meaning of the Fourth Amendment is likely to be an issue in increasing numbers of cases.

Background information on law enforcement and the drug problem can be found on the Web site of the Drug Enforcement Administration of the U.S. Department of Justice at http://www.justice.gov/dea/. The thermal imaging issue is discussed in Kathleen A. Lomas, "Bad Physics and Bad Law: A Review of the Constitutionality of Thermal Imagery Surveillance After *United States v. Elkins,*" 34 *University of San Francisco Law Review* 799 (2000). Other articles about new technologies and the Fourth Amendment are Tobias W. Mock, "The TSA's New X-Ray Vision: The Fourth Amendment Implications of 'Body-Scan' Searches at Domestic Airport Security Checkpoints," 49 *Santa Clara L. Rev.* 213 (2009) and Ian James Samuel, "Warrantless Location Tracking," 83 *N.Y.U.L. Rev.* 1324 (2008). A report on the oral argument in the *Redding* case is Dahlia Lithwick, "Search Me: The Supreme Court Is Neither Hot nor Bothered by Strip Searches," *Slate* (http://www.slate.com/id/2216608).

ISSUE 13

Does the "Cruel and Unusual Punishment" Clause of the Eighth Amendment Bar the Imposition of the Death Penalty on Juveniles?

YES: Anthony Kennedy, from Majority Opinion, *Roper v. Simmons,* U.S. Supreme Court (March 1, 2005)

NO: Antonin Scalia, from Dissenting Opinion, *Roper v. Simmons,* U.S. Supreme Court (March 1, 2005)

ISSUE SUMMARY

YES: Supreme Court Justice Anthony Kennedy holds that the Constitution prohibits the execution of a person who was under the age of 18 at the time of the offense.

NO: Supreme Court Justice Antonin Scalia believes that the Constitution does not preclude the execution of a juvenile.

The questions of how a society punishes its wrongdoers, and to what extent it does so, are central to the very structure of social organization. These questions are particularly complex in democratic societies. Modern states, democratic or not, claim a monopoly over the use of violence. When democratic states punish, they do so in the name of its citizens. Such questions are particularly urgent when they deal with capital punishment. Death, it is often said, is different. If someone takes a life, should the state take his or hers in return? These questions are informed by centuries of debate. For example, in 428 B.C.E., Thucydides recorded the following arguments by Cleon in support of the death penalty:

> Punish them as they deserve, and teach your other allies by a striking example that the penalty of rebellion is death. Let them once understand this and you will not so often have to neglect your enemies while you are fighting with your confederates.

In response, Diodotus wrote:

All states and individuals are alike prone to err, and there is no law that will prevent them, or why should men have exhausted the list of punishments in search of enactments to protect them from evildoers? It is probable that in early times the penalties for the greatest offenses were less severe, and that as these were disregarded, the penalty of death has been by degrees in most cases arrived at, which is itself disregarded in like manner. Either some means of terror more terrible than this must be discovered, or it must be owned that this restraint is useless. . . . We must make up our minds to look for our protection not to legal terrors but to careful administration.

During the last four decades, the United States Supreme Court has been confronted with death penalty cases almost every term. The most significant was that of *Furman v. Georgia,* 408 U.S. 238 (1972). Furman, a 26-year-old African American, had killed a homeowner during a break-in and was sentenced to death. In a 5-4 decision, the Court overturned the sentence. It held that the procedure used by Georgia (and most other states at the time) was "cruel and unusual" and, therefore, a violation of the Eighth Amendment of the Constitution. Two justices, Thurgood Marshall and William Brennan, believed that at that point in the development of American society, infliction of the death penalty under any circumstances violated the Cruel and Unusual Punishments Clause of the Eighth Amendment. The three other justices in the *Furman* majority, however, held that the death penalty was not inherently unconstitutional, but that the procedures through which it was applied in that specific case were. In particular, Georgia law left it to the discretion of the jury to decide whether or not capital punishment was appropriate in each case, leading the death penalty to be administered in an arbitrary and potentially discriminatory fashion. *Furman* resulted in a nationwide moratorium on capital punishment that lasted until the Supreme Court revisited the issue in 1976 in *Gregg v. Georgia,* 428 U.S. 153. In *Gregg,* the Court upheld a revised Georgia death penalty statute that, in keeping with the *Furman* guidelines, was intended to limit the capital jury's discretion. The process effected a bifurcated trial—divided into a "guilt phase" and a "penalty phase"—that aimed at greater equalization of punishment, while, at the same time, remaining sensitive to the unique characteristics of the individual defendant and the circumstances of the crime.

Actual executions resumed in 1977 and 34 states currently have a death penalty. From the 1970s to the present, the United States Supreme Court has continued to examine various aspects of the administration of capital punishment, but a majority of the Court has continued to find that the death penalty in itself is consistent with the requirements of the Eighth Amendment. A majority of the Court has also held, however, that the meaning of the Eighth Amendment is not fixed but continues to evolve. Accordingly, in 2002, the Court found in *Atkins v. Virginia,* 536 U.S. 304, that a "national consensus" had evolved against the execution of the mentally retarded and held that such punishment now violates the Eighth Amendment's prohibition of cruel and unusual punishment.

YES ↵

Anthony Kennedy

Majority Opinion, *Donald P. Roper, Superintendent, Potosi Correctional Center, Petitionern v. Christopher Simmons*

JUSTICE KENNEDY delivered the opinion of the Court.

This case requires us to address, for the second time in a decade and a half, whether it is permissible under the Eighth and Fourteenth Amendments to the Constitution of the United States to execute a juvenile offender who was older than 15 but younger than 18 when he committed a capital crime. In *Stanford v. Kentucky*, 492 U.S. 361 (1989), a divided Court rejected the proposition that the Constitution bars capital punishment for juvenile offenders in this age group. We reconsider the question. . . .

◦◦◦

After these proceedings in Simmons' case had run their course, this Court held that the Eighth and Fourteenth Amendments prohibit the execution of a mentally retarded person. *Atkins v. Virginia*, 536 U.S. 304 (2002). Simmons filed a new petition for state postconviction relief, arguing that the reasoning of *Atkins* established that the Constitution prohibits the execution of a juvenile who was under 18 when the crime was committed.

The Missouri Supreme Court agreed. *State ex rel. Simmons v. Roper*, 112 S. W. 3d 397 (2003) (en banc). It held that since *Stanford*,

> "a national consensus has developed against the execution of juvenile offenders, as demonstrated by the fact that eighteen states now bar such executions for juveniles, that twelve other states bar executions altogether, that no state has lowered its age of execution below 18 since *Stanford*, that five states have legislatively or by case law raised or established the minimum age at 18, and that the imposition of the juvenile death penalty has become truly unusual over the last decade." 112 S. W. 3d, at 399.

From Supreme Court of the United States, March 1, 2005.

On this reasoning it set aside Simmons' death sentence and resentenced him to "life imprisonment without eligibility for probation, parole, or release except by act of the Governor." *Id.*, at 413.

We granted certiorari, 540 U.S. 1160 (2004), and now affirm.

⋯⟡⋯

The Eighth Amendment provides: "Excessive bail shall not be required, nor excessive fines imposed, nor cruel and unusual punishments inflicted." The provision is applicable to the States through the Fourteenth Amendment. As the Court explained in *Atkins,* the Eighth Amendment guarantees individuals the right not to be subjected to excessive sanctions. The right flows from the basic "'precept of justice that punishment for crime should be graduated and proportioned to [the] offense.'" By protecting even those convicted of heinous crimes, the Eighth Amendment reaffirms the duty of the government to respect the dignity of all persons.

The prohibition against "cruel and unusual punishments," like other expansive language in the Constitution, must be interpreted according to its text, by considering history, tradition, and precedent, and with due regard for its purpose and function in the constitutional design. To implement this framework we have established the propriety and affirmed the necessity of referring to "the evolving standards of decency that mark the progress of a maturing society" to determine which punishments are so disproportionate as to be cruel and unusual.

In *Thompson v. Oklahoma*, 487 U.S. 815 (1988), a plurality of the Court determined that our standards of decency do not permit the execution of any offender under the age of 16 at the time of the crime. *Id.*, at 818–838. The plurality opinion explained that no death penalty State that had given express consideration to a minimum age for the death penalty had set the age lower than 16. *Id.*, at 826–829. The plurality also observed that "[t]he conclusion that it would offend civilized standards of decency to execute a person who was less than 16 years old at the time of his or her offense is consistent with the views that have been expressed by respected professional organizations, by other nations that share our Anglo-American heritage, and by the leading members of the Western European community." *Id.*, at 830. . . .

The next year, in *Stanford v. Kentucky,* the Court, . . . referred to contemporary standards of decency in this country and concluded the Eighth and Fourteenth Amendments did not proscribe the execution of juvenile offenders over 15 but under 18. . . . A plurality of the Court also "emphatically reject[ed]" the suggestion that the Court should bring its own judgment to bear on the acceptability of the juvenile death penalty.

The same day the Court decided *Stanford,* it held that the Eighth Amendment did not mandate a categorical exemption from the death penalty for the mentally retarded. *Penry v. Lynaugh,* 492 U.S. 302 (1989). In reaching this conclusion it stressed that only two States had enacted laws banning the imposition of the death penalty on a mentally retarded person convicted of a capital offense. *Id.*, at 334. According to the Court, "the two state statutes prohibiting execution of the mentally retarded, even when added to the 14 States that have rejected capital punishment completely, [did] not provide sufficient evidence at present of a national consensus." *Ibid.*

Three Terms ago the subject was reconsidered in *Atkins*. We held that standards of decency have evolved since *Penry* and now demonstrate that the execution of the mentally retarded is cruel and unusual punishment. The Court noted objective indicia of society's standards, as expressed in legislative enactments and state practice with respect to executions of the mentally retarded. When *Atkins* was decided only a minority of States permitted the practice, and even in those States it was rare. 536 U.S., at 314–315. On the basis of these indicia the Court determined that executing mentally retarded offenders "has become truly unusual, and it is fair to say that a national consensus has developed against it." *Id.,* at 316. . . .

The *Atkins* Court neither repeated nor relied upon the statement in *Stanford* that the Court's independent judgment has no bearing on the acceptability of a particular punishment under the Eighth Amendment. Instead we returned to the rule, established in decisions predating *Stanford*, that "'the Constitution contemplates that in the end our own judgment will be brought to bear on the question of the acceptability of the death penalty under the Eighth Amendment.'" . . . Based on these considerations and on the finding of national consensus against executing the mentally retarded, the Court ruled that the death penalty constitutes an excessive sanction for the entire category of mentally retarded offenders, and that the Eighth Amendment "'places a substantive restriction on the State's power to take the life' of a mentally retarded offender."

Just as the *Atkins* Court reconsidered the issue decided in *Penry,* we now reconsider the issue decided in *Stanford*. The beginning point is a review of objective indicia of consensus, as expressed in particular by the enactments of legislatures that have addressed the question. This data gives us essential instruction. We then must determine, in the exercise of our own independent judgment, whether the death penalty is a disproportionate punishment for juveniles.

⚜

The evidence of national consensus against the death penalty for juveniles is similar, and in some respects parallel, to the evidence *Atkins* held sufficient to demonstrate a national consensus against the death penalty for the mentally retarded. . . .

Though less dramatic than the change from *Penry* to *Atkins* . . . we still consider the change from *Stanford* to this case to be significant. . . . The number of States that have abandoned capital punishment for juvenile offenders since *Stanford* is smaller than the number of States that abandoned capital punishment for the mentally retarded after *Penry;* yet we think the same consistency of direction of change has been demonstrated. Since *Stanford*, no State that previously prohibited capital punishment for juveniles has reinstated it. This fact, coupled with the trend toward abolition of the juvenile death penalty, carries special force in light of the general popularity of anti-crime legislation, and in light of the particular trend in recent years toward cracking down on juvenile crime in other respects. . . .

As in *Atkins,* the objective indicia of consensus in this case—the rejection of the juvenile death penalty in the majority of States; the infrequency of its use even where it remains on the books; and the consistency in the trend toward abolition of the practice—provide sufficient evidence that today our society views juveniles, in the words *Atkins* used respecting the mentally retarded, as "categorically less culpable than the average criminal." 536 U.S., at 316.

⋅◐⋅

A majority of States have rejected the imposition of the death penalty on juvenile offenders under 18, and we now hold this is required by the Eighth Amendment.

Because the death penalty is the most severe punishment, the Eighth Amendment applies to it with special force. Capital punishment must be limited to those offenders who commit "a narrow category of the most serious crimes" and whose extreme culpability makes them "the most deserving of execution." . . .

Three general differences between juveniles under 18 and adults demonstrate that juvenile offenders cannot with reliability be classified among the worst offenders. First, . . .

The second area of difference . . .

The third broad difference . . .

These differences render suspect any conclusion that a juvenile falls among the worst offenders. The susceptibility of juveniles to immature and irresponsible behavior means "their irresponsible conduct is not as morally reprehensible as that of an adult." *Thompson, supra,* at 835 (plurality opinion). Their own vulnerability and comparative lack of control over their immediate surroundings mean juveniles have a greater claim than adults to be forgiven for failing to escape negative influences in their whole environment. See *Stanford,* 492 U.S., at 395 (Brennan, J., dissenting). The reality that juveniles still struggle to define their identity means it is less supportable to conclude that even a heinous crime committed by a juvenile is evidence of irretrievably depraved character. From a moral standpoint it would be misguided to equate the failings of a minor with those of an adult, for a greater possibility exists that a minor's character deficiencies will be reformed. Indeed, "[t]he relevance of youth as a mitigating factor derives from the fact that the signature qualities of youth are transient; as individuals mature, the impetuousness and recklessness that may dominate in younger years can subside." *Johnson, supra,* at 368; see also Steinberg & Scott 1014 ("For most teens, [risky or antisocial] behaviors are fleeting; they cease with maturity as individual identity becomes settled. Only a relatively small proportion of adolescents who experiment in risky or illegal activities develop entrenched patterns of problem behavior that persist into adulthood"). . . .

Once the diminished culpability of juveniles is recognized, it is evident that the penological justifications for the death penalty apply to them with lesser force than to adults. We have held there are two distinct social purposes served by the death penalty: "'retribution and deterrence of capital crimes by prospective offenders.'" As for retribution, we remarked in *Atkins* that "[i]f the culpability of the average murderer is insufficient to justify the most extreme sanction available to the State, the lesser culpability of the mentally retarded offender surely does not merit that form of retribution." The same conclusions follow from the lesser culpability of the juvenile offender. Whether viewed as an attempt to express the community's moral outrage or as an attempt to right the balance for the wrong to the victim, the case for retribution is not as strong with a minor as with an adult. Retribution is not proportional if the law's most severe penalty is imposed on one whose culpability or blameworthiness is diminished, to a substantial degree, by reason of youth and immaturity.

As for deterrence, it is unclear whether the death penalty has a significant or even measurable deterrent effect on juveniles, as counsel for the petitioner acknowledged at oral argument. . . .

In concluding that neither retribution nor deterrence provides adequate justification for imposing the death penalty on juvenile offenders, we cannot deny or overlook the brutal crimes too many juvenile offenders have committed. . . .

Drawing the line at 18 years of age is subject, of course, to the objections always raised against categorical rules. The qualities that distinguish juveniles from adults do not disappear when an individual turns 18. By the same token, some under 18 have already attained a level of maturity some adults will never reach. For the reasons we have discussed, however, a line must be drawn. The plurality opinion in *Thompson* drew the line at 16. In the intervening years the *Thompson* plurality's conclusion that offenders under 16 may not be executed has not been challenged. The logic of *Thompson* extends to those who are under 18. The age of 18 is the point where society draws the line for many purposes between childhood and adulthood. It is, we conclude, the age at which the line for death eligibility ought to rest. . . .

Our determination that the death penalty is disproportionate punishment for offenders under 18 finds confirmation in the stark reality that the United States is the only country in the world that continues to give official sanction to the juvenile death penalty. This reality does not become controlling, for the task of interpreting the Eighth Amendment remains our responsibility. Yet at least from the time of the Court's decision in *Trop,* the Court has referred to the laws of other countries and to international authorities as instructive for its interpretation of the Eighth Amendment's prohibition of "cruel and unusual punishments." . . .

As respondent and a number of *amici* emphasize, Article 37 of the United Nations Convention on the Rights of the Child, which every country in the world has ratified save for the United States and Somalia, contains an express prohibition on capital punishment for crimes committed by juveniles under 18. . . .

Respondent and his *amici* have submitted, and petitioner does not contest, that only seven countries other than the United States have executed juvenile offenders since 1990: Iran, Pakistan, Saudi Arabia, Yemen, Nigeria, the Democratic Republic of Congo, and China. Since then each of these countries has either abolished capital punishment for juveniles or made public disavowal of the practice. Brief for Respondent 49–50. In sum, it is fair to say that the United States now stands alone in a world that has turned its face against the juvenile death penalty. . . .

It is proper that we acknowledge the overwhelming weight of international opinion against the juvenile death penalty, resting in large part on the understanding that the instability and emotional imbalance of young people may often be a factor in the crime. See Brief for Human Rights Committee of the Bar of England and Wales et al. as *Amici Curiae* 10–11. The opinion of the world community, while not controlling our outcome, does provide respected and significant confirmation for our own conclusions.

Over time, from one generation to the next, the Constitution has come to earn the high respect and even, as Madison dared to hope, the veneration of the American people. See The Federalist No. 49, p. 314 (C. Rossiter ed. 1961). The document sets forth, and rests upon, innovative principles original to the American experience, such as federalism; a proven balance in political mechanisms through separation of powers; specific guarantees for the accused in criminal cases; and broad provisions to secure individual freedom and preserve human dignity. These doctrines and guarantees are central to the American experience and remain essential to our present-day self-definition and national identity. Not the least of the reasons we honor the Constitution, then, is because we know it to be our own. It does not lessen our fidelity to the Constitution or our pride in its origins to acknowledge that the express affirmation of certain fundamental rights by other nations and peoples simply underscores the centrality of those same rights within our own heritage of freedom.

The Eighth and Fourteenth Amendments forbid imposition of the death penalty on offenders who were under the age of 18 when their crimes were committed. The judgment of the Missouri Supreme Court setting aside the sentence of death imposed upon Christopher Simmons is affirmed.

It is so ordered.

Antonin Scalia

→ NO

Minority Opinion, *Donald P. Roper, Superintendent, Potosi Correctional Center, Petitioner v. Christopher Simmons*

J USTICE SCALIA, with whom THE CHIEF JUSTICE and JUSTICE THOMAS join, dissenting.

In urging approval of a constitution that gave life-tenured judges the power to nullify laws enacted by the people's representatives, Alexander Hamilton assured the citizens of New York that there was little risk in this, since "[t]he judiciary ... ha[s] neither FORCE nor WILL but merely judgment." The Federalist No. 78, p. 465 (C. Rossiter ed. 1961). But Hamilton had in mind a traditional judiciary, "bound down by strict rules and precedents which serve to define and point out their duty in every particular case that comes before them." *Id.*, at 471. Bound down, indeed. What a mockery today's opinion makes of Hamilton's expectation, announcing the Court's conclusion that the meaning of our Constitution has changed over the past 15 years—not, mind you, that this Court's decision 15 years ago was *wrong,* but that the Constitution *has changed.* The Court reaches this implausible result by purporting to advert, not to the original meaning of the Eighth Amendment, but to "the evolving standards of decency," *ante,* at 6 (internal quotation marks omitted), of our national society. It then finds, on the flimsiest of grounds, that a national consensus which could not be perceived in our people's laws barely 15 years ago now solidly exists. Worse still, the Court says in so many words that what our people's laws say about the issue does not, in the last analysis, matter: "[I]n the end our own judgment will be brought to bear on the question of the acceptability of the death penalty under the Eighth Amendment." *Ante,* at 9 (internal quotation marks omitted). The Court thus proclaims itself sole arbiter of our Nation's moral standards—and in the course of discharging that awesome responsibility purports to take guidance from the views of foreign courts and legislatures. Because I do not believe that the meaning of our Eighth Amendment, any more than the meaning of other provisions of our Constitution, should be determined by the subjective views of five Members of this Court and like-minded foreigners, I dissent. . . .

From Supreme Court of the United States, March 1, 2005.

We have held that this determination should be based on "objective indicia that reflect the public attitude toward a given sanction"—namely, "statutes passed by society's elected representatives." As in *Atkins v. Virginia*, 536 U.S. 304, 312 (2002), the Court dutifully recites this test and claims half-heartedly that a national consensus has emerged since our decision in *Stanford*, because 18 States—or 47% of States that permit capital punishment—now have legislation prohibiting the execution of offenders under 18, and because all of four States have adopted such legislation since *Stanford*.

Words have no meaning if the views of less than 50% of death penalty States can constitute a national consensus. Our previous cases have required overwhelming opposition to a challenged practice, generally over a long period of time. . . .

In an attempt to keep afloat its implausible assertion of national consensus, the Court throws overboard a proposition well established in our Eighth Amendment jurisprudence. "It should be observed," the Court says, "that the *Stanford* Court should have considered those States that had abandoned the death penalty altogether as part of the consensus against the juvenile death penalty . . . ; a State's decision to bar the death penalty altogether of necessity demonstrates a judgment that the death penalty is inappropriate for all offenders, including juveniles." The insinuation that the Court's new method of counting contradicts only "the *Stanford* Court" is misleading. *None* of our cases dealing with an alleged constitutional limitation upon the death penalty has counted, as States supporting a consensus in favor of that limitation, States that have eliminated the death penalty entirely. And with good reason. Consulting States that bar the death penalty concerning the necessity of making an exception to the penalty for offenders under 18 is rather like including old-order Amishmen in a consumer-preference poll on the electric car. Of *course* they don't like it, but that sheds no light whatever on the point at issue. That 12 States favor no executions says something about consensus against the death penalty, but nothing—absolutely nothing—about consensus that offenders under 18 deserve special immunity from such a penalty. In repealing the death penalty, those 12 States considered *none* of the factors that the Court puts forth as determinative of the issue before us today—lower culpability of the young, inherent recklessness, lack of capacity for considered judgment, etc. What might be relevant, perhaps, is how many of those States permit 16- and 17-year-old offenders to be treated as adults with respect to non-capital offenses. (They all do;[1] indeed, some even *require* that juveniles as young as 14 be tried as adults if they are charged with murder.[2]) The attempt by the Court to turn its remarkable minority consensus into a faux majority by counting Amishmen is an act of nomological desperation. . . .

The Court's reliance on the infrequency of executions, for under-18 murderers, *ante,* at 10–11, 13, credits an argument that this Court considered and explicitly rejected in *Stanford*. That infrequency is explained, we accurately said, both by "the undisputed fact that a far smaller percentage of capital crimes are committed by persons under 18 than over 18," 492 U.S., at 374, and by the fact that juries are required at sentencing to consider the offender's youth as a mitigating factor. Thus, "it is not only possible, but overwhelmingly probable, that the very considerations which induce [respondent] and [his] supporters to believe that death should *never* be imposed on offenders under 18 cause prosecutors and juries to believe that it should *rarely* be imposed." *Stanford, supra,* at 374. . . .

◆

Of course, the real force driving today's decision is not the actions of four state legislatures, but the Court's " ' "own judgment" ' " that murderers younger than 18 can never be as morally culpable as older counterparts. The Court claims that this usurpation of the role of moral arbiter is simply a "retur[n] to the rul[e] established in decisions predating *Stanford*." That supposed rule—which is reflected solely in dicta and never once in a *holding* that purports to supplant the consensus of the American people with the Justices' views[3]—was repudiated in *Stanford* for the very good reason that it has no foundation in law or logic. If the Eighth Amendment set forth an ordinary rule of law, it would indeed be the role of this Court to say what the law is. But the Court having pronounced that the Eighth Amendment is an ever-changing reflection of "the evolving standards of decency" of our society, it makes no sense for the Justices then to *prescribe* those standards rather than discern them from the practices of our people. On the evolving-standards hypothesis, the only legitimate function of this Court is to identify a moral consensus of the American people. By what conceivable warrant can nine lawyers presume to be the authoritative conscience of the Nation?[4]

The reason for insistence on legislative primacy is obvious and fundamental: "'[I]n a democratic society legislatures, not courts, are constituted to respond to the will and consequently the moral values of the people.'" *Gregg v. Georgia,* 428 U.S. 153, 175–176 (1976) (joint opinion of Stewart, Powell, and STEVENS, JJ.) (quoting *Furman v. Georgia,* 408 U.S. 238, 383 (1972) (Burger, C. J., dissenting)). For a similar reason we have, in our determination of society's moral standards, consulted the practices of sentencing juries: Juries "'maintain a link between contemporary community values and the penal system'" that this Court cannot claim for itself. *Gregg, supra,* at 181 (quoting *Witherspoon v. Illinois,* 391 U.S. 510, 519, n. 15 (1968)).

Today's opinion provides a perfect example of why judges are ill equipped to make the type of legislative judgments the Court insists on making here. To support its opinion that States should be prohibited from imposing the death penalty on anyone who committed murder before age 18, the Court looks to scientific and sociological studies, picking and choosing those that support its position. It never explains why those particular studies are methodologically sound; none was ever entered into evidence or tested in an adversarial proceeding. . . .

In other words, all the Court has done today, to borrow from another context, is to look over the heads of the crowd and pick out its friends. . . .

That "almost every State prohibits those under 18 years of age from voting, serving on juries, or marrying without parental consent," *ante,* at 15, is patently irrelevant—and is yet another resurrection of an argument that this Court gave a decent burial in *Stanford*. . . . As we explained in *Stanford*, it is "absurd to think that one must be mature enough to drive carefully, to drink responsibly, or to vote intelligently, in order to be mature enough to understand that murdering another human being is profoundly wrong, and to conform one's conduct to that most minimal of all civilized standards." Serving on a jury or entering into marriage also involve decisions far more sophisticated than the simple decision not to take another's life. . . .

The Court's contention that the goals of retribution and deterrence are not served by executing murderers under 18 is also transparently false. The argument that "[r]etribution is not proportional if the law's most severe penalty is imposed on one whose culpability or blameworthiness is diminished," is simply an extension of the earlier, false generalization that youth *always* defeats culpability. The Court claims that "juveniles will be less susceptible to deterrence," *ante*, at 18, because "'[t]he likelihood that the teenage offender has made the kind of cost-benefit analysis that attaches any weight to the possibility of execution is so remote as to be virtually nonexistent.'" The Court unsurprisingly finds no support for this astounding proposition, save its own case law. The facts of this very case show the proposition to be false. Before committing the crime, Simmons encouraged his friends to join him by assuring them that they could "get away with it" because they were minors. This fact may have influenced the jury's decision to impose capital punishment despite Simmons' age. Because the Court refuses to entertain the possibility that its own unsubstantiated generalization about juveniles could be wrong, it ignores this evidence entirely.

❧

Though the views of our own citizens are essentially irrelevant to the Court's decision today, the views of other countries and the so-called international community take center stage.

The Court begins by noting that "Article 37 of the United Nations Convention on the Rights of the Child, entered into force Sept. 2, 1990, which every country in the world has ratified save *for the United States* and Somalia, contains an express prohibition on capital punishment for crimes committed by juveniles under 18.". . .

Unless the Court has added to its arsenal the power to join and ratify treaties on behalf of the United States, I cannot see how this evidence favors, rather than refutes, its position. That the Senate and the President—those actors our Constitution empowers to enter into treaties, see Art. II, §2—have declined to join and ratify treaties prohibiting execution of under-18 offenders can only suggest that *our country* has either not reached a national consensus on the question, or has reached a consensus contrary to what the Court announces. . . .

More fundamentally, however, the basic premise of the Court's argument—that American law should conform to the laws of the rest of the world—ought to be rejected out of hand. In fact the Court itself does not believe it. In many significant respects the laws of most other countries differ from our law—including not only such explicit provisions of our Constitution as the right to jury trial and grand jury indictment, but even many interpretations of the Constitution prescribed by this Court itself. The Court-pronounced exclusionary rule, for example, is distinctively American. . . .

The Court has been oblivious to the views of other countries when deciding how to interpret our Constitution's requirement that "Congress shall make no law respecting an establishment of religion. . . ."

And let us not forget the Court's abortion jurisprudence, which makes us one of only six countries that allow abortion on demand until the point of viability. . . .

The Court should either profess its willingness to reconsider all these matters in light of the views of foreigners, or else it should cease putting forth foreigners' views as part of the *reasoned basis* of its decisions. To invoke alien law when it agrees with one's own thinking, and ignore it otherwise, is not reasoned decisionmaking, but sophistry.[5]

To add insult to injury, the Court affirms the Missouri Supreme Court without even admonishing that court for its flagrant disregard of our precedent in *Stanford*. Until today, we have always held that "it is this Court's prerogative alone to overrule one of its precedents." . . . Today, however, the Court silently approves a state-court decision that blatantly rejected controlling precedent.

One must admit that the Missouri Supreme Court's action, and this Court's indulgent reaction, are, in a way, understandable. In a system based upon constitutional and statutory text democratically adopted, the concept of "law" ordinarily signifies that particular words have a fixed meaning. Such law does not change, and this Court's pronouncement of it therefore remains authoritative until (confessing our prior error) we overrule. The Court has purported to make of the Eighth Amendment, however, a mirror of the passing and changing sentiment of American society regarding penology. The lower courts can look into that mirror as well as we can; and what we saw 15 years ago bears no necessary relationship to what they see today. Since they are not looking at the same text, but at a different scene, why should our earlier decision control their judgment?

However sound philosophically, this is no way to run a legal system. We must disregard the new reality that, to the extent our Eighth Amendment decisions constitute something more than a show of hands on the current Justices' current personal views about penology, they purport to be nothing more than a snapshot of American public opinion at a particular point in time (with the timeframes now shortened to a mere 15 years). We must treat these decisions just as though they represented *real* law, *real* prescriptions democratically adopted by the American people, as conclusively (rather than sequentially) construed by this Court. Allowing lower courts to reinterpret the Eighth Amendment whenever they decide enough time has passed for a new snapshot leaves this Court's decisions without any force—especially since the "evolution" of our Eighth Amendment is no longer determined by objective criteria. To allow lower courts to behave as we do, "updating" the Eighth Amendment as needed, destroys stability and makes our case law an unreliable basis for the designing of laws by citizens and their representatives, and for action by public officials. The result will be to crown arbitrariness with chaos.

Notes

1. See Alaska Stat. §47.12.030 (Lexis 2002); Haw. Rev. Stat. §571-22 (1999); Iowa Code §232.45 (2003); Me. Rev. Stat. Ann., Tit. 15, §3101(4) (West 2003); Mass. Gen. Laws Ann., ch. 119, §74 (West 2003); Mich. Comp. Laws Ann. §764.27 (West 2000); Minn. Stat. §260B.125 (2002); N. D. Cent. Code §27-20-34 (Lexis Supp. 2003); R. I. Gen. Laws §14-1-7 (Lexis 2002); Vt. Stat. Ann., Tit. 33, §5516 (Lexis 2001); W. Va. Code §49-5-10 (Lexis 2004); Wis. Stat. §938.18 (2003–2004); see also National Center for Juvenile Justice, Trying and Sentencing Juveniles as Adults: An Analysis of State Transfer and Blended Sentencing Laws 1 (Oct. 2003). The District of Columbia is the only jurisdiction without a death penalty that specifically exempts under-18 offenders from its harshest sanction—life imprisonment without parole. See D. C. Code §22-2104 (West 2001).

2. See Mass. Gen. Laws Ann., ch. 119, §74 (West 2003); N. D. Cent. Code §27-20-34 (Lexis Supp. 2003); W. Va. Code §49-5-10 (Lexis 2004).

3. See, e.g., *Enmund v. Florida,* 458 U.S. 782, 801 (1982) ("[W]e have no reason to disagree with th[e] judgment [of the state legislatures] for purposes of construing and applying the Eighth Amendment"); *Coker v. Georgia,* 433 U.S. 584, 597 (1977) (plurality opinion) ("[T]he legislative rejection of capital punishment for rape strongly confirms our own judgment").

4. JUSTICE O'CONNOR agrees with our analysis that no national consensus exists here, *ante,* at 8–12 (dissenting opinion). She is nonetheless prepared (like the majority) to override the judgment of America's legislatures if it contradicts her own assessment of "moral proportionality," *ante,* at 12. She dissents here only because it does not. The votes in today's case demonstrate that the offending of selected lawyers' moral sentiments is not a predictable basis for law—much less a democratic one.

5. JUSTICE O'CONNOR asserts that the Eighth Amendment has a "special character," in that it "draws its meaning directly from the maturing values of civilized society." *Ante,* at 19. Nothing in the text reflects such a distinctive character—and we have certainly applied the "maturing values" rationale to give brave new meaning to other provisions of the Constitution, such as the Due Process Clause and the Equal Protection Clause. See, *e.g., Lawrence v. Texas,* 539 U.S. 558, 571–573 (2003); *United States v. Virginia,* 518 U.S. 515, 532–534 (1996); *Planned Parenthood of Southeastern Pa. v. Casey,* 505 U.S. 833, 847–850 (1992). Justice O'Connor asserts that an international consensus can at least "serve to confirm the reasonableness of a consonant and genuine American consensus." *Ante,* at 19. Surely not unless it can also demonstrate the unreasonableness of such a consensus. Either America's principles are its own, or they follow the world; one cannot have it both ways. Finally, Justice O'Connor finds it unnecessary to

consult foreign law in the present case because there is "no . . . domestic consensus" to be confirmed. *Ibid.* But since she believes that the Justices can announce their own requirements of "moral proportionality" despite the absence of consensus, why would foreign law not be relevant to *that* judgment? If foreign law is powerful enough to supplant the judgment of the American people, surely it is powerful enough to change a personal assessment of moral proportionality.

POSTSCRIPT

Does the "Cruel and Unusual Punishment" Clause of the Eighth Amendment Bar the Imposition of the Death Penalty on Juveniles?

Roper v. Simmons presented the United States Supreme Court with the question of whether or not the execution of someone who was 16 or 17 at the time of their capital offense is "cruel and unusual." Clearly, the Eighth Amendment does not explicitly prohibit capital punishment. What is far less clear is what the language of that amendment *means* when we attempt to apply it under ever-changing historical and cultural conditions. Does the language of the Eighth Amendment mean today what it meant at the end of the eighteenth century when it was written? If not, what is the proper mechanism for determining its changed meaning? And, who shall be the authoritative agent for interpreting this change? Congress? the Courts? the people themselves?

The interpretive problems that attend the meaning of the Eighth Amendment are one manifestation of more general disagreements about constitutional interpretation. Justice Kennedy assumes a central role for the courts—the Supreme Court in particular—in determining the meaning of the Eighth Amendment. Kennedy's interpretive approach requires the courts to "read" public opinion, to comprehend dominant trends in state legislative enactments, and to be aware of comparative legal developments in the international arena. Justice Scalia, however, believes that each of these moves is but a part of a more general problem of misunderstanding the proper nature of the judicial role, a misunderstanding that risks the legitimacy of the court itself. Who is correct? How do we adjudicate the different approaches to determining what the Constitution—here, the Eighth Amendment—means?

The literature on capital punishment is enormous. Perhaps one of the best places to begin is with Stuart Banner's history of capital punishment, *The Death Penalty: An American History* (Harvard, 2003). Hugo Adam Bedau, a long time opponent of capital punishment, has published two useful collections. The first, *Debating the Death Penalty* (Oxford, 2003), provides a collection of arguments for and against capital punishment. The second, *The Death Penalty in America* (Oxford, 1998), provides a comprehensive overview of the subject. For useful background information on capital punishment in the United States, one should consult the Web site of the Death Penalty Information Center at http://www.deathpenaltyinfo.org.

One of the central points contested by Justices Kennedy and Scalia is the proper place of foreign legal developments in our understanding of the death penalty in the United States. In an important and widely cited book, James Q. Whitman addresses the differences in approach to capital punishment between the United States and selected European nations. See *Harsh Justice: Capital Punishment and the Widening Divide Between America and Europe* (Oxford, 2003). Additionally, there are two books of note that deal with the question of capital punishment from slightly different yet equally challenging perspectives. The first, by Timothy Kaufman-Osborn, *From Noose to Needle: Capital Punishment and the Late Liberal State* (Michigan, 2002), approaches the subject from the perspective of a critique of liberal political thought. The second, by Austin Sarat, *When the State Kills: Capital Punishment and the American Condition* (Princeton, 2002), provides an analysis of the reciprocal relationship between capital punishment and American culture.

ISSUE 14

Is a Sentence of Life in Prison for Stealing $150 Worth of Videotapes Constitutional?

YES: Sandra Day O'Connor, from Majority Opinion, *Lockyer v. Andrade*, U.S. Supreme Court (March 5, 2003)

NO: David Souter, from Dissenting Opinion, *Lockyer v. Andrade*, U.S. Supreme Court (March 5, 2003)

ISSUE SUMMARY

YES: Supreme Court Justice Sandra Day O'Connor rules that a decision in a case involving the theft of $150 worth of merchandise that resulted in two consecutive terms of 25 years to life in prison for a "third strike" conviction was not "grossly disproportional" to the crime nor "contrary to, or an unreasonable application of, clearly established federal law."

NO: Supreme Court Justice David Souter argues that under several prior Supreme Court decisions, the "third strike" punishment in this case was grossly disproportional to the crime committed.

> My object all sublime
> I shall achieve in time—
> To let the punishment fit the crime—
> The punishment fit the crime.
>
> —William S. Gilbert and Arthur Sullivan, *The Mikado*

Should the punishment fit the crime, so that all persons who commit the same crime receive comparable sentences? Or should the punishment fit the criminal by taking into account such factors as likelihood of rehabilitation and prior record? Focusing on the offense is generally thought to lead to more consistent sentencing. This goal is important, considering that discrimination in sentencing has occurred in the past. On the other hand, focusing on the person who has committed the crime allows some flexibility in considering the likely impact of incarceration on that person, including the possibility of rehabilitation.

The practice in most of the United States is to try to achieve a balance between letting the punishment fit the crime and letting it fit the criminal. Thus, many states establish guidelines and formulas for sentencing while, allowing judges to individualize a sentence if clear and public reasons are given. The three-strikes laws that are of concern in the following case are unusual in that they shift the balance over to a "punishment to fit the criminal" model but take away discretion to consider individual circumstances.

Three-strikes laws typically provide for much more severe penalties if the offender has several prior convictions. Under such laws, a recidivist might receive a very different sentence than someone who has committed the same offense but who has no prior convictions. In some instances the differences in sentencing may be quite extreme.

In 1980 the Supreme Court decided that the Eighth Amendment prohibition against cruel and unusual punishment was not violated when a third felony led to a sentence of life imprisonment with the possibility of parole. In that case, *Rummel v. Estelle,* 445 U.S. 263, the defendant had been sentenced to such a harsh punishment because he had been convicted once for fraudulent use of a credit card to obtain $80 worth of goods or services, once for passing a forged check in the amount of $28.36, and a third time for obtaining $120.75 by false pretenses.

In *Solem v. Helm,* 463 U.S. 277 (1983), the Supreme Court decided by a 5–4 vote that a life sentence without possibility of parole for a seventh nonviolent felony violated the Eighth Amendment prohibition against cruel and unusual punishment. The defendant, Jerry Helm, had previously been convicted of six nonviolent felonies—three third-degree burglaries, grand larceny, driving while intoxicated, and obtaining money under false pretenses. The final crime was bouncing a check, which normally would have had a maximum penalty of five years' imprisonment and a $5,000 fine. Unlike in *Rummel,* the Court found the life sentence to be "grossly disproportionate to the nature of the offense."

Seven years later, in *Harmelin v. Michigan,* 501 U.S. 957 (1991), the Court upheld a life sentence for a defendant convicted of possession of more than 650 grams of cocaine. Justice Anthony Kennedy wrote that sentences may be evaluated as to whether they are "grossly disproportionate" to the crime, but, given the seriousness of the defendant's crime, the sentence was not disproportionate.

In the following case, *Lockyer v. Andrade,* the defendant was convicted of stealing videotapes worth approximately $150, and he received a sentence of two consecutive terms of 25 years to life. To which of the previous cases is this fact pattern most similar? Can there be any formula to determine whether or not a sentence is "grossly disproportionate"?

YES

Sandra Day O'Connor

Majority Opinion, *Lockyer v. Andrade*

JUSTICE O'CONNOR delivered the opinion of the Court.

This case raises the issue whether the United States Court of Appeals for the Ninth Circuit erred in ruling that the California Court of Appeal's decision affirming Leandro Andrade's two consecutive terms of 25 years to life in prison for a "third strike" conviction is contrary to, or an unreasonable application of, clearly established federal law as determined by this Court within the meaning of 28 U.S.C. §2254(d)(1).

I

A

On November 4, 1995, Leandro Andrade stole five videotapes worth $84.70 from a Kmart store in Ontario, California. Security personnel detained Andrade as he was leaving the store. On November 18, 1995, Andrade entered a different Kmart store in Montclair, California, and placed four videotapes worth $68.84 in the rear waistband of his pants. Again, security guards apprehended Andrade as he was exiting the premises. Police subsequently arrested Andrade for these crimes.

These two incidents were not Andrade's first or only encounters with law enforcement. According to the state probation officer's presentence report, Andrade has been in and out of state and federal prison since 1982. In January 1982, he was convicted of a misdemeanor theft offense and was sentenced to 6 days in jail with 12 months' probation. Andrade was arrested again in November 1982 for multiple counts of first-degree residential burglary. He pleaded guilty to at least three of those counts, and in April of the following year he was sentenced to 120 months in prison. In 1988, Andrade was convicted in federal court of "[t]ransportation of [m]arijuana," App. 24, and was sentenced to eight years in federal prison. In 1990, he was convicted in state court for a misdemeanor petty theft offense and was ordered to serve 180 days in jail. In September 1990, Andrade was convicted again in federal court for the same felony of "[t]ransportation of [m]arijuana," and was sentenced to 2,191 days in federal prison. And in 1991, Andrade was arrested for a state parole violation—escape from federal prison. He was paroled from the state penitentiary system in 1993.

From Supreme Court of the United States, March 5, 2003.

A state probation officer interviewed Andrade after his arrest in this case. The presentence report notes:

> "The defendant admitted committing the offense. The defendant further stated he went into the K-Mart Store to steal videos. He took four of them to sell so he could buy heroin. He has been a heroin addict since 1977. He says when he gets out of jail or prison he always does something stupid. He admits his addiction controls his life and he steals for his habit."

Because of his 1990 misdemeanor conviction, the State charged Andrade in this case with two counts of petty theft with a prior conviction, in violation of Cal. Penal Code Ann. §666 (West Supp. 2002). Under California law, petty theft with a prior conviction is a so-called "wobbler" offense because it is punishable either as a misdemeanor or as a felony. The decision to prosecute petty theft with a prior conviction as a misdemeanor or as a felony is in the discretion of the prosecutor. The trial court also has discretion to reduce the charge to a misdemeanor at the time of sentencing.

Under California's three strikes law, any felony can constitute the third strike, and thus can subject a defendant to a term of 25 years to life in prison. See Cal. Penal Code Ann. §667(e)(2)(A) (West 1999). In this case, the prosecutor decided to charge the two counts of theft as felonies rather than misdemeanors. The trial court denied Andrade's motion to reduce the offenses to misdemeanors, both before the jury verdict and again in state habeas proceedings.

A jury found Andrade guilty of two counts of petty theft with a prior conviction. According to California law, a jury must also find that a defendant has been convicted of at least two serious or violent felonies that serve as qualifying offenses under the three strikes regime. In this case, the jury made a special finding that Andrade was convicted of three counts of first-degree residential burglary. A conviction for first-degree residential burglary qualifies as a serious or violent felony for the purposes of the three strikes law. As a consequence, each of Andrade's convictions for theft under Cal. Penal Code Ann. §666 (West Supp. 2002) triggered a separate application of the three strikes law. Pursuant to California law, the judge sentenced Andrade to two consecutive terms of 25 years to life in prison. See §§667(c)(6), 667(e)(2)(B). The State stated at oral argument that under the decision announced by the Supreme Court of California in *People v. Garcia,* 20 Cal. 4th 490, 976 P.2d 831 (1999)—a decision that postdates his conviction and sentence—it remains "available" for Andrade to "file another State habeas corpus petition" arguing that he should serve only one term of 25 years to life in prison because "sentencing courts have a right to dismiss strikes on a count-by-count basis." Tr. of Oral Arg. 24.

B

On direct appeal in 1997, the California Court of Appeal affirmed Andrade's sentence of two consecutive terms of 25 years to life in prison. It rejected Andrade's claim that his sentence violates the constitutional prohibition against cruel and unusual punishment. The court stated that "the proportionality analysis" of *Solem v. Helm,* 463 U.S. 277 (1983), "is questionable in light of" *Harmelin v. Michigan,* 501 U.S. 957 (1991). App. to Pet. for Cert. 76. The court then applied our decision in *Rummel v. Estelle,* 445 U.S. 263 (1980), where we rejected the defendant's claim that a life sentence was "'grossly disproportionate' to the three felonies that formed the predicate for his sentence." *Id.,* at 265. The California Court of Appeal then examined Andrade's claim in light of the facts in *Rummel:* "Comparing [Andrade's] crimes and criminal history with that of defendant Rummel, we cannot say the sentence of 50 years to life at issue in this case is disproportionate and constitutes cruel and unusual punishment under the United States Constitution." App. to Pet. for Cert. 76–77.

After the Supreme Court of California denied discretionary review, Andrade filed a petition for a writ of habeas corpus in Federal District Court. The District Court denied his petition. The Ninth Circuit granted Andrade a certificate of appealability as to his claim that his sentence violated the Eighth Amendment, and subsequently reversed the judgment of the District Court. 270 F. 3d 743 (2001).

The Ninth Circuit first noted that it was reviewing Andrade's petition under the Antiterrorism and Effective Death Penalty Act of 1996 (AEDPA), 110 Stat. 1214. Applying its own precedent, the Ninth Circuit held that an unreasonable application of clearly established federal law occurs "when our independent review of the legal question 'leaves us with a "firm conviction" that one answer, the one rejected by the [state] court, was correct and the other, the application of the federal law that the [state] court adopted, was erroneous—in other words that clear error occurred.'" 270 F. 3d, at 753 (alteration in original) (quoting *Van Tran v. Lindsey,* 212 F. 3d 1143, 1153–1154 (CA9 2000)).

The court then reviewed our three most recent major precedents in this area—*Rummel v. Estelle, supra, Solem v. Helm, supra,* and *Harmelin v. Michigan, supra.* The Ninth Circuit "follow[ed] the test prescribed by Justice Kennedy in *Harmelin,*" concluding that "both *Rummel* and *Solem* remain good law and are instructive in *Harmelin*'s application." 270 F. 3d, at 766. It then noted that the California Court of Appeal compared the facts of Andrade's case to the facts of *Rummel,* but not *Solem.* 270 F. 3d, at 766. The Ninth Circuit concluded that it should grant the writ of habeas corpus because the state court's "disregard for *Solem* results in an unreasonable application of clearly established Supreme Court law," and "is irreconcilable with . . . *Solem,*" thus constituting "clear error." *Id.,* at 766–767.

Judge Sneed dissented in relevant part. He wrote that "[t]he sentence imposed in this case is not one of the 'exceedingly rare' terms of imprisonment prohibited by the Eighth Amendment's proscription against cruel and unusual punishment." *Id.,* at 767 (quoting *Harmelin v. Michigan, supra,* at 1001 (KENNEDY, J., concurring in part and concurring in judgment)). Under his view, the state court decision upholding Andrade's sentence was thus "not an unreasonable application of clearly established federal law." 270 F. 3d, at 772. We granted certiorari, 535 U.S. 969 (2002), and now reverse.

II

Andrade's argument in this Court is that two consecutive terms of 25 years to life for stealing approximately $150 in videotapes is grossly disproportionate in violation of the Eighth Amendment. Andrade similarly maintains that the state court decision affirming his sentence is "contrary to, or involved an unreasonable application of, clearly established Federal law, as determined by the Supreme Court of the United States." 28 U.S.C. §2254(d)(1).

AEDPA circumscribes a federal habeas court's review of a state-court decision. Section 2254 provides:

> "(d) An application for a writ of habeas corpus on behalf of a person in custody pursuant to the judgment of a State court shall not be granted with respect to any claim that was adjudicated on the merits in State court proceedings unless the adjudication of the claim—
> "(1) resulted in a decision that was contrary to, or involved an unreasonable application of, clearly established Federal law, as determined by the Supreme Court of the United States."

The Ninth Circuit requires federal habeas courts to review the state court decision *de novo* before applying the AEDPA standard of review. See, e.g., *Van Tran v. Lindsey, supra,* at 1154–1155; *Clark v. Murphy,* 317 F. 3d 1038, 1044, n. 3 (CA9 2003). We disagree with this approach. AEDPA does not require a federal habeas court to adopt any one methodology in deciding the only question that matters under §2254(d)(1)—whether a state court decision is contrary to, or involved an unreasonable application of, clearly established Federal law. In this case, we do not reach the question whether the state court erred and instead focus solely on whether §2254(d) forecloses habeas relief on Andrade's Eighth Amendment claim.

III

A

As a threshold matter here, we first decide what constitutes "clearly established Federal law, as determined by the Supreme Court of the United States." §2254(d)(1). Andrade relies upon a series of precedents from this Court— *Rummel v. Estelle,* 445 U.S. 263 (1980), *Solem v. Helm,* 463 U.S. 277 (1983), and *Harmelin v. Michigan,* 501 U.S. 957 (1991)—that he claims clearly establish a principle that his sentence is so grossly disproportionate that it violates the Eighth Amendment. Section 2254(d)(1)'s "clearly established" phrase "refers to the holdings, as opposed to the dicta, of this Court's decisions as of the time of the relevant state-court decision." *Williams v. Taylor,* 529 U.S. 362, 412 (2000). In other words, "clearly established Federal law" under §2254(d)(1) is the governing legal principle or principles set forth by the Supreme Court at the time the state court renders its decision. In most situations, the task of determining what we have clearly established will be straightforward. The difficulty with Andrade's position, however, is that our precedents in this area have not been a model of clarity. See *Harmelin v. Michigan*, 501 U.S., at 965 (opinion of Scalia, J.); *id.*, at 996, 998 (KENNEDY, J., concurring in part and concurring in judgment). Indeed, in determining whether a particular sentence for a term of years can violate the Eighth Amendment, we have not established a clear or consistent path for courts to follow.

B

Through this thicket of Eighth Amendment jurisprudence, one governing legal principle emerges as "clearly established" under §2254(d)(1): A gross disproportionality principle is applicable to sentences for terms of years.

Our cases exhibit a lack of clarity regarding what factors may indicate gross disproportionality. In *Solem* (the case upon which Andrade relies most heavily), we stated: "It is clear that a 25-year sentence generally is more severe than a 15-year sentence, but in most cases it would be difficult to decide that the former violates the Eighth Amendment while the latter does not." 463 U.S., at 294 (footnote omitted). And in *Harmelin,* both JUSTICE KENNEDY and JUSTICE SCALIA repeatedly emphasized this lack of clarity: that "*Solem* was scarcely the expression of clear . . . constitutional law," 501 U.S., at 965 (opinion of Scalia, J.), that in "adher[ing] to the narrow proportionality principle . . . our proportionality decisions have not been clear or consistent in all respects," *id.*, at 996 (Kennedy, J., concurring in part and concurring in judgment), that "we lack clear objective standards to distinguish between sentences for different terms of years," *id.*, at 1001 (KENNEDY, J., concurring in part and concurring in judgment), and that the "precise contours" of the proportionality principle "are unclear," *id.*, at 998 (KENNEDY, J., concurring in part and concurring in judgment).

Thus, in this case, the only relevant clearly established law amenable to the "contrary to" or "unreasonable application of" framework is the gross disproportionality principle, the precise contours of which are unclear, applicable only in the "exceedingly rare" and "extreme" case. *Id.*, at 1001 (KENNEDY, J., concurring in part and concurring in judgment) (internal quotation marks omitted); see also *Solem v. Helm, supra,* at 290; *Rummel v. Estelle, supra,* at 272.

IV

The final question is whether the California Court of Appeal's decision affirming Andrade's sentence is "contrary to, or involved an unreasonable application of," this clearly established gross disproportionality principle.

First, a state court decision is "contrary to our clearly established precedent if the state court applies a rule that contradicts the governing law set forth in our cases" or "if the state court confronts a set of facts that are materially indistinguishable from a decision of this Court and nevertheless arrives at a result different from our precedent." *Williams v. Taylor, supra,* at 405–406; see also *Bell v. Cone, supra,* at 694. In terms of length of sentence and availability of parole, severity of the underlying offense, and the impact of recidivism, Andrade's sentence implicates factors relevant in both *Rummel* and *Solem*. Because *Harmelin* and *Solem* specifically stated that they did not overrule *Rummel*, it was not contrary to our clearly established law for the California Court of Appeal to turn to *Rummel* in deciding whether a sentence is grossly disproportionate. See *Harmelin, supra,* at 998 (Kennedy, J., concurring in part and concurring in judgment); *Solem, supra,* at 288, n. 13, 303–304, n. 32. Indeed, *Harmelin* allows a state court to reasonably rely on *Rummel* in determining whether a sentence is grossly disproportionate. The California Court of Appeal's decision was therefore not "contrary to" the governing legal principles set forth in our cases.

Andrade's sentence also was not materially indistinguishable from the facts in *Solem*. The facts here fall in between the facts in *Rummel* and the facts in *Solem*. *Solem* involved a sentence of life in prison without the possibility of parole. 463 U.S., at 279. The defendant in *Rummel* was sentenced to life in prison with the possibility of parole. 445 U.S., at 267. Here, Andrade retains the possibility of parole. *Solem* acknowledged that *Rummel* would apply in a "similar factual situation." 463 U.S., at 304, n. 32. And while this case resembles to some degree both *Rummel* and *Solem*, it is not materially indistinguishable from either. Cf. *Ewing v. California, ante,* at __ (slip op., at 6) (BREYER, J., dissenting) (recognizing a "twilight zone between *Solem* and *Rummel*"). Consequently, the state court did not "confron[t] a set of facts that are materially indistinguishable from a decision of this Court and nevertheless arriv[e] at a result different from our precedent." *Williams v. Taylor,* 529 U.S., at 406.[1]

Second, "[u]nder the 'unreasonable application' clause, a federal habeas court may grant the writ if the state court identifies the correct governing legal principle from this Court's decisions but unreasonably applies that principle to the facts of the prisoner's case." *Id.,* at 413. The "unreasonable application" clause requires the state court decision to be more than incorrect or erroneous. *Id.,* at 410, 412. The state court's application of clearly established law must be objectively unreasonable. *Id.,* at 409.

The Ninth Circuit made an initial error in its "unreasonable application" analysis. In *Van Tran v. Lindsey,* 212 F. 3d, at 1152–1154, the Ninth Circuit defined "objectively unreasonable" to mean "clear error." These two standards, however, are not the same. The gloss of clear error fails to give proper deference to state courts by conflating error (even clear error) with unreasonableness. See *Williams v. Taylor, supra,* at 410; *Bell v. Cone,* 535 U.S., at 699.

It is not enough that a federal habeas court, in its "independent review of the legal question" is left with a "'firm conviction'" that the state court was "'erroneous'" 270 F. 3d, at 753 (quoting *Van Tran v. Lindsey, supra,* at 1153–1154). We have held precisely the opposite: "Under §2254(d)(1)'s 'unreasonable application' clause, then, a federal habeas court may not issue the writ simply because that court concludes in its independent judgment that the relevant state-court decision applied clearly established federal law erroneously or incorrectly." *Williams v. Taylor,* 529 U.S., at 411. Rather, that application must be objectively unreasonable. *Id.,* at 409; *Bell v. Cone, supra,* at 699; *Woodford v. Visciotti,* 537 U.S. __, __ (2002) (*per curiam*) (slip op., at 6).

Section 2254(d)(1) permits a federal court to grant habeas relief based on the application of a governing legal principle to a set of facts different from those of the case in which the principle was announced. See, *e.g., Williams v. Taylor, supra,* at 407 (noting that it is "an unreasonable application of this Court's precedent if the state court identifies the correct governing legal rule from this Court's cases but unreasonably applies it to the facts of the particular state prisoner's case"). Here, however, the governing legal principle gives legislatures broad discretion to fashion a sentence that fits within the scope of the proportionality principle—the "precise contours" of which "are unclear." *Harmelin v. Michigan,* 501 U.S., at 998 (KENNEDY, J., concurring in part and concurring in judgment). And it was not objectively unreasonable for the California Court of Appeal to conclude that these "contours" permitted an affirmance of Andrade's sentence.

Indeed, since *Harmelin,* several Members of this Court have expressed "uncertainty" regarding the application of the proportionality principle to the California three strikes law. *Riggs v. California,* 525 U.S. 1114, 1115 (1999) (STEVENS, J., joined by SOUTER and GINSBURG, JJ., respecting denial of certiorari) ("[T]here is some uncertainty about how our cases dealing with the punishment of recidivists should apply"); see also *id.,* at 1116 ("It is thus unclear how, if at all, a defendant's criminal record beyond the requisite two prior 'strikes' . . . affects the constitutionality of his sentence"); cf. *Durden v. California,* 531 U.S. 1184 (2001) (SOUTER, J., joined by BREYER, J., dissenting from denial of certiorari) (arguing that the Court should hear the three strikes gross disproportionality issue on direct review because of the "potential for disagreement over application of" AEDPA).[2]

The gross disproportionality principle reserves a constitutional violation for only the extraordinary case. In applying this principle for §2254(d)(1) purposes, it was not an unreasonable application of our clearly established law for the California Court of Appeal to affirm Andrade's sentence of two consecutive terms of 25 years to life in prison.

V

The judgment of the United States Court of Appeals for the Ninth Circuit, accordingly, is reversed.

It is so ordered.

Notes

1. JUSTICE SOUTER argues that the possibility of Andrade's receiving parole in 50 years makes this case similar to the facts in *Solem v. Helm,* 463 U.S. 227 (1983). *Post,* at 2 (dissenting opinion). Andrade's sentence, however, is also similar to the facts in *Rummel v. Estelle,* 445 U.S. 263 (1980), a case that is also "controlling." *Post,* at 2. Given the lack of clarity of our precedents in *Solem, Rummel,* and *Harmelin v. Michigan,* 501 U.S. 957 (1991), we cannot say that the state court's affirmance of two sentences of 25 years to

life in prison was contrary to our clearly established precedent. And to the extent that JUSTICE SOUTER is arguing that the similarity of *Solem* to this case entitles Andrade to relief under the unreasonable application prong of §2254(d), we reject his analysis for the reasons given *infra*, at 11–12. Moreover, it is not true that Andrade's "sentence can only be understood as punishment for the total amount he stole." *Post,* at 2. To the contrary, California law specifically provides that *each* violation of Cal. Penal Code Ann. §666 (West Supp. 2002) triggers a separate application of the three strikes law, if the different felony counts are "not arising from the same set of operative facts." §667(c)(6); see also §667(e)(2)(B). Here, Andrade was sentenced to two consecutive terms under California law precisely because the two thefts of two different Kmart stores occurring two weeks apart were two distinct crimes.

JUSTICE SOUTER, relying on *Robinson v. California,* 370 U.S. 660 (1962), also argues that in this case, it is "unrealistic" to think that a sentence of 50 years to life for Andrade is not equivalent to life in prison without parole. *Post,* at 3. This argument, however, misses the point. Based on our precedents, the state court decision was not contrary to, or an unreasonable application of, our clearly established law. Moreover, JUSTICE SOUTER's position would treat a sentence of life without parole for the 77-year-old person convicted of murder as equivalent to a sentence of life with the possibility of parole in 10 years for the same person convicted of the same crime. Two different sentences do not become materially indistinguishable based solely upon the age of the persons sentenced.

2. JUSTICE SOUTER would hold that Andrade's sentence also violates the unreasonable application prong of §2254(d)(1). *Post,* at 3–6. His reasons, however, do not change the "uncertainty" of the scope of the proportionality principle. We cannot say that the state court decision was an unreasonable application of this principle.

David Souter   ➡ **NO**

Dissenting Opinion
Lockyer v. Andrade

J USTICE SOUTER, with whom JUSTICE STEVENS, JUSTICE GINSBURG, and JUSTICE BREYER join, dissenting.

The application of the Eighth Amendment prohibition against cruel and unusual punishment to terms of years is articulated in the "clearly established" principle acknowledged by the Court: a sentence grossly disproportionate to the offense for which it is imposed is unconstitutional. See *ante,* at 4; *Harmelin v. Michigan,* 501 U.S. 957 (1991); *Solem v. Helm,* 463 U.S. 277 (1983); *Rummel v. Estelle,* 445 U.S. 263 (1980). For the reasons set forth in JUSTICE BREYER's dissent in *Ewing v. California, ante,* at ___, which I joined, Andrade's sentence cannot survive Eighth Amendment review. His criminal history is less grave than Ewing's, and yet he received a prison term twice as long for a less serious triggering offense. To be sure, this is a habeas case and a prohibition couched in terms as general as gross disproportion necessarily leaves state courts with much leeway under the statutory criterion that conditions federal relief upon finding that a state court unreasonably applied clear law, see 28 U.S.C. §2254(d). This case nonetheless presents two independent reasons for holding that the disproportionality review by the state court was not only erroneous but unreasonable, entitling Andrade to relief. I respectfully dissent accordingly.

The first reason is the holding in *Solem,* which happens to be our most recent effort at proportionality review of recidivist sentencing, the authority of which was not left in doubt by *Harmelin,* see 501 U.S., at 998. Although *Solem* is important for its instructions about applying objective proportionality analysis, see 463 U.S., at 290–292, the case is controlling here because it established a benchmark in applying the general principle. We specifically held that a sentence of life imprisonment without parole for uttering a $100 "no account" check was disproportionate to the crime, even though the defendant had committed six prior nonviolent felonies. In explaining our proportionality review, we contrasted the result with *Rummel's* on the ground that the life sentence there had included parole eligibility after 12 years, *Solem,* 463 U.S., at 297.

The facts here are on all fours with those of *Solem* and point to the same result. Andrade, like the defendant in *Solem,* was a repeat offender who committed theft of fairly trifling value, some $150, and their criminal records are comparable, including burglary (though Andrade's were residential), with no violent crimes or crimes against the person. The respective sentences, too,

From Supreme Court of the United States, March 5, 2003.

are strikingly alike. Although Andrade's petty thefts occurred on two separate occasions, his sentence can only be understood as punishment for the total amount he stole. The two thefts were separated by only two weeks; they involved the same victim; they apparently constituted parts of a single, continuing effort to finance drug sales; their seriousness is measured by the dollar value of the things taken; and the government charged both thefts in a single indictment. Cf. United States Sentencing Commission, Guidelines Manual §3D1.2 (Nov. 2002) (grouping temporally separated counts as one offense for sentencing purposes). The state court accordingly spoke of his punishment collectively as well, carrying a 50-year minimum before parole eligibility, see App. to Pet. for Cert. 77 ("[W]e cannot say the sentence of 50 years to life at issue in this case is disproportionate"), and because Andrade was 37 years old when sentenced, the substantial 50-year period amounts to life without parole. *Solem, supra,* at 287 (quoting *Robinson v. California,* 370 U.S. 660, 667 (1962) (when considering whether a punishment is cruel or unusual "'the questions cannot be considered in the abstract'")); cf. *Rummel, supra,* at 280–281 (defendant's eligibility for parole in 12 years informs a proper assessment of his cruel and unusual punishment claim). The results under the Eighth Amendment should therefore be the same in each case. The only ways to reach a different conclusion are to reject the practical equivalence of a life sentence without parole and one with parole eligibility at 87, see *ante,* at 9, ("Andrade retains the possibility of parole"), or to discount the continuing authority of *Solem*'s example, as the California court did, see App. to Pet. for Cert. 76 ("[T]he current validity of the Solem proportionality analysis is questionable.") The former is unrealistic; an 87-year-old man released after 50 years behind bars will have no real life left, if he survives to be released at all. And the latter, disparaging *Solem* as a point of reference on Eighth Amendment analysis, is wrong as a matter of law.

The second reason that relief is required even under the §2254(d) unreasonable application standard rests on the alternative way of looking at Andrade's 50-year sentence as two separate 25-year applications of the three-strikes law, and construing the challenge here as going to the second, consecutive 25-year minimum term triggered by a petty theft. To understand why it is revealing to look at the sentence this way, it helps to recall the basic difficulty inherent in proportionality review. We require the comparison of offense and penalty to disclose a truly gross disproportionality before the constitutional limit is passed, in large part because we believe that legislatures are institutionally equipped with better judgment than courts in deciding what penalty is merited by particular behavior. In this case, however, a court is substantially aided in its reviewing function by two determinations made by the State itself.

The first is the State's adoption of a particular penalogical theory as its principal reason for shutting a three-strikes defendant away for at least 25 years. Although the State alludes in passing to retribution or deterrence (see Brief for Petitioner 16, 24; Reply Brief for Petitioner 10), its only serious justification for the 25-year minimum treats the sentence as a way to incapacitate a given defendant from further crime; the underlying theory is the need to protect the public from a danger demonstrated by the prior record of violent and serious crime. See Brief for Petitioner 17 ("significant danger to society such that [defendant] must be imprisoned for no less than twenty-five years to life"); *id.*, at 21 ("statute carefully tailored to address . . . defendants that pose the greatest danger"); *id.*, at 23 ("isolating such a defendant for a substantial period of time"); Reply Brief for Petitioner 11 ("If Andrade's reasoning were accepted, however, California would be precluded from incapacitating him"). See also *Rummel,* 445 U.S., at 284 ("purpose of a recidivist statute . . . [is] to segregate").[1] The State, in other words has not chosen 25 to life because of the inherent moral or social reprehensibility of the triggering offense in isolation; the triggering offense is treated so seriously, rather, because of its confirmation of the defendant's danger to society and the need to counter his threat with incapacitation. As to the length of incapacitation, the State has made a second helpful determination, that the public risk or danger posed by someone with the specified predicate record is generally addressed by incapacitation for 25 years before parole eligibility. Cal. Penal Code Ann. §667(e)(2)(A)(ii) (West 1999). The three-strikes law, in sum, responds to a condition of the defendant shown by his prior felony record, his danger to society, and it reflects a judgment that 25 years of incapacitation prior to parole eligibility is appropriate when a defendant exhibiting such a condition commits another felony.

Whether or not one accepts the State's choice of penalogical policy as constitutionally sound, that policy cannot reasonably justify the imposition of a consecutive 25-year minimum for a second minor felony committed soon after the first triggering offense. Andrade did not somehow become twice as dangerous to society when he stole the second handful of videotapes; his dangerousness may justify treating one minor felony as serious and warranting long incapacitation, but a second such felony does not disclose greater danger warranting substantially longer incapacitation. Since the defendant's condition has not changed between the two closely related thefts, the incapacitation penalty is not open to the simple arithmetic of multiplying the punishment by two, without resulting in gross disproportion even under the State's chosen benchmark. Far from attempting a novel penal theory to justify doubling the sentence, the California Court of Appeal offered no comment at all as to the particular penal theory supporting such a punishment. Perhaps even more tellingly, no one could seriously argue that the second theft of videotapes provided any basis to think that Andrade would be so dangerous after 25 years, the date on which the consecutive sentence would begin to run, as to require at least 25 years more. I know of no jurisdiction that would add 25 years of imprisonment simply to reflect the fact that the two temporally related thefts took place on two separate occasions, and I am not surprised that California has found no such case, not even under its three-strikes law. In sum, the argument that repeating a trivial crime justifies doubling a 25-year minimum incapacitation sentence based on a threat to the public does not raise a seriously debatable point on which judgments might reasonably differ. The argument is irrational, and the state court's acceptance of it in response to a facially gross disproportion between triggering offense and penalty was unreasonable within the meaning of §2254(d).

This is the rare sentence of demonstrable gross disproportionality, as the California Legislature may well have recognized when it specifically provided that a prosecutor may move to dismiss or strike a prior felony conviction "in the furtherance of justice." Cal. Penal Code Ann. §667(f) (2) (West 1999). In this case, the statutory safeguard failed, and the state court was left to ensure that the Eighth Amendment prohibition on grossly disproportionate sentences was met. If Andrade's sentence is not grossly disproportionate, the principle has no meaning. The California court's holding was an unreasonable application of clearly established precedent.

Note

1. Implicit in the distinction between future dangerousness and repunishment for prior crimes is the notion that the triggering offense must, within some degree, be substantial enough to bear the weight of the sentence it elicits. As triggering offenses become increasingly minor and recidivist sentences grow, the sentences advance toward double jeopardy violations. When defendants are parking violators or slow readers of borrowed library books, there is not much room for belief, even in light of a past criminal record, that the State is permanently incapacitating the defendant because of future dangerousness rather than resentencing for past offenses.

   That said, I do not question the legitimacy of repeatedly sentencing a defendant in light of his criminal record: the Federal Sentencing Guidelines provide a prime example of how a sentencing scheme may take into account a defendant's criminal history without resentencing a defendant for past convictions, *Witte v. United States,* 515 U.S. 389, 403 (1995) (the triggering offense determines the range of possible sentences, and the past criminal record affects an enhancement of that sentence). The point is merely that the triggering offense must reasonably support the weight of even the harshest possible sentences.

POSTSCRIPT

Is a Sentence of Life in Prison for Stealing $150 Worth of Videotapes Constitutional?

According to law professor Bernard E. Harcourt, in "The Shaping of Chance: Actuarial Models and Criminal Profiling at the Turn of the Twenty-First Century," 70 *University of Chicago Law Review* 105 (2003),

> The turn of the twentieth century marked a new era of individualization in the field of criminal law. Drawing on the new science of positivist criminology, legal scholars called for diagnosis of the causes of delinquence and for imposition of individualized courses of remedial treatment specifically adapted to these individual diagnoses. . . . At the close of the century, the contrast could hardly have been greater. The rehabilitative project had been largely displaced by a model of criminal law enforcement that emphasized mandatory sentences, fixed guidelines, and sentencing enhancements for designated classes of crimes. The focus of criminal sentencing had become the category of crime, rather than the individual characteristics and history of the convicted person, with one major exception for prior criminal conduct. Incapacitation theory—the idea that incarcerating serious and repeat criminal offenders for lengthy sentences will significantly impact crime rates— had replaced the rehabilitative model. In the area of policing, the dominant strategy shifted from the model of the professional police force rapidly responding to 911 emergency calls to a more forward-looking crime prevention model that relied heavily on criminal profiling.

Along with a shift in sentencing practices, there has been enormous growth in the prison population in the United States. This did not happen immediately or quickly. Incarceration rates averaged 110 state and federal prisoners per 100,000 people until 1970. Between 1970 and 2001, however, federal and state prison populations nationwide grew from less than 200,000 to more than 1,300,000, with another 630,000 persons being held in local jails. The current rate of incarceration in prison is 743 per 100,000. This is 6–10 times the incarceration rate of Western European countries, and it means that a higher proportion of the adult population of America is incarcerated than that of any other country in the world. The United States, with 5 percent of the world's population, has 25 percent of the world's prisoners.

It is not clear that the three-strikes movement has had any significant impact on crime rates. Such rates did decline in the 1990s, but they had already begun declining before any of the three-strikes laws were enacted. The only jurisdiction in which three strikes has involved significant numbers is California. The federal government and many other states require that the third strike involve a violent or serious felony. As *Lockyer v. Andrade* illustrates, in California third-strike sentences can be applied even if the third felony conviction is for a relatively minor crime, such as petty theft.

Some recommended additional readings are Franklin E. Zimring, Gordon Hawkins, and Sam Kamin, *Punishment and Democracy: Three Strikes and You're Out in California* (Oxford University Press, 2003); Marie Gottschalk, "Black Flower: Prisons and the Future of Incarceration," 582 *Annals of the American Academy of Political and Social Science* 195, 197 (2002); Randal S. Jeffrey, "Restricting Prisoners' Equal Access to the Federal Courts: The Three Strikes Provision of the Prison Litigation Reform Act and Substantive Equal Protection," 49 *Buffalo Law Review* 1099 (2001); and James Q. Whitman, *Harsh Justice: Criminal Punishment and the Widening Divide Between America and Europe* (New York: Oxford University Press, 2003).

ISSUE 15

Can Noise Coming from Inside an Apartment and Which the Police Believe Involves the Destruction of Drugs Constitute "Exigent Circumstances" That Allow Police Officers to Enter and Search a Home Without a Warrant?

YES: **Samuel Alito,** from Majority Opinion, *Kentucky v. King,* U.S. Supreme Court (May 16, 2011)

NO: **Ruth Bader Ginsburg**, from Dissenting Opinion, *Kentucky v. King,* U.S. Supreme Court (May 16, 2011)

ISSUE SUMMARY

YES: Justice Samuel Alito holds that a warrant is unnecessary when "exigent circumstances" exist and the police have not created them.

NO: Justice Ruth Bader Ginsburg believes that the "exigent circumstances" must exist before the police arrive and that in this case a warrant should have been obtained before entry into the apartment.

In Issue 16, the police conducted a search for marijuana in a residence. They had been stationed outside the residence with equipment that showed very high heat levels inside and they used this information to persuade a judge that the high temperatures recorded on the equipment constituted sufficient probable cause to believe marijuana was being grown and a search warrant should be issued. When the police officers used the warrant to enter the home, they did indeed find marijuana growing. When the case got to the Supreme Court, a majority of the court ruled that the use of the thermal imaging equipment constituted an unlawful search in that it provided information about a place where the occupants had an "expectation of privacy." The search warrant was invalid since an illegal search had turned up the information needed to obtain the warrant.

In the following readings about the legality of a search for drugs, the step of obtaining a search warrant is skipped altogether. Indeed, the central issue is whether the police action falls within one of the categories for which a warrant is not required. When there is an arrest, for example, a search can be made without obtaining a warrant. If something illegal is in plain view, a warrant is also not required. As discussed earlier in this book, students may enjoy a lesser protection against searches and seizures and a warrant may not be needed to search a school locker.

This case involved a sting operation that did not go according to plan. The police had arranged for an undercover officer to buy crack cocaine. A second police officer sat in a car with a view of the transaction. Several more police officers who were nearby waited to be told by the officer in the car that the sale had taken place and that they could arrest the seller. When the officer in the car saw that the sale had been completed, he radioed the other policemen that they could make the arrest. He also told them that the seller was escaping through a breezeway in an apartment building. They then left so quickly that they did not hear the officer in the car say that the seller had entered an apartment on the right side of the breezeway. The officers in pursuit did not see whether the seller had entered the apartment on the right or the apartment on the left. However, when trying to figure out which apartment the seller went into, they smelled marijuana from the apartment on the left. They therefore knocked on the door and announced themselves as the police. After doing so, they heard noises coming from inside the apartment and assumed that the noises they were hearing meant that those inside were destroying drugs. They then forcibly entered the apartment and saw and seized marijuana and cocaine. Later, they found the original drug dealer in the apartment on the right. Ironically, and for some reason that has not been reported, this individual was never prosecuted.

Were the police acting lawfully when they knocked down the door after hearing movement inside the apartment and announcing themselves as police? Did this fall in the category of "exigent circumstances," meaning that there was imminent danger of people being harmed, of evidence being destroyed or of a suspect escaping? At the center of these questions is the issue of the police not simply finding themselves in exigent circumstances but of actually creating the emergency by announcing their presence. If police can avoid the need for a warrant by actually creating "exigent circumstances," it would open up many opportunities for police to avoid getting a warrant. The case was decided by the Court by an 8-1 vote. Only Justice Ginsberg felt that the police had gone too far.

YES ↩   Samuel Alito

Majority Opinion, *Kentucky v. King*

J USTICE ALITO delivered the opinion of the Court.

It is well established that "exigent circumstances," including the need to prevent the destruction of evidence, permit police officers to conduct an otherwise permissible search without first obtaining a warrant. In this case, we consider whether this rule applies when police, by knocking on the door of a residence and announcing their presence, cause the occupants to attempt to destroy evidence. The Kentucky Supreme Court held that the exigent circumstances rule does not apply in the case at hand because the police should have foreseen that their conduct would prompt the occupants to attempt to destroy evidence. We reject this interpretation of the exigent circumstances rule. The conduct of the police prior to their entry into the apartment was entirely lawful. They did not violate the Fourth Amendment or threaten to do so. In such a situation, the exigent circumstances rule applies.

. . .

II

A

The Fourth Amendment provides:

> "The right of the people to be secure in their persons, houses, papers, and effects, against unreasonable searches and seizures, shall not be violated, and no Warrants shall issue, but upon probable cause, supported by Oath or affirmation, and particularly describing the place to be searched, and the persons or things to be seized."

The text of the Amendment thus expressly imposes two requirements. First, all searches and seizures must be reasonable. Second, a warrant may not be issued unless probable cause is properly established and the scope of the authorized search is set out with particularity. See *Payton v. New York*, 445 U.S. 573, 584 (1980).

Although the text of the Fourth Amendment does not specify when a search warrant must be obtained, this Court has inferred that a warrant must generally be secured. "It is a 'basic principle of Fourth Amendment law,'" we have often said, "'that searches and seizures inside a home without a warrant

Supreme Court of the United States, March 16, 2011.

are presumptively unreasonable.'" *Brigham City v. Stuart,* 547 U.S. 398, 403 (2006) (quoting *Groh v. Ramirez,* 540 U.S. 551, 559 (2004)). But we have also recognized that this presumption may be overcome in some circumstances because "[t]he ultimate touchstone of the Fourth Amendment is 'reasonable-ness.'" *Brigham City, supra,* at 403; see also *Michigan v. Fisher,* 558 U.S. ___, ___ (2009) *(per curiam)* (slip op., at 2). Accordingly, the warrant requirement is subject to certain reasonable exceptions. *Brigham City, supra,* at 403.

One well-recognized exception applies when "'the exigencies of the situa-tion' make the needs of law enforcement so compelling that [a] warrantless search is objectively reasonable under the Fourth Amendment." *Mincey v. Arizona,* 437 U.S. 385, 394 (1978); see also *Payton, supra,* at 590 ("[T]he Fourth Amendment has drawn a firm line at the entrance to the house. Absent exigent circumstances, that threshold may not reasonably be crossed without a warrant").

This Court has identified several exigencies that may justify a warrantless search of a home. See *Brigham City,* 547 U.S., at 403. Under the "emergency aid" exception, for example, "officers may enter a home without a warrant to render emergency assistance to an injured occupant or to protect an occupant from imminent injury." *Ibid.;* see also, *e.g., Fisher, supra,* at ___ (slip op., at 5) (upholding warrantless home entry based on emergency aid exception). Police officers may enter premises without a warrant when they are in hot pursuit of a fleeing suspect. See *United States v. Santana,* 427 U.S. 38, 42–43 (1976). And— what is relevant here—the need "to prevent the imminent destruction of evi-dence" has long been recognized as a sufficient justification for a warrantless search. *Brigham City, supra,* at 403; see also *Georgia v. Randolph,* 547 U.S. 103, 116, n. 6 (2006); *Minnesota v. Olson,* 495 U.S. 91, 100 (1990).[1]

B

Over the years, lower courts have developed an exception to the exigent cir-cumstances rule, the so-called "police-created exigency" doctrine. Under this doctrine, police may not rely on the need to prevent destruction of evidence when that exigency was "created" or "manufactured" by the conduct of the police. See, *e.g., United States v. Chambers,* 395 F. 3d 563, 566 (CA6 2005) ("[F]or a warrantless search to stand, law enforcement officers must be responding to an unanticipated exigency rather than simply creating the exigency for themselves"); *United States v. Gould,* 364 F. 3d 578, 590 (CA5 2004) (en banc) ("[A]lthough exigent circumstances may justify a warrantless probable cause entry into the home, they will not do so if the exigent circumstances were manufactured by the agents" (internal quotation marks omitted)).

In applying this exception for the "creation" or "manufacturing" of an exigency by the police, courts require something more than mere proof that fear of detection by the police caused the destruction of evidence. An additional showing is obviously needed because, as the Eighth Circuit has recognized, "in some sense the police always create the exigent circumstances." *United States v. Duchi,* 906 F. 2d 1278, 1284 (CA8 1990). That is to say, in the vast majority of cases in which evidence is destroyed by persons who are engaged in ille-gal conduct, the reason for the destruction is fear that the evidence will fall into the hands of law enforcement. Destruction of evidence issues probably occur most frequently in drug cases because drugs may be easily destroyed by flushing them down a toilet or rinsing them down a drain. Persons in possession of valuable drugs are unlikely to destroy them unless they fear discovery by the police. Consequently, a rule that precludes the police from making a warrantless entry to prevent the destruction of evidence whenever their conduct causes the exigency would unreasonably shrink the reach of this well-established exception to the warrant requirement.

Presumably for the purpose of avoiding such a result, the lower courts have held that the police-created exigency doctrine requires more than simple causation, but the lower courts have not agreed on the test to be applied. Indeed, the petition in this case maintains that "[t]here are currently five different tests being used by the United States Courts of Appeals," Pet. for Cert. 11, and that some state courts have crafted additional tests, *id.*, at 19–20.

III

A

Despite the welter of tests devised by the lower courts, the answer to the question presented in this case follows directly and clearly from the principle that permits warrantless searches in the first place. As previously noted, warrantless searches are allowed when the circumstances make it reasonable, within the meaning of the Fourth Amendment, to dispense with the warrant requirement. Therefore, the answer to the question before us is that the exigent circumstances rule justifies a warrantless search when the conduct of the police preceding the exigency is reasonable in the same sense. Where, as here, the police did not create the exigency by engaging or threatening to engage in conduct that violates the Fourth Amendment, warrantless entry to prevent the destruction of evidence is reasonable and thus allowed.[2]

We have taken a similar approach in other cases involving warrantless searches. For example, we have held that law enforcement officers may seize evidence in plain view, provided that they have not violated the Fourth Amendment in arriving at the spot from which the observation of the evidence is made. See *Horton v. California*, 496 U.S. 128, 136–140 (1990). As we put it in *Horton*, "[i]t is . . . an essential predicate to any valid warrantless seizure of incriminating evidence that the officer did not violate the Fourth Amendment in arriving at the place from which the evidence could be plainly viewed." *Id.*, at 136. So long as this prerequisite is satisfied, however, it does not matter that the officer who makes the observation may have gone to the spot from which the evidence was seen with the hope of being able to view and seize the evidence. See *id.*, at 138 ("The fact that an officer is interested in an item of evidence and fully expects to find it in the course of a search should not invalidate its seizure"). Instead, the Fourth Amendment requires only that the steps preceding the seizure be lawful. See *id.*, at 136–137.

Similarly, officers may seek consent-based encounters if they are lawfully present in the place where the consensual encounter occurs. See *INS v. Delgado*,

466 U.S. 210, 217, n. 5 (1984) (noting that officers who entered into consent-based encounters with employees in a factory building were "lawfully present [in the factory] pursuant to consent or a warrant"). If consent is freely given, it makes no difference that an officer may have approached the person with the hope or expectation of obtaining consent. See *id.*, at 216 ("While most citizens will respond to a police request, the fact that people do so, and do so without being told they are free not to respond, hardly eliminates the consensual nature of the response").

B

Some lower courts have adopted a rule that is similar to the one that we recognize today. See *United States v. MacDonald*, 916 F. 2d 766, 772 (CA2 1990) (en banc) (law enforcement officers "do not impermissibly create exigent circumstances" when they "act in an entirely lawful manner"); *State v. Robinson*, 2010 WI 80, ¶32, 327 Wis. 2d 302, 326–328, 786 N. W. 2d 463, 475–476 (2010). But others, including the Kentucky Supreme Court, have imposed additional requirements that are unsound and that we now reject.

Bad faith. Some courts, including the Kentucky Supreme Court, ask whether law enforcement officers "'deliberately created the exigent circumstances with the bad faith intent to avoid the warrant requirement.'" 302 S. W. 3d, at 656 (quoting *Gould*, 364 F. 3d, at 590); see also, *e.g., Chambers*, 395 F. 3d, at 566; *United States v. Socey*, 846 F. 2d 1439, 1448 (CADC 1988); *United States v. Rengifo*, 858 F. 2d 800, 804 (CA1 1988).

This approach is fundamentally inconsistent with our Fourth Amendment jurisprudence. "Our cases have repeatedly rejected" a subjective approach, asking only whether "the circumstances, viewed *objectively,* justify the action." *Brigham City*, 547 U.S., at 404 (alteration and internal quotation marks omitted); see also *Fisher*, 558 U.S., at ___ (slip op., at 3–5). Indeed, we have never held, outside limited contexts such as an "inventory search or administrative inspection . . . , that an officer's motive invalidates objectively justifiable behavior under the Fourth Amendment." *Whren v. United States*, 517 U.S. 806, 812 (1996); see also *Brigham City, supra,* at 405.

The reasons for looking to objective factors, rather than subjective intent, are clear. Legal tests based on reasonableness are generally objective, and this Court has long taken the view that "evenhanded law enforcement is best achieved by the application of objective standards of conduct, rather than standards that depend upon the subjective state of mind of the officer." *Horton, supra,* at 138.

Reasonable foreseeability. Some courts, again including the Kentucky Supreme Court, hold that police may not rely on an exigency if "it was reasonably foreseeable that the investigative tactics employed by the police would create the exigent circumstances." 302 S. W. 3d, at 656 (quoting *Mann v. State*, 357 Ark. 159, 172, 161 S. W. 3d 826, 834 (2004)); see also, *e.g., United States v. Mowatt*, 513 F. 395, 402 (CA4 2008). Courts applying this test have invalidated warrantless home searches on the ground that it was reasonably foreseeable that police officers, by knocking on the door and announcing their presence, would lead a drug suspect to destroy evidence. See, *e.g., id.,* at 402–403; 302 S. W. 3d, at 656.

Contrary to this reasoning, however, we have rejected the notion that police may seize evidence without a warrant only when they come across the evidence by happenstance. In *Horton,* as noted, we held that the police may seize evidence in plain view even though the officers may be "interested in an item of evidence and fully expec[t] to find it in the course of a search." 496 U.S., at 138.

Adoption of a reasonable foreseeability test would also introduce an unacceptable degree of unpredictability. For example, whenever law enforcement officers knock on the door of premises occupied by a person who may be involved in the drug trade, there is *some* possibility that the occupants may possess drugs and may seek to destroy them. Under a reasonable foreseeability test, it would be necessary to quantify the degree of predictability that must be reached before the police-created exigency doctrine comes into play.

A simple example illustrates the difficulties that such an approach would produce. Suppose that the officers in the present case did not smell marijuana smoke and thus knew only that there was a 50% chance that the fleeing suspect had entered the apartment on the left rather than the apartment on the right. Under those circumstances, would it have been reasonably foreseeable that the occupants of the apartment on the left would seek to destroy evidence upon learning that the police were at the door? Or suppose that the officers knew only that the suspect had disappeared into one of the apartments on a floor with 3, 5, 10, or even 20 units? If the police chose a door at random and knocked for the purpose of asking the occupants if they knew a person who fit the description of the suspect, would it have been reasonably foreseeable that the occupants would seek to destroy evidence?

We have noted that "[t]he calculus of reasonableness must embody allowance for the fact that police officers are often forced to make split-second judgments—in circumstances that are tense, uncertain, and rapidly evolving." *Graham v. Connor,* 490 U.S. 386, 396–397 (1989). The reasonable foreseeability test would create unacceptable and unwarranted difficulties for law enforcement officers who must make quick decisions in the field, as well as for judges who would be required to determine after the fact whether the destruction of evidence in response to a knock on the door was reasonably foreseeable based on what the officers knew at the time.

Probable cause and time to secure a warrant. Some courts, in applying the police-created exigency doctrine, fault law enforcement officers if, after acquiring evidence that is sufficient to establish probable cause to search particular premises, the officers do not seek a warrant but instead knock on the door and seek either to speak with an occupant or to obtain consent to search. See, *e.g., Chambers, supra,* at 569 (citing "[t]he failure to seek a warrant in the face of plentiful probable cause" as a factor indicating that the police deliberately created the exigency).

This approach unjustifiably interferes with legitimate law enforcement strategies. There are many entirely proper reasons why police may not want to seek a search warrant as soon as the bare minimum of evidence needed to establish probable cause is acquired. Without attempting to provide a comprehensive list of these reasons, we note a few.

First, the police may wish to speak with the occupants of a dwelling before deciding whether it is worthwhile to seek authorization for a search. They may think that a short and simple conversation may obviate the need to apply for and execute a warrant. See *Schneckloth v. Bustamonte,* 412 U.S. 218, 228 (1973). Second, the police may want to ask an occupant of the premises for consent to search because doing so is simpler, faster, and less burdensome than applying for a warrant. A consensual search also "may result in considerably less inconvenience" and embarrassment to the occupants than a search conducted pursuant to a warrant. *Ibid.* Third, law enforcement officers may wish to obtain more evidence before submitting what might otherwise be considered a marginal warrant application. Fourth, prosecutors may wish to wait until they acquire evidence that can justify a search that is broader in scope than the search that a judicial officer is likely to authorize based on the evidence then available. And finally, in many cases, law enforcement may not want to execute a search that will disclose the existence of an investigation because doing so may interfere with the acquisition of additional evidence against those already under suspicion or evidence about additional but as yet unknown participants in a criminal scheme.

We have said that "[l]aw enforcement officers are under no constitutional duty to call a halt to criminal investigation the moment they have the minimum evidence to establish probable cause." *Hoffa v. United States,* 385 U.S. 293, 310 (1966). Faulting the police for failing to apply for a search warrant at the earliest possible time after obtaining probable cause imposes a duty that is nowhere to be found in the Constitution.

Standard or good investigative tactics. Finally, some lower court cases suggest that law enforcement officers may be found to have created or manufactured an exigency if the court concludes that the course of their investigation was "contrary to standard or good law enforcement practices (or to the policies or practices of their jurisdictions)." *Gould,* 364 F. 3d, at 591. This approach fails to provide clear guidance for law enforcement officers and authorizes courts to make judgments on matters that are the province of those who are responsible for federal and state law enforcement agencies.

C

Respondent argues for a rule that differs from those discussed above, but his rule is also flawed. Respondent contends that law enforcement officers impermissibly create an exigency when they "engage in conduct that would cause a reasonable person to believe that entry is imminent and inevitable." Brief for Respondent 24. In respondent's view, relevant factors include the officers' tone of voice in announcing their presence and the forcefulness of their knocks. But the ability of law enforcement officers to respond to an exigency cannot turn on such subtleties.

Police officers may have a very good reason to announce their presence loudly and to knock on the door with some force. A forceful knock may be necessary to alert the occupants that someone is at the door. Cf. *United*

States v. Banks, 540 U.S. 31, 33 (2003) (Police "rapped hard enough on the door to be heard by officers at the back door" and announced their presence, but defendant "was in the shower and testified that he heard nothing"). Furthermore, unless police officers identify themselves loudly enough, occupants may not know who is at their doorstep. Officers are permitted—indeed, encouraged—to identify themselves to citizens, and "in many circumstances this is cause for assurance, not discomfort." *United States v. Drayton,* 536 U.S. 194, 204 (2002). Citizens who are startled by an unexpected knock on the door or by the sight of unknown persons in plain clothes on their doorstep may be relieved to learn that these persons are police officers. Others may appreciate the opportunity to make an informed decision about whether to answer the door to the police.

If respondent's test were adopted, it would be extremely difficult for police officers to know how loudly they may announce their presence or how forcefully they may knock on a door without running afoul of the police-created exigency rule. And in most cases, it would be nearly impossible for a court to determine whether that threshold had been passed. The Fourth Amendment does not require the nebulous and impractical test that respondent proposes.[3]

D

For these reasons, we conclude that the exigent circumstances rule applies when the police do not gain entry to premises by means of an actual or threatened violation of the Fourth Amendment. This holding provides ample protection for the privacy rights that the Amendment protects.

When law enforcement officers who are not armed with a warrant knock on a door, they do no more than any private citizen might do. And whether the person who knocks on the door and requests the opportunity to speak is a police officer or a private citizen, the occupant has no obligation to open the door or to speak. Cf. *Florida v. Royer,* 460 U.S. 491, 497–498 (1983). ("[H]e may decline to listen to the questions at all and may go on his way".) When the police knock on a door but the occupants choose not to respond or to speak, "the investigation will have reached a conspicuously low point," and the occupants "will have the kind of warning that even the most elaborate security system cannot provide." *Chambers,* 395 F. 3d, at 577 (Sutton, J., dissenting). And even if an occupant chooses to open the door and speak with the officers, the occupant need not allow the officers to enter the premises and may refuse to answer any questions at any time.

Occupants who choose not to stand on their constitutional rights but instead elect to attempt to destroy evidence have only themselves to blame for the warrantless exigent-circumstances search that may ensue.

IV

We now apply our interpretation of the police-created exigency doctrine to the facts of this case.

A

We need not decide whether exigent circumstances existed in this case. Any warrantless entry based on exigent circumstances must, of course, be supported by a genuine exigency. See *Brigham City,* 547 U.S., at 406. The trial court and the Kentucky Court of Appeals found that there was a real exigency in this case, but the Kentucky Supreme Court expressed doubt on this issue, observing that there was "certainly some question as to whether the sound of persons moving [inside the apartment] was sufficient to establish that evidence was being destroyed." 302 S. W. 3d, at 655. The Kentucky Supreme Court "assum[ed] for the purpose of argument that exigent circumstances existed," *ibid.,* and it held that the police had impermissibly manufactured the exigency.

We, too, assume for purposes of argument that an exigency existed. We decide only the question on which the Kentucky Supreme Court ruled and on which we granted certiorari: Under what circumstances do police impermissibly create an exigency? Any question about whether an exigency actually existed is better addressed by the Kentucky Supreme Court on remand. See *Kirk v. Louisiana,* 536 U.S. 635, 638 (2002) (*per curiam*) (reversing state-court judgment that exigent circumstances were not required for warrantless home entry and remanding for state court to determine whether exigent circumstances were present).

B

In this case, we see no evidence that the officers either violated the Fourth Amendment or threatened to do so prior to the point when they entered the apartment. Officer Cobb testified without contradiction that the officers "banged on the door as loud as [they] could" and announced either "'Police, police, police'" or " 'This is the police.'" App. 22–23. This conduct was entirely consistent with the Fourth Amendment, and we are aware of no other evidence that might show that the officers either violated the Fourth Amendment or threatened to do so (for example, by announcing that they would break down the door if the occupants did not open the door voluntarily).

Respondent argues that the officers "demanded" entry to the apartment, but he has not pointed to any evidence in the record that supports this assertion. He relies on a passing statement made by the trial court in its opinion denying respondent's motion to suppress. . . . In recounting the events that preceded the search, the judge wrote that the officers "banged on the door of the apartment on the back left of the breezeway identifying themselves as police officers and *demanding* that the door be opened by the persons inside." . . . However, at a later point in this opinion, the judge stated that the officers "initially knock[ed] on the door of the apartment unit and await[ed] the response or consensual entry." . . . This later statement is consistent with the testimony at the suppression hearing and with the findings of the state appellate courts. See 302 S. W. 3d, at 651 (The officers "knocked loudly on the back left apartment door and announced 'police'"); App. to Pet. for Cert. 14a (The officers "knock[ed] on the door and announc[ed] themselves as police"); App. 22–24. There is no evidence of a "demand" of any sort, much less a demand that amounts to a threat to violate the Fourth Amendment. If there is contradictory evidence that has not been brought to our attention, the state court may elect to address that matter on remand.

Finally, respondent claims that the officers "explained to [the occupants that the officers] were going to make entry inside the apartment," *id.*, at 24, but the record is clear that the officers did not make this statement until after the exigency arose. As Officer Cobb testified, the officers "knew that there was possibly something that was going to be destroyed inside the apartment," and "*[a]t that point,* . . . [they] explained . . . [that they] were going to make entry." *Ibid.* (emphasis added). Given that this announcement was made *after* the exigency arose, it could not have created the exigency.

*   *   *

Like the court below, we assume for purposes of argument that an exigency existed. Because the officers in this case did not violate or threaten to violate the Fourth Amendment prior to the exigency, we hold that the exigency justified the warrantless search of the apartment.

The judgment of the Kentucky Supreme Court is reversed, and the case is remanded for further proceedings not inconsistent with this opinion.

It is so ordered.

Notes

1. Preventing the destruction of evidence may also justify dispensing with Fourth Amendment requirements in other contexts. See, *e.g., Richards v. Wisconsin,* 520 U.S. 385, 395–396 (1997) (failure to comply with the knock-and-announce requirement was justified because "the circumstances . . . show[ed] that the officers had a reasonable suspicion that [a suspect] might destroy evidence if given further opportunity to do so"); *Schmerber v. California,* 384 U.S. 757, 770–771 (1966) (warrantless testing for blood-alcohol content was justified based on potential destruction of evidence); cf. *United States v. Banks,* 540 U.S. 31, 37–40 (2003) (15 to 20 seconds was a reasonable time for officers to wait after knocking and announcing their presence where there was a risk that suspect would dispose of cocaine).

2. There is a strong argument to be made that, at least in most circumstances, the exigent circumstances rule should not apply where the police, without a warrant or any legally sound basis for a warrantless entry, threaten that they will enter without permission unless admitted. In this case, however, no such actual threat was made, and therefore we have no need to reach that question.

3. Contrary to respondent's argument, see Brief for Respondent 13–18, *Johnson v. United States,* 333 U.S. 10 (1948), does not require affirmance in this case. In *Johnson,* officers noticed the smell of burning opium emanating from a hotel room. They then knocked on the door and demanded entry. Upon seeing that Johnson was the only occupant of the room, they placed her under arrest, searched the room, and discovered opium and drug paraphernalia. *Id.*, at 11.

Defending the legality of the search, the Government attempted to justify the warrantless search of the room as a valid search incident to a lawful arrest. See Brief for United States in *Johnson v. United States,* O. T. 1947, No. 329, pp. 13, 16, 36. The Government did not contend that the officers entered the room in order to prevent the destruction of evidence. Although the officers said that they heard a "'shuffling'" noise inside the room after they knocked on the door, 333 U.S., at 12, the Government did not claim that this particular noise was a noise that would have led a reasonable officer to think that evidence was about to be destroyed. Thus, *Johnson* is simply not a case about exigent circumstances. See *id.,* at 14–15 (noting that if "exceptional circumstances" existed—for example, if a "suspect was fleeing or likely to take flight" or if "evidence or contraband was threatened with removal or destruction"—then "it may be contended that a magistrate's warrant for search may be dispensed with").

Ruth Bader Ginsburg ➡ NO

Dissenting Opinion, *Kentucky v. King*

J USTICE GINSBURG, dissenting.

The Court today arms the police with a way routinely to dishonor the Fourth Amendment's warrant requirement in drug cases. In lieu of presenting their evidence to a neutral magistrate, police officers may now knock, listen, then break the door down, nevermind that they had ample time to obtain a warrant. I dissent from the Court's reduction of the Fourth Amendment's force.

The Fourth Amendment guarantees to the people "[t]he right . . . to be secure in their . . . houses . . . against unreasonable searches and seizures." Warrants to search, the Amendment further instructs, shall issue only upon a showing of "probable cause" to believe criminal activity is afoot. These complementary provisions are designed to ensure that police will seek the authorization of a neutral magistrate before undertaking a search or seizure. Exceptions to the warrant requirement, this Court has explained, must be "few in number and carefully delineated," if the main rule is to remain hardy. *United States v. United States Dist. Court for Eastern Dist. of Mich.*, 407 U.S. 297, 318 (1972); see *Kyllo v. United States*, 533 U.S. 27, 31 (2001).

This case involves a principal exception to the warrant requirement, the exception applicable in "exigent circumstances." . . . "[C]arefully delineated," the exception should govern only in genuine emergency situations. Circumstances qualify as "exigent" when there is an imminent risk of death or serious injury, or danger that evidence will be immediately destroyed, or that a suspect will escape. *Brigham City v. Stuart*, 547 U.S. 398, 403 (2006). The question presented: May police, who could pause to gain the approval of a neutral magistrate, dispense with the need to get a warrant by themselves creating exigent circumstances? I would answer no, as did the Kentucky Supreme Court. The urgency must exist, I would rule, when the police come on the scene, not subsequent to their arrival, prompted by their own conduct.

I

Two pillars of our Fourth Amendment jurisprudence should have controlled the Court's ruling: First, "whenever practical, [the police must] obtain advance judicial approval of searches and seizures through the warrant procedure," *Terry v. Ohio*, 392 U.S. 1, 20 (1968); second, unwarranted "searches and seizures inside a home" bear heightened scrutiny, *Payton v. New York*, 445 U.S. 573,

Supreme Court of the United States, March 16, 2011.

586 (1980). The warrant requirement, Justice Jackson observed, ranks among the "fundamental distinctions between our form of government, where officers are under the law, and the police-state where they are the law." *Johnson v. United States,* 333 U.S. 10, 17 (1948). The Court has accordingly declared warrantless searches, in the main, *"per se* unreasonable." *Mincey v. Arizona,* 437 U.S. 385, 390 (1978); see also *Groh v. Ramirez,* 540 U.S. 551, 559 (2004). "[T]he police bear a heavy burden," the Court has cautioned, "when attempting to demonstrate an urgent need that might justify warrantless searches." *Welsh v. Wisconsin,* 466 U.S. 740, 749–750 (1984).

That heavy burden has not been carried here. There was little risk that drug-related evidence would have been destroyed had the police delayed the search pending a magistrate's authorization. As the Court recognizes, "[p]ersons in possession of valuable drugs are unlikely to destroy them unless they fear discovery by the police." . . . Nothing in the record shows that, prior to the knock at the apartment door, the occupants were apprehensive about police proximity.

In no quarter does the Fourth Amendment apply with greater force than in our homes, our most private space which, for centuries, has been regarded as "'entitled to special protection.'" *Georgia v. Randolph,* 547 U.S. 103, 115, and n. 4 (2006); *Minnesota v. Carter,* 525 U.S. 83, 99 (1998) (KENNEDY, J., concurring). Home intrusions, the Court has said, are indeed "the chief evil against which . . . the Fourth Amendment is directed." *Payton,* 445 U.S., at 585 (internal quotation marks omitted); see *Silverman v. United States,* 365 U.S. 505, 511 (1961) ("At [the Fourth Amendment's] very core stands the right of a man to retreat to his own home and there be free from unreasonable governmental intrusion."). "'[S]earches and seizures inside a home without a warrant are [therefore] presumptively unreasonable.'" *Brigham City,* 547 U.S., at 403 (quoting *Groh,* 540 U.S., at 559). How "secure" do our homes remain if police, armed with no warrant, can pound on doors at will and, on hearing sounds indicative of things moving, forcibly enter and search for evidence of unlawful activity?

II

As above noted, to justify the police activity in this case, Kentucky invoked the once-guarded exception for emergencies "in which the delay necessary to obtain a warrant . . . threaten[s] 'the destruction of evidence.'" *Schmerber v. California,* 384 U.S. 757, 770 (1966) (quoting *Preston v. United States,* 376 U.S. 364, 367 (1964)). To fit within this exception, "police action literally must be [taken] 'now or never' to preserve the evidence of the crime." *Roaden v. Kentucky,* 413 U.S. 496, 505 (1973).

The existence of a genuine emergency depends not only on the state of necessity at the time of the warrantless search; it depends, first and foremost, on "actions taken by the police *preceding* the warrantless search." *United States v. Coles,* 437 F. 3d 361, 367 (CA3 2006). See also *United States v. Chambers,* 395 F. 3d 563, 565 (CA6 2005) ("[O]fficers must seek a warrant based on probable cause when they believe in advance they will find contraband or evidence of a crime."). "[W]asting a clear opportunity to obtain a warrant," therefore, "disentitles the officer from relying on subsequent exigent circumstances." S. Saltz burg & D. Capra, American Criminal Procedure 376 (8th ed. 2007).

Under an appropriately reined-in "emergency" or "exigent circumstances" exception, the result in this case should not be in doubt. The target of the investigation's entry into the building, and the smell of marijuana seeping under the apartment door into the hallway, the Kentucky Supreme Court rightly determined, gave the police "probable cause . . . sufficient . . . to obtain a warrant to search the . . . apartment." 302 S. W. 3d 649, 653 (2010). As that court observed, nothing made it impracticable for the police to post officers on the premises while proceeding to obtain a warrant authorizing their entry. *Id.*, at 654. Before this Court, Kentucky does not urge otherwise. See Brief for Petitioner 35, n. 13 (asserting "[i]t should be of no importance whether police could have obtained a warrant").

In *Johnson*, the Court confronted this scenario: standing outside a hotel room, the police smelled burning opium and heard "some shuffling or noise" coming from the room. 333 U.S., at 12 (internal quotation marks omitted). Could the police enter the room without a warrant? The Court answered no. Explaining why, the Court said:

> "The right of officers to thrust themselves into a home is . . . a grave concern, not only to the individual but to a society which chooses to dwell in reasonable security and freedom from surveillance. When the right of privacy must reasonably yield to the right of search is, as a rule, to be decided by a judicial officer, not a policeman . . . .

> "If the officers in this case were excused from the constitutional duty of presenting their evidence to a magistrate, it is difficult to think of [any] case in which [a warrant] should be required." *Id.*, at 14–15.

I agree, and would not allow an expedient knock to override the warrant requirement.[1] Instead, I would accord that core requirement of the Fourth Amendment full respect. When possible, "a warrant must generally be secured," the Court acknowledges. . . . There is every reason to conclude that securing a warrant was entirely feasible in this case, and no reason to contract the Fourth Amendment's dominion.

Note

1. The Court in Johnson was informed that "when [the officer] knocked on [Johnson's] door the 'first thing that naturally struck [her]' was to conceal the opium and the equipment for smoking it." See Brief for United States in *Johnson v. United States*, O. T. 1947, No. 329, p. 17, n. 6. Had the Government in Johnson urged that the "shuffling or noise" indicated evidence was at risk, would the result have changed? Justice Jackson's recognition of the primacy of the warrant requirement suggests not. But see ante, at 15, n. 5 (distinguishing Johnson on the ground that the Government did not contend "that the officers entered the room in order to prevent the destruction of evidence").

POSTSCRIPT

Can Noise Coming from Inside an Apartment and Which the Police Believe Involves the Destruction of Drugs Constitute "Exigent Circumstances" That Allow Police Officers to Enter and Search a Home Without a Warrant?

In expressing concern over using "exigent circumstances" to get around the requirement of obtaining a search warrant from a judge, law professor Oren Kerr has written that

> [t]o see why this exception exists, imagine the police are outside a home of a person whom they suspect has drugs inside. The police ordinarily need a warrant to enter the home. If the police decide to light the home on fire, however, they can manufacture an exigency: The fire will mean that they have an emergency justifying a warrant-less entry, both to save the person inside and to seize the drugs (so they are not burned up by the fire and the evidence is lost). If the police can create an emergency in this way, the police can circumvent the warrant requirement by just creating the exigency and then searching without a warrant.

The Supreme Court, in recent years, has been more tolerant of police searches and, in that sense, the decision in this case is more representative of the trend of decisions in the Fourth Amendment area than is the Kyllo case (Issue 16). Underlying almost all Fourth Amendment decisions is the controversial topic of the exclusionary rule. Almost 100 years ago, the Supreme Court ruled that illegally seized evidence cannot be used at trial in the Federal courts. In *Mapp v. Ohio*, 367 U.S. 643 (1961), the Court required state courts to also apply the exclusionary rule. The Court cited a well-known statement by Justice Louis D. Brandeis that "if the government becomes a lawbreaker, it breeds contempt for the law; it invites every man to become a law unto himself; it invites anarchy."

Over time, the exclusionary rule has become a principal means of deterring unlawful searches. It has also become a target of the more conservative justices on the Court and whether the exclusionary rule should continue is likely to be the focal point of some future case.

An interesting argument by a conservative in support of the exclusionary rule is "In Defense of the Exclusionary Rule," by Timothy Lynch, available at http://www.cato.org/pubs/pas/pa-319es.html. Relevant recent articles include Matthew Allan Josephson, "To Exclude or Not to Exclude: The Future of the Exclusionary Rule After *Herring v. United States 43 Creighton L. Rev.* (2009), and Craig M. Bradley, "Reconceiving the Fourth Amendment and the Exclusionary Rule," *73 Law & Contemp. Prob.* 211 (2010). A review of recent cases involving searches and exigent circumstances is given in Katherine A. Carmon, "Don't Act Like You Smell Pot! (At Least, Not in the Fourth Circuit): Police-Created Exigent Circumstances in Fourth Amendment Jurisprudence," *87 North Carolina L. Rev.* (2009).

ISSUE 16

Is the Fourth Amendment Search and Seizure Guaranty Violated by the Use of High-Technology Thermal Imaging Devices?

YES: Antonin Scalia, from Majority Opinion, *Danny Lee Kyllo v. United States,* U.S. Supreme Court (June 11, 2001)

NO: John Paul Stevens, from Dissenting Opinion, *Danny Lee Kyllo v. United States,* U.S. Supreme Court (June 11, 2001)

ISSUE SUMMARY

YES: Supreme Court Justice Antonin Scalia maintains that thermal imaging devices reveal information "that would previously have been unknowable without physical intrusion" and that using such devices for surveillance without a warrant constitutes a violation of the Fourth Amendment.

NO: Supreme Court Justice John Paul Stevens asserts that the Court's application of search and seizure rules to new technology is too broad and that collecting thermal imaging data from outside the home is not a violation of privacy rights.

In 1991 agent William Elliott of the U.S. Department of the Interior became suspicious that marijuana was being grown in the home of Danny Kyllo. Indoor marijuana growth typically requires high-intensity lamps, and at 3:20 a.m. on January 16, 1992, Elliott scanned Kyllo's home with a thermal imaging device. Such devices can detect infrared radiation, which virtually all objects emit but which is not visible to the naked eye. The imager converts radiation into images based on relative warmth—black is cool, white is hot, and shades of gray connote relative differences.

The scan of Kyllo's home took only a few minutes. It showed that the roof over the garage and a side wall of the home were relatively hot compared to the rest of the home and substantially warmer than neighboring homes. Elliott concluded that Kyllo was using special lamps to grow marijuana in his house. Based on tips from informants, utility bills, and the thermal imaging, a warrant was issued authorizing a search of Kyllo's home, where the agents found more than 100 plants being grown. Kyllo was indicted on one count of manufacturing marijuana. He unsuccessfully moved to suppress the evidence seized from his home and then entered a conditional guilty plea.

The Fourth Amendment to the Constitution requires authorities to obtain a search warrant before conducting a search. In order to do this, they must first persuade a judge that probable cause exists that a crime has been committed and that the evidence sought will be found in the place to be searched. The warrant requirement is the key constitutional element restricting the power of the police to decide unilaterally to invade the privacy of someone's home.

There are exceptions to this requirement. The Court has held that search warrants are not required for school officials to search school lockers if there are reasonable grounds for believing that the search will reveal evidence of criminal behavior (*New Jersey v. T. L. O., A Juvenile,* 105 S. Ct. 733, [1985]), nor are search warrants required when a person is searched after an arrest or when the object seized is in plain view. Technological advances, however, are posing new challenges. We are developing technological capabilities to do things at a distance and to obtain information that previously would have required entering a physical location. The *Kyllo* case is a perfect example of this.

The lower court ruled against Kyllo and found that the thermal imager "is a nonintrusive device which emits no rays or beams and shows a crude visual image of the heat being radiated from the outside of the house"; it "did not show any people or activity within the walls of the structure"; "the device used cannot penetrate walls or windows to reveal conversations or human activities"; and "no intimate details of the home were observed." Kyllo appealed to the Court of Appeals and then to the U.S. Supreme Court, which ruled in his favor. The following selections are from the majority and dissenting opinions in the case, as delivered by Justice Antonin Scalia and Justice John Paul Stevens, respectively.

Thermal imaging is only the latest technological challenge to the Fourth Amendment. In *Katz v. United States,* 389 U.S. 347 (1967), the Court held that wiretapping without a warrant could violate the search and seizure clause. It was not necessary for the police to enter someone's property physically to "search" something. Rather, "once it is recognized that the Fourth Amendment protects people—and not simply 'areas'—against unreasonable searches and seizures, it becomes clear that the reach of [the Fourth] Amendment cannot turn upon the presence or absence of a physical intrusion into any given enclosure."

Thermal imaging has been used by law enforcement authorities for some time, and *Kyllo* was not the first case in which a lower court ruled on its use. As it often does, the Supreme Court agreed to hear the *Kyllo* case because various lower courts had come to different conclusions about the constitutionality of using this technology without first obtaining a warrant. As new technological applications that assist law enforcement and also invade privacy are perfected, the opinions covered by the following selections are likely to be referred to often.

YES

Antonin Scalia

Majority Opinion,
Kyllo v. United States

J USTICE SCALIA delivered the opinion of the Court. . . .

I

In 1991 Agent William Elliott of the United States Department of the Interior came to suspect that marijuana was being grown in the home belonging to petitioner Danny Kyllo, part of a triplex on Rhododendron Drive in Florence, Oregon. Indoor marijuana growth typically requires high-intensity lamps. In order to determine whether an amount of heat was emanating from petitioner's home consistent with the use of such lamps, at 3:20 a.m. on January 16, 1992, Agent Elliott and Dan Haas used an Agema Thermovision 210 thermal imager to scan the triplex. . . .

II

The Fourth Amendment provides that "[t]he right of the people to be secure in their persons, houses, papers, and effects, against unreasonable searches and seizures, shall not be violated." "At the very core" of the Fourth Amendment "stands the right of a man to retreat into his own home and there be free from unreasonable governmental intrusion." *Silverman v. United States,* 365 U.S. 505, 511 (1961). With few exceptions, the question whether a warrantless search of a home is reasonable and hence constitutional must be answered no. See *Illinois v. Rodriguez,* 497 U.S. 177, 181 (1990); *Payton v. New York,* 445 U.S. 573, 586 (1980).

On the other hand, the antecedent question of whether or not a Fourth Amendment "search" has occurred is not so simple under our precedent. The permissibility of ordinary visual surveillance of a home used to be clear because, well into the 20th century, our Fourth Amendment jurisprudence was tied to common-law trespass. . . . Visual surveillance was unquestionably lawful because " 'the eye cannot by the laws of England be guilty of a trespass.'" *Boyd v. United States,* 116 U.S. 616, 628 (1886) (quoting *Entick v. Carrington,* 19 How. St. Tr. 1029, 95 Eng. Rep. 807 (K. B. 1765)). We have since decoupled violation of a person's Fourth Amendment rights from trespassory violation of his property, see *Rakas v. Illinois,* 439 U.S. 128, 143 (1978), but the lawfulness of warrantless

Supreme Court of the United States, June 11, 2001.

visual surveillance of a home has still been preserved. As we observed in *California v. Ciraolo,* 476 U.S. 207, 213 (1986), "[t]he Fourth Amendment protection of the home has never been extended to require law enforcement officers to shield their eyes when passing by a home on public thoroughfares."

One might think that the new validating rationale would be that examining the portion of a house that is in plain public view, while it is a "search" despite the absence of trespass, is not an "unreasonable" one under the Fourth Amendment. See *Minnesota v. Carter,* 525 U.S. 83, 104 (1998) (BREYER, J., concurring in judgment). But in fact we have held that visual observation is no "search" at all—perhaps in order to preserve somewhat more intact our doctrine that warrantless searches are presumptively unconstitutional. See *Dow Chemical Co. v. United States,* 476 U.S. 227, 234–235, 239 (1986). In assessing when a search is not a search, we have applied somewhat in reverse the principle first enunciated in *Katz v. United States,* 389 U.S. 347 (1967). *Katz* involved eavesdropping by means of an electronic listening device placed on the outside of a telephone booth—a location not within the catalog ("persons, houses, papers, and effects") that the Fourth Amendment protects against unreasonable searches. We held that the Fourth Amendment nonetheless protected Katz from the warrantless eavesdropping because he "justifiably relied" upon the privacy of the telephone booth. *Id.,* at 353. As Justice Harlan's oft-quoted concurrence described it, a Fourth Amendment search occurs when the government violates a subjective expectation of privacy that society recognizes as reasonable. See *id.,* at 361. We have subsequently applied this principle to hold that a Fourth Amendment search does *not* occur—even when the explicitly protected location of a *house* is concerned—unless "the individual manifested a subjective expectation of privacy in the object of the challenged search," and "society [is] willing to recognize that expectation as reasonable." *Ciraolo, supra,* at 211. We have applied this test in holding that it is not a search for the police to use a pen register at the phone company to determine what numbers were dialed in a private home, *Smith v. Maryland,* 442 U.S. 735, 743–744 (1979), and we have applied the test on two different occasions in holding that aerial surveillance of private homes and surrounding areas does not constitute a search, *Ciraolo, supra; Florida v. Riley,* 488 U.S. 445 (1989).

The present case involves officers on a public street engaged in more than naked-eye surveillance of a home. We have previously reserved judgment as to how much technological enhancement of ordinary perception from such a vantage point, if any, is too much. While we upheld enhanced aerial photography of an industrial complex in *Dow Chemical,* we noted that we found "it important that this is *not* an area immediately adjacent to a private home, where privacy expectations are most heightened," 476 U.S., at 237, n. 4 (emphasis in original).

III

It would be foolish to contend that the degree of privacy secured to citizens by the Fourth Amendment has been entirely unaffected by the advance of technology. For example, as the cases discussed above make clear, the technology enabling human flight has exposed to public view (and hence, we have said, to official observation) uncovered portions of the house and its curtilage that once were private. See *Ciraolo, supra,* at 215. The question we confront today is what limits there are upon this power of technology to shrink the realm of guaranteed privacy.

The *Katz* test—whether the individual has an expectation of privacy that society is prepared to recognize as reasonable—has often been criticized as circular, and hence subjective and unpredictable. See 1 W. LaFave, *Search and Seizure* §2.1(d), pp. 393–394 (3d ed. 1996); Posner, The Uncertain Protection of Privacy by the Supreme Court, 1979 *S. Ct. Rev.* 173, 188; *Carter, supra,* at 97 (SCALIA, j., concurring). But see *Rakas, supra,* at 143–144, n. 12. While it may be difficult to refine Katz when the search of areas such as telephone booths, automobiles, or even the curtilage and uncovered portions of residences are at issue, in the case of the search of the interior of homes—the prototypical and hence most commonly litigated area of protected privacy—there is a ready criterion, with roots deep in the common law, of the minimal expectation of privacy that *exists,* and that is acknowledged to be *reasonable.* To withdraw protection of this minimum expectation would be to permit police technology to erode the privacy guaranteed by the Fourth Amendment. We think that obtaining by sense-enhancing technology any information regarding the interior of the home that could not otherwise have been obtained without physical "intrusion into a constitutionally protected area," *Silverman,* 365 U.S., at 512, constitutes a search—at least where (as here) the technology in question is not in general public use. This assures preservation of that degree of privacy against government that existed when the Fourth Amendment was adopted. On the basis of this criterion, the information obtained by the thermal imager in this case was the product of a search.[1]

The Government maintains, however, that the thermal imaging must be upheld because it detected "only heat radiating from the external surface of the house," Brief for United States 26. The dissent makes this its leading point, see *post,* at 1, contending that there is a fundamental difference between what it calls "off-the-wall" observations and "through-the-wall surveillance." But just as a thermal imager captures only heat emanating from a house, so also a powerful directional microphone picks up only sound emanating from a house—and a satellite capable of scanning from many miles away would pick up only visible light emanating from a house. We rejected such a mechanical interpretation of the Fourth Amendment in *Katz,* where the eavesdropping device picked up only sound waves that reached the exterior of the phone booth. Reversing that approach would leave the homeowner at the mercy of advancing technology—including imaging technology that could discern all human activity in the home. While the technology used in the present case was relatively crude, the rule we adopt must take account of more sophisticated systems that are already in use or in development.[2] The dissent's reliance on the distinction between "off-the-wall" and "through-the-wall" observation is entirely incompatible with the dissent's belief, which we discuss below, that thermal-imaging observations of the intimate details of a home are impermissible. The most sophisticated thermal imaging devices continue to measure heat "off-the-wall" rather than "through-the-wall"; the dissent's disapproval of those more sophisticated thermal-imaging devices, see *post,* at 10, is an acknowledgement that there is no substance to this distinction. As for the dissent's extraordinary assertion that anything learned through "an inference" cannot be a search, see *post,* at 4–5, that would validate even the "through-the-wall" technologies that the dissent purports to disapprove. Surely the dissent does not believe that the through-the-wall radar or ultrasound technology produces an 8-by-10 Kodak glossy that needs no analysis (*i.e.,* the making of inferences). And, of course, the novel proposition that inference insulates a search is blatantly contrary to *United States v. Karo,* 468 U.S. 705 (1984), where the police "inferred" from the activation of a beeper that a certain can of ether was in the home. The police activity was held to be a search, and the search was held unlawful.[3]

The government also contends that the thermal imaging was constitutional because it did not "detect private activities occurring in private areas," Brief for United States 22. It points out that in *Dow Chemical* we observed that the enhanced aerial photography did not reveal any "intimate details." 476 U.S., at 238. *Dow Chemical,* however, involved enhanced aerial photography of an industrial complex, which does not share the Fourth Amendment sanctity of the home. The Fourth Amendment's protection of the home has never been tied to measurement of the quality or quantity of information obtained. In *Silverman,* for example, we made clear that any physical invasion of the structure of the home, "by even a fraction of an inch," was too much, 365 U.S., at 512, and there is certainly no exception to the warrant requirement for the officer who barely cracks open the front door and sees nothing but the nonintimate rug on the vestibule floor. In the home, our cases show, *all* details are intimate details, because the entire area is held safe from prying government eyes. Thus, in *Karo, supra,* the only thing detected was a can of ether in the home; and in *Arizona v. Hicks,* 480 U.S. 321 (1987), the only thing detected by a physical search that went beyond what officers lawfully present could observe in "plain view" was the registration number of a phonograph turntable. These were intimate details because they were details of the home, just as was the detail of how warm—or even how relatively warm—Kyllo was heating his residence.[4]

Limiting the prohibition of thermal imaging to "intimate details" would not only be wrong in principle; it would be impractical in application, failing to provide "a workable accommodation between the needs of law enforcement and the interests protected by the Fourth Amendment," *Oliver v. United States,* 466 U.S. 170, 181 (1984). To begin with, there is no necessary connection between the sophistication of the surveillance equipment and the "intimacy" of the details that it observes—which means that one cannot say (and the police cannot be assured) that use of the relatively crude equipment at issue here will always be lawful. The Agema Thermovision 210 might disclose, for example, at what hour each night the lady of the house takes her daily sauna and bath—a detail that many would consider "intimate"; and a much more sophisticated system might detect nothing more intimate than the fact that someone left a closet light on. We could not, in other words, develop a rule approving only that through-the-wall surveillance which identifies objects no smaller than 36 by 36 inches, but would have to develop a jurisprudence specifying which home activities are "intimate" and which are not. And even when (if ever) that jurisprudence were fully developed, no police officer would be able to know in *advance* whether his through-the-wall surveillance picks up "intimate" details—and thus would be unable to know in advance whether it is constitutional.

The dissent's proposed standard—whether the technology offers the "functional equivalent of actual presence in the area being searched," *post,* at 7—would seem quite similar to our own at first blush. The dissent concludes that *Katz* was such a case, but then inexplicably asserts that if the same listening device only revealed the volume of the conversation, the surveillance would be permissible, *post,* at 10. Yet if, without technology, the police could not discern volume without being actually present in the phone booth, JUSTICE STEVENS should conclude a search has occurred. Cf. *Karo, supra,* at 735 (STEVENS, J., concurring in part and dissenting in part) ("I find little comfort in the Court's notion that no invasion of privacy occurs until a listener obtains some significant information by use of the device. . . . A bathtub is a less private area when the plumber is present even if his back is turned"). The same should hold for the interior heat of the home if only a person present in the home could discern the heat. Thus the driving force of the dissent, despite its recitation of the above standard, appears to be a distinction among different types of information—whether the "homeowner would even care if anybody noticed," *post,* at 10. The dissent offers no practical guidance for the application of this standard, and for reasons already discussed, we believe there can be none. The people in their houses, as well as the police, deserve more precision.[5]

We have said that the Fourth Amendment draws "a firm line at the entrance to the house," *Payton,* 445 U.S., at 590. That line, we think, must be not only firm but also bright—which requires clear specification of those methods of surveillance that require a warrant. While it is certainly possible to conclude from the videotape of the thermal imaging that occurred in this case that no "significant" compromise of the homeowner's privacy has occurred, we must take the long view, from the original meaning of the Fourth Amendment forward.

> "The Fourth Amendment is to be construed in the light of what was deemed an unreasonable search and seizure when it was adopted, and in a manner which will conserve public interests as well as the interests and rights of individual citizens." *Carroll v. United States,* 267 U.S. 132, 149 (1925).

Where, as here, the Government uses a device that is not in general public use, to explore details of the home that would previously have been unknowable without physical intrusion, the surveillance is a "search" and is presumptively unreasonable without a warrant.

Since we hold the Thermovision imaging to have been an unlawful search, it will remain for the District Court to determine whether, without the evidence it provided, the search warrant issued in this case was supported by probable cause—and if not, whether there is any other basis for supporting admission of the evidence that the search pursuant to the warrant produced.

✦

The judgment of the Court of Appeals is reversed; the case is remanded for further proceedings consistent with this opinion.

It is so ordered.

Notes

1. The dissent's repeated assertion that the thermal imaging did not obtain information regarding the interior of the home, *post,* at 3, 4 (opinion of STEVENS, J.), is simply inaccurate. A thermal imager reveals the relative heat of various rooms in the home. The dissent may not find that information particularly private or important, see *post,* at 4, 5, 10, but there is no basis for saying it is not information regarding the interior of the home. The dissent's comparison of the thermal imaging to various circumstances in which outside observers might be able to perceive, without technology, the heat of the home—for example, by observing snowmelt on the roof, *post,* at 3—is quite irrelevant. The fact that equivalent information could sometimes be obtained by other means does not make lawful the use of means that violate the Fourth Amendment. The police might, for example, learn how many people are in a particular house by setting up year-round surveillance; but that does not make breaking and entering to find out the same information lawful. In any event, on the night of January 16, 1992, no outside observer could have discerned the relative heat of Kyllo's home without thermal imaging.

2. The ability to "see" through walls and other opaque barriers is a clear, and scientifically feasible, goal of law enforcement research and development. The National Law Enforcement and Corrections Technology Center, a program within the United States Department of Justice, features on its Internet Website projects that include a "Radar-Based Through-the-Wall Surveillance System," "Handheld Ultrasound Through the Wall Surveillance," and a "Radar Flashlight" that "will enable law officers to detect individuals through interior building walls." . . . (visited May 3, 2001). Some devices may emit low levels of radiation that travel "through-the-wall," but others, such as more sophisticated thermal imaging devices, are entirely passive, or "off-the-wall" as the dissent puts it.

3. The dissent asserts, *post,* at 5, n. 3, that we have misunderstood its point, which is not that inference *insulates* a search, but that inference alone is *not* a search. If we misunderstood the point, it was only in a good-faith effort to render the point germane to the case at hand. The issue in this case is not the police's allegedly unlawful inferencing, but their allegedly unlawful thermal-imaging measurement of the emanations from a house. We say such measurement is a search; the dissent says it is not, because an inference is not a search. We took that to mean that, since the

technologically enhanced emanations had to be the basis of inferences before anything inside the house could be known, the use of the emanations could not be a search. But the dissent certainly knows better than we what it intends. And if it means only that an inference is not a search, we certainly agree. That has no bearing, however, upon whether hi-tech measurement of emanations from a house is a search.

4. The Government cites our statement in *California v. Ciraolo,* 476 U.S. 207 (1986), noting apparent agreement with the state of California that aerial surveillance of a house's curtilage could become "invasive" if "modern technology" revealed "those intimate associations, objects or activities otherwise imperceptible to police or fellow citizens." *Id.,* at 215, n. 3 (quoting brief of the state of California). We think the Court's focus in this second-hand dictum was not upon intimacy but upon otherwise-imperceptibility, which is precisely the principle we vindicate today.

5. The dissent argues that we have injected potential uncertainty into the constitutional analysis by noting that whether or not the technology is in general public use may be a factor. See *post,* at 7–8. That quarrel, however, is not with us but with this Court's precedent. See *Ciraolo, supra,* at 215 ("In an age where private and commercial flight in the public airways is routine, it is unreasonable for respondent to expect that his marijuana plants were constitutionally protected from being observed with the naked eye from an altitude of 1,000 feet"). Given that we can quite confidently say that thermal imaging is not "routine," we decline in this case to reexamine that factor.

John Paul Stevens  **NO**

Dissenting Opinion
of John Paul Stevens

JUSTICE STEVENS, with whom THE CHIEF JUSTICE, JUSTICE O'CONNOR, and JUSTICE KENNEDY join, dissenting.

There is, in my judgment, a distinction of constitutional magnitude between "through-the-wall surveillance" that gives the observer or listener direct access to information in a private area, on the one hand, and the thought processes used to draw inferences from information in the public domain, on the other hand. The Court has crafted a rule that purports to deal with direct observations of the inside of the home, but the case before us merely involves indirect deductions from "off-the-wall" surveillance, that is, observations of the exterior of the home. Those observations were made with a fairly primitive thermal imager that gathered data exposed on the outside of petitioner's home but did not invade any constitutionally protected interest in privacy.[1] Moreover, I believe that the supposedly "bright-line" rule the Court has created in response to its concerns about future technological developments is unnecessary, unwise, and inconsistent with the Fourth Amendment.

I

There is no need for the Court to craft a new rule to decide this case, as it is controlled by established principles from our Fourth Amendment jurisprudence. One of those core principles, of course, is that "searches and seizures *inside a home* without a warrant are presumptively unreasonable." *Payton v. New York,* 445 U.S. 573, 586 (1980) (emphasis added). But it is equally well settled that searches and seizures of property in plain view are presumptively reasonable. See *id.,* at 586–587.[2] Whether that property is residential or commercial, the basic principle is the same: "What a person knowingly exposes to the public, even in his own home or office, is not a subject of Fourth Amendment protection." *California v. Ciraolo,* 476 U.S. 207, 213 (1986) (quoting *Katz v. United States,* 389 U.S. 347, 351 (1967)); see *Florida v. Riley,* 488 U.S. 445, 449–450 (1989); *California v. Greenwood,* 486 U.S. 35, 40–41 (1988); *Dow Chemical Co. v. United States,* 476 U.S. 227, 235–236 (1986); *Air Pollution Variance Bd. of Colo. v. Western Alfalfa Corp.,* 416 U.S. 861, 865 (1974). That is the principle implicated here.

Supreme Court of the United States, June 11, 2001.

While the Court "take[s] the long view" and decides this case based largely on the potential of yet-to-be-developed technology that might allow "through-the-wall surveillance," this case involves nothing more than off-the-wall surveillance by law enforcement officers to gather information exposed to the general public from the outside of petitioner's home. All that the infrared camera did in this case was passively measure heat emitted from the exterior surfaces of petitioner's home; all that those measurements showed were relative differences in emission levels, vaguely indicating that some areas of the roof and outside walls were warmer than others. As still images from the infrared scans show, no details regarding the interior of petitioner's home were revealed. Unlike an x-ray scan, or other possible "through-the-wall" techniques, the detection of infrared radiation emanating from the home did not accomplish "an unauthorized physical penetration into the premises," *Silverman v. United States,* 365 U.S. 505, 509 (1961), nor did it "obtain information that it could not have obtained by observation from outside the curtilage of the house," *United States v. Karo,* 468 U.S. 705, 715 (1984).

Indeed, the ordinary use of the senses might enable a neighbor or passerby to notice the heat emanating from a building, particularly if it is vented, as was the case here. Additionally, any member of the public might notice that one part of a house is warmer than another part or a nearby building if, for example, rainwater evaporates or snow melts at different rates across its surfaces. Such use of the senses would not convert into an unreasonable search if, instead, an adjoining neighbor allowed an officer onto her property to verify her perceptions with a sensitive thermometer. Nor, in my view, does such observation become an unreasonable search if made from a distance with the aid of a device that merely discloses that the exterior of one house, or one area of the house, is much warmer than another. Nothing more occurred in this case.

Thus, the notion that heat emissions from the outside of a dwelling is a private matter implicating the protections of the Fourth Amendment (the text of which guarantees the right of people "to be secure *in* their . . . houses" against unreasonable searches and seizures (emphasis added)) is not only unprecedented but also quite difficult to take seriously. Heat waves, like aromas that are generated in a kitchen, or in a laboratory or opium den, enter the public domain if and when they leave a building. A subjective expectation that they would remain private is not only implausible but also surely not "one that society is prepared to recognize as 'reasonable.'" *Katz,* 389 U.S., at 361 (HARLAN, J., concurring).

To be sure, the homeowner has a reasonable expectation of privacy concerning what takes place within the home, and the Fourth Amendment's protection against physical invasions of the home should apply to their functional equivalent. But the equipment in this case did not penetrate the walls of petitioner's home, and while it did pick up "details of the home" that were exposed to the public, *ante,* at 10, it did not obtain "any information regarding the *interior* of the home," *ante,* at 6 (emphasis added). In the Court's own words, based on what the thermal imager "showed" regarding the outside of petitioner's home, the officers "concluded" that petitioner was engaging in illegal activity inside the home. It would be quite absurd to characterize their thought processes as "searches," regardless of whether they inferred (rightly) that petitioner was growing marijuana in his house, or (wrongly) that "the lady of the house [was taking] her daily sauna and bath." In either case, the only conclusions the officers reached concerning the interior of the home were at least as indirect as those that might have been inferred from the contents of discarded garbage, see *California v. Greenwood,* 486 U.S. 35 (1988), or pen register data, see *Smith v. Maryland,* 442 U.S. 735 (1979), or, as in this case, subpoenaed utility records, see 190 F. 3d 1041, 1043 (CA9 1999). For the first time in its history, the Court assumes that an inference can amount to a Fourth Amendment violation.

Notwithstanding the implications of today's decision, there is a strong public interest in avoiding constitutional litigation over the monitoring of emissions from homes, and over the inferences drawn from such monitoring. Just as "the police cannot reasonably be expected to avert their eyes from evidence of criminal activity that could have been observed by any member of the public," *Greenwood,* 486 U.S., at 41, so too public officials should not have to avert their senses or their equipment from detecting emissions in the public domain such as excessive heat, traces of smoke, suspicious odors, odorless gases, airborne particulates, or radioactive emissions, any of which could identify hazards to the community. In my judgment, monitoring such emissions with "sense-enhancing technology," and drawing useful conclusions from such monitoring, is an entirely reasonable public service.

On the other hand, the countervailing privacy interest is at best trivial. After all, homes generally are insulated to keep heat in, rather than to prevent the detection of heat going out, and it does not seem to me that society will suffer from a rule requiring the rare homeowner who both intends to engage in uncommon activities that produce extraordinary amounts of heat, and wishes to conceal that production from outsiders, to make sure that the surrounding area is well insulated. Cf. *United States v. Jacobsen,* 466 U.S. 109, 122 (1984) ("The concept of an interest in privacy that society is prepared to recognize as reasonable is, by its very nature, critically different from the mere expectation, however well justified, that certain facts will not come to the attention of the authorities.") The interest in concealing the heat escaping from one's house pales in significance to the "chief evil against which the wording of the Fourth Amendment is directed," the "physical entry of the home," *United States v. United States Dist. Court for Eastern Dist. of Mich.,* 407 U.S. 297, 313 (1972), and it is hard to believe that it is an interest the Framers sought to protect in our Constitution.

Since what was involved in this case was nothing more than drawing inferences from off-the-wall surveillance, rather than any "through-the-wall" surveillance, the officers' conduct did not amount to a search and was perfectly reasonable.[3]

II

Instead of trying to answer the question whether the use of the thermal imager in this case was even arguably unreasonable, the Court has fashioned a rule that is intended to provide essential guidance for the day when "more sophisticated systems" gain the "ability to 'see' through walls and other opaque barriers." The newly minted rule encompasses "obtaining [1] by sense-enhancing technology [2] any information regarding the interior of the home [3] that could not otherwise have been obtained without physical intrusion into a constitutionally protected area . . . [4] at least where (as here) the technology in question is not in general public use." In my judgment, the Court's new rule is at once too broad and too narrow, and is not justified by the Court's explanation for its adoption. As I have suggested, I would not erect a constitutional impediment to the use of sense-enhancing technology unless it provides its user with the functional equivalent of actual presence in the area being searched.

Despite the Court's attempt to draw a line that is "not only firm but also bright," the contours of its new rule are uncertain because its protection apparently dissipates as soon as the relevant technology is "in general public use." Yet how much use is general public use is not even hinted at by the Court's opinion, which makes the somewhat doubtful assumption that the thermal imager used in this case does not satisfy that criterion.[4] In any event, putting aside its lack of clarity, this criterion is somewhat perverse because it seems likely that the threat to privacy will grow, rather than recede, as the use of intrusive equipment becomes more readily available.

It is clear, however, that the category of "sense-enhancing technology" covered by the new rule is far too broad. It would, for example, embrace potential mechanical substitutes for dogs trained to react when they sniff narcotics. But in *United States v. Place,* 462 U.S. 696, 707 (1983), we held that a dog sniff that "discloses only the presence or absence of narcotics" does "not constitute a 'search' within the meaning of the Fourth Amendment," and it must follow that sense-enhancing equipment that identifies nothing but illegal activity is not a search either. Nevertheless, the use of such a device would be unconstitutional under the Court's rule, as would the use of other new devices that might detect the odor of deadly bacteria or chemicals for making a new type of high explosive, even if the devices (like the dog sniffs) are "so limited in both the manner in which" they obtain information and "in the content of the information" they reveal. If nothing more than that sort of information could be obtained by using the devices in a public place to monitor emissions from a house, then their use would be no more objectionable than the use of the thermal imager in this case.

The application of the Court's new rule to "any information regarding the interior of the home," is also unnecessarily broad. If it takes sensitive equipment to detect an odor that identifies criminal conduct and nothing else, the fact that the odor emanates from the interior of a home should not provide it with constitutional protection. The criterion, moreover, is too sweeping in that information "regarding" the interior of a home apparently is not just information obtained through its walls, but also information concerning the outside of the building that could lead to (however many) inferences "regarding" what might be inside. Under that expansive view, I suppose, an officer using an infrared camera to observe a man silently entering the side door of a house at night carrying a pizza might conclude that its interior is now occupied by someone who likes pizza, and by doing so the officer would be guilty of conducting an unconstitutional "search" of the home.

Because the new rule applies to information regarding the "interior" of the home, it is too narrow as well as too broad. Clearly, a rule that is designed to protect individuals from the overly intrusive use of sense-enhancing equipment should not be limited to a home. If such equipment did provide its user with the functional equivalent of access to a private place—such as, for example, the telephone booth involved in *Katz*, or an office building—then the rule should apply to such an area as well as to a home. See *Katz*, 389 U.S., at 351 ("[T]he Fourth Amendment protects people, not places").

The final requirement of the Court's new rule, that the information "could not otherwise have been obtained without physical intrusion into a constitutionally protected area," *ante*, at 6 (internal quotation marks omitted), also extends too far as the Court applies it. As noted, the Court effectively treats the mental process of analyzing data obtained from external sources as the equivalent of a physical intrusion into the home. As I have explained, however, the process of drawing inferences from data in the public domain should not be characterized as a search.

The two reasons advanced by the Court as justifications for the adoption of its new rule are both unpersuasive. First, the Court suggests that its rule is compelled by our holding in *Katz*, because in that case, as in this, the surveillance consisted of nothing more than the monitoring of waves emanating from a private area into the public domain. Yet there are critical differences between the cases. In *Katz*, the electronic listening device attached to the outside of the phone booth allowed the officers to pick up the content of the conversation inside the booth, making them the functional equivalent of intruders because they gathered information that was otherwise available only to someone inside the private area; it would be as if, in this case, the thermal imager presented a view of the heat-generating activity inside petitioner's home. By contrast, the thermal imager here disclosed only the relative amounts of heat radiating from the house; it would be as if, in Katz, the listening device disclosed only the relative volume of sound leaving the booth, which presumably was discernible in the public domain.[5] Surely, there is a significant difference between the general and well-settled expectation that strangers will not have direct access to the contents of private communications, on the one hand, and the rather theoretical expectation that an occasional homeowner would even care if anybody noticed the relative amounts of heat emanating from the walls of his house, on the other. It is pure hyperbole for the Court to suggest that refusing to extend the holding of *Katz* to this case would leave the homeowner at the mercy of "technology that could discern all human activity in the home." *Ante*, at 8.

Second, the Court argues that the permissibility of "through-the-wall surveillance" cannot depend on a distinction between observing "intimate details" such as "the lady of the house [taking] her daily sauna and bath," and noticing only "the nonintimate rug on the vestibule floor" or "objects no smaller than 36 by 36 inches." *Ante*, at 10–11. This entire argument assumes, of course, that the thermal imager in this case could or did perform "through-the-wall surveillance" that could identify any detail "that would previously have been unknowable without physical intrusion." In fact, the device could not, and did not, enable its user to identify either the lady of the house, the rug on the vestibule floor, or anything else inside the house, whether smaller or larger than 36 by 36 inches. Indeed, the vague thermal images of petitioner's home that are reproduced in the Appendix were submitted by him to the District Court as part of an expert report raising the question whether the device could even take "accurate, consistent infrared images" of the *outside* of his house. Defendant's Exhibit 107, p. 4. But even if the device could reliably show extraordinary differences in the amounts of heat leaving his home, drawing the inference that there was something suspicious occurring inside the residence—a conclusion that officers far less gifted than Sherlock Holmes would readily draw—does not qualify as "through-the-wall surveillance," much less a Fourth Amendment violation.

III

Although the Court is properly and commendably concerned about the threats to privacy that may flow from advances in the technology available to the law enforcement profession, it has unfortunately failed to heed the tried and true counsel of judicial restraint. Instead of concentrating on the rather mundane issue that is actually presented by the case before it, the Court has endeavored to craft an all-encompassing rule for the future. It would be far wiser to give legislators an unimpeded opportunity to grapple with these emerging issues rather than to shackle them with prematurely devised constitutional constraints.

I respectfully dissent.

Notes

1. After an evidentiary hearing, the District Court found:

   "[T]he use of the thermal imaging device here was not an intrusion into Kyllo's home. No intimate details of the home were observed, and there was no intrusion upon the privacy of the individuals within the home. The device used cannot penetrate walls or windows to reveal conversations or human activities. The device recorded only the heat being emitted from the home." Supp. App. to Pet. for Cert. 40.

2. Thus, for example, we have found consistent with the Fourth Amendment, even absent a warrant, the search and seizure of garbage left for collection outside the curtilage of a home, *California v. Greenwood,* 486 U.S. 35 (1988); the aerial surveillance of a fenced-in backyard from an altitude of 1,000 feet, *California v. Ciraolo,* 476 U.S. 207 (1986); the aerial observation of a partially exposed interior of a residential greenhouse from 400 feet above, *Florida v. Riley,* 488 U.S. 445 (1989); the aerial photography of an industrial complex from several thousand feet above, *Dow Chemical Co. v. United States,* 476 U.S. 227 (1986); and the observation of smoke emanating from chimney stacks, *Air Pollution Variance Bd. of Colo. v. Western Alfalfa Corp.,* 416 U.S. 861 (1974).

3. This view comports with that of all the Courts of Appeals that have resolved the issue. See 190 F. 3d 1041 (CA9 1999); *United States v. Robinson,* 62 F. 3d 1325

(CA11 1995) (upholding warrantless use of thermal imager); *United States v. Myers*, 46 F. 3d 668 (CA7 1995) (same); *United States v. Ishmael*, 48 F. 3d 850 (CA5 1995) (same); *United States v. Pinson*, 24 F. 3d 1056 (CA8 1994) (same). But see *United States v. Cusumano*, 67 F. 3d 1497 (CA10 1995) (warrantless use of thermal imager violated Fourth Amendment), vacated and decided on other grounds, 83 F. 3d 1247 (CA10 1996) (en banc).

4. The record describes a device that numbers close to a thousand manufactured units; that has a predecessor numbering in the neighborhood of 4,000 to 5,000 units; that competes with a similar product numbering from 5,000 to 6,000 units; and that is "readily available to the public" for commercial, personal, or law enforcement purposes, and is just an 800-number away from being rented from "half a dozen national companies" by anyone who wants one. App. 18. Since, by virtue of the Court's new rule, the issue is one of first impression, perhaps it should order an evidentiary hearing to determine whether these facts suffice to establish "general public use."

5. The use of the latter device would be constitutional given *Smith v. Maryland*, 442 U.S. 735, 741 (1979), which upheld the use of pen registers to record numbers dialed on a phone because, unlike "the listening device employed in *Katz* . . . pen registers do not acquire the *contents* of communications."

POSTSCRIPT

Is the Fourth Amendment Search and Seizure Guaranty Violated by the Use of High-Technology Thermal Imaging Devices?

Even though Antonin Scalia's opinion is a strong statement about the need for protecting privacy in a technological era, there will certainly be more cases in which challenging issues will be presented. Law enforcement's ability to invade privacy at a distance is increasing, and the Supreme Court has not, as it did in this case, always sided with the individual. Indeed, the Court has upheld various novel search techniques in other Fourth Amendment cases. Consider the following:

- *Dow Chemical Co. v. United States,* 476 U.S. 227 (1986)—The Court allowed aerial pictures taken by the Environmental Protection Agency (EPA) even though the company had refused to allow inspectors to enter.
- *Florida v. Riley,* 488 U.S. 445, 450 (1989)—The Court allowed a search in which a police officer in a helicopter looked into a greenhouse from a height of 400 feet and observed through openings in the roof what he thought was marijuana.
- *California v. Ciraolo,* 476 U.S. 207, 213–214 (1986)—The Court held that police officers were not "searching" when they flew over the defendant's property and observed marijuana growing.
- *Smith v. Maryland,* 442 U.S. 735, 742–744 (1979)—The Court allowed the authorities to look at "pen registers," or records of telephone numbers dialed, without a warrant.

Scalia does not mention the use of trained dogs to sniff out the presence of drugs at airports and other public places. The Court, in *United States v. Place,* 462 U.S. 696 (1983), allowed the use of dogs when the sniff "discloses only the presence or absence of narcotics." John Paul Stevens raises the interesting question of whether or not "mechanical substitutes for dogs trained to react when they sniff narcotics" would be lawful. Since technology allows information to be obtained at a distance, often without a person feeling that his or her privacy has been invaded, we can expect additional cases in which the lawful use of "mechanical substitutes" is the main issue.

Background information on law enforcement and the drug problem can be found on the Web site of the Drug Enforcement Administration of the U.S. Department of Justice at http://www.usdoj.gov/dea/. Readings on the thermal imaging issue are Kathleen A. Lomas, "Bad Physics and Bad Law: A Review of the Constitutionality of Thermal Imagery Surveillance after *United States v. Elkins*," *University of San Francisco Law Review* (vol. 34, p. 799, 2000); Jennifer Murphy, "Trash, Thermal Imagers, and the Fourth Amendment: The New Search and Seizure," *Southern Methodist University Law Review* (vol. 53, p. 1645, 2000); and Jeffrey P. Campisi, "The Fourth Amendment and New Technologies: The Constitutionality of Thermal Imaging," *Villanova Law Review* (vol. 46, p. 241, 2001).

Internet References . . .

The Brady Campaign to Prevent Gun Violence

News about gun control.

http://www.bradycampaign.org

Politics1.com

This site links to organizations—representing the Left, the Right, and the middle—that are working on many controversial legal issues.

http://www.politics1.com/issues.htm

Law.com

At Law.com you can read about recent cases as well as current legal issues in the news.

http://www.lawnewsnetwork.com

Law and the Community

*W*hile we are all citizens of a state, we are also participants in various communities whose members generally hold shared values and hope to satisfy shared goals. The challenge of finding appropriate relationships among the individual, the state, and the community is examined in this section.

- Is There a Constitutional Right to Possess a Firearm for Private Use?

- Are Blanket Prohibitions on Cross Burnings Unconstitutional?

- Should Same-Sex Couples Receive Constitutional Protection?

- Do Race-Conscious Programs in Public University Admissions Policies Violate the Fourteenth Amendment's Guarantee of Equal Protection Under the Law?

ISSUE 17

Is There a Constitutional Right to Possess a Firearm for Private Use?

YES: Antonin Scalia, from Majority Opinion, *District of Columbia, et al., v. Dick Anthony Heller,* U.S. Supreme Court (June 26, 2008)

NO: John Paul Stevens, from Dissenting Opinion, *District of Columbia, et al., v. Dick Anthony Heller,* U.S. Supreme Court (June 26, 2008)

ISSUE SUMMARY

YES: Supreme Court Justice Antonin Scalia argues that the Second Amendment protects the right of a private citizen to own a handgun for self-defense.

NO: Supreme Court Justice John Paul Stevens argues that a previous case, *United States v. Miller,* held that the Second Amendment did not protect the right of a private citizen to own a handgun for self-defense.

$\mathbf{T}$he Supreme Court routinely hears cases requiring it to interpret the vague language of the Bill of Rights and determine how to apply the often-abstract principles to concrete situations in modern American society. The Court frequently addresses the meaning of the First Amendment guarantee of freedom of speech, the Fifth Amendment right to due process, the Eighth Amendment prohibition on cruel and unusual punishment, and numerous other constitutional guarantees of individual rights and civil liberties. The Second Amendment, however, has historically been conspicuously absent from the Court's docket. The Court has addressed the Second Amendment so rarely that until 2008, more than two centuries after ratification of the Bill of Rights, the Court had never even made a definitive statement about what the right to "bear arms" encompassed—and what government action would violate that right.

As law professor Sanford Levinson once wryly noted, "No one has ever described the Constitution as a marvel of clarity, and the Second Amendment is perhaps one of the worst drafted of all its provisions."[1] The Second Amendment states, "A well regulated militia, being necessary to the security of a free

---

[1] Levinson, "The Embarrassing Second Amendment," 99 *Yale L. J.* 637 (1989).

state, the right of the people to keep and bear arms, shall not be infringed." One of the central questions in interpreting the amendment is how to understand the connection between its two clauses. Is the first clause intended to limit the right to bear arms to military situations or military-type weapons, or is it simply announcing a purpose and not otherwise circumscribing the right? (Those who endorse the latter view claim that the first clause is merely "prefatory.") Is the "right to keep and bear arms" one that even applies to individual persons, or does the language about the militia in the first clause turn it into a "collective" right that is relevant only to a group?

The amendment's confusing language has led to other interpretive debates. Are all "arms" protected under the amendment, or only certain types of weapons? Who is prohibited from infringing on the right to bear arms: Congress? the individual states? Does the right belong to everyone—including, say, dangerous criminals? Do gun-control laws that regulate but do not outlaw gun ownership, such as licensing requirements, constitute infringement?

The Supreme Court was forced to grapple with these issues in the 2008 case of *District of Columbia v. Heller.* Washington, D.C., had one of the strictest gun-control laws in the country, and Robert Levy, a Washington lawyer affiliated with the libertarian Cato Institute, decided to organize and bankroll a legal challenge to the constitutionality of the D.C. gun law. Levy found six D.C. residents who were willing to serve as plaintiffs in a lawsuit against the District; one of them was Dick Heller, a D.C. police officer who wanted to purchase a handgun to keep in his home for self-defense. Although an appeals court dismissed the other five plaintiffs from the lawsuit, it allowed Heller's case to go forward and sided with his argument that the D.C. law violated the Second Amendment. Faced with losing what its leaders saw as an important tool for fighting crime, the District appealed the decision to the Supreme Court, which agreed to hear the case.

In the readings that follow, Justices Stevens and Scalia provide two strikingly different interpretations of the Second Amendment. Both agree on the importance, in interpreting the text of the amendment, of looking at how it would have been understood at the time it was drafted and ratified. However, by relying on different historical sources and putting emphasis on different pieces of evidence, the two justices reach very divergent conclusions about the "original" meaning of the amendment. Furthermore, the justices disagree about how to interpret the Court's decision in a prior Second Amendment case, *United States v. Miller* (307 U.S. 174, 1939), and how much weight to assign that decision. While Justice Scalia, writing for the five-person majority, asserts that *Miller* supports his argument that the Second Amendment protects the right of a private citizen like Heller to own a handgun for self-defense, Justice Stevens claims that the majority is ignoring *Miller's* clear holding to the contrary, simply because it does not agree with the prior Court's decision.

YES ⤶

Majority Opinion, *District of Columbia, et al., v. Heller*

J USTICE SCALIA delivered the opinion of the Court.

We consider whether a District of Columbia prohibition on the possession of usable handguns in the home violates the Second Amendment to the Constitution.

I

. . .

II

We turn first to the meaning of the Second Amendment. . . .

The two sides in this case have set out very different interpretations of the Amendment. Petitioners and today's dissenting Justices believe that it protects only the right to possess and carry a firearm in connection with militia service. . . . Respondent argues that it protects an individual right to possess a firearm unconnected with service in a militia, and to use that arm for traditionally lawful purposes, such as self-defense within the home. . . .

Presser said nothing about the Second Amendment's meaning or scope, beyond the fact that it does not prevent the prohibition of private paramilitary organizations.

JUSTICE STEVENS places overwhelming reliance upon this Court's decision in *United States v. Miller*, 307 U.S. 174 (1939). "[H]undreds of judges," we are told, "have relied on the view of the amendment we endorsed there," *post*, at 2, and "[e]ven if the textual and historical arguments on both sides of the issue were evenly balanced, respect for the well-settled views of all of our predecessors on this Court, and for the rule of law itself . . . would prevent most jurists from endorsing such a dramatic upheaval in the law," *post*, at 4. And what is, according to JUSTICE STEVENS, the holding of *Miller* that demands such obeisance? That the Second Amendment "protects the right to keep and bear arms for certain military purposes, but that it does not curtail the legislature's power to regulate the nonmilitary use and ownership of weapons." *Post*, at 2.

From Supreme Court of the United States, June 26, 2008.

Nothing so clearly demonstrates the weakness of JUSTICE STEVENS' case. *Miller* did not hold that and cannot possibly be read to have held that. The judgment in the case upheld against a Second Amendment challenge two men's federal convictions for transporting an unregistered short-barreled shotgun in interstate commerce, in violation of the National Firearms Act, 48 Stat. 1236. It is entirely clear that the Court's basis for saying that the Second Amendment did not apply was *not* that the defendants were "bear[ing] arms" not "for . . . military purposes" but for "nonmilitary use," *post,* at 2. Rather, it was that the *type of weapon at issue* was not eligible for Second Amendment protection: "In the absence of any evidence tending to show that the possession or use of a [short-barreled shotgun] at this time has some reasonable relationship to the preservation or efficiency of a well regulated militia, we cannot say that the Second Amendment guarantees the right to keep and bear *such an instrument.*" 307 U.S., at 178 (emphasis added). "Certainly," the Court continued, "it is not within judicial notice that this weapon is any part of the ordinary military equipment or that its use could contribute to the common defense." *Ibid.* Beyond that, the opinion provided no explanation of the content of the right.

This holding is not only consistent with, but positively suggests, that the Second Amendment confers an individual right to keep and bear arms (though only arms that "have some reasonable relationship to the preservation or efficiency of a well regulated militia"). Had the Court believed that the Second Amendment protects only those serving in the militia, it would have been odd to examine the character of the weapon rather than simply note that the two crooks were not militiamen. JUSTICE STEVENS can say again and again that *Miller* did "not turn on the difference between muskets and sawed-off shotguns, it turned, rather, on the basic difference between the military and nonmilitary use and possession of guns," *post,* at 42–43, but the words of the opinion prove otherwise. The most JUSTICE STEVENS can plausibly claim for *Miller* is that it declined to decide the nature of the Second Amendment right, despite the Solicitor General's argument (made in the alternative) that the right was collective, see Brief for United States, O. T. 1938, No. 696, pp. 4–5. *Miller* stands only for the proposition that the Second Amendment right, whatever its nature, extends only to certain types of weapons.

It is particularly wrongheaded to read *Miller* for more than what it said, because the case did not even purport to be a thorough examination of the Second Amendment. JUSTICE STEVENS claims, *post,* at 42, that the opinion reached its conclusion "[a]fter reviewing many of the same sources that are discussed at greater length by the Court today." Not many, which was not entirely the Court's fault. The respondent made no appearance in the case, neither filing a brief nor appearing at oral argument; the Court heard from no one but the Government (reason enough, one would think, not to make that case the beginning and the end of this Court's consideration of the Second Amendment). See Frye, The Peculiar Story of *United States v. Miller,* 3 N. Y. U. J. L. & Liberty 48, 65–68 (2008). The Government's brief spent two pages discussing English legal sources, concluding "that at least the carrying of weapons without lawful occasion or excuse was always a crime" and that (because of the class-based restrictions and the prohibition on terrorizing people with dangerous or unusual weapons) "the early English law did not guarantee an unrestricted right to bear arms." Brief for United States, O. T. 1938, No. 696, at 9–11. It then went on to rely primarily on the discussion of the English right to bear arms in *Aymette v. State,* 21 Tenn. 154, for the proposition that the only uses of arms protected by the Second Amendment are those that relate to the militia, not self-defense. See Brief for United States, O. T. 1938, No. 696, at 12–18. The final section of the brief recognized that "some courts have said that the right to bear arms includes the right of the individual to have them for the protection of his person and property," and launched an alternative argument that "weapons which are commonly used by criminals," such as sawed-off shotguns, are not protected. See *id.,* at 18–21. The Government's *Miller* brief thus provided scant discussion of the history of the Second Amendment—and the Court was presented with no counterdiscussion. As for the text of the Court's opinion itself, that discusses *none* of the history of the Second Amendment. It assumes from the prologue that the Amendment was designed to preserve the militia, 307 U.S., at 178 (which we do not dispute), and then reviews some historical materials dealing with the nature of the militia, and in particular with the nature of the arms their members were expected to possess, *id.,* at 178–182. Not a word *(not a word)* about the history of the Second Amendment. This is the mighty rock upon which the dissent rests its case.[1]

We may as well consider at this point (for we will have to consider eventually) *what* types of weapons *Miller* permits. Read in isolation, *Miller's* phrase "part of ordinary military equipment" could mean that only those weapons useful in warfare are protected. That would be a startling reading of the opinion, since it would mean that the National Firearms Act's restrictions on machineguns (not challenged in *Miller*) might be unconstitutional, machineguns being useful in warfare in 1939. We think that *Miller's* "ordinary military equipment" language must be read in tandem with what comes after: "[O]rdinarily when called for [militia] service [able-bodied] men were expected to appear bearing arms supplied by themselves and of the kind in common use at the time." 307 U.S., at 179. The traditional militia was formed from a pool of men bringing arms "in common use at the time" for lawful purposes like self-defense. "In the colonial and revolutionary war era, [small-arms] weapons used by militiamen and weapons used in defense of person and home were one and the same." *State v. Kessler,* 289 Ore. 359, 368, 614 P. 2d 94, 98 (1980) (citing G. Neumann, Swords and Blades of the American Revolution 6–15, 252–254 (1973)). Indeed, that is precisely the way in which the Second Amendment's operative clause furthers the purpose announced in its preface. We therefore read *Miller* to say only that the Second Amendment does not protect those weapons not typically possessed by law-abiding citizens for lawful purposes, such as short-barreled shotguns. That accords with the historical understanding of the scope of the right, see Part III, *infra.*[2]

We conclude that nothing in our precedents forecloses our adoption of the original understanding of the Second Amendment. It should be unsurprising that such a significant matter has been for so long judicially unresolved. For most of our history, the Bill of Rights was not thought applicable to the States, and the Federal Government did not significantly regulate the possession of firearms by law-abiding citizens. Other provisions of the Bill of Rights have similarly remained unilluminated for lengthy periods. This Court first held a law to violate the First Amendment's guarantee of freedom of speech in 1931, almost 150 years after the Amendment was ratified, see *Near v. Minnesota ex rel. Olson,* 283 U.S. 697 (1931), and it was not until after World War II that we held a law invalid under the Establishment Clause, see *Illinois ex rel. McCollum v. Board of Ed. of School Dist. No. 71, Champaign Cty.,* 333 U.S. 203 (1948). Even a question as basic as the scope of proscribable libel was not addressed by this Court until 1964, nearly two centuries after the founding. See *New York Times Co. v. Sullivan,* 376 U.S. 254 (1964). It is demonstrably not true that, as JUSTICE STEVENS claims, *post,* at 41–42, "for most of our history, the invalidity of Second-Amendment-based objections to firearms regulations has been well settled and uncontroversial." For most of our history the question did not present itself.

III

Like most rights, the right secured by the Second Amendment is not unlimited. From Blackstone through the 19th-century cases, commentators and courts routinely explained that the right was not a right to keep and carry any weapon whatsoever in any manner whatsoever and for whatever purpose. See, *e.g., Sheldon,* in 5 Blume 346; Rawle 123; Pomeroy 152–153; Abbott 333. For example, the majority of the 19th-century courts to consider the question held that prohibitions on carrying concealed weapons were lawful under the Second Amendment or state analogues. See, *e.g., State v. Chandler,* 5 La. Ann., at 489–490; *Nunn v. State,* 1 Ga., at 251; see generally 2 Kent *340, n. 2; The American Students' Blackstone 84, n. 11 (G. Chase ed. 1884). Although we do not undertake an exhaustive historical analysis today of the full scope of the Second Amendment, nothing in our opinion should be taken to cast doubt on longstanding prohibitions on the possession of firearms by felons and the mentally ill, or laws forbidding the carrying of firearms in sensitive places such as schools and government buildings, or laws imposing conditions and qualifications on the commercial sale of arms.[3]

We also recognize another important limitation on the right to keep and carry arms. *Miller* said, as we have explained, that the sorts of weapons protected were those "in common use at the time." 307 U.S., at 179. We think that limitation is fairly supported by the historical tradition of prohibiting the carrying of "dangerous and unusual weapons." See 4 Blackstone 148–149 (1769); 3 B. Wilson, Works of the Honourable James Wilson 79 (1804); J. Dunlap, The New-York Justice 8 (1815); C. Humphreys, A Compendium of the Common Law in Force in Kentucky 482 (1822); 1 W. Russell, A Treatise on Crimes and Indictable Misdemeanors 271–272 (1831); H. Stephen, Summary of the Criminal Law 48 (1840); E. Lewis, An Abridgment of the Criminal Law of the United States 64 (1847); F. Wharton, A Treatise on the Criminal Law of the United States 726 (1852). See also *State v. Langford,* 10 N. C. 381, 383–384 (1824); *O'Neill v. State,* 16 Ala. 65, 67 (1849); *English v. State,* 35 Tex. 473, 476 (1871); *State v. Lanier,* 71 N. C. 288, 289 (1874).

It may be objected that if weapons that are most useful in military service—M-16 rifles and the like—may be banned, then the Second Amendment right is completely detached from the prefatory clause. But as we have said, the conception of the militia at the time of the Second Amendment's ratification was the body of all citizens capable of military service, who would bring the sorts of lawful weapons that they possessed at home to militia duty. It may well be true today that a militia, to be as effective as militias in the 18th century, would require sophisticated arms that are highly unusual in society at large. Indeed, it may be true that no amount of small arms could be useful against modern-day bombers and tanks. But the fact that modern developments have limited the degree of fit between the prefatory clause and the protected right cannot change our interpretation of the right.

IV

We turn finally to the law at issue here. As we have said, the law totally bans handgun possession in the home. It also requires that any lawful firearm in the home be disassembled or bound by a trigger lock at all times, rendering it inoperable.

As the quotations earlier in this opinion demonstrate, the inherent right of self-defense has been central to the Second Amendment right. The handgun ban amounts to a prohibition of an entire class of "arms" that is overwhelmingly chosen by American society for that lawful purpose. The prohibition extends, moreover, to the home, where the need for defense of self, family, and property is most acute. Under any of the standards of scrutiny that we have applied to enumerated constitutional rights,[4] banning from the home "the most preferred firearm in the nation to 'keep' and use for protection of one's home and family," 478 F. 3d, at 400, would fail constitutional muster.

Few laws in the history of our Nation have come close to the severe restriction of the District's handgun ban. And some of those few have been struck down. In *Nunn v. State*, the Georgia Supreme Court struck down a prohibition on carrying pistols openly (even though it upheld a prohibition on carrying concealed weapons). See 1 Ga., at 251. In *Andrews v. State*, the Tennessee Supreme Court likewise held that a statute that forbade openly carrying a pistol "publicly or privately, without regard to time or place, or circumstances," 50 Tenn., at 187, violated the state constitutional provision (which the court equated with the Second Amendment). That was so even though the statute did not restrict the carrying of long guns. *Ibid.* See also *State v. Reid*, 1 Ala. 612, 616–617 (1840) ("A statute which, under the pretence of regulating, amounts to a destruction of the right, or which requires arms to be so borne as to render them wholly useless for the purpose of defence, would be clearly unconstitutional").

It is no answer to say, as petitioners do, that it is permissible to ban the possession of handguns so long as the possession of other firearms (*i.e.*, long guns) is allowed. It is enough to note, as we have observed, that the American people have considered the handgun to be the quintessential self-defense weapon. There are many reasons that a citizen may prefer a handgun for home defense: It is easier to store in a location that is readily accessible in an emergency; it cannot easily be redirected or wrestled away by an attacker; it is easier to use for those without the upper-body strength to lift and aim a long gun; it can be pointed at a burglar with one hand while the other hand dials the police. Whatever the reason, handguns are the most popular weapon chosen by Americans for self-defense in the home, and a complete prohibition of their use is invalid.

We must also address the District's requirement (as applied to respondent's handgun) that firearms in the home be rendered and kept inoperable at all times. This makes it impossible for citizens to use them for the core lawful purpose of self-defense and is hence unconstitutional. The District argues that we should interpret this element of the statute to contain an exception for self-defense. See Brief for Petitioners 56–57. But we think that is precluded by the unequivocal text, and by the presence of certain other enumerated exceptions: "Except for law enforcement personnel . . . , each registrant shall keep any firearm in his possession unloaded and disassembled or bound by a trigger lock or similar device unless such firearm is kept at his place of business, or while being used for lawful recreational purposes within the District of Columbia." D. C. Code §7–2507.02. The nonexistence of a self-defense exception is also suggested by the D. C. Court of Appeals' statement that the statute forbids residents to use firearms to stop intruders, see *McIntosh v. Washington*, 395 A. 2d 744, 755–756 (1978).[5]

Apart from his challenge to the handgun ban and the trigger-lock requirement respondent asked the District Court to enjoin petitioners from enforcing the separate licensing requirement "in such a manner as to forbid the carrying of a firearm within one's home or possessed land without a license." App. 59a. The Court of Appeals did not invalidate the licensing requirement, but held only that the District "may not prevent [a handgun] from being moved throughout one's house." 478 F. 3d, at 400. It then ordered the District Court to enter summary judgment "consistent with [respondent's] prayer for relief." *Id.*, at 401. Before this Court petitioners have stated that "if the handgun ban is struck down and respondent registers a handgun, he could obtain a license, assuming he is not otherwise disqualified," by which they apparently mean if he is not a felon and is not insane. Brief for Petitioners 58. Respondent conceded at oral argument that he does not "have a problem with . . . licensing" and that the District's law is permissible so long as it is "not enforced in an arbitrary and capricious manner." Tr. of Oral Arg. 74–75. We therefore assume that petitioners' issuance of a license will satisfy respondent's prayer for relief and do not address the licensing requirement.

JUSTICE BREYER has devoted most of his separate dissent to the handgun ban. He says that, even assuming the Second Amendment is a personal guarantee of the right to bear arms, the District's prohibition is valid. He first tries to establish this by founding-era historical precedent, pointing to various restrictive laws in the colonial period. These demonstrate, in his view, that the District's law "imposes a burden upon gun owners that seems proportionately no greater than restrictions in existence at the time the Second Amendment was adopted." *Post*, at 2. Of the laws he cites, only one offers even marginal support for his assertion. A 1783 Massachusetts law forbade the residents of Boston to "take into" or "receive into" "any Dwelling House, Stable, Barn, Out-house, Ware-house, Store, Shop or other Building" loaded firearms, and permitted the seizure of any loaded firearms that "shall be found" there. Act of Mar. 1, 1783, ch. 13, 1783 Mass. Acts p. 218. That statute's text and its prologue, which makes clear that the purpose of the prohibition was to eliminate the danger to firefighters posed by the "depositing of loaded Arms" in buildings, give reason to doubt that colonial Boston authorities would have enforced that general prohibition against someone who temporarily loaded a firearm to confront an intruder (despite the law's application in that case). In any case, we would not stake our interpretation of the Second Amendment upon a single law, in effect in a single city, that contradicts the overwhelming weight of other evidence regarding the right to keep and bear arms for defense of the home. The other laws JUSTICE BREYER cites are gunpowder-storage laws that he concedes did not clearly prohibit loaded weapons, but required only that excess gunpowder be kept in a special container or on the top floor of the home. *Post,* at 6–7. Nothing about those fire-safety laws undermines our analysis; they do not remotely burden the right of self-defense as much as an absolute ban on handguns. Nor, correspondingly, does our analysis suggest the invalidity of laws regulating the storage of firearms to prevent accidents.

JUSTICE BREYER points to other founding-era laws that he says "restricted the firing of guns within the city limits to at least some degree" in Boston, Philadelphia and New York. *Post,* at 4 (citing Churchill, Gun Regulation, the Police Power, and the Right to Keep Arms in Early America, 25 Law & Hist. Rev. 139, 162 (2007)). Those laws provide no support for the severe restriction in the present case. The New York law levied a fine of 20 shillings on anyone who fired a gun in certain places (including houses) on New Year's Eve and the first two days of January, and was aimed at preventing the "great Damages . . . frequently done on [those days] by persons going House to House, with Guns and other Firearms and being often intoxicated with Liquor." 5 Colonial Laws of New York 244–246 (1894). It is inconceivable that this law would have been enforced against a person exercising his right to self-defense on New Year's Day against such drunken hooligans. The Pennsylvania law to which JUSTICE BREYER refers levied a fine of 5 shillings on one who fired a gun or set off fireworks in Philadelphia without first obtaining a license from the governor. See Act of Aug. 26, 1721, §4, in 3 Stat. at Large 253–254. Given Justice Wilson's explanation that the right to self-defense with arms was protected by the Pennsylvania Constitution, it is unlikely that this law (which in any event amounted to at most a licensing regime) would have been enforced against a person who used firearms for self-defense. JUSTICE BREYER cites a Rhode Island law that simply levied a 5-shilling fine on those who fired guns in *streets* and *taverns,* a law obviously inapplicable to this case. See An Act for preventing Mischief being done in the town of Newport, or in any other town in this Government, 1731, Rhode Island Session Laws. Finally, JUSTICE BREYER points to a Massachusetts law similar to the Pennsylvania law, prohibiting "discharg[ing] any Gun or Pistol charged with Shot or Ball in the Town of *Boston."* Act of May 28, 1746, ch. X, Acts and Laws of Mass. Bay 208. It is again implausible that this would have been enforced against a citizen acting in self-defense, particularly given its preambulatory reference to "the *indiscreet* firing of Guns." *Ibid,* (preamble) (emphasis added).

A broader point about the laws that JUSTICE BREYER cites: All of them punished the discharge (or loading) of guns with a small fine and forfeiture of the weapon (or in a few cases a very brief stay in the local jail), not with significant criminal penalties.[6] They are akin to modern penalties for minor public-safety infractions like speeding or jaywalking. And although such public-safety laws may not contain exceptions for self-defense, it is inconceivable that the threat of a jaywalking ticket would deter someone from disregarding a "Do Not Walk" sign in order to flee an attacker, or that the Government would enforce those laws under such circumstances. Likewise, we do not think that a law imposing a 5-shilling fine and forfeiture of the gun would have prevented a person in the founding era from using a gun to protect himself or his family from violence, or that if he did so the law would be enforced against him. The District law, by contrast, far from imposing a minor fine, threatens citizens with a year in prison (five years for a second violation) for even obtaining a gun in the first place. See D. C. Code §7-2507.06.

JUSTICE BREYER moves on to make a broad jurisprudential point: He criticizes us for declining to establish a level of scrutiny for evaluating Second Amendment restrictions. He proposes, explicitly at least, none of the traditionally expressed levels (strict scrutiny, intermediate scrutiny, rational basis), but rather a judge-empowering "interest-balancing inquiry" that "asks whether the statute burdens a protected interest in a way or to an extent that is out of proportion to the statute's salutary effects upon other important governmental interests." *Post,* at 10. After an exhaustive discussion of the arguments for and against gun control, JUSTICE BREYER arrives at his interest-balanced answer: because handgun violence is a problem, because the law is limited to an urban area, and because there were somewhat similar restrictions in the founding period (a false proposition that we have already discussed), the interest-balancing inquiry results in the constitutionality of the handgun ban. QED.

We know of no other enumerated constitutional right whose core protection has been subjected to a freestanding "interest-balancing" approach. The very enumeration of the right takes out of the hands of government— even the Third Branch of Government—the power to decide on a case-by-case basis whether the right is *really worth* insisting upon. A constitutional guarantee subject to future judges' assessments of its usefulness is no constitutional guarantee at all. Constitutional rights are enshrined with the scope they were understood to have when the people adopted them, whether or not future legislatures or (yes) even future judges think that scope too broad. We would not apply an "interest-balancing" approach to the prohibition of a peaceful neo-Nazi march through Skokie. See *National Socialist Party of America v. Skokie,* 432 U.S. 43 (1977) *(per curiam).* The First Amendment contains the freedom-of-speech guarantee that the people ratified, which included exceptions for obscenity, libel, and disclosure of state secrets, but not for the expression of extremely unpopular and wrong-headed views. The Second Amendment is no different. Like the First, it is the very *product* of an interest-balancing by the people—which JUSTICE BREYER would now conduct for them anew. And whatever else it leaves to future evaluation, it surely elevates above all other interests the right of law-abiding, responsible citizens to use arms in defense of hearth and home.

JUSTICE BREYER chides us for leaving so many applications of the right to keep and bear arms in doubt, and for not providing extensive historical justification for those regulations of the right that we describe as permissible. See *post,* at 42–43. But since this case represents this Court's first in-depth examination of the Second Amendment, one should not expect it to clarify the entire field, any more than *Reynolds v. United States,* 98 U.S. 145 (1879), our first in-depth Free Exercise Clause case, left that area in a state of utter certainty. And there will be time enough to expound upon the historical justifications for the exceptions we have mentioned if and when those exceptions come before us.

In sum, we hold that the District's ban on handgun possession in the home violates the Second Amendment, as does its prohibition against rendering any lawful firearm in the home operable for the purpose of immediate self-defense. Assuming that Heller is not disqualified from the exercise of Second Amendment rights, the District must permit him to register his handgun and must issue him a license to carry it in the home.

⚜

We are aware of the problem of handgun violence in this country, and we take seriously the concerns raised by the many *amici* who believe that prohibition of handgun ownership is a solution. The Constitution leaves the District of Columbia a variety of tools for combating that problem, including some measures regulating handguns, see *supra,* at 54–55, and n. 26. But the enshrinement of constitutional rights necessarily takes certain policy choices off the table. These include the absolute prohibition of handguns held and used for self-defense in the home. Undoubtedly some think that the Second Amendment is outmoded in a society where our standing army is the pride of our Nation, where well-trained police forces provide personal security, and where gun violence is a serious problem. That is perhaps debatable, but what is not debatable is that it is not the role of this Court to pronounce the Second Amendment extinct.

We affirm the judgment of the Court of Appeals.

It is so ordered.

Notes

[1.] As for the "hundreds of judges," *post,* at 2, who have relied on the view of the Second Amendment JUSTICE STEVENS claims we endorsed in *Miller:* If so, they overread *Miller.* And their erroneous reliance upon an uncontested and virtually unreasoned case cannot nullify the reliance of millions of Americans (as our historical analysis has shown) upon the true meaning of the right to keep and bear arms. In any event, it should not be thought that the cases decided by these judges would necessarily have come out differently under a proper interpretation of the right.

[2.] *Miller* was briefly mentioned in our decision in *Lewis v. United States,* 445 U.S. 55 (1980), an appeal from a conviction for being a felon in possession of a firearm. The challenge was based on the contention that the prior felony conviction had been unconstitutional. No Second Amendment claim was raised or briefed by any party. In the course of rejecting the asserted challenge, the Court commented gratuitously, in a footnote, that "[t]hese legislative restrictions on the use of firearms are neither based upon constitutionally suspect criteria, nor do they trench upon any constitutionally protected liberties. See *United States v. Miller* . . . (the Second Amendment guarantees no right to keep and bear a firearm that does not have 'some reasonable relationship to the preservation or efficiency of a well regulated militia')." *Id.,* at 65–66, n. 8. The footnote then cites several Court of Appeals cases to the same effect. It is inconceivable that we would rest our interpretation of the basic meaning of any guarantee of the Bill of Rights upon such a footnoted dictum in a case where the point was not at issue and was not argued.

[3.] We identify these presumptively lawful regulatory measures only as examples; our list does not purport to be exhaustive.

[4.] JUSTICE BREYEE correctly notes that this law, like almost all laws, would pass rational-basis scrutiny. *Post,* at 8. But rational-basis scrutiny is a mode of analysis we have used when evaluating laws under constitutional commands that are themselves prohibitions on irrational laws. See, *e.g., Engquist v. Oregon Dept. of Agriculture,* 553 U.S. ___, ___ (2008) (slip op., at 9–10). In those cases, "rational basis" is not just the standard of scrutiny, but the very substance of the constitutional guarantee. Obviously, the same test could not be used to evaluate the extent to which a legislature may regulate a specific, enumerated right, be it the freedom of speech, the guarantee against double jeopardy, the right to counsel, or the right to keep and bear arms. See *United States v. Carolene Products Co.,* 304 U.S. 144, 152, n. 4 (1938) ("There may be narrower scope for operation of the presumption of constitutionality [*i.e.,* narrower than that provided by rational-basis review] when legislation appears on its face to be within a specific prohibition of the Constitution, such as those of the first ten amendments. . ."). If all that was required to overcome the right to keep and bear arms was a rational basis, the Second Amendment would be redundant with the separate constitutional prohibitions on irrational laws, and would have no effect.

[5.] *McIntosh* upheld the law against a claim that it violated the Equal Protection Clause by arbitrarily distinguishing between residences and businesses. See 395 A. 2d, at 755. One of the rational bases listed for that distinction was the legislative finding "that for each intruder stopped by a firearm there are four gun-related accidents within the home." *Ibid.* That tradeoff would not bear mention if the statute did not prevent stopping intruders by firearms.

[6.] The Supreme Court of Pennsylvania described the amount of five shillings in a contract matter in 1792 as "nominal consideration." *Morris's Lessee v. Smith,* 4 Dall. 119, 120 (Pa. 1792). Many of the laws cited punished violation with fines in a similar amount; the 1783 Massachusetts gunpowder-storage law carried a somewhat larger fine of £10 (200 shillings) and forfeiture of the weapon.

Dissenting Opinion, *District of Columbia, et al., v. Heller*

J USTICE STEVENS, with whom JUSTICE SOUTER, JUSTICE GINSBURG, and JUSTICE BREYER join, dissenting.

The question presented by this case is not whether the Second Amendment protects a "collective right" or an "individual right." Surely it protects a right that can be enforced by individuals. But a conclusion that the Second Amendment protects an individual right does not tell us anything about the scope of that right.

Guns are used to hunt, for self-defense, to commit crimes, for sporting activities, and to perform military duties. The Second Amendment plainly does not protect the right to use a gun to rob a bank; it is equally clear that it *does* encompass the right to use weapons for certain military purposes. Whether it also protects the right to possess and use guns for nonmilitary purposes like hunting and personal self-defense is the question presented by this case. The text of the Amendment, its history, and our decision in *United States v. Miller*, 307 U.S. 174 (1939), provide a clear answer to that question.

The Second Amendment was adopted to protect the right of the people of each of the several States to maintain a well-regulated militia. It was a response to concerns raised during the ratification of the Constitution that the power of Congress to disarm the state militias and create a national standing army posed an intolerable threat to the sovereignty of the several States. Neither the text of the Amendment nor the arguments advanced by its proponents evidenced the slightest interest in limiting any legislature's authority to regulate private civilian uses of firearms. Specifically, there is no indication that the Framers of the Amendment intended to enshrine the common-law right of self-defense in the Constitution.

In 1934, Congress enacted the National Firearms Act, the first major federal firearms law. Upholding a conviction under that Act, this Court held that, "[i]n the absence of any evidence tending to show that possession or use of a 'shotgun having a barrel of less than eighteen inches in length' at this time has some reasonable relationship to the preservation or efficiency of a well regulated militia, we cannot say that the Second Amendment guarantees the right to keep and bear such an instrument." *Miller*, 307 U.S., at 178. The view of the Amendment we took in *Miller*—that it protects the right to keep and bear arms for certain military purposes, but that it does not curtail the Legislature's

From Supreme Court of the United States, June 26, 2008.

power to regulate the nonmilitary use and ownership of weapons—is both the most natural reading of the Amendment's text and the interpretation most faithful to the history of its adoption.

Since our decision in *Miller,* hundreds of judges have relied on the view of the Amendment we endorsed there;[1] we ourselves affirmed it in 1980. See *Lewis v. United States,* 445 U.S. 55, 65–66, n. 8 (1980).[2] No new evidence has surfaced since 1980 supporting the view that the Amendment was intended to curtail the power of Congress to regulate civilian use or misuse of weapons. Indeed, a review of the drafting history of the Amendment demonstrates that its Framers *rejected* proposals that would have broadened its coverage to include such uses.

The opinion the Court announces today fails to identify any new evidence supporting the view that the Amendment was intended to limit the power of Congress to regulate civilian uses of weapons. Unable to point to any such evidence, the Court stakes its holding on a strained and unpersuasive reading of the Amendment's text; significantly different provisions in the 1689 English Bill of Rights, and in various 19th-century State Constitutions; postenactment commentary that was available to the Court when it decided *Miller;* and, ultimately, a feeble attempt to distinguish *Miller* that places more emphasis on the Court's decisional process than on the reasoning in the opinion itself.

Even if the textual and historical arguments on both sides of the issue were evenly balanced, respect for the well-settled views of all of our predecessors on this Court, and for the rule of law itself, see *Mitchell v. W. T. Grant Co.,* 416 U.S. 600, 636 (1974) (Stewart, J., dissenting), would prevent most jurists from endorsing such a dramatic upheaval in the law.[3] As Justice Cardozo observed years ago, the "labor of judges would be increased almost to the breaking point if every past decision could be reopened in every case, and one could not lay one's own course of bricks on the secure foundation of the courses laid by others who had gone before him." The Nature of the Judicial Process 149 (1921).

In this dissent I shall first explain why our decision in *Miller* was faithful to the text of the Second Amendment and the purposes revealed in its drafting history. I shall then comment on the postratification history of the Amendment, which makes abundantly clear that the Amendment should not be interpreted as limiting the authority of Congress to regulate the use or possession of firearms for purely civilian purposes. . . .

II

The proper allocation of military power in the new Nation was an issue of central concern for the Framers. The compromises they ultimately reached, reflected in Article I's Militia Clauses and the Second Amendment, represent quintessential examples of the Framers' "splitting the atom of sovereignty."[4]

Two themes relevant to our current interpretive task ran through the debates on the original Constitution. "On the one hand, there was a widespread fear that a national standing Army posed an intolerable threat to individual liberty and to the sovereignty of the separate States." *Perpich v. Department of Defense,* 496 U.S. 334, 340 (1990).[5] Governor Edmund Randolph, reporting on the Constitutional Convention to the Virginia Ratification Convention, explained: "With respect to a standing army, I believe there was not a member in the federal Convention, who did not feel indignation at such an institution." 3 J. Elliot, Debates in the Several State Conventions on the Adoption of the Federal Constitution 401 (2d ed. 1863) (hereinafter Elliot). On the other hand, the Framers recognized the dangers inherent in relying on inadequately trained militia members "as the primary means of providing for the common defense," *Perpich,* 496 U.S., at 340; during the Revolutionary War, "[t]his force, though armed, was largely untrained, and its deficiencies were the subject of bitter complaint." Wiener, The Militia Clause of the Constitution, 54 Harv. L. Rev. 181, 182 (1940).[6] In order to respond to those twin concerns, a compromise was reached: Congress would be authorized to raise and support a national Army and Navy, and also to organize, arm, discipline, and provide for the calling forth of "the Militia." U.S. Const., Art. I, §8, cls. 12–16. The President, at the same time, was empowered as the "Commander in Chief of the Army and Navy of the United States, and of the Militia of the several States, when called into the actual Service of the United States." Art. II, §2. But, with respect to the militia, a significant reservation was made to the States: Although Congress would have the power to call forth, organize, arm, and discipline the militia, as well as to govern "such Part of them as may be employed in the Service of the United States," the States respectively would retain the right to appoint the officers and to train the militia in accordance with the discipline prescribed by Congress. Art. I, §8, cl. 16.

But the original Constitution's retention of the militia and its creation of divided authority over that body did not prove sufficient to allay fears about the dangers posed by a standing army. For it was perceived by some that Article I contained a significant gap: While it empowered Congress to organize, arm, and discipline the militia, it did not prevent Congress from providing for the militia's disarmament. As George Mason argued during the debates in Virginia on the ratification of the original Constitution:

> "The militia may be here destroyed by that method which has been practiced in other parts of the world before; that is, by rendering them useless—by disarming them. Under various pretences, Congress may neglect to provide for arming and disciplining the militia; and the state governments cannot do it, for Congress has the exclusive right to arm them." . . .

This sentiment was echoed at a number of state ratification conventions; indeed, it was one of the primary objections to the original Constitution voiced by its opponents. The Anti-Federalists were ultimately unsuccessful in persuading state ratification conventions to condition their approval of the Constitution upon the eventual inclusion of any particular amendment. But a number of States did propose to the first Federal Congress amendments reflecting a desire to ensure that the institution of the militia would remain protected under the new Government. The proposed amendments sent by the States of Virginia, North Carolina, and New York focused on the importance of preserving the state militias and reiterated the dangers posed by standing armies. New Hampshire sent a proposal that differed significantly from the others; while also invoking the dangers of a standing army, it suggested that the Constitution should more broadly protect the use and possession of weapons, without tying such a guarantee expressly to the maintenance of the militia. The States of Maryland, Pennsylvania, and Massachusetts sent no relevant proposed amendments to Congress, but in each of those States a minority of the delegates advocated related amendments. While the Maryland minority proposals were exclusively concerned with standing armies and conscientious objectors, the unsuccessful proposals in both Massachusetts and Pennsylvania would have protected a more broadly worded right, less clearly tied to service in a state militia. Faced with all of these options, it is telling that James Madison chose to craft the Second Amendment as he did.

The relevant proposals sent by the Virginia Ratifying Convention read as follows:

> "17th, That the people have a right to keep and bear arms; that a well regulated Militia composed of the body of the people trained to arms is the proper, natural and safe defence of a free State. That standing armies are dangerous to liberty, and therefore ought to be avoided, as far as the circumstances and protection of the Community will admit; and that in all cases the military should be under strict subordination to and be governed by the civil power." Elliot 659.
>
> "19th. That any person religiously scrupulous of bearing arms ought to be exempted, upon payment of an equivalent to employ another to bear arms in his stead." *Ibid.*

North Carolina adopted Virginia's proposals and sent them to Congress as its own, although it did not actually ratify the original Constitution until Congress had sent the proposed Bill of Rights to the States for ratification. . . .

New York produced a proposal with nearly identical language. It read:

> "That the people have a right to keep and bear Arms; that a well regulated Militia, including the body of the People capable of bearing Arms, is the proper, natural, and safe defence of a free State. . . . That standing Armies, in time of Peace, are dangerous to Liberty, and ought not to be kept up, except in Cases of necessity; and that at all times, the Military should be kept under strict Subordination to the civil Power." 2 Schwartz 912.

Notably, each of these proposals used the phrase "keep and bear arms," which was eventually adopted by Madison. And each proposal embedded the phrase within a group of principles that are distinctly military in meaning. . . .

Madison, charged with the task of assembling the proposals for amendments sent by the ratifying States, was the principal draftsman of the Second Amendment. He had before him, or at the very least would have been aware of, all of these proposed formulations. In addition, Madison had been a member, some years earlier, of the committee tasked with drafting the Virginia Declaration of Rights. That committee considered a proposal by Thomas Jefferson that would have included within the Virginia Declaration the following language: "No freeman shall ever be debarred the use of arms [within his own lands or tenements]." 1 Papers of Thomas Jefferson 363 (J. Boyd ed. 1950). But the committee rejected that language, adopting instead the provision drafted by George Mason.[7]

With all of these sources upon which to draw, it is strikingly significant that Madison's first draft omitted any mention of nonmilitary use or possession of weapons. Rather, his original draft repeated the essence of the two proposed amendments sent by Virginia, combining the substance of the two provisions succinctly into one, which read: "The right of the people to keep and bear arms shall not be infringed; a well armed, and well regulated militia being the best security of a free country; but no person religiously scrupulous of bearing arms, shall be compelled to render military service in person." . . .

Madison's decision to model the Second Amendment on the distinctly military Virginia proposal is therefore revealing, since it is clear that he considered and rejected formulations that would have unambiguously protected civilian uses of firearms. When Madison prepared his first draft, and when that draft was debated and modified, it is reasonable to assume that all participants in the drafting process were fully aware of the other formulations that would have protected civilian use and possession of weapons and that their choice to craft the Amendment as they did represented a rejection of those alternative formulations. . . .

The history of the adoption of the Amendment thus describes an overriding concern about the potential threat to state sovereignty that a federal standing army would pose, and a desire to protect the States' militias as the means by which to guard against that danger. But state militias could not effectively check the prospect of a federal standing army so long as Congress retained the power to disarm them, and so a guarantee against such disarmament was needed. As we explained in *Miller:* "With obvious purpose to assure the continuation and render possible the effectiveness of such forces the declaration and guarantee of the Second Amendment were made. It must be interpreted and applied with that end in view." 307 U.S., at 178. The evidence plainly refutes the claim that the Amendment was motivated by the Framers' fears that Congress might act to regulate any civilian uses of weapons. And even if the historical record were genuinely ambiguous, the burden would remain on the parties advocating a change in the law to introduce facts or arguments "'newly ascertained,'" *Vasquez,* 474 U.S., at 266; the Court is unable to identify any such facts or arguments. . . .

[F]or most of our history, the invalidity of Second-Amendment-based objections to firearms regulations has been well settled and uncontroversial. Indeed, the Second Amendment was not even mentioned in either full House of Congress during the legislative proceedings that led to the passage of the 1934 Act. Yet enforcement of that law produced the judicial decision that confirmed the status of the Amendment as limited in reach to military usage.

After reviewing many of the same sources that are discussed at greater length by the Court today, the *Miller* Court unanimously concluded that the Second Amendment did not apply to the possession of a firearm that did not have "some reasonable relationship to the preservation or efficiency of a well regulated militia." 307 U.S., at 178.

The key to that decision did not, as the Court belatedly suggests, . . . turn on the difference between muskets and sawed-off shotguns; it turned, rather, on the basic difference between the military and nonmilitary use and possession of guns. Indeed, if the Second Amendment were not limited in its coverage to military uses of weapons, why should the Court in *Miller* have suggested that some weapons but not others were eligible for Second Amendment protection? If use for self-defense were the relevant standard, why did the Court not inquire into the suitability of a particular weapon for self-defense purposes? . . .

The Court is simply wrong when it intones that *Miller* contained *"not a word"* about the Amendment's history. . . . The Court plainly looked to history to construe the term "Militia," and, on the best reading of *Miller,* the entire guarantee of the Second Amendment. After noting the original Constitution's grant of power to Congress and to the States over the militia, the Court explained:

> "With obvious purpose to assure the continuation and render possible the effectiveness of such forces the declaration and guarantee of the Second Amendment were made. It must be interpreted and applied with that end in view.
>
> "The Militia which the States were expected to maintain and train is set in contrast with Troops which they were forbidden to keep without the consent of Congress. The sentiment of the time strongly disfavored standing armies; the common view was that adequate defense of country and laws could be secured through the Militia—civilians primarily, soldiers on occasion.
>
> "The signification attributed to the term Militia appears from the debates in the Convention, the history and legislation of Colonies and States, and the writings of approved commentators." *Miller,* 307 U.S., at 178–179.

The majority cannot seriously believe that the *Miller* Court did not consider any relevant evidence; the majority simply does not approve of the conclusion the *Miller* Court reached on that evidence. Standing alone, that is insufficient reason to disregard a unanimous opinion of this Court, upon which substantial reliance has been placed by legislators and citizens for nearly 70 years.

V

The Court concludes its opinion by declaring that it is not the proper role of this Court to change the meaning of rights "enshrine[d]" in the Constitution. *Ante,* at 64. But the right the Court announces was not "enshrined" in the Second Amendment by the Framers; it is the product of today's law-changing decision. The majority's exegesis has utterly failed to establish that as a matter of text or history, "the right of law-abiding, responsible citizens to use arms in defense of hearth and home" is "elevate[d] above all other interests" by the Second Amendment. . . .

Until today, it has been understood that legislatures may regulate the civilian use and misuse of firearms so long as they do not interfere with the preservation of a well-regulated militia. The Court's announcement of a new constitutional right to own and use firearms for private purposes upsets that settled understanding, but leaves for future cases the formidable task of defining the scope of permissible regulations. Today judicial craftsmen have confidently asserted that a policy choice that denies a "law-abiding, responsible citize[n]" the right to keep and use weapons in the home for self-defense is "off the table." . . . Given the presumption that most citizens are law abiding, and the reality that the need to defend oneself may suddenly arise in a host of locations outside the home, I fear that the District's policy choice may well be just the first of an unknown number of dominoes to be knocked off the table.

I do not know whether today's decision will increase the labor of federal judges to the "breaking point" envisioned by Justice Cardozo, but it will surely give rise to a far more active judicial role in making vitally important national policy decisions than was envisioned at any time in the 18th, 19th, or 20th centuries.

The Court properly disclaims any interest in evaluating the wisdom of the specific policy choice challenged in this case, but it fails to pay heed to a far more important policy choice—the choice made by the Framers themselves. The Court would have us believe that over 200 years ago, the Framers made a choice to limit the tools available to elected officials wishing to regulate civilian uses of weapons, and to authorize this Court to use the common-law process of case-by-case judicial lawmaking to define the contours of acceptable gun control policy. Absent compelling evidence that is nowhere to be found in the Court's opinion, I could not possibly conclude that the Framers made such a choice.

For these reasons, I respectfully dissent.

Notes

[1.] Until the Fifth Circuit's decision in *United States v. Emerson*, 270 F. 3d 203 (2001), every Court of Appeals to consider the question had understood *Miller* to hold that the Second Amendment does not protect the right to possess and use guns for purely private, civilian purposes. See, *e.g.*, *United States v. Haney*, 264 F. 3d 1161, 1164–1166 (CA10 2001); *United States v. Napier*, 233 F. 3d 394, 402–404 (CA6 2000); *Gillespie v. Indianapolis*, 185 F. 3d 693, 710–711 (CA7 1999); *United States v. Scanio*, No. 97-1584, 1998 WL 802060, *2 (CA2, Nov. 12, 1998) (unpublished opinion); *United States v. Wright*, 117 F. 3d 1265, 1271–1274 (CA11 1997); *United States v. Rybar*, 103 F. 3d 273, 285–286 (CA3 1996); *Hickman v. Block*, 81 F. 3d 98, 100–103 (CA9 1996); *United States v. Hale*, 978 F. 2d 1016, 1018–1020 (CA8 1992); *Thomas v. City Council of Portland*, 730 F. 2d 41, 42 (CA1 1984) *(per curiam); United States v. Johnson*, 497 F. 2d 548, 550 (CA4 1974) *(per curiam); United States v.*

Johnson, 441 F. 2d 1134, 1136 (CA5 1971); see also *Sandidge v. United States,* 520 A. 2d 1057, 1058–1059 (DC App. 1987). And a number of courts have remained firm in their prior positions, even after considering *Emerson.* See, *e.g., United States v. Lippman,* 369 F. 3d 1039, 1043–1045 (CA8 2004); *United States v. Parker,* 362 F. 3d 1279, 1282–1284 (CA10 2004); *United States v. Jackubowski,* 63 Fed. Appx. 959, 961 (CA7 2003) (unpublished opinion); *Silveira v. Lockyer,* 312 F. 3d 1052, 1060–1066 (CA9 2002);. *United States v. Milheron,* 231 F. Supp. 2d 376, 378 (Me. 2002); *Bach v. Pataki,* 289 F. Supp. 2d 217, 224–226 (NDNY 2003); *United States v. Smith,* 56 M. J. 711, 716 (C. A. Armed Forces 2001).

[2.] Our discussion in *Lewis* was brief but significant. Upholding a conviction for receipt of a firearm by a felon, we wrote: "These legislative restrictions on the use of firearms are neither based upon constitutionally suspect criteria, nor do they entrench upon any constitutionally protected liberties. See *United States v. Miller,* 307 U.S. 174, 178 (1939) (the Second Amendment guarantees no right to keep and bear a firearm that does not have 'some reasonable relationship to the preservation or efficiency of a well regulated militia')." 445 U.S., at 65, n. 8.

[3.] See *Vasquez v. Hillery,* 474 U.S. 254, 265, 266 (1986) ("*[Stare decisis]* permits society to presume that bedrock principles are founded in the law rather than in the proclivities of individuals, and thereby contributes to the integrity of our constitutional system of government, both in appearance and in fact. While *stare decisis* is not an inexorable command, the careful observer will discern that any detours from the straight path of *stare decisis* in our past have occurred for articulable reasons, and only when the Court has felt obliged 'to bring its opinions into agreement with experience and with facts newly ascertained.' *Burnet v. Coronado Oil & Gas Co.,* 285 U.S. 393, 412 (1932) (Brandeis, J., dissenting)"); *Pollock v. Farmers' Loan & Trust Co.,* 157 U.S. 429, 652 (1895) (White, J., dissenting) ("The fundamental conception of a judicial body is that of one hedged about by precedents which are binding on the court without regard to the personality of its members. Break down this belief in judicial continuity and let it be felt that on great constitutional questions this Court is to depart from the settled conclusions of its predecessors, and to determine them all according to the mere opinion of those who temporarily fill its bench, and our Constitution will, in my judgment, be bereft of value and become a most dangerous instrument to the rights and liberties of the people").

[4.] By "'splitt[ing] the atom of sovereignty,'" the Framers created "'two political capacities, one state and one federal, each protected from incursion by the other. The resulting Constitution created a legal system unprecedented in form and design, establishing two orders of government, each with its own direct relationship, its own privity, its own set of mutual rights and obligations to the people who sustain it and are governed by it.'" *Saenz v. Roe,* 526 U.S. 489, 504, n. 17 (1999) (quoting *U.S. Term Limits, Inc. v. Thornton,* 514 U.S. 779, 838 (1995) (KENNEDY, J., concurring)).

[5.] Indeed, this was one of the grievances voiced by the colonists: Paragraph 13 of the Declaration of Independence charged of King George, "He has kept among us, in times of peace, Standing Armies without the Consent of our legislatures."

[6.] George Washington, writing to Congress on September 24, 1776, warned that for Congress "[t]o place any dependance upon Militia, is, assuredly, resting upon a broken staff." 6 Writings of George Washington 106, 110 (J. Fitzpatrick ed. 1932). Several years later he reiterated this view in another letter to Congress: "Regular Troops alone are equal to the exigencies of modern war, as well for defence as offence. . . . *No Militia* will ever acquire the habits necessary to resist a regular force. . . . The firmness requisite for the real business of fighting is only to be attained by a constant course of discipline and service." 20 *id.,* at 49, 49–50 (Sept. 15, 1780). And Alexander Hamilton argued this view in many debates. In 1787, he wrote:

> "Here I expect we shall be told that the militia of the country is its natural bulwark, and would be at all times equal to the national defense. This doctrine, in substance, had like to have lost us our independence. . . . War, like most other things, is a science to be acquired and perfected by diligence, by perseverance, by time, and by practice." The Federalist No. 25, p. 166 (C. Rossiter ed. 1961).

[7.] The adopted language, Virginia Declaration of Rights ¶13 (1776), read as follows: "That a well-regulated Militia, composed of the body of the people, trained to arms, is the proper, natural, and safe defence of a free State; that Standing Armies, in time of peace, should be avoided as dangerous to liberty; and that, in all cases, the military should be under strict subordination to, and governed by, the civil power." 1 Schwartz 234.

POSTSCRIPT

Is There a Constitutional Right to Possess a Firearm for Private Use?

Justice Scalia has long been an advocate of "originalism," the idea that the Constitution is properly interpreted by looking at how its provisions were "originally" understood when it was drafted and ratified. He relies on this methodology in his *Heller* opinion to determine the meaning of the Second Amendment. While Justice Stevens has never been a committed originalist, he attempts to rebut much of Justice Scalia's argument using originalist arguments. For Justice Stevens, the primary problem with Justice Scalia's opinion is not that the interpretive method is wrong, but that Justice Scalia relies on the wrong historical evidence in trying to use that method to understand the Second Amendment.

One could, however, also object to Justice Scalia's argument on methodological grounds: instead of arguing about who is correct with historical details, one could claim that the historical details are not the most important determinant of how the Constitution should be interpreted. In a separate dissent, Justice Stephen Breyer makes just such a claim. As he sees it,

> The majority's conclusion is wrong for two independent reasons. The first reason is that set forth by Justice Stevens—namely, that the Second Amendment protects militia-related, not self-defense-related, interests. . . . The second independent reason is that the protection the Amendment provides is not absolute. The Amendment permits government to regulate the interests that it serves. Thus, irrespective of what those interests are—whether they do or do not include an independent interest in self-defense—the majority's view cannot be correct unless it can show that the District's regulation is unreasonable or inappropriate in Second Amendment terms. This the majority cannot do.

In Justice Breyer's view, the Court should not be relying solely on originalism to determine the scope of the Second Amendment. Instead, the Court should be considering the governmental interests at stake, taking into account that violent crime in urban areas like Washington, D.C., is a significant problem today but was not when the Second Amendment was drafted. For Breyer, history may be illuminating, but the meaning of the Constitution is not fixed at the time it was written; rather, the text sets out broad principles that can be interpreted in various ways, and it is the job of the courts to determine how those principles can be best applied to the specific circumstances of modern-day America.

Three leading constitutional scholars—Akhil Amar, Reva Siegel, and Cass Sunstein—provide their analyses of the *Heller* opinions in the November 2008 issue of the *Harvard Law Review* (Vol. 122, No. 1). The practical implications of *Heller* for gun control laws across the country are discussed by law professor Sanford Levinson in "For Whom is the Heller Decision Important and Why?" 13 *Lewis & Clark L. Rev.* 315 (2009). For more on the history of the Second Amendment and the right to bear arms in Anglo-American law, see Saul Cornell, *A Well-Regulated Militia: The Founding Fathers and the Origins of Gun Control in America* (Oxford University Press, 2008); and Joyce Lee Malcolm, *To Keep and Bear Arms: The Origins of an Anglo-American Right* (Harvard University Press, 1996).

ISSUE 18

Are Blanket Prohibitions on Cross Burnings Unconstitutional?

YES: Sandra Day O'Connor, from Majority Opinion, *Virginia v. Black, et al.,* U.S. Supreme Court (April 7, 2003)

NO: Clarence Thomas, from Dissenting Opinion, *Virginia v. Black, et al.,* U.S. Supreme Court (April 7, 2003)

ISSUE SUMMARY

YES: Supreme Court Justice Sandra Day O'Connor argues that a Virginia statute proscribing all forms of cross burning is unconstitutional because symbolic speech can only be prohibited when done with the intent to intimidate, and such an intent cannot be inferred solely from the type of symbolic speech used.

NO: Supreme Court Justice Clarence Thomas argues that the history and nature of cross burning in the United States inextricably links the act to threatening and menacing violence and that the intent to intimidate can therefore be inferred solely from the act of cross burning itself.

We do not live in tranquil, quiet, and harmonious times. Terrorism, as a domestic threat, is a fairly new challenge for the United States. Hate crimes, however, have occurred throughout the nation's history. The Community Relations Service of the U.S. Department of Justice has defined hate crime as "the violence of intolerance and bigotry, intended to hurt and intimidate someone because of their race, ethnicity, national origin, religion, sexual orientation, or disability."

Since 1991 the Hate Crimes Statistics Act has required the FBI to keep statistics on hate crimes (http://www2.fbi.gov/ucr/hc2009/index.html). In general, these crimes are not separate, distinct crimes but traditional offenses, such as assault, that are motivated by the offender's bias. The following readings, which are from a case involving cross burning, focus on a criminal statute that explicitly targets bias activities.

In the United States, among the few categories of speech that can be constitutionally prohibited are "fighting words," defined by the Supreme Court as statements "which by their very utterance inflict injury or tend to incite an immediate breach of the peace" (see *Chaplinsky v. New Hampshire*, 315 U.S. 568, 1942). The "fighting words" exception applies not only to actual speech but also to "symbolic" speech, actions that are not speech per se but convey certain messages and thus, the Supreme Court has held, deserve the same First Amendment protection as audible words. Because of the importance of free speech to political discourse and debate, the "fighting words" prohibition has been narrowly construed throughout its history: The government can only prohibit speech that constitutes an immediate threat, and even calls for violence may be permissible if they are rhetorical in nature and will probably not incite any actual violence.

In *R. A. V. v. City of St. Paul*, 505 U.S. 377 (1992), the Supreme Court applied the "fighting words" doctrine to one particularly controversial form of symbolic speech: cross burning. St. Paul, Minnesota, had passed a city ordinance that outlawed "plac[ing] on public or private property a symbol . . . including, but not limited to, a burning cross or Nazi swastika, which one knows or has reasonable grounds to know arouses anger, alarm or resentment in others on the basis of race, color, creed, religion or gender." The Supreme Court struck down the ordinance, ruling that to be constitutionally permissible, speech codes regulating "fighting words" must address only the *outcome* of the speech: whether it is foreseeable that the speech will make others feel threatened or encourage physical violence. Writing for the majority, Justice Antonin Scalia noted that "[t]he First Amendment generally prevents government from proscribing speech . . . or even expressive conduct [i.e., symbolic speech] . . . because of disapproval of the ideas expressed. Content-based regulations are presumptively invalid." According to the majority, the problem with the St. Paul ordinance was that it focused only on speech that "insult[s] or provoke[s] violence, 'on the basis of race, color, creed, religion, or gender.'" To fulfill the demands of content neutrality, however, the ordinance would have to outlaw *all* speech that provoked violence; the ordinance could not specify that some subject matter, such as race or gender, was prohibited, while ignoring, in the words of the Court, "those who wish to use 'fighting words' in connection with other ideas—to express hostility, for example, on the basis of political affiliation, union membership, or homosexuality."

In the case that follows, the Supreme Court once again addresses constitutionality of laws intended to outlaw cross burnings. Under the *R. A. V.* precedent, legislatures are allowed to outlaw symbolic speech, such as cross burnings, as long as such prohibitions are content-neutral and apply only to speech that constitutes "fighting words" (or one of the other limited categories of speech that fall outside constitutional protection). In *Virginia v. Black*, the Court addresses the question of whether the intent to intimidate—a prerequisite for establishing "fighting words" status—can be inferred from the nature of the act itself. In so doing, the Court tackles not only the philosophical nature of symbolic actions but also the social history of such acts as cross burning that help define what they stand for in the specific context of twenty-first-century America.

YES ↩   Sandra Day O'Connor

Plurality Opinion, *Virginia v. Black*

In this case we consider whether the Commonwealth of Virginia's statute banning cross burning with "an intent to intimidate a person or group of persons" violates the First Amendment. We conclude that while a State, consistent with the First Amendment, may ban cross burning carried out with the intent to intimidate, the provision in the Virginia statute treating any cross burning as prima facie evidence of intent to intimidate renders the statute unconstitutional in its current form.

I

Respondents Barry Black, Richard Elliott, and Jonathan O'Mara were convicted separately of violating Virginia's cross-burning statute, §18.2–423. That statute provides:

> "It shall be unlawful for any person or persons, with the intent of intimidating any person or group of persons, to burn, or cause to be burned, a cross on the property of another, a highway or other public place. Any person who shall violate any provision of this section shall be guilty of a Class 6 felony.
>
> "Any such burning of a cross shall be prima facie evidence of an intent to intimidate a person or group of persons."

On August 22, 1998, Barry Black led a Ku Klux Klan rally in Carroll County, Virginia. Twenty-five to thirty people attended this gathering, which occurred on private property with the permission of the owner, who was in attendance. The property was located on an open field just off Brushy Fork Road (State Highway 690) in Cana, Virginia.

When the sheriff of Carroll County learned that a Klan rally was occurring in his county, he went to observe it from the side of the road. During the approximately one hour that the sheriff was present, about 40 to 50 cars passed the site, a "few" of which stopped to ask the sheriff what was happening on the property. Eight to ten houses were located in the vicinity of the rally. Rebecca Sechrist, who was related to the owner of the property where the rally took place, "sat and watched to see wha[t] [was] going on" from the lawn of her in-laws' house. She looked on as the Klan prepared for the gathering and subsequently conducted the rally itself.

During the rally, Sechrist heard Klan members speak about "what they were" and "what they believed in." The speakers "talked real bad about the

From Supreme Court of the United States, April 7, 2003.

blacks and the Mexicans." One speaker told the assembled gathering that "he would love to take a .30/.30 and just random[ly] shoot the blacks." The speakers also talked about "President Clinton and Hillary Clinton," and about how their tax money "goes to . . . the black people." Sechrist testified that this language made her "very . . . scared."

At the conclusion of the rally, the crowd circled around a 25- to 30-foot cross. The cross was between 300 and 350 yards away from the road. According to the sheriff, the cross "then all of a sudden . . . went up in a flame." As the cross burned, the Klan played Amazing Grace over the loudspeakers. Sechrist stated that the cross burning made her feel "awful" and "terrible."

When the sheriff observed the cross burning, he informed his deputy that they needed to "find out who's responsible and explain to them that they cannot do this in the State of Virginia." The sheriff then went down the driveway, entered the rally, and asked "who was responsible for burning the cross." Black responded, "I guess I am because I'm the head of the rally." The sheriff then told Black, "[T]here's a law in the State of Virginia that you cannot burn a cross and I'll have to place you under arrest for this."

Black was charged with burning a cross with the intent of intimidating a person or group of persons, in violation of §18.2-423. At his trial, the jury was instructed that "intent to intimidate means the motivation to intentionally put a person or a group of persons in fear of bodily harm. Such fear must arise from the willful conduct of the accused rather than from some mere temperamental timidity of the victim." The trial court also instructed the jury that "the burning of a cross by itself is sufficient evidence from which you may infer the required intent." When Black objected to this last instruction on First Amendment grounds, the prosecutor responded that the instruction was "taken straight out of the [Virginia] Model Instructions." The jury found Black guilty, and fined him $2,500. The Court of Appeals of Virginia affirmed Black's conviction.

On May 2, 1998, respondents Richard Elliott and Jonathan O'Mara, as well as a third individual, attempted to burn a cross on the yard of James Jubilee. Jubilee, an African-American, was Elliott's next-door neighbor in Virginia Beach, Virginia. Four months prior to the incident, Jubilee and his family had moved from California to Virginia Beach. Before the cross burning, Jubilee spoke to Elliott's mother to inquire about shots being fired from behind the Elliott home. Elliott's mother explained to Jubilee that her son shot firearms as a hobby, and that he used the backyard as a firing range.

On the night of May 2, respondents drove a truck onto Jubilee's property, planted a cross, and set it on fire. Their apparent motive was to "get back" at Jubilee for complaining about the shooting in the backyard. Respondents were not affiliated with the Klan. The next morning, as Jubilee was pulling his car out of the driveway, he noticed the partially burned cross approximately 20 feet from his house. After seeing the cross, Jubilee was "very nervous" because he "didn't know what would be the next phase," and because "a cross burned in your yard . . . tells you that it's just the first round."

Elliott and O'Mara were charged with attempted cross burning and conspiracy to commit cross burning. O'Mara pleaded guilty to both counts, reserving the right to challenge the constitutionality of the cross-burning statute. The judge sentenced O'Mara to 90 days in jail and fined him $2,500. The judge also suspended 45 days of the sentence and $1,000 of the fine.

At Elliott's trial, the judge originally ruled that the jury would be instructed "that the burning of a cross by itself is sufficient evidence from which you may infer the required intent." At trial, however, the court instructed the jury that the Commonwealth must prove that "the defendant intended to commit cross burning," that "the defendant did a direct act toward the commission of the cross burning," and that "the defendant had the intent of intimidating any person or group of persons." The court did not instruct the jury on the meaning of the word "intimidate," nor on the prima facie evidence provision of §18.2-423. The jury found Elliott guilty of attempted cross burning and acquitted him of conspiracy to commit cross burning. It sentenced Elliott to 90 days in jail and a $2,500 fine. The Court of Appeals of Virginia affirmed the convictions of both Elliott and O'Mara.

Each respondent appealed to the Supreme Court of Virginia, arguing that §18.2-423 is facially unconstitutional. The Supreme Court of Virginia consolidated all three cases, and held that the statute is unconstitutional on its face. It held that the Virginia cross-burning statute "is analytically indistinguishable from the ordinance found unconstitutional in *R. A. V.* [*v. St. Paul*]. The Virginia statute, the court held, discriminates on the basis of content since it "selectively chooses only cross burning because of its distinctive message." The court also held that the prima facie evidence provision renders the statute overbroad because "[t]he enhanced probability of prosecution under the statute chills the expression of protected speech."

Three justices dissented, concluding that the Virginia cross-burning statute passes constitutional muster because it proscribes only conduct that constitutes a true threat. The justices noted that unlike the ordinance found unconstitutional in *R. A. V. v. St. Paul,* the Virginia statute does not just target cross burning "on the basis of race, color, creed, religion or gender." Rather, "the Virginia statute applies to any individual who burns a cross for any reason provided the cross is burned with the intent to intimidate." The dissenters also disagreed with the majority's analysis of the prima facie provision because the inference alone "is clearly insufficient to establish beyond a reasonable doubt that a defendant burned a cross with the intent to intimidate." The dissent noted that the burden of proof still remains on the Commonwealth to prove intent to intimidate. We granted certiorari.

II

Cross burning originated in the 14th century as a means for Scottish tribes to signal each other. . . . Cross burning in this country, however, long ago became unmoored from its Scottish ancestry. Burning a cross in the United States is inextricably intertwined with the history of the Ku Klux Klan.

The first Ku Klux Klan began in Pulaski, Tennessee, in the spring of 1866. Although the Ku Klux Klan started as a social club, it soon changed into something far different. The Klan fought Reconstruction and the corresponding drive to allow freed blacks to participate in the political process. Soon the Klan imposed "a veritable reign of terror" throughout the South. The Klan employed tactics such as whipping, threatening to burn people at the stake, and murder. The Klan's victims included blacks, southern whites who disagreed with the Klan, and "carpetbagger" northern whites.

The activities of the Ku Klux Klan prompted legislative action at the national level. In 1871, "President Grant sent a message to Congress indicating that the Klan's reign of terror in the Southern States had rendered life and property insecure." In response, Congress passed what is now known as the Ku Klux Klan Act. President Grant used these new powers to suppress the Klan in South Carolina, the effect of which severely curtailed the Klan in other States as well. By the end of Reconstruction in 1877, the first Klan no longer existed.

The genesis of the second Klan began in 1905, with the publication of Thomas Dixon's The Clansmen: An Historical Romance of the Ku Klux Klan. Dixon's book was a sympathetic portrait of the first Klan, depicting the Klan as a group of heroes "saving" the South from blacks and the "horrors" of Reconstruction. Although the first Klan never actually practiced cross burning, Dixon's book depicted the Klan burning crosses to celebrate the execution of former slaves. Cross burning thereby became associated with the first Ku Klux Klan. When D. W. Griffith turned Dixon's book into the movie The Birth of a Nation in 1915, the association between cross burning and the Klan became indelible. In addition to the cross burnings in the movie, a poster advertising the film displayed a hooded Klansman riding a hooded horse, with his left hand holding the reins of the horse and his right hand holding a burning cross above his head. Soon thereafter, in November 1915, the second Klan began.

From the inception of the second Klan, cross burnings have been used to communicate both threats of violence and messages of shared ideology. The first initiation ceremony occurred on Stone Mountain near Atlanta, Georgia. While a 40-foot cross burned on the mountain, the Klan members took their oaths of loyalty. This cross burning was the second recorded instance in the United States. The first known cross burning in the country had occurred a little over one month before the Klan initiation, when a Georgia mob celebrated the lynching of Leo Frank by burning a "gigantic cross" on Stone Mountain that was "visible throughout" Atlanta.

The new Klan's ideology did not differ much from that of the first Klan. As one Klan publication emphasized, "We avow the distinction between [the] races, . . . and we shall ever be true to the faithful maintenance of White Supremacy and will strenuously oppose any compromise thereof in any and all things." Violence was also an elemental part of this new Klan. By September 1921, the New York World newspaper documented 152 acts of Klan violence, including 4 murders, 41 floggings, and 27 tar-and-featherings.

Often, the Klan used cross burnings as a tool of intimidation and a threat of impending violence. For example, in 1939 and 1940, the Klan burned crosses in front of synagogues and churches. After one cross burning at a synagogue, a Klan member noted that if the cross burning did not "shut the Jews up, we'll cut a few throats and see what happens." In Miami in 1941, the Klan burned four crosses in front of a proposed housing project, declaring, "We are here to keep niggers out of your town. . . . When the law fails you, call on us." And in Alabama in 1942, in "a whirlwind climax to weeks of flogging and terror," the Klan burned crosses in front of a union hall and in front of a union leader's home on the eve of a labor election. These cross burnings embodied threats to people whom the Klan deemed antithetical to its goals. And these threats had special force given the long history of Klan violence.

The Klan continued to use cross burnings to intimidate after World War II. In one incident, an African-American "school teacher who recently moved his family into a block formerly occupied only by whites asked the protection of city police . . . after the burning of a cross in his front yard." And after a cross burning in Suffolk, Virginia, during the late 1940's, the Virginia Governor stated that he would "not allow any of our people of any race to be subjected to terrorism or intimidation in any form by the Klan or any other organization." These incidents of cross burning, among others, helped prompt Virginia to enact its first version of the cross-burning statute in 1950.

The decision of this Court in *Brown v. Board of Education,* 347 U.S. 483 (1954), along with the civil rights movement of the 1950's and 1960's, sparked another outbreak of Klan violence. These acts of violence included bombings, beatings, shootings, stabbings, and mutilations. Members of the Klan burned crosses on the lawns of those associated with the civil rights movement, assaulted the Freedom Riders, bombed churches, and murdered blacks as well as whites whom the Klan viewed as sympathetic toward the civil rights movement.

Throughout the history of the Klan, cross burnings have also remained potent symbols of shared group identity and ideology. The burning cross became a symbol of the Klan itself and a central feature of Klan gatherings. According to the Klan constitution (called the kloran), the "fiery cross" was the "emblem of that sincere, unselfish devotedness of all klansmen to the sacred purpose and principles we have espoused." And the Klan has often published its newsletters and magazines under the name The Fiery Cross.

At Klan gatherings across the country, cross burning became the climax of the rally or the initiation. Posters advertising an upcoming Klan rally often featured a Klan member holding a cross. Typically, a cross burning would start with a prayer by the "Klavern" minister, followed by the singing of Onward Christian Soldiers. The Klan would then light the cross on fire, as the members raised their left arm toward the burning cross and sang The Old Rugged Cross. Throughout the Klan's history, the Klan continued to use the burning cross in their ritual ceremonies.

For its own members, the cross was a sign of celebration and ceremony. During a joint Nazi-Klan rally in 1940, the proceeding concluded with the wedding of two Klan members who "were married in full Klan regalia beneath a blazing cross." In response to antimasking bills introduced in state legislatures after World War II, the Klan burned crosses in protest. On March 26, 1960, the Klan engaged in rallies and cross burnings throughout the South in an attempt to recruit 10 million members. Later in 1960, the Klan became an issue in the third debate between Richard Nixon and John Kennedy, with both candidates renouncing the Klan. After this debate, the Klan reiterated its support for Nixon by burning crosses. And cross burnings featured prominently in

Klan rallies when the Klan attempted to move toward more nonviolent tactics to stop integration. In short, a burning cross has remained a symbol of Klan ideology and of Klan unity.

To this day, regardless of whether the message is a political one or whether the message is also meant to intimidate, the burning of a cross is a "symbol of hate." And while cross burning sometimes carries no intimidating message, at other times the intimidating message is the *only* message conveyed. For example, when a cross burning is directed at a particular person not affiliated with the Klan, the burning cross often serves as a message of intimidation, designed to inspire in the victim a fear of bodily harm. Moreover, the history of violence associated with the Klan shows that the possibility of injury or death is not just hypothetical. The person who burns a cross directed at a particular person often is making a serious threat, meant to coerce the victim to comply with the Klan's wishes unless the victim is willing to risk the wrath of the Klan. Indeed, as the cases of respondents Elliott and O'Mara indicate, individuals without Klan affiliation who wish to threaten or menace another person sometimes use cross burning because of this association between a burning cross and violence.

In sum, while a burning cross does not inevitably convey a message of intimidation, often the cross burner intends that the recipients of the message fear for their lives. And when a cross burning is used to intimidate, few if any messages are more powerful.

III

A

The First Amendment, applicable to the States through the Fourteenth Amendment, provides that "Congress shall make no law . . . abridging the freedom of speech." The hallmark of the protection of free speech is to allow "free trade in ideas"—even ideas that the overwhelming majority of people might find distasteful or discomforting. Thus, the First Amendment "ordinarily" denies a State "the power to prohibit dissemination of social, economic and political doctrine which a vast majority of its citizens believes to be false and fraught with evil consequence." The First Amendment affords protection to symbolic or expressive conduct as well as to actual speech.

The protections afforded by the First Amendment, however, are not absolute, and we have long recognized that the government may regulate certain categories of expression consistent with the Constitution. The First Amendment permits "restrictions upon the content of speech in a few limited areas, which are 'of such slight social value as a step to truth that any benefit that may be derived from them is clearly outweighed by the social interest in order and morality.'"

Thus, for example, a State may punish those words "which by their very utterance inflict injury or tend to incite an immediate breach of the peace." We have consequently held that fighting words—"those personally abusive epithets which, when addressed to the ordinary citizen, are, as a matter of common knowledge, inherently likely to provoke violent reaction"—are generally proscribable under the First Amendment. Furthermore, "the constitutional guarantees of free speech and free press do not permit a State to forbid or proscribe advocacy of the use of force or of law violation except where such advocacy is directed to inciting or producing imminent lawless action and is likely to incite or produce such action." And the First Amendment also permits a State to ban a "true threat."

"True threats" encompass those statements where the speaker means to communicate a serious expression of an intent to commit an act of unlawful violence to a particular individual or group of individuals. The speaker need not actually intend to carry out the threat. Rather, a prohibition on true threats "protect[s] individuals from the fear of violence" and "from the disruption that fear engenders," in addition to protecting people "from the possibility that the threatened violence will occur." Intimidation in the constitutionally proscribable sense of the word is a type of true threat, where a speaker directs a threat to a person or group of persons with the intent of placing the victim in fear of bodily harm or death. Respondents do not contest that some cross burnings fit within this meaning of intimidating speech, and rightly so. As noted in Part II, *supra,* the history of cross burning in this country shows that cross burning is often intimidating, intended to create a pervasive fear in victims that they are a target of violence.

B

The Supreme Court of Virginia ruled that in light of *R. A. V. v. City of St. Paul,* even if it is constitutional to ban cross burning in a content-neutral manner, the Virginia cross-burning statute is unconstitutional because it discriminates on the basis of content and viewpoint. It is true, as the Supreme Court of Virginia held, that the burning of a cross is symbolic expression. The reason why the Klan burns a cross at its rallies, or individuals place a burning cross on someone else's lawn, is that the burning cross represents the message that the speaker wishes to communicate. Individuals burn crosses as opposed to other means of communication because cross burning carries a message in an effective and dramatic manner.[1]

The fact that cross burning is symbolic expression, however, does not resolve the constitutional question. The Supreme Court of Virginia relied upon *R. A. V. v. City of St. Paul* to conclude that once a statute discriminates on the basis of this type of content, the law is unconstitutional. We disagree.

In *R. A. V.,* we held that a local ordinance that banned certain symbolic conduct, including cross burning, when done with the knowledge that such conduct would "'arouse anger, alarm or resentment in others on the basis of race, color, creed, religion or gender'" was unconstitutional. We held that the ordinance did not pass constitutional muster because it discriminated on the basis of content by targeting only those individuals who "provoke violence" on a basis specified in the law. The ordinance did not cover "[t]hose who wish to use 'fighting words' in connection with other ideas—to express hostility, for example, on the basis of political affiliation, union membership, or homosexuality."

This content-based discrimination was unconstitutional because it allowed the city "to impose special prohibitions on those speakers who express views on disfavored subjects."

We did not hold in *R. A. V.* that the First Amendment prohibits *all* forms of content-based discrimination within a proscribable area of speech. Rather, we specifically stated that some types of content discrimination did not violate the First Amendment:

> "When the basis for the content discrimination consists entirely of the very reason the entire class of speech at issue is proscribable, no significant danger of idea or viewpoint discrimination exists. Such a reason, having been adjudged neutral enough to support exclusion of the entire class of speech from First Amendment protection, is also neutral enough to form the basis of distinction within the class."

Indeed, we noted that it would be constitutional to ban only a particular type of threat: "[T]he Federal Government can criminalize only those threats of violence that are directed against the President . . . since the reasons why threats of violence are outside the First Amendment . . . have special force when applied to the person of the President." And a State may "choose to prohibit only that obscenity which is the most patently offensive *in its prurience*—i.e., that which involves the most lascivious displays of sexual activity." Consequently, while the holding of *R. A. V.* does not permit a State to ban only obscenity based on "offensive *political* messages" or "only those threats against the President that mention his policy on aid to inner cities," the First Amendment permits content discrimination "based on the very reasons why the particular class of speech at issue . . . is proscribable."

Similarly, Virginia's statute does not run afoul of the First Amendment insofar as it bans cross burning with intent to intimidate. Unlike the statute at issue in *R. A. V.,* the Virginia statute does not single out for opprobrium only that speech directed toward "one of the specified disfavored topics." It does not matter whether an individual burns a cross with intent to intimidate because of the victim's race, gender, or religion, or because of the victim's "political affiliation, union membership, or homosexuality." Moreover, as a factual matter it is not true that cross burners direct their intimidating conduct solely to racial or religious minorities. Indeed, in the case of Elliott and O'Mara, it is at least unclear whether the respondents burned a cross due to racial animus.

The First Amendment permits Virginia to outlaw cross burnings done with the intent to intimidate because burning a cross is a particularly virulent form of intimidation. Instead of prohibiting all intimidating messages, Virginia may choose to regulate this subset of intimidating messages in light of cross burning's long and pernicious history as a signal of impending violence. Thus, just as a State may regulate only that obscenity which is the most obscene due to its prurient content, so too may a State choose to prohibit only those forms of intimidation that are most likely to inspire fear of bodily harm. A ban on cross burning carried out with the intent to intimidate is fully consistent with our holding in *R. A. V.* and is proscribable under the First Amendment.

IV

The Supreme Court of Virginia ruled in the alternative that Virginia's cross-burning statute was unconstitutionally overbroad due to its provision stating that "[a]ny such burning of a cross shall be prima facie evidence of an intent to intimidate a person or group of persons." The Commonwealth added the prima facie provision to the statute in 1968. The court below did not reach whether this provision is severable from the rest of the cross-burning statute under Virginia law. In this Court, as in the Supreme Court of Virginia, respondents do not argue that the prima facie evidence provision is unconstitutional as applied to any one of them. Rather, they contend that the provision is unconstitutional on its face.

The Supreme Court of Virginia has not ruled on the meaning of the prima facie evidence provision. It has, however, stated that "the act of burning a cross alone, with no evidence of intent to intimidate, will nonetheless suffice for arrest and prosecution and will insulate the Commonwealth from a motion to strike the evidence at the end of its case-in-chief." The jury in the case of Richard Elliott did not receive any instruction on the prima facie evidence provision, and the provision was not an issue in the case of Jonathan O'Mara because he pleaded guilty. The court in Barry Black's case, however, instructed the jury that the provision means: "The burning of a cross, by itself, is sufficient evidence from which you may infer the required intent."

The prima facie evidence provision, as interpreted by the jury instruction, renders the statute unconstitutional. Because this jury instruction is the Model Jury Instruction, and because the Supreme Court of Virginia had the opportunity to expressly disavow the jury instruction, the jury instruction's construction of the prima facie provision "is a ruling on a question of state law that is as binding on us as though the precise words had been written into" the statute. As construed by the jury instruction, the prima facie provision strips away the very reason why a State may ban cross burning with the intent to intimidate. The prima facie evidence provision permits a jury to convict in every cross-burning case in which defendants exercise their constitutional right not to put on a defense. And even where a defendant like Black presents a defense, the prima facie evidence provision makes it more likely that the jury will find an intent to intimidate regardless of the particular facts of the case. The provision permits the Commonwealth to arrest, prosecute, and convict a person based solely on the fact of cross burning itself.

It is apparent that the provision as so interpreted "'would create an unacceptable risk of the suppression of ideas.'" The act of burning a cross may mean that a person is engaging in constitutionally proscribable intimidation. But that same act may mean only that the person is engaged in core political speech. The prima facie evidence provision in this statute blurs the line between these two meanings of a burning cross. As interpreted by the jury instruction, the provision chills constitutionally protected political speech because of the possibility that a State will prosecute—and potentially convict—somebody engaging only in lawful political speech at the core of what the First Amendment is designed to protect.

As the history of cross burning indicates, a burning cross is not always intended to intimidate. Rather, sometimes the cross burning is a statement of ideology, a symbol of group solidarity. It is a ritual used at Klan gatherings, and it is used to represent the Klan itself. Thus, "[b]urning a cross at a political rally would almost certainly be protected expression." Indeed, occasionally a person who burns a cross does not intend to express either a statement of ideology or intimidation. Cross burnings have appeared in movies such as *Mississippi Burning*, and in plays such as the stage adaptation of Sir Walter Scott's *The Lady of the Lake*.

The prima facie provision makes no effort to distinguish among these different types of cross burnings. It does not distinguish between a cross burning done with the purpose of creating anger or resentment and a cross burning done with the purpose of threatening or intimidating a victim. It does not distinguish between a cross burning at a public rally or a cross burning on a neighbor's lawn. It does not treat the cross burning directed at an individual differently from the cross burning directed at a group of like-minded believers. It allows a jury to treat a cross burning on the property of another with the owner's acquiescence in the same manner as a cross burning on the property of another without the owner's permission. To this extent I agree with Justice Souter that the prima facie evidence provision can "skew jury deliberations toward conviction in cases where the evidence of intent to intimidate is relatively weak and arguably consistent with a solely ideological reason for burning."

It may be true that a cross burning, even at a political rally, arouses a sense of anger or hatred among the vast majority of citizens who see a burning cross. But this sense of anger or hatred is not sufficient to ban all cross burnings. As Gerald Gunther has stated, "The lesson I have drawn from my childhood in Nazi Germany and my happier adult life in this country is the need to walk the sometimes difficult path of denouncing the bigot's hateful ideas with all my power, yet at the same time challenging any community's attempt to suppress hateful ideas by force of law." The prima facie evidence provision in this case ignores all of the contextual factors that are necessary to decide whether a particular cross burning is intended to intimidate. The First Amendment does not permit such a shortcut.

For these reasons, the prima facie evidence provision, as interpreted through the jury instruction and as applied in Barry Black's case, is unconstitutional on its face. We recognize that the Supreme Court of Virginia has not authoritatively interpreted the meaning of the prima facie evidence provision. Unlike Justice Scalia, we refuse to speculate on whether any interpretation of the prima facie evidence provision would satisfy the First Amendment. Rather, all we hold is that because of the interpretation of the prima facie evidence provision given by the jury instruction, the provision makes the statute facially invalid at this point. We also recognize the theoretical possibility that the court, on remand, could interpret the provision in a manner different from that so far set forth in order to avoid the constitutional objections we have described. We leave open that possibility. We also leave open the possibility that the provision is severable, and if so, whether Elliott and O'Mara could be retried under §18.2–423.

V

With respect to Barry Black, we agree with the Supreme Court of Virginia that his conviction cannot stand, and we affirm the judgment of the Supreme Court of Virginia. With respect to Elliott and O'Mara, we vacate the judgment of the Supreme Court of Virginia, and remand the case for further proceedings.

It is so ordered.

Note

1. Justice Thomas argues in dissent that cross burning is "conduct, not expression." While it is of course true that burning a cross is conduct, it is equally true that the First Amendment protects symbolic conduct as well as pure speech. As Justice Thomas has previously recognized, a burning cross is a "symbol of hate," and a "a symbol of white supremacy."

Dissenting Opinion
Virginia v. Black

J ustice Thomas, dissenting.

In every culture, certain things acquire meaning well beyond what outsiders can comprehend. That goes for both the sacred and the profane. I believe that cross burning is the paradigmatic example of the latter.

I

Although I agree with the majority's conclusion that it is constitutionally permissible to "ban . . . cross burning carried out with intent to intimidate," I believe that the majority errs in imputing an expressive component to the activity in question (relying on one of the exceptions to the First Amendment's prohibition on content-based discrimination outlined in *R. A. V. v. St. Paul*). In my view, whatever expressive value cross burning has, the legislature simply wrote it out by banning only intimidating conduct undertaken by a particular means. A conclusion that the statute prohibiting cross burning with intent to intimidate sweeps beyond a prohibition on certain conduct into the zone of expression overlooks not only the words of the statute but also reality.

A

"In holding [the ban on cross burning with intent to intimidate] unconstitutional, the Court ignores Justice Holmes' familiar aphorism that 'a page of history is worth a volume of logic.'"

To me, the majority's brief history of the Ku Klux Klan only reinforces [the] common understanding of the Klan as a terrorist organization, which, in its endeavor to intimidate, or even eliminate those it dislikes, uses the most brutal of methods.

Such methods typically include cross burning—"a tool for the intimidation and harassment of racial minorities, Catholics, Jews, Communists, and any other groups hated by the Klan." For those not easily frightened, cross burning has been followed by more extreme measures, such as beatings and murder. As the Solicitor General points out, the association between acts of intimidating cross burning and violence is well documented in recent American history. Indeed, the connection between cross burning and violence is well ingrained, and lower courts have so recognized. . . .

From Supreme Court of the United States, April 7, 2003.

But the perception that a burning cross is a threat and a precursor of worse things to come is not limited to blacks. Because the modern Klan expanded the list of its enemies beyond blacks and "radical[s]," to include Catholics, Jews, most immigrants, and labor unions, a burning cross is now widely viewed as a signal of impending terror and lawlessness. I wholeheartedly agree with the observation made by the Commonwealth of Virginia that

> "A white, conservative, middle-class Protestant, waking up at night to find a burning cross outside his home, will reasonably understand that someone is threatening him. His reaction is likely to be very different than if he were to find, say, a burning circle or square. In the latter case, he may call the fire department. In the former, he will probably call the police." Brief of Petitioner, at 26.

In our culture, cross burning has almost invariably meant lawlessness and understandably instills in its victims well-grounded fear of physical violence.

B

Virginia's experience has been no exception. In Virginia, though facing wide-spread opposition in 1920s, the KKK developed localized strength in the southeastern part of the State, where there were reports of scattered raids and floggings. Although the KKK was disbanded at the national level in 1944, a series of cross burnings in Virginia took place between 1949 and 1952.

Most of the crosses were burned on the lawns of black families, who either were business owners or lived in predominantly white neighborhoods. At least one of the cross burnings was accompanied by a shooting. The crosses burned near residences were about five to six feet tall; while a "huge cross reminiscent of the Ku Klux Klan days" burned "atop a hill" as part of the initiation ceremony of the secret organization of the Knights of Kavaliers, was twelve feet tall. These incidents were, in the words of the time, "*terroristic* [sic] . . . un-American act[s], designed to *intimidate* Negroes from seeking their rights as citizens."

In February 1952, in light of this series of cross burnings and attendant reports that the Klan, "long considered dead in Virginia, is being revitalized in Richmond," Governor Battle announced that "Virginia 'might well consider passing legislation' to restrict the activities of the Ku Klux Klan." As newspapers reported at the time, the bill was "to ban the burning of crosses and other similar evidences of *terrorism*." The bill was presented to the House of Delegates by a former FBI agent and future two-term Governor, Delegate Mills E. Godwin, Jr. "Godwin said law and order in the State were impossible if organized groups could *create fear by intimidation*."

That in the early 1950s the people of Virginia viewed cross burning as creating an intolerable atmosphere of terror is not surprising: Although the cross took on some religious significance in the 1920's when the Klan became connected with certain southern white clergy, by the postwar period it had reverted to its original function "as an instrument of intimidation."

Strengthening Delegate Godwin's explanation, as well as my conclusion, that the legislature sought to criminalize terrorizing *conduct* is the fact that at the time the statute was enacted, racial segregation was not only the prevailing practice, but also the law in Virginia. And, just two years after the enactment of this statute, Virginia's General Assembly embarked on a campaign of "massive resistance" in response to *Brown v. Board of Education.*

It strains credulity to suggest that a state legislature that adopted a litany of segregationist laws self-contradictorily intended to squelch the segregationist message. Even for segregationists, violent and terroristic conduct, the Siamese twin of cross burning, was intolerable. The ban on cross burning with intent to intimidate demonstrates that even segregationists understood the difference between intimidating and terroristic conduct and racist expression. It is simply beyond belief that, in passing the statute now under review, the Virginia legislature was concerned with anything but penalizing conduct it must have viewed as particularly vicious.

Accordingly, this statute prohibits only conduct, not expression. And, just as one cannot burn down someone's house to make a political point and then seek refuge in the First Amendment, those who hate cannot terrorize and intimidate to make their point. In light of my conclusion that the statute here addresses only conduct, there is no need to analyze it under any of our First Amendment tests.

II

Even assuming that the statute implicates the First Amendment, in my view, the fact that the statute permits a jury to draw an inference of intent to intimidate from the cross burning itself presents no constitutional problems. Therein lies my primary disagreement with the plurality.

A

"The threshold inquiry is ascertaining the constitutional analysis applicable to [a jury instruction involving a presumption] is to determine the nature of the presumption it describes." We have categorized the presumptions as either permissive inferences or mandatory presumptions.

To the extent we do have a construction of this statute by the Virginia Supreme Court, we know that both the majority and the dissent agreed that the presumption was "a statutorily supplied *inference.*" Under Virginia law, the term "inference" has a well-defined meaning and is distinct from the term "presumption."

> A presumption is a rule of law that compels the fact finder to draw a certain conclusion or a certain inference from a given set of facts. [FN1: In contrast, *an inference,* sometimes loosely referred to as a presumption of fact, *does not compel a specific conclusion. An inference merely applies to the rational potency or probative value of an evidentiary fact to which the fact finder may attach whatever force or weight it deems best.*] The primary

significance of a presumption is that it operates to shift to the opposing party the burden of producing evidence tending to rebut the presumption. [FN2: *An inference, on the other hand, does not invoke this procedural consequence of shifting the burden of production.*] No presumption, however, can operate to shift the ultimate burden of persuasion from the party upon whom it was originally cast.

Both the majority and the dissent below classified the clause in question as an "inference," and I see no reason to disagree, particularly in light of the instructions given to the jury in Black's case, requiring it to find guilt beyond a reasonable doubt both as to the fact that "the defendant burned or caused to burn a cross in a public place," and that "he did so with the intent to intimidate any person or persons."

Even though under Virginia law the statutory provision at issue here is characterized as an "inference," the Court must still inquire whether the label Virginia attaches corresponds to the categorization our cases have given such clauses. In this respect, it is crucial to observe that what Virginia law calls an "inference" is what our cases have termed "a permissive inference or presumption."[1] Given that this Court's definitions of a "permissive inference" and a "mandatory presumption" track Virginia's definitions of "inference" and "presumption," the Court should judge the Virginia statute based on the constitutional analysis applicable to "inferences:" they raise no constitutional flags unless "no rational trier could make a connection permitted by the inference." As explained in Part I, *not* making a connection between cross burning and intimidation would be irrational.

But even with respect to statutes containing a mandatory irrebuttable presumption as to intent, the Court has not shown much concern. For instance, there is no scienter requirement for statutory rape. That is, a person can be arrested, prosecuted, and convicted for having sex with a minor, without the government ever producing any evidence, let alone proving beyond a reasonable doubt, that a minor did not consent. In fact, "[f]or purposes of the child molesting statute . . . consent is irrelevant. The legislature has determined in such cases that children under the age of sixteen (16) cannot, as a matter of law, consent to have sexual acts performed upon them, or consent to engage in a sexual act with someone over the age of sixteen (16)." The legislature finds the behavior so reprehensible that the intent is satisfied by the mere act committed by a perpetrator. Considering the horrific effect cross burning has on its victims, it is also reasonable to presume intent to intimidate from the act itself.

Statutes prohibiting possession of drugs with intent to distribute operate much the same way as statutory rape laws. Under these statutes, the intent to distribute is effectively satisfied by possession of some threshold amount of drugs. As with statutory rape, the presumption of intent in such statutes is irrebuttable—not only can a person be arrested for the crime of possession with intent to distribute (or "trafficking") without any evidence of intent beyond quantity of drugs, but such person cannot even mount a defense to the element of intent. However, as with statutory rape statutes, our cases do not reveal any controversy with respect to the presumption of intent in these drug statutes.

Because the prima facie clause here is an inference, not an irrebuttable presumption, there is all the more basis under our Due Process precedents to sustain this statute.

B

The plurality, however, is troubled by the presumption because this is a First Amendment case. The plurality laments the fate of an innocent cross-burner who burns a cross, but does so without an intent to intimidate. The plurality fears the chill on expression because, according to the plurality, the inference permits "the Commonwealth to arrest, prosecute and convict a person based solely on the fact of cross burning itself." First, it is, at the very least, unclear that the inference comes into play during arrest and initiation of a prosecution, that is, prior to the instructions stage of an actual trial. Second, as I explained above, the inference is rebuttable and, as the jury instructions given in this case demonstrate, Virginia law still requires the jury to find the existence of each element, including intent to intimidate, beyond a reasonable doubt.

Moreover, even in the First Amendment context, the Court has upheld such regulations where conduct that initially appears culpable, ultimately results in dismissed charges. A regulation of pornography is one such example. While possession of child pornography is illegal, possession of adult pornography, as long as it is not obscene, is allowed. As a result, those pornographers trafficking in images of adults who look like minors, may be not only deterred but also arrested and prosecuted for possessing what a jury might find to be legal materials. This "chilling" effect has not, however, been a cause for grave concern with respect to overbreadth of such statutes among the members of this Court.

That the First Amendment gives way to other interests is not a remarkable proposition. What is remarkable is that, under the plurality's analysis, the determination of whether an interest is sufficiently compelling depends not on the harm a regulation in question seeks to prevent, but on the area of society at which it aims. For instance, in *Hill v. Colorado,* the Court upheld a restriction on protests near abortion clinics, explaining that the State had a legitimate interest, which was sufficiently narrowly tailored, in protecting those seeking services of such establishments "from unwanted advice" and "unwanted communication." In so concluding, the Court placed heavy reliance on the "vulnerable physical and emotional conditions" of patients. Thus, when it came to the rights of those seeking abortions, the Court deemed restrictions on "unwanted advice," which, notably, can be given only from a distance of at least 8 feet from a prospective patient, justified by the countervailing interest in obtaining abortion. Yet, here, the plurality strikes down the statute because one day an individual might wish to burn a cross, but might do so without an intent to intimidate anyone. That cross burning subjects its targets, and, sometimes, an unintended audience, to extreme emotional distress, and is virtually never viewed merely as "unwanted communication," but rather, as a physical threat, is of no concern to the plurality. Henceforth, under the plurality's view, physical safety will be valued less than the right to be free from unwanted communications.

III

Because I would uphold the validity of this statute, I respectfully dissent.

Note

1. As the Court explained in [*County Court of Ulster City v.*] *Allen,* a permissive inference or presumption "allows—but does not require—the trier of fact to infer the elemental fact from proof by the prosecutor of the basic one and which places no burden of any kind on the defendant. In that situation the basic fact may constitute prima facie evidence of the elemental fact. . . . Because this permissive presumption leaves the trier of fact free to credit or reject the inference and does not shift the burden of proof, it affects the application of the 'beyond a reasonable doubt' standard only if, under the facts of the case, there is no rational way the trier could make the connection permitted by the inference." *Id.* at 157 (internal citations omitted). By contrast, "a mandatory presumption . . . may affect not only the strength of the 'no reasonable doubt' burden but also the placement of that burden; it tells the trier that he or they *must* find the elemental fact upon proof of the basic fact, at least unless the defendant has come forward with some evidence to rebut the presumed connection between the two facts." *Id.*

POSTSCRIPT

Are Blanket Prohibitions on Cross Burnings Unconstitutional?

Cross burning and other acts of "symbolic speech" straddle the poorly defined line that distinguishes speech from conduct. In the history of the Supreme Court, this distinction has been a central cause of controversy surrounding what does and does not deserve First Amendment protection. According to Justice Thomas, it is one of the key issues in *Virginia v. Black*: He asserts that the majority reaches the wrong conclusion because it refuses to recognize cross burning as "conduct" that the state may constitutionally outlaw. "A conclusion," he writes, "that the statute prohibiting cross burning with intent to intimidate sweeps beyond a prohibition on certain conduct into the zone of expression overlooks not only the words of the statute but also reality."

Justice Thomas's argument suggests one solution: Limit First Amendment protection only to actual speech. Such an approach to the First Amendment might be consistent with its actual words—that "Congress shall make no law . . . abridging the freedom of speech"—but could undermine some of the greater ends that the First Amendment attempts to accomplish, such as allowing citizens to express their objections to government policies with which they disagree. In some instances, symbolic speech may better express political ideas than actual words ever could. Take, for example, the 1969 case of *Tinker v. Des Moines*, in which the Supreme Court had to consider whether students who wore black armbands to school to protest the Vietnam War were engaging in a form of protected symbolic speech. An important aspect of the Court's decision in favor of the students was that wearing armbands in class was a "silent, passive expression of opinion, unaccompanied by any disorder or disturbance." Actual speech, yelled in the middle of a school class, would probably have been viewed as disruptive, perhaps even creating the type of "breach of the peace" that would make it fall under the "fighting words" exception to the First Amendment. Symbolic speech, by contrast, allowed the students to effectively convey their political views in a calm, peaceful fashion, one that the Supreme Court recognized as precisely the type of dissent that the First Amendment was designed to protect.

Recommended readings include Wyn Craig Wade, *The Fiery Cross: The Ku Klux Klan in America* (Simon & Schuster, 1987); Frederick Schauer, *Free Speech: A Philosophical Enquiry* (Cambridge University Press, 1982); Randall P. Bezanson, *Speech Stories: How Free Can Speech Be?* (New York University Press, 1998); Edward J. Cleary, *Beyond the Burning Cross: The First Amendment and the Landmark R A. V. Case* (Random House, 1994); and Steven Gey, "The Nuremberg Files and the First Amendment Value of Threats," 78 *Texas Law Review*

541 (2000). For a look at how the First Amendment has fared during times of conflict, including the war on terror, see Geoffrey R. Stone, *Perilous Times: Free Speech in Wartime from the Sedition Act of 1789 to the War on Terrorism* (W. W. Norton & Co., 2004). Finally, an interesting case concerning speech, threats, and the Internet is *Planned Parenthood v. American Coalition of Life Activists,* 290 F.3d 1058 (9th Cir. 2002).

ISSUE 19

Should Same-Sex Couples Receive Constitutional Protection?

YES: Margaret Marshall, from Majority Opinion, *Goodridge, et al., v. Department of Public Health*, Massachusetts Supreme Judicial Court (2003)

NO: Robert Cordy, from Minority Opinion, *Goodridge, et al., v. Department of Public Health*, Massachusetts Supreme Judicial Court (2003)

ISSUE SUMMARY

YES: Massachusetts Supreme Judicial Court Chief Justice Margaret Marshall rules that prohibiting same-sex couples from marrying causes hardship to a segment of the population for no rational reason.

NO: Massachusetts Supreme Judicial Court Justice Robert Cordy, in dissent, holds that a statute banning same-sex marriage is a valid exercise of the state's police power.

In spring 2001, seven same-sex couples in Massachusetts unsuccessfully applied for marriage licenses from their respective town clerks. The clerks all denied the requests because the applicants were same-sex couples. As a result, the couples filed suit in the Massachusetts Superior Court (trial court), claiming that the clerks' actions violated the equal protection clause of the Massachusetts Constitution. That clause provides, "All people are born free and equal and have certain natural, essential and unalienable rights; among which may be reckoned the right of enjoying and defending their lives and liberties; that of acquiring, possessing and protecting property; in fine, that of seeking and obtaining their safety and happiness. Equality under the law shall not be denied or abridged because of sex, race, color, creed or national origin" (Mass. Const. Pt. 1, Art. 1). The trial court rejected the same-sex couples' claims and held that the state's prohibition of same-sex marriages was constitutionally permissible because it advanced the state's interest in protecting the primary purpose of the institution of marriage: procreation.

All sides agreed that the issue's importance was of sufficient magnitude to warrant bypassing the intermediate appellate court and, instead, called for direct appeal to the Massachusetts Supreme Judicial Court. There, in a sharply divided 4–3 decision, the Supreme Judicial Court vacated the trial court's ruling, holding that the prohibition of same-sex marriages was unconstitutional. The high court did not, however, order the state to begin to issue marriage licenses to the same-sex applicants but, instead, remanded the case back to the Superior Court with a stay for 180 days to allow the Massachusetts legislature to take appropriate action.

The Massachusetts Court was immediately caught up in the political storm surrounding the question of gay rights in particular and the question of "moral values" and contemporary society more generally. The Court was both reviled and praised. Little more than a year away from the presidential elections, the Court and its decision were pulled into the national political debates. Was this decision the fair and just thing to do, treating all, regardless of their sexual orientation, to the benefits of the institution of marriage? Or is marriage an historically unique social institution, intended to recognize only the union between a man and a woman? With upwards of 50 percent of all marriages in the United States ending in divorce, would this decision further contribute to the fragility of a social institution that, historically, has been central to the organization and stability of society? Or would it have the opposite effect: reaffirming the centrality of marriage, whether it be formed by same- or opposite-sex couples? Finally, was this decision yet one more example of a highly politicized, "activist" judiciary usurping the law-making function and "legislating" from the bench? Or was this a situation where the judiciary properly used its power of judicial review to protect the rights of a traditionally marginalized minority group? These issues are contested in the following opinions by Justices Marshall and Cordy from the *Goodridge* decision.

YES ↙   Margaret Marshall

Majority Opinion *Goodridge et al. v. Department of Public Health*

Marriage is a vital social institution. The exclusive commitment of two individuals to each other nurtures love and mutual support; it brings stability to our society. For those who choose to marry, and for their children, marriage provides an abundance of legal, financial, and social benefits. In return it imposes weighty legal, financial, and social obligations. The question before us is whether, consistent with the Massachusetts Constitution, the Commonwealth may deny the protections, benefits, and obligations conferred by civil marriage to two individuals of the same sex who wish to marry. We conclude that it may not. The Massachusetts Constitution affirms the dignity and equality of all individuals. It forbids the creation of second-class citizens. In reaching our conclusion we have given full deference to the arguments made by the Commonwealth. But it has failed to identify any constitutionally adequate reason for denying civil marriage to same-sex couples.

We are mindful that our decision marks a change in the history of our marriage law. Many people hold deep-seated religious, moral, and ethical convictions that marriage should be limited to the union of one man and one woman, and that homosexual conduct is immoral. Many hold equally strong religious, moral, and ethical convictions that same-sex couples are entitled to be married, and that homosexual persons should be treated no differently than their heterosexual neighbors. Neither view answers the question before us. Our concern is with the Massachusetts Constitution as a charter of governance for every person properly within its reach. "Our obligation is to define the liberty of all, not to mandate our own moral code." *Lawrence v. Texas*, 123 S.Ct. 2472, 2480 (2003) (*Lawrence*), quoting *Planned Parenthood of Southeastern Pa. v. Casey*, 505 U.S. 833, 850 (1992).

Whether the Commonwealth may use its formidable regulatory authority to bar same-sex couples from civil marriage is a question not previously addressed by a Massachusetts appellate court. It is a question the United States Supreme Court left open as a matter of Federal law in *Lawrence, supra* at 2484, where it was not an issue. There, the Court affirmed that the core concept of common human dignity protected by the Fourteenth Amendment to the United States Constitution precludes government intrusion into the deeply personal realms of consensual adult expressions of intimacy and one's choice of an intimate partner. The Court also reaffirmed the central role that decisions whether to marry or have children bear in shaping one's identity. *Id.* at 2481. The Massachusetts Constitution

Majority Opinion, SJC-08860, March 4, 2003–November 18, 2003. Some case citations omitted.

is, if anything, more protective of individual liberty and equality than the Federal Constitution; it may demand broader protection for fundamental rights; and it is less tolerant of government intrusion into the protected spheres of private life. . . .

Barred access to the protections, benefits, and obligations of civil marriage, a person who enters into an intimate, exclusive union with another of the same sex is arbitrarily deprived of membership in one of our community's most rewarding and cherished institutions. That exclusion is incompatible with the constitutional principles of respect for individual autonomy and equality under law. . . .

❦

The plaintiffs include business executives, lawyers, an investment banker, educators, therapists, and a computer engineer. Many are active in church, community, and school groups. They have employed such legal means as are available to them—for example, joint adoption, powers of attorney, and joint ownership of real property—to secure aspects of their relationships. Each plaintiff attests a desire to marry his or her partner in order to affirm publicly their commitment to each other and to secure the legal protections and benefits afforded to married couples and their children. . . .

The department, represented by the Attorney General, admitted to a policy and practice of denying marriage licenses to same-sex couples. It denied that its actions violated any law or that the plaintiffs were entitled to relief. The parties filed cross motions for summary judgment.

A Superior Court judge ruled for the department. In a memorandum of decision and order dated May 7, 2002, he dismissed the plaintiffs' claim that the marriage statutes should be construed to permit marriage between persons of the same sex, holding that the plain wording of G.L. c. 207, as well as the wording of other marriage statutes, precluded that interpretation. Turning to the constitutional claims, he held that the marriage exclusion does not offend the liberty, freedom, equality, or due process provisions of the Massachusetts Constitution, and that the Massachusetts Declaration of Rights does not guarantee "the fundamental right to marry a person of the same sex." He concluded that prohibiting same-sex marriage rationally furthers the Legislature's legitimate interest in safeguarding the "primary purpose" of marriage, "procreation." The Legislature may rationally limit marriage to opposite-sex couples, he concluded, because those couples are "theoretically . . . capable of procreation," they do not rely on "inherently more cumbersome" noncoital means of reproduction, and they are more likely than same-sex couples to have children, or more children. . . .

❦

In short, for all the joy and solemnity that normally attend a marriage, G.L. c. 207, governing entrance to marriage, is a licensing law. The plaintiffs argue that because nothing in that licensing law specifically prohibits marriages between persons of the same sex, we may interpret the statute to permit "qualified same sex couples" to obtain marriage licenses, thereby avoiding the question whether the law is constitutional. . . . This claim lacks merit. . . .

❦

The larger question is whether, as the department claims, government action that bars same-sex couples from civil marriage constitutes a legitimate exercise of the State's authority to regulate conduct, or whether, as the plaintiffs claim, this categorical marriage exclusion violates the Massachusetts Constitution. We have recognized the long-standing statutory understanding, derived from the common law, that "marriage" means the lawful union of a woman and a man. But that history cannot and does not foreclose the constitutional question.

The plaintiffs' claim that the marriage restriction violates the Massachusetts Constitution can be analyzed in two ways. Does it offend the Constitution's guarantees of equality before the law? Or do the liberty and due process provisions of the Massachusetts Constitution secure the plaintiffs' right to marry their chosen partner? In matters implicating marriage, family life, and the upbringing of children, the two constitutional concepts frequently overlap, as they do here. . . .

We begin by considering the nature of civil marriage itself. Simply put, the government creates civil marriage. In Massachusetts, civil marriage is, and since pre-Colonial days has been, precisely what its name implies: a wholly secular institution. . . . No religious ceremony has ever been required to validate a Massachusetts marriage.

In a real sense, there are three partners to every civil marriage: two willing spouses and an approving State. . . . While only the parties can mutually assent to marriage, the terms of the marriage—who may marry and what obligations, benefits, and liabilities attach to civil marriage—are set by the Commonwealth. Conversely, while only the parties can agree to end the marriage (absent the death of one of them or a marriage void ab initio), the Commonwealth defines the exit terms.

Civil marriage is created and regulated through exercise of the police power. . . . "Police power" (now more commonly termed the State's regulatory authority) is an old-fashioned term for the Commonwealth's lawmaking authority, as bounded by the liberty and equality guarantees of the Massachusetts Constitution and its express delegation of power from the people to their government. In broad terms, it is the Legislature's power to enact rules to regulate conduct, to the extent that such laws are "necessary to secure the health, safety, good order, comfort, or general welfare of the community." . . .

Without question, civil marriage enhances the "welfare of the community." It is a "social institution of the highest importance." Civil marriage anchors an ordered society by encouraging stable relationships over transient ones. It is central to the way the Commonwealth identifies individuals, provides for the orderly distribution of property, ensures that children and adults are cared for and supported whenever possible from private rather than public funds, and tracks important epidemiological and demographic data.

Marriage also bestows enormous private and social advantages on those who choose to marry. Civil marriage is at once a deeply personal commitment to another human being and a highly public celebration of the ideals of mutuality, companionship, intimacy, fidelity, and family. "It is an association that promotes a way of life, not causes; a harmony in living, not political faiths; a bilateral loyalty, not commercial or social projects." *Griswold v. Connecticut,* 381 U.S. 479, 486 (1965). Because it fulfils yearnings for security, safe haven, and connection that express our common humanity, civil marriage is an esteemed institution, and the decision whether and whom to marry is among life's momentous acts of self-definition.

Tangible as well as intangible benefits flow from marriage. The marriage license grants valuable property rights to those who meet the entry requirements, and who agree to what might otherwise be a burdensome degree of government regulation of their activities. . . . The Legislature has conferred on "each party [in a civil marriage] substantial rights concerning the assets of the other which unmarried cohabitants do not have." . . .

⚜

For decades, indeed centuries, in much of this country (including Massachusetts) no lawful marriage was possible between white and black Americans. That long history availed not when the Supreme Court of California held in 1948 that a legislative prohibition against interracial marriage violated the due process and equality guarantees of the Fourteenth Amendment, *Perez v. Sharp,* 32 Cal.2d 711, 728 (1948), or when, nineteen years later, the United States Supreme Court also held that a statutory bar to interracial marriage violated the Fourteenth Amendment, *Loving v. Virginia,* 388 U.S. 1 (1967). As both *Perez* and *Loving* make clear, the right to marry means little if it does not include the right to marry the person of one's choice, subject to appropriate government restrictions in the interests of public health, safety, and welfare. See *Perez v. Sharp, supra* at 717 ("the essence of the right to marry is freedom to join in marriage with the person of one's choice"). See also *Loving v. Virginia, supra* at 12. In this case, as in *Perez* and *Loving,* a statute deprives individuals of access to an institution of fundamental legal, personal, and social significance—the institution of marriage—because of a single trait: skin color in *Perez* and *Loving,* sexual orientation here. As it did in *Perez* and *Loving,* history must yield to a more fully developed understanding of the invidious quality of the discrimination.

The Massachusetts Constitution protects matters of personal liberty against government incursion as zealously, and often more so, than does the Federal Constitution, even where both Constitutions employ essentially the same language. See *Planned Parenthood League of Mass., Inc., v. Attorney Gen.,* 424 Mass. 586, 590 (1997); *Corning Glass Works v. Ann & Hope, Inc., of Danvers,* 363 Mass. 409, 416 (1973). That the Massachusetts Constitution is in some instances more protective of individual liberty interests than is the Federal Constitution is not surprising. Fundamental to the vigor of our Federal system of government is that "state courts are absolutely free to interpret state constitutional provisions to accord greater protection to individual rights than do similar provisions of the United States Constitution." *Arizona v. Evans,* 514 U.S. 1, 8 (1995).

The individual liberty and equality safeguards of the Massachusetts Constitution protect both "freedom from" unwarranted government intrusion into protected spheres of life and "freedom to" partake in benefits created by the State for the common good. See *Bachrach v. Secretary of the Commonwealth,* 382 Mass. 268, 273 (1981); *Dalli v. Board of Educ.,* 358 Mass. 753, 759 (1971). Both freedoms are involved here. Whether and whom to marry, how to express sexual intimacy, and whether and how to establish a family—these are among the most basic of every individual's liberty and due process rights. See, e.g., *Lawrence, supra* at 2481; *Planned Parenthood of Southeastern Pa. v. Casey,* 505 U.S. 833, 851 (1992); *Zablocki v. Redhail,* 434 U.S. 374, 384 (1978); *Roe v. Wade,* 410 U.S. 113, 152–153 (1973); *Eisenstadt v. Baird,* 405 U.S. 438, 453 (1972); *Loving v. Virginia, supra.* And central to personal freedom and security is the assurance that the laws will apply equally to persons in similar situations. "Absolute equality before the law is a fundamental principle of our own Constitution." *Opinion of the Justices,* 211 Mass. 618, 619 (1912). The liberty interest in choosing whether and whom to marry would be hollow if the Commonwealth could, without sufficient justification, foreclose an individual from freely choosing the person with whom to share an exclusive commitment in the unique institution of civil marriage. . . .

The plaintiffs challenge the marriage statute on both equal protection and due process grounds. With respect to each such claim, we must first determine the appropriate standard of review. Where a statute implicates a fundamental right or uses a suspect classification, we employ "strict judicial scrutiny." *Lowell v. Kowalski,* 380 Mass. 663, 666 (1980). For all other statutes, we employ the "'rational basis' test." *English v. New England Med. Ctr.,* 405 Mass. 423, 428 (1989). For due process claims, rational basis analysis requires that statutes "bear[ ] a real and substantial relation to the public health, safety, morals, or some other phase of the general welfare." *Coffee-Rich, Inc., v. Commissioner of Pub. Health, supra,* quoting *Sperry & Hutchinson Co. v. Director of the Div. on the Necessaries of Life,* 307 Mass. 408, 418 (1940). For equal protection challenges, the rational basis test requires that "an impartial lawmaker could logically believe that the classification would serve a legitimate public purpose that transcends the harm to the members of the disadvantaged class." *English v. New England Med. Ctr., supra* at 429, quoting *Cleburne v. Cleburne Living Ctr., Inc.,* 473 U.S. 432, 452 (1985) (Stevens, J., concurring).

The department argues that no fundamental right or "suspect" class is at issue here, and rational basis is the appropriate standard of review. For the reasons we explain below, we conclude that the marriage ban does not meet the rational basis test for either due process or equal protection. Because the statute does not survive rational basis review, we do not consider the plaintiffs' arguments that this case merits strict judicial scrutiny.

The department posits three legislative rationales for prohibiting same-sex couples from marrying: (1) providing a "favorable setting for procreation"; (2) ensuring the optimal setting for child rearing, which the department defines as "a two-parent family with one parent of each sex"; and (3) preserving scarce State and private financial resources. We consider each in turn. . . .

Our laws of civil marriage do not privilege procreative heterosexual intercourse between married people above every other form of adult intimacy and every other means of creating a family. General Laws c. 207 contains no requirement that the applicants for a marriage license attest to their ability or intention to conceive children by coitus. Fertility is not a condition of marriage, nor is it grounds for divorce. People who have never consummated their marriage, and never plan to, may be and stay married. . . . People who cannot stir from their deathbed may marry. See G.L. c. 207, § 28A. While it is certainly true that many, perhaps most, married couples have children together (assisted or unassisted), it is the exclusive and permanent commitment of the marriage partners to one another, not the begetting of children, that is the sine qua non of civil marriage.

Moreover, the Commonwealth affirmatively facilitates bringing children into a family regardless of whether the intended parent is married or unmarried, whether the child is adopted or born into a family, whether assistive technology was used to conceive the child, and whether the parent or her partner is heterosexual, homosexual, or bisexual. If procreation were a necessary component of civil marriage, our statutes would draw a tighter circle around the permissible bounds of nonmarital child bearing and the creation of families by noncoital means. The attempt to isolate procreation as "the source of a fundamental right to marry," *post* at (Cordy, J., dissenting), overlooks the integrated way in which courts have examined the complex and overlapping realms of personal autonomy, marriage, family life, and child rearing. Our jurisprudence recognizes that, in these nuanced and fundamentally private areas of life, such a narrow focus is inappropriate.

The "marriage is procreation" argument singles out the one unbridgeable difference between same-sex and opposite-sex couples, and transforms that difference into the essence of legal marriage . . . and full access to the political process, the marriage restriction impermissibly "identifies persons by a single trait and then denies them protection across the board." *Romer v. Evans,* 517 U.S. 620, 633 (1996). In so doing, the State's action confers an official stamp of approval on the destructive stereotype that same-sex relationships are inherently unstable and inferior to opposite-sex relationships and are not worthy of respect.

The department's first stated rationale, equating marriage with unassisted heterosexual procreation, shades imperceptibly into its second: that confining marriage to opposite-sex couples ensures that children are raised in the "optimal" setting. Protecting the welfare of children is a paramount State policy. Restricting marriage to opposite-sex couples, however, cannot plausibly further this policy. . . .

The department has offered no evidence that forbidding marriage to people of the same sex will increase the number of couples choosing to enter into opposite-sex marriages in order to have and raise children. There is thus no rational relationship between the marriage statute and the Commonwealth's proffered goal of protecting the "optimal" child rearing unit. Moreover, the department readily concedes that people in same-sex couples may be "excellent" parents. These couples (including four of the plaintiff couples) have children for the reasons others do—to love them, to care for them, to nurture them. But the task of child rearing for same-sex couples is made infinitely harder by their status as outliers to the marriage laws. . . . Given the wide range of public benefits reserved only for married couples, we do not credit the department's contention that the absence of access to civil marriage amounts to little more than an inconvenience to same-sex couples and their children. Excluding same-sex couples from civil marriage will not make children of opposite-sex marriages more secure, but it does prevent children of same-sex couples from enjoying the immeasurable advantages that flow from the assurance of "a stable family structure in which children will be reared, educated, and socialized." . . .

In this case, we are confronted with an entire, sizeable class of parents raising children who have absolutely no access to civil marriage and its protections because they are forbidden from procuring a marriage license. It cannot be rational under our laws, and indeed it is not permitted, to penalize children by depriving them of State benefits because the State disapproves of their parents' sexual orientation.

The third rationale advanced by the department is that limiting marriage to opposite-sex couples furthers the Legislature's interest in conserving scarce State and private financial resources. The marriage restriction is rational, it argues, because the General Court logically could assume that same-sex couples are more financially independent than married couples and thus less needy of public marital benefits, such as tax advantages, or private marital benefits, such as employer-financed health plans that include spouses in their coverage.

An absolute statutory ban on same-sex marriage bears no rational relationship to the goal of economy. First, the department's conclusory generalization—that same-sex couples are less financially dependent on each other than opposite-sex couples—ignores that many same-sex couples, such as many of the plaintiffs in this case, have children and other dependents (here, aged parents) in their care. The department does not contend, nor could it, that these dependents are less needy or deserving than the dependents of married couples. Second, Massachusetts marriage laws do not condition receipt of public and private financial benefits to married individuals on a demonstration of financial dependence on each other; the benefits are available to married couples regardless of whether they mingle their finances or actually depend on each other for support. . . .

Here, the plaintiffs seek only to be married, not to undermine the institution of civil marriage. They do not want marriage abolished. They do not attack the binary nature of marriage, the consanguinity provisions, or any of the other gate-keeping provisions of the marriage licensing law. Recognizing the right of an individual to marry a person of the same sex will not diminish the validity or dignity of opposite-sex marriage, any more than recognizing the right of an individual to marry a person of a different race devalues the marriage of a person who marries someone of her own race. If anything, extending civil marriage to same-sex couples reinforces the importance of marriage to individuals and communities. That same-sex couples are willing to embrace marriage's solemn obligations of exclusivity, mutual support, and commitment to one another is a testament to the enduring place of marriage in our laws and in the human spirit. . . .

The marriage ban works a deep and scarring hardship on a very real segment of the community for no rational reason. The absence of any reasonable relationship between, on the one hand, an absolute disqualification of same-sex couples who wish to enter into civil marriage and, on the other, protection of public health, safety, or general welfare, suggests that the marriage restriction is rooted in persistent prejudices against persons who are (or who are believed to be) homosexual. "The Constitution cannot control such prejudices but neither can it tolerate them. Private biases may be outside the reach of the law, but the law cannot, directly or indirectly, give them effect." Limiting the protections, benefits, and obligations of civil marriage to opposite-sex couples violates the basic premises of individual liberty and equality under law protected by the Massachusetts Constitution.

<hr />

We consider next the plaintiffs' request for relief. We preserve as much of the statute as may be preserved in the face of the successful constitutional challenge. . . .

Here, no one argues that striking down the marriage laws is an appropriate form of relief. Eliminating civil marriage would be wholly inconsistent with the Legislature's deep commitment to fostering stable families and would dismantle a vital organizing principle of our society. . . .

We construe civil marriage to mean the voluntary union of two persons as spouses, to the exclusion of all others. This reformulation redresses the plaintiffs' constitutional injury and furthers the aim of marriage to promote stable, exclusive relationships. It advances the two legitimate State interests the department has identified: providing a stable setting for child rearing and conserving State resources. It leaves intact the Legislature's broad discretion to regulate marriage. . . .

So ordered. . . .

Robert Cordy

→ **NO**

Minority Opinion *Goodridge v. Department of Public Health*

. . . The court's opinion concludes that the Department of Public Health has failed to identify any "constitutionally adequate reason" for limiting civil marriage to opposite-sex unions, and that there is no "reasonable relationship" between a disqualification of same-sex couples who wish to enter into a civil marriage and the protection of public health, safety, or general welfare. Consequently, it holds that the marriage statute cannot withstand scrutiny under the Massachusetts Constitution. Because I find these conclusions to be unsupportable in light of the nature of the rights and regulations at issue, the presumption of constitutional validity and significant deference afforded to legislative enactments, and the "undesirability of the judiciary substituting its notions of correct policy for that of a popularly elected Legislature" responsible for making such policy, *Zayre Corp. v. Attorney Gen.*, 372 Mass. 423, 433 (1977), I respectfully dissent. Although it may be desirable for many reasons to extend to same-sex couples the benefits and burdens of civil marriage (and the plaintiffs have made a powerfully reasoned case for that extension), that decision must be made by the Legislature, not the court. . . .

A. *Limiting marriage to the union of one man and one woman does not impair the exercise of a fundamental right.* Civil marriage is an institution created by the State. In Massachusetts, the marriage statutes are derived from English common law. . . . They were enacted to secure public interests and not for religious purposes or to promote personal interests or aspirations. As the court notes in its opinion, the institution of marriage is "the legal union of a man and woman as husband and wife," *ante* at, and it has always been so under Massachusetts law, colonial or otherwise.

The plaintiffs contend that because the right to choose to marry is a "fundamental" right, the right to marry the person of one's choice, including a member of the same sex, must also be a "fundamental" right. While the court stops short of deciding that the right to marry someone of the same sex is "fundamental" such that strict scrutiny must be applied to any statute that impairs it, it nevertheless agrees with the plaintiffs that the right to choose to marry is of fundamental importance . . . and would be "hollow" if an individual was foreclosed from "freely choosing the person with whom to share . . . the . . . institution of civil marriage." Hence, it concludes that a marriage

Minority Opinion, SJC-08860, March 4, 2003–November 18, 2003.

license cannot be denied to an individual who wishes to marry someone of the same sex. In reaching this result the court has transmuted the "right" to marry into a right to change the institution of marriage itself. This feat of reasoning succeeds only if one accepts the proposition that the definition of the institution of marriage as a union between a man and a woman is merely "conclusory," rather than the basis on which the "right" to partake in it has been deemed to be of fundamental importance. In other words, only by assuming that "marriage" includes the union of two persons of the same sex does the court conclude that restricting marriage to opposite-sex couples infringes on the "right" of same-sex couples to "marry."

The plaintiffs ground their contention that they have a fundamental right to marry a person of the same sex in a long line of Supreme Court decisions that discuss the importance of marriage. In context, all of these decisions and their discussions are about the "fundamental" nature of the institution of marriage as it has existed and been understood in this country, not as the court has redefined it today. Even in that context, its "fundamental" nature is derivative of the nature of the interests that underlie or are associated with it. An examination of those interests reveals that they are either not shared by same-sex couples or not implicated by the marriage statutes.

Supreme Court cases that have described marriage or the right to marry as "fundamental" have focused primarily on the underlying interest of every individual in procreation, which, historically, could only legally occur within the construct of marriage because sexual intercourse outside of marriage was a criminal act. . . . Because same-sex couples are unable to procreate on their own, any right to marriage they may possess cannot be based on their interest in procreation, which has been essential to the Supreme Court's denomination of the right to marry as fundamental.

Supreme Court cases recognizing a right to privacy in intimate decision-making . . . have also focused primarily on sexual relations and the decision whether or not to procreate, and have refused to recognize an "unlimited right" to privacy. . . .

What the *Griswold* Court found "repulsive to the notions of privacy surrounding the marriage relationship" was the prospect of "allow[ing] the police to search the sacred precincts of marital bedrooms for telltale signs of the use of contraceptives." . . . When Justice Goldberg spoke of "marital relations" in the context of finding it "difficult to imagine what is more private or more intimate than a husband and wife's marital relations[hip]," he was obviously referring to sexual relations. Similarly, in *Lawrence v. Texas*, 123 S.Ct. 2472 (2003), it was the criminalization of private sexual behavior that the Court found violative of the petitioners' liberty interest. . . .

The marriage statute, which regulates only the act of obtaining a marriage license, does not implicate privacy in the sense that it has found constitutional protection under Massachusetts and Federal law. . . . It does not intrude on any right that the plaintiffs have to privacy in their choices regarding procreation, an intimate partner or sexual relations. The plaintiffs' right to privacy in such matters does not require that the State officially endorse their choices in order for the right to be constitutionally vindicated.

Although some of the privacy cases also speak in terms of personal autonomy, no court has ever recognized such an open-ended right. "That many of the rights and liberties protected by the Due Process Clause sound in personal autonomy does not warrant the sweeping conclusion that any and all important, intimate, and personal decisions are so protected. . . ." *Washington v. Glucksberg,* 521 U.S. 702, 727 (1997). Such decisions are protected not because they are important, intimate, and personal, but because the right or liberty at stake is "so deeply rooted in our history and traditions, or so fundamental to our concept of constitutionally ordered liberty" that it is protected by due process. *Id.* Accordingly, the Supreme Court has concluded that while the decision to refuse unwanted medical treatment is fundamental, *Cruzan v. Director, Mo. Dep't of Health,* 497 U.S. 261, 278 (1990), because it is deeply rooted in our nation's history and tradition, the equally personal and profound decision to commit suicide is not because of the absence of such roots. *Washington v. Glucksberg, supra.*

While the institution of marriage is deeply rooted in the history and traditions of our country and our State, the right to marry someone of the same sex is not. No matter how personal or intimate a decision to marry someone of the same sex might be, the right to make it is not guaranteed by the right of personal autonomy. . . .

Unlike opposite-sex marriages, which have deep historic roots, or the parent-child relationship, which reflects a "strong tradition" founded on "the history and culture of Western civilization" and "is now established beyond debate as an enduring American tradition," or extended family relationships, which have been "honored throughout our history," same-sex relationships, although becoming more accepted, are certainly not so "deeply rooted in this Nation's history and tradition" as to warrant such enhanced constitutional protection.

Although "expressions of emotional support and public commitment" have been recognized as among the attributes of marriage, which, "*[t]aken together* . . . form a constitutionally protected marital relationship," those interests, standing alone, are not the source of a fundamental right to marry. . . .

Finally, the constitutionally protected interest in child rearing . . . is not implicated or infringed by the marriage statute here. The fact that the plaintiffs cannot marry has no bearing on their independently protected constitutional rights as parents which, as with opposite-sex parents, are limited only by their continued fitness and the best interests of their children. . . .

Because the rights and interests discussed above do not afford the plaintiffs any fundamental right that would be impaired by a statute limiting marriage to members of the opposite sex, they have no fundamental right to be declared "married" by the State.

Insofar as the right to marry someone of the same sex is neither found in the unique historical context of our Constitution nor compelled by the meaning ascribed by this court to the liberty and due process protections contained within it, should the court nevertheless recognize it as a fundamental right? The consequences of deeming a right to be "fundamental" are profound, and this court, as well as the Supreme Court, has been very cautious in recognizing them. Such caution is required by separation of powers principles. If a right is found to be "fundamental," it is, to a great extent, removed from "the arena of public debate and legislative action"; utmost care must be taken when breaking new ground in this field "lest the liberty protected by the Due Process Clause be subtly transformed into the policy preferences of [judges]." . . .

Although public attitudes toward marriage in general and same-sex marriage in particular have changed and are still evolving, "the asserted contemporary concept of marriage and societal interests for which [plaintiffs] contend" are "manifestly [less] deeply founded" than the "historic institution" of marriage. . . .

Given this history and the current state of public opinion, as reflected in the actions of the people's elected representatives, it cannot be said that "a right to same-sex marriage is so rooted in the traditions and collective conscience of our people that failure to recognize it would violate the fundamental principles of liberty and justice that lie at the base of all our civil and political institutions. . . .

"[I]t is not the court's function to launch an inquiry to resolve a debate which has already been settled in the legislative forum. '[I]t [is] the judge's duty . . . to give effect to the will of the people as expressed in the statute by their representative body. It is in this way . . . that the doctrine of separation of powers is given meaning.' . . .

The court's opinion concedes that the civil marriage statute serves legitimate State purposes . . .

Civil marriage is the institutional mechanism by which societies have sanctioned and recognized particular family structures, and the institution of marriage has existed as one of the fundamental organizing principles of human society. . . . Marriage has not been merely a contractual arrangement for legally defining the private relationship between two individuals (although that is certainly part of any marriage). Rather, on an institutional level, marriage is the "very basis of the whole fabric of civilized society," . . . and it serves many important political, economic, social, educational, procreational, and personal functions.

Paramount among its many important functions, the institution of marriage has systematically provided for the regulation of heterosexual behavior, brought order to the resulting procreation, and ensured a stable family structure in which children will be reared, educated, and socialized. Admittedly, heterosexual intercourse, procreation, and child care are not necessarily conjoined (particularly in the modern age of widespread effective contraception and supportive social welfare programs), but an orderly society requires some mechanism for coping with the fact that sexual intercourse commonly results in pregnancy and childbirth. The institution of marriage is that mechanism.

The institution of marriage provides the important legal and normative link between heterosexual intercourse and procreation on the one hand and family responsibilities on the other. The partners in a marriage are expected to engage in exclusive sexual relations, with children the probable result and paternity presumed. . . . Whereas the relationship between mother and child is demonstratively and predictably created and recognizable through the biological process of pregnancy and childbirth, there is no corresponding process for creating a relationship between father and child. Similarly, aside from an act of heterosexual intercourse nine months prior to childbirth, there is no process for creating a relationship between a man and a woman as the parents of a particular child. The institution of marriage fills this void by formally binding the husband-father to his wife and child, and imposing on him the responsibilities of fatherhood. . . . The alternative, a society without the institution of marriage, in which heterosexual intercourse, procreation, and child care are largely disconnected processes, would be chaotic.

The marital family is also the foremost setting for the education and socialization of children. Children learn about the world and their place in it primarily from those who raise them, and those children eventually grow up to exert some influence, great or small, positive or negative, on society. The institution of marriage encourages parents to remain committed to each other and to their children as they grow, thereby encouraging a stable venue for the education and socialization of children. See P. Blumstein & P. Schwartz, *supra* at 26; C.N. Degler, *supra* at 61; S.L. Nock, *supra* at 2–3; C. Lasch, *supra* at 81; M.A. Schwartz & B.M. Scott, *supra* at 6–7. More macroscopically, construction of a family through marriage also formalizes the bonds between people in an ordered and institutional manner, thereby facilitating a foundation of inter-connectedness and interdependency on which more intricate stabilizing social structures might be built. See M. Grossberg, Governing the Hearth: Law and Family in Nineteenth-Century America 10 (1985); C. Lasch, *supra;* L. Saxton, *supra* at 260; J.Q. Wilson, *supra* at 221. . . .

It is undeniably true that dramatic historical shifts in our cultural, political, and economic landscape have altered some of our traditional notions about marriage, including the interpersonal dynamics within it, the range of responsibilities required of it as an institution, and the legal environment in which it exists. Nevertheless, the institution of marriage remains the principal weave of our social fabric. . . .

It is difficult to imagine a State purpose more important and legitimate than ensuring, promoting, and supporting an optimal social structure within which to bear and raise children. At the very least, the marriage statute continues to serve this important State purpose.

. . . The question we must turn to next is whether the statute, construed as limiting marriage to couples of the opposite sex, remains a rational way to further that purpose. Stated differently, we ask whether a conceivable rational basis exists on which the Legislature could conclude that continuing to limit the institution of civil marriage to members of the opposite sex furthers the legitimate purpose of ensuring, promoting, and supporting an optimal social structure for the bearing and raising of children.

In considering whether such a rational basis exists, we defer to the decision-making process of the Legislature, and must make deferential assumptions about the information that it might consider and on which it may rely. . . .

There is no reason to believe that legislative processes are inadequate to effectuate legal changes in response to evolving evidence, social values, and views of fairness on the subject of same-sex relationships. Deliberate consideration of, and incremental responses to rapidly evolving scientific and social understanding is the norm of the political process—that it may seem painfully slow to those who are already persuaded by the arguments in favor of change is not a sufficient basis to conclude that the processes are constitutionally infirm. . . . The Legislature is the appropriate branch, both constitutionally and practically, to consider and respond to it. It is not enough that we as Justices might be personally of the view that we have learned enough to decide what is best. So long as the question is at all debatable, it must be the Legislature that decides. The marriage statute thus meets the requirements of the rational basis test. . . .

POSTSCRIPT

Should Same-Sex Couples Receive Constitutional Protection?

After the Massachusetts Supreme Judicial Court decided *Goodridge*, the state senate requested an advisory opinion from the Court as to whether a pending "civil union" bill would satisfy the requirements of the Massachusetts Constitution. The bill would provide same-sex couples with the same benefits, protections, and responsibilities that a traditional marriage then provided to opposite-sex couples. In response, the Court held that only the recognition of same-sex marriages would prove constitutionally satisfactory. In May 2004, Massachusetts began issuing marriage certificates to same-sex couples, becoming the first state in the nation to do so. Although same-sex-marriage opponents have vowed to override the *Goodridge* decision by amending the Massachusetts state constitution, they have repeatedly failed to get the necessary votes in the state legislature to put a constitutional amendment up for a vote in a ballot initiative.

Beyond the borders of Massachusetts, the *Goodridge* decision generated a wave of legal and political activity, much of it timed to the 2004 presidential election. Both major candidates, Bush and Kerry, voiced their opposition to same-sex marriage. Although the Massachusetts senator moderated his opposition by supporting the notion of same-sex civil unions, he insisted that a "marriage" must remain between a man and a woman. President Bush pushed the point further and, during the later phases of the campaign, called for a constitutional amendment (one that would seem to "constitutionalize" the basic points of the federal Defense of Marriage Act, 28 U.S.C. 1738C (2004)) declaring that a "marriage" was the union between a man and a woman. It was suggested that Bush's harder line was calculated for political appeal to an important part of his political base. Whether this issue played a decisive role in the election is much more difficult to determine. What we do know is that the November 2004 election saw eleven states (Arkansas, Georgia, Kentucky, Michigan, Mississippi, Montana, North Dakota, Oklahoma, Oregon, Ohio, and Utah) overwhelmingly pass ballot initiatives that contained same-sex marriage bans.

More recent developments have signaled greater acceptance of same-sex marriage. In particular, after same-sex marriage became legal in Iowa, Connecticut, and California through judicial decisions similar to Goodridge, Vermont, Maine, New Hampshire, and, most recently, New York—successively instituted same-sex marriage through legislation. By relying on the legislatures to change the state marriage statutes, same-sex marriage proponents in those states undercut one of the main arguments of many same-sex marriage opponents: In decisions such as Goodridge, judges were "legislating from the bench" and usurping the prerogative of the legislature to set marriage policy. Same-sex marriage opponents, however, won a large victory in the 2008 elections when Californian voters passed Proposition 8, amending the state constitution to limit marriage to heterosexual couples and overturning the California Supreme Court's 2007 decision extending marriage to same-sex couples. On August 4, 2010, U.S. district court Judge Vaughn R. Walker overturned Proposition 8 in the case *Perry v. Schwarzenegger,* ruling that it violated both the Due Process and Equal Protection clauses of the U.S. Constitution. Judge Walker issued an injunction against enforcing Proposition 8 and a stay to determine suspension of his ruling pending appeal. The Ninth Circuit Court of Appeals continued the stay, keeping Judge Walker's ruling on hold pending appeal.

A comprehensive overview of the same-sex-marriage debate and the constitutional issues it raises is provided by Evan Gerstmann in *Same-Sex Marriage and the Constitution,* 2nd ed. (Cambridge University Press, 2008).

For an analysis of the virtues of marriage for both same- and opposite-sex couples, see Jonathan Rauch, *Gay Marriage: Why It Is Good for Gays, Good for Straights, and Good for America* (Times Books, 2004). A counterpoint from the conservative perspective is offered by Maggie Gallagher, "What Marriage Is For," *Weekly Standard* (August 4–11, 2003) and Stanley Kurtz, "The End of Marriage in Scandinavia," *Weekly Standard* (February 2, 2004). Finally, historian Stephanie Coontz provides an illuminating perspective on how the meaning of marriage has changed over time in *Marriage, A History: How Love Conquered Marriage* (Penguin, 2006).

ISSUE 20

Do Race-Conscious Programs in Public University Admissions Policies Violate the Fourteenth Amendment's Guarantee of Equal Protection Under the Law?

YES: Clarence Thomas, from Dissenting Opinion, *Barbara Grutter v. Lee Bollinger et al.*, U.S. Supreme Court (June 23, 2003)

NO: Sandra Day O'Connor, from Majority Opinion, *Barbara Grutter v. Lee Bollinger et al.*, U.S. Supreme Court (June 23, 2003)

ISSUE SUMMARY

YES: Supreme Court Justice Clarence Thomas argues that the University of Michigan Law School's admissions policy discriminates on the basis of race and is therefore in violation of the Fourteenth Amendment's equal protection clause.

NO: Supreme Court Justice Sandra Day O'Connor holds that the admissions policy of the University of Michigan Law School, which makes race one factor among many in the process of creating a diverse student body, does not violate the Constitution's guarantee of equal protection under the law.

$\mathbf{A}$ffirmative action continues to be one of the most hotly debated issues in the United States. Proponents justify the use of affirmative action policies by arguing that government should utilize race-conscious programs both to redress the continuing effects of past racial discrimination and to achieve more racially diverse educational and work environments. Opponents of affirmative action view it as unnecessary and unfair, arguing that it is, in essence, nothing more than "reverse discrimination" and, as such, a violation of the Fourteenth Amendment's guarantee of equal protection under the law. Opponents also assert that affirmative action policies stigmatize the beneficiaries of such programs, marking them as unable to succeed on their own merits.

For the past 25 years, since the U.S. Supreme Court's decision in *Regents of the University of California v. Bakke*, 438 U.S. 265 (1978) held that race could be taken into account in a public university's admissions decisions, opponents of affirmative action have pressed their challenge to its legality. In other words, rather than settling the matter, the *Bakke* decision only seems to have provided both sides in this debate with the resources for its continuation. Why? The *Bakke* Court was deeply divided, producing six separate opinions, none of which were able to garner a majority of the Court. Justice Lewis F. Powell was joined by four other members of the Court in invalidating the admissions policy of the University of California at Davis Medical School—a race-based "set aside" policy—on the grounds that it constituted an impermissible racial classification. However, Powell was joined by four different members of the Court in holding that public universities may nonetheless use race as one factor in the admissions decision. Because of the splintered nature of the Court's statement on affirmative action, and because of the inherently contested nature of the problem of race in American law and politics, further litigation was almost inevitable. And while the Court did not revisit the specific question presented in *Bakke* for another 25 years, it did speak to several closely related legal questions. In two important cases in the intervening decades, *City of Richmond v. J. A. Croson Co.,* 488 U.S. 469 (1989) and *Adarand Constructors, Inc. v. Pena*, 515 U.S. 200 (1995), the Court held that the only constitutionally legitimate use of racial preferences was to remedy historically specific instances of racial discrimination.

In 1996 Barbara Grutter, a state resident, applied for admission to the University of Michigan Law School. When filling out her application form, Grutter identified herself as "white" in response to a question that asked each applicant to disclose his or her race. Although she was initially placed on a waiting list, Grutter was ultimately denied admission to the school. Six months later, Grutter filed a class action suit in federal district court on behalf of herself and all others from "disfavored racial groups" who had been denied admission to the law school because of its policy and practice of applying different admissions standards depending upon the race of the applicant. Grutter contended that the law school's admissions policy discriminated against her on the basis of race, thereby denying her equal protection under the law in violation of the Fourteenth Amendment.

After a 13-day trial, the District Court for the Eastern District of Michigan concluded that the law school's use of race as a factor in its admissions decisions was unconstitutional. During the spring of 2002, the U.S. Court of Appeals for the Sixth Circuit reversed the lower court's decision, holding that the law school could consider race as one factor in the admissions process in order to advance the compelling state interest of achieving a diverse student population. With a conflicting interpretation of a similar admissions policy coming from the Fifth Circuit, the stage was set for the U.S. Supreme Court to speak once again to this issue. The following readings are from Justices Clarence Thomas's and Sandra Day O'Connor's opinions from the case.

YES

Clarence Thomas

Dissenting Opinion, *Grutter v. Bollinger*

Frederick Douglass, speaking to a group of abolitionists almost 140 years ago, delivered a message lost on today's majority:

> "[I]n regard to the colored people, there is always more that is benevolent, I perceive, than just, manifested towards us. What I ask for the negro is not benevolence, not pity, not sympathy, but simply *justice*. The American people have always been anxious to know what they shall do with us. . . . I have had but one answer from the beginning. Do nothing with us! Your doing with us has already played the mischief with us. Do nothing with us! If the apples will not remain on the tree of their own strength, if they are worm-eaten at the core, if they are early ripe and disposed to fall, let them fall! . . . And if the negro cannot stand on his own legs, let him fall also. All I ask is, give him a chance to stand on his own legs! Let him alone! . . . [Y]our interference is doing him positive injury." What the Black Man Wants: An Address Delivered in Boston, Massachusetts, on 26 January 1865, reprinted in 4 The Frederick Douglass Papers 59, 68 (J. Blassingame & J. McKivigan eds. 1991) (emphasis in original).

Like Douglass, I believe blacks can achieve in every avenue of American life without the meddling of university administrators. Because I wish to see all students succeed whatever their color, I share, in some respect, the sympathies of those who sponsor the type of discrimination advanced by the University of Michigan Law School (Law School). The Constitution does not, however, tolerate institutional devotion to the status quo in admissions policies when such devotion ripens into racial discrimination. Nor does the Constitution countenance the unprecedented deference the Court gives to the Law School, an approach inconsistent with the very concept of "strict scrutiny."

No one would argue that a university could set up a lower general admission standard and then impose heightened requirements only on black applicants. Similarly, a university may not maintain a high admission standard and grant exemptions to favored races. The Law School, of its own choosing, and for its own purposes, maintains an exclusionary admissions

From Supreme Court of the United States, June 23, 2003.

system that it knows produces racially disproportionate results. Racial discrimination is not a permissible solution to the self-inflicted wounds of this elitist admissions policy.

The majority upholds the Law School's racial discrimination not by interpreting the people's Constitution, but by responding to a faddish slogan of the cognoscenti. Nevertheless, I concur in part in the Court's opinion. First, I agree with the Court insofar as its decision, which approves of only one racial classification, confirms that further use of race in admissions remains unlawful. Second, I agree with the Court's holding that racial discrimination in higher education admissions will be illegal in 25 years. See *ante,* at 31 (stating that racial discrimination will no longer be narrowly tailored, or "necessary to further" a compelling state interest, in 25 years). I respectfully dissent from the remainder of the Court's opinion and the judgment, however, because I believe that the Law School's current use of race violates the Equal Protection Clause and that the Constitution means the same thing today as it will in 300 months.

I

. . . The Constitution abhors classifications based on race, not only because those classifications can harm favored races or are based on illegitimate motives, but also because every time the government places citizens on racial registers and makes race relevant to the provision of burdens or benefits, it demeans us all. "Purchased at the price of immeasurable human suffering, the equal protection principle reflects our Nation's understanding that such classifications ultimately have a destructive impact on the individual and our society." *Adarand Construction, Inc. v. Peña,* 515 U.S. 200, 240 (1995) (Thomas, J., concurring in part and concurring in judgment).

II

Unlike the majority, I seek to define with precision the interest being asserted by the Law School before determining whether that interest is so compelling as to justify racial discrimination. The Law School maintains that it wishes to obtain "educational benefits that flow from student body diversity," Brief for Respondents Bollinger et al. 14. This statement must be evaluated carefully, because it implies that both "diversity" and "educational benefits" are components of the Law School's compelling state interest. Additionally, the Law School's refusal to entertain certain changes in its admissions process and status indicates that the compelling state interest it seeks to validate is actually broader than might appear at first glance.

Undoubtedly there are other ways to "better" the education of law students aside from ensuring that the student body contains a "critical mass" of underrepresented minority students. Attaining "diversity," whatever it means, is the mechanism by which the Law School obtains educational benefits, not an end of itself. The Law School, however, apparently believes that only a racially mixed student body can lead to the educational benefits it seeks. How, then, is the Law School's interest in these allegedly unique educational "benefits" *not* simply the forbidden interest in "racial balancing," *ante,* at 17, that the majority expressly rejects?

A distinction between these two ideas (unique educational benefits based on racial aesthetics and race for its own sake) is purely sophistic—so much so that the majority uses them interchangeably. The Law School's argument, as facile as it is, can only be understood in one way: Classroom aesthetics yields educational benefits, racially discriminatory admissions policies are required to achieve the right racial mix, and therefore the policies are required to achieve the educational benefits. It is the *educational benefits* that are the end, or allegedly compelling state interest, not "diversity."

One must also consider the Law School's refusal to entertain changes to its current admissions system that might produce the same educational benefits. The Law School adamantly disclaims any race-neutral alternative that would reduce "academic selectivity," which would in turn "require the Law School to become a very different institution, and to sacrifice a core part of its educational mission." Brief for Respondents Bollinger et al. 33–36. In other words, the Law School seeks to improve marginally the education it offers without sacrificing too much of its exclusivity and elite status.

The proffered interest that the majority vindicates today, then, is not simply "diversity." Instead the Court upholds the use of racial discrimination as a tool to advance the Law School's interest in offering a marginally superior education while maintaining an elite institution. Unless each constituent part of this state interest is of pressing public necessity, the Law School's use of race is unconstitutional. I find each of them to fall far short of this standard.

III

A

A close reading of the Court's opinion reveals that all of its legal work is done through one conclusory statement: The Law School has a "compelling interest in securing the educational benefits of a diverse student body." *Ante,* at 21. No serious effort is made to explain how these benefits fit with the state interests the Court has recognized (or rejected) as compelling, see Part I, *supra,* or to place any theoretical constraints on an enterprising court's desire to discover still more justifications for racial discrimination. In the absence of any explanation, one might expect the Court to fall back on the judicial policy of *stare decisis.* But the Court eschews even this weak defense of its holding, shunning an analysis of the extent to which Justice Powell's opinion in *Regents of Univ. of Cal. v. Bakke,* 438 U.S. 265 (1978), is binding, *ante,* at 13, in favor of an unfounded wholesale adoption of it.

Justice Powell's opinion in *Bakke* and the Court's decision today rest on the fundamentally flawed proposition that racial discrimination can be contextualized so that a goal, such as classroom aesthetics, can be compelling in one context but not in another. This "we know it when we see it" approach to evaluating state interests is not capable of judicial application. Today, the

Court insists on radically expanding the range of permissible uses of race to something as trivial (by comparison) as the assembling of a law school class. I can only presume that the majority's failure to justify its decision by reference to any principle arises from the absence of any such principle. . . .

IV

The interest in remaining elite and exclusive that the majority thinks so obviously critical requires the use of admissions "standards" that, in turn, create the Law School's "need" to discriminate on the basis of race. The Court validates these admissions standards by concluding that alternatives that would require "a dramatic sacrifice of . . . the academic quality of all admitted students" need not be considered before racial discrimination can be employed.[1] In the majority's view, such methods are not required by the "narrow tailoring" prong of strict scrutiny because that inquiry demands, in this context, that any race-neutral alternative work "'about as well.'" The majority errs, however, because race-neutral alternatives must only be "workable" and do "about as well" *in vindicating the compelling state interest.* The Court never explicitly holds that the Law School's desire to retain the status quo in "academic selectivity" is itself a compelling state interest, and, as I have demonstrated, it is not. Therefore, the Law School should be forced to choose between its classroom aesthetic and its exclusionary admissions system—it cannot have it both ways.

With the adoption of different admissions methods, such as accepting all students who meet minimum qualifications, the Law School could achieve its vision of the racially aesthetic student body without the use of racial discrimination. The Law School concedes this, but the Court holds, implicitly and under the guise of narrow tailoring, that the Law School has a compelling state interest in doing what it wants to do. I cannot agree. First, under strict scrutiny, the Law School's assessment of the benefits of racial discrimination and devotion to the admissions status quo are not entitled to any sort of deference, grounded in the First Amendment or anywhere else. Second, even if its "academic selectivity" must be maintained at all costs along with racial discrimination, the Court ignores the fact that other top law schools have succeeded in meeting their aesthetic demands without racial discrimination. . . .

V

Putting aside the absence of any legal support for the majority's reflexive deference, there is much to be said for the view that the use of tests and other measures to "predict" academic performance is a poor substitute for a system that gives every applicant a chance to prove he can succeed in the study of law. The rallying cry that in the absence of racial discrimination in admissions there would be a true meritocracy ignores the fact that the entire process is poisoned by numerous exceptions to "merit." For example, in the national debate on racial discrimination in higher education admissions, much has been made of the fact that elite institutions utilize a so-called "legacy" preference to give the children of alumni an advantage in admissions. This, and other, exceptions to a "true" meritocracy give the lie to protestations that merit admissions are in fact the order of the day at the Nation's universities. The Equal Protection Clause does not, however, prohibit the use of unseemly legacy preferences or many other kinds of arbitrary admissions procedures. What the Equal Protection Clause does prohibit are classifications made on the basis of race. So while legacy preferences can stand under the Constitution, racial discrimination cannot.[2] I will not twist the Constitution to invalidate legacy preferences or otherwise impose my vision of higher education admissions on the Nation. The majority should similarly stay its impulse to validate faddish racial discrimination the Constitution clearly forbids.

In any event, there is nothing ancient, honorable, or constitutionally protected about "selective" admissions. The University of Michigan should be well aware that alternative methods have historically been used for the admission of students, for it brought to this country the German certificate system in the late-19th century. See H. Wechsler, The Qualified Student 16–39 (1977) (hereinafter Qualified Student). Under this system, a secondary school was certified by a university so that any graduate who completed the course offered by the school was offered admission to the university. The certification regime supplemented, and later virtually replaced (at least in the Midwest), the prior regime of rigorous subject-matter entrance examinations. The facially race-neutral "percent plans" now used in Texas, California, and Florida are in many ways the descendents of the certificate system.

Certification was replaced by selective admissions in the beginning of the 20th century, as universities sought to exercise more control over the composition of their student bodies. Since its inception, selective admissions has been the vehicle for racial, ethnic, and religious tinkering and experimentation by university administrators. The initial driving force for the relocation of the selective function from the high school to the universities was the same desire to select racial winners and losers that the Law School exhibits today. Columbia, Harvard, and others infamously determined that they had "too many" Jews, just as today the Law School argues it would have "too many" whites if it could not discriminate in its admissions process. See Qualified Student 155–168 (Columbia); H. Broun & G. Britt, Christians Only: A Study in Prejudice 53–54 (1931) (Harvard).

. . . [N]o modern law school can claim ignorance of the poor performance of blacks, relatively speaking, on the Law School Admissions Test (LSAT). Nevertheless, law schools continue to use the test and then attempt to "correct" for black underperformance by using racial discrimination in admissions so as to obtain their aesthetic student body. The Law School's continued adherence to measures it knows produce racially skewed results is not entitled to deference by this Court. The Law School itself admits that the test is imperfect, as it must, given that it regularly admits students who score at or below 150 (the national median) on the test. See App. 156–203 (showing that, between 1995 and 2000, the Law School admitted 37 students—27 of whom were black; 31 of whom were "underrepresented minorities"—with LSAT scores of 150 or lower). And the Law School's *amici* cannot seem to agree on the fundamental question whether the test itself is useful. Compare Brief for Law School Admission

Council as *Amicus Curiae* 12 ("LSAT scores . . . are an effective predictor of students' performance in law school") with Brief for Harvard Black Law Students Association et al. as *Amici Curiae* 27 ("Whether [the LSAT] measure[s] objective merit . . . is certainly questionable").

Having decided to use the LSAT, the Law School must accept the constitutional burdens that come with this decision. The Law School may freely continue to employ the LSAT and other allegedly merit-based standards in whatever fashion it likes. What the Equal Protection Clause forbids, but the Court today allows, is the use of these standards hand-in-hand with racial discrimination. An infinite variety of admissions methods are available to the Law School. Considering all of the radical thinking that has historically occurred at this country's universities, the Law School's intractable approach toward admissions is striking.

The Court will not even deign to make the Law School try other methods, however, preferring instead to grant a 25-year license to violate the Constitution. And the same Court that had the courage to order the desegregation of all public schools in the South now fears, on the basis of platitudes rather than principle, to force the Law School to abandon a decidedly imperfect admissions regime that provides the basis for racial discrimination.

VI

The absence of any articulated legal principle supporting the majority's principal holding suggests another rationale. I believe what lies beneath the Court's decision today are the benighted notions that one can tell when racial discrimination benefits (rather than hurts) minority groups, see *Adarand*, 515 U.S., at 239 (Scalia, J., concurring in part and concurring in judgment), and that racial discrimination is necessary to remedy general societal ills. This Court's precedents supposedly settled both issues, but clearly the majority still cannot commit to the principle that racial classifications are *per se* harmful and that almost no amount of benefit in the eye of the beholder can justify such classifications. . . .

The silence in this case is deafening to those of us who view higher education's purpose as imparting knowledge and skills to students, rather than a communal, rubber-stamp, credentialing process. The Law School is not looking for those students who, despite a lower LSAT score or undergraduate grade point average, will succeed in the study of law. The Law School seeks only a facade—it is sufficient that the class looks right, even if it does not perform right.

The Law School tantalizes unprepared students with the promise of a University of Michigan degree and all of the opportunities that it offers. These overmatched students take the bait, only to find that they cannot succeed in the cauldron of competition. And this mismatch crisis is not restricted to elite institutions. See T. Sowell, Race and Culture 176–177 (1994) ("Even if most minority students are able to meet the normal standards at the 'average' range of colleges and universities, the systematic mismatching of minority students begun at the top can mean that such students are generally overmatched throughout all levels of higher education"). Indeed, to cover the tracks of the aestheticists, this cruel farce of racial discrimination must continue—in selection for the Michigan Law Review, see University of Michigan Law School Student Handbook 2002–2003, pp. 39–40 (noting the presence of a "diversity plan" for admission to the review), and in hiring at law firms and for judicial clerkships—until the "beneficiaries" are no longer tolerated. While these students may graduate with law degrees, there is no evidence that they have received a qualitatively better legal education (or become better lawyers) than if they had gone to a less "elite" law school for which they were better prepared. And the aestheticists will never address the real problems facing "underrepresented minorities," instead continuing their social experiments on other people's children. . . .

[T]he majority has placed its *imprimatur* on a practice that can only weaken the principle of equality embodied in the Declaration of Independence and the Equal Protection Clause. "Our Constitution is color-blind, and neither knows nor tolerates classes among citizens." *Plessy v. Ferguson,* 163 U.S. 537, 559 (1896) (Harlan, J., dissenting). It has been nearly 140 years since Frederick Douglass asked the intellectual ancestors of the Law School to "[d]o nothing with us!" and the Nation adopted the Fourteenth Amendment. Now we must wait another 25 years to see this principle of equality vindicated. I therefore respectfully dissent from the remainder of the Court's opinion and the judgment.

Notes

1. The Court refers to this component of the Law School's compelling state interest variously as "academic quality," avoiding "sacrifice [of] a vital component of its educational mission," and "academic selectivity." *Ante,* at 27–28.

2. Were this Court to have the courage to forbid the use of racial discrimination in admissions, legacy preferences (and similar practices) might quickly become less popular—a possibility not lost, I am certain, on the elites (both individual and institutional) supporting the Law School in this case.

NO

Majority Opinion, *Grutter v. Bollinger*

Justice O'Connor delivered the opinion of the Court.

This case requires us to decide whether the use of race as a factor in student admissions by the University of Michigan Law School (Law School) is unlawful.

I

A

The Law School ranks among the Nation's top law schools. It receives more than 3,500 applications each year for a class of around 350 students. Seeking to "admit a group of students who individually and collectively are among the most capable," the Law School looks for individuals with "substantial promise for success in law school" and "a strong likelihood of succeeding in the practice of law and contributing in diverse ways to the well-being of others." App. 110. More broadly, the Law School seeks "a mix of students with varying backgrounds and experiences who will respect and learn from each other." *Ibid.* In 1992, the dean of the Law School charged a faculty committee with crafting a written admissions policy to implement these goals. In particular, the Law School sought to ensure that its efforts to achieve student body diversity complied with this Court's most recent ruling on the use of race in university admissions. See *Regents of Univ. of Cal. v. Bakke,* 438 U.S. 265 (1978). Upon the unanimous adoption of the committee's report by the Law School faculty, it became the Law School's official admissions policy.

The hallmark of that policy is its focus on academic ability coupled with a flexible assessment of applicants' talents, experiences, and potential "to contribute to the learning of those around them." The policy requires admissions officials to evaluate each applicant based on all the information available in the file, including a personal statement, letters of recommendation, and an essay describing the ways in which the applicant will contribute to the life and diversity of the Law School. In reviewing an applicant's file, admissions officials must consider the applicant's undergraduate grade point average (GPA) and Law School Admissions Test (LSAT) score because they are important (if imperfect) predictors of academic success in law school. The policy stresses

From Supreme Court of the United States, June 23, 2003.

that "no applicant should be admitted unless we expect that applicant to do well enough to graduate with no serious academic problems."

The policy makes clear, however, that even the highest possible score does not guarantee admission to the Law School. Nor does a low score automatically disqualify an applicant. Rather, the policy requires admissions officials to look beyond grades and test scores to other criteria that are important to the Law School's educational objectives. So-called "'soft' variables" such as "the enthusiasm of recommenders, the quality of the undergraduate institution, the quality of the applicant's essay, and the areas and difficulty of undergraduate course selection" are all brought to bear in assessing an "applicant's likely contributions to the intellectual and social life of the institution."

The policy aspires to "achieve that diversity which has the potential to enrich everyone's education and thus make a law school class stronger than the sum of its parts." The policy does not restrict the types of diversity contributions eligible for "substantial weight" in the admissions process, but instead recognizes "many possible bases for diversity admissions." The policy does, however, reaffirm the Law School's longstanding commitment to "one particular type of diversity," that is, "racial and ethnic diversity with special reference to the inclusion of students from groups which have been historically discriminated against, like African-Americans, Hispanics and Native Americans, who without this commitment might not be represented in our student body in meaningful numbers." By enrolling a "'critical mass' of [underrepresented] minority students," the Law School seeks to "ensur[e] their ability to make unique contributions to the character of the Law School."

The policy does not define diversity "solely in terms of racial and ethnic status." Nor is the policy "insensitive to the competition among all students for admission to the [L]aw [S]chool." Rather, the policy seeks to guide admissions officers in "producing classes both diverse and academically outstanding, classes made up of students who promise to continue the tradition of outstanding contribution by Michigan Graduates to the legal profession."

B

. . . We granted certiorari, 537 U.S. 1043 (2002), to resolve the disagreement among the Courts of Appeals on a question of national importance: Whether diversity is a compelling interest that can justify the narrowly tailored use of race in selecting applicants for admission to public universities. Compare *Hopwood v. Texas,* 78 F.3d 932 (CA5 1996) (*Hopwood I*) (holding that diversity is not a compelling state interest), with *Smith v. University of Wash. Law School,* 233 F.3d 1188 (CA9 2000) (holding that it is).

II . . .

B

The Equal Protection Clause provides that no State shall "deny to any person within its jurisdiction the equal protection of the laws." U.S. Const., Amdt.

14, §2. Because the Fourteenth Amendment "protect[s] *persons*, not *groups*," all "governmental action based on race—a *group* classification long recognized as in most circumstances irrelevant and therefore prohibited—should be subjected to detailed judicial inquiry to ensure that the *personal* right to equal protection of the laws has not been infringed." *Adarand Constructors, Inc. v. Peña*, 515 U.S. 200, 227 (1995) (emphasis in original; internal quotation marks and citation omitted). We are a "free people whose institutions are founded upon the doctrine of equality." *Loving v. Virginia*, 388 U.S. 1, 11 (1967) (internal quotation marks and citation omitted). It follows from that principle that "government may treat people differently because of their race only for the most compelling reasons." *Adarand Constructors, Inc. v. Peña*, 515 U.S., at 227.

We have held that all racial classifications imposed by government "must be analyzed by a reviewing court under strict scrutiny." This means that such classifications are constitutional only if they are narrowly tailored to further compelling governmental interests. "Absent searching judicial inquiry into the justification for such race-based measures," we have no way to determine what "classifications are 'benign' or 'remedial' and what classifications are in fact motivated by illegitimate notions of racial inferiority or simple racial politics." *Richmond v. J. A. Croson Co.*, 488 U.S. 469, 493 (1989) (plurality opinion). We apply strict scrutiny to all racial classifications to "'smoke out' illegitimate uses of race by assuring that [government] is pursuing a goal important enough to warrant use of a highly suspect tool." *Ibid.*

Strict scrutiny is not "strict in theory, but fatal in fact." *Adarand Constructors, Inc. v. Peña, supra*, at 237 (internal quotation marks and citation omitted). Although all governmental uses of race are subject to strict scrutiny, not all are invalidated by it. As we have explained, "whenever the government treats any person unequally because of his or her race, that person has suffered an injury that falls squarely within the language and spirit of the Constitution's guarantee of equal protection." 515 U.S., at 229–230. But that observation "says nothing about the ultimate validity of any particular law; that determination is the job of the court applying strict scrutiny." *Id.*, at 230. When race-based action is necessary to further a compelling governmental interest, such action does not violate the constitutional guarantee of equal protection so long as the narrow-tailoring requirement is also satisfied.

Context matters when reviewing race-based governmental action under the Equal Protection Clause. See *Gomillion v. Lightfoot*, 364 U.S. 339, 343–344 (1960) (admonishing that, "in dealing with claims under broad provisions of the Constitution, which derive content by an interpretive process of inclusion and exclusion, it is imperative that generalizations, based on and qualified by the concrete situations that gave rise to them, must not be applied out of context in disregard of variant controlling facts"). In *Adarand Constructors, Inc. v. Peña*, we made clear that strict scrutiny must take "'relevant differences' into account." 515 U.S., at 228. Indeed, as we explained, that is its "fundamental purpose." *Ibid.* Not every decision influenced by race is equally objectionable and strict scrutiny is designed to provide a framework for carefully examining the importance and the sincerity of the reasons advanced by the governmental decisionmaker for the use of race in that particular context.

III

A

With these principles in mind, we turn to the question whether the Law School's use of race is justified by a compelling state interest. Before this Court, as they have throughout this litigation, respondents assert only one justification for their use of race in the admissions process: obtaining "the educational benefits that flow from a diverse student body." Brief for Respondents Bollinger et al. i. In other words, the Law School asks us to recognize, in the context of higher education, a compelling state interest in student body diversity.

We first wish to dispel the notion that the Law School's argument has been foreclosed, either expressly or implicitly, by our affirmative-action cases decided since *Bakke.* It is true that some language in those opinions might be read to suggest that remedying past discrimination is the only permissible justification for race-based governmental action. See, *e.g., Richmond v. J. A. Croson Co., supra,* at 493 (plurality opinion) (stating that unless classifications based on race are "strictly reserved for remedial settings, they may in fact promote notions of racial inferiority and lead to a politics of racial hostility"). But we have never held that the only governmental use of race that can survive strict scrutiny is remedying past discrimination. Nor, since *Bakke,* have we directly addressed the use of race in the context of public higher education. Today, we hold that the Law School has a compelling interest in attaining a diverse student body.

The Law School's educational judgment that such diversity is essential to its educational mission is one to which we defer. The Law School's assessment that diversity will, in fact, yield educational benefits is substantiated by respondents and their *amici.* Our scrutiny of the interest asserted by the Law School is no less strict for taking into account complex educational judgments in an area that lies primarily within the expertise of the university. Our holding today is in keeping with our tradition of giving a degree of deference to a university's academic decisions, within constitutionally prescribed limits.

We have long recognized that, given the important purpose of public education and the expansive freedoms of speech and thought associated with the university environment, universities occupy a special niche in our constitutional tradition. In announcing the principle of student body diversity as a compelling state interest, Justice Powell invoked our cases recognizing a constitutional dimension, grounded in the First Amendment, of educational autonomy: "The freedom of a university to make its own judgments as to education includes the selection of its student body." *Bakke, supra,* at 312. From this premise, Justice Powell reasoned that by claiming "the right to select those students who will contribute the most to the 'robust exchange of ideas,'" a university "seek[s] to achieve a goal that is of paramount importance in the fulfillment of its mission." 438 U.S., at 313 (quoting *Keyishian v. Board of Regents of Univ. of State of N.Y., supra,* at 603). Our conclusion that the Law School has a compelling interest in a diverse student body is informed by our view that attaining a diverse student body is at the heart of the Law School's proper institutional mission, and that "good faith" on the part of a university is "presumed" absent "a showing to the contrary." 438 U.S., at 318–319.

As part of its goal of "assembling a class that is both exceptionally academically qualified and broadly diverse," the Law School seeks to "enroll a 'critical mass' of minority students." Brief for Respondents Bollinger et al. 13. The Law School's interest is not simply "to assure within its student body some specified percentage of a particular group merely because of its race or ethnic origin." *Bakke,* 438 U.S., at 307 (opinion of Powell, J.). That would amount to outright racial balancing, which is patently unconstitutional. *Ibid.; Freeman v. Pitts,* 503 U.S. 467, 494 (1992) ("Racial balance is not to be achieved for its own sake"); *Richmond v. J. A. Croson Co.,* 488 U.S., at 507. Rather, the Law School's concept of critical mass is defined by reference to the educational benefits that diversity is designed to produce.

These benefits are substantial. As the District Court emphasized, the Law School's admissions policy promotes "cross-racial understanding," helps to break down racial stereotypes, and "enables [students] to better understand persons of different races." App. to Pet. for Cert. 246a. These benefits are "important and laudable," because "classroom discussion is livelier, more spirited, and simply more enlightening and interesting" when the students have "the greatest possible variety of backgrounds."

The Law School's claim of a compelling interest is further bolstered by its *amici,* who point to the educational benefits that flow from student body diversity. In addition to the expert studies and reports entered into evidence at trial, numerous studies show that student body diversity promotes learning outcomes, and "better prepares students for an increasingly diverse workforce and society, and better prepares them as professionals." Brief for American Educational Research Association et al. as *Amici Curiae* 3; see, *e.g.,* W. Bowen & D. Bok, The Shape of the River (1998); Diversity Challenged: Evidence on the Impact of Affirmative Action (G. Orfield & M. Kurlaender eds. 2001); Compelling Interest: Examining the Evidence on Racial Dynamics in Colleges and Universities (M. Chang, D. Witt, J. Jones, & K. Hakuta eds. 2003).

These benefits are not theoretical but real, as major American businesses have made clear that the skills needed in today's increasingly global marketplace can only be developed through exposure to widely diverse people, cultures, ideas, and viewpoints. Brief for 3M et al. as *Amici Curiae* 5; Brief for General Motors Corp. as *Amicus Curiae* 3–4. What is more, high-ranking retired officers and civilian leaders of the United States military assert that, "[b]ased on [their] decades of experience," a "highly qualified, racially diverse officer corps . . . is essential to the military's ability to fulfill its principle mission to provide national security." Brief for Julius W. Becton, Jr. et al. as *Amici Curiae* 27. The primary sources for the Nation's officer corps are the service academies and the Reserve Officers Training Corps (ROTC), the latter comprising students already admitted to participating colleges and universities. *Id.,* at 5. At present, "the military cannot achieve an officer corps that is *both* highly qualified *and* racially diverse unless the service academies and the ROTC used limited race-conscious recruiting and admissions policies." *Ibid.* (emphasis in original). To fulfill its mission, the military "must be selective in admissions for training and education for the officer corps, *and* it must train and educate a highly qualified, racially diverse officer corps in a racially diverse setting." *Id.,* at 29 (emphasis in original). We agree that "[i]t requires only a small step from this analysis to conclude that our country's other most selective institutions must remain both diverse and selective." *Ibid.*

We have repeatedly acknowledged the overriding importance of preparing students for work and citizenship, describing education as pivotal to "sustaining our political and cultural heritage" with a fundamental role in maintaining the fabric of society. *Plyler v. Doe,* 457 U.S. 202, 221 (1982). This Court has long recognized that "education . . . is the very foundation of good citizenship." *Brown v. Board of Education,* 347 U.S. 483, 493 (1954). For this reason, the diffusion of knowledge and opportunity through public institutions of higher education must be accessible to all individuals regardless of race or ethnicity. The United States, as *amicus curiae,* affirms that "[e]nsuring that public institutions are open and available to all segments of American society, including people of all races and ethnicities, represents a paramount government objective." Brief for United States as *Amicus Curiae* 13. And, "[n]owhere is the importance of such openness more acute than in the context of higher education." *Ibid.* Effective participation by members of all racial and ethnic groups in the civic life of our Nation is essential if the dream of one Nation, indivisible, is to be realized.

Moreover, universities, and in particular, law schools, represent the training ground for a large number of our Nation's leaders. *Sweatt v. Painter,* 339 U.S. 629, 634 (1950) (describing law school as a "proving ground for legal learning and practice"). Individuals with law degrees occupy roughly half the state governorships, more than half the seats in the United States Senate, and more than a third of the seats in the United States House of Representatives. See Brief for Association of American Law Schools as *Amicus Curiae* 5–6. The pattern is even more striking when it comes to highly selective law schools. A handful of these schools accounts for 25 of the 100 United States Senators, 74 United States Courts of Appeals judges, and nearly 200 of the more than 600 United States District Court judges. *Id.,* at 6.

In order to cultivate a set of leaders with legitimacy in the eyes of the citizenry, it is necessary that the path to leadership be visibly open to talented and qualified individuals of every race and ethnicity. All members of our heterogeneous society must have confidence in the openness and integrity of the educational institutions that provide this training. As we have recognized, law schools "cannot be effective in isolation from the individuals and institutions with which the law interacts." See *Sweatt v. Painter, supra,* at 634. Access to legal education (and thus the legal profession) must be inclusive of talented and qualified individuals of every race and ethnicity, so that all members of our heterogeneous society may participate in the educational institutions that provide the training and education necessary to succeed in America.

The Law School does not premise its need for critical mass on "any belief that minority students always (or even consistently) express some characteristic minority viewpoint on any issue." Brief for Respondent Bollinger et al. 30. To the contrary, diminishing the force of such stereotypes is both a crucial part of the Law School's mission, and one that it cannot accomplish with only token numbers of minority students. Just as growing up in a particular region or having particular professional experiences is likely to affect an individual's views, so too is one's own, unique experience of being a racial minority in a society, like our own, in which race unfortunately still matters. The Law School has determined, based on its experience and expertise, that a "critical mass" of underrepresented minorities is necessary to further its compelling interest in securing the educational benefits of a diverse student body.

B

Even in the limited circumstance when drawing racial distinctions is permissible to further a compelling state interest, government is still "constrained in how it may pursue that end: [T]he means chosen to accomplish the [government's] asserted purpose must be specifically and narrowly framed to accomplish that purpose." *Shaw v. Hunt,* 517 U.S. 899, 908 (1996) (internal quotation marks and citation omitted). The purpose of the narrow tailoring requirement is to ensure that "the means chosen 'fit' . . . th[e] compelling goal so closely that there is little or no possibility that the motive for the classification was illegitimate racial prejudice or stereotype."

Since *Bakke,* we have had no occasion to define the contours of the narrow-tailoring inquiry with respect to race-conscious university admissions programs. That inquiry must be calibrated to fit the distinct issues raised by the use of race to achieve student body diversity in public higher education. Contrary to Justice Kennedy's assertions, we do not "abandon[ ] strict scrutiny," see *post,* at 8 (dissenting opinion). Rather, as we have already explained, *ante,* at 15, we adhere to *Adarand*'s teaching that the very purpose of strict scrutiny is to take such "relevant differences into account."

To be narrowly tailored, a race-conscious admissions program cannot use a quota system—it cannot "insulat[e] each category of applicants with certain desired qualifications from competition with all other applicants." *Bakke, supra,* at 315 (opinion of Powell, J.). Instead, a university may consider race or ethnicity only as a "'plus' in a particular applicant's file," without "insulat[ing] the individual from comparison with all other candidates for the available seats." In other words, an admissions program must be "flexible enough to consider all pertinent elements of diversity in light of the particular qualifications of each applicant, and to place them on the same footing for consideration, although not necessarily according them the same weight."

We find that the Law School's admissions program bears the hallmarks of a narrowly tailored plan. As Justice Powell made clear in *Bakke,* truly individualized consideration demands that race be used in a flexible, nonmechanical way. It follows from this mandate that universities cannot establish quotas for members of certain racial groups or put members of those groups on separate admissions tracks. Nor can universities insulate applicants who belong to certain racial or ethnic groups from the competition for admission. *Ibid.* Universities can, however, consider race or ethnicity more flexibly as a "plus" factor in the context of individualized consideration of each and every applicant.

. . . The importance of this individualized consideration in the context of a race-conscious admissions program is paramount.

. . . Unlike the program at issue in *Gratz v. Bollinger,* the Law School awards no mechanical, predetermined diversity "bonuses" based on race or ethnicity. . . .

We also find that, like the Harvard plan Justice Powell referenced in *Bakke,* the Law School's race-conscious admissions program adequately ensures that all factors that may contribute to student body diversity are meaningfully considered alongside race in admissions decisions. With respect to the use of race itself, all underrepresented minority students admitted by the Law School have been deemed qualified. By virtue of our Nation's struggle with racial inequality, such students are both likely to have experiences of particular importance to the Law School's mission, and less likely to be admitted in meaningful numbers on criteria that ignore those experiences.

The Law School does not, however, limit in any way the broad range of qualities and experiences that may be considered valuable contributions to student body diversity. To the contrary, the 1992 policy makes clear "[t]here are many possible bases for diversity admissions," and provides examples of admittees who have lived or traveled widely abroad, are fluent in several languages, have overcome personal adversity and family hardship, have exceptional records of extensive community service, and have had successful careers in other fields. The Law School seriously considers each "applicant's promise of making a notable contribution to the class by way of a particular strength, attainment, or characteristic—*e.g.,* an unusual intellectual achievement, employment experience, nonacademic performance, or personal background." *Id.,* at 83–84. All applicants have the opportunity to highlight their own potential diversity contributions through the submission of a personal statement, letters of recommendation, and an essay describing the ways in which the applicant will contribute to the life and diversity of the Law School.

What is more, the Law School actually gives substantial weight to diversity factors besides race. The Law School frequently accepts nonminority applicants with grades and test scores lower than underrepresented minority applicants (and other nonminority applicants) who are rejected. This shows that the Law School seriously weighs many other diversity factors besides race that can make a real and dispositive difference for nonminority applicants as well. By this flexible approach, the Law School sufficiently takes into account, in practice as well as in theory, a wide variety of characteristics besides race and ethnicity that contribute to a diverse student body. . . .

We are mindful, however, that "[a] core purpose of the Fourteenth Amendment was to do away with all governmentally imposed discrimination based on race." *Palmore v. Sidoti,* 466 U.S. 429, 432 (1984). Accordingly, race-conscious admissions policies must be limited in time. This requirement reflects that racial classifications, however compelling their goals, are potentially so dangerous that they may be employed no more broadly than the interest demands. Enshrining a permanent justification for racial preferences would offend this fundamental equal protection principle. We see no reason to exempt race-conscious admissions programs from the requirement that all governmental use of race must have a logical end point. The Law School, too, concedes that all "race-conscious programs must have reasonable durational limits."

In the context of higher education, the durational requirement can be met by sunset provisions in race-conscious admissions policies and periodic reviews to determine whether racial preferences are still necessary to achieve student body diversity. . . .

We take the Law School at its word that it would "like nothing better than to find a race-neutral admissions formula" and will terminate its race-conscious admissions program as soon as practicable. It has been 25 years since Justice Powell first approved the use of race to further an interest in student body diversity in the context of public higher education. Since that time, the number of minority applicants with high grades and test scores has indeed increased. We expect that 25 years from now, the use of racial preferences will no longer be necessary to further the interest approved today.

IV

In summary, the Equal Protection Clause does not prohibit the Law School's narrowly tailored use of race in admissions decisions to further a compelling interest in obtaining the educational benefits that flow from a diverse student body. Consequently, petitioner's statutory claims based on Title VI and 42 U.S.C. §1981 also fail. The judgment of the Court of Appeals for the Sixth Circuit, accordingly, is affirmed.

It is so ordered.

POSTSCRIPT

Do Race-Conscious Programs in Public University Admissions Policies Violate the Fourteenth Amendment's Guarantee of Equal Protection Under the Law?

In 1954 the landmark civil rights case *Brown v. Board of Education*, 347 U.S. 483 (1954) was decided. *Brown* was the culmination of the desegregation strategy of the National Association for the Advancement of Colored People (NAACP) Legal Defense Fund; it promised the beginning of a new era of equal justice under law for America's racial minorities. For many, the promise of *Brown* was a nation that had overcome the vestiges of past practices of racial discrimination and that stood at the threshold of a truly color-blind society. But that promise has been elusive. Not too long after *Brown* was decided, it became apparent to some that in order to bring about racial justice, it would still be necessary to continue to take race into account in many important public policy decisions. The late justice Harry A. Blackmun lent an eloquent voice to this position in his opinion in *Regents of the University of California v. Bakke*, 438 U.S. 265 (1978). There he announced that he yielded

> to no one in [his] earnest hope that the time will come when an "affirmative action" program is unnecessary, and is, in truth, only a relic of the past. . . . At some time, beyond any period of what some would claim is only transitional inequality, the United States must and will reach a stage of maturity where action along this line is no longer necessary. Then persons will be regarded as persons, and discrimination of the type we address today will be an ugly feature of history that is instructive but that is behind us.

For some, race-conscious remedies designed to cure the ills of past discrimination have done nothing to ease racial tensions and have resulted only in creating new problems, such as punishing "innocent" people—Barbara Grutter, for example—for the sins of others. For others, race-conscious programs have threatened the very integrity of the Constitution, risking one of its most sacred principles: that all stand equal before the law, regardless of race, class, or other personal characteristics. Yet the fact remains that, nearly half a century after *Brown*, far too many of America's colleges and universities would remain predominantly white but for race-conscious admissions programs of the sort at issue in *Grutter v. Bollinger*. None of the Supreme Court justices seem to disagree on that single point; the question is what to do about it.

Prior to the decision in *Grutter*, it was unclear whether the Court would continue to allow race to be taken into account for any purpose other than providing a remedy for past discrimination. Indeed, many have argued that race can be taken into account only for such purposes. The *Grutter* majority breaks rank with this, however, and says that forward-looking, utilitarian justifications are also sufficient to justify race-conscious college admissions policies; that is, the achievement of *diversity* in the university classroom is a compelling state interest. Even after *Grutter*, however, it is still not entirely clear what the Court means by "diversity." Furthermore, one might reasonably question whether such diversity policies are synonymous with *affirmative action*. Wasn't the original goal of affirmative action to "level the playing field," to offer opportunities to those who have not had them? More specifically, wasn't the original goal of affirmative action to remedy the present effects of past discrimination? According to the *Grutter* majority, diversity is justified because it will be good for all students—the white majority as well as underrepresented groups—and for the educational institution as a whole. One might reasonably ask whether the Court is authorizing the university to use underrepresented students of color for purely instrumental reasons.

Grutter may have answered a few questions concerning the use of race in college admissions, but it left open how race might be used in other contexts. As a result, the Supreme Court continues to be faced with challenges to policies that take race into account. In *Parents Involved in Community Schools v. Seattle School District No. 1* (2007), for example, race was an element that could affect which school a child attended. The Court, by a 5–4 vote, declared the practice unlawful. In *Ricci v. Destefano* (2009), the city of New Haven gave a test to fire fighters who wished to be promoted. The results of the test showed that white candidates outperformed minority candidates and that, even in a city that had a minority population over 60 percent, no minority members would be promoted. The Supreme Court, again by a 5–4 vote, held that New Haven's throwing out the result of the test was impermissible.

Those who wish to read further on this issue might begin with a study by Derek Bok and William Bowen, former presidents of Harvard and Princeton Universities: *The Shape of the River: Long-Term Consequences of Considering Race in College and University Admissions* (Princeton University Press, 1998). In addition, Michel Rosenfeld's *Affirmative Action and Justice: A Philosophical and Constitutional Inquiry* (Yale University Press, 1991) provides a thoughtful and challenging study of many of the important issues involved here. Further, readers might be interested in visiting the Web site of the Center for Individual Rights (CIR) at http://www.cir-usa.org. The CIR is a nonprofit, tax-exempt public interest law firm, which provided legal representation for Grutter in her suit against the University of Michigan Law School. Finally, visit the University of Michigan Web site http://www.umich.edu/~urel/admissions/legal/grutter for useful information about *Grutter* and for many of the legal documents filed in this case.

Contributors to This Volume

EDITOR

M. ETHAN KATSH is professor of legal studies and director of the Center for Information Technology and Dispute Resolution at the University of Massachusetts at Amherst (www.odr.info). A graduate of the Yale Law School, he has authored three books on law and technology: *Law in a Digital World* (Oxford University Press, 1995), *The Electronic Media and the Transformation of Law* (Oxford University Press, 1989), and, with Professor Janet Rifkin, *Online Dispute Resolution: Resolving Conflicts in Cyberspace* (2001). Professor Katsh conducted the pilot online dispute-resolution project for eBay and is involved in many activities designed to resolve disputes using the Internet. He may be reached at Katsh@legal.umass.edu.

AUTHORS

STEPHEN BREYER is an associate justice of the U.S. Supreme Court. He received an A.B. from Stanford University, a B.A. from Magdalen College, Oxford, and an LL.B. from Harvard Law School. He served as a law clerk to Justice Arthur Goldberg of the Supreme Court of the United States during the 1964 term. Prior to being appointed as a judge of the United States Court of Appeals for the First Circuit, he was a professor at Harvard Law School. From 1990 to 1994, he served as chief judge for the First Circuit Court of Appeals. President Clinton nominated him as an associate justice of the Supreme Court in 1994.

ROBERT CORDY is associate justice of the Massachusetts Supreme Judicial Court. He received a J.D. from Harvard Law School in 1974. Prior to being appointed to the bench, he was a partner at the law firm of McDermott, Will & Emery.

CHARLES GARDNER GEYH is Associate Dean for Research and professor of Law at Indiana University–Bloomington. Professor Geyh's teaching and scholarship focus on the operation of state and federal courts in relation to the political branches of government and the legal profession. He is the author of *When Courts and Congress Collide: The Struggle for Control of America's Judicial System* (University of Michigan Press, 2006), coauthor of *Judicial Conduct and Ethics* (4th ed., Lexis Law Publishing, 2007) (with Alfini, Lubet, and Shaman), and *Disqualification: An Analysis Under Federal Law* (2nd ed. Federal Judicial Center, forthcoming 2010).

RUTH BADER GINSBURG is an associate justice of the U.S. Supreme Court. She graduated at the top of her law school class at Columbia University and taught at Rutgers and Columbia Law Schools. She served as director of the ACLU Women's Rights Project, and between 1972 and 1978 she argued six cases involving sex-role stereotyping before the Court and won five. She was appointed to the Supreme Court by President Bill Clinton in 1993.

ANTHONY KENNEDY is an associate justice of the U.S. Supreme Court. He received his LL.B. from Harvard Law School in 1961 and worked for law firms in San Francisco and Sacramento, California, until he was nominated by President Gerald Ford to the U.S. Court of Appeals for the Ninth Circuit in 1975. He was nominated by President Ronald Reagan to the Supreme Court in 1988.

MARGARET MARSHALL is chief justice of the Massachusetts Supreme Judicial Court. A native of South Africa, she graduated from Witwatersrand University in Johannesburg in 1966 and later received a J.D. from Yale Law School. Before her appointment to the Supreme Judicial Court, she was vice president and general counsel of Harvard University. She was appointed as an associate justice of the Supreme Judicial Court in November 1996 and named chief justice in September 1999.

SANDRA DAY O'CONNOR was an associate justice of the U.S. Supreme Court. She worked in various legal capacities both in the United States and in

Germany until she was appointed to the Arizona State Senate in 1969. She served as a state senator for 4 years and served in the Arizona judiciary for 6 years before she was nominated to the Supreme Court by President Ronald Reagan in 1981.

MICHAEL R. DIMINO, SR., is an associate professor of law on Widener's Harrisburg Campus. Professor Dimino is an honors-program graduate of the State University of New York at Buffalo, where he earned baccalaureate degrees, summa cum laude, in political science and history (1998); and a cum laude graduate of Harvard Law School (J.D., 2001), where he was articles editor of the Harvard Journal of Law & Public Policy.

WILLIAM H. REHNQUIST (1924–2005) became the 16th chief justice of the U.S. Supreme Court in 1986. He engaged in a general practice of law with primary emphasis on civil litigation for 16 years before being appointed assistant attorney general, Office of Legal Counsel, by President Richard Nixon in 1969. He was nominated by Nixon to the Supreme Court in 1972.

STEPHEN REINHARDT is a judge on the U.S. Court of Appeals for the Ninth Circuit in Seattle, Washington.

JOHN ROBERTS is the current chief justice of the U.S. Supreme Court. He received an A.B. from Harvard College in 1976 and a J.D. from Harvard Law School in 1979. He served as a law clerk for former U.S. Supreme Court Chief Justice William H. Rehnquist during the 1980 term, and in various other legal capacities until his appointment to the U.S. Court of Appeals for the District of Columbia Circuit in 2003. President George W. Bush nominated him as chief justice in 2005.

ANTONIN SCALIA is an associate justice of the U.S. Supreme Court. He taught law at the University of Virginia, the American Enterprise Institute, Georgetown University, and the University of Chicago before being nominated to the U.S. Court of Appeals by President Ronald Reagan in 1982. He served in that capacity until he was nominated by Reagan to the Supreme Court in 1986.

DAVID SOUTER retired as an associate justice of the U.S. Supreme Court in June 2009. Prior to his appointment to the Supreme Court he was a former judge for the U.S. Court of Appeals for the First Circuit in Boston, Massachusetts. He was nominated by President George H. W. Bush to the Supreme Court in 1990.

JOHN PAUL STEVENS retired as an associate justice of the U.S. Supreme Court in June 2010. He worked in law firms in Chicago, Illinois, for 20 years before being nominated by President Richard Nixon to the U.S. Court of Appeals in 1970. He served in that capacity until he was nominated to the Supreme Court by President Gerald Ford in 1975.

CLARENCE THOMAS is an associate justice of the U.S. Supreme Court. A former judge on the U.S. Court of Appeals for the District of Columbia, he was nominated by President George H. W. Bush to the Supreme Court in 1991. He received his J.D. from the Yale University School of Law in 1974.

THE UNITED STATES DEPARTMENT OF JUSTICE has a mission to enforce the law and defend the interests of the United States according to the law, to ensure public safety against threats foreign and domestic, to provide federal leadership in preventing and controlling crime, to seek just punishment for those guilty of unlawful behavior, and to ensure fair and impartial administration of justice for all Americans.